The Enabling Pov

Volume 3

Series editor
Claire Wyatt-Smith, Faculty of Education and Arts, Australian Catholic University, Brisbane, Queensland, Australia

This series heralds the idea that new times call for new and different thinking about assessment and learning, the identities of teachers and students, and what is involved in using and creating new knowledge. Its scope is consistent with a view of assessment as inherently connected with cultural, social practices and contexts. Assessment is a shared enterprise where teachers and students come together to not only develop knowledge and skills, but also to use and create knowledge and identities. Working from this position, the series confronts some of the major educational assessment issues of our times.

More information about this series at http://www.springer.com/series/13204

Shelleyann Scott • Donald E. Scott
Charles F. Webber
Editors

Leadership of Assessment, Inclusion, and Learning

🐎 Springer

Editors
Shelleyann Scott
Werklund School of Education
University of Calgary
Calgary, AB, Canada

Donald E. Scott
Werklund School of Education
University of Calgary
Calgary, AB, Canada

Charles F. Webber
Faculty of Continuing Education
  and Extension
Mount Royal University
Calgary, AB, Canada

ISSN 2198-2643   ISSN 2198-2651 (electronic)
The Enabling Power of Assessment
ISBN 978-3-319-37079-8   ISBN 978-3-319-23347-5 (eBook)
DOI 10.1007/978-3-319-23347-5

Springer Cham Heidelberg New York Dordrecht London
© Springer International Publishing Switzerland 2016
Softcover re-print of the Hardcover 1st edition 2016
This work is subject to copyright. All rights are reserved by the Publisher, whether the whole or part of the material is concerned, specifically the rights of translation, reprinting, reuse of illustrations, recitation, broadcasting, reproduction on microfilms or in any other physical way, and transmission or information storage and retrieval, electronic adaptation, computer software, or by similar or dissimilar methodology now known or hereafter developed.
The use of general descriptive names, registered names, trademarks, service marks, etc. in this publication does not imply, even in the absence of a specific statement, that such names are exempt from the relevant protective laws and regulations and therefore free for general use.
The publisher, the authors and the editors are safe to assume that the advice and information in this book are believed to be true and accurate at the date of publication. Neither the publisher nor the authors or the editors give a warranty, express or implied, with respect to the material contained herein or for any errors or omissions that may have been made.

Springer International Publishing AG Switzerland is part of Springer Science+Business Media (www.springer.com)

Contents

1 **Reconceptualising Instructional Leadership: Exploring the Relationships Between Leadership, Instructional Design, Assessment, and Student Needs**.. 1
Shelleyann Scott

Part I Pragmatics of Assessment Leadership – What Leaders Need to Know About Assessment

2 **Educational Renovations: Nailing Down Terminology in Assessment**.. 25
Michelle McKean and E. Nola Aitken

3 **Assessment and Cooperative Learning: The Missing Think** 45
Barrie Bennett

Part II Pragmatics of Assessment Leadership in the Disciplines

4 **Rubrics and Exemplars in Writing Assessment**.................................. 89
Johanna de Leeuw

5 **Arts-Inspired Performance Assessment Considerations for Educational Leaders**.. 111
Matthew J. Meyer

6 **Assessment for Learning in a Math Classroom** 141
Sharon Friesen

7 **Supporting Optimal Student Assessment Practices in Science as a Core Subject Area** 171
Ann Sherman and Leo MacDonald

Part III Pragmatics of Assessment Leadership for Inclusion

8 **Effective Leadership for Inclusionary Practice: Assessment Considerations for Cognitively Challenged Students** 199
Elaine Fournier, Shelleyann Scott, and Donald E. Scott

9 **Assessing Bilingual and Multilingual Learners in Mainstream Classrooms** 225
Sylvie Roy

10 **Leading Assessment for Gifted and Talented Students: The Pursuit of Mediocrity of Excellence?** 243
Shelleyann Scott, Donald E. Scott, and Leanne Longmire

11 **Fairer Assessment for Indigenous Students: An Australian Perspective** 273
Val Klenowski

12 **Challenges, Tensions and Possibilities: An Analysis of Assessment Policy and Practice in New Zealand** 287
Bronwen Cowie and Dawn Penney

13 **First Nations Assessment Issues** 305
David F. Philpott

14 **Assessment Practices and Aboriginal Students** 327
Jacqueline Ottmann and Joan Jeary

Index 365

Contributors

E. Nola Aitken Faculty of Education, University of Lethbridge, Lethbridge, AB, Canada

Barrie Bennett Ontario Institute for Studies in Education, University of Toronto (OISE/UT), Toronto, ON, Canada

Bronwen Cowie Faculty of Education, The University of Waikato, Hamilton, New Zealand

Johanna de Leeuw Founder & President, Visible Assessment for Learning Inc., Calgary, AB, Canada

Elaine Fournier Bancroft, ON, Canada

Sharon Friesen Werklund School of Education, University of Calgary, Calgary, AB, Canada

Joan Jeary Werklund School of Education, University of Calgary, Calgary, AB, Canada

Val Klenowski School of Learning and Professional Studies, Faculty of Education, Queensland University of Technology, Brisbane, QLD, Australia

Leanne Longmire Department of Education Western Australia, Perth, Australia

Leo MacDonald Faculty of Education, St. Francis Xavier University, Antigonish, NS, Canada

Michelle McKean Faculty of Education, University of Lethbridge, Lethbridge, AB, Canada

Matthew J. Meyer Faculty of Education, St. Francis Xavier University, Antigonish, NS, Canada

Jacqueline Ottmann Werklund School of Education, University of Calgary, Calgary, AB, Canada

Dawn Penney Faculty of Education, Monash University, Frankston, VIC, Australia

David F. Philpott Faculty of Education, Memorial University of Newfoundland, St. John's, NL, Canada

Sylvie Roy Werklund School of Education, University of Calgary, Calgary, AB, Canada

Donald E. Scott Werklund School of Education, University of Calgary, Calgary, AB, Canada

Shelleyann Scott Werklund School of Education, University of Calgary, Calgary, AB, Canada

Ann Sherman Faculty of Education, University of New Brunswick, Fredericton, NB, Canada

About the Editors and Contributors

Editors

Shelleyann Scott is a Professor in the leadership, policy, and governance specialisation in the Werklund School of Education, University of Calgary. She has held numerous leadership roles in Canada and Australia including most recently Associate Dean of Professional and Community Engagement and Director of Graduate Programmes. Shelleyann's work experience spans the contexts of business, government, and medical research and includes tertiary and secondary contexts, professional development, quality assurance, district school leadership, and serving as a business and government consultant. Her research interests include capacity building of leaders, educators, staff, and organisations within the contexts of K–12 and higher education and promoting instructional capacity that encompasses pedagogical strategies, assessment approaches and practices, and learning technologies. Shelleyann has published numerous articles and book chapters and serves on a number of editorial boards.

Donald E. Scott is an Assistant Professor in the leadership, policy, and governance specialisation in the Werklund School of Education, University of Calgary. His professional experience includes university educator, school teacher, and school network administrator. His research interests encompass postsecondary teaching and learning, professional development of teachers and faculty, school and university leadership development, and ICT integration within educational environments. He has authored many journal papers and chapters and is on the editorial board of a number of journals.

Charles F. Webber is Professor and Dean of the Faculty of Continuing Education and Extension, Mount Royal University, Calgary, Alberta, Canada. His current research interest focuses on the influences of school leaders on student achievement and on cross-cultural leadership development including technology-mediated leadership development. During his career as an educator, he has served as a classroom teacher, curriculum consultant, principal, professor, associate dean, and dean. His work appears in international and national journals, and he has served as invited presenter in conferences, seminars, and workshops in North America, Europe, Asia, Africa, the Middle East, New Zealand, and Australia. He is the past academic editor of *Educational Forum*, a scholarly journal published by the American educational honour society Kappa Delta Pi based in Indianapolis.

Contributors

E. Nola Aitken began her career as a schoolteacher teaching students from Kindergarten to Grade 9 for over two decades. Following her teaching career she was a mathematics test development specialist and was further involved in the diagnostic mathematics programme for 5 years at the Student Evaluation Branch, Alberta Education, Canada. Following her work in those two areas, she taught assessment and evaluation of student learning in undergraduate and graduate programmes from 1992 to 2011 in the Faculty of Education at the University of Lethbridge, Alberta. Nola's research areas were student assessment, mathematics education, and higher education.

Nola has received several research grants including an award of a $40,000 research grant to serve as Director to establish the Centre for Assessment Research in Education (CARE). In addition she received a $43,000 Social Sciences and Human Research Count grant for her study on *Native Reserve Students' and Native Public School Students' Ways of Knowing and Doing Mathematics*. Also, Nola was part of a tri-university research team funded by Alberta Education to investigate assessment practices in Alberta.

Nola has published two coedited books and several journal articles and book chapters on assessment, mathematics education, and higher education.

Since she retired as Professor Emerita in 2011, Nola has continued to write in the education field and has pursued recreation activities such as music, art, and golf in Alberta and Phoenix.

Barrie Bennett is Professor Emeritus at the Ontario Institute for Studies in Education at the University of Toronto (OISE/UT). His research work focuses primarily on the design of powerful learning environments for students and teachers through the process of systemic change. He is currently working in districts in three countries (Australia, Ireland, and Canada) on long-term projects related to instructional intelligence and systemic change. Instructional intelligence involves intersecting the current research on curriculum, assessment, and instruction guided by what is known about how students and teachers learn. That intersection is being driven by what is known about change and systemic change. He also assists teachers, schools, and districts with issues related to classroom management and school-wide discipline. Barrie has taught at the elementary and secondary levels, as well as having worked in group homes, prisons, and security units for juvenile offenders. He has written six books: *Cooperative Learning: Where Heart Meet Mind*; *Classroom Management: A Thinking and Caring Approach*; *Beyond Monet: The*

Artful Science of Instructional Integration; *Graphic Intelligence: Playing with Possibilities*; and most recently *Power Plays*. Currently he is completing a text on assessment titled *Assessment: The Missing Think*.

Bronwen Cowie is a Professor of education and Associate Dean of Research in the Faculty of Education at the University of Waikato. She is director of the Wilf Malcolm Institute of Educational Research, which provides the research infrastructure for the Faculty. Bronwen is a former secondary school teacher of maths and physics. Her research interests include assessment for learning, curriculum implementation, student voice, and the role of ICTs in education. She has worked on a number of large national research projects including the *Laptops for teacher's evaluations* and the *Curriculum Exploratory Studies* projects. She has extensive experience in classroom-based research using video, teacher and student interviews, and the analysis of teacher and student work. Her research is characterised by close collaboration with teachers within an action research frame. Bronwen is codirector of the Science Learning Hub, which is a Ministry of Business, Innovation and Employment initiative to make New Zealand science accessible to New Zealand teachers via a multimedia web-based resource.

Johanna de Leeuw is the Director and Assessment Research Consultant for Visible Assessment for Learning Inc., a professional learning organisation dedicated to promoting innovative inquiry and student peer and self-assessment strategies in critical thinking and writing. Johanna completed her PhD in assessment and instructional design and her MA on musically gifted adolescents from the University of Calgary, where she is teaching a winter session graduate course in gifted education. For Calgary Board of Education (CBE), Johanna held positions as system assistant principal (where she coordinated the CBE's Alberta Initiative for School Improvement Cycle 5 project), research specialist, English curriculum leader, humanities teacher, and music and fine arts specialist. She has had over 30 years of teaching experience at all grade levels both with the Calgary Board of Education and Mount Royal Conservatory of Music (now University), Calgary. Johanna continues professional development throughout Alberta in cross-jurisdictional, collaborative assessment practices at the high school level. Johanna has presented at numerous refereed (Canadian Society for the Study of Education, John Hattie's Visible Learning**plus** in Australia, Alberta Assessment Consortium) and non-refereed conferences on the assessment of writing. Johanna is currently designing and developing *PeerVision®*, a formative assessment software application for peer and self-assessment.

Elaine Fournier is an elementary school principal and the coordinator for the New Teacher Induction Programme in her district. Her doctoral study explored the topic of how preservice education affects a novice elementary teacher's experience with mainstreamed special needs students. She is also a researcher and lecturer with interest and expertise in the areas of leadership, special education, and novice teachers. With over 20 years' experience in public education, she has provided leadership in the school board and in the county serving on various committees such as The Principal's Advisory Group for Special Education and the Children's Mental Health Steering Committee.

Sharon Friesen is the Vice Dean and the Associate Dean of Professional and Community Engagement in the Werklund School of Education at the University of Calgary. She is also the president of the Galileo Educational Network. Her research interest is focused on the educational relevance of recent developments in the cognitive and complexity sciences and includes the ways in which K–12 educational structures, curriculum, and learning need to be reinvented for a knowledge/learning society. She has specific interests in and a deep passion for: (i) the promotion of deep intellectual engagement, (ii) the ability to create learning environments that require sustained work with ideas, and (iii) the pervasiveness of networked digital technologies that open up new ways of knowing, leading, teaching, working, and living in the world. She has co-authored three books. Sharon has received numerous awards for her research and teaching practice.

Joan Jeary is retired from academic life and now works as a full-time gardener in her yard and as a companion for her Border collie, Rufus. In her professional life Joan spent over 35 years working as a school psychologist, teacher, principal, district administrator, and university professor. Immediately prior to retirement, Joan served as director of the University of Calgary Applied Educational and Psychological Services and was employed as assistant professor in the Faculty of Education at the University of Calgary.

Val Klenowski is Professor of education at the Queensland University of Technology in Brisbane, Australia. She has research interests in curriculum and assessment reform, evaluation, social justice, assessment, and learning. Recent research and evaluation have been conducted in the fields of fairness and equity in classroom assessment, teacher judgment, and social moderation in the context of standards-driven reform, assessment, and student diversity. Val has published in the fields of assessment, pedagogy, curriculum, and evaluation. She has held academic positions at the Hong Kong Institute of Education and the Institute of Education, University of London, and is currently visiting professor at the University of Bristol.

Leanne Longmire is awaiting the conferral of a master's in education (gifted education) and a postgraduate certificate in gifted education from GERRIC, UNSW. She is an educator and leader in the Department of Education in Western Australia. She has served as an educator for over 25 years and has taught across all socio-economic demographics including elite and extremely low SES schools in private and public education systems. She was appointed *Level 3 Exemplar Teacher* (DETWA) 12 years ago in recognition of the quality of her pedagogical leadership. Her leadership roles have included head of department (English), year coordinator, and student services manager. Her leadership in the service of gifted and talented (G&T) education encompassed the role of academic extension coordinator and challenge programme coordinator (Gifted and Talented Education programme) and spanned two decades. Leanne is a professional developer specialising in G&T education including: identifying characteristics of G&T students, differentiated instruction and assessment, negotiating assessment, and establishing optimal classroom environments. She has also conducted professional development on curriculum and instruction in English. Leanne has served as secretary and conference convener of the Australian Association for Pastoral Care in Education and committee member and conference co-convener of the English Teachers' Association of WA, the Gifted and Talented Children's Association of WA, and the Association for Philosophy in Schools (WA). In pursuing fun strategies to promote higher-order thinking, Leanne, in collaboration with her colleagues, conceptualised a competition in philosophy, coining the *Philosothon*, an interschool philosophy competition which has now spread across Australia and into Asia and the UK. She has received a National Excellence in Teaching Award (NEiTA) and the Western Australian Department of Education and Training West Coast District Award for excellence in teaching for her innovative programmes with gifted and 'at-risk' students.

Leo MacDonald is a full professor at St. Francis Xavier University in Nova Scotia where he teaches science education at the BEd level and curriculum courses at the graduate level. Leo completed an MSc in physics from St. Francis Xavier University in 1985. He then graduated with his BEd from St. Francis Xavier University in 1988 and began teaching high school physics for 2 years. He completed his PhD in science education from the University of Alberta in 1997 and has taught at StFX since 1996 and is heavily involved in science education research, particularly with elementary teachers. He recently completed a million dollar project funded by the Canadian government and is examining ways consultants and principals can support upper elementary teachers in science and mathematics. He also holds an Imperial Oil Grant that is supporting the production of science kits for use in elementary classrooms and the corresponding research.

Michelle McKean completed her undergraduate degree in education at the University of Alberta with a major in elementary education and a minor in educational psychology. She subsequently worked for 3 years as a teacher both in Grade 1 and teaching junior high language arts and social studies in her third year. She then left the classroom to complete a master's degree in education specialising in counselling psychology. During her second year of graduate studies, she worked as a research assistant on the Alberta Student Assessment Study project gathering information for a literature review of educational leadership and general classroom assessment theory and practice. She currently enjoys doing intake interviews for a counselling centre.

Matthew J. Meyer is an Associate Professor of education in the Faculty of Education at St. Francis Xavier University (Antigonish, Nova Scotia, Canada). His areas of research lie primarily in three genres: educational leadership (administrator succession, administration ethics); the use of performing arts in educational research, teacher, and administrator professional development; and drama and theatre arts pedagogy, evaluation, and programme development. He received his PhD in educational administration from McGill University, Montréal. Matthew has presented scholarly papers at local, national, and international conferences and has published articles and chapters in a number of different media. Prior to his university career, he spent over 24 years as a secondary school teacher in theatre arts and English literature, served as a performing arts department head, and directed over 225 theatrical productions. During that time, he toured extensively, nationally, and internationally, for over 16 years with his advanced secondary school drama students. Prior to his teaching and directing career, he was a professional musician and playwright.

Jacqueline Ottmann is Anishinaabe (Saulteaux) originally from Saskatchewan. After elementary and secondary teaching in public, separate, and private systems, Ottmann entered the graduate programme where she received an MEd degree and a PhD after completing research on First Nations spirituality and leadership and First Nations leadership development. Since 2004, Jacqueline has been Associate Professor at the University of Calgary in the Werklund School of Education where she instructs in both the teacher preparation and the graduate programmes. In this context, Ottmann has also been active in research and publications that focus on successes of Indigenous education, language, and literacy, Indigenous leadership and governance, organisational culture and change, and intercultural leadership. Through her research and publications, Ottmann has been invited to present at numerous conferences and consequently has established collegial and collaborative scholarly and educational relationships in Canada, the United States, New Zealand, and Australia.

Dawn Penney gained her PhD from the University of Southampton in 1994 and worked in universities in the UK and Australia before being appointed to the University of Waikato in 2010. Dawn's research and teaching interests are in policy and curriculum development in health and physical education and equity and inclusion in education and sport. Dawn has led research projects focusing on national curriculum developments, senior secondary schooling, pedagogy and assessment in physical education, and the Specialist Sports Colleges initiative in England. Her most recent book is titled *Assessment in Physical Education: A Socio-Cultural Perspective* (Routledge, 2013) and was co-authored with Peter Hay (University of Queensland). In January 2014 Dawn took up a position as professor of physical education and sport pedagogy with Monash University, Australia.

David F. Philpott can best be described as a tireless advocate for vulnerable children and their families, having enjoyed a 30-year career in education and community activism. Ranging from involvement in the closure of Exon House, the province's last residential facility for children with disabilities, in the mid-1980s to recent Pan-Canadian research projects, he has been at the forefront of informing societal approaches to supporting families with exceptional children. He joined MUN's Faculty of Education in 2000 following a 15-year career in the public education system. He has worked in a wide range of teaching and management positions in special education, including private consulting/counselling and educational assessment. He was promoted to full Professor at Memorial University in 2011 and also maintains adjunct professor status with the Faculty of Medicine, University of Calgary, where he teaches on child-centred, family-focused support planning. His research has informed provincial and territorial models of special services, including Nunavut's approach to inclusive education and Newfoundland's recent review of support services. He led the project that resulted in the Innu's attainment of self-government and the development of a bicultural model of education for their children. He has been involved in countless provincial and national organisations, is an international speaker on approaches to supporting children and families, and is a recognised advocate for vulnerable youth. He was actively involved in a 2011 national report on early child care (Early Years Study 3) through his involvement with private family foundations. His latest work with vulnerable children has led to his involvement in Memorial University's Teaching and Learning Framework as lead researcher on supporting academically at-risk students. While his contribution to knowledge creation and dissemination has been outstanding, he continues to maintain a private practice working with children, which grounds him in the reality of families and directs his research and teaching. He holds degrees in education, special education, and educational psychology from Memorial University and a doctorate of education from the University of Calgary.

Sylvie Roy is an Associate Professor in the Werklund School of Education, University of Calgary. Her research interests are in sociolinguistics for change, teaching and learning a second and additional languages, discourse analysis, Francophone minorities, and teaching French in a content-based programme. She was the past president of the Canadian Applied Linguistics Association. She is the chair of the Languages and Diversity Educational Studies in her university. She has written articles related to language ideologies, bilingualism, and linguistic varieties. She is now completing a book on sociolinguistics for change in French immersion.

Ann Sherman is currently the Dean of Education at the Faculty of Education at the University of New Brunswick. She graduated with a bachelor of science education degree in 1977 after which she taught high school mathematics and science for 2 years and then elementary school (Grades K to 6) for 13 years. She was an elementary school administrator in Fort McMurray for the last 3 years of her public school teaching career. She completed a Master of Education degree in curriculum and teaching from the University of New Brunswick and then a PhD in early childhood education in 1997 from the University of Nottingham in the UK. Since 1997 she has taught at three universities in Canada where she has served in several administrative roles. Her research interests include instructional leadership and pedagogical support of teachers. She recently completed two large research projects. One, a million dollar project funded by the Canadian government, examined the ways in which consultants and principals can support upper elementary teachers in science and mathematics. The second project, funded by a $500,000 Imperial Oil Foundation grant, examined the teaching of STEM (science, technology, engineering, and Mathematics) in upper elementary and middle schools. She continues to do individual research on school leadership.

Chapter 1
Reconceptualising Instructional Leadership: Exploring the Relationships Between Leadership, Instructional Design, Assessment, and Student Needs

Shelleyann Scott

Abstract This chapter introduces the notion that current definitions of instructional leadership, while generally useful, need to be reconceptualised to acknowledge the power of assessment in its many forms. In this chapter a discussion of various definitions of instructional leadership is examined to identify common dimensions of this leadership orientation. The argument is further developed in describing the changes in thinking related to instructional design and the pivotal role assessment should now play in designing appropriate and educational learning experiences. Assessment and inclusion are examined as another key dimension, and one that is frequently overlooked or addressed as a separate issue for leaders, rather than an embedded component of instructional leadership. The final dimension offered as part of this new conceptualisation is to examine how assessment influences the motivation of students and their teachers and is used within socio-political debates. Overall these dimensions are discussed in order to highlight their importance and the need for leaders to acknowledge the power of assessment within their instructional leadership responsibilities.

Keywords Globalisation • Instructional leadership • Instructional design • Assessment • Student needs • Inclusion • Power of assessment • Socio-political context • Accountability • Student motivation • Teacher motivation • Assessment efficacy • Professional development • Student learning

---

S. Scott (✉)
Werklund School of Education, University of Calgary,
2500 University Drive NW, Calgary, AB T2N 1N4, Canada
e-mail: sscott@ucalgary.ca

© Springer International Publishing Switzerland 2016
S. Scott et al. (eds.), *Leadership of Assessment, Inclusion, and Learning*,
The Enabling Power of Assessment 3, DOI 10.1007/978-3-319-23347-5_1

1.1 The Complexity of Leading in Contemporary Educational Contexts

Public schools and school systems, as they are presently constituted, are simply not led in ways that enable them to respond to the increasing demands they face under standards-based reform [i.e., schools and school systems should be held accountable for their contributions to student learning]. Further, if schools, school systems, and their leaders respond to standards-based reforms the way they have responded to other attempts at broad scale reform of public education over the past century, they will fail massively and visibly, with an attendant loss of public confidence and serious consequences for public education. The way out of this problem is through the large scale improvement of instruction, something public education has been unable to do to date, but which is possible with dramatic changes in the way public schools define and practice leadership… Schools are being asked by elected officials—policy leaders, if you will—to do things they are largely unequipped to do. School leaders are being asked to assume responsibilities they are largely unequipped to assume, and the risks and consequences of failure are high for everyone, but especially high for children. (Elmore, 2000, p. 2)

This book aims to be a useful source of information for leaders – both formal and informal – who are charged with guiding instructional practices that support learning for all, that is, students and their teachers, in pursuit of enhanced educational outcomes for students. This book has three main themes that illustrate the pragmatics of leading assessment in contemporary schools: what leaders need to know about assessment to create a change vision and promote a culture of success in their schools; understanding how assessment may vary within different disciplines; and highlights the role of assessment within the frame of inclusion. In addition to highlighting some of the excellent information and interesting key points that our authors have included in their chapters, I wanted to examine established understandings of instructional leadership against contemporary expectations on leaders as "leaders of learning" in schools – emphasising the important role that assessment plays but is frequently not well understood.

Educational leaders, teacher-leaders, and teachers are faced with increasingly complex classroom environments, with the complexity demonstrated in terms of: the range of roles and responsibilities demanded of them; the increasing variety of instructional and assessment approaches that can be, and should be, utilised within classrooms; the changing nature of knowledge and curriculum developments; the ever changing, but nevertheless impactful nature of technology (including technology for teaching and learning, management and reporting, communication, and for information literacy); and the considerable variety of the student population encompassing differing ability levels, racial, ethnic, and religious backgrounds, linguistic diversity, socio-economic status, as well as students' prior learning experiences and educational efficacy.

The roles of leaders and teacher-leaders have widened to encompass not only that of head teacher, but now include expectations to fulfill the role of professional developers, managers, marketers, economic forecasters, as well as social workers, counsellors, mediators, negotiators, surrogate parents/caregivers, and so on. Hence, leaders are expected to be all things to all people, accountable to their superiors for the performance of others over whom they may have limited influence, and to do more with fewer resources and supports. This has spawned the leadership field of study, with what Mulford (2008) aptly described as "adjectival" leadership theories that seek to describe and capture these complexities but which actually offer "a monocular view of leadership, by taking just one slice of what leaders do and implying that this is the whole of leadership" (p. iii). Leaders are frequently charged with being instructional leaders; that is, to lead their staff in instruction and assessment within the context of an innovation boom in instruction and assessment strategies and approaches. For example, these innovations may include cooperative learning, inquiry and problem-based learning, discovery learning, project-based learning, models of teaching, universal design for learning, assessment *for* learning, authentic assessment, problem-based assessment, portfolio assessment, and outcomes-based assessment to name a few. Further compounding the complexity of instructional leadership is the rapid development and dissemination of knowledge – the realities of living in the Information Age – and this means that knowledge is changing at a rapid pace, access to new knowledge and information is easier but sources are not always credible or formal, and curriculum is struggling to keep pace with these influences. An essential dimension of the Information Age is technology and this has impacted almost all aspects of leadership and teaching. Technology, with its associated software, hardware, social media, information access and dissemination portals, is ubiquitous in contemporary education contexts and has become integrated in all aspects of leading, teaching, and learning. In addition to these aforementioned complexities, many countries have experienced the impact of migration in pursuit of employment opportunities. Simultaneously, the influence of societal unrest and terrorism has resulted in many fleeing their homes to seek safety and better lives in more stable and/or affluent nations. These economic and societal trends illustrate the impact of globalisation and present new and very different challenges to leaders and educators in most nations including significant changes in the demographics of their societies, naturally reflected in considerably more diverse school populations to those of a decade or more ago. With these global influences it is hardly surprising that society and politicians are demanding schools change to ensure greater success for all with the long-term view of meeting the challenges of uncertain economic futures, professions, and employment markets.

Individually these complexities may be quantifiable and manageable, however as a milieu they can be taxing, and for some educators and leaders, overwhelming – evident in the dwindling pools of aspiring school and educational leaders in many contexts. There is considerable literature that discusses how the world has changed particularly in terms of the expectations societies have of education, but many education systems and schools remain locked into old models of traditional education that simply do not work for our young people in twenty-first century globalised societies. Hence, this means that educators and their leaders must re-examine their knowledge, skills, and attitudes in order to engage with change and innovation that will enable them to nimbly adjust practices and policies to provide optimal learning environments for all learners. Our leaders must re-examine what it means to be a leader of learning and consider how to use their expertise to facilitate and drive positive change.

1.2 Instructional Leadership

Duke, Grogan, Tucker, and Heinecke (2003) believe that while true instructional leadership has been an aspiration of principals for many years, the demands of the job have made it a difficult goal to realise. Studies they reviewed dating back 20 years showed principals express a preference for spending more time on instructional leadership, but analyses of daily activities have consistently shown that the time dedicated to it is limited. Hallinger (2007) notes the absence of any empirical evidence that principals spend more time directly observing and supervising classroom instruction than they did 25 years ago. Australian research on eight Western Australian (Wildy & Dimmock, 1993) and 131 Tasmanian (Mulford et al., 2007b) schools found that principals do not assume instructional leadership responsibilities by themselves, nor do they assume a great degree of responsibility for instructional leadership, especially in secondary schools. In particular, principals are perceived as doing little monitoring of teaching performance or providing recognition for high-quality teaching. … This situation is worrying, given the Queensland School Reform Longitudinal Study [Hayes et al., 2004] finding that improved student outcomes occur when pedagogies are a priority of the school within a culture of care. (Mulford, 2008, pp. 40–41)

1.2.1 Traditional Conceptualisations of Instructional Leadership?

It became clear during the editing of this book that we needed to include a chapter that explored current conceptualisations of instructional leadership, as this is one of the most favoured definitions of leadership which many system administrators and policy makers advocate as the most likely form of leadership to make a significant difference to student success. Hence, I examined some of the key authors in the leadership field to explore their conceptualisations of instructional leadership with the view to identifying the emphasis and role that assessment plays in leading learning. This section provides a brief outline of some of the definitions of instructional leadership.

Mulford (2008) and Siccone (2012) explained that the term instructional leadership emerged from the effective school movement that was popular during the

1970–1980s. During that decade there was concern expressed with the tensions that many principals experienced between their managerial and administrative duties with their leadership responsibilities. Along with this tension was the increasing socio-political concern that education was not meeting the needs of students and society and that change was needed, so attention was turned to how school leaders could focus more closely on the core business of schools – teaching and learning.

Krug (1992) indicated a positive relationship between instructional leadership and student achievement. He identified five main aspects of instructional leadership: *defining a mission* through shaping school goals and purpose; *managing curriculum and instruction* which was important for teachers' planning and execution of appropriate instructional and assessment approaches; *supervising and supporting teaching* as well as providing appropriate *professional development*; and *monitoring student progress* which is more about what teachers can do to support student learning rather than summative forms of assessment. Krug also emphasised instructional climate or culture wherein he stated "effective leaders nurture and develop a climate in which learning is valued" (p. 2).

Similar to Krug's early research, Hallinger (2003) highlighted the same three main aspects of instructional leadership: (1) defining a school mission, (2) managing the instructional programme including supervising and evaluating instruction, coordinating curriculum, and monitoring student progress, and (3) promoting positive school learning climates. Hallinger also included some useful pragmatic advice related to protecting instructional time, promoting effective professional development, providing incentives for teachers to engage with instructional improvement, developing high expectations, and potentially very important, the principal remaining highly visible and invested in learning and enhancement. Robinson, Lloyd, Hohepa, and Rowe (2007) added to Krug's and Hallinger's (2005) conceptualisations of instructional leadership by also including strategic resourcing, leaders promoting professional development by participating with their teachers, and ensuring orderly and supportive environments so teachers have optimal conditions for learning and teaching. Leithwood, Seashore Louis, Anderson, and Wahlstrom (2004) found that leadership was crucial to student success, secondary only to the influence of the classroom teacher. Their categorisation followed the pattern from Krug, Hallinger, and Robinson and her associates with the three elements of: (1) setting directions, (2) developing people, and (3) redesigning the organisation.

Darling-Hammond, Lapointe, Meyerson, and Orr (2010) indicated that the most important elements of instructional leadership revolved around enhancing instructional capacity through professional development. They also indicated that leaders could influence overall staff capacity through more discerning selection processes so that effective teachers were appointed rather than expending time, money, and effort on poorly skilled or less qualified teachers. They too endorsed the importance of promoting positive change through the creation of optimal organisational cultures. The Wallace Foundation (2011) provided a contemporary and comprehensive review of the research in instructional leadership and identified five functions of effective school leaders:

- Shaping a vision of academic success for all students, one based on high standards;
- Creating a climate hospitable to education in order that safety, a cooperative spirit and other foundations of fruitful interaction prevail;
- Cultivating leadership in others so that teachers and other adults assume their part in realising the school vision;
- Improving instruction to enable teachers to teach at their best and students to learn at their utmost; and
- Managing people, data and processes to foster school improvement. (p. 4)

Hoy and Hoy (2013) explored instructional leadership and identified many dimensions of psychology as it applied to teaching, learning, and leading. They listed seven elements of instructional leadership which resonated with understanding the influence that motivation has on teachers, students, and school cultures. Principals need to take the lead in celebrating educational achievement among students which reinforces positive school cultures, as well as leaders developing a "culture of optimism" where teacher collective efficacy is high, student collaboration around academic tasks is the norm, and perseverance "in spite of obstacles" is encouraged (p. 3). For example, they indicated academic excellence should be a strong motivating force in the school citing research where academic emphasis was linked to student achievement. They also underlined the importance of leaders' high but realistic expectations and the belief that all can learn as crucial to setting the tone of the school. Similar to the other authors in instructional leadership, Hoy and Hoy reinforced the importance of pursuing teacher instructional excellence and continuous improvement and capacity, as teachers are the individuals who have the most direct influence on student learning and motivation. Leaders must ensure that resourcing is in place for maximum benefit in the classroom. Their final three elements focused on leaders' knowledge and intellectual capacity and their motivation to "remain abreast of the latest developments in teaching, learning, motivation, classroom management, and assessment, as well as share best practices in each area with teachers" (p. 3).

Therefore, from these varied definitions of instructional leadership there is considerable alignment between the elements identified as crucial to effective leaders of learning; that is, the need to have a clear vision for student achievement, ensuring optimal and ordered schooling environments, professional development designed to enhance teachers' instructional capacities, and the establishment of positive school cultures focused on high expectations and quality learning outcomes for students. Other aspects of instructional leadership that were identified by some but not others touched on leaders' capacity to motivate staff and facilitate high teacher efficacy (regarding the impact of instructional leadership behaviours and teacher efficacy also see Calik, Sezgin, Kavgaci, & Cagatay Kilinc, 2012), leaders' ability to obtain the necessary resources for teaching and learning, and to monitor school and curricular improvement efforts and effectiveness, which implies a level of assessment literacy and evidenced-based decision making.

What is interesting in reviewing these definitions that have stood the test of time is that 'assessment' appears to be largely subsumed into assumptions about teachers' instructional capacity and curricular foci. Considering this book is devoted to assessment and in particular what leaders, both formal and informal, need to know about assessment in order to be instructional leaders in a broader sense, I searched for references to instructional leadership that did overtly mention or emphasise assessment. To this end I found that most definitions and explanations ignored or simply mentioned assessment in passing almost as a tack-on concept loosely connected with instruction or discussed in relation to monitoring and accountability measures. However, Darling-Hammond et al. (2010), Cordeiro and Cunningham (2013), and not surprisingly Stiggins and Duke (2008), given their considerable research and interest in assessment, did overtly emphasise and in some cases explain indepth, the link between instructional leadership and assessment.

Drawing upon Leithwood and Jantzi's and others' research, Darling-Hammond et al. (2010) discussed instructional leadership in terms of the following and highlighted the differences to more traditional conceptualisations of leadership with its focus on more transactional, administrative duties:

- Working with teachers to enable them to be more effective in their classrooms including supervision, modelling, evaluation, and other forms of support;
- Providing resources and professional development focused on enhancing teachers' instructional approaches;
- Coordinating and evaluating curriculum, instruction, and assessment;
- Regularly monitoring student progress, which implies considering student assessment as an important aspect but also being able to use data to inform teaching and learning and school improvement efforts; and
- Developing and maintaining shared norms and expectations with stakeholders.

Similarly, Cordeiro and Cunningham (2013) defined instructional leadership as:

> Instructional leadership is focused on curriculum and instructional development; staff development; instructional supervision; program, teacher, and **student evaluation**; research and experimentation; provision of resources; and the continuous improvement of teaching and learning.... Research tends to suggest that principals must first and primarily be the instructional leader, but not at the expense of effectively managing the school. (p. 121, emphasis added)

In their exploration of the theme of effective leadership, their work went on to include entire sections that explicate curriculum development and assessment, programme improvement and evaluation, and assessing student progress – discussing portfolios and exhibitions, assessing student performance, reporting student progress, and presenting student outcomes to the community. Hence, their perception is a more well-rounded understanding of the role assessment plays in instructional leadership effectiveness.

Stiggins and Duke (2008) devoted an entire article to linking instructional leadership directly with assessment leadership. They too argued that curriculum, instruction, evaluation and supervision of teaching does not fully encapsulate true instructional leadership and that what is just as crucial is "an understanding of the role of sound assessment in efforts to improve teaching and learning" (p. 286). They continued by stating that "the well-prepared principal is ready to ensure that assessments are of high quality and used effectively" – pivotal in promoting effective teacher instruction (p. 286). Similar to Halverson, Grigg, Prichett, and Thomas' (2007) perceptions that principals must "build data-driven instructional systems" and "develop a collaborative cycle for collecting, reflecting on, and acting on feedback data", Stiggins and Duke also indicated principals must understand the different users and uses of assessment information. For example, uses include classroom-level assessment for informing teaching and learning, and programme-level assessment for informing teacher leaders and teams about programme effectiveness; while instructionalaccountability and policy-level assessments inform school, district, and community leaders about learners, school success and needs, and resources needed to support the work of schools. They indicated that many principals did not have sufficient background knowledge about sound assessment from preservice education which may be further compounded by a lack of professional development to fill this deficit. They also contended that many professors who offer graduate programs may not have sufficient background in sound assessment theory and practice to offer or even recognise the importance of leading assessment within the leadership of learning. They posited that there may be the mistaken notion that assessment is not within the domain of the principal, rather:

> conventional wisdom in schools has been that 'assessment people,' not principals, do the assessment work. ... This belief, too, is unfounded ... the classroom level falls to teachers under the direct supervision of their principal. This means principals must be sufficiently assessment literate to fulfill these growing responsibilities. If they are not, it is a barrier to sound practice ... the answer is to promote an understanding of sound assessment practice among school leaders ... The stronger the assessment literacy background for new and practicing school leaders, the more able they will be to develop or arrange for the professional development their colleagues need to find remedies to their problems. (pp. 289–290)

Hence, when considering the many and varied definitions and explanations of instructional leadership, assumptions are clearly made related to leaders' understanding of assessment, their capacity to be assessment leaders, their ability to use a range of data to inform their own and to guide teachers' decision making, and to perceive the important motivational role assessment plays for both students and teachers. For example, assumptions include that leaders must have a deep understanding of: the crucial role of assessment in the instructional design process; how various forms of data are important in monitoring programme effectiveness; the uses of different forms of assessment; the dangers of misusing data; the usefulness of using data to evaluate staff instructional effectiveness; and to be able to guide professional development programming to meet staff needs. However, in many authors' discussions on instructional leadership these direct linkages to assessment are not overt or highlighted. To further compound this ambiguity within conceptualisation of instructional leadership, we found in previous research that many leaders and teachers lacked confidence with assessment in its many forms, frequently had limited understanding of varied assessment purposes and influences on students', teachers', parents', and leaders' motivations, and decision-making capacities

(Webber, Aitken, Lupart, & Scott, 2009). This is not to say that teachers and leaders are to blame for these deficiencies in understanding and capacity as we also found that preservice teacher preparation programmes, professional development, as well as leadership development programming are frequently deficit in the depth and breadth of assessment content (Scott, Webber, Aitken, & Lupart, 2011). Even worse, some programmes may include skewed content that underpins prevailing political rhetoric of the day (Webber, Lupart, & Scott, 2012) rather than seeking praxis between scholarly rigorous theory and practical applications aimed at creating thought provoking and constructive debate and change – important for reinforcing the fabric of civil societies (Webber & Scott, 2010).

We know that the principalship is a highly complex and challenging position and that system leaders expect more from school leaders than ever before, so I felt it was important to consider some of the pragmatics principals need to know in order to be effective leaders of learning in contemporary school environments. Therefore, in this text we have included chapters that explicate some of the common terminology related to assessment and provide a firm evidence base for these terms to ensure that leaders are working with and using accurate information when leading their staff discussions. We also included a chapter on how cooperative learning and assessment align, as cooperative learning is a key constructivist approach that is pervasive within all levels of education. We also felt that it would be useful for leaders to have exposure to classroom assessment within the disciplines; this is important as most leaders generally only had one discipline specialisation and limited exposure to others when they were teachers, but as leaders they are expected to lead all disciplines and year levels within their leadership portfolio. The most contemporary theme, and one that many teachers as well as leaders find extremely difficult, is assessment within an inclusionary classroom, as this means assessment needs to be considered as an important component of differentiation to meet students' particular needs. With this in mind, the following sections aim to highlight additional dimensions of assessment that should be overtly included in conceptualisations of instructional leadership; for example, elements in instructional design with a particular emphasis on the role assessment plays; how leaders need to understand the motivational influence that assessment exerts on students and teachers within fraught socio-political contexts; and assessment dimensions within the inclusionary class setting.

1.3 Understanding the Role of Assessment in Instructional Leadership for Enhancing Student Outcomes

As leaders of learning, principals need to have a clear understanding of the importance assessment plays within the instructional design process (see Fig. 1.1). While many principals understand this from their own teaching background, in the past the focus has been on increasing student engagement through more interesting and fun learning experiences and activities, technologies, and resources. This was important and valuable as many students find school boring and irrelevant to the world of

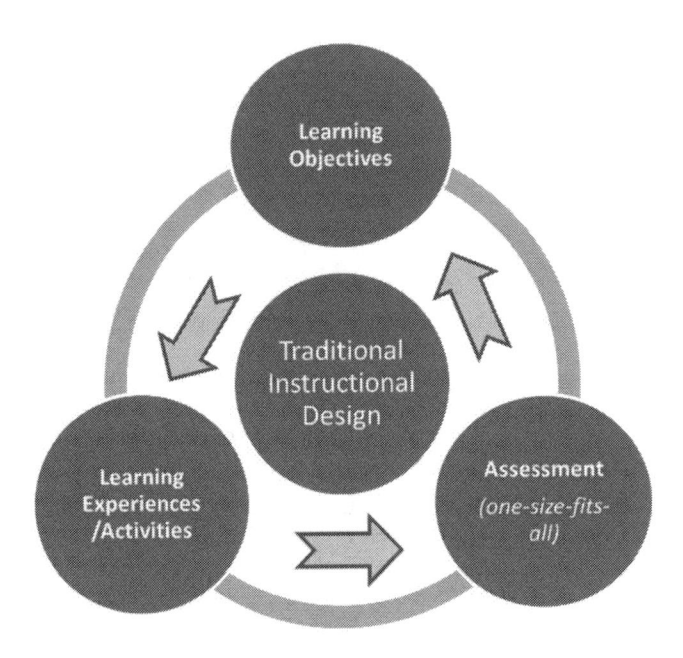

Fig. 1.1 Traditional conceptualisations of instructional design

work; therefore it is important to consider learning experiences as crucial to student engagement. This is discussed at length in Bennett's chapter on cooperative learning but he also highlights the importance of teachers demonstrating "instructional intelligence" – having a wide repertoire of instructional strategies **and** a deep understanding of how these complex strategies interplay with assessment within the instructional process. While a focus on engaging learning experiences is not wrong, this may inadvertently relegate the assessment of the objectives to that of testing the knowledge students should have attained as a result of these exciting learning experiences. In these traditional conceptualisations of instructional design (see Fig. 1.1), learning objectives represent an 'input foci' wherein the teacher identified, from the curriculum documents or syllabus, what he/she was going to teach (rather than what students needed to learn or be able to do), then selected learning experiences and resources that would support students' learning, and then identified a way to test students' understandings of the objectives (Arends, 2012; Barry & King, 1998; Smith & Ragan, 2005).

More recently though, with a focus on assessment as an educative component (as part of the assessment *for* learning and assessment *as* learning movement) there has been increased scrutiny of the important role assessment plays within the learning cycle (Black, Harrison, Lee, & Wiliam, 2004; Earl, 2007; Earl & Katz, 2006; Sackney & Mergel, 2007). Figure 1.2 displays the subtle differences in emphasis wherein the teacher identifies from the curriculum what outcomes (output foci) in terms of knowledge, skills, and attitudes/attributes the students need to attain and demonstrate, then selects or designs educative and innovative assessments that will

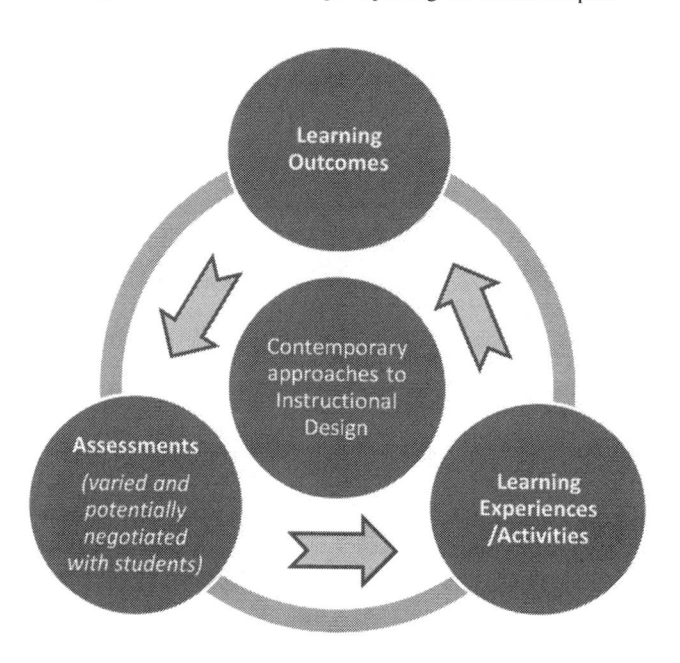

Fig. 1.2 Contemporary conceptualisations of instructional design

engage students in the learning process but also enable them to demonstrate their learning outcomes, followed by the learning experiences and/or activities that align with the outcomes and assessment tasks. It should be noted that this is not a one-size-fits-all approach, so teachers would consider the varied needs and capacities of the students in the class within the design process. In traditional instructional approaches the teacher designed a lesson, taught it, and if the students did not learn or learn well, or demonstrate their learning adequately, that was deemed to be the shortcoming of the students and a natural phenomenon in the classroom. This is no longer an option for contemporary educators or permissible for leaders who must account for the learning of all students in the school.

An example of this more contemporary approach to instructional design is articulated in Friesen's chapter in this book where she examines the Universal Design for Learning (UDL) instructional design approach and articulates the role of assessment as embedded in the learning – therefore assessment becomes an educative process – and enables students "*multiple means of expression*, to provide learners alternatives for demonstrating what they know" (Friesen, Chap. 6). This UDL was a key approach to addressing the complexity of inclusion and facilitates teachers' consideration of students' needs within the design and execution of teaching, learning, and assessment. Similarly, Wiggins and McTighe (2005) coined the phrase "backward design" in relation to the process whereby a teacher identifies the end goal(s) or outcome(s) (what students need to know or be able to do and what should be assessed), then identifies the evidence (forms of assessment) that will best enable the teacher to identify if the students have achieved the outcome(s), and subsequently the learning experiences students will need in order to support the attainment of the learning outcome(s). Both UDL and Backward Design indicate a reversal of traditional conceptualisations of the importance of assessment in the instructional design process, wherein designing for desired learning is based upon the end point and places assessment, preferably authentic assessment, in the spotlight as pivotal in the instructional design process. Hence, in order for principals to promote these more enlightened approaches to teaching, learning, and assessment, they themselves need to have not only a reasonable understanding of these nouveauinstructional design approaches, but also the terminology to be able to effectively communicate their expectations for assessment "renovation", as described by McKean and Aitken in their chapter.

1.4 Assessment and Inclusion

The emphasis in today's world is on all young people, not some. Access, participation and equity take on new meaning; they make economic sense just as much as they accord with the dictates of common justice. The consignment to marginality of large numbers of people, young or old, by an outdated education model represents an enormous economic waste. … It also exacts an enormous cost on society that simply cannot be afforded. It is no longer acceptable or defensible on economic, social or moral grounds. It is time as a nation we admitted that, identified the real causes and stopped putting the blame for failure on the victims… The core business of schooling is learning, and the quality of learning experienced by all learners should be the standard against which performance is measured. The product of schooling is not the student, but … about developing the knowledge, skills and values students need to be successful in their lives after school, including within the labour market. (Hood, 1998, pp. 19–22)

As discussed in the introduction to this chapter, principals are leading in complex school environments which are very different to those of their counterparts of even two decades ago. For example, with globalisation we have seen the impact of worker migration and international terror (refugees) wherein the student demographic in many Western schools is now highly diverse in terms of race, home language, intellectual capacity, prior educational background, and religion. Additionally, with many countries establishing legislation to include students with special needs in regular classrooms, many educators are facing increasing demands to meet diverse student learning needs for which many teachers were never adequately trained. The other major impact on education has been the advent of information communication technologies which have radically influenced the way teachers teach, assess, and access information; monitor and report on student progress; communicate with students and parents and their colleagues; and accommodate for student intellectual or physical challenges. Therefore, leaders of learning are now expected to be leaders of learning for **all** students.

What is the difference, then, in being a leader of learning and a leader of learning for **all** students? Principals now need to have different attitudes, knowledge, and skills to meet the varied needs of students within their care. Previously we identified that "leaders must have a strong moral compass that guides their approaches to leading positive change … the values framework held by educational leaders must be informed by theoretical and empirical knowledge about current assessment practices and policies" (Webber, Scott, Aitken, Lupart, & Scott, 2013, p. 12). We also identified in our expansion of the 4L (Life-Long Learning Leader) framework (Scott, Scott, & Webber, 2016) that assessment leaders needed to enhance their ethic of care as a dimension of social justice alongside conceptualisations of fairness and equity:

> School leaders must navigate and mediate contentions between students, parents, teachers, superordinates, and policy decision makers, all the while maintaining an ethic of care and commitment to social justice for all students. … There is no doubt that the ethic of care, in concert with leaders' knowledge of and belief in fairness and equity, is influential in establishing authentic leadership in order to build trusting relationships with students, teachers, parents/caregivers, and the wider community. …Equity is one of the most poorly understood concepts in assessment with non-equitable approaches frequently rationalised by teachers in terms of: preparation of students for the workplace, teaching life skills, perceptions of being seen to be fair to all in the class by treating all the same, and so on. Leaders must understand that equity is not the same as equality, indeed, while equality means being treated the same as everyone else, equity means meeting the unique needs of the individual student which may be quite different to others in the class. Leaders need to be able to understand and communicate this simple complexity in order to educate others, especially teachers, who do not perceive the nuances of this 'equity/equality' construct. In leading their school to examine current assessment practices and become more innovative, to interrogate their assumptions, and resolve conflict that can arise over assessment issues, leaders need to also have courage and commitment – courage to stand against the prevailing traditions or norms and commitment to protecting the vulnerable, usually the students – to ensure that educators do the right thing founded upon deep theoretical understandings of principled assessment. (n.p.)

In our chapter on leading assessment for gifted and talented students (Scott, Scott, & Longmire) we identified that:

> to expect an average principal to be an expert on gifted education, psychological testing for giftedness, or to be highly competent in teaching G&T students him or herself is unreasonable. What we do expect is for principals to know enough about differentiated instruction and assessment to be able to select the optimal teacher to support these students within the school.

So leaders of learning must have a strong ethic of care and be reasonably aware of student differences, know how to seek assistance in identifying particular problems, and be proactive in selecting the right teacher for the job or providing appropriate and targeted professional development to enhance teacher instructional and assessment capacity. This was a theme which resonated in most of the inclusionary chapters in this book.

Along with notions of fairness and equity and how these may play out in the classroom and within assessment approaches, it is also important to include technology in this discussion. For example, some teachers reject the idea of using technologies to support students' learning and/or for accommodating students' learning and assessment needs, and may actually justify this as unfair to the other students. Hence, leaders need to have a clear understanding of not only innovative forms of assessment that will promote student learning, engagement, and motivation, but also they need to be aware of the power of various technologies, and advocate for their use in supporting students, especially those with special needs who **need** to use these technologies, in their learning and assessment tasks. Indeed, Friesen discusses the uses of technology within the UDL approach stating: "effective use of technology enables all students to represent, express and engage with ideas in multiple ways not generally seen in conventional classrooms", while Bausch and Hasselbring (2005) posit that "technology can be the difference between students with special needs sitting in a classroom watching others participate and all students participating fully" (p. 9). Therefore, there is more to assessment leadership than simply facilitating teachers' development of knowledge and expertise in innovative and sound assessment.

In traditional descriptions of instructional leaders' responsibilities such as: "managing curriculum and instruction" (Krug, 1992, p. 5); "managing the instructional program including supervising and evaluating instruction, coordinating curriculum, and monitoring student progress" (Hallinger, 2003, p. 332); and "improving instruction to enable teachers to teach at their best and students to learn at their utmost and managing people, data and processes to foster school improvement" (Wallace Foundation, 2011, p. 4), the nuances of overseeing optimal inclusionary efforts are couched in vague terms of enabling students to learn at their utmost or monitoring student progress. This is a significant oversight in conceptualisations and descriptions of instructional leadership whereby leading inclusionary strategies and differentiated assessment is lumped in with curriculum, instruction, and assessment and yet requires vastly different skills and attitudes to traditional forms of teaching and assessment.

1.5 Understanding Assessment Motivation, Learning, and the Socio-political Context

Assessment is one of the most contentious and emotive subjects in education (Webber et al., 2012). It has the power to rouse anger and frustration or alternatively excitement or satisfaction in students and teachers alike. The other powerful aspect of assessment is its capacity to influence motivation. Drawing upon Fulmer and Frijter's (2009) definition Snowman, McCown, and Biehler (2012) defined motivation as "the selection, persistence, intensity, and direction of behavior" (p. 367) and within a more pragmatic frame of reference "motivation is simply the willingness of a person to expend a certain amount of effort to achieve a particular goal under a particular set of circumstances" (p. 367). This section examines the other aspect that is not overtly included in current understandings of instructional leadership; that is, the motivational dimensions of assessment and how these should be considered and can be harnessed by innovative instructional leaders. It is well-established that assessment has a significant influence on students' motivation to engage with or withdraw from their learning and assessment tasks (Brookhart, 2004; Crooks, 1988; Stiggins, Arter, Chappuis, & Chappuis, 2005). Linked to motivation is students' efficacy, and assessment can also influence this psychological dimension as well (Chow & Yong, 2013; Panadero, Tapia, & Huertas, 2012). Bandura (1986, 1997) defined self-efficacy as a judgment of one's ability to organise and execute given types of performances. He indicated that even though an individual may possess adequate skills to successfully perform, it is his/her personal belief about his/her ability that may impact the consequent performance. Therefore, success in a particular performance will motivate the student, through experiencing the positive reinforcement of success, to persevere and/or to expand their performance to other tasks. In other words, success breeds success with a resultant increase in self-efficacy beliefs. Similarly in considering teachers, classroom and standardised assessment are also used within socio-political debates related to system performance and accountability, and as a corollary can influence teacher motivation and efficacy related to their teaching and assessment approaches (Harris & Brown, 2009; Wang, Beckett, & Brown, 2006). Hence, motivation and assessment are important elements of instructional leadership as these influence student learning, engagement, and perseverance, as well as teachers' instructional capacities and willingness to engage in professional development, and innovative practice.

1.5.1 Assessment and Student Motivation for Learning, Perseverance, Efficacy

Given Bandura's (1986, 1997) definition of self-efficacy as articulated previously when we consider students and assessment, we see the seriousness of ensuring that teachers utilise not only fair and equitable assessment approaches, but also include a range of different forms of assessment within their classroom assessment regime so that students have a greater chance of success and can engage in interesting and educative assessment processes. If teachers work with students to develop clear outcome criteria, rubrics, and provide assessment tasks that engage students in interesting and informative processes with different assessment tasks and students achieve a measure of success, these factors will foster positive self-efficacy beliefs and encourage positive motivation to engage with the learning and assessment tasks. Conversely, if students' experiences of assessment are ambiguous, frightening, or unfair, it is likely they will perceive assessment processes to be constant sources of failure and degradation, which will reinforce negative self-efficacy and may lead to a lack of motivation to engage with school in general, and learning specifically.

There is considerable discussion in assessment literature that lays blame for fear of assessment and disenfranchisement of students at the door of standardised assessments (Beghetto, 2005; Gipps, 1999; Haertel, 2013; Harris & Brown, 2009; Klinger, Maggi, & D'Angiulli, 2011; Wang et al., 2006). As Gipps (1999) stated, "the way students respond to assessment is subject to social and cultural influences" (p. 355). Many authors discuss standardised tests as "high stakes" for students and teachers, which in the case of final exams that are used for gatekeeping processes is true; however, Crooks (1988) seminal analysis of assessment impacting motivation stated that classroom assessment has the potential to exert considerably more influence over students' motivation than a one-shot standardised test. The significant motivational import of classroom assessment is largely attributable to: the amount of time expended on classroom assessment compared with standardised tests; the greater proportion of impact on the overall grade; issues related to the validity and reliability of teacher judgments; and the opportunities these offer for learning, feedback, and greater cultural sensitivity (Bolt, 2011; Crooks, 1988; Harlen, 2005; Klenowski, 2009; Tierney, Simon, & Charland, 2011). Therefore, it is crucial to students' academic and emotional wellbeing and efficacy for classroom assessment to be an educative, engaging, and viable activity. This means teachers must have the knowledge and expertise with both their curriculum content but also in a range of assessment approaches including more innovative and authentic forms of assessment. It also means teachers must be skilled in devising and marking assessments as well as making sound and fair judgments about students. Hence, teachers must have assessment efficacy based upon sound understandings of optimal assessment practices.

1.5.2 Assessment and Teacher Motivation for Optimal Instructional Design and Professional Growth

Teaching is hard work. Teachers develop their approaches to teaching out of their prior experience as students and out of their experience in solving problems on a daily basis in their classrooms. These approaches to teaching tend to be relatively stable once they are established, and they are relatively immune except in rare cases, to exhortations from policymakers and administrators to teach differently. Teachers are now being asked by education reformers to teach more ambitious content to larger and larger numbers of student, but these reforms do not provide teachers with access to the knowledge or support they need to practice differently. Simply changing the structure of relationships in schools does not change the knowledge of practice that teachers bring to their work. The primary problem of school reform, then, is knowledge and its development, use, and deployment in the classroom. (Elmore, 2007, p. 195)

We know that teachers are the most powerful influence in the classroom – for good or bad. We also know that most teachers enter teaching with humanistic and altruistic motivations – that is, to be able to help their students to learn and be successful. Teachers though are not immune to the influences of the socio-political contexts within which they work; hence many feel inadequate or emasculated by the repeated calls for accountability, teacher evaluation, and demands for increased professionalism. Frequently, it is teachers' capacity to assess appropriately, fairly, and innovatively that comes under scrutiny when there are discussions about teacher effectiveness and yet much of the professional development that is available focuses on instructional rather than assessment strategies. This focus on instruction provides teachers the opportunity to play to their strengths and interests and to further neglect their weaknesses, creating a cyclical instructional design problem. That is, as described earlier in the chapter, if teachers are to identify the desired outcomes first, then consider the assessment approaches that best match the selected outcomes before moving to considerations of learning experiences, they will encounter difficulties unless they have expertise in more authentic and variable assessment approaches.

To further compound this problem in deficient professional learning opportunities, we found that many teachers articulated concerns with the amount of emphasis on optimal assessment, particularly the pragmatics of designing effective assessments, within their preservice education programmes (Scott et al., 2011). Teachers who do not perceive their assessment knowledge and expertise to be comprehensive tend to have poor assessment efficacy. This may lead teachers to continue to use safe and familiar traditional forms of assessment rather than taking a more risky pathway by venturing into trialling authentic and problem-based assessment forms. It also creates an assessment culture of isolation and defensiveness rather than one of transparency, open communication, and innovation. Therefore teachers' motivation levels are influenced by their self-efficacy with assessment. The higher their efficacy, the greater their motivation to design more engaging and optimal, but sometimes complex and challenging, forms of assessment. The implication for instructional leaders then, is to determine the assessment capacity of the staff and to provide systematic and supportive professional development opportunities that facilitate teachers' assessment efficacy – a precursor to enhanced teacher motivation to adopt more innovative and engaging assessment approaches. This is a theme we described in our previous chapter on the assessment knowledge, skills and attitudes (KSA) learning journey as our updated thoughts on expanding the 4L – Life-Long Learning Leader Framework (Scott et al., 2016).

1.5.3 Assessment and the Socio-political Context Linked with Accountability

Gipps' (1999) commentary about the influence of social and cultural context on assessment resonates as a truism within most Western societies. We see many emotive discussions surrounding testing and school and teacher accountability with some stakeholders advocating for standardised testing programmes as a valuable measure of system and curriculum effectiveness, and national competitiveness;

while opponents argue that the inherent evaluative nature of standardised tests damages student morale due to potential punitive results of these "high stakes" tests and the eroding impact on teacher professionalism and autonomy. It is refreshing to find authors within the assessment literature who explicate balanced arguments related to the purpose, value, and uses of standardised tests and classroom assessment particularly within societies that are increasingly demanding high quality education systems, excellence in leadership, expert teachers, and positive outcomes for all students (Barber, 2004; Brookhart, 2004; Garner, 2013; Harlen, 2005; Klinger et al., 2011). Hence it is important for instructional leaders to understand the socio-cultural influences that are in play within their educational context and to understand the motivational impact these influences are likely to exert on their teachers, students, and community. As knowledge is power, effective instructional leaders are able to articulate and explain these debates and harness these to influence teacher engagement with professional development that will promote their assessment and instructional capacities. This is not just about traditional conceptualisations of instructional leadership – that is, supporting and organising professional development or influencing school missions and cultures and operations – it is about having a deep understanding of the implications and importance assessment plays within socio-political debates and how these connect to the day-to-day work of teaching, learning, and leadership in schools. It is the wise instructional leader who is able to harness the positive motivational influence of these arguments to create the impetus for change within their school, and to create an environment where balanced dialogue is possible, along with a culture of innovation and experimentation for the ultimate benefit of students.

1.6 Future Directions

Renaissance leaders recognize that current and past policies may represent decades-old institutional needs and may no longer be appropriate. In fact, new leaders will seek constructive disruption of practices and policies that may institutionalize damaging or limiting approaches to schooling and which should be interrogated for contemporary relevance. Included in the role of constructive disruptor is the ability to differentiate the need for sustainability from the need for change. (Webber & Scott, 2013, p. 102)

No one can deny that the concept of instructional leadership is a laudable leadership orientation for all principals considering its emphasis on learning as the core business of schools, and on student achievement and teacher instructional capacity. What remains contentious is whether leaders are able to expend significant amounts of time engaged in instructional leadership related activities with the overriding system demands for paperwork, people management, and administrivia. For example, Elmore (2000) stated that "administration in education, then, has come to mean not the management of instruction but the management of the structures and processes around instruction" where he described leaders' roles as "buffering" or "protecting teachers from outside intrusions into their highly uncertain and murky work", and secondly creating "the appearance of rational management of the technical core [the core business of teaching and learning], so as to allay the uncertainties of the public about the actual quality of legitimacy of what is happening in the technical core" (p. 6). Duke et al. (2003) also identified that instructional leadership was a difficult role to assume as the management elements of school operations tended to crowd out time for other instructionally focused activities. Wildy and Dimmock (1993) also indicated that principals did not tend to assume sole responsibility for instructional leadership rather this was distributed to others particularly within secondary schools. So clearly, instructional leadership is a pragmatically contentious form of leadership which may need to be shared with other leaders in the school.

While I wholeheartedly agree that 'instructional leadership' as: *shaping a vision of academic success for all students, creating a climate hospitable to education, cultivating distributed leadership, improving instruction, and managing people, data and processes to foster school improvement* (Wallace Foundation, 2011) are all critical, I also feel these elements fall short in one crucial aspect – the focus on the importance of assessment. I would argue that instructional leadership definitions need to be reconceptualised with an overt lens on the power of assessment, as opposed to a general focus on the importance of instruction. For example, the powerful role assessment plays ininstructional design is crucial to understanding not only how to design optimal opportunities for student learning but also overtly acknowledges the dominant motivational influence that assessment can exert. It is also an important consideration in terms of leading inclusion. Many educators are still struggling with the pragmatics of differentiation and do not necessarily perceive the pivotal role assessment plays. The authors in this book articulate the importance of valid assessment data that informs and provides the impetus for continuing with change initiatives and for meeting the needs of the varied student demographic in inclusive classrooms. Indeed, Prytula, Noonan, and Hellsten (2013) indicated that a new focus on standardised assessments appeared to have catalysed some principals towards instructional leadership activities, although this was not necessarily widespread. They reported that "Some responded by using the assessment to improve practice, some responded by empowering teachers to do the same, and others responded by buffering their staffs from the change" (n.p.), indicating that instructional leadership remains an elusive capacity for many principals; however, focusing on assessment can be a force for positive change. Hence, I agree with Newton, Tunison, and Viczko's (2010) contention:

> Principals in this study suggested that the current context of large scale assessment and accountability has resulted in their roles being redefined. In particular, they suggested that it is the principal's role to teach other staff members about assessment, to advocate for assessment, and to organize and manage data. We argue that these emerging roles have the potential to redefine instructional leadership in schools. (n.p.)

As a final thought this book aims to provide formal leaders and those who have assumed distributed leadership roles with useful information and guidance in using assessment to drive positive educational change in their schools. We have focused on the *power of assessment* to: guide leaders' understanding about assessment terminology; the role of assessment within instructional design processes as well across the disciplines; to increase student and teacher motivation; to provide valuable information to monitor change efforts and to celebrate achievements; and to inform effective inclusionary approaches. I trust the chapters we, as editors, have selected for inclusion in this volume will be helpful in your change efforts and will expand your expertise in your own teaching and leadership practices.

References

Arends, R. (2012). *Learning to teach* (10th ed.). Boston, MA: McGraw-Hill Companies.
Bandura, A. (1986). *Social foundations of thought and action: A social cognitive theory*. Englewood Cliffs, NJ: Prentice-Hall.
Bandura, A. (1997). *Self-efficacy: The exercise of control*. New York, NY: W.H. Freeman and Company.
Barber, M. (2004). The virtue of accountability: System redesign, inspection, and incentives in the era of informed professionalism. *Journal of Education, 185*(1), 7–900.
Barry, K., & King, L. (1998). *Beginning teaching and beyond* (3rd ed.). Katoomba, Australia: Social Sciences Press.
Bausch, M., & Hasselbring, T. (2005). Using AT: Is it working? *Thresholds, 2*(1), 7–9.
Beghetto, R. A. (2005). Does assessment kill student creativity? *The Educational Forum, 69*(3), 254–263. doi:10.1080/00131720508984694.
Black, P., Harrison, C., Lee, C., & Wiliam, D. (2004). Working inside the black box: Assessment for learning in the classroom. *Phi Delta Kappan, 86*(1), 8–21.
Bolt, S. (2011). Making consistent judgements. A professional development program based on using teacher judgement to assess student attainment of systemic achievement targets. *Educational Forum, 75*(2), 157–172. doi:10.1080/00131725.2011.552694.
Brookhart, S. M. (2004). Classroom assessment: Tensions and intersections in theory and practice. *Teachers College Record, 106*(3), 429–458. doi:10.1111/j.1467-9620.2004.00346.x.
Calik, T., Sezgin, F., Kavgaci, H., & Cagatay Kilinc, A. (2012). Examination of relationships between instructional leadership of school principals and self-efficacy of teachers and collective teacher efficacy. *Educational Sciences: Theory and Practice, 12*(4), 2498–2504.
Chow, S. J., & Yong, B. C. S. (2013). Secondary school students' motivation and achievement in combined science. *US-China Education Review, 3*(4), 213–228.
Cordeiro, P. A., & Cunningham, W. G. (2013). *Educational leadership. A bridge to improved practice* (5th ed.). Upper Saddle River, NJ: Pearson Education.
Crooks, T. J. (1988). The impact of classroom evaluation practices on students. *Review of Educational Research, 58*(4), 438–481.
Darling-Hammond, L., Lapointe, M., Meyerson, D., & Orr, M. T. (2010). *Preparing principals for a changing world: Lessons from effective school leadership programs*. San Francisco, CA: Jossey-Bass.
Duke, D., Grogan, M., Tucker, P., & Heinecke, W. (Eds.). (2003). *Educational leadership in an age of accountability: The Virginia experience*. Albany, NY: State University of New York Press.
Earl, L. (2007). Assessment as learning. In W. D. Hawley (Ed.), *The keys to effective schools: Educational reform as continuous improvement* (2nd ed., pp. 85–98). Thousand Oaks, CA: Corwin.
Earl, L. M., & Katz, S. (2006). *Rethinking classroom assessment with purpose in mind: Assessment for learning, assessment as learning, assessment of learning*. Winnipeg, MB, Canada: Manitoba Education. Retrieved from http://www.edu.gov.mb.ca/k12/assess/wncp/rethinking_assess_mb.pdf.

Elmore, R. (2000). *Building a new structure for school leadership*. Washington, DC: The Albert Shanker Institute.

Elmore, R. (2007). Local school districts and instructional improvements. In W. D. Hawley & D. L. Rollie (Eds.), *The keys to effective schools: Educational reform as continuous improvement* (2nd ed., pp. 189–201). Thousand Oaks, CA: Corwin Press.

Garner, M. (2013). Lies, damn lies, and tests. *Measurement Interdisciplinary Research and Perspectives, 11*(1–2), 36–39. doi:10.1080/15366367.2013.784159.

Gipps, C. (1999). Socio-cultural aspects of assessment. *Review of Research in Education, 24*, 355–392.

Haertel, E. (2013). How is testing supposed to improve schooling? *Measurement Interdisciplinary Research and Perspectives, 11*(1–2), 1–18. doi:10.1080/15366367.2013.783752.

Hallinger, P. (2003). Leading educational change: Reflections on the practice of instructional and transformational leadership. *Cambridge Journal of Education, 33*(3), 329–351.

Hallinger, P. (2005). Instructional leadership and the school principal: A passing fancy that refuses to fade away. *Leadership and Policy in Schools, 4*(3), 221–239.

Halverson, R., Grigg, J., Prichett, R., & Thomas, C. (2007). The new instructional leadership: Creating data-driven instructional systems in school. *Journal of School Leadership, 17*(3), 159–194.

Harlen, W. (2005). Trusting teachers' judgement: Research evidence of the reliability and validity of teachers' assessment used for summative purposes. *Research Papers in Education, 20*(3), 245–270. doi:10.1080/02671520500193744.

Harris, L. R., & Brown, G. T. L. (2009). The complexity of teachers' conceptions of assessment: Tensions between the needs of schools and students. *Assessment in Education Principles, Policy and Practice, 16*(3), 365–381. doi:10.1080/09695940903311974.

Hood, D. (1998). *Our secondary schools don't work anymore. Why and how New Zealand schools must change for the 21st century*. Auckland, New Zealand: Profile Books.

Hoy, A., & Hoy, W. K. (2013). *Instructional leadership. A research-based guide to learning in schools*. Upper Saddle River, NJ: Pearson Education.

Klenowski, V. (2009). Australian Indigenous students: Addressing equity issues in assessment. *Teaching Education, 20*(1), 77–93. doi:10.1080/10476210802681741.

Klinger, D. A., Maggi, S., & D'Angiulli, A. (2011). School accountability and assessment: Should we put the roof up first? *The Educational Forum, 75*(2), 114–128. doi:10.1080/00131725.2011.552671.

Krug, S. (1992). *Instructional leadership, school instructional climate, and student learning outcomes. Project report*. Urbana, IL: National Center for School Leadership.

Leithwood, K., Seashore Louis, K., Anderson, S., & Wahlstrom, K. (2004). *How leadership influences student learning*. New York, NY: Wallace Foundation.

Mulford, B. (2008). *The leadership challenge: Improving learning in schools*. Camberwell, Australia: Australian Council for Educational Research.

Newton, P., Tunison, S., & Viczko, M. (2010). The school principal's role in large-scale assessment. *Canadian Journal of Educational Administration and Policy, 105*, 1–24.

Panadero, E., Tapia, J. A., & Huertas, J. A. (2012). Rubrics and self-assessment scripts effects on self-regulation, learning and self-efficacy in secondary education. *Learning and Individual Differences, 22*(6), 806–813. doi:10.1016/j.lindif.2012.04.007.

Prytula, M., Noonan, B., & Hellsten, L. (2013). Toward instructional leadership: Principals' perceptions of large-scale assessment in schools. *Canadian Journal of Educational Administration and Policy*, (140), 1–30.

Robinson, V., Lloyd, C., Hohepa, M., & Rowe, K. (2007, April). *The impact of leadership on student outcomes: An analysis of effects from international research*. Paper presented at AERA, Chicago, IL.

Sackney, L., & Mergel, B. (2007). Contemporary learning theories, instructional design and leadership. In J. M. Burger, C. F. Webber, & P. Klinck (Eds.), *Intelligent leadership*. (Vol. 6, pp. 67–98). Dordrecht, The Netherlands: Springer.

Scott, S., Scott, D. E., & Webber, C. F. (2016). The assessment KSA learning journey: Expanding the 4L – Life-Long Learning Leader – Framework. In S. Scott, D. E. Scott, & C. F. Webber (Eds.), *Assessment in education: Implications for leadership*. Dordrecht, The Netherlands: Springer.

Scott, S., Webber, C. F., Aitken, N., & Lupart, J. (2011). Developing teachers' knowledge, beliefs, and expertise: Findings from the Alberta Student Assessment Study. *The Educational Forum, 75*(2), 96–113. doi:10.1080/00131725.2011.552594.

Siccone, F. (2012). *Essential skills for effective school leadership*. Upper Saddle River, NJ: Pearson Education.

Smith, P. L., & Ragan, T. J. (2005). *Instructional design* (3rd ed.). New York, NY: Wiley Publishing.

Snowman, J., McCown, R., & Biehler, R. (2012). *Psychology applied to teaching* (13th ed.). Belmont, CA: Wadsworth Cengage Learning.

Stiggins, R., & Duke, D. (2008). Effective instructional leadership requires assessment leadership. *Phi Delta Kappan, 90*(4), 285–291.

Stiggins, R. J., Arter, J., Chappuis, J., & Chappuis, S. (2005). *Classroom assessment for student learning: Doing it right-using it well*. Kingston, ON, Canada: Educational Testing Service.

Tierney, R., Simon, M., & Charland, J. (2011). Being fair: Teachers' interpretations of principles for standards-based grading. *The Educational Forum, 75*(3), 210–227.

Wallace Foundation. (2011). *The school principal as leader: Guiding schools to better teaching and learning*. New York, NY: Wallace Foundation.

Wang, L., Beckett, G. H., & Brown, L. (2006). Controversies of standardized assessment in school accountability reform: A critical synthesis of multidisciplinary research evidence. *Applied Measurement in Education, 19*(4), 305–328. doi:10.1207/s15324818ame1904_5.

Webber, C. F., Aitken, N., Lupart, J., & Scott, S. (2009). *The Alberta Student Assessment Study: Final report*. Edmonton, AB, Canada: The Government of Alberta.

Webber, C. F., Lupart, J., & Scott, S. (2012). The ecology of student assessment. In C. F. Webber & J. Lupart (Eds.), *Leading student assessment* (pp. 283–297). Dordrecht, The Netherlands: Springer.

Webber, C. F., & Scott, S. (2010). Mapping principal preparation in Alberta, Canada. *Journal of Education and Humanities Theory and Practice, 1*, 75–96.

Webber, C. F., & Scott, S. (2013). Principles for principal preparation. In C. L. Slater & S. Nelson (Eds.), *Understanding the principalship: An international guide to principal preparation* (Vol. 19, pp. 95–124). Bingley, UK: Emerald.

Webber, C. F., Scott, S., Aitken, N., Lupart, J., & Scott, D. E. (2013). Leading assessment for enhanced student outcomes. *School Leadership and Management, 33*(3), 240–255. doi:10.1080/13632434.2013.773885.

Wiggins, G., & McTighe, J. (2005). *Understanding by design*. Alexandria, VA: Association for Supervision and Curriculum Development.

Wildy, H., & Dimmock, C. (1993). Instructional leadership in primary and secondary schools in Western Australia. *Journal of Educational Administration, 31*(2), 43–62.

Part I
Pragmatics of Assessment Leadership – What Leaders Need to Know About Assessment

Chapter 2
Educational Renovations: Nailing Down Terminology in Assessment

Michelle McKean and E. Nola Aitken

Abstract There is currently a great deal of variation in the assessment terminology used by researchers and educators alike. Consistency of vocabulary is necessary for productive dialogue to occur between professionals. Well-defined assessment terminology contributes significantly to how educators and researchers conceptualise, and subsequently implement assessment processes. A brief history of assessment terminology is explored to provide a clearer comprehension of how our current understanding of assessment has been influenced. Using a cyclical model of assessment modified from previous work by Wiliam and Black, Harlen, and the Alberta Assessment Consortium, the authors define both assessment and evaluation and then proceed to further explore the various purposes and functions of assessment. Bidirectionality of feedback between external organisational-driven assessment and internal student-driven assessment is discussed as being essential to maintaining the formative intent of assessment while simultaneously meeting accountability needs. Other assessment terms are finally explored in the framework of these discussions.

Keywords Assessment • Evaluation • Nature of assessment • Nature of evaluation • Educational terminology • Purpose of assessment • Purpose of evaluation • Function of assessment • Function of evaluation • Formative assessment • Summative assessment • Assessment for learning • Assessment of learning • Assessment as learning • Defining assessment and evaluation

2.1 Educational Renovations: Nailing Down Terminology in Assessment

Over the past two decades there has been a radical shift in educators' views of assessment and evaluation. At first glance it seems as though assessment and evaluation concepts ought to be straightforward, and yet when examined microscopically the intricate interconnectedness of sustaining systems becomes readily apparent. The

M. McKean • E.N. Aitken (✉)
Faculty of Education, University of Lethbridge, Lethbridge, AB, Canada
e-mail: mckean@live.com; nola.aitken@uleth.ca

1990s saw a profound shift in focus from summative to formative assessment, and both theorists and practitioners became more concerned with validity and authenticity issues in the classroom (Black, 1993; Dassa, Vazquez-Abad, & Ajar, 1993; Daws & Singh, 1996; Haney, 1991; Maeroff, 1991; Meyer, 1992; Newmann, Secada, & Wehlage, 1995; Perrenoud, 1991; Rothman, 1990; Sadler, 1989; Sutton, 1995; Wiggins, 1993; Wiliam & Black, 1996; Willis, 1990). Shifting conceptualisations of assessment have caused the educational equivalent of the demolition phase of a renovation, yet current frameworks designed to replace their predecessors "perpetuate an understanding which is confused and illogical" (Taras, 2008b, p. 175). Indeed, running the term "assessment" through the ERIC database alone revealed tens of thousands of articles to review, with each scholar choosing to focus on a different aspect of evaluation or assessment and disagreement on the theoretical frameworks of assessment proliferating. Although the segmentation of assessment into differing purposes has provided helpful information and could contribute significantly to a strong, cohesive model, such a coherent theoretical framework remains to be established. Unless the different segments begin to coalesce into a unified picture of what evaluation and assessment are, educational dialogue will continue to be confused and progress towards better classroom practice will be inhibited.

Consistent definitions of terminology pertaining to classroom assessment are lacking (Frey & Schmitt, 2007). Taras (2008b) concurred with this conclusion, noting the lack of alignment in formative and summative definitions and their relationship to each other, as well as theoretical gaps resulting in a divergence between theory and practice (2008a). In 2008, Gallagher and Worth (2008) certainly observed differences in definition and interpretation among merely five states in the United States of America that were examined in their research. Understanding assessment terminology and its framework is essential not only for intelligent dialogue among researchers and teachers (Frey & Schmitt, 2007), but also it is important for discourse with educational leadership and policy makers (Broadfoot & Black, 2004; Taras, 2008b) and for the research quality and subsequent empirical evidence outlining best practices in formative assessment (Dunn & Mulvenon, 2009). Consequently, the intent of this article is to dissect the concepts of assessment and evaluation in an attempt to create both an educational understanding of related terminology and a framework of the interconnected system we call assessment.

2.2 History of Assessment

Warmington and Rouse (1956) cite the earliest known recorded assessment term as "test", provided by Socrates as he explained the need for testing to Glaucon in order to establish the highest echelon of Guardians:

> [W]e must examine who are best guardians of their resolution that they must do whatever they think from time to time to be best for the city. They must be watched from childhood up; we must set them tests in which a man would be most likely to forget such a resolution or to be deceived, and we must choose the one who remembers well and is not easily deceived, and reject the rest. (p. 213)

This example is the first documented indication of humans making the assumption that knowledge and ability are measurable attributes. Uninfluenced by Socrates' philosophies, the Chinese had similar ideas somewhat later and what would now be termed "performance assessment" (see later in this article for further discussion) formed the basis of Chinese civil examinations possibly as early as approximately 200 years BCE (Frey & Schmitt, 2007). In 1200 AD, the first doctoral examination was conducted in Italy at the University of Bologna, and marked the first instance of academic measurement in Western civilization (Linden & Linden, 1968). Five hundred years later this practice reached the Master degree level at Cambridge University in England. It was not until the early 1800s that performance-based methods of examination were used in common schooling practices at lower educational levels (Frey & Schmitt, 2007).

Although tests of performance have been used for centuries, Francis Galton was the first to attempt the scientific development of mental tests in the 1870s, and Binet carried out similar research in the early 1900s (Berlak et al., 1992; Eisner, 1985). Even though the Thorndike Handwriting Scale was successfully produced and implemented in 1909 specifically for school use, and was followed by a number of achievement and aptitude tests (Perrone, 1991), World War I provided the perfect opportunity to capitalize on the research by Galton and Binet by testing potential soldiers' mental skill and aptitude. As a result of military drafts, Robert Yerkes found himself chairing a committee intended to devise a group intelligence test (Yoakum & Yerkes, 1920). After much debate, persuasion, and tireless research the Army Alpha and Army Beta tests were spawned – largely based on the research of Binet and A.S. Otis from Stanford University. The objective of examination procedures was initially to increase efficiency of military operations; however, the impact these tests had on both military operations and later educational uses (such as the Scholastic Aptitude Test [SAT]) forever changed the face of assessment (Black, 2001). With the adaptation of standardised testing for educational purposes, large-scale summative assessments and multiple-choice response formats became the testing methods of choice – chiefly because they were highly efficient and cost-effective when assessing large groups of people from a diversity of geographical regions.

Despite the negative consequences and drawbacks of this form of testing (often called traditional assessment), the time-efficient ease of the tests' administration, scoring, and interpretation minimised financial costs and thus caused it to survive in the face of heavy criticism.

In the late 1960s Scriven (1967) began writing about what he termed "formative" and "summative evaluation". Originally Scriven shared his thoughts about formative and summative evaluation with the intention that these terms be applied to programme evaluation; however, he quickly broadened his focus to include educational practices as well. Wiliam and Black (1996) noted that Bloom, Hastings, and Madaus (1971) were the first to extend the terms "formative" and "summative" to the currently understood and accepted educational uses of the terms. As Wiliam and Black (2003) carefully relayed, the purposes behind the forms of assessment were most important.

Madaus and Dwyer (1999) noted the return of performance assessment in the early 1980s, around the same time as authentic assessment was possibly first referenced (likely by Archbald and Newman (1988) according to Frey and Schmitt 2007). Similarly, the term "alternative assessment" was also brandished in the 1980s possibly first by Murphy and Torrance in 1988 (Buhagiar, 2007). As a method of authentic evaluation, portfolio assessment was later detailed by Sulzby (1990) and then further elaborated by Bauer (1993). Most recently Perie, Marion, and Gong (2009) have added to Wiliam and Black's (1996) concept of formative and summative assessment by detailing a third intermediary that they label "interim assessment", and in addition to this there appears to be a resurgence in the study and application of "dynamic assessment" (e.g., Crick, 2007; Poehner & Lantolf, 2005, 2010; Yeomans, 2008). Somewhere along the way many of the aforementioned terms began to be used interchangeably and connoted different meanings to different people. The intent of the next three sections is therefore to explore the often-confused terms of assessment and evaluation in the hope of clarifying discrepancies.

2.3 Assessment Versus Evaluation

Quite often when reading articles on assessment and/or evaluation, it seemed as if the terms assessment and evaluation were used either interchangeably or were distinctly defined and separated from one another. For example, Scriven (1967) described what most educators and researchers today would call assessment, yet he refers to it as evaluation. Savickiene (2011) uses the term "evaluation" in much the same way as Scriven; however, she refers to evaluation as the process of making a decision based on assessment data, while assessment is the "collection, classification, and analysis of data on student learning achievements" (p. 75). Taras (2005) noted the common use of the terms assessment and evaluation; however, she distinguished between the two concepts by using "'assessment' … to refer to judgements of students' work, and 'evaluation' to refer to judgements regarding courses or course delivery, or the process of making such judgements" (p. 467). Hosp and Ardoin (2008) utilise much the same definitions of assessment and evaluation as Taras. Similarly, Harlen (2007) used assessment in a manner that focused on students while evaluation was used to refer to the aspects of education that did not directly affect or refer to student achievement. In contrast to Taras and Harlen, Trevisan (2007) used the terms differently by referring to the purpose of "evaluability assessment" as assessing readiness for evaluation whereas "evaluation" (specifically programme evaluation) was portrayed as having a greater sense of finality. More recently Dunn and Mulvenon (2009) have suggested that it is most helpful to separate formative assessment and formative evaluation by an object-use paradigm where a formative assessment is the test and an evaluation speaks to the use of data. The aforementioned articles highlight the terminology confusion that results largely from semantic discrepancies and confusion of method, use, and purpose. With such disparity, how do we create a common consensus on terminology that is both straightforward and practical? Although arriving at such unanimity is no small feat, perhaps it is most helpful to turn to Paul Black and his various associated counterparts for further clarification. As one of the leading authorities in assessment with at least 49 publications in the field, his contributions arguably reframed the way we view assessment today.

In educational circles the concepts that Trevisan (2007) discussed as assessment and evaluation are often referred to as formative and summative assessment respectively – terminology brought to prominence by Black (1993). According to Black and Wiliam (2003), the distinction between formative and summative assessment lies primarily in the function of the assessment, with formative assessments narrowing the gap between a student's current versus expected knowledge (also referred to as assessment *for* learning), and summative assessments providing a description of a student's performance without providing opportunity for further learning (referred to also as assessment *of* learning). Wiliam and Black (1996) conceptualised summative and formative assessment as being linked and simply on opposite ends of a continuum; however, significantly the process of assessment itself was viewed as cyclical in nature. Irving, Harris, and Peterson (2011) attribute this cycle to an interplay between what they term "assessment and feedback" (p. 415); however, in the context of this article the terminology we apply to the same concepts would be evaluation and communication as being the two key propellants in the assessment cycle.

Although copious numbers of articles have been written surrounding formative assessment and its distinction from summative assessment, Taras (2005) pointed out that researchers may have lost Scriven's original vision of bringing the dimension of formative assessment to educators' attention in their haste to distinguish between formative and summative assessment. Indeed Taras noted that the separation between formative and summative assessment "has been self-destructive and self-defeating" (p. 476). Despite her strong position about separating formative and summative assessment completely, Taras (2007) later points out difficulties that arise because formative and summative assessments lack differentiation in the assessment literature, yet what if the two were never intended to be separated? Perhaps the following argument oversimplifies the issue; however, if researchers return to the fundamental nature and purposes of assessment and of evaluation it is possible that the issue may be clarified further.

2.4 Nature of Assessment and Evaluation

The Oxford English Dictionary defined evaluation as "the making of a judgement about the amount, number, or value of something; assessment". When reading this description, two concepts that arose were: (a) a sense of exacting a judgment (possibly numerical and value laden), and (b) an atmosphere of finality to the verdict reached. A process to reach such a judgment is implicated; however, the focus appears to be on a conclusive outcome. Interestingly, the finality of what is termed "evaluation" parallels common conceptions of what is labelled summative assessment. For example, Taras (2005) described summative assessment as "a judgment which encapsulates all the evidence up to a given point" (p. 468). It seems that the terms "evaluation" (Trevisan, 2007) and "summative assessment" (Taras, 2005; Wiliam & Black, 1996) are both referring to a similar concept and have been used interchangeably. Even the perceptions of educators were that summative assessment had an air of finality or an end point (Taras, 2008b).

Illustrating the difficulty in distinguishing between assessment and evaluation, the Oxford Dictionary defines assessment as: "the evaluation or estimation of the nature, quality, or ability of someone or something". Confusion arises largely from the interchangeability of the terms and their use to define one another, yet definitions and descriptions of assessment in educational research describe assessment in a manner altered from the Oxford Dictionary definition. Harlen (2006) described assessment as "deciding, collecting and making judgments about evidence relating to the goals of the learning being assessed" (p. 103). This explanation fits with Wiliam and Black's (1996) portrayal of the assessment cycle, which consists of (a) eliciting evidence (deciding what evidence is desired and how it can best be obtained and observed), and (b) interpretation (decoding the information that has been obtained as a result of elicitation, and taking action based on this understanding). More recently, Taras (2008b) affirmed perceptions that assessment is more than making a judgment, and involves a cyclical process with "formative and summative assessment feed[ing] into each other" (p. 183). Based on the work of Wiliam and Black, Harlen, and a cyclical model of assessment put forth by the Alberta Assessment Consortium (2005), we would like to suggest the following cyclical stages of assessment:

- deciding what information is desired, how best to obtain such information, and what will indicate learning has taken place (planning);
- actively eliciting desired information (elicitation);
- interpreting the data (interpretation);
- making a judgment based on one's interpretation (evaluation);
- communicating this interpretation (communication); and
- deciding what the next steps in learning should be (reflection).

Evaluation still involves judgment; however, it implies action to improve learning by providing feedback and opportunity for reflection, which both influence the planning phase of the next revolution in the cycle (see Fig. 2.1).

Inherently cyclical (Harlen, 2000; Wiliam & Black, 1996), it is the nature of assessment that clarifies the relationship between assessment and evaluation. If assessment is viewed as a cyclical process and evaluation is viewed merely as a stage in this sequence, then the philosophical implication is that learning is continuous, lifelong, and does not have a definitive endpoint. For example, Black, Harrison, Lee, Marshall, and Wiliam (2004), Stiggins and Chappuis (2005), and Taras (2009) highlight a shift in educational practices to use summative assessments in formative ways – illustrating a desire for all assessment to contain some formative aspects despite alternate purposes. Kealey (2010) uses the term "feedback loop" to describe

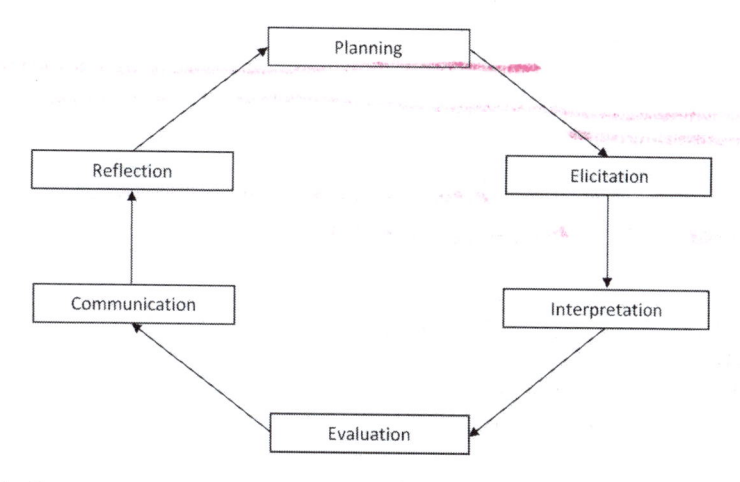

Fig. 2.1 Contemporary assessment cycle (Modified from the work of the Alberta Assessment Consortium (2005), Harlen (2006), and Wiliam and Black (1996))

this concept in her review for social work education and assessment, and Segers, Dochy, and Gijbels (2010) describe it as a feedback and feedforward loop that ultimately results in what they term "pure assessment". An advantage to viewing the relationship between assessment and evaluation in this manner is that the neutrality of the oft-disparaged summative assessment has the potential to be restored as it would no longer be viewed with the same finality; rather, summative assessment could be viewed as a higher order cyclical process that feeds *both* educational administration and student learning needs. Wehlburg (2007) captures the spirit of continuity in assessment by describing an "assessment spiral" (p. 1) in which each cycle of assessment is monitored and increased in its quality. Cyclical models have already been suggested for use with students on Individual Education Programs (IEPs) (Thomson, Bachor, & Thomson, 2002), implemented in engineering education programs (Christoforou & Yigit, 2008), and are recommended when applied to regular classroom assessment as well (Alberta Assessment Consortium, 2005). Viewing assessment and evaluation in a cyclical framework removes the need for distinction between assessment and evaluation: there is simply assessment albeit assessment with varying purposes.

2.5 Definitions of Assessment and Evaluation

Having addressed the nature of assessment, we now move on to developing concise definitions of assessment and evaluation. For the purposes of this chapter, assessment is defined as: a cyclical learning process of planning, elicitation, interpretation, evaluation, communication, and reflection. Notice that this definition is not specific to student achievement as this definition can be used not only for students, but also for teachers, schools, and even workplace assessments. With the definition of assessment in mind, evaluation is defined as: a stage in the assessment cycle characterised by making a judgment about learning based on an interpretation of elicited information.

Although these definitions address continual attempts to distinguish between assessment and evaluation, they fail to address the spirit that lies behind such attempts – namely, the purposes of assessment. Therefore, the next section attempts to construct a theoretical framework that uses our definitions, yet also addresses concerns of purpose or function.

2.6 Function Versus Purpose of Assessment

Further characterisation of the assessment process is made possible by exploring the purpose of assessment. Taras (2007) points out that the terms "purpose" and "function" are used interchangeably; however, upon examination subtle differences exist that distinguish between the purpose of assessment and its function. Newton (2007) lists the difficulties in assessment purpose as being primarily those of definition and of use categorisation. While he links purpose chiefly to the decision level of assessment (and therefore to the use to which assessment is applied), further reflection challenges this conclusion. It seems as though what Newton labels as purpose, is actually function, evidenced by the following quotation:

> This [the decision level] is taken to be the most significant usage of the term "assessment purpose" since it seems to be the level that is most frequently associated with it in the technical literature. For this reason, and for the sake of clarity, if the term "purpose" is to be retained as a feature of assessment discourse – as it will be in the remainder of this paper – it ought to be restricted to the decision level. (p. 150)

For the sake of clarity, in this chapter when we refer to the purpose of assessment we are describing *why* the assessment was performed, while function describes *how* the assessment is used in order to meet the established purpose. This distinction will be expanded upon in the following two sections.

2.7 Purposes of Assessment

Ultimately the primary purpose of assessment is to enhance learning. Beneficiaries of learning may vary; however, learning ideally is the focus of all assessment. In 2006, the Western and Northern Canadian Protocol for Collaboration in Education (WNCP) put forth a document that summarised three purposes of assessment, namely, (a) Assessment for Learning, (b) Assessment as Learning, and (c) Assessment of Learning. Although we will deviate slightly from the descriptions in the WNCP, these concepts provide the most helpful basis on which to form a discussion on purpose and so we now turn to them.

2.7.1 Assessment for Learning

The term "assessment for learning" is often used interchangeably with "formative assessment" as is evidenced by both Black and Wiliam's (2006) chapter surrounding formative assessment practices entitled "Assessment for Learning in the Classroom" and Harlen's (2006) stated use of the terms. According to Harlen, what matters most is not the *kind* of assessment used, but the *purpose* of its use. Black and Wiliam's reflections capture the learning-focused purpose of formative assessment while providing details on the process of assessment and its constructivist nature. Taras (2010) disagrees and clarifies that regardless of how the work is used, "the *process* of formative assessment can only be said to have taken place when feedback has been used to improve the work" (p. 3021). She feels that formative assessment (or assessment for learning) is a process of the interplay between what she refers to as summative assessment and feedback – yet when she is referring to summative assessment, she is referring specifically to the fact that a judgment must be made about learning and knowledge, much the same as the stage of evaluation in our cycle. It may be most helpful to thus conceptualise assessment for learning as embodying the primary purpose of assessment (the enhancement of learning), yet primarily as the general process of assessment enacted or supported by other purposes of assessment such as assessment of learning or summative assessment. As all assessment ought to be for learning, it is hoped the necessity for the use of this terminology will eventually be antiquated.

2.7.2 Assessment as Learning

Assessment as learning is formative in nature; however, it specifically refers to the task of metacognitive learning. Overall, the general aim of assessment as learning is to eventually bridge and shift ownership of learning from the teacher to the student – in other words from external to internal monitoring. Salient examples of assessment as learning include elements of what Boekaerts and Corno (2005) and Clark (2012) discuss as self-regulated learning and what Brookhart (2001) describes as student self-assessment. Boekaerts and Corno paint a portrait of a self-regulating student as follows: "All theorists assume that students who self-regulate their learning are engaged actively and constructively in a process of meaning generation and that they adapt their thoughts, feelings, and actions as needed to affect their learning and motivation" (p. 201).

Although they explore student self-regulation in far more depth than we are able to capture here, this description beautifully portrays the intent of assessment as learning. In the words of Black and Wiliam (1998), "the ultimate user of assessment information that is elicited in order to improve learning is the pupil" (p. 142). For this reason, assessment as learning is of crucial importance to student outcomes because it engages students, motivates them, and supports eventual transition to lifelong learner.

2.7.3 Assessment of Learning

Assessment of learning is often used as another label for summative assessment. Under the assumption that all assessment ought to be formative in nature (i.e., assessment for learning), does assessment of learning still deserve to be a purpose of assessment? In its traditional role, assessment of learning was used primarily for both political and educational decision making, thus connoting a large degree of control over students (Taras, 2008a). There has therefore been an outcry against summative assessment in general, particularly as a result of both perceived and actual misuse – despite research suggesting that large-scale summative assessments are still a necessity (Brookhart, 2013). Newton (2007) pointed out that in the manner that the term "summative" is used it has no purpose and only characterises a type of judgment. The truth inherent in this statement lies in a traditionally problematic approach to assessment that either interrupted the assessment cycle at the evaluation stage or shuffled the information to external organisational agencies without feedback returned to the student. As Taras (2008b) dissects this issue, she draws attention to the fact that judgments are naturally occurring and necessary, albeit sometimes misused. Yet if approached properly, assessment of learning can be a valuable tool to summarise a collection of assessment cycle rotations. Conceptualise it as a geological core sample that communicates a student's learning over a period of time. It accomplishes on a macroscale what occurs on a microcosmic level in the classroom all the time. When used appropriately, this feedback can provide a student with a greater sense of accomplishment, at an organisational level can provide learning opportunities for teachers and administrators concerning how to support further student learning; and at a political/societal level can provide potential information that, when used correctly can contribute to vital decision making processes.

2.8 Functions of Assessment

One of the most helpful descriptions of assessment function comes from Newton (2007). Although Newton used the term "purpose", we argue that he is really addressing assessment "function" (how an assessment is used), and helpfully provides a list of various functions of assessments. Perhaps first and foremost, an important aspect of this chapter is that there may be both student and organisational uses of assessment. Newton's use of learning classifications of formative, placement, diagnosis, guidance, and student monitoring are all examples of student-focused functions of assessment. Harlen (2005) would use the term "internal" (p. 208) to refer to a similar concept (she used it specifically when dealing with formative and summative assessment; however, we find the language use helpful for our purposes so forgive the license taken here). Returning to Newton, institution monitoring, resource allocation, organisational intervention, system monitoring, and comparability illustrate the conjoint functions of organisational assessment. Borrowing from Harlen, we will use the term "external" to describe this as well. Distinguishing between the two fundamental functions and describing potential uses within these frameworks is helpful insofar as it points toward

2 Educational Renovations: Nailing Down Terminology in Assessment   35

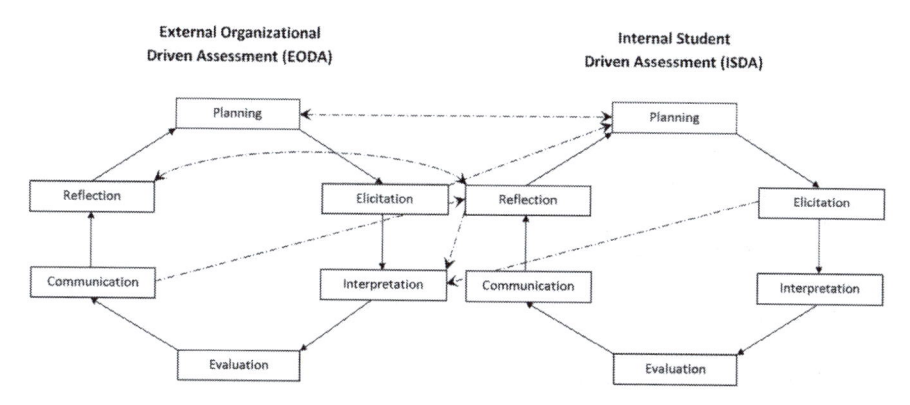

Fig. 2.2 Bidirectional examples between EODA and ISDA. In Fig. 2.2, the *broken arrows* indicate some possibilities for exchange of information between cycles to take place. Following informational exchange, regular rotation of cycles is assumed

the primary directional flow of information while still challenging educators and administrators to keep as much bidirectional flow as possible (see Fig. 2.2).

Depending on the desired function of assessment, the exchange of information between cycles may occur at different points in the cycle. Figure 2.2 is intended to illustrate the bidirectional flow of information in assessment practices where External Organizational Driven Assessment (EODA) involvement is necessary; however, it is not to be assumed that this is always the case, and there may be instances of Internal Student Driven Assessment (ISDA) independent cycling. Ultimately, for EODA to be used in a formative manner there must be effective and helpful feedback into the ISDA assessment cycle. For some examples of lower order assessment functions (modified and extended from Newton, 2007) as well as the primary cycle in which they operate, see Fig. 2.3.

There are many aspects of Fig. 2.3 that are worthy of note. Although organisational intervention, system monitoring, institution monitoring, and resource allocation affect students, direct student learning is not as much a priority for these functions. Conversely, although EODA involvement may play a role in guidance, diagnostic, placement, student monitoring, and selection functions, less bidirectional flow of information is required for these functions than those categorised as both ISDA and EODA. Although this is a rough division of various functions and certainly not intended as an exhaustive list, it is hoped it will provide a springboard for further discussion and debate.

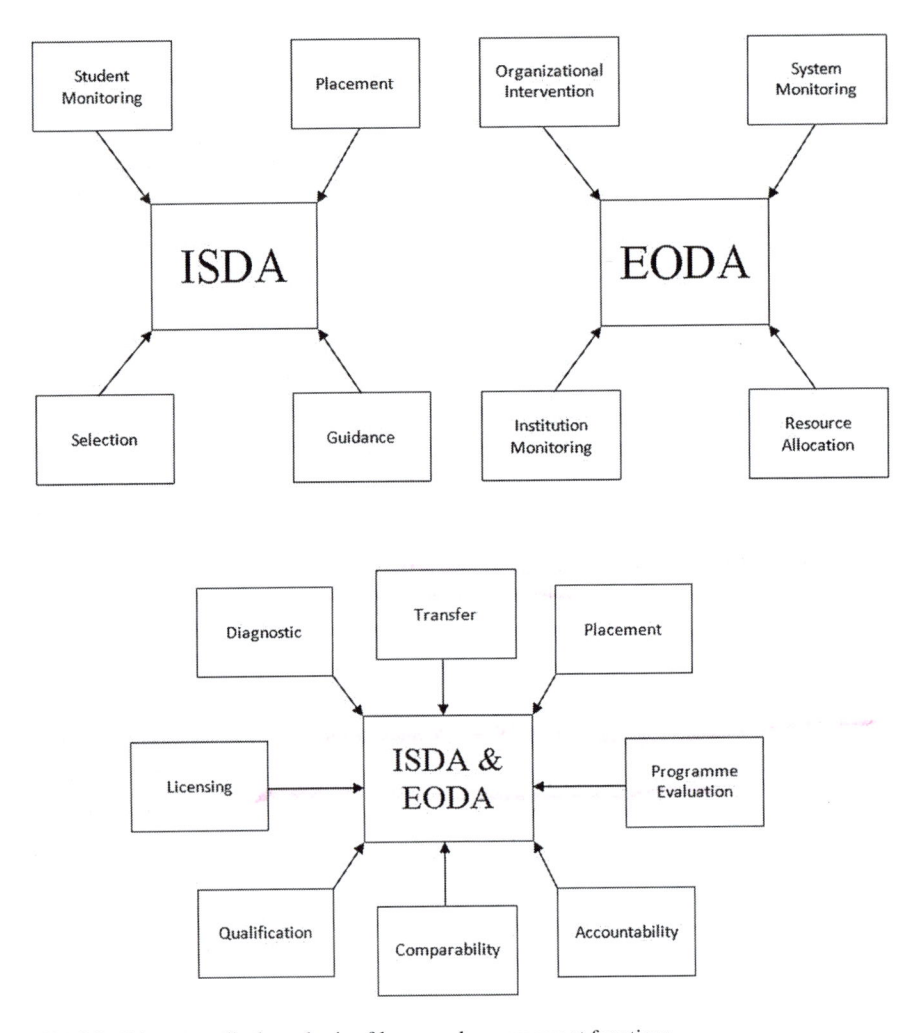

Fig. 2.3 Primary cyclical emphasis of lower order assessment functions

2.9 Conceptualising Other Terminology

As alluded to in the beginning of this chapter, there is an excessive number of terms brandished about without a reliable level of comprehension among researchers. Although we have already focused on many such terms, we feel it is beneficial to explore a few in our discussion.

2.9.1 Authentic Assessment

The term "authentic assessment" speaks not so much to the purpose of assessment as to its contributions to quality and validity. "Alternative assessment", "direct assessment", or "performance assessment" are sometimes used interchangeably with the term "authentic assessment" (National Center for Fair and Open Testing, 1992); however, this can be understandably confusing and it can be helpful to reconceptualise the relationship between these terms based on nature, purpose, and function.

Instead of viewing "authentic assessment" as a separate type of assessment, it seems logical that authentic is used as an adjective. Segers et al. (2010) helpfully outline four criteria for an assessment to be authentic: representativeness (adequately assessing the scope of the domain at stake); meaningfulness ("assessing relevant and worthwhile contributions of the learner," [p. 200]); cognitive complexity (higher order skills present); and content coverage (breadth of material included). When viewing "authentic assessment" in this light, it is possible for a wide variety of assessment tools and processes to be authentic.

Perhaps the best way to facilitate comprehension of authentic assessment is to provide a practical example of an authentic assessment scenario that might unfold in any classroom. Following is a brief depiction of an authentic assessment in a Junior High Language Arts classroom.

Ms Woods would like to teach her students the components of a short story as well as encourage their ability to apply this knowledge to their own writing. She decides that ultimately the most authentic way to teach such knowledge and skill is to have the students write a short story; however, she feels they should be involved in the assessment process as well so that they can truly understand what they are supposed to be learning and doing. Ms Woods begins by dividing up the various parts of a short story and using cooperative learning groups to have the students teach each other about the various components. Once the class has learned about the various segments, then she lays before them the task of writing a short story themselves and helps them brainstorm rubric requirements by which the short story will be marked as well as their participation in the editing process with their classmates. After this process has been completed the final drafts of their stories will be placed in their portfolios and they will complete further self-evaluation at the end of the term.

In this example, the scope of the assessment is aligned with what Ms Woods wishes to assess, the activity is meaningful in the respect that learners are contributing their thoughts at a number of different levels in a variety of ways, there is good cognitive complexity, and the content coverage is appropriate for the desired outcome. Because these four criteria are satisfied, it can be said that this assessment activity is authentic.

2.9.2 Alternative Assessment

Similarly, "alternative assessment" is a term of description that simply refers to approaching student-driven assessment in a manner that is different than that which has traditionally been done – usually in reference to strict pencil-and-paper testing. Stobart and Gipps (2010) outline three levels of alternative assessment that refer to different facets or applications of the word "alternative". Firstly they describe "alternative assessment" in the context of alternative formats. An alternative format could include administering a test on computer instead of by paper-and-pencil (with the content and scope remaining entirely the same) or it could refer to the use of open-ended written-response questions in contrast to traditional strictly multiple-choice examinations. Alternative formats are seen as the most basic level of alternative assessment. Secondly, Stobart and Gipps described alternative models of assessment. When referring to alternative models of assessment, they described simply the use of a different approach to assessment including examples of "performance assessment" and alternative educational assessment (including extended projects/assignments, "portfolio assessment", and assessments by teachers for external purposes). Finally Stobart and Gipps addressed alternative purposes of assessment – referring to the use of assessment for formative and diagnostic purposes as an alternative to a focus only on summative assessment. Formative and diagnostic purposes are thought to dovetail with one another as diagnostic assessment identifies learner knowledge that is currently present and gaps that are present between current and desired understanding of material, while formative assessment seeks to close gaps and increase learning primarily through the use of feedback. "Dynamic assessment" was seen to be an alternative form of "diagnostic assessment" based on the sociocultural theories of Vygotsky (1978) which uses a one-to-one learner-facilitator model which focuses on how effectively students learn when assisted. (See the sections on diagnostic and dynamic assessment later in this article for more information on these areas.)

In addition to the simple distinction of "alternative assessment" as being something other than what was traditionally done, it is also helpful to examine the assumptions made by an alternative assessment as they prove useful in further delineating the concept of "alternative assessment". Anderson (1998) pointed out that alternative assessment assumes that:

- there are multiple meanings of knowledge;
- learning is actively constructed;
- process and product are paramount;
- inquiry is central;
- there is a focus on multimodal abilities;
- it is subjective;
- power and control of learning is shared by the teacher and the student – it is a collaborative process; and
- the primary purpose is to facilitate learning.

Note the consistency of these assumptions with the assessment terminology described by Stobart and Gipps (2010). Such characteristics also fit nicely with Newton's (2007) descriptions of various uses of assessment, and the view of learning as a central focus of assessment.

2.9.3 Diagnostic Assessment

Turner, VanderHeide, and Fynewever (2011) discuss diagnostic assessment in a similar manner as we would discuss a summative assessment used for a formative purpose. They distinguish diagnostic assessment from summative assessment by pointing out that a diagnostic assessment is used in a formative fashion while a summative assessment is used as a summary at the end of instruction. While this contributes to the furthering of utilising summative assessment for formative purposes, this description is contrary to the definitions supported in this article and as such we are not considering this as helpful for our purposes. Instead, when discussing diagnostic assessment we are referring primarily to assessment streamlined to describe cognitive functioning in students. Diagnostic assessment is performed with the underlying purposes of (a) providing information so that instruction can be altered and student learning improved, as well as (b) providing students with greater insight so that they can maximise their strengths and support any areas of weakness they may have. Its use is intervention-focused and less frequently employed than other forms of assessment (Newton, 2007). For our purposes, diagnostic uses are typically both student-centred and organisationally focused because feedback is provided and used in both spheres. Diagnostic assessments are intended to be repeated periodically so that the feedback may be used to streamline student instruction, optimise student-learning potential, and to provide a certain level of accountability at an organisational level.

2.9.4 Dynamic Assessment

Dynamic assessment outlines a certain methodological and philosophical approach to assessment defined as the "dialectical unity of instruction and assessment" by Poehner and Lantolf (2010). Based on Vygotsky's zone of proximal development (Leung, 2007), dynamic assessment is a social constructionist form of assessment that is "both retrospective (diagnostic and reflective) and prospective (formative and motivational)" (Crick, 2007, p. 139). The basic premises for dynamic assessment are that the social environment is key to development (Poehner, 2008), intelligence is a product of both biological predisposition and social construction (Yeomans, 2008), and that supportive interactions or interventions with others foster learning (Leung, 2007; Yeomans, 2008). It implies a specific interaction between the person assessing and the person being assessed, with particular attention paid to a type of scaffolding interaction that is based within – sometimes described as a "test-train-test design" (DÖrfler, Golke, & Artelt, 2009). In this model feedback is very important, particularly when it is detailed and learning-oriented. Also common in dynamic assessment is the concept of collaboration between peers in a more group-based than individually-based form of assessment. In practical terms, dynamic assessment describes a specific interplay between student and teacher/mediator whereby the cycle of assessment is navigated by both parties in a predominantly metacognitive fashion.

2.9.5 Self-Assessment and Integrative Assessment

While the implementation of self-assessment follows the same cycle as regular assessment, the student is placed in the role of assessor and follows a specific self-assessment subcycle. Self-assessment in reality speaks not to a new form of assessment, but rather it specifies who is performing the act of assessment. More specifically, McMillan and Hearn (2008) define self-assessment as "a process by which students (1) monitor and evaluate the quality of their thinking and behavior when learning, and (2) identify strategies that improve their understanding and skills" (p. 40). According to McMillan and Hearn, self-assessment is described as a formative use of assessment involving a cyclical process of identifying learning targets and instructional correctives, self-monitoring, and self-judgment.

In their interview study of teachers in Canada, Volante and Beckett (2011) suggested that in order for self-assessment to be valuable as a formative use of assessment, students must understand both the aims of the assessment and the criteria for assessment. The inherent value of having students engage in their own assessment is explored in detail by Brookhart (2001); however, generally speaking self-assessment is a vital tool used to meet the purpose of assessment as learning.

Another term used somewhat interchangeably with self-assessment is "integrative assessment". Crisp (2012) discusses the two primary purposes of integrative assessment as being to enhance students' learning approaches in the future and to reward them for their growth and insight in their approach to learning in contrast to the actual learning itself. It would be this use of assessment in which students would actively participate in the structuring of the task itself, thus encouraging students to take responsibility for their own learning. Crisp's description of integrative assessment fits well with current definitions of self-assessment; however, self-assessment at present seems to be a term more commonly used than integrative assessment.

2.9.6 Self-Evaluation

Based on our discussion of assessment and evaluation, this term is unnecessary. Self-evaluation does not speak to a new type of assessment, it simply points out who is performing the evaluation phase of assessment, which is already specified if using the term "self-assessment".

Although there are more terms that are used in respect to assessment and evaluation, they cannot all be covered due to space constraints. Still, the basic case has been woven and the groundwork of a foundation for conceptualisation of terms has been built. Perhaps most important is that we are conscious of being specific not only in the use of the assessment terms, but also in describing:

- their particular purpose and function(s);
- who is performing the assessment or evaluation;
- who or what is being assessed or evaluated; and
- the process that was followed to reach assessment conclusions.

2.10 Conclusion

The purpose of this chapter is to encourage more specific use of our language and to promote common understanding as educators and researchers; hence, we have attempted to advance an awareness of the following:

- the cyclical nature of assessment creating a spiral formation of learning;
- evaluation as a component of assessment;
- the various purposes and functions of assessment;
- the importance of authenticity in assessment as it contributes to validity;
- the integral role feedback plays in assessment;
- the formative nature of assessment; and
- the flow of information between Internal Student Driven Assessment and External Organizational Driven Assessment cycles.

Such common understandings as these allow educators to better address the needs of students and be more purposeful in assessment design and implementation. In addition, these concepts serve as primary considerations when establishing an assessment model in a school as well as for establishing policies regarding general school assessments and accountability measures. In an evidence-based society, it is imperative that educators not only strive to increase learning and communicate outcomes, but also ensure that what we are encouraging and communicating is reliable and valid. If we clarify our dialogue and can create methods of assessment that are specific to the function for which they were intended, validity will be further promoted and the value of educational systems will be made more apparent.

References

Alberta Assessment Consortium. (2005). *A framework for student assessment* (2nd ed.). Retrieved from: http://www.aac.ab.ca/framework_blue.html

Anderson, R. S. (1998). Why talk about different ways to grade? The shift from traditional assessment to alternative assessment. *New Directions for Teaching and Learning, 74*, 5–16.

Archbald, D. A., & Newmann, F. M. (1988). *Beyond standardized testing: Assessing authentic academic achievement in the secondary school*. Reston, VA: National Association of Secondary School Principals.

Assessment. (2010). *OxfordDictionaries.com*. Oxford University Press. Retrieved from: http://oxforddictionaries.com/view/entry/m_en_us1223361

Bauer, N. J. (1993, April). *Instructional designs, portfolios and the pursuit of authentic assessment.* Paper presented at the spring conference of the New York State Association of Teacher Educators, Syracuse, NY.

Berlak, H., Newmann, F. M., Adams, E., Archbald, D. A., Burgess, T., Raven, J., et al. (1992). *Toward a new science of educational testing and assessment.* New York, NY: SUNY.

Black, P. (1993). Formative and summative assessment by teachers. *Studies in Science Education, 21*(1), 49–97.

Black, P. (2001). Dreams, strategies and systems: Portraits of assessment past, present and future. *Assessment in Education: Principles, Policy & Practice, 8*(1), 65–85.

Black, P., Harrison, C., Lee, C., Marshall, B., & Wiliam, D. (2004). Working inside the black box: Assessment for learning in the classroom. *Phi Delta Kappan, 86*, 8–21.

Black, P., & Wiliam, D. (1998). Inside the black box: Raising standards through classroom assessment. *Phi Delta Kappan, 80*(2), 139–148.

Black, P., & Wiliam, D. (2003). In praise of educational research: Formative assessment. *British Educational Research Journal, 29*, 623–637.

Black, P., & William, D. (2006). Assessment for learning in the classroom. In J. Gardner (Ed.), *Assessment and learning* (pp. 9–26). London, UK: Sage Publications.

Bloom, B. S., Hastings, J. T., & Madaus, G. F. (1971). *Handbook on formative and summative evaluation of student learning.* New York, NY: McGraw-Hill.

Boekaerts, M., & Corno, L. (2005). Self-regulation in the classroom: A perspective on assessment and intervention. *Applied Psychology: An International Review, 54*(2), 199–231.

Broadfoot, P., & Black, P. (2004). Redefining assessment? The first ten years of assessment in education. *Assessment in Education: Principles, Policy & Practice, 11*(1), 7–27.

Brookhart, S. M. (2001). Successful students' formative and summative uses of assessment information. *Assessment in Education: Principles, Policy & Practice, 8*(2), 153–169.

Brookhart, S. M. (2013). The use of teacher judgement for summative assessment in the USA. *Assessment in Education: Principles, Policy & Practice, 20*(1), 69–90.

Buhagiar, M. A. (2007). Classroom assessment within the alternative assessment paradigm: Revisiting the territory. *The Curriculum Journal, 18*(1), 39–56.

Christoforou, A. P., & Yigit, A. S. (2008). Improving teaching and learning in engineering education through a continuous assessment process. *European Journal of Engineering Education, 33*(1), 105–116.

Clark, I. (2012). Formative assessment: Assessment is for self-regulated learning. *Educational Psychological Review, 24*, 205–249.

Crick, R. D. (2007). Learning how to learn: The dynamic assessment of learning power. *Curriculum Journal, 18*(2), 135–153.

Crisp, G. T. (2012). Integrative assessment: Reframing assessment practice for current and future learning. *Assessment & Evaluation in Higher Education, 37*(1), 33–43.

Dassa, C., Vazquez-Abad, J., & Ajar, D. (1993). Formative assessment in a classroom setting: From practice to computer innovations. *Alberta Journal of Educational Research, 39*, 116.

Daws, N., & Singh, B. (1996). Formative assessment: To what extent is its potential to enhance pupils' science being realized? *School Science Review, 77*, 99.

Dörfler, T., Golke, S., & Artelt, C. (2009). Dynamic assessment and its potential for the assessment of reading competence. *Studies in Educational Evaluation, 35*, 77–82.

Dunn, K. E., & Mulvenon, S. W. (2009). A critical review of the research on formative assessment: The limited scientific evidence of the impact of formative assessment in education. *Practical Assessment, Research & Evaluation, 14*(7), 1–11. Retrieved from: http://pareonline.net/pdf/v14n7.pdf.

Eisner, E. W. (1985). *The art of educational evaluation.* Philadelphia, PA: Falmer Press.

Evaluation. (2010). *OxfordDictionaries.com.* Oxford University Press. Retrieved from: http://oxforddictionaries.com/view/entry/m_en_us1417730

Frey, B. B., & Schmitt, V. L. (2007). Coming to terms with classroom assessment. *Journal of Advanced Academics, 18*(3), 402–423.

Gallagher, C., & Worth, P. (2008). *Formative assessment policies, programs, and practices in the southwest region* (Issues & Answers Report, REL 2008–No. 041). Washington, DC: U.S. Department of Education, Institute of education Sciences, National Center for Education

Evaluation and Regional Assistance, Regional Educational Laboratory Southwest. Retrieved from: http://ies.ed.gov/ncee/edlabs/projects/project.asp?ProjectID=150.

Haney, W. (Ed.). (1991). *We must take care: Fitting assessments to function*. Alexandria, VA: Association for Supervision and Curriculum Development.

Harlen, W. (2000). *Teaching, learning and assessing science* (3rd ed.). Thousand Oaks, CA: Sage.

Harlen, W. (2005). Teachers' summative practices and assessment for learning: Tensions and synergies. *Curriculum Journal, 16*(2), 207–223.

Harlen, W. (2006). On the relationship between assessment for formative and summative purposes. In J. Gardner (Ed.), *Assessment and learning* (pp. 103–117). London, UK: Sage.

Harlen, W. (2007). Criteria for evaluating systems for student assessment. *Studies in Educational Evaluation, 33*, 15–28.

Hosp, J. L., & Ardoin, S. P. (2008). Assessment for instructional planning. *Assessment for Effective Intervention, 33*, 69–77.

Irving, S. E., Harris, L. R., & Peterson, E. R. (2011). 'One assessment doesn't serve all the purposes or does it?' New Zealand teachers describe assessment and feedback. *Asia Pacific Education Review, 12*, 413–426.

Kealey, E. (2010). Assessment and evaluation in social work education: Formative and summative approaches. *Journal of Teaching in Social Work, 30*, 64–74.

Leung, C. (2007). Dynamic assessment: Assessment *for* and *as* teaching? *Language Assessment Quarterly, 4*(3), 257–278.

Linden, J. D., & Linden, K. W. (1968). *Tests on trial*. Boston, MA: Houghton Mifflin.

Madaus, G. F., & Dwyer, L. M. (1999). Short history of performance assessment: Lessons learned. *Phi Delta Kappan, 80*, 688–695.

Maeroff, G. I. (1991). Assessing alternative assessment. *Phi Delta Kappan, 73*(4), 273–281.

McMillan, J. H., & Hearn, J. (2008). Student self-assessment: The key to stronger student motivation and higher achievement. *Educational Horizons, 87*(1), 40–49.

Meyer, C. A. (1992). What's the difference between authentic and performance assessment? *Educational Leadership, 49*(8), 39–40.

Murphy, R., & Torrance, H. (1988). *The changing face of educational assessment*. Milton Keynes, UK: Open University Press.

National Center for Fair and Open Testing. (1992). *What is authentic evaluation?* Cambridge, MA: Author.

Newmann, F. M., Secada, W. G., & Wehlage, G. G. (1995). *A guide to authentic instruction and assessment: Vision, standards and scoring*. Madison, WI: Wisconsin Center for Education Research.

Newton, P. E. (2007). Clarifying the purposes of educational assessment. *Assessment in Education: Principles, Policy and Practice, 14*(2), 149–170.

Perie, M., Marion, S., & Gong, B. (2009). Moving toward a comprehensive assessment system: A framework for considering interim assessments. *Educational Measurement: Issues and Practice, 28*(3), 5–13.

Perrenoud, P. (1991). Towards a pragmatic approach to formative evaluation. In P. Weston (Ed.), *Assessment of pupils' achievement: Motivation and school success* (p. 92). Amsterdam, The Netherlands: Swets and Zeitlinger.

Perrone, V. (1991). *ACEI position paper on standardized testing* (Available from the Association for Childhood Educational International, 17904 Georgia Ave, Suite 215, Olney, Maryland 20832). Retrieved from: http://uee.uabc.mx/valora/infoEvaluacion/criticaapruebas.pdf

Poehner, M. E. (2008). *Dynamic assessment: A Vygotskian approach to understanding and promoting L2 development*. New York, NY: Springer.

Poehner, M. E., & Lantolf, J. P. (2005). Dynamic assessment in the language classroom. *Language Teaching Research, 9*(3), 233–265.

Poehner, M. E., & Lantolf, J. P. (2010). Vygotsky's teaching-assessment dialectic and L2 education: The case for dynamic assessment. *Mind, Culture, and Activity, 17*(4), 312–330.

Rothman, R. (1990). New tests based on performance raise questions. *Education Week, 10*(2), 1.

Sadler, R. (1989). Formative assessment and the design of instructional systems. *Instructional Science, 18*, 119–144.

Savickiene, I. (2011). Designing of student learning achievement evaluation. *Quality of Higher Education, 8*, 74–93.

Scriven, M. (1967). The methodology of evaluation. In R. Tyler, R. Gagne, & M. Scriven (Eds.), *Perspectives of curriculum evaluation* (pp. 39–83). Chicago, IL: Rand McNally.

Segers, M., Dochy, F., & Gijbels, D. (2010). Impact of assessment on students' learning strategies and implications for judging assessment quality. In P. Peterson, E. Baker, & B. McGaw (Eds.), *International encyclopedia of education* (3rd ed., pp. 196–201). Oxford, UK: Elsevier.

Stiggins, R. J., & Chappuis, S. (2005). Putting testing in perspective: It's for learning. *Principal Leadership, 6*(2), 16–20.

Stobart, G., & Gipps, C. (2010). Alternative assessment. In B. McGraw, E. Baker, & P. Peterson (Eds.), *International encyclopedia of education* (3rd ed., pp. 202–208). Oxford, UK: Elsevier.

Sulzby, E. (1990). Qualities of a school district culture that support a dynamic process of assessment. In J. A. Roderick (Ed.), *Context-responsive approaches to assessing children's language* (pp. 97–104). Urbana, IL: National Conference on Research in English.

Sutton, R. (1995). *Assessment for learning*. Salford, UK: RS.

Taras, M. (2005). Assessment – Summative and formative – Some theoretical reflections. *British Journal of Educational Studies, 53*(4), 466–478.

Taras, M. (2007). Machinations of assessment: Metaphors, myths and realities. *Pedagogy, Culture & Society, 15*(1), 55–69.

Taras, M. (2008a). Assessment for learning: Sectarian divisions of terminology and concepts. *Journal of Further and Higher Education, 32*(4), 389–397.

Taras, M. (2008b). Summative and formative assessment: Perceptions and realities. *Active Learning in Higher Education, 9*(2), 172–192.

Taras, M. (2009). Summative assessment: The missing link for formative assessment. *Journal of Further and Higher Education, 33*(1), 57–69.

Taras, M. (2010). Assessment for learning: Assessing the theory and evidence. *Procedia Social and Behavioral Sciences, 2*, 3015–3022.

Thomson, K., Bachor, D., & Thomson, G. (2002). The development of individualised educational programmes using a decision-making model. *British Journal of Special Education, 29*(1), 37–43.

Trevisan, M. S. (2007). Evaluability assessment from 1986 to 2006. *American Journal of Evaluation, 28*(3), 290–303.

Turner, M., VanderHeide, K., & Fynewever, H. (2011). Motivations for and barriers to the implementation of diagnostic assessment practices – A case study. *Chemistry Education Research and Practice, 12*, 142–157.

Volante, L., & Beckett, D. (2011). Formative assessment and the contemporary classroom: Synergies and tensions between research and practice. *Canadian Journal of Education, 34*(2), 239–255.

Vygotsky, L. (1978). *Mind in society*. Cambridge, MA: Harvard University Press.

Warmington, E. H., & Rouse, P. G. (1956). *Great dialogues of Plato*. Toronto, ON, Canada: The New English Library.

Wehlburg, C. M. (2007). Closing the feedback loop is not enough: The assessment spiral. *Assessment Update, 19*(2), 1–2, 15.

Western and Northern Canadian Protocol for Collaboration in Education. (2006). *Rethinking classroom assessment with purpose in mind: Assessment for learning, assessment as learning, assessment of learning*. Retrieved from: http://www.wncp.ca/media/40539/rethink.pdf

Wiggins, G. P. (1993). Assessment: Authenticity, context, and validity. *Phi Delta Kappan, 75*(3), 200–214.

Wiliam, D., & Black, P. (1996). Meanings and consequences: A basis for distinguishing formative and summative functions of assessment. *British Educational Research Journal, 22*, 537–548.

Wiliam, D., & Black, P. (2003). In praise of educational research: Formative assessment. *British Educational Research Journal, 29*, 623–637.

Willis, S. (1990). Transforming the test. ASCD update. *Association for Supervision and Curriculum Development, 32*(7), 3–6.

Yeomans, J. (2008). Dynamic assessment practice: Some suggestions for ensuring follow-up. *Educational Psychology in Practice, 24*(2), 105–114.

Yoakum, C. S., & Yerkes, R. M. (1920). *Army mental tests*. New York, NY: Holt.

Chapter 3
Assessment and Cooperative Learning: The Missing Think

Barrie Bennett

Abstract Cooperative learning facilitates the design of effective group work; but effective group work is more complex than attending to the research on cooperative learning. This chapter illustrates some of the missing thinks in the application of effective group work and how leadership at the school and district levels positively impacts instructional change. Key to effective group work is understanding how different cooperative learning methods might intersect with each other, as well as with other instructional methods outside of cooperative learning. For example, intersecting the Johnsons' five basic elements as students do an Academic Controversy or intersecting Think Pair Share and Place Mat to complete phase two of Concept Attainment. That intersection of multiple methods allows teachers to combine the effect sizes of those innovations; by combining innovations we impact learning and assessment. The idea of how effectively teachers apply aspects of cooperative learning is also explored through the research on Levels of Use on an innovation that emerged from the work of Gene Hall and Shirley Hord on the Concerns Based Adoption Model (CBAM). Here teachers are reminded that until they and their students are skilled at implementing effective group work, they need to understand that student learning is going to be minimal. Obviously, we must consider the teachers' and students' skill level with all instructional innovations before making 'assessment' decisions about student learning.

Keywords Assessment • CBAM • Change • Cooperative learning • Effective group work • Instruction • Leadership • Levels of use

3.1 Introduction

This chapter is not about a 'best answer' or 'best practice' concerning the relationship between assessment and cooperative learning. The quality of any practice emerges and/or disappears over the intersection of time and collective effort. In this

---

B. Bennett (✉)
Ontario Institute for Studies in Education, University of Toronto (OISE/UT),
252 Bloor St W, Toronto, on M5S 1V6, Canada
e-mail: b.bennett@utoronto.ca

© Springer International Publishing Switzerland 2016
S. Scott et al. (eds.), *Leadership of Assessment, Inclusion, and Learning*,
The Enabling Power of Assessment 3, DOI 10.1007/978-3-319-23347-5_3

chapter, I focus on how those two concepts might emerge over time within a complex learning environment. As you read this chapter, I invite you to consider the possibility that I may be completely wrong.

The first iteration of this chapter focused on what I was asked to do: explore the intersection between assessment and cooperative learning. That said, I realised that, although I was doing what was asked, I was missing the mark. To only focus on the relationship between those two concepts is folly (*folly* meaning pursuing a course of action that evidence shows is incorrect).

The second iteration of this chapter focused on how assessment and cooperative learning must be thought of as interacting organically with other facets of the teaching and learning process, such as instruction, curriculum, and how students learn. But, that focus implied that we know what we are doing with all those facets – and that is an 'assumptive think' nested within the process of folly.

This third iteration resulted when I sensed a 'missing think'. Although the first two attempts were, from my experience and reading, correct, an issue emerged: our failure to collectively understand, apply, and research the intersection of assessment, cooperative learning, instruction and how students learn *guided by what is understood about change and systemic change*. The change piece was missing. Keep in mind that change and systemic change imply the idea of leadership and more specifically instructional leadership. Why instructional leadership? Leithwood, Day, Sammons, Harris, and Hopkins (2007) identified principal support of teachers becoming instructionally skilled as the second most powerful predictor of student achievement (teachers' instructional repertoire being the most powerful predictor). Total leadership accounted for a quite significant 27 % of the variation in student achievement across schools (p. 11).

As an example, in 2012 (the seventh year of a systemic change project focused on instruction) the Medicine Hat School District in Alberta, Canada, ran a 4-day cooperative learning training programme, during the academic year designed to create safer classrooms. The training involved all teachers in the district, including school administration and all central office administration (assistant superintendents and the superintendent). Here you start to sense the district as the unit of analysis.

In this chapter, I look at the familiar in an unfamiliar way to create clarity through complexity. By 'familiar' I refer to the extensive research and writing on assessment and cooperative learning. We have all heard about assessment *of, for,* and *as* learning (Earl, 2004) as well as 'knowledge of results' and 'feedback'. Hattie (2012) posits 'feedback' as one of the most powerful processes related to student achievement. Tangentially, we sense how assessment connects to, or simply re-labels, what we know as summative and formative evaluation (Scriven, 1967). We have all heard of Think Pair Share and Jigsaw, and most of you have likely heard of Tribes and the Johnsons' Five Basic Elements of effective group work. Most of you have likely (knowingly or unknowingly) played with Kagan's (2009) structures, such as Round Robin and Numbered Heads. That said, understanding and applying those cooperative-learning structures (and the literature must contain at least 200 small group structures) is a small part of the teaching and learning process (including the cooperative learning process). Our concern should be the disconnect between instruction, curriculum, assessment, how students learn, change and systemic change by educators who live their professional lives almost completely focused on only one of those six areas. I understand those educators may 'talk' about other areas, but we seldom see evidence of a 'practical' connection. Of course the flip side is that we would not have such a deep grasp of those areas if those individuals had not focused so intensely in those areas. So the tragic flaw slices both ways. Those who intersect struggle to get to those deeper levels; those have a focused inquiry struggle to enact the intersection of multiple areas.

To expand our thinking about the intersection of assessment and cooperative learning, I focus on five concerns. Each of the five sections of this chapter covers one concern. In addition, the five sections fit within two dimensions of understanding assessment and cooperative learning: (1) classroom practice, and (2) leadership around the process of educational change/support within a district. The first dimension aligns with this scenario: it's 9.00 a.m., Monday morning. How do I, as a teacher, effectively enact cooperative learning and assessment in my classroom? The second dimension aligns with the teacher's level of skill: "How do I get better at this over time?" The mistake, I argue, is to continually operate in only one of those dimensions. Those two dimensions, classroom practice and educational change/support, will appear in all five sections of this chapter. In Sects. 3.2, 3.3, and 3.4, I deal with classroom teaching. In Sects. 3.5 and 3.6, I deal with the processes of leadership/support within the process of school and systemic change.

In Sect. 3.2, I argue that we do not understand, nor effectively enact, instruction in the classroom; and, tangentially, we fail to assess the integrative reality of instruction (Bennett, 1996; Bennett et al., 1996). By not grasping this integrative reality, we fail to wisely act on what is known or understood about assessment and cooperative learning. Obviously, assessment and cooperative learning are both embedded in that 'integrative reality' of the teaching and learning process. Logic would tell us that a teacher's classroom application of assessment and cooperative learning essentially depends on their overall instructional efficacy.

In Sect. 3.3, I focus more closely on the multiple processes contained in assessment and cooperative learning that play out what we understand about assessment and cooperative learning. Because we do not clearly grasp those two concepts and the processes that enact them, we unwittingly inaccurately assess their impact in the teaching and learning process. This includes not understanding the concept of *effect size* as a way of valuing the diverse possibilities of the cooperative learning literature, and as a result, making unintentionally inaccurate judgments about the usefulness or lack of usefulness of all instructional innovations.

In Sect. 3.4, I merge the concepts of assessment and cooperative learning to illustrate how they might play out in the classroom. Here the focus is on how cooperative learning facilitates a richer variety of ways of assessing *for* and *as* learning.

In Sect. 3.5, I posit that we have a naïve grasp of what it means to demonstrate expert instructional behaviour. When we research (assess) the impact of an innovation, such as cooperative learning, on student learning, we seldom, if ever, assess the innovation's levels of use before determining its impact – which is absurd. This is where leadership within the school determines whether or not teachers become instructionally efficacious. In this section I also connect to research on Levels of Use of an innovation, one component of Hall and Hord's (2011) research on the Concerns Based Adoption Model (CBAM). Again, this illustrates how school culture/leadership impacts level of use.

In Sect. 3.6, I briefly discuss how most school districts do not take systemic action to more effectively merge cooperative learning and assessment, or any other instructional innovations. Hargreaves and Fullan (2012) state that the idea of building human and social capital systemically is essential (p. 4). As examples, I share the actions taken by two large Canadian school districts over time to increase preservice and inservice teachers' sense of efficacy in cooperative learning and assessment: Ontario's Durham Board of Education and the York Region District School Board. I also briefly illustrate how this led to change in Germany and to our current work with the Ministry of Education in Ireland.

Each of the five sections also contains one or more concept maps (Novak & Gowan, 1984) that organise most of the key ideas in that section. As you work your way through this chapter, think of the process as an archaeological dig. Before I begin the first section, I am going to set the stage by stating what this chapter is *not* about. Then I will go on what I call an introductory ramble, designed to foreshadow the five sections.

3.1.1 What This Chapter Is Not About

Although I briefly share some of the research results from the literature on assessment and cooperative learning later in this chapter, this chapter is not a review of the research intended to convince you to act. We know that assessment and cooperative learning work; that should not be an issue. That said, if you are new to teaching and require a sense of the research/history of research on cooperative learning, the following review articles would be practical places to start: Ellis (2001), Hattie (2012), Johnson and Johnson (1989, 1999), Marzano and Kendall (2008), Schmuck and Schmuck (1998), Slavin (1980). In those reviews you will find not only the foundational constructs of cooperative learning but also bibliographies containing hundreds of research articles, all reporting the impact of cooperative learning on students' social and academic learning. If you want to read about the impact of assessment, see Black, Harrison, Lee, Marshall, and Wiliam (2004), Black and Wiliam (1998), Dufour, Eaker, and Dufour (2005), Earl (2004), Marzano (2000), Stiggins (2004, 2005).

Clearly, so much has been written about cooperative learning and assessment that another indepth analysis of research on them is not going to add much to what we already understand; and, tangentially, the literature and research on the two areas overwhelmingly indicates that they both powerfully affect student learning. Unfortunately, our zeal for researching assessment and cooperative learning is far greater than our willingness to collectively understand and act on what we've learned from that research.

3   Assessment and Cooperative Learning: The Missing Think

3.1.2 Introductory Ramble

Here I chat a bit about the importance of enjoying the processes of thinking. If we do not enjoy thinking or value it, we will not evolve in our understanding of assessment and cooperative learning. One of my graduate students who teaches in Comox, British Columbia, Canada, did a 2-year analysis of the effect of graphic organisers on her Grade 12 English students, and found that, by using concept maps, she encouraged her students to think – which, interestingly, led to them to *wanting* to edit their work (Peacock, 2005).

In a visit to Rossmoyne Secondary High School in Perth, Australia in November of 2013, I visited Karri, who is in her fourth year of teaching. Interestingly, she teaches the Johnson's 'five basic elements' to her students to not only have them self-assess (evaluate) all their group projects, but also as a lens for students to assess political parties' challenges related to social issues. She has shifted beyond the teacher as 'user' of an innovation to applying that innovation as a shift towards student self-assessment and students' assessment of group processes outside the classroom. Very sophisticated thinking.

Do you believe that the following is possible? If you do not enjoy thinking, you will most likely not enjoy editing your writing, because editing one's work is a form of personal assessment – assessment as learning. Personally, from kindergarten through my first degree, I did not enjoy writing, and I did not enjoy thinking, especially when it came to writing about topics that had no connection to my lived experience. What if you do not understand thinking? How can you enjoy what you don't understand?

Let's prove a point about how much you don't know about thinking. Table 3.1 is a data set, my guess is that you will not get the answer. (Table 3.1 is based on the work of Bruner, 1966).

Focus Statement: How are all the instructional methods on the left side the same? How are all the instructional methods on the right side the same? Note that every instructional method in the world, by default, will fit on the Left or Right side because of Bloom's Taxonomy. Note that complex instructional methods fit on the left and the right side including cooperative learning structures; but virtually all

Table 3.1 Data set

Left side	Right side
Group investigation	Jigsaw
Academic controversy	Teams games tournament
Mind maps	Johnsons five basic elements
Concept maps	Place mat
Venn diagrams	Think pair share
Ranking ladders	Framing questions
Concept attainment	Lecture
Concept formation	Lesson design (Madeline Hunter's work)
Plus minus interesting (PMI)	Know want to know learned (KWL)

cooperative-learning structures will fit on the right side. One side is not 'better' than the other. Nonetheless, the implication for assessment is massive. I will not give you the answer; and you are unlikely to see it.

Where would you put project based learning (PBL), Synectics, Flow Charts, the Picture Word Inductive Model, Brainstorming, Value Lines, etc.

Until you do find the answer, you will be missing a key link between cooperative learning, assessment, student learning, and research ... including effect size. Hattie (2012) also misses this piece in all his research; along with other key pieces ... so don't feel bad. Sometimes it is good not to know ... for a while.

Why would students' unwillingness to think change simply because we put them in small cooperative groups? Who cares about pronoun-referent problems or misplaced modifiers or run-on sentences when you do not enjoy thinking ... regardless of whether or not you're in groups? And conversely, if teachers do not care about student learning, why would they care about the quality of their assessments of students' efforts? Getting a mark of 7/10 or a B+ on an essay – with a few general comments, such as "Well done" or "You should have done another draft" – does not show much *assessment character* (concern for student learning). Basically, it represents meaningless assessment of learning. So when we as teachers assess students' work, regardless of whether it is before, during, or after learning – or *for, as,* or *of* learning, etc. – our feedback is less likely to impact learners if their minds and hearts are not involved in that work. Combine that with failing to really care about the quality of the assessment, and you, by default, get caught up in what I call *shadow assessment*: assessment done, yes, but meaningless, valueless, and usually failing to understand or reflect the student as learner.

The idea of focusing on the student, as well as on the interaction between students and the roles of instruction and assessment, is not new; John Dewey and Evelyn Dewey, in their 1914 book *Schools of Tomorrow*, urged educators to design learning so that it is steeped in learners' experiences. Here are two interesting quotes:

> Since a child lives in a social world, where even the simplest act or word is bound up with the words and acts of his neighbors (p. 138) ... If every pupil has an opportunity to express himself, to show what are his particular qualities, the teacher will have material on which to base her plans of instruction. (p. 138)

A hundred years earlier, Charles Dickens, who studied with Froebel in the early 1800s (Froebel created kindergartens) made many astute observations as he visited classrooms. Dickens spoke of the "need of practicing the fundamental law of cooperation and the sharing of responsibilities and duties, as the foundation for the true comprehension of the law of community" (Huges, 1901, p. 7).

As you read the first section of this chapter, about understanding instruction, please keep in mind that, if teachers do not enjoy and understand thinking, the chances are slim that they will think deeply about instruction. Do you yourself really understand instruction? Does your understanding of instruction affect how you think about, and enact, assessment and cooperative learning?

As an educator who still has a lot to learn, I have an ever-growing understanding and appreciation of how much I do *not* know. I taught for 10 years in secondary, junior high, and elementary schools, then for 6 years was a school-district consultant focused on instruction. Now having taught instruction at the Ontario Institute for Studies in Education of the University of Toronto (OISE/UT) for 26 years, I am acutely aware, when it comes to expert knowledge in specific areas, of how smart I am *not* and how smart others are. Nonetheless, my strength has always been my ability and willingness to learn from others, and to merge multiple processes and multiple voices. In terms of cooperative learning, for example, 2 weeks before writing this chapter, I completed the 4-day Tribes training (a cooperative learning approach to creating safe, inclusive environments) for my sixth time in about 13 years. That is 24 days of training to understand Tribes. I wrote a book on cooperative learning with several colleagues, and I work with graduate students who are exploring and assessing the effects of different aspects of cooperative learning on student learning. The bother in all this is that, the more I learn, the more doors open. And behind each door is a world I've yet to explore.

I currently work in 11 districts in 3 countries on large-scale, systemic school reform. A lot of that work is based on Fullan's synthesis of change research (2001, 2011). Most of these districts are working effectively; two are struggling to sustain their reform after 5 years of intensive effort. Cooperative learning and assessment are key pieces in the quilt of their efforts. Previously, I worked in a district that had focused on cooperative learning for 16 years. In the tenth year, they won a $300,000 international award as one of the best districts in the world (Bennett & Green, 1995). I talk about this district's efforts to implement cooperative learning further in Sect. 3.6. In the 16th year their systemic effort ended; they lost what they had. The message in this district's loss is that all innovation in assessment and cooperative learning, in terms of impact over time, comes down to leadership; to the collective wisdom of central office and the *will* and *skill* of principals in helping teachers extend and refine their classroom practice. I've come to realise that if a district is not going to innovate effectively, then why bother innovating at all. You will also see this in our current project in Ireland (O'Murchu, Russell, & Bennett, 2013). We are now in our sixth year and have approximately 25 % of 720 schools involved in the project.

3.2 Understanding Instruction and Situating Assessment and Cooperative Learning in Instruction

In this section I briefly share the experience that led to my work on Instructional Intelligence and its role in student learning. This leads to the first reason why educators do not collectively understand instruction. Currently, we have no practical theory about explaining how instructional methods interact with one another. (This was argued by Jerome Bruner in 1996). For example, how Framing Questions, Wait Time, Bloom's Taxonomy, Think Pair Share, Place Mat, Round Robin, Numbered Heads, the Five Basic Elements and Tribes all intersect to facilitate learning – in about 5 min. As a result, given that assessment and cooperative learning are part of instruction, we fail to (collectively) act wisely in enacting cooperative learning and assessment. In response to this issue of integrating instructional methods, I clarify Instructional Intelligence and also provide a concept map that situates both cooperative learning and assessment in my work on Instructional Intelligence.

Instructional Intelligence is an amorphous concept that incorporates the concepts of cooperative learning and assessment. And, like assessment and cooperative learning, Instructional Intelligence is not absolutely clear – which, you will see, is somewhat of a godsend. No group or person owns the definition of the concept *intelligence*; ergo, no one owns the definition of Instructional Intelligence. This means we can play/evolve with Instructional Intelligence forever (as we have with the concepts *love* and *motivation*). Not knowing fuels inquiry.

That said, I share one perspective on intelligence for the purpose of this chapter: David Perkins' (1995) definition of *intelligent behaviour* from his book *Outsmarting IQ: The Emerging Science of Learnable Intelligence*. Perkins argues that IQ scores are a poor predictor of intelligent behaviour; in response, he identifies four factors that *do* predict intelligent behaviour.

1. Experience that results in the development of patterns.
2. Constant reflection to create and connect patterns.
3. A repertoire of strategies to respond to those patterns.
4. Sufficient neurons to carry out thinking and action.

My own experience tells me that what we seek in education (from students, parents, teachers, consultants, administrators, university lecturers, union representatives, ministries of education, etc.) is collective intelligent behaviour – action that pushes beyond mediocrity. Who among us wants a mediocre cup of coffee, electrician, surgeon, haircut, pilot, or pizza? So, why would we want a mediocre teacher playing with assessment and cooperative learning in a mediocre way?

In our use of cooperative learning and assessment we are looking for intelligent (above mediocre) or, hopefully, expert behaviour from all education stakeholders in enacting those two concepts. For example, look at the current lack of interaction between teacher unions, faculties of education, ministries of education, and school districts? Do those agencies cooperate to improve the life and learning chances of students? If our leaders don't, where is the impetus for teachers and students to work more responsibly?

Look in your classroom(s). Is it possible that 90 % (or more) of teachers do not structure group work effectively? How would you know? Of what value is attending to assessment if group work is ineffective? In terms of effectiveness in applying cooperative learning and assessment, where would you place yourself, or teachers in your school or district? What we are after is expert behaviour (see Berieter & Scardamalia, 1993 for the research on how experts become experts). When you shift in the direction of applying group work effectively, you shift towards being Instructionally Intelligent. Take a look at Table 3.2, a rubric that uses five of the many variables to assess group work.

Where would you place your current level of skill in the identified attributes?

So what is Instructional Intelligence, and where do the concepts of assessment and cooperative learning fit within the structure of instructional intelligence?

3 Assessment and Cooperative Learning: The Missing Think

Table 3.2 Sample rubric for assessing group effectiveness using five criteria

Attributes	Level 1	Level 2	Level 3	Level 4
Group size	No attention to group size. Teacher does not sense that group size is relevant. Often more than four students per group	Some attention to group size, but some groups unnecessarily bigger than they need be, given the skill level of the students. May be two to four per group, but some groups still more than four	Group size is considered in most situations, although group size at times does not match the size needed for the academic task or skill level of the group	Group size always considered. Group size reflects the skill level of the students and the needs of the academic task. Teacher rarely uses group larger than four, unless necessary to successfully complete the task
Group structure	No attention to how groups are chosen – usually friendship or location groups. Teacher has no idea that, or fails to act, on the idea that, different group structures exist, such as friendship, random assignment, and teacher selected	Some attention to who works with who, but again, mostly friendship groups. Teacher not very aware of different ways to structure groups	Teacher attends to how groups are structured and will usually carefully use teacher-selected groups or, at times, random assignment to groups. Will seldom use friendship groups	Teacher is conscious of the need to structure group work carefully, that teacher-structured groups are usually the most effective; next is random assignment to groups. Teacher will let students work with friends at times, once they have proved they can work effectively will all students in the class
Readiness for group work	Students are placed in groups with no opportunity to acquire the skills needed to work together effectively. Teacher has no idea that collaborative skills can be classified into social, communication, and critical thinking skills	Teacher may explain skills, but students do not understand what those skills look like and sound like. Teacher still has no idea that collaborative skills can be classified into social, communication, and critical thinking skills	Students are taught the appropriate skills needed to complete the task. The teacher is still most likely not acting on how social skills, communication skills, and critical thinking skills play off each other	Students are taught the appropriate collaborative skills needed to complete the task. Teacher is very much aware of how social skills, communication skills, and critical thinking skills play off each other

(continued)

Table 3.2 (continued)

Attributes	Level 1	Level 2	Level 3	Level 4
Individual accountability	Teacher may think about individual accountability but do little to nothing to enact it	Teacher is beginning to think about individual accountability and periodically invokes it; often the attempt is made too late in the group activity	Teacher invokes individual accountability; that said, it still may be possible for a student to not be involved or to take over, and/or do more than they should	Teacher effectively invokes individual accountability and students find it difficult to 'escape' being involved or to take over and not let others be involved
Clear meaningful task	Task not clear; if it is, the task is often not amenable to group work.	Task is somewhat clear and somewhat meaningful to some students and worth completing in groups	Task is clear and meaningful to most students and worth completing in groups	Task is very clear and meaningful to most to all students and clearly worth completing in groups
Collaborative skills	Not taught and not discussed/ processed	Mentioned and possibly discussed/ processed	Taught and usually discussed/ processed	Effectively taught and always discussed/ processed

(For clarification on understanding our thinking around 'concepts' see Perkins (1991) text, Knowledge as Design.)

The concept map in Fig. 3.1 illustrates how I position cooperative learning in the design of learning environments and how it relates to other instructional methods. Later, you will see how this concept map illustrates the imprecision of research on the application of cooperative learning methods in classroom learning, as well as, how that imprecision clearly impacts how we interpret assessment results.

The six key components of Instructional Intelligence are curriculum, assessment, instruction, how students learn, classroom and school change, and systemic change. If any one of those components is not wisely understood and enacted, then expert behaviour in any of them is unlikely. And, by default, so is intelligent behaviour in enacting cooperative learning and assessment. As Ruth Sutton stated about 10 years ago at an assessment conference, "Weighing the pig does not increase the weight of the pig." Assessment in the absence of a range of instructional options and a deep grasp of the curriculum and how students learn is rather naïve.

Figure 3.1, also shows that, whereas assessment is one of the six essential components of Instructional Intelligence, cooperative learning is a subcomponent of another essential component: instruction. That said, the literature on cooperative learning is one of the most, if not *the* most, extensive of literature on all approaches to learning. Without question, some of cooperative-learning methods collectively have one of the most powerful impacts of all instructional approaches on higher-level thinking, social learning, and learning overall.

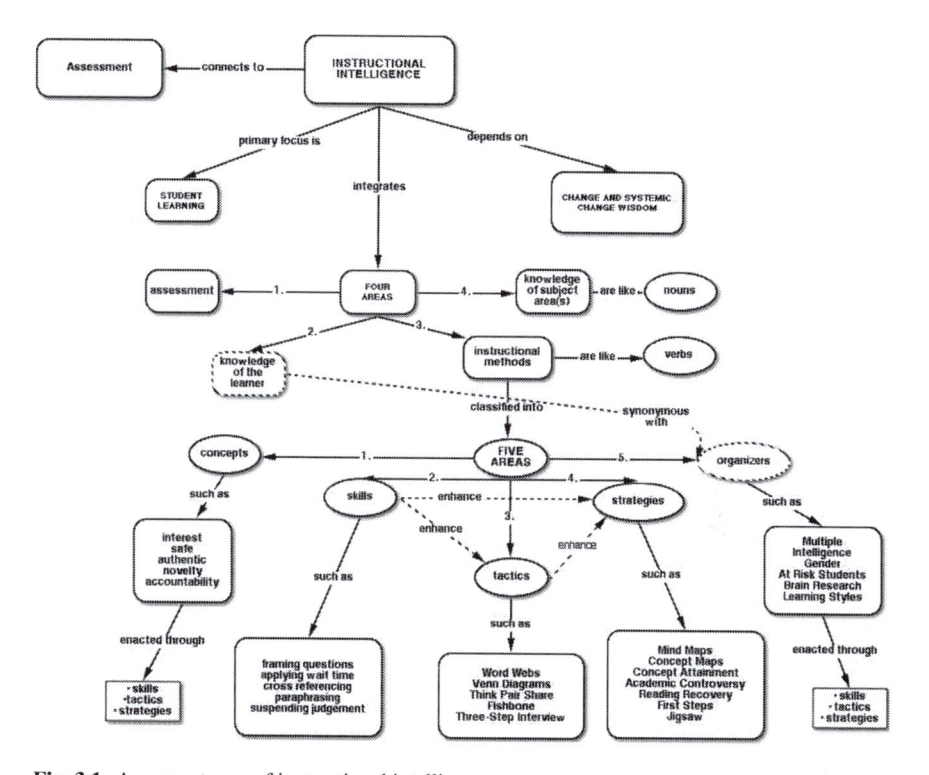

3   Assessment and Cooperative Learning: The Missing Think   55

Fig. 3.1 A concept map of instructional intelligence

Note that, in Fig. 3.1, instruction is classified into six [Five] areas: concepts, skills, tactics, strategies, and organisers. Those six areas are developed around the framework provided in Perkins (1991) text, Knowledge as Design. Classification allows us to be more specific when we communicate, when we plan, when we teach, and when we assess the effect of our efforts or those of our students. For example, at a simple level, we classify utensils into knives, forks, and spoons; or clothing into pants, shirts, socks, dresses, etc.; or transportation into land, sea, air, and space. At a more complex level, we have periodic tables and taxonomies of thinking. Virtually every concept we have is the result of classification.

The cooperative-learning literature contains approximately 200 approaches to group learning: I would classify 190 of those 'approaches' as tactics (less complex and less powerful) and about 10 as strategies (more complex and more powerful). For example, cooperative-learning tactics would include the following processes: Think Pair Share, Place Mat, Four Corners, and 2-3-4 Person Interview. Cooperative-learning strategies would include: Teams Games Tournament, Jigsaw, Academic Controversy, and Group Investigation. Whereas few tactics have a research base, strategies do; some strategies have quite an extensive research base. Again, if we look at research about impact on student learning, strategies are likely to have a larger impact than tactics. That said, what if we merged three or more tactics

Table 3.3 Sample classification of instructional approaches

Concepts	Skills	Tactics	Strategies	Organisers
Safety	Taking turns	Place mat	Jigsaw	Multiple intelligences
Authentic	Wait time	Round robin	Group investigation	Learning styles
Meaningful	Framing questions	4 corners	Academic controversy	Autism
Interesting	Paraphrasing	Community circle	Teams games	Critical thinking
Success	Sharing the objective and purpose of the lesson	Think pair share	Tournament	Cooperative-learning research
Summative		Venn diagrams	Team analysis	
Feedback		Mind maps	Concept attainment	

simultaneously? Would the combined effect be more powerful than one strategy applied in isolation? It might, but we don't know.

By classifying instructional approaches (see Table 3.3), I attempt to focus our understanding of instruction, so that we are more likely to demonstrate intelligent or expert behaviour in the design and assessment of learning environments. Of course, in this chapter, the instructional approach of concern is cooperative learning.

The rationale for the classification in Table 3.3 is that we do not have a clearly articulated theory for explaining instruction's interactive nature. This is what I have been developing for the last 26 years (Bennett, 1996; Bennett et al., 1996). I propose a theory of *instructional integration*, a way of thinking about what happens when we merge two or more instructional processes, guided by what we know about how we learn.

A theory must explain something and be generalisable to other areas. In this chapter, the theory of instructional integration explains how labels – concept, skills, tactics, strategies, and organisers – are applied to research on cooperative learning and assessment, and its application in classrooms. Note that cooperative learning and assessment both contain numerous tactics and/or strategies; however, in the literature on cooperative learning and assessment, tactics and strategies (as labels) also act as organisers to guide teachers in selecting and enacting specific examples of tactics and strategies in their classrooms. When we select and apply a variety of tactics and strategies with little or no grasp of what they are designed to accomplish then we risk enacting them in less effective ways. That of course impacts our research on the effects of those methods.

Tangentially, you can sense how other instructional organisers influence how cooperative learning and assessment tactics and strategies play out – organisers such as Multiple Intelligences, learning styles, gender, culture, learning disabilities, taxonomies of thinking, critical thinking, and, perhaps most important, research on effective group work. Can you effectively apply critical thinking in the absence of effective group work? And, conversely, can you apply effective group work in the absence of critical thinking?

Key to how I classify instructional approaches is the shift from less complex and powerful impact on learning, to more complex and powerful impact. Here is an analogy. In basketball, two concepts would be *fitness* and *sportspersonship*. Basketball players do not enact those concepts directly; rather, their behaviour plays out the concepts. Now, if a coach is going to apply a particular basketball strategy, say the *1-3-1 offence*, the team's players must be able to apply a less complex behaviour (tactic) a give-and-go. That tactic, in turn, requires integrating two less complex behaviours (skills) passing and catching a basketball. The less-complex behaviour makes the more-complex behaviour possible. Attempting to apply a *1-3-1 offence* when players cannot pass, catch, and shoot a basketball is somewhat absurd.

The above analogy, showing how skills, tactics, and strategies intersect, has implications not only for basketball coaches but for how we, as teachers, assess students. Imagine researching the effectiveness of the *1-3-1 offence* (a strategy) if the players could not do a give-and-go, and could not pass, catch, and shoot a basketball, and were poor sports refusing to share. Can you sense the connection between this sports analogy and a teacher running a strategy of Jigsaw, Group Investigation, or Academic Controversy when the students cannot effectively complete such simple tactics as Think Pair Share and Four Corners, because they cannot attentively listen, paraphrase, suspend judgment, seek clarification, probe, accept and extend the ideas of others, or disagree agreeably? What we are assessing – in too many instances – is the ineffective application of the cooperative-learning process.

The above idea of less complex behaviour driving more complex behaviour plays out everywhere. Think, for example, of building a house from a blueprint (the strategy). Good luck building the house if you cannot square the foundation (a tactic) and you cannot hammer, saw, and measure (skills). Those involved in leadership positions are unlikely to be in a position to support teachers growth in cooperative learning if they fail to grasp that complex interdependency between less and more complex instructional methods.

Now let's return to cooperative learning. Asking students to apply or engage in a complex strategy, such as Academic Controversy, when they cannot effectively complete Four Corners is akin to asking someone to run the Boston Marathon when they struggle to run around a city block. Again, this has implications for both classroom practice and assessment. When we decide to assess the concept of cooperative learning, having selected cooperative-learning structures that are not complex and not powerful, and then conclude that cooperative learning did not have a meaningful effect on student learning, we are assessment naïve. In fact, the cooperative learning methods did exactly what they were designed to do: they yielded a small effect size.

You can sense why, in this section, I have said that cooperative learning is an inert concept; you cannot directly 'do it'. Something has to happen to make it come alive; that something is determined by the selection and enactment of those tactics and strategies. Making broad statements about the effect of cooperative learning without knowing its impact is unwise. Hattie (2012) lumps cooperative learning methods into one effect size. The downside of that approach is that you get regression toward the mean and more effective methods look less effective and less effective methods look more effective.

At this point, I will reconnect to my assertion that most teachers are not effective implementers of effective group work. Although most teachers play with what they think is group work, their efforts rarely contain the researched attributes of effective group work. In addition, they apply a limited range of less powerful group structures and do not use those structures to drive other more powerful instructional strategies, such as the Jurisprudential Model of Teaching, Concept Attainment, Concept Formation, Concept Mapping, and Mind Mapping. (See Joyce and Weil, 2000 text Models of Teaching for a description of the more complex instructional strategies.) And, of course, this applies even more to university instructors. Perhaps the most insidious miss-think is the answer to the Concept Attainment data set that all of you did not get. (Don't you just hate arrogance). I did not get it for 40 years … it simply jumped out at me.

That said, how do we encourage educators to shift their thinking and action? We can argue the research, but teachers will argue that they do not have time for group work or that they are preparing students for university and life. Well, I have played in this world of effective group work for over 30 years, and group work structured effectively speeds up the learning process. The problem is, most teachers have no effective training in group-work, and (the literature is clear here) ineffective group work is one of the least effective of all instructional processes.

In response to teachers' argument that they are preparing their students for university, here is another take: "I am going to teach ineffectively at the secondary level so that students can survive ineffective tertiary teaching." This is the incompetence-justifies-incompetence argument. Teachers who choose not to use group work (when appropriate) are not preparing their students for any occupation that I am aware of. Look at the job ads; none that I've seen say, "Wanted: employees who can sit in a row, work on their own and, when stuck on a problem, will put up their hands and wait for the boss to come around and solve their problems." Most employers demand employees who are highly skilled at working with all stakeholders, have evident communication and interpersonal skills, and who can work as part of a team. Most relationships, including marriage, work better when the partners demonstrate appropriate social, communication, and critical-thinking skills, such as taking turns, attentive listening, and suspending judgment. These can all be learned through group work.

3.2.1 Situating Cooperative Learning and Assessment in Lesson Design

Below is an example showing how a preservice teacher used her understanding of connections between multiple areas related to teaching and learning when she designed lessons.

Figure 3.2 illustrates how concepts, skills, tactics, strategies, and organisers interact in the design of learning environments. Of course, it is one thing to understand the factors and how they relate; enacting them is another.

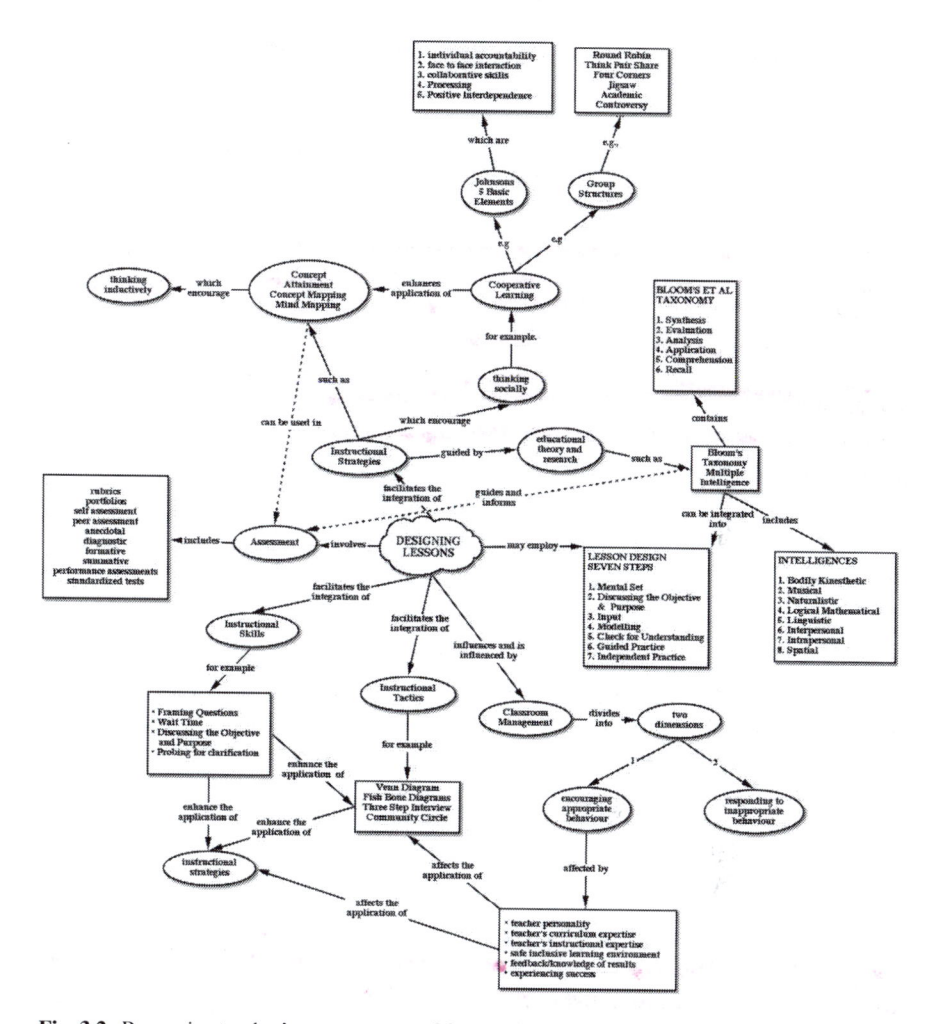

Fig. 3.2 Preservice teacher's concept map of factors that impact lesson design

Sternberg and Horvath (1995), in their article on a prototype of effective teaching, push the idea that, to understand a problem, experts look for complexity rather than attempting to simply clarify or reduce it. Sternberg and Horvath also say that expert teachers have a way of organising what they do: a way of planning lessons that facilitates coherence.

Figure 3.2 is a concept map done by one of my Bachelor of Education (BEd) students. She looked at the factors that she felt should be considered when designing a lesson. When you look carefully at Fig. 3.2, you will sense the complexity of the lesson planning process, as well as how this emerging teacher situates assessment and cooperative learning. How can we as educators meaningfully research assessment and cooperative learning divorced from those other areas such as those identified on her concept map?

In the next section, I focus more specifically on cooperative learning and assessment.

3.3 Understanding Cooperative Learning and Assessment

In this chapter, *cooperative learning* refers to students working effectively in small groups for the purpose of both academic and social learning. *Assessment* refers to the appropriate feedback the students receive (from themselves and from others) on their efforts at academic and social learning. Of course, the above suggests that we understand the attributes of effective group work so that we can recognise the difference between effective and less effective group work; additionally, that we can situate the appropriate forms of assessment within the process of cooperative learning. If we fail to attend to the difference between effective and less effective group work, we'll get caught trying to cut wood with a hammer and then complaining that the hammer fails to effectively cut wood. You won't think this 'tool metaphor' so silly as you delve deeper into this section.

In this section, I first position our understanding of how cooperative learning and assessment play out in the classroom. I then play with each in isolation. Then I merge cooperative learning and assessment. I end this section with a discussion how the effect-size statistic relates to cooperative learning and how we make instructional and assessment decisions.

3.3.1 Positioning Cooperative Learning and Assessment

We do not *do* cooperative learning or assessment any more than we *do* whole language, motivation, constructivism, interest, or safety. Cooperative learning and assessment are not strategies; they are labels for a class of things that can happen in the name of cooperative learning and assessment. Assessment and cooperative learning are inert and connect to other valuably inert concepts, such as safety, respect, and motivation. We do not enter a room and say, "Okay you're motivated, respected, and safe" and then expect the learners to feel or believe they are now motivated, respected, and safe just because we say they are. Ditto for cooperative learning and assessment. Something has to happen in order for cooperative learning and assessment to effectively play out in a learning environment.

Herbert Blumer (1954) positioned how we understand concepts more clearly. He classified concepts into two groups: definitive and sensitising. *Definitive concepts* have absolute clarity (e.g., truck, window, fork, table). We seldom have differences of opinion over definitive concepts. When we see a truck, we don't argue about whether or not it is a truck – for the most part, a truck is a truck. *Sensitising concepts*, on the other hand, are more amorphous (e.g., love, motivation, justice, democracy). We often have differences of opinion over sensitising concepts. In fact, one could study a particular sensitising concept (e.g., motivation or beauty) for the rest of one's life and still not have a locally or globally accepted definition of that concept.

So, where would you position the two concepts of *cooperative learning* and *assessment* – in the definitive or sensitising group? In this chapter, I treat them both as sensitising concepts, because they do not allow absolute clarity. In the literature and research on cooperative learning and assessment we can find multiple interpretations of those two concepts. We will most likely study both concepts for the rest of our professional lives and still not *own* them. As a result of this positioning of cooperative learning and assessment as sensitising concepts we accept different perspectives. Some of those perspectives have a substantial research base, and some have none. The result, however, is a richer understanding of those two concepts.

Let's start with cooperative learning. We see an extensive research base underlying the approaches of Robert Slavin (1995) and David and Roger Johnson (1989) in their work on cooperative learning. As of yet, we don't see a similarly extensive research base underlying Spencer Kagan's (2009) work on cooperative learning structures and Jeanne Gibbs' (2001) work on creating safer and more inclusive environments. Importantly, cooperative learning and assessment contain hundreds of things one can do in the name of assessment and cooperative learning; some are effective, others not so effective. So, when you say you are assessing student work or having students work in groups, is what you're doing effective or not so effective? And, moreover, how would you know?

Cooperative learning is a belief system, grounded in social theory, which in the United States was introduced in the 1960s to facilitate social learning. Interestingly, as an instructional process, cooperative learning predates Christ. And it has one of the largest research bases of all instructional processes.

In this subsection, I first work at clarifying the concept of cooperative learning. I also define the statistical term *effect size* and show how it explains expected results for different applications of cooperative learning. I argue that, if we do not understand this statistical term, we increase the chances of making mistaken assessments of cooperative learning's impact on student learning.

Please note that working cooperatively is only one of three options for structuring classroom learning environments. The other two options are working individually and working competitively. When deciding which one to apply, a colleague of mine, who has applied cooperative learning for over 20 years, always asks himself first, "Is cooperative learning the best way to engage the students in learning this topic?" If that answer is no, he does not enact cooperative learning. In terms of the art and science of teaching, *science* is the research, along with all the components of cooperative learning, and *art* is the how, when, what, where, and why they are being applied. The cooperative learning literature is only one of many knowledge-bases that inform group-work practices.

For example, understanding the research on students with autism will guide your decisions about including such students in the group-work process. In addition, in Fig. 3.2 you can see that classroom management is part of effective group work. Just because we put students in cooperative-learning groups does not mean they will cooperate. One of the reasons that cooperative learning emerged in the United States was to resolve conflicts between different racial/cultural groups. My experience with cooperative learning informs me that if teachers are not experiencing conflict when implementing cooperative learning they are most likely not implementing it properly. Michael Fullan, a renowned researcher and writer on educational change, said in one of his workshops about 15 years ago that "smooth early use is a sure sign that you are not doing it right." So understanding autism, classroom management, Multiple Intelligences, learning styles, change (and numerous other factors) is part of being skilled at cooperative learning.

Figure 3.3 summarises some of the key ideas of cooperative learning.

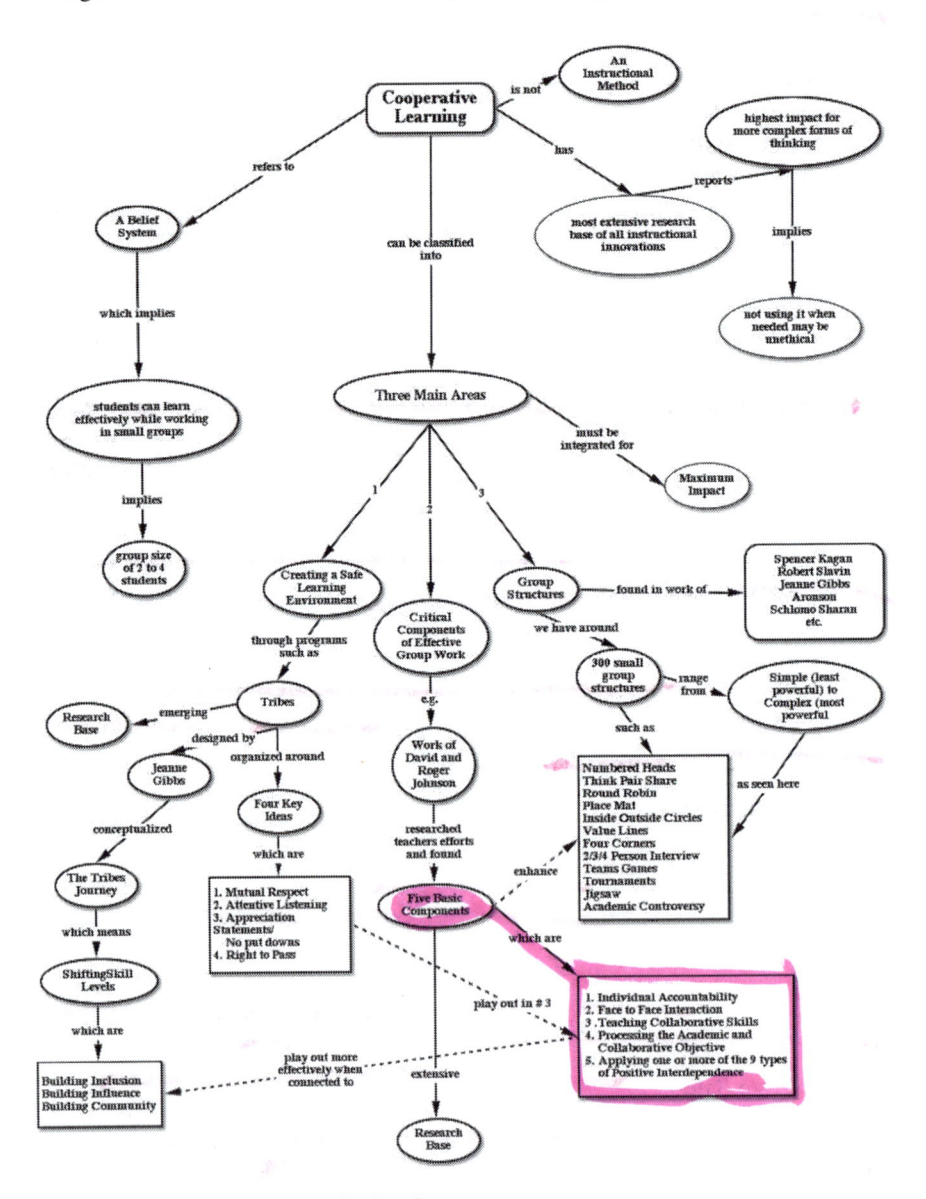

Fig. 3.3 Concept map of cooperative learning

3   Assessment and Cooperative Learning: The Missing Think

Over the years, cooperative learning has also been supported by an esteemed group of thinkers; for example, Lev Vygotsky, Jean Piaget, Paulo Freire, John Dewey, B.F. Skinner, and Howard Gardner. They support the idea that learning is socially constructed. For example, Vygotsky's Zone of Proximal Development focuses on learning from and with another person. One could argue that Vygotsky's work is the foundation for work on mentoring and peer coaching. Howard Gardner (1985) argues, in his theory of Multiple Intelligences, that interpersonal intelligence has a synergistic effect on all the other intelligences and is also the number one predictor of success in each culture studied. Currently, neurologists report that talk is essential for intellectual development.

As I mentioned earlier, cooperative learning has been studied by a variety of researchers, and they and educators have different interpretations as to how cooperative learning plays out. For convenience, we could classify the researchers into three groups: (1) those that focus on building inclusion and safety in group work, such as Jeanne Gibbs' (1995, 2001) Tribes programme; (2) those that focus on how groups function in order to work effectively, such as David and Roger Johnson (1989) and Elizabeth Cohen (1994); and (3) those who provide a variety of structures (from less powerful to more powerful) designed to meet different needs in a classroom, such as Robert Slavin's (1995) Student Teams-Achievement Division, Aronson and Patnoe's (1997) Jigsaw, and Kagan's (1994) Three Step Interview. It may be useful to liken those three groups to layers on a cake, with safety/inclusion on the bottom, then the research on how groups function, and on the top the variety of structures (see Fig. 3.4).

Two of most prolific writers and researchers of the essence of cooperative learning are David and Roger Johnson. Together, they have written hundreds of articles, research papers, and books based on their inquiry into cooperative learning. They identified the five basic elements of effective group work: (1) individual accountability, (2) promoting face-to-face interaction in groups of 2 to 4, (3) teaching the required collaborative skills, (4) processing both the academic and collaborative

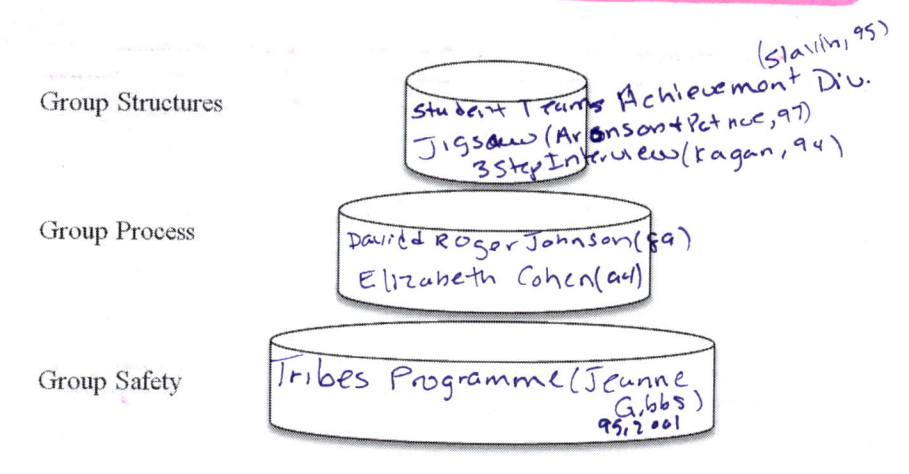

Fig. 3.4 The three layers of cooperative learning

objectives of the lesson, and (5) applying one or more of the nine types of positive interdependence. Of those nine types of positive interdependence, only goal positive interdependence is essential; the other eight are selected according to need. In summary, two of the Johnsons' five basic elements are essential: individual accountability and one of the nine types of positive interdependence: Goal Positive Interdependence (the idea that the group's task is clear, meaningful, and worth doing in a group).

So, we now have a sense of the attributes of effective group work. And more important, the attributes David and Roger Johnson (1989) identified emerged from their qualitative research examining classrooms where group work was effective and those where it was not. However, to assess the impact of cooperative learning in the classroom, simply finding evidence of those attributes of effective group work is insufficient. It is critical to assess how well the teacher and the students use those attributes. If the attributes are not present, or if they are present but not applied at a high enough level of efficacy, then any assessment will report on a non-event or an unskilled application of those attributes. In Sect. 3.5, I include a rubric designed by preservice students to self-assess their application of these attributes.

Effect size is a statistic that indicates how much impact an innovation has on student learning. Conceptually, effect size relates to assessment *of* learning. We often hear or read about the significance of research results. *Significance* refers to the level of confidence you have in rejecting what is called a null hypothesis – which simply states that an innovation will *not* have an impact. Here is an example of a null hypothesis: "Mind Maps will not significantly affect student memory." Now, if the level of significance you set is .05 and your result is significant at that level, then that means that, if you replicated this study, 95 times out of a hundred you would be able to reject the null hypothesis of *no* effect – which actually means that Mind Maps had a positive effect (much like the double negative "I have not got no friends," which means you have friends). So significance tells you that you had an effect (with confidence); effect size tells you how much of a different and gives you more confidence in selecting an innovation to impact student learning.

Significance has two problems. First, it does not tell you *how much* of a difference an innovation made. Second, the decision to accept or reject the null hypothesis is affected by the number of participants in the study. If you only have a few subjects, and you get impressive results – say a shift from the 50th to the 80th percentile – the results might be *not* significant because the numbers are too low and that the results may have happened by chance. So you have to accept the null hypothesis of *no* effect. On the other hand, you could have had minimal results – say a shift from the 50th to the 53rd percentile. However, because you had a high number of participants, you can say your results are significant and so you can reject the null hypothesis. You can see the problem for teachers and staff developers who use significance for making decisions about which innovations to select for professional development.

Effect size is part of the analytical process known as meta-analysis, which allows educators to combine all studies where results are reported as correlations, or F scores, or t scores, etc., regardless of the number of participants in the studies, and to calculate an overall effect. (For an example of a meta-analysis focused on cooperative learning, see Rolheiser-Bennett, 1986). So we can now combine all the small and large studies. And, although all effect sizes are useful information, anything over .5 of a standard deviation is considered powerful. The standard deviation simply refers to how much the mean score of one group differs from the mean score of another group (see Eq.3.1).

Let's take an example. In one of your classes, you try an approach that involves effective structuring of a mostly teacher-led discussion, where students work on their own with no effectively structured group work (the control group). In another class, you have some teacher-led discussion but students also have the opportunity to work effectively in groups for an appropriate amount of time (the experimental group). Now, if the two groups are equal (let's say you put them into the two groups randomly) and you then give them a test at the end of a unit, you could find the classes' average or mean score on the test. To find the effect size, you would use the formula in Eq. 3.1.

Equation 3.1 Formula for calculating effect size $ES = \dfrac{MS_e - MS_c}{SD_c}$
Where

MS = mean score,
SD = standard deviation
e = experimental group, c = control group

I now illustrate this with two overlapping normal curves, to illustrate how far the mean score of the experimental group shifted from the control group's mean score (the standard deviation). You can see in Fig. 3.5 that each line represents the containment of a percentage. One standard deviation in any direction equals approximately 34 %; the next standard deviation 12 %; the next one 3 %. After the third standard deviation, you can see the percentage becomes minimal.

Note that the standard deviation is a constant; it is roughly 34 %, 13 %, 2 % and as stated above, any less than 1 % does not mean much. So, for cooperative learning, the effect size on higher-level thinking is 1.25 standard deviations from the mean. To determine the percentage effect size, do the following calculation:

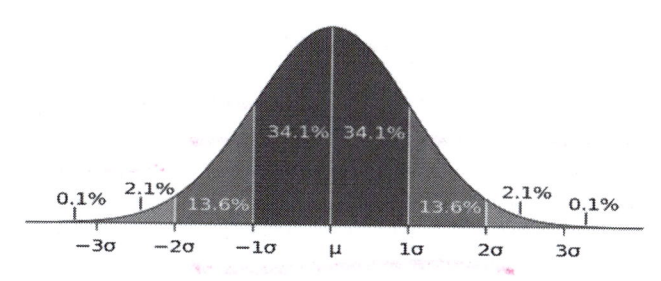

Fig. 3.5 Normal curve

$$50\% + 34\% \text{ (the first standard deviation)}$$
$$+ 3\% \text{ (.25 of the second standard deviation)} = 87\%.$$

So that means, for higher-level thinking, if your class had no cooperative learning, your students' mean score would be at the 50th percentile (the mean) for higher-level thinking. If your other class experienced effectively structured group work, your students' mean would be at the 87th percentile for higher-level thinking. The standard deviation of 1.25 is, of course, an average based on numerous studies; variations will occur between classes. Nonetheless, if you were a parent, which teaching option would you want your child's teacher to use? In addition to cooperative learning's larger effect size on higher-level thinking, its effect size on social learning is .95 standard deviations (.95 of 34 % + 50 %). This is a shift in the mean from the 50 to the 82 percentile.

As for peer coaching as a way for teachers to engage students in cooperative learning, the effect size of having teachers from one school train in teams with their principal and then having follow-up support as they implement peer coaching, compared with teachers attending the training alone with no follow-up support, is 2.23 standard deviations (Bennett, 1987). That is a shift in the mean from the 50th to the 98th percentile.

So, look at the one-shot workshops in your school district and assess their impact. Do teachers attend in school teams with the principal? Is there follow-up support? Are there at least a couple of opportunities to watch each other teach and have follow-up conversations? Are you a principal who sends a teacher or two to a workshop or course, on the condition they come back and do a workshop for the rest of your staff? If the answer is yes, rethink this action. Why would you send someone to a workshop on how to play the violin and then, before they get a chance to practice, have them run a workshop? That is another form of folly. When you do that, you chose not to attend to the critical attribute of being professional: paying attention to what research tells us we need to do. You have chosen expediency and folly over wisdom. You are pursuing the path of becoming accidentally adequate, an option that would not impress the parents of your school's students. Leithwood et al. (2007) identified that school leadership is second only to classroom teaching as an influence on student learning.

That said, you see in Sect. 3.4 most assessments of the effect of cooperative learning, and indeed most instructional innovations, are flawed. This has to become a critical concern for all educators wanting to merge assessment and cooperative learning, or assessment with any other instructional innovations.

Assessment as I said earlier, is feedback students get from their own effort, and from peers or teachers during and/or after the effort. Two of the most common assessment terms that have been applied over the years are *formative* and *summative* (which Michael Scriven coined in 1967). Those assessment processes (minus the labels) have most likely been used for thousands of years. More recently, educators are employing the terms *for learning* and *as learning* as subsets and at times in lieu of formative assessment, and *of learning* in lieu of summative assessment. Again, even though the terms *for*, *as*, and *of learning* are more recent, the assessment processes they label have no doubt been used for centuries. Black et al. (2004) situate those three positions of assessment in saying, "Students can achieve a learning goal only if they understand that goal and can assess what they need to do to reach it. So self-assessment is essential to learning" (p. 14). Hattie (2012) shows the effect size of having students understand the learning objective.

Figure 3.6 is a concept map summarising how I conceptualise assessment in this chapter.

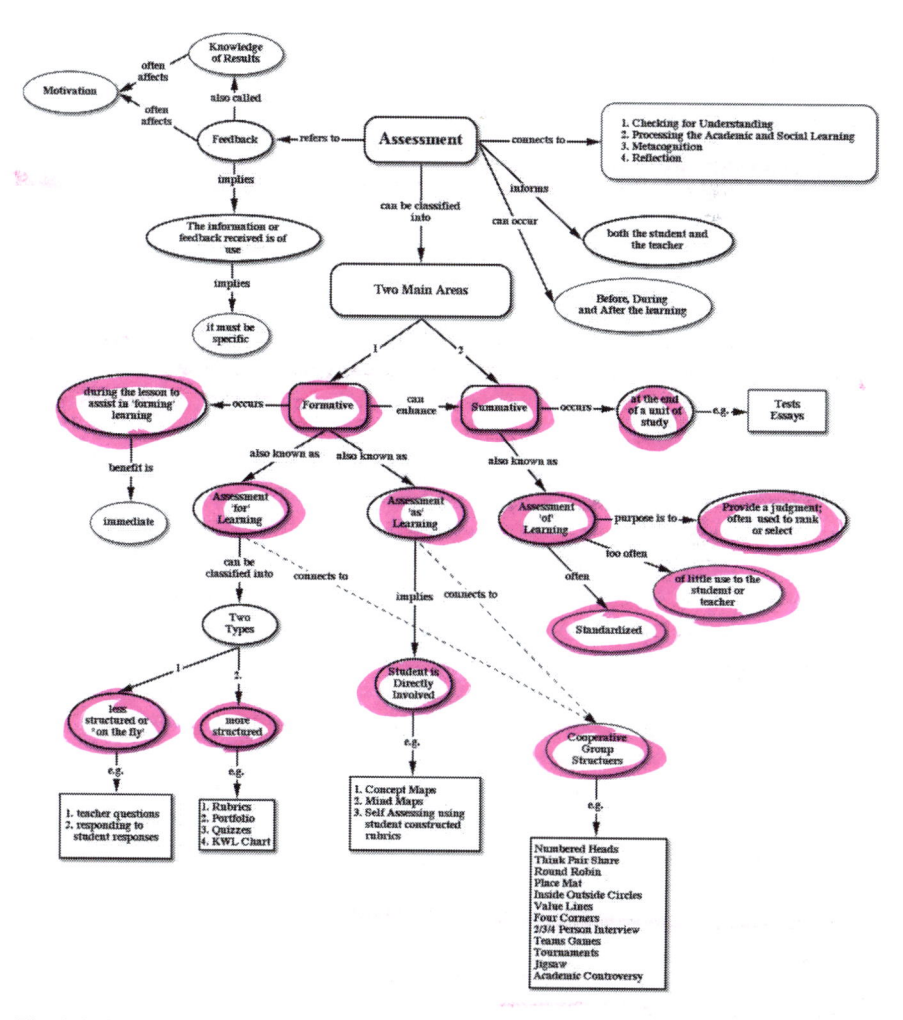

Fig. 3.6 Concept map of my current perspective on assessment. *Note*: this concept map is not the only way of organising assessment. It simply represents my thinking at the time of writing this paper. This map will have no doubt changed by the time this book is published. That is part of playing with such a complex concept as assessment, integrated into the even-more-complex process of teaching and learning

As I said at the start of the chapter, assessment (feedback) is integral to life. We live in a democracy – we assess politicians' platforms and vote. We go out on dates – and assess. We buy cars based on consumer reports. In sports, would many of us continue to go bowling if the ball we bowled disappeared behind an opaque sheet, and we heard a noise but had no idea how many or which pins we knocked down? What would be the motivation to pick up and bowl a second ball? By reflecting on life, we sense that motivation and its subsets – such as interest, meaning, success, positive feeling, tone, and knowledge of results – are key to assessment. Interestingly, those are all concepts that were integral to Madeline Hunter's (1987) work in the 1970s and 1980s.

In this part of Sect. 3.3, I briefly share key ideas about assessment to position it within cooperative learning. Note that I discussed some of these ideas in previous sections. You can also information on assessment on the Web. Start with http://en.wikipedia.org/wiki/Formative_assessment.

Formative assessment was designed to help *form* student thinking and action. Obviously, that is a key part of the teaching and learning process. Stiggins (2004) posits that the "instructional decisions that have the greatest impact are made day to day in the classroom" (p. 25). Madeline Hunter (1987) discussed the teacher's role as one of monitoring students' learning and adjusting their teaching, regardless of whether the students were working alone or in small, cooperative groups. Monitoring and adjusting our teaching is a key part of assessment *for* learning. Hunter also found that effective teachers checked for understanding at appropriate times during the lesson. This implies being in the moment when it comes to merging the processes of instruction (cooperative learning) and assessment.

But are you effective at assessing in the moment? Watch teachers as they check for understanding. I often hear, "Now, does everyone understand what I said? [followed by a brief pause and scan of the classroom, with no student response] Good, okay, let's move on." Or "Could someone in your group explain what this means? Okay, Cameron [Cameron explains]. Okay, now does everyone understand what Cameron said? Are you sure? [brief pause and scan]. Okay, great, let's move on to Question Two." All the teacher knows for sure about the first example is that the teacher understands. In the second example, all the teacher knows is that the teacher and Cameron understand. So, if teachers are not effective at checking for understanding (assessment *for* learning) when students are working alone or a large group, why would they suddenly be better when students work in small, cooperative groups? The literature is clear: four or five kids will answer around 80 % of questions if teachers let them.

Summative refers to assessment after learning. There is not a lot of difference, conceptually, between the definitions of *summative assessment* and assessment *of* learning. This type of assessment plays out, at the end of a unit and/or the end of a year, as tests or exams to determine, for example, whether students will get an A, B, etc., on their test or essay or report card; or pass a driver's test, or get into university. Summative assessment has little instructional value for students who have completed a unit of study or course. The benefit, if any, will be for the teachers, and the students taught the following year – this backward effect is often known as 'backwash' and is not all that useful. Black et al. (2004) discuss the formative use of summative-assessment results to help students identify what they need work to study for upcoming tests. So we see that summative assessment results can stimulate formative assessment. We need to design tests that are responsive to instruction, but that implies teachers have an effective and extensive instructional repertoire. In this chapter, that repertoire refers to the effective application of cooperative learning. The New Frontier School District in Quebec, Canada is shifting their thinking towards doing their summative assessment at the start of the year.

One safe way of using tests to increase student participation in class is the collaborative quiz. Students are placed in groups of two to four (roll a die, if you like, to determine the group size and randomly assign students to groups) or use already established exam partners. Give the student groups each a quiz. The first student reads the first question and provides what they think is the best answer. Then, each member of the group shares his or her response. The first student then summarises what was said and writes down the answer. The second student follows the same procedure for the second question, and the process continues until all questions are answered. If you want to mark the quizzes *for* learning, you'll have fewer quizzes to mark with a group quiz. Of course, the students can mark each other's quizzes or be given sample answers and mark their own. Any group that gets more than 80 % gets an incentive – perhaps no homework the next day. The group quiz can be a pre-test for summative, end-of-unit test, where students are tested individually.

One subtle shift regarding involving students in assessment is assessment *as learning* (Earl, 2004). For example, when we have students create a concept map on the key idea of a study unit, as part of an exam or simply as an assignment, we are shifting to assessment *for* and *as* learning. The following is a comment by a colleague (who is a teacher) related to a comment by her son who was in Grade 12 at the time. The teachers of her son introduced concept maps as a way to organise information when studying for exams. He came home one day and said to his teacher-mother, "If I see one more concept map, I'm going to be ill!" Months later, he was studying for his final math exam. His mother noticed that he had a big piece of paper out and was concept-mapping his math course. His mother said, "I thought you hated them." He responded, "I do, but they work." Now studying engineering, he shows other university students how to use concept maps.

Here's another example. My graduate students work in groups on concept maps that summarise the key ideas in their course. Their final mark for that course is based on a rubric and scoring sheet I give them before starting the activity. They self-assess their concept map with other students in the class before handing it in. I only change the mark if I think that they scored themselves too low or too high. If after the group share, they feel they need to rework it, they hand it in the following week. This saves me a lot of time assessing/providing feedback on their work.

In parallel with assessment *for*, *as*, and *of* learning, there is also assessment *before*, *during*, and *after* learning. This is a common, everyday practice. When we go into a restaurant, we assess the ambience of the restaurant before eating. When we get our order, we assess it during the eating. Finally, after all is eaten and the bill paid, we assess the overall effect of the experience. The same holds true for secondary students: they assess *before* learning (when they walk into the classroom) regarding its ambience, *during* learning (when students experience the personality and pedagogy of the teacher), and *after* learning (when the students make the final assessment of that learning experience).

As adults, we can choose to return or not to a particular restaurant – and we can spread the word. Unfortunately for secondary students, most classrooms and schools are the only restaurant in town. Nonetheless, students share their assessments of their classrooms and schools with others. If a teacher does not structure group work effectively, the students will spread the word that group work does not work.

I have talked with secondary teachers who have invested time and inquiry into effective group work over the years. They find that their students learn more, learn faster, and that neither students nor parents complain about group work. But, when group work is *in*effective, students and parents do complain. And *in*effectively assessing ineffective group work does *not* produce a positive result, no matter how well you understand the multiplication of negative integers.

We can illustrate assessment *before* and *after* learning when we employ an organiser such as the KWL chart (Know Before Starting, Want to Learn, What Was Learned). The KWL chart provides the teacher with information about what students understand before a unit of study and, after the unit, what they have learned. Portfolios serve a similar reflective purpose. That said, KWL charts are often integrated into portfolios – individually, cooperatively, or as a combination of the two. The teacher can create a Place Mat, and have students complete their own *before* assessment (the K part of the KWL chart). Then they do a Round Robin of their ideas. In the middle, they come up with some things the group would like to learn about that topic (the W part). At the end of the unit, students can take time to pull together all their ideas, say on a Mind Map or Fish Bone Diagram or a Concept Map, and then a Three Step Interview of what they've learned. When they finish the unit, they can do a Ranking Ladder, rating the top ten ideas in the unit after generating criteria for their ranking. This is the *after* assessment. All of these instructional methods are ways to push the idea of assessment *for* and *as* learning. More important, they set students up for success in the summative, individual assessment *of* learning.

3.4 Merging Assessment and Cooperative Learning

We know that formative assessment is divided into assessment *for* and *as* learning – meaning that it occurs during the learning. We also have summative assessment (or assessment *of* learning) that occurs at the end of a unit or course of study. And we have assessment *before, during,* and *after* learning. Let's take a peek into a classroom.

If the teacher is effectively checking for understanding during group work, we might first see the following: each student works on a problem individually. They share how they arrived at their answers and then take time to think individually about what they now know about that problem. The teacher randomly calls on

3 Assessment and Cooperative Learning: The Missing Think

students from the groups to explain. Or, the teacher might inform them in advance that one person from each group will have to put the answer on the board, so the students need to make sure everyone in their group understands. They need to know anyone can be picked. Now the teacher has invoked the concepts of accountability and level of concern. As the teacher walks around, she gets a sense of who understands. If she numbers the students off in the same pattern (Numbered Heads is one tactic) then she knows which number belongs to each person in each group. Now she can select a student from each group who will be successful; students will not know that she is selecting the student who is in most need of the question. Following the students working at the board, the teacher has the students observe what is on the board, discuss it, and then once again randomly calling on them to respond to what they see.

Some of you have invoked Teams Games Tournaments (TGT, an instructional strategy) to have students compete cooperatively. One of my graduate students at OISE/UT, is investigating the effects of TGT in her high-school algebra class in the Thames Valley District School Board, in London, Ontario. In her district, secondary teachers have been placing tournament questions in all subject areas on the Board website for several years. This means the teachers do not spend an inordinate amount of time preparing questions for tournaments.[1] TGT is an effective instructional strategy for students to take responsibility for checking for each other's understanding. Once students are skilled in TGT, teachers often have them make up tournament questions in order to have the students attempt to predict the assessment *of* learning. The key message here is that instructional methods can provide powerful feedback to students in a variety of ways that respect student's need to show how they learn and what they know.

Table 3.4 is a rubric one of my graduate students, designed to assess how effectively the Johnsons' Five Basic Elements of effective group work played out in his lessons.

Can you sense the folly of assessing the impact of cooperative learning when students fail to sense its value, and when students get little or no useful feedback on their cooperative learning? Remember what I said earlier: one of the Five Basic Elements of effective group work is processing students' efforts at working together as well as their academic effort. That specific component of *processing* represents an opportunity for assessment *for* and *of* learning.

The rubric in Table 3.4 is useful, but when you observe a lesson where the Johnsons' Five Basic Elements are integrated with many other processes you see so much more than those five elements. For example, here are the instructional methods I employed in a 45 min lesson to teach congruency to Grade 2 students (working in groups of four):

Place Mat, Round Robin, Numbered Heads, Concept Attainment, the Five Basic Elements, Equal Voice, Attentive Listening, One Stray the Rest Stay, framing questions, and wait time. I invoked the concepts of safety, accountability, and active

---

[1] See Bennett and Rolheiser (2001) for an explanation of the process and examples of TGT question sets.

Table 3.4 Rubric for teacher self-assessment

Attribute	Level 1	Level 2	Level 3	Level 4
Individual accountability	Little or no evidence that students are all accountable	Emerging evidence that some students are accountable	Clear evidence that most students are accountable	Clear evidence that all students are accountable
Promoting face-to-face interaction	Students are not sitting in a way that promotes this attribute	Some students are sitting correctly, but group size is too large	Most students are sitting appropriately and group size also appropriate	All students are sitting appropriately and group size is appropriate
Teaching appropriate collaborative skill	No evidence of a relevant skill being introduced or taught	Skill mentioned but not taught; skill not always appropriate to the task; at times too many skills mentioned	Skill taught and, for the most part, relates to the academic task; may mention 1 or 2 others but focuses on one	Skill or skills taught meaningfully relate to the academic task; teacher checks to make sure all students understand the skill
Processing the academic and social objective	Little or no evidence that students reflected on or processed their academic or social learning	Some evidence, but most processing is done by the teacher	Clear evidence that students reflected on or processed their academic and social learning	Clear evidence that students and teacher effectively processed the academic and social learning
Positive Interdependence (PI)	No evidence of PI; no clear goal stated; task usually not appropriate for group work	Some evidence of PI; goal not stated as clearly or meaningfully as it goal not discussed with student	Clear evidence of PI; goal stated, brief discussion with students; appropriate types of PI selected	Clear evidence of PI; goal clearly stated and relevance discussed appropriate type of PI selected

participation. This class was also a Tribes classroom; the teacher had completed the 4-day Tribes training programme. I pushed the Analysis level of Bloom's Taxonomy and addressed inter- and intrapersonal intelligences, linguistic intelligence, and logical mathematical intelligence from Gardner's work on Multiple Intelligence.

You can sense the complexity of assessing the impact of effective group work when it is embedded in multiple other processes. Researching the effects of cooperative learning in this context is messy – but rich. You can also see that if the principal does not attend the workshops with teachers, he or she will be challenged to support their efforts.

If we take the above lesson and shift to students assessing how they work collaboratively, we imply that the teacher and students focused on, and understood, the required collaborative skills. This opens another door to analysis and assessment. Collaborative skills can be classified as social skills (e.g., taking turns, using quiet voices), communication skills (e.g., attentive listening, paraphrasing), and critical thinking skills (e.g., suspending judgment and examining both sides of an issue). Why critical thinking is complex relates to attempting to have students apply critical thinking skills without the requisite social and communication skills. If these are not in place, then critical thinking skills will not play out effectively.

Once again, less complex processes drive more complex processes. For example, how can students 'Examine Both Sides' (EBS) of an issue (a critical thinking skill from de Bono's CoRT programme) if they do not invoke equal voice, listen attentively, and suspend judgment? Too often I go into classrooms, especially secondary classrooms, and I see little or no evidence that the teacher even senses this complexity. And you can see that the group process is not working effectively; it's akin to having a Lamborghini with two flat tires. That failure to act on the interdependence of social, communication, and critical thinking skills has implications for assessing how critical thinking impacts student learning – especially if the critical-thinking process is immersed in the cooperative-learning process. Each is essential to the other; I cannot imagine implementing critical thinking in the absence of cooperative learning nor cooperative learning in the absence of critical thinking. They both exist because of each other.

Shifting back to assessment, a teacher's assessment of what students can do on their own happens once the students have demonstrated they can shift to more independent work. Madeline Hunter (1987) presented two types of teaching practice: guided (with support – akin to assessment *for* learning) and independent (students working on their own, which could be both assessment *as* or *of* learning). Both of these are discussed in Hattie (2012).

When students work together on a project that plays out over time, the key mistake teachers make is not assessing student progress at various points during the project. Finding out at the end of the project that one or two students did all the work is the teacher's fault, not the students'. Students are usually not skilled at group work and will, at times – like electrons – take the path of least resistance. Here you have to set the social, communication, and critical-thinking skills the students must demonstrate in the project by taking the time to teach these skills, and to build in individual accountability. Otherwise, one person can hitchhike on the coattails of others, or take over and do all the work. Students need to know that they are all accountable for the completion of the project and that their marks will be based both on their individual and group skills – like real life. Then, during the project, you stop a few times to have the students reflect on how they are doing and give their groups a *progression score*. The teacher also provides each group a progression score, and then the class discusses what they can do better in the next phase of the project. After each group presents its project, the group gets a mark in addition to each group member's mark. Teachers develop protocols for students to self-assess their academic and collaborative work, to assess their group's work, and another group's work.

All parents want their sons and daughters to be successful; they want to know how they are progressing academically. That implies that parents want to know what their children can do on their own, and, as educators, we need to provide that information. Informed parents should also be just as curious about how well their children are functioning socially – especially given that social and emotional intelligence are the number one predictors of success in life (Gardner, 1985; Goleman, 1998). For example, below is part of a recent job advertisement from the *Toronto Star*: Ryerson University: Dean, Faculty of Engineering and Architectural Science:

> He/She will possess an open and collegial style, outstanding management, communication and interpersonal skills ... a creative and entrepreneurial approach to problem solving and the ability to inspire ... experience in building collaborative teams ... relating to range of internal and external partners.

Connected to that job ad, cooperative learning, fundamentally, allows students to develop the collaborative skills to do academic work more effectively on their own. Of course, working alone or collaboratively is not the issue; the issue is engaging in both effectively.

In our book *Cooperative Learning: Where Heart Meets Mind* (Bennett, Rolheiser, & Stevahn, 1991) we included a chapter on the assessment or evaluation of student learning during cooperative learning. For the most part, this involves assessment of both the collaborative and academic tasks during and after the learning – assessment *for* learning, and *of* learning. That said, when it comes to students, teachers and parents needing to know exactly what students can do on their own, I suggest a shift to individual assessment. In addition, when it comes to assessment *for* learning, students also need to work on their own. This also applies to the preservice teacher-training programme at OISE/UT. Teacher educators need to know what preservice teachers can do with others and on their own.

3.5 Levels of Use of an Innovation

In this section, I briefly illustrate the need to understand not only how we as teachers include all the attributes of the innovation we are attempting to implement, but just as important, our level of skill in applying those attributes. Table 3.5 is an example of a rubric designed collaboratively by a team of three OISE/UT Bachelor of Education students. It is not meant to be 'the' rubric; just their first attempt at creating one to assess their group work. They created the rubric and applied it in their teaching practicum, to assess their use of the Johnsons' Five Basic Elements. Their associate teacher also used the rubric to give the student teachers feedback and to guide the reflective discussion after each lesson they taught during their practicum. In Table 3.5 you can also see that, in this case, Processing (one of the Johnsons' five basic elements) refers to the student teachers self-assessing their efforts.

3   Assessment and Cooperative Learning: The Missing Think   75

Table 3.5 Rubric for assessing the five basic elements of effective group work

Area	Level One	Level Two	Level Three	Level Four
Cooperative learning	Individual accountability is rarely observed	Individual accountability is sometimes observed	Individual accountability is usually observed	Individual accountability is always observed
	Most students not sitting in a way that facilitates face-to-face interaction	Some students sitting in a way to facilitate face-to-face interaction	Most students sitting in a way to facilitate face-to-face interaction	All students sitting in a way to facilitate face-to-face interaction
	Collaborative skill mentioned but not taught or reviewed	Collaborative skill mentioned and explained	Appropriate collaborative skill taught or reviewed	Appropriate collaborative skill effectively taught or reviewed
	Few if any students processing the academic and collaborative work	Some students involved in processing the academic and collaborative work	Most students involved in processing their academic and collaborative work	All students involved in processing their academic and collaborative work
	Positive interdependence happens by default if at all; task is not clear to all group members	Positive interdependence is sometimes practiced; task is somewhat clear to most group members	Positive interdependence is applied; task is meaningful and clear to all group members	Positive interdependence is applied effectively and the task is meaningful and very clear to all group members

Using rubrics is one way teachers self-assess how well they attend to the essential attributes of an innovation. Another way is to self-assess the *level of skill* that the teacher models with that innovation. This form of assessment is particularly critical to the impact of any innovation – in the case of this chapter, the impact of cooperative learning. Levels of skill relate to the Levels of Use of an innovation, a concept developed by Susan Loucks and described in Hall and Hord (2006). Levels of Use of an innovation is one part of a larger framework developed by Hall and Hord (2006). That framework is known as the Concerns Based Adoption Model (CBAM).

Levels of Use measures teachers' and students' skill shift at eight levels, shown in Table 3.6. The first three levels describe non-use of the innovation, and the last five describe increasingly skilled use.

Hord, Hall, and Loucks-Horsley have researched the Levels of Use model over the last 35 years, and their research shows that, until teachers and students reach the 'Routine' level of use, the innovation has little effect on student learning. For the fundamental work on Levels of Use see Loucks, Newlove, and Hall (1975).

In a conversation with Susan Loucks-Horsley approximately 14 years ago, she told me that in their research on instructional methods in secondary-school science classrooms, they rarely found teachers even at the Mechanical level of use with any research-based instructional innovation. The CBAM literature shows that until

Table 3.6 Levels of use of an innovation

1. Nonuser	You are not using the innovation, but you may have heard of it
2. Orientating	You are interested, and you are seeking out more information
3. Preparing	You are getting ready to apply the innovation for the first time
4. Mechanical	You are applying the innovation in your classroom, but your application is clunky
5. Routine	You have applied the innovation for enough time that it is working smoothly
6. Refined	You are extending how you apply the innovation into new areas
7. Integrative	You are connecting the innovation to other innovations
8. Refocusing	You are searching for other innovations

Source: Hall and Hord (2006, 2011)

students and teachers get to the Routine level of use, little or no evidence exists of an innovation's impact on student learning. From a change perspective, students and the teacher at the mechanical level are in the *implementation dip*; things are actually getting worse rather than better. You can see that if teachers or researchers attempt to assess the impact of cooperative learning on student learning without first assessing the teachers' and students' level of use of this innovation, they will not accurately assess the innovation's impact on student learning.

The Levels of Use framework and related research provide a precise and thorough approach to analysing and assessing the evolving skill level of teachers as they implement innovations (Craib, 2006). More importantly, the Levels of Use also applies to students.

Interestingly, from my experience with the implementation of instructional innovations, each Level of Use engenders another implementation dip; the dips don't go away, they simply become progressively more complex. You can see CBAM being applied in Saunder's (2012a, 2012b) work related to the implementation and assessing of instructional change in Western Australia at the tertiary level. She won the Dissertation of the Year award at AERA (2012) for her research.

Table 3.7 is a rubric I use in my research that illustrates how three of the Levels of Use (Mechanical, Routine, and Refined) relate to the Five Basic Elements of effective group work. How many teachers do you think are Routine or higher users of cooperative learning? What would it take to get to the Routine and Refined levels?

Understanding instruction is more complex than we realise. For that reason, we have no option but to think and act more wisely within and between educational systems. The following section illustrates two examples of school districts working more intentionally over time: respecting educational research to extend and refine teachers' instructional repertoire.

3 Assessment and Cooperative Learning: The Missing Think

Table 3.7 How levels of use relate to the five basic elements in cooperative learning

Mechanical	Routine	Refined
Teacher has notes reminding how and when to apply the Five Basic Elements	Teacher may have a few notes to refer to, but for the most part, smoothly plays with the Five Basic Elements	Teacher does not need notes; clearly and effectively applies the Five Basic Elements
Accountability not as high as it should be; not all students are involved, some students are still buying in; others may be taking over	Most students are accountable. Periodically, one or two students take over and do more	All students, most of the time, are accountable and actively involved
Discussion of the academic goal happens, but is not as meaningful to students as it could be. Students find it somewhat strange	The academic goal is discussed and is, for the most part, meaningful. Students expect this to happen – still need to be reminded. Narrow range of collaborative skills used	Academic goal is discussed, is meaningful and of interest, clearly worth doing in a group. Students do it naturally. Wide range of appropriate collaborative skills used
Students are not very skilled at processing their academic and social task	Most students can process the academic and social task – although the social task is sometimes not processed	Students skilfully process their academic and collaborative tasks
Students have few skills to confront and resolve conflict. Students struggle to work with some other students	Students beginning dealing with their own conflicts but may need help at times. Students can work with most students in the class	Few conflicts; if they occur, students usually deal with them. Students easily work with all students in the class
Teacher does not merge Five Basic Elements with other instructional methods	Teacher beginning to connect the Five Basic Elements to other instructional methods, but those methods are less complex methods	Teacher, when appropriate, easily and effectively integrates the Five Basic Elements into other instructional methods, including more complex strategies

3.6 Leadership Within Districts Working at Systemic Change

Most school staff are not positioned to sustain their efforts at extending and refining instructional practice. Principals or other key people leave, and good intentions dissolve. Cuban and Usdan (2003) summarise this dilemma regarding systemic change in the United States in their book *Large Scale Reform with Shallow Roots*. They found the innovations selected for implementation never evolved; there were great intentions but limited change skills. The No Child Left Behind Act exemplifies the failure to implement systemically. Currently, we have few, if any, books about how a large school district focuses on instructional change over time (say for 5 or more years). That said, however, we know systemic change happens, we just don't see the research (for example, see the Durham District School Board's efforts in Ontario, Canada discussed later in this section).

Ellis (2001) describes three levels of educational research. The first is Level 1 – this research is qualitative and looks at patterns and relationships – often known as *grounded research*. It precedes the design of specific innovations. Howard Gardner's (1985) work on Multiple Intelligence is Level 1 research. His work also exemplifies how Level 1 research leads to Level 2 research – this research can be both qualitative and quantitative and focuses on the implementation of an innovation in classrooms or a school. A teacher or group of teachers in a school doing action research on an innovation such as Mind Mapping or Teams Games Tournaments in their classroom would be Level 2 research.

Level 3 research shifts to the systemic implementation of an innovation and can also employ both qualitative and quantitative approaches. For example, in the 1990s, the government of Australia attempted to create a national curriculum based on Gardner's work. If this initiative had succeeded, it would be an example of Level 3 research, which looks at the impact of an innovation throughout an education system. I was invited to talk to 200 educators from around Australia who were responsible for implementing the Australia-wide innovation. My message was that, although it was a good idea, the Australian teachers did not have the instructional repertoire to pull it off, nor did the Ministry of Education have any training mechanism to reach teachers across Australia. Millions of dollars were spent on planning the national curriculum, and it was never implemented. Again, the systemic innovation was well intentioned but ill positioned. The government attempting to implement it did not have the necessary systemic-change skills. Leadership rarely understands or acts upon what we understand about the process of classroom, school, and district change.

Cooperative learning emerged from Level 1 research grounded in social theory. Perhaps the key book in this area is Schmuck and Schmuck's (1998) *Group Processes in the Classroom*. Their research over the last 40 years has led to a plethora of cooperative-learning tactics and strategies that teachers have been applying in their classrooms. This success points out that the issue for assessment is not whether or not one teacher improves; it is how you shift all teachers in an education system over time.

In 1996, the Durham District School Board in Oshawa, Ontario won a $300,000 prize as one of the top school districts in the world, awarded by Europe's Bertlesman Foundation. The Foundation spent a year selecting and identifying a district that was highly successful at implementing change over time. The Durham Board was able to demonstrate through Level 3 research how they had pushed the implementation of instructional innovations (the focus being cooperative learning) for 10 years. They were one of four districts that came together to form the Learning Consortium in the Toronto area, and the only one of the four that was able to push instruction innovations systemically. I was hired to provide the initial training and demonstration lessons on cooperative learning in the Consortium's four districts.

Interestingly, in the mid-1980s, just before the start of the Learning Consortium, Ontario's Ministry of Education identified the Durham Board as one of the worst school districts of its size in Ontario. That begs the question, 'How does a district shift to being "worst" in Ontario to "best" in the world in 10 years?' The answer is quite simple: the leadership paid attention to the research on change. Michael Fullan was one of the key designers of the Learning Consortium, so the change piece was central to its work. A few key players at the Durham Board's central office (Norm Green and Pauline Lang) and a few Board consultants, supported school-staff professional development, which teachers found made a difference. The leadership worked at merging top-down and bottom-up change; they focused on one innovation that research showed made a difference at all grade levels and in all subject areas: cooperative learning.

During the first 4 years of the project in Durham, I ran approximately 16, 4-day workshops with teams of teachers and their principals; we limited the number to approximately 125 participants per workshop. In the workshops, they applied Joyce and Shower's (1996; Joyce, Weil, & Calhoun 2000, 2004) skill-training model: presentation of theory, demonstrations, the chance to practice with feedback, and then the peer coaching in study teams follow-up sessions throughout the school year. In addition, the workshop instructor went into kindergarten to Grade 12 classrooms to do demonstration lessons.

After the first 4 years, teachers and board consultants continued to run these workshops – again, limited to approximately 125 participants per workshop. The number of workshops per year constantly increased and, eventually, the District adapted them for specific subjects, such as French and Math. In addition, they designed workshops that integrated other instructional methods with cooperative learning. By the tenth year, District teachers were instructing all the workshops including those not specifically related to cooperative learning. They also continued to provide the follow-up support in the classroom and at evening review and sharing sessions. The Durham District had built the internal capacity to deal with instructional change.

The Durham Board effectively initiated and implemented cooperative learning and other instructional innovations (the change piece). They developed curriculum and videos, and began sending teachers to school districts across Canada and around the world as consultants. The Board began to generate money for its own staff's professional development through this consulting. It also made money from visitors from other districts within and beyond Canada coming to see why the Durham Board was so successful.

Shifting away from Canada: the Durham educators had a powerful effect on the implementation of cooperative learning in Germany. As a result of the work in Germany, Ireland established its own project, different from, but based on the Durham experience. Currently, we are in the sixth year of an instructional leadership process with the ministry in Ireland. We have approximately 750 teacher/principal teams from around Ireland involved (about 25 % of 720 secondary schools). Cooperative learning, assessment, and the process of change are key components of this project. Key to our current success has been the leadership provided by teachers, principals, inspectors, and ministry personnel. We have created rubrics on how we assess ourselves on the factors that influence the initiation, implementation, and sustaining of change. Our understanding of how we lead change is critical. For more information on the project and how we are attending to the research on educational and systemic change, you can see O'Murchu et al. (2013). This is a paper we presented in Zug, Switzerland at a conference focused on school improvement and school effectiveness.

Shifting back to Durham, central office administration, collectively, never developed norms of collaboration and collegiality with each other or with school-based administration, nor did they research the impact of their change efforts. Key superintendents continued to vie for turf (money), chose not to be involved and, at times, unwittingly worked at undermining the change project. The Director and the staff development officer had a few key players on their side, but not all the players. From my experience working in districts, the lack of a common cohesive stance in central office is usually the norm. Nonetheless, when the two key players, the director of education (CEO) of the Durham Board left and (more importantly) the director of staff development left, their systemic change effort ended. Importantly, no one at central office (including me) enacted what was understood about systemic change; this systemic change literature was just starting to emerge. Collectively, we just did not know.

The new director of education did not understand change or systemic change; the new director of staff development was likewise not skilled at change and did not have the skills to sustain systemic change and push the District forward. This person was a master workshop presenter but, unfortunately, not a skilled change agent (and at that time, neither was I). The central-office once again balkanised, and 16 years of change ended.

Interestingly, at the time Durham's effort was flagging, the York Region District School Board (YRDSB), decided to build on the work of the Durham District School Board. The difference was that YRDSB involved all board consultants (about 25) from the beginning. In 1997, they met for a 2-day workshop to experience the possibilities of what might be possible around instruction if they were to start a systemic initiative. Those consultants then decided whether a systemic change initiative was worth doing and how it should play out. After the consultants decided to go ahead, the Board's superintendents were invited to a 1-day workshop on the possibilities of the project. (Note that in Ontario the CEO is the Director, whereas in most districts the CEO is the Superintendent.) The project thus became a district-wide initiative, supported by all consultants and superintendents. Since then, the change project's initiators have recruited extensive support from teachers and principals throughout the Board, and from central office staff. YRDSB educators have developed the internal capacity to sustain systemic change. You can see the difference related to leadership and how key players were in on the initiation.

The York Region Board's change project now focuses on instructional innovations other than cooperative learning, but implemented through various cooperative group processes. For example, the Board now has over 3000 teachers trained in Jeanne Gibbs' Tribes programme. They have completed action research, some of it on aspects of cooperative learning. They are also seen as one of the most progressive districts in Canada related to literacy.

The York Region district, 2 years after the project started, connected with OISE/UT to create a Bachelor of Education (BEd) preservice option (called the Doncrest Option) that runs out of Doncrest Public School (K-8). We also have a secondary option at Emily Carr Secondary School. Those two programs involve about 70 and 35 BEd students, respectively. The BEd students take most of their courses at Doncrest. I will briefly describe the Doncrest Option, because that is the one in which I am more involved.

The Doncrest Option students develop the same skills that YRDSB teachers developed through the Instructional Intelligence project. This means that when the BEd students begin their practicums in the York Region Board, they have a common instructional and assessment language with their associate teachers. For example, in September of each year (beginning of the school year in Canada), the Doncrest Option (which is 1 of 28 BEd, options at OISE/UT) had students involved in 2 weeks of intensive group work. They spent 4 days becoming certified in Tribes and 4 days merging the Johnsons' Five Basic Elements with other small-group structures – mostly the work of Spencer Kagan. Doncrest Public School is where the BEd students also do demonstration lessons and begin creating rubrics on different instructional methods, so that they can self-assess and plan their lessons and units. Again, because the students and their associate teachers have a common language, the practicum experience is much richer.

The York Region Board consultants also come to Doncrest Public School to provide workshops on such topics as Literacy, Science, the Arts, etc. Two of the full-time instructors in the Doncrest Option are seconded York Region Board teachers with Master's degrees from OISE/UT, who were interviewed in competitions for the positions. Interestingly, the current Doncrest Option BEd students are now being mentored by graduates of the Doncrest Option who were hired by the York Region Board 5 or 6 years ago. So, in the York Region Board, you sense the power of systems working systemically to make change over time. The larger Board-wide initiative, which has shifted more into differentiated instruction, is also impacting the university/school district partnership. You sense that cooperative learning is one part of a rich quilt of possibilities, and that richness makes assessment so much more doable and meaningful.

3.7 Summary

In this chapter, I have connected assessment and cooperative learning at both the classroom and district levels. Key to our work has been our respect for the process of change and the role school administration played/plays in both the transfer and on-going skill development and complexity of thinking. This connection was divided into two dimensions: (1) how we assess student efforts in the classroom connected to their cooperative learning and (2) how we assess the implementation of cooperative learning in the classroom, to ensure that we are assessing *effective* implementation of cooperative learning.

In the first dimension, I proposed that cooperative learning plays out most appropriately in terms of when we focus on assessment *for* and *as* learning (two components of formative assessment). Assessment *of* learning (summative assessment) aligns more with students working individually. Key here is that students who work better collaboratively usually work better individually – so assessment *for* and *as* learning impacts assessment *of* learning. Another key point is that certain components of effective group work tie directly into assessment. For example, in the Johnsons' Learning Together strategy, students must process (or assess) their academic and collaborative learning. With one strategy, Teams Games Tournament, groups of students respond to test-like questions. If we realise that cooperative learning is akin to mentoring, peer coaching, guided practice, or Vygotsky's Zone of Proximal Development, we will think more deeply about cooperative learning's impact on student learning.

In the second dimension, I proposed that, in assessing the implementation of cooperative learning, we ensure that we, in fact, assess what we intend. That implies being able to differentiate effective group work from less effective group work. We also need to make sure that all the attributes of effective group work are present if we want to meaningfully assess the impact of cooperative learning. Additionally, we have to keep in mind that not all cooperative-learning processes are of equal power in affecting student learning. When assessing, we must make sure that we note whether the cooperative learning methods in use are less or more complex. Taking this to a more complex level, we have to remember that cooperative-learning methods can be integrated with each other, as well as with other instructional methods. This makes assessing the impact of cooperative learning even more complex. Of course all of this is dependent on both the teachers' and students' skill levels in applying cooperative learning. Here, the concept *Levels of Use* of an innovation helps determine the skill levels of teachers and students. In the absence of support from school and district leadership, Levels of Use is of no value as not much happens.

From my experience, more time and effort should be spent on making sure we wisely select appropriate cooperative learning methods and implement them effectively before we assess the effects of cooperative learning on student learning. More attention needs to be paid to how leadership supports teachers' efforts to improve their instructional repertoire. Why assess a naïve or incomplete application of cooperative learning? Faculties of education and school-district staff-development programs must work together to provide higher quality opportunities to acquire the requisite cooperative learning skills. A good place to start would be to minimise one-shot inservice workshops with no follow-up support and replace them with more collaborative relationships between faculties of education and school districts. This will develop a common language between teachers in the districts as well as between teachers and faculty of education students. That is unlikely to happen in the absence of leadership. In one of the Instructional Intelligence projects in the North Vancouver School District, the University of British Columbia and the school district leadership designed a Master's degree for educators in the district focused on instructional leadership. Of about 700 teachers, close to 90 have that degree.

Much is possible when we work collectively to make a difference in the life chances and learning chances of students. If not for students, we would have no faculties of education, ministries of education, teacher unions, and school districts. One would think that all of us would work together to make that happen.

References

Aronson, E., & Patnoe, S. (1997). *The Jigsaw classroom*. New York, NY: Addison-Wesley Longman.
Bennett, B. (1987). *The effectiveness of staff development training practices: A meta-analysis*. Unpublished PhD Thesis.
Bennett, B. (1996, April). *The effects of integrating pedagogy on student learning: An experimental study*. Paper presented at the annual meeting of the American Educational Research Association, Chicago, IL.
Bennett, B., Anderson, S., & Evans, M. (1996, April). *Towards a theory of instructional acquisition*. Paper presented at the annual meeting of the American Educational Research Association, Chicago, IL.
Bennett, B., & Green, N. (1995). The effect of the learning consortium: One district's journey. *School Effectiveness and School Improvement: An International Journal of Research, Policy and Practice, 6*(3), 247–264.
Bennett, B., & Rolheiser, C. (2001). *Beyond Monet: The artful science of instructional integration*. Ajax, ON: Bookation.
Bennett, B., Rolheiser, C., & Stevahn, L. (1991). *Cooperative learning: Where heart meets mind*. Toronto, ON: Educational Connections.
Berieter, C., & Scardamalia, M. (1993). *Surpassing ourselves: An inquiry into the nature and implications of expertise*. Chicago, IL: Open Court.
Black, P., Harrison, C., Lee, C., Marshall, B., & Wiliam, D. (2004). Working inside the black box: Assessment for learning in the classroom. *Phi Delta Kappan, 86*, 9–21.
Black, P., & Wiliam, D. (1998). Inside the black box: Raising standards through classroom assessment. *Phi Delta Kappan, 80*(1), 139–148.
Blumer, H. (1954). What is wrong with social theory? *American Sociological Review, 19*, 3–10.
Bruner, J. (1966). *Towards a theory of instruction*. Cambridge, MA: Harvard University Press.
Cohen, E. (1994). *Designing group work: Strategies for the heterogeneous classroom*. New York, NY: Teachers College Press.
Craib, G. W. (2006). *Measuring the tacit knowledge of practicing teachers*. Doctoral dissertation, Ontario Institute for Studies in Education, University of Toronto, Toronto, ON, Canada.
Cuban, L., & Usdan, M. (2003). *Powerful reforms with shallow roots: Improving America's urban schools*. New York, NY: Teachers College Press.
Dewey, J., & Dewey, E. (1914). *Schools of tomorrow*. New York, NY: E.P. Dutton.
Dufour, R., Eaker, R., & Dufour, R. (Eds.). (2005). *On common ground: The power of professional learning communities*. Bloomington, IN: Solution Tree.
Earl, L. M. (2004). *Assessment as learning: Using classroom assessment to maximize student learning*. Thousand Oaks, CA: Corwin.
Ellis, A. K. (2001). *Research on educational innovations* (3rd ed.). Larchmont, NY: Eye on Education.
Fullan, M. (2001). *The new meaning of educational change*. New York, NY: Teachers College Press.

Fullan, M. (2011). *Choosing the wrong drivers for whole system reform* (Centre for Strategic Education: Seminar Series Paper No. 204). Melbourne, Australia.

Gardner, H. (1985). *Multiple intelligences: The theory in practice*. New York, NY: Basic Books.

Gibbs, J. (1995). *Tribes: A new way of learning together*. Sausalito, CA: Center Source Systems.

Gibbs, J. (2001). *Tribes: A new way of learning together*. Sausalito, CA: Center Source Systems.

Goleman, D. (1998). *Working with emotional intelligence*. New York, NY: Bantam Books.

Hall, G. E., & Hord, S. M. (2006). *Implementing change: Patterns, principles, and potholes*. New York, NY: Pearson Education.

Hall, G. E., & Hord, S. M. (2011). *Implementing change: Patterns, principles, and potholes* (3rd ed.). New York, NY: Pearson Education.

Hargreaves, A., & Fullan, M. (2012). *Professional capital: Transforming teaching in every school*. New York, NY: Teachers College Press.

Hattie, J. (2012). *Visible learning for teachers: Maximizing impact on learning*. New York, NY: Routledge.

Huges, J. L. (1901). *Dickens as an educator*. New York, NY: D. Appleton.

Hunter, M. (1987). *Enhancing teaching*. New York, NY: Macmillan College.

Johnson, D. W., & Johnson, R. T. (1989). *Cooperation and competition: Theory and research*. Edina, MN: Interaction Book Company.

Johnson, D. W., & Johnson, R. T. (1999). *Learning together and alone: Cooperative, competitive and individualistic learning* (5th ed.). Boston, MA: Allyn & Bacon.

Joyce, B., & Showers, B. (1996). The evolution of peer coaching. *Educational Leadership, 53*(6), 12–16.

Joyce, B., & Weil, M. (2000). *Models of teaching*. New York, NY: Allyn & Bacon.

Joyce, B., Weil, M., & Calhoun, E. (2004). *Models of teaching* (7th ed.). New York, NY: Allyn & Bacon.

Kagan, S. (1994). *Cooperative learning*. San Juan Capistrano, CA: Kagan Cooperative Learning.

Kagan, S. (2009). *Cooperative learning*. San Juan Capistrano, CA: Kagan Cooperative Learning.

Leithwood, K., Day, C., Sammons, P., Harris, A., & Hopkins, D. (2007). *Seven strong claims about successful school leadership*. Nottingham, UK: National College for School Leadership.

Loucks, S. F., Newlove, B. W., & Hall, G. E. (1975). *Measuring levels of use of the innovation: A manual for trainers, interviewers and raters*. Austin, TX: Research and Development Center for Teacher Education, University of Texas.

Marzano, R. J. (2000). *Transforming classroom grading*. Alexandria, VA: Association for Supervision and Curriculum Development.

Marzano, R. J., & Kendall, J. S. (2008). *Designing & assessing educational objectives: Applying the new taxonomy*. Thousand Oaks, CA: Corwin.

Novak, J. D., & Gowan, B. E. (1984). *Learning how to learn*. New York, NY: Cambridge University Press.

O'Murchu, F., Russell, J., & Bennett, B. (2013). *A system learning: Five years into a systemic change project, a focus on classroom practice in secondary schools*. In School leadership symposium 2013, Zug, Switzerland.

Peacock, J. (2005). *Graphic organizers: Their implementation and impact on student learning and writing in senior English*. Unpublished Master of Education thesis, Ontario Institute for Studies in Education of the University of Toronto, Toronto, ON, Canada.

Perkins, D. (1991). *Knowledge as design*. Hillsdale, NJ: Lawrence Erlbaum.

Perkins, D. (1995). *Outsmarting IQ. The emerging science of learnable intelligence*. New York, NY: Free Press.

Rolheiser-Bennett, C. (1986). *Four models of teaching: A meta-analysis of student outcomes*. Unpublished doctoral dissertation, University of Oregon, Eugene, OR.

Saunders, R. (2012a, August). The role of teacher emotions in change: Experiences, patterns and implications for professional development. *Journal of Educational Change*, online.

Saunders, R. (2012b). Assessment of professional development for teachers in the vocational education and training sector: An examination of the Concerns Based Adoption Model. *Australian Journal of Education, 56*(2), 182–204.

Schmuck, D. H., & Schmuck, P. (1998). *Group processes in the classroom*. Dubuque, IA: Wm. C. Brown.

Scriven, M. (1967). The methodology of evaluation. In R. W. Tyler, R. M. Gagne, & M. Scriven (Eds.), *Perspectives of curriculum evaluation* (pp. 39–83). Chicago, IL: Rand McNally.

Slavin, R. (1980). *Cooperative learning: Theory, research and practice*. Needham Heights, MA: Allyn & Bacon.

Slavin, R. (1995). *Cooperative learning*. Needham Heights, MA: Allyn & Bacon.

Sternberg, R. J., & Horvath, J. A. (1995). A prototype of expert teaching. *Educational Researcher, 24*(6), 9–17.

Stiggins, R. (2004). New assessment beliefs for a new school mission. *Phi Delta Kappan, 86*, 23–27.

Stiggins, R. (2005). Assessment for learning: Building a culture of confident learners. In R. Dufour, R. Eaker, & R. Dufour (Eds.), *On common ground: The power of professional learning communities*. Bloomington, IN: Solution Tree.

Part II
Pragmatics of Assessment Leadership in the Disciplines

Chapter 4
Rubrics and Exemplars in Writing Assessment

Johanna de Leeuw

Abstract The use of rubrics for performance assessment as opposed to holistic methods is widely accepted as current enlightened practice and continues to receive considerable attention particularly in the current drive for increased accountability for student achievement. This has resulted in extensive discussion regarding their appropriateness, use and misuse, particularly in the assessment of writing. In order to understand the basis of the conflicting viewpoints that have characterised the rubrics debate in assessment of writing over the last decade, its historical roots and philosophical underpinnings are considered. A critical analysis of the scholarly literature on the role of rubrics and their relationship with writing exemplars provides the context for a discussion of current trends in assessment for learning and increased emphasis on student peer and self-assessment.

Keywords Rubrics • Assessment • Formative • Summative • Criterion-referenced • Norm-referenced • Outcomes • Measures • Achievement • Accountability • Policies • Practice • Standardised testing • Performance assessment • Authentic assessment

4.1 Introduction

Rubrics are seen as essential tools in standards-based education and have been credited with the capacity to perform multi-faceted functions such as providing reliable scores with efficiency and accuracy, useful instructional feedback to students, and enabling focussed curriculum planning for teachers (Arter & McTighe, 2001; Brookhart, 2013; Goodrich Andrade, 2005; Popham, 1997; Spandel, 2006; Yoshina & Harada, 2007). In the area of writing assessment, this remains a hotly debated issue and every aspect of how rubrics are used as well as claims to their reliability, validity, efficiency and effectiveness, has been called into question (Kohn, 2006;

J. de Leeuw (✉)
Founder & President, Visible Assessment for Learning Inc.,
Calgary, AB, Canada
e-mail: djohanna@visibleassessment.ca

Mabry, 1999, 2004; Wilson, 2007b). Despite these stated shortcomings, despite additional concerns that rubrics-based writing assessment may be misguided and potentially counterproductive, and despite the claim that the age of rubrics has passed (Broad, 2002), their successes and benefits in the classroom, particularly in the context of standardised tests, has ensured the endurance of rubrics as a tool for writing assessment.

Scoring guides or writing scales, with the intended purpose of providing a standardised and more 'objective' way of judging student level of attainment, have been around for the better part of the twentieth century (Towne, 1918; Turley & Gallagher, 2008). It is unclear when the term "rubric" – originally meaning decorative, red lettering in fifteenth century manuscripts, or directions for a divine service in a liturgical book (Canadian Oxford Dictionary of English) – began to be used for such scoring guides. Popham (2003) suggests (perhaps somewhat tongue-in-cheek) that "all specialist fields love to have their own special terminology, and 'rubric' is sufficiently opaque to be a terrific turn on to the measurement community" (p. 96). Rubrics as we understand them today are used in performance assessment, situations where students are asked to construct a response to a given question or task such as in written compositions, oral or multi-media presentations and research projects in various subject areas. Constructed responses provide valuable material for both formative and summative student assessment because they require the range of thinking and performance skills that can provide a fuller, perhaps closer measure of student ability than conventional forms such as multiple choice testing. Tasks requiring a range of constructed responses encourage students to problem-solve, think creatively, deal with ambiguity, and manage the social, emotional complexities of human relationships (Eisner, 1999, p. 658).

Asking students to make meaning of, and construct responses to authentic tasks reflects a change in the beliefs about the nature of learning and knowledge creation. The behaviourist view evident in the early twentieth century work of educational psychologist Edward Thorndike and later promoted by Skinner in the 1960s, conceives learning as knowledge acquisition and assumes that "by controlling the stimulus, learning can be shaped and modified to predetermined intentions" (Dann, 2002, p. 12). Here the learner is objectified; a receptacle for information, an agent who will demonstrate acquisition of pre-set learning objectives. In this context, the role of engagement, initiation and motivation in the learning process is minimised (p. 13). By contrast, the emergence of a constructivist approach shifted the emphasis on the centrality of the learner as actively, intentionally, and cognitively engaged in making sense of her/his environment, to where context matters; judgment counts; and opportunities to act and speculate are of critical importance. As teachers, "we are shapers of the environment, stimulators, motivators, guides, consultants, resources … in the end, what children make of what we provide is a function of what they construe from what we offer" (Eisner, 1999, p. 658). The claim to authenticity lies in contextualising the task in apparently 'real' rather than artificial situations and requires a performance response that integrates knowledge with applications in a holistic rather than component skill manner (Cumming & Maxwell, 1999). The mastery of higher order thinking and problem-solving capacities is seen to be both more meaningful and possess more ready transfer from life in the classroom to the changing demands of modern society (Newmann & Archibald, 1992, cited in Cumming & Maxwell, 1999; Redecker & Johannessen, 2013). The terms authentic and performance assessment are not used with consistency in the research literature. Some scholars see the terms as synonymous arguing that performance by its nature is authentic, while others maintain that not all performance assessment is or need be authentic for this depends, in part, on its purpose (Frey & Schmitt, 2007).

These distinctions may be understood or determined in different ways but the consistent element is that assessment of performance, whether authentic, formative or summative in purpose, has always presented a challenge. Performance assessment involves making skilled judgments regarding quality of student responses which in turn involves determining which aspects of a given response receive more or less value in the making of that judgment. Judgments are seen to be both valid (because of the integrity of the construct by which a judgment has been made) and reliable (because several different assessors would arrive at a similar judgment), when they can assume a common understanding among qualified professionals of varying levels of performance. In writing assessment, efforts to make evaluation criteria explicit as well as address inter-rater agreement appeared as early as the 1920s in the form of scoring guides (Hudelson, 1923). Despite these efforts, for the better part of the last century, holistic rather than analytic grading remained the predominant means by which student writing was assessed. Holistic grading places the emphasis on global judgment and allows the assessor to build up "a complex mental response to student work [by] attending to particular aspects that draw attention to themselves, and allowing an appreciation of the quality of the work as a whole to emerge" (Sadler, 2009, p. 161). This judgment is then correlated to a mark on a grading scale. In contrast, analytic grading focuses on the components or criteria of a given work and it is this practice that is represented in the use of rubrics. Here, evaluative criteria along with quality descriptors for varying levels of achievement with an assigned value or weight are established ahead of time and made explicit. Judgments are made for each criterion and then combined and converted into a score. The score or evaluative judgment is the sum of the component parts.

In the area of writing assessment, analytic versus holistic grading continues to be debated particularly as the latter form has, since the 1990s, increased in favour and dominated the assessment agenda. Though the two approaches come to the same task with completely different processes, it could be argued that when followed meticulously, each system can be seen to have its own methodological and critical integrity. Provided attention is paid to the integrity of each process, the results of the differing grading processes should approximate one another and therefore be equally reliable and valid. Ongoing debate on the issue suggests that this is not the case. The question is "Which process provides the most accurate evaluation for summative purposes and which process yields the most accurate evaluation and analysis for formative or instructional purposes?" Those in favour of rubrics point to the analytical capacities of this tool to provide accurate assessment and indepth information for instructional purposes (Saddler & Andrade, 2004).

Despite the original intent of rubrics use as a means to provide 'objectivity', the term as it is used today indicates more than a scoring guide for presumed accurate evaluation. An appropriately designed rubric can also function as an "instructional illuminator" (Popham, 1997), a tool that has the capacity to convey to the student the specifics of both the criteria of a given performance that will be evaluated, as well as the quality levels for each criterion (Goodrich Andrade, 2005). In this instance, the rubric is transformed from a scoring guide for summative purposes to an instructional tool for formative uses, and is created specifically to give feedback to students regarding their progress towards attaining the outlined criteria as well as providing information to teachers allowing for modification of instruction to better meet student needs. Such rubrics may be co-created with students and can also facilitate peer and self-assessment, in essence becoming a tool for teaching and learning with assessment embedded in the process (Andrade, 2006; Goodrich Andrade, 2005; Yoshina & Harada, 2007; Andrade et al., 2009).

The conflicting views that characterise the rubrics debate in writing assessment hinge on two distinct but interrelated assertions. First, the promise to deliver a more 'objective' means to score student work thereby increasing inter-rater reliability, arose as a corrective to the 'subjective' or holistic method; this development may be best understood when examined from a historical perspective. Second, by deconstructing the elements of a performance, rubrics provide an insider's view of the 'building bricks' of composition setting the stage for more specific, targeted assessment and instruction; the arguments opposing this position question the validity of the rubric construct (Sadler, 2009) and require an investigation into their philosophical underpinnings. Viewing these positions within a philosophical and historical framework may reveal a clearer understanding of what exactly rubrics can and cannot do and leads to implications for the role of student exemplars in both formative and summative assessment.

4.2 Historical Perspectives

In their initial inception, scoring guides, the precursor of rubrics, were used primarily for summative evaluation and developed with the specific aim of providing a means for accurate, objective measurement of student writing. At this time, there was no notion of using scoring guides as instructional tools for addressing student needs. As early as 1923 Hudelson wrote: "Composition scales will not improve writing ability. They never were designed to do this directly, and any who attempt to employ them for such a purpose are certain to be disappointed" (p. 163). His list of seven reasons for developing composition scales ranged from judging teaching methods, enabling and judging teacher reliability in marking, to establishing norms and rating student performance against these norms. Interest in the promised capacity of composition scales to provide objectivity grew out of the dismay "on the part of educational scientists of the discouraging lack of agreement among teachers as to the merit of their pupils' writing when scored by personal subjective standards and expressed in percentile terms" (p. 164). This belief is based on the premise that anything that exists can be measured and that "the subjective aspect of composition can be stripped of its formal impersonal elements and these elements measured objectively", reducing the chance of unreliable marking (p. 164). The drive for a positivistic, exact measurement of student writing was not a new development. Hudelson (1923) added his own scale to the elaborate 'scientific' scales that were aligned with benchmark-setting student exemplars developed by Rice (1903), Hillegas (1912), Thorndike (1915), and Hudelson (1923). Parker's (1919) comments suggested that objections to such developments were also not new:

> As your committee sees the matter, composition has at least two large phases: First it is the science of expression rigidly encased in a body of rules ... as such it is definitely measurable. Second, it is also an art with all the intangible graces and beauty which reside in that realm; as such it is not only not definitely measurable but the attempt to make it so may result in positive harm. (p. 204)

Ironically, it was at almost exactly the same time when a change in philosophical thought began to challenge the traditional concept of an objective reality that Ernest C. Noyes (1912) announced a call to pay attention to "a new science of education based upon exact measurement and judgment by ascertained facts" (p. 532). He saw the problem as residing in the fact that "present methods of measuring compositions are controlled too much by personal opinion, [and the] vagueness with which standards have been defined" (p. 534). By 1913, many schools regularly used the *Scale for Measurement of Quality in English Composition by Young People* or the Hillegas Scale, which had teachers scoring student writing by comparing it with rated samples. As Turley and Gallagher (2008) commented, this practice was informed by the belief that assessment of student writing could be translated into a number and quantified: "The Hillegas Scale and the others that followed, answered the call for a scientific tool that could eliminate teacher subjectivity for an objective and exact numerical measurement of student writing" (p. 88).

Renewed efforts to address inter-rater reliability were undertaken by a team of researchers from the American organisation created in 1947, the Educational Testing Service (ETS). Diederich, French, and Carlton (1961) set out to "reveal the differences of opinion that prevail in uncontrolled grading – both in the academic community and in the educated public" (abstract). The premise on which these researchers operated was fundamentally positivistic. The aim of their study, which involved "53 distinguished readers, representing six different fields [including] college English teachers, social scientists, natural scientists, writers and editors, lawyers, and business executives" (abstract), was not to investigate the how and why of the disparities in their judgments of writing, but rather to find a positivistic paradigm that would eliminate bias, reduce discrepancies and promote consistent responses (inter-rater reliability). These researchers, working from a psychometric premise that validity in assessment depended on reliability, believed that an objective truth was obtainable provided the correct conditions for such an event were created. Using factor analysis or correlations among the grades of the 53 readers, they were disturbed to find that "no paper received less than five different grades;

and that the median correlation between readers was .31" (abstract). Follow up research saw the team collecting responses and comments, repeatedly classifying and codifying them until five factors were distilled that reflected what seemed to be the essence of the core values in writing. They were:

- Ideas: relevance, clarity, quantity, development, persuasiveness
- Form: organization and analysis
- Flavor: style, interest, sincerity
- Mechanics: specific errors in punctuation, grammar, etc.
- Wording: choice and arrangement of words. (Diederich, French, & Carlton, cited in Broad, 2002, p. 6)

This amounted to a five-point rubric that has remained virtually standard in writing assessment to this day. From Broad's (2002) perspective, the ETS research team's focus on creating "a simplified, ordered, well-controlled representation that would keep the future of writing assessment efforts clean of such disturbing features as dissent, diversity, context-sensitivity, and ambiguity" in order to avoid confronting "an apparent wilderness of rhetorical values" was misguided. Their extensive and comprehensive research missed an "historic opportunity" (p. 6) to discover what is at the heart of writing assessment:

> The ETS team of researchers achieved the chance to show the world what real experts working in real professions in the real world valued in real college students' writing. This is the truth and the reality they discovered, and it could have provided them and us with a powerful authority and reference point for understanding writing assessment. Their positivist presuppositions and methods, however, compelled them in a different direction. Decrying their findings as 'disturbing' and full of evaluators' 'error,' Diederich, French, and Carlton traded in the rhetorical truth confronting them (that readers value texts differently) in exchange for the grail of high inter-rater agreement. (Broad, 2002, pp. 7–8)

What the ETS research team did contribute is the writing assessment rubric as it is known today. Though it has undergone countless variations, the core idea has remained much as it was put forward in 1961 and the fact that it continues to be used in some form speaks to its fundamental success. Though much has been written that has questioned their value, particularly in the last two decades as their popularity has increased (Broad, 2002; Kohn, 2006; Mabry, 1999, 2004; Sadler, 2008; Wilson, 2007a), considerably more has been written on rubrics than any other tool, on how they are able to benefit writing instruction and assessment (Andrade, 2006; Arter & McTighe, 2001; Popham, 2003; Wiggins, 1991). Ongoing research continues to refine their potential strengths while also paying heed to the flaws that can diminish a rubric's value (Popham, 1997, 2003). It is evident that the assets rubrics bring to instruction and assessment, particularly large scale assessment – notably accountability, efficiency and legitimacy (Brown et al., 2014) – ensure that they will most likely become a permanent fixture in assessment. If the strength of rubrics "lies in what they include [and] their great weakness is what they leave out"; if they have the power to either "prevent us from telling the truth about what we believe, what we teach, what we value" (Broad, 2002, p. 2) or the opposite, to "echo our beliefs" (Spandel, 2006, p. 21), then an inquiry into these claims is needed. Such understandings could provide a foundation on which to continue to build and refine the process of evaluating student writing in schools and may assist in making informed decisions regarding both the power and limitations of this tool. It is apparent that fundamentally different philosophical positions underlie the rubrics debate.

4.3 Philosophical Underpinnings

The epistemological framework that governs standardised testing, rankings and ratings can be seen to be in direct conflict with the belief that assessment of student achievement is a complex, multi-faceted affair that defies quantification and objectification (Kohn, 2006; Wilson, 2007a). Nowhere is this more evident than in assessment of writing where determining the level of accomplishment relies upon (the unpredictable nature of) human judgment: "the history of direct writing skill assessment is a bleak one. As far back as 1880 it was recognised that the essay exam was beset with the curse of unreliability" (Breland, 1983, p. 1). The idea that human judgment is subjective by nature, too easily influenced by unpredictable and uncontrollable factors, essentially 'flawed' and therefore not able to make objective decisions, has led to efforts to remove as much of the human subjective element as possible in order to arrive at an objective 'truth' (Hudelson, 1923). Furthermore, a standardised method of marking favours standardising the skill that it is attempting to assess; since writing is both a skill and an expressive art, such standardisation compromises the very nature and integrity of the activity: "The standardization of a skill that is fundamentally self-expressive and individualistic obstructs its assessment. And rubrics standardise the teaching of writing, which jeopardizes the learning and understanding of writing" (Mabry, 1999, p. 674). As in most disagreements that are based on ideological differences, attempts to find a resolution or compromise rest on an increased understanding of the principles on which the diverging views are based.

Yancey (1999) suggests two different lenses through which to historicize the writing assessment debate. One is located in method (objective tests, holistically scored essays, portfolios, rubrics). Another is located in the defining concepts of reliability and validity and the differing interpretations between psychometricians (the old experts) and teachers (the new non-experts). Yancey characterises the history of writing assessment as the struggle between these two groups as follows:

> From this perspective, the last 50 years of writing assessment can be narrativized as the teacher-layperson (often successfully) challenging the (psychometric) expert, developing and then applying both expertise and theory located not in psychometrics, but in rhetoric, in reading and hermeneutics, and, increasingly, in writing practice. (p. 484)

When Wilson (2007b) states that she "won't be using rubrics to respond to student writing" (p. 62) because she believes we need "to look at the piece of writing itself to suggest its own evaluative criteria" (p. 42), her argument is rooted in a phenomenological perspective that calls for a "return to the things themselves" (Husserl, cited in Moran & Mooney, 2002, p. 1). Husserl's loss of faith in the ability of objectified scientific facts to provide meaningful and significant answers for human life as a whole and its inability to cope with the problems of absolute truth and validity led to a call for a philosophical overhaul: "The need for an utterly original philosophy has re-emerged, the need of a philosophy that ... seeks ... to penetrate to that primal ground on whose basis (philosophical) problems must find whatever solution is genuinely scientific" (Husserl, cited in Moran & Mooney, 2002, p. 124). Husserl's focus on the "life-world" of human experience as "a realm of original self-evidences" arose as a corrective to the notion that scientific truth lies in the objective world detached from human experience. Accordingly, 'objective reality' is a contradiction in terms because what is real must be experienced in order to be real, and all experiences are subjective:

> The contrast between the subjectivity of the life-world and the 'objective', the 'true' world, lies in the fact that the latter is a logical substruction of something that is in principle not perceivable...not experienceable in its own proper being, whereas the subjective in the life-world, is distinguished in all respects precisely by its being actually experienceable. (Husserl, cited in Moran & Mooney, 2002, p. 167)

This philosophical reorganisation is Husserl's response to the prevailing pre twentieth century view of Descartes' mind-body dualism where the idea of reality is a dichotomy between physical matter and spiritual or mental matter. The core understanding is that consciousness does not exist as an entity isolated from the object of which it is conscious. Because consciousness exists only in its capacity to be always aware of something, mind and matter are interrelated, thus the dichotomy between thought and the object of thought, between mind and matter is artificial, arbitrary and contradictory: "The recognition that consciousness is intentional implies that such distinctions are misdirected. An unknowable reality is unthinkable...a completely empty consciousness closed in upon itself is inconceivable" (Stewart & Mickunas, 1990, p. 9). This is the philosophical basis for Wilson's (2007b) objections to rubrics. She is ideologically unwilling to dissect student writing into its component parts for 'objective' analysis because to do so, in her view, compromises the integrity of the student work as well as compromising her integrity as the recipient of and participant in that work:

> The way that rubrics attempt to facilitate my responses to students – by asking me to choose from [a pre-constructed] menu of responses – troubles me ... rubrics and their "menu" of generic comments are clumsy in practice and in theory; they tear at the foundations of the rhetorical art of writing, reducing student essays and our responses to an exercise in purposelessness. (Wilson, 2007b, p. 63)

The loss to which Wilson (2007b) and Broad (2002) allude to is a loss of belief in the ability to objectify created work by deconstructing it into component parts for the purpose of appraisal or appreciation. They argue that rubrics, whether externally imposed or internally created, rest on a pre twentieth century paradigm that is "trapped in a positivist/behaviorist ideological framework in which they were conceived" (Turley & Gallagher, 2008, p. 89). By remaining trapped in the "egocentric predicament" of the Cartesian tradition, the rubrics way of thinking denies the capacity to enter a world in common, an opportunity to question the meaning of what appears in consciousness thereby seeking to understand the truth as it is perceived. In essence, this argument sees using rubrics for instruction and assessment as the prevention of capturing true responses or expressing what is truly valued in a piece of writing. Because values are at the heart of all human enterprise, this factor alone is seen as sufficient grounds not to use rubrics at all. Values are what drive the human quest to arrive at understandings of the world which according to Gadamer (1975), occurs primarily through the use of language, by directing our "gaze on the things themselves" (p. 267). These understandings include recognising that presuppositions are brought to a given situation which paradoxically is the "recognition that all understanding inevitably involves some prejudice" (p. 270). Thus language, interpretation and understanding are inextricably intertwined within an essential interpretive or hermeneutic conversation. The complexity of this exchange is expressed by Gadamer (1975) in this way:

> A person who is trying to understand a text is always projecting. He projects a meaning for the text as a whole as soon as some initial meaning emerges in the text. Again, the initial meaning emerges only because he is reading the text with particular expectations in regard to certain meaning. Working out this fore-projection, which is constantly revised in terms of what emerges as he penetrates into meaning, is understanding what is there. (p. 267)

4.3.1 The Rubrics Debate

According to Broad (2002), the only way we can recover this loss and "reclaim what rhetoric and composition lost half a century ago when it adopted rubrics" is to move beyond rubrics (p. 5). This view is echoed by Kohn (2006) who sees the promotion of rubrics as instruments that promise objectivity, validity and reliability in marking student writing as an illusion, allowing teachers to "pretend that what they are doing is exact and objective" (p. 13). His arguments opposing rubrics are supported with such rhetorical statements as: [they are] "above all a tool to promote standardisation", can become a "handy strategy of self-justification during parent teacher conferences" and "turn teachers into grading machines" (p. 12). In addition to the erroneous notion of viewing objectivity as the desired goal, Kohn views the attempt to "deny the subjectivity of human judgment" as objectionable and harmful. The desire for this kind of definition leads to a rubric design that focuses on assessing the isolated parts of writing rather than the expression and artistry of the whole (Kohn, 2006, p. 13). Each component is linked to a scorable standard allowing for standardised ratings, in turn encouraging standardised writing, thereby increasing the production of formulaic prose: "high scores on a list of criteria for excellence in essay writing do not mean that the essay is any good because quality is more than the sum of its rubicized parts" (p. 14). Clearly, Kohn is challenging the assumption that knowledge or truth can be gained by disconnecting ourselves from the subject (the piece of writing), breaking it down into manageable component parts or objects (through rubrics) and reconnecting with the components for the purpose of analysis.

Spandel (2006) moves the argument away from reaching for the elusive goal of objectivity by accepting that 'objective marking' is probably impossible. Acknowledging that subjectivity is neither wrong nor harmful "unless we use it as an excuse not to make our scores or grade defensible" (p. 21), she creates the space for an exploration of the potential uses as well as limitations of rubrics. Her focus is on the instructional benefits of thoughtfully crafted rubrics that "cause us to go deep inside the performance and question our traditional belief about what we define as proficient" (p. 19). She admits that not all aspects of writing can be captured by simple rubrics terms: "no assessment (score, grade, narrative description, or conference) reveals *everything* – but each offers useful insights" (p. 19). Livingston (2012) argues that rubrics are more likely to draw attention to the multiple complexities of good writing rather than "any traditional number-out-of-the-grading-ether method of assessment" (p. 109). Key to this understanding is ensuring that the rubric construct is not assigned with attributes that are not inherent in its design, namely, the power to confer objectivity on the act of scoring and grading writing or the capacity to assess qualities of performance that lie beyond its scope. Expert use of rubrics requires seeing them as a springboard for further thought rather than a prescriptive device, requiring interaction as well as interpretation and professional judgment.

This kind of skilled, qualitative judgment is what is required when a work is to be assessed holistically. Among Mabry's (1999) concerns is the confusion surrounding the terms 'holistic' or 'analytic' with reference to rubrics. The relatively recent development of using the term 'holistic' to describe some rubrics is, according to her, erroneous. 'Holistic' implies an emphasis on the total effect of a piece of writing, "the irreducibility of the whole" (p. 675). Arter and McTighe (2001) define a holistic rubric as one that "gives a single score or rating for an entire product or performance based on an overall impression of a student's work. In essence, one combines all the important ingredients of a performance or product to arrive at an overall, single judgment of quality" (p. 18). Similarly, Brookhart (2013) describes a holistic rubric as "applying all the criteria at the same time and enabling an overall judgement about the quality of the work" (p. 6). Sadler (2009) refines the distinction by focusing on intent; the extended verbal descriptions in a so-called holistic rubric are "intended as indicative rather than definitive or prescriptive. The descriptions invariably contain embedded or implied references to multiple criteria, but do not necessarily refer to the same criteria at all grade levels" (p. 6). Mabry contends that once criteria are specified, attention has been taken away from the overall effect and the focus is redirected to the components of the writing performance: "although it is possible to derive a holistic score from a list of discrete criteria, strategies that focus on criteria are fundamentally analytic in character because they focus on components" (p. 675).

The solution for Arter and McTighe (2001) is that the rater is instructed to consider all the traits (such as understanding, sophistication and communication, organisation, conventions), "mentally weigh them and decide on a score that best suits the overall performance" (p. 18). On the surface this may seem straightforward, but in reality, it may not proceed so smoothly. Arter and McTighe's "overall impression" assumes implicit rather than explicit reference to criteria for assessing a work and could be seen as a haphazard and random way of arriving at a judgment. The implication is that making a judgment would include reference to criteria whether explicitly stated or implied. Does weighing up the components or traits (just in our heads this time but not on paper) constitute holistic assessment? A true overall impression suggests, as Mabry (1999) pointed out earlier, the 'irreducibility' of the performance into traits or components, or as Sadler (2009) implies, particular aspects are considered not because this has been pre-decided but because they draw attention to themselves. The understanding is that true appreciation means preserving the integrity of the whole, while allowing awareness of these elements to emerge in the critical appraisal process, rather than engaging with a work through a list of pre-determined criteria. There is an elusive, artistically creative factor in performances and compositions, whether musical, painted or written, that resists separating parts from the whole. That is why producing a single score by combining traits, either in our heads or on paper, is not considered by Mabry to be holistic marking. For her, engaging in holistic assessment stands as a separate enterprise. A rubric by nature is an instrument that first identifies the parts of something before considering the whole; calling a rubric holistic is conferring on the instrument a quality not inherent in its design. It is a contradiction in terms: "because rubrics to assess writing prescribe the criteria by which papers are to be judged, claims of their holism rarely survive analysis" (p. 675).

Mabry's second main concern is with validity and reliability. The fact that rubrics improve inter-rater reliability may ironically undermine their validity. Scorers are limited by the criteria they have been directed to use for evaluation and are trained to use rubrics uniformly. This can result in discounting a student response that happens to elude pre-set criteria: "writing rubrics can fail to predict the actual features of a student's writing, thereby creating a mismatch between scoring criteria and actual performance…the score will not support valid inferences about the student's achievement" (p. 675). The reverse situation can also occur. "Forced attention to features anticipated by the rubric" can lead to artificially inflated scores. In addition, the standardisation feature of rubrics fails to address creative expression which is the essence of writing: "the standardization of any skill that is fundamentally individual obstructs its assessment…and this presents a validity problem … more specifically, it is a problem of construct validity" (p. 678).

Balancing the twin concepts of validity and reliability is commonly seen as core to writing assessment with the understanding that "validity means you are measuring what you intend to measure, reliability that you can measure it consistently" (Yancey, 1999, p. 487). As seen earlier in this paper, reliability dominated the writing assessment agenda for the first 50 years of the last century, operating under the assumption that higher inter-rater reliability meant greater validity. The shift to direct assessment (as in a constructed response such as an essay) from indirect (as in multiple choice, which can only test writing support skills) resulted in a shift to a different concern with validity – are we measuring what we teach? The intent was to replicate the reliability found in multiple choice tests to a performance situation (constructed response). The appeal of the rubric as a scoring guide as a means to address these concerns becomes apparent. Arter and McTighe (2001) articulate how a scoring rubric can become a multi-purpose instruction and assessment tool. They claim that rubrics can:

> Clarify the targets of instruction, especially those that are complex and hard to define; provide valid and reliable assessment of student learning of these same complex and hard to assess outcomes; improve student motivation and achievement by helping students understand the nature of quality for performance and products. (p. ix)

Instructional methods that promote 'teaching with the end in mind' or 'the backward design process' (McTighe & Wiggins, 1999) places greater emphasis on making explicit the criteria as defined by a rubric ahead of time rather than demonstrating or modelling as is the traditional apprenticeship method. Replacing the complexity of shared learning through modelling and critique of the work itself with focus on making criteria explicit can be seen as potentially reductionist. This raises the questions: what happens when criteria emerge that do not fit in the pre-set model? Does making the criteria explicit limit as well as define? How is our view of the literary performance as a whole impacted when we consider the parts piece-meal first?

In his landmark 1989 article (re-published, 2008), Sadler faces these issues directly and in doing so, addresses many of the arguments levied against the use of analytic scoring rubrics for evaluation. He explicates how understanding these issues lead to informed ways of making judgments of student work and in turn transforms this knowledge into a proposed instructional design for formative assessment. The first issue he considers is the making of qualitative judgments. The capacity to make qualitative judgments is a pre-requisite for all performance assessments and necessitates clarity regarding what is involved (Sadler, 2010). Sadler (2008, p. 8) outlines five essential points in his analysis and these can be summarised as follows:

1. Performances involve multiple criteria and expert appraisal requires awareness of these criteria. Criteria possess individual dimensions that interlock. The overall configuration amounts to more than a sum of its parts and decomposing the configuration tends to reduce the validity of an appraisal.
2. Some criteria are fuzzy rather than sharp. Sharp criteria can be defined as separate and discontinuous whereas a fuzzy criterion is an abstract mental construct denoted by a linguistic term which has no absolute or unambiguous meaning independent of its context. Fuzzy criteria are characterised by a continuous gradation from one state to another.
3. At any one appraisal, only a subset of a large pool of legitimate criteria is typically used. These may not be able to be specified ahead of time but the competent judge is able to decide which criteria are relevant and be able to substantiate that decision. Professional judgement requires knowing the rules.
4. There is often no independent method or means of confirming whether a judgement is correct. Having two persons instead of one to mark an essay does not constitute independent methods. An example of two independent ways of marking an essay could be by person and then with a computer.
5. In making qualitative judgments, the final decision is never arrived at by counting things. Marks are assigned after the judgement is made. (Sadler, 2008, p. 8)

Sadler's (2009) conclusion, that a properly executed holistic approach provides a truer assessment than an analytical (rubric based) one, is based on a theoretical analysis of the structural adequacy of the rubric construct rather than its practical applications in a classroom setting:

The answer lies in the form of potential structural adequacy, which is an aspect of validity rather than an aspect of reliability. The argument in this article has been that the analytic approach is theoretically and practically deficient on two grounds. By limiting itself to preset criteria, it cannot take into account all the necessary nuances of expert judgments. Neither can analytic appraisal, when using a simplistic combination rule, represent the complex ways in which criteria are actually used. In principle, properly done holistic appraisals can do both. Therefore, the 'truer' representation is the 'fuller' of the two. (p. 177)

Despite this conclusion, Sadler (2009) admits that traditional holistic methods of assessment "are not up to the task" (p. 174) since this approach is equally subject to significant shortcomings as is the analytic approach. Briefly summarised, he proposes a way of moving forward that focusses on students themselves being engaged in making "multiple holistic judgements on complex works, the source material being the work of their peers and the anonymised teacher's response to the same task" (p. 176). In essence, Sadler is speaking about students learning the language and art of appraisal through critically analysing multiple examples of constructed responses. Students learn through peer assessment to monitor and self-evaluate "developing evaluative expertise through guided practice … [equipping] learners to become self-critical and able to self-monitor their own work while it is in production, which ultimately is the very point at which it can make a difference to the work's quality" (p. 177).

4.3.2 Rubrics and Exemplars in Writing Assessment

This scenario represents a challenge for communicating standards to students. Knowledge resident in the head of the expert (teacher) must somehow be manifested externally to be of use to the learner. One way is to employ verbal descriptions, but these are open to endless interpretations and negotiating a common understanding becomes a cumbersome and impractical solution. An answer, as introduced by Hillegas in the 1920s (Turley & Gallagher, 2008) is to link these descriptions to exemplars: "a combination of verbal descriptions and associated exemplars provides a practical and efficient means of externalising a reference level" (Sadler, 2008, p. 169). The current emphasis on formative assessment has led educators to see the value of using writing exemplars for instructional purposes (Limbrick & Knight, 2005). Of importance is noting the dual role that exemplars would play; that of conveying a standard, but also providing a concrete illustration that conveys the 'how and why', providing an anchor for the assessment (Wiggins, 1996). Ideally, a written exemplar that functions as an illustration could be annotated, thus incorporating a verbal description alongside the text. Students would preferably have access to a variety of both professional and peer exemplars that consider the optimum gap between the learner's level and their aspirations (Sadler, 2008, p. 14). A music instruction comparison is the practice of the 'master class' where students take turns in performing in front of an expert musician and his/her peers. The performances are followed by conversation, critique and sometimes an expert performance of the same or different piece of music, thus exposing students to a variety of amateur and professional illustrations along with 'annotations'. This process is described as follows:

> Knowledge of the criteria is 'caught' through experience, not defined. It is developed through an inductive process which involves prolonged engagement in evaluative activity shared with and under the tutelage of a person who is already something of a connoisseur. By so doing 'the apprentice unconsciously picks up the roles of the art', including those which are not explicitly known to the master … Connoisseurship … can only be communicated through example, not by precept. (Polyani, cited in Sadler, 2008, p. 19)

Wiggins (1991) maintains that we must provide "specific examples of excellence on the tasks we value" (p. 19) pointing to the numerous and varied 'exemplars' of excellence that are available to musicians through performances of artists such as Yo-Yo Ma and Wynton Marsalis. He differentiates between the importance of setting standards as opposed to standardisation of performances and responses: "there is no single model of excellence …excellence is not a mere uniform correctness but the ability to unite personal style with the mastery of a subject in a product or performance of one's design" (p. 19). Wiggins appears to focus on how exemplars function as benchmarks but he also refers to them as goals that represent values. He is critical of current evaluation practices that rely on "vague statements of value or intent, providing neither exemplars of them nor insight into how the standard might be met" (p. 19). His main argument is one that could be seen to support the role of the exemplar as an instructional illuminator. For Wiggins, standards are synonymous with exemplars and in the context of formative assessment they represent the "intellectual virtues such as craftsmanship, self-criticism and persistence" that are the hallmark of quality performances (p. 19).

Spandel (2006) supports this notion by preferring to see the rubric as part of a writing guide with three parts: written criteria; examples of the criteria in action; the reader interpreter. Andrade and Boulay (2003) had Grade 3 and 4 students study model stories or essays and create a list of criteria that indicated desirable writing qualities. These lists resembled the rubrics that were to be used for marking their writing assignments. The study was designed to address the question: "Is there a main effect of a model, generating criteria, and rubric-referenced self-assessment on scores assigned to students' writing?" (p. 5). Student achievement was seen to improve as a result of three interconnected factors: studying and using model papers; generating criteria that resembled the rubric used to mark their assignments and self-assessing their first drafts. Though it is not clear from this study whether students received an opportunity to revise after the self-assessment, the report indicates that significant improvement was made in all areas except sentence structure and conventions. Recommendations for further studies included researching the effect of providing students with multiple strong models particularly in secondary education.

An earlier study (Orsmond, Merry, & Reiling, 2002) with first year undergraduate biology students yielded similar results. These researchers also commented on the lack of literature on instructional strategies that involved exemplars, and research on the effect such strategies might have on student achievement. Though the student assignments involved poster creation rather than written essay-like responses, their results can be summarised as follows: (1) the use of exemplars can help students demonstrate greater understanding of both marking criteria and subject standards; (2) the use of exemplars can help student's learning so that higher quality outcomes are produced; (3) the use of exemplars forms a focus for meaningful formative feedback; (4) when students are asked to assess a product the peer assessor is able to make a more objective assessment of the product than the self-assessor.

Drawing on the work in the last three decades of scholars, theorists in education, as well as linguists (Halliday) and psychologists (Vygotsky), Morgan and Wyatt-Smith (2000) described how through the concept of apprenticeship or modelling, literacy teachers …

> are expected to adopt or model a metalanguage or a portable language through which to talk about language itself [providing] linguistic information about language choices and assessment expectations…Adult and child engage in carefully calibrated interactions [where] the adult simultaneously assists the child to accomplish tasks that lie outside her capabilities, while modelling culturally appropriate ways of accomplishing a goal. (p. 128)

Referring to the work of Sadler, and Black and Wiliam (cited in Morgan & Wyatt-Smith, 2000, p. 129) discuss notions of feedback, induction, and apprenticeship in a teacher-learner contract that form the basis of how we have come to understand formative assessment. They further point out that while improvement is linked to student empowerment through assessment knowledge, teacher feedback alone does not necessarily lead to improved performance. As in the guild or apprentice relationship where a variety of desirable performances are modelled, knowledge or assessment standards need to be made explicit and available to students. For improvement to occur, students need to be familiar with the accepted norms against which their work is to be judged and also to be taught how to use these norms, and thus "be able to judge the quality of their work in progress and completion" (p. 131). In their critical-theoretical discussion of the social, political and intellectual implications of this dialogic relationship between teacher and student, they show how knowledge transfer is not enough:

> the teacher's goal is to interrogate the workings of language and power with the ultimate aim of transforming students and their understandings of themselves, their worlds and their capacities to act in and on these worlds … [with a] renewed vision of a participatory democratic society. (p. 132)

In the guild concept, mastery and excellence are modelled creating the space for engagement with evaluative activities shared between master and apprentice. Mastery learning is more than skill acquisition. Timperley and Parr (2009) describe the power of mastery learning as involving the learner in developing an "understanding of what success in that task might look like and receiving instruction and feedback directly related to it" (p. 45). They maintain that research reviews assessing the effect of mastery learning show a significant impact on student achievement. Mastery learning enables the development of a socio-political, critical consciousness (Morgan & Wyatt-Smith, 2000) and in addition, creates the space necessary for the creative and aesthetic component essential in good teaching. Eisner (2002) articulates how multiple ways of knowing, multiple ways of constructing this knowledge through the "interactive nature of all human experience" and multiple ways of representing this knowledge influences "not only what one is able to say but what one is able to see ... [and gives] permission to use new tools and new forms of representations [enabling] us to look for different things and ask new questions" (p. 380). These generalisations, Eisner observes, reside in the particular and these particulars are what is enacted in our classrooms. While pointing out that no one method describes how understanding is advanced, one consistent point is that teaching depends on artistry and "that sense has to do with the place of aesthetic experience in its pursuit" (p. 380). By moving from episteme (the theoretical and philosophical principles) to phronesis (the particular, practical and performing or producing) and artistry, a learning environment is created that moves skill acquisition to levels of a shared critique of ourselves and the world around us. This is the guild experience.

4.4 Current Trends in Writing Assessment

Seen in this context where holistic assessment holds the theoretical upper hand, the charges made against the use of analytic scoring rubrics could be seen as substantive enough that they should not be used at all. In practice, theoretical understandings have yet to undermine the ongoing use of rubrics for analytical assessment; in fact, these efforts have served to shift the design and use of rubrics to become effective tools for assessment for learning. The original positivist notion of rubrics that arose from a desire to measure and rank students and evaluate teacher effectiveness has for the most part receded and been replaced by investigations as to how the formative use of rubrics may mediate improved performance (Panadero & Jonsson, 2013), self-assessment and metacognition or self-regulation (Panadero & Alonso-Tapia, 2013) and peer assessment strategies (Panadero, Romero, & Strijbos, 2013). Rubrics used in their former narrower sense continue to receive a reputation for reductionist methodology and pedagogy. Extensive research in the last decades (Arter & McTighe, 2001; Black & Wiliam, 1998; Popham, 1997) has seen a reinvention of both their uses and variety of designs. These developments come with many cautions regarding their potential misuse, but as research teams develop more sensitive instruments (Brookhart, 2013; Davies, 2000; McTighe & Wiggins, 1999; Popham, 2003) and teacher knowledge and expertise increases, multiple ways of creating flexible designs to meet learner needs are emerging.

The focus in this chapter has been on examining the use of rubrics in writing assessment, and their origins and development throughout the past decades. Despite the vigorous debate that has accompanied their rise in popularity, rubrics-based assessment, particularly of writing, is generally accepted as preferred practice. Recent developments, spurred in part by the current drive for curriculum redesign in jurisdictions within Canada as well as international jurisdictions, has led to a call for 'balanced assessments' that take into account multiple ways of knowing and representing and framing learning outcomes in the broader context of cross curricular competencies. International environmental e-scans (Parsons & Beauchamp, 2012) of curriculum redesign in Australia, Finland, New Zealand, and the Republic of Korea coupled with information from the Organisation for Economic Co-operation and Development (OECD), the International Review of Curriculum and Assessment Frameworks Internet Archive, and the United Nations Educational, Scientific, and Cultural Organization (UNESCO), indicate increased focus on engagement of students in their own assessments and a priority on assessment for learning rather than summative assessments. The implications for writing assessment show a focus on student centred learning, providing students with more explicit examples of writing linked to benchmarks or standards, creating the conditions for student self-evaluation and self-monitoring of progress.

This trend however, does not resolve the tension between assessment for learning and accountability measures where they exist, such as jurisdiction or school leaving exams when students are being assessed for achievement standards (Slomp, 2008; Crooks, 2011). State or jurisdiction exams aside, a focus on assessment for learning requires a standards based approach that reveals benchmarks along a learning continuum. However, instead of a focus on external standardised tests, the call is for a balanced or integrated approach where the assessment system "would redesign the summative tests used for accountability purposes and embed them in a comprehensive and coherent system in which curriculum, instruction, and assessment are intertwined" (Rothman, 2010, p. 2). Using a wheel analogy, Rothman depicts benchmarked standards at the hub with the spokes denoting summative and formative assessments, curriculum tasks and instructional tools and professional learning for teachers: "In such a system, assessments are not separate and apart from classroom instruction, they are integral to it. All forms of assessment provide an ongoing information loop to teachers, school leaders, parents, policymakers, and the public" (p. 3).

Darling-Hammond's (2010) international analysis of effective assessment systems echoes the call for a balanced and integrated approach. She cites high achieving jurisdictions such as Finland, Australia and Hong Kong that complement open ended items such as essays and problem solutions that require students to analyse, apply knowledge, and write extensively in exam settings with school-based projects and tasks. In writing assessment, rubrics still play a prominent role enabling "comparability in scoring" through the use of standardised rubrics as well as extensive teacher involvement in "training and moderation systems that enable scorers to use the same standards in consistent ways that result in reliable scores" (Darling-Hammond, 2010, p. 3).

An effort to address the holistic versus analytic dilemma when grading student writing is addressed in the Western Australian Literacy and Numeracy Assessment (WALNA) marking guide (Government of Western Australia, 2007). The marking guide "is a curriculum-based and criterion referenced assessment that tests students' knowledge and skills" (p. 3) and as such, stands as an analytic guide. The marking guide consists of criteria and annotated exemplars. Directions for marking are extensive and very specific and are intended to result in less inter-dependency of criteria, that is, the grade for one criteria is not to be influenced by the grade of another: "Markers are required to make 10 independent judgements of students' writing and to score each script carefully using the 10 marking criteria and the accompanying exemplars" (p. 4). In addition, each criterion is a developmental continuum rather than a unit. Holistic marking is addressed by what is termed "on balance judgement" (OBJ). The directions for OBJ suggest:

> Use this to make a holistic judgement of the script. The category descriptors are very broad descriptions of achievement—the range of performance within a category is considerable … Each category will cover several years of schooling and will encompass many different types of scripts … Sometimes a judgement call is needed. (Government of Western Australia, 2007, p. 4)

In providing an OBJ markers are asked to consider three broad categories: text form (narrative conventions); purpose and audience (contextual understandings); and writing conventions, and they are asked to do this before the analytic assessment takes place. It is questionable whether this version of holistic assessment would be considered holistic according to Sadler's (2009) concept. What is apparent is that WALNA is a very comprehensive marking guide and serves as an excellent instructional tool.

The drive to promote integrated, balanced assessment practices in classrooms has led the New Zealand Ministry of Education to develop an extensive website based on their position paper on assessment (New Zealand Ministry of Education, n.d.). This public website is replete with information for teachers providing the tools and resources to enable student engagement as well as practical application of student involvement in holistic (Overall Teacher Judgment or OTJ) assessment. Writing assessment resources include a well-developed bank of benchmarked annotated exemplars that makes explicit the level attained and explanations, enabling students and teachers to answer the three feedback questions identified by Hattie and Timperley (2007): Where am I going? How am I going? Where to next? (p. 88). Further, the development of the online Assessment Tools for Teaching and Learning (e-asTTle) contains prompts, rubrics and annotated exemplars allowing teachers to assess student level of achievement along a developmental continuum. Unlike many other jurisdictions (including Alberta, Canada) where the date and content of standardised tests are set by a provincial or jurisdictional ministry, e-asTTle provides the resources for teachers to select the testing items appropriate to their context and timeline. Teacher marked student writing scores derived from analytic, criterion-reference marking rubric are entered into a digital application that generates interactive graphic reports allowing teachers to analyse student achievement against curriculum levels, curriculum objectives, and population norms.

4.5 Conclusion

For the purposes of formative assessment, feedback can be provided in numerous ways (Hattie & Timperley, 2007) and is always open for revisions and clarification. With regards to holistic versus analytic assessment, it may not be necessary to make a firm decision in favour of one or the other except that the information outcome needs to be accessible to the student for formative purposes. Despite the criticisms mounted against the analytical scoring rubric, the upsurge and popularity of analytical evaluation in the form of rubrics suggests that traditional approaches to holistic assessment have not served that purpose very well. In his 1989 article, Sadler (2008) suggested that if new approaches to holistic appraisal could be devised, there would be a prospect of moving forward. Much of the research literature published on holistic assessment is theoretically rather than empirically based (Huot, 1990, 2002; Sadler, 2009) implying that this is no easy undertaking. Broad's 2002 empirical study is evidence of the complexity and enormity of such a task. His answer, Dynamic Criteria Mapping (DCM) appears to be an extremely detailed, multifaceted account of all the values that could be held for a given task and comes dangerously close to representing yet another mega-rubric (p. 33). Sadler's suggestions on how to best communicate holistic feedback to students is theoretically based; and these theories hold promise but they still remain in theory and have yet to be successfully demonstrated in empirical research.

Although formative assessment has received a great deal of press as well as being the subject of an increasing number of instructional manuals, this literature survey indicates that much of what is being put forward as good instructional practice is based more on intuition rather than actual research (Andrade, Du, & Wang, 2008). The focus of the research to date has been in two main areas: the use of rubrics for instruction and the role of feedback. Other aspects of formative assessment could well deserve more attention (Panadero & Jonsson, 2013), such as student self-assessment, peer critique, and the role of exemplars as instructional tools, not only as benchmark providers for summative measures. Such research in the formative assessment of writing could examine the impact of powerful models on actual achievement in writing. Recent studies in the use of rubrics in combination with peer and self-assessment have indicated that students experience increased understanding of marking criteria leading to improved performance (Panadero & Alonso-Tapia, 2013; Panadero et al., 2013). The same could well apply to the use of exemplars, and how such a tool could be used to improve achievement requires further examination. In addition, research on the role of exemplars could examine whether students derive any benefit from studying work that is not powerful. Davies (2000) advocates using exemplars of varying quality to clarify students' understanding of different levels of achievement. This may be a persuasive theory. However, the traditional artistic guild model for learning, the accepted model for the successful training of artists and musicians, suggests that powerful work is inspired by powerful examples.

References

Andrade, H. L. (2006). The trouble with a narrow view of rubrics. *English Journal, 95*(6), 9–9.
Andrade, H. L., & Boulay, B. A. (2003). Role of rubric-referenced self-assessment in learning to write. *Journal of Educational Research, 97*(1), 21–34.

Andrade, H. L., Du, Y., & Wang, X. (2008). Putting rubrics to the test: The effect of a model, criteria generation, and rubric-referenced self-assessment on elementary school students' writing. *Educational Measurement: Issues and Practice, 27*(2), 3–13.

Andrade, H. L., Wang, X., Du, Y., & Akawi, R. L. (2009). Rubric-referenced self-assessment and self-efficacy for writing. *Journal of Educational Research, 102*(4), 287–302.

Arter, J., & McTighe, J. (2001). *Scoring rubrics in the classroom*. Thousand Oakes, CA: Sage Publications.

Black, P., & Wiliam, D. (1998). Inside the black box. *Phi Delta Kappan, 80*(2), 139.

Breland, H. M. (1983). *The direct assessment of writing skill: A measurement review*. New York, NY: College Board Report, No. 83-6. (ETS RR No. 83-32).

Broad, B. (2002). *What we really value beyond rubrics in teaching and assessing writing*. Logan, UT: Utah State, UP.

Brookhart, S. M. (2013). *How to create rubrics for formative assessment and grading*. Alexandria, VA: Association for Supervision and Curriculum Development (ASCD).

Brown, G. T. L., Glasswell, K., & Harland, D. (2014). Accuracy in the scoring of writing: Studies of reliability and validity using a New Zealand writing assessment system. *Assessing Writing, 9*(2), 105–121.

Crooks, T. (2011). Assessment for learning in the accountability era: New Zealand. *Studies in Educational Evaluation, 37*(1), 71–77.

Cumming, J. J., & Maxwell, G. S. (1999). Contextualising authentic assessment. *Assessment in Education: Principles, Policy and Practice, 6*(2), 177.

Dann, R. (2002). *Promoting assessment as learning*. New York, NY: RoutledgeFalmer.

Darling-Hammond, L. (2010). *Performance counts: Assessment systems that support high-quality learning*. Washington, DC: Council of Chief State School Officers. Retrieved from: http://www.hewlett.org/library/grantee-publication/performance-counts-assessment-systems-support-high-quality-learning

Davies, A. (2000). *Making classroom assessment work*. Courtney, BC, Canada: Connections Publishing Co.

Diederich, P. B., French, J. W., & Carlton, S. T. (1961). *Factors in judgments of writing ability* (ETS Research Bulletin 61-15). Princeton, NJ: Educational Testing Service.

Eisner, E. (2002, May). From episteme to phronesis to artistry in the study and improvement of teaching. *Teaching and Teacher Education, 18*(4), 375.

Eisner, E. W. (1999). The uses and limits of performance assessment. *Phi Delta Kappan, 80*(9), 658.

Frey, B. B., & Schmitt, V. L. (2007). Coming to terms with classroom assessment. *Journal of Advanced Academics, 18*(3), 402–423.

Gadamer, H. G. (1975). *Truth and method*. New York, NY: The Continuum Publishing Company.

Goodrich Andrade, H. (2005). Teaching with rubrics. *College Teaching, 53*(1), 27–30.

Goodrich Andrade, H. L., & Du, Y. (2005). Student perspectives on rubric-referenced assessment. *Practical Assessment, Research and Evaluation, 10*, 1–11.

Government of Western Australia. (2007). *Writing and marking guide: Western Australian literacy and numeracy assessment*. Perth, Australia: Department of Education and Training.

Hattie, J., & Timperley, H. (2007). The power of feedback. *Review of Educational Research, 77*, 81–112.

Hillegas, M. B. (1912). *A scale for the measurement of quality in English composition for young people*. New York, NY: Bureau of Publications, Teachers College, Columbia University.

Hudelson, E. (1923). The development and comparative values of composition scales. *English Journal, 12*(3), 163–168.

Huot, B. (1990). The literature of direct writing assessment: Major concerns and prevailing trends. *Review of Educational Research, 60*(2), 237–263.

Huot, B. (2002). *(Re)Articulating writing assessment*. Logan, UT: Utah State University Press.

Kohn, A. (2006). The trouble with rubrics. *English Journal, 95*(4), 12–15.

Limbrick, L., & Knight, N. (2005). Close reading of students' writing: What teachers learn about writing. *English Teaching: Practice and Critique, 4*(2), 5–22.

Livingston, M. (2012). The infamy of grading rubrics. *English Journal, 102*(2), 108–113.
Mabry, L. (1999). Writing to the rubric. *Phi Delta Kappan, 80*(9), 673.
Mabry, L. (2004). Strange, yet familiar: Assessment-driven education. In K. A. Sirotnik (Ed.), *Holding accountability accountable: What ought to matter in public education*. New York, NY: Teachers College Press.
McTighe, J., & Wiggins, G. (1999). *The understanding by design handbook*. Alexandria, VA: Association for Supervision and Curriculum Development (ASCD).
Moran, D., & Mooney, T. (2002). *The phenomenological reader*. London, UK: Routledge.
Morgan, W., & Wyatt-Smith, C. (2000). Im/proper accountability: Towards a theory of critical literacy and assessment. *Assessment in Education: Principles, Policy and Practice, 7*(1), 123–142.
New Zealand Ministry of Education. (n.d.). *Assessment online*. Retrieved from: http://assessment.tki.org.nz/
Noyes, E. C. (1912). Progress in standardizing the measurement of composition. *The English Journal, 1*(9), 532–536.
Orsmond, P., Merry, S., & Reiling, K. (2002). The use of exemplars and formative feedback when using student derived marking criteria in peer and self-assessment. *Assessment & Evaluation in Higher Education, 27*(4), 309–323.
Panadero, E., & Alonso-Tapia, J. (2013). Self-assessment: Theoretical and practical connotations. When it happens, how is it acquired and what to do to develop it in our students. *Electronic Journal of Research in Educational Psychology, 11*(2), 551–576.
Panadero, E., & Jonsson, A. (2013). The use of scoring rubrics for formative assessment purposes revisited: A review. *Educational Research Review, 9*, 129–144.
Panadero, E., Romero, M., & Strijbos, J. (2013). The impact of a rubric and friendship on peer assessment: Effects on construct validity, performance, and perceptions of fairness and comfort. *Studies in Educational Evaluation, 39*(4), 195–203.
Parker, F. E. (1919). The measurement of composition in English classes. *The English Journal, 98*(4), 203–208.
Parsons, J., & Beauchamp, L. (2012). *From knowledge to action: Shaping the future of curriculum development in Alberta*. Edmonton, AB, Canada: Alberta Education. Retrieved: http://education.alberta.ca/department/ipr/curriculum/research/knowledgetoaction.aspx
Popham, J. W. (1997). What's wrong – And what's right – With rubrics. *Educational Leadership, 12*, 72–75.
Popham, J. W. (2003). *Test better, teach better*. Alexandria, VA: Association for Curriculum Development.
Redecker, C., & Johannessen, O. (2013). Changing assessment: Towards a new assessment paradigm using ICT. *European Journal of Education, 48*(1), 79–96.
Rice, J. M. (1903). English: The need of a new basis in education. *Forum, October, 35*, 269–293.
Rothman, R. (2010). *Policy brief: Principles for a comprehensive assessment system*. Washington, DC: Alliance for Excellent Education. Retrieved from: http://all4ed.org/wp-content/uploads/ComprehensiveAssessmentSystem.pdf
Saddler, B., & Andrade, H. (2004). The writing rubric. *Educational Leadership, 62*(2), 48–52.
Sadler, D. R. (2008). Formative assessment and the design of instructional systems. In W. Harlen (Ed.), *Student assessment and testing* (pp. 3–28). Thousand Oakes, CA: Sage.
Sadler, D. R. (2009). Indeterminacy in the use of preset criteria for assessment and grading. *Assessment & Evaluation in Higher Education, 34*(2), 159–179.
Sadler, D. R. (2010). Beyond feedback: Developing student capability in complex appraisal. *Assessment & Evaluation in Higher Education, 35*(5), 535–550.
Slomp, D. H. (2008). Harming not helping: The impact of a Canadian standardized writing assessment on curriculum and pedagogy. *Assessing Writing, 13*(3), 180–200.
Spandel, V. (2006). In defense of rubrics. *English Journal, 96*(1), 19–22.
Stewart, D., & Mickunas, A. (1990). *Exploring phenomenology*. Athens, OH: Ohio University Press.

Thorndike, E. L. (1915). *Thorndike extension of the Hillegas scale*. New York, NY: Bureau of Publications, Teachers College, Columbia University.

Timperley, H. S., & Parr, J. M. (2009). What is this lesson about? Instructional processes and student understandings in writing classrooms. *Curriculum Journal, 20*(1), 43–60.

Towne, C. F. (1918). Making a scale for the measurement of English composition. *The Elementary School Journal, 19*(1), 41–53.

Turley, E. D., & Gallagher, C. W. (2008). On the uses of rubrics: Refraining the great rubric debate. *English Journal, 97*(4), 87–92.

Wiggins, G. (1991). Standards, not standardization: Evoking quality student work. (Cover story). *Educational Leadership, 48*(5), 18–25.

Wiggins, G. (1996). Anchoring assessment with exemplars: Why students and teachers need models. *Gifted Child Quarterly, 40*(2), 66.

Wilson, M. (2007a). The view from somewhere. *Educational Leadership, 65*(4), 76–80.

Wilson, M. (2007b). Why I won't be using rubrics to respond to students' writing. *English Journal, 96*(4), 62–66.

Yancey, K. B. (1999). Looking back as we look forward: Historicizing writing assessment. *College Composition and Communication, 50*(3), 483–503.

Yoshina, J. M., & Harada, V. H. (2007). Involving students in learning through rubrics. *Library Media Connection, 25*(5), 10–14.

Chapter 5
Arts-Inspired Performance Assessment Considerations for Educational Leaders

Matthew J. Meyer

Abstract Assessment in the visual and performance arts has always been a challenge in its attempt to balance content, performance, and participation for students. This chapter focuses on some of these issues employing the drama constituency as the medium for discussion. Some rubrics and curriculum content are discussed from both Canada and the United States.

Keywords Visual and performing arts • Assessment • Drama interpretation for assessment

5.1 Introduction

Study the following work of visual art.

M.J. Meyer (✉)
Faculty of Education, St. Francis Xavier University,
Xavier Hall, West Street, Antigonish, NS B2G 2W5, Canada
e-mail: mmeyer@stfx.ca

© Springer International Publishing Switzerland 2016
S. Scott et al. (eds.), *Leadership of Assessment, Inclusion, and Learning*,
The Enabling Power of Assessment 3, DOI 10.1007/978-3-319-23347-5_5

What type of critical examination or criteria would you use to evaluate its worth to you? Do you find it pleasing? Do you find it aggravating? Or perhaps simply a bunch of messed up lines, drawn by a crazed artist or brilliant genius from beyond the norm of everyday media artists? These are only a few of the questions teachers and educators ask every day as they approach and employ performance assessment in the classroom. In this chapter, we will approach some of these types of queries. By the way, the piece is Pablo Picasso's *Guernica*, created to commemorate the late 1930s Basque city of the same name by the Nazis and fascists to assist Franco in his quest for rule in Spain.

From about the mid-1970s onward, there was a great movement in education curriculum to include not only Visual and Performing Arts as singular, stand-alone academic subjects; there was also a movement to use some of their respective teaching methodologies in classrooms that taught subjects other than the Arts. I define Visual Arts as those areas that include Three-dimensional Drawing, Sculpture, Design, Pottery, and such Plastic Arts as Photography, Film, and Video. Performing Arts include Drama/theatre, Music, and Dance.

There are many forms of performance assessment activities, both from the assigning perspective and from the assessing perspective such as portfolios. However for this chapter, I will only focus on live drama-like presentation activities. However, much of the content presented here can also be associated within the more generic performing arts purview that include such genres as dramatic, dance, or music presentation activities. In a non-art setting, this could be an activity such as a debate, historical representation, or a literary original work activity to assist and expand the experiential and collaborative learning event.

These are only several of many areas to focus on how school leaders can support optimal student assessment practices using arts-based performance assessment. It is implicit that arts teachers and school administrators believe that arts are an integral part of the learning and school experience either by belief or as is by legislation. Needless to say, I advocate for as much arts experiences in schooling. Given that foundation, my position is:

1. arts performance assessment is not unique to the arts;
2. the unique nature of assessment in the arts can be employed across the more general curriculum.

Embedded within these are issues of:

- instructional leadership in the arts
- leadership preparation implications
- professional development implications for educators
- implications for student-parent-community communication
- governance policy implications for arts programs administration.

Art-based performance assessment is the thread that sews all these issues together. I will use several examples to help illustrate these connections – more for awareness than anything else. Understanding these connections during the current emphasis on accountability might aid us in furthering our understanding in arts programs' assessment.

The Arts have always been an enigma to most educators. In many cases it has also pitted working artists against many Arts teachers who perhaps have not experienced the same professional levels of success and excellence as professional working artists. This conflict of the expectation of excellence has been similarly seen between highly trained Arts teachers and those dilettantes who dabble in the Arts and from this dabbling believe they are experts in the field. The ultimate question, and not for discussion in this chapter, is whether or not liking and enjoying the Arts or even reading and watching plays or going to art galleries qualifies one to teach Arts. Perhaps more challenging a question is why many school administrators assign someone to teach an Arts course who does not have the background or qualifications to teach that Arts course. The rationale may be one of expedience, need or whatever, and it may not necessarily be best for the school or the students.

There has also been much speculation that students who have studied in the visual and fine Arts also show academic success in typical academic subjects. There are many behaviours that may be linked with the Arts and which serve to enhance multiple other behaviours such as fine and gross motor skills, verbal and auditory acuteness, visual and emotional growth, and social adaptation. There have been many studies that have shown that those students who have participated in the Arts have had great academic crossovers and success in other subject areas. It is not the purpose of this chapter to either reassert or further prove this. The purpose here is to further explore the challenges in appraisal and assessment both in the presentation and participation of arts assignments and/or in arts-related assignments in other subject areas. This becomes somewhat more complex when considering the Alberta Student Assessment Study's (Webber, Aitken, Lupart, Runté, & Scott, 2008) society-perceived paradigms, i.e., "the complexity of assessment resulting from the 'different paradigms' held by society" (p. 22). These four paradigms were branded as:

1. the assessment of knowledge;
2. the view that schools should prepare students for their places in society and to manifest "good citizenship";
3. that schools should "prepare students for the world of work"; and
4. "developing the natural talents of students". (pp. 22–23)

The quest for both subject knowledge and its subsequent applications for real-world and daily-life interactions with both people and the environment seems to be a critical success indicator of knowledge acquisition (hence, teaching) and knowledge application (hence, learning). It is my view, biased as it is, that Arts education, with its subsequent applications is the most direct, immediate, and long-term vehicle for such knowledge attainment and knowledge relevance. This is in addition to the widely acclaimed and accepted world view that education in the Arts contributes to the spirituality and cohesion of nations and their cultures. Just think for a moment about the impact on a nation's national anthem, flag, or oaths of office. The national anthem is a music medium; the flag is a visual arts medium, and an oath of office is a dramatic scripted act. Observers of these patriotic demonstrations, (similar to audience members) through the association of the act itself – become part of the ceremony; or part of the experience. Ethereally or spiritually there is a unification of mind, body, and spirit. This fusion, so to speak, creates the citizenship or bonding of the participants. The goals of the four paradigms are fulfilled in these communal acts of art.

This is all well and good for national/community unity and pride. However, the issue may be rather more complex when parents are choosing course programs for their children's school exiting requirements. The Arts knowledge disciplines are usually reduced to content subject credits and many times lose their lustre. Regardless of such parental and academic choices, school legislation requires some Arts knowledge and experience is required to fulfil the K-12 curriculum. For our purposes here in exploring issues of performance assessment, I take the more pragmatic view and assume that Arts education, either in terms of subject discipline or in terms of general awareness, is a sought and required aspect of the school curriculum. The teaching methodologies of the Arts can be adapted and serve as pedagogical vehicles in many other subject areas. These other subjects may not have the same intentions or goals as those of the Arts, but for students the Arts-like experience may serve as a vehicle for knowledge-acquisition as well as for experiential self-learning.

In addition to the above statement that "arts performance assessment is not unique to the arts": yes, many state and/or provincial education departments require performance assessment protocols for school systems to adjudicate grading systems in order to judge whether or not students have fulfilled specific subject requirements. Many subject teachers can employ quantitative or Likert-like assessments, or highly rubric grading guidelines for literary type questions (either on-going or exam inclusive). Arts' performance phenomena also include actual performance (physical acting, dancing, music playing), psycho-motor coordination, voice and aural presentation, and the like activities. The difference here between Visual and Performing Arts assessments and typical liberal Arts and/or Science assessments is in perception and execution. Hence, it is the definition and application of *uniqueness* that is translucent to many non-visual and performing Arts teachers and administrators (and probably politicians who create education policy). Herein lies the on-going discussion of whether or not assessments are all the same or serve the same purpose. Unfortunately, there is not enough space in this chapter to take this discussion further.

5.2 The Unique Nature of Assessment in the Arts

To begin this journey of knowledge, please read aloud the following monolog from Ben Johnson's (1606/2013) neo-Classical play, *Volpone*:

(ENTER MOSCA, Volpone's servant, alone, on a street)
MOS: I fear, I shall begin to grow in love

With my dear self, and my most prosperous parts,
They do so spring and burgeon; I can feel
A whimsy in my blood: I know not how,
Success hath made me wanton. I could skip
Out of my skin, now, like a subtle snake,
I am so limber. O! your parasite
Is a most precious thing, dropt from above,
Not bred 'mongst clods, and clodpoles, here on earth.
I muse, the mystery was not made a science,
It is so liberally profest! almost
All the wise world is little else, in nature,
But parasites, or sub-parasites. – And yet,
I mean those that have not your bare town-art,
To know who's fit to feed them; have no house,
No family, no care, and therefore mould
Tales for men's ears, to bait that sense; or get
Kitchen-invention, and some stale receipts
To please the belly, and the groin; nor those,
With their court dog-tricks, that can fawn and fleer,
Make their revenue out of legs and faces,
Echo my lord, and lick away a moth:
But your fine elegant rascal, that can rise,
And stoop, almost together, like an arrow;
Shoot through the air as nimbly as a star;
Turn short as doth a swallow; and be here,
And there, and here, and yonder, all at once;
Present to any humour, all occasion;
And change a visor, swifter than a thought!
This is the creature had the art born with him;
Toils not to learn it, but doth practise it
Out of most excellent nature: and such sparks
Are the true parasites, others but their zanis.

(From Act 3, Scene 3.1)

Recite it again putting dramatic emphasis on all pronouns and the words in bold, and slow the pronunciation of the italicised verbs.

MOS: **I** fear, **I** shall *begin* **to grow in love**
With **my** dear self, and **my** most prosperous parts,
They *do* so spring and burgeon; *I can feel*
A **whimsy** in my blood: I know not how,
Success hath *made* **me** wanton. I *could skip*
Out of **my** skin, now, like a subtle snake,
I *am* so limber. O! your parasite
Is a most precious thing, *dropt* from above,
Not *bred* 'mongst clods, and clodpoles, here on earth.
I muse, the mystery was not made a science,
It is so liberally profest! almost
All the wise world *is little else*, in nature,
But parasites, or sub-parasites.– And yet,
I mean those that have not your bare town-art,
To know *who's* fit to feed them; *have* no house,
No family, no care, and therefore *mould*

> *Tales* for men's ears, *to bait* that sense; or *get*
> Kitchen-invention, and some stale receipts
> To please the belly, and the groin; nor those,
> With their court dog-tricks, that *can fawn and flee*,
> *Make* their revenue out of legs and faces,
> *Echo* my lord, and *lick* away a moth:
> But your fine elegant rascal, that *can rise*,
> And *stoop*, almost together, like an arrow;
> *Shoot through* the air as nimbly as a star;
> *Turn short* as doth a swallow; and *be here*,
> And there, and here, and yonder, all at once;
> *Present* to any humour, all occasion;
> And *change* a visor, swifter than a thought!
> *This is* the creature had the art born with him;
> *Toils not* to learn it, but doth practise it
> Out of most excellent nature: and such sparks
> Are the true parasites, others but their zanis.

How would you assess your two presentations: by your acting ability, presentation ability, or dramatic emphasis? Or do you assess its success level by counting the number of speech or pronunciation errors, or just merely the fact that it was completed?

The above exercise raises at least one issue: what is the purpose of this type of performance assessment? Unlike typical academic subjects such as Mathematics, Language Arts, or Science, Visual and Performing Arts clearly have content and context components. More complex, however, are the presentation components. These presentation components consist of such aesthetic parameters that frequently transcend the content and context components. Presentational components also elicit emotional responses from both the presenter and audience members. This is not usually an assessment component in other subject areas. Assessment standards have prescribed objectives and outcomes. Emotional components do not fall easily within this realm.

Assessment can be based on historical presentations such as presentations that have moved past audiences. There are moral and value associations as to what constitutes "good or bad" or "acceptable and unacceptable" or "permissible and not permissible". Success consequently lies in the eyes, ears, and emotional hearts of the beholders. This is hardly fair. With this in mind, can you fairly and objectively assess your performance of the Mosca monolog? Can this assessment be measured? If so, within what parameters can we construct such an assessment? Let us begin to answer these questions with a general definition of educational measurement:

> Educational measurement is ... an inference-making enterprise in which we formally collect **overt**, test-based evidence from students to arrive at what we hope are accurate inferences about students' status with respect to **covert**, educationally important variables: reading ability, knowledge of history, ability to solve simultaneously equations, interest in. (Popham, 2003, p. 4, emphasis added)

5.2.1 Inference-Making Enterprise

What a bizarre concept, "to derive from reasoning; conclude or judge from premises or evidence … to guess; speculate; surmise … to draw a conclusion, as by reasoning" (Stein, 1971, p. 729). Clearly, assessment here is not absolute. In fact it is merely an assertion about what is perhaps acceptable or plausible or perhaps simply pleasant, in an acceptable manner to the adjudicator. So how do we assess a performance? The assessment literature would classify this under the banner of *Performance Assessment*. One working definition of performance assessment is "any form of assessment in which students carry out an activity or produce a product in order to demonstrate learning" (Airasian et al., 2007, p. 148). A general definition indeed! How about this one:

> Performance assessment is one in which the teacher observes and makes a judgment about the student's demonstration of a skill or competency in creating a product, constructing a response, or making a presentation … The emphasis is on the student's ability to perform tasks by producing their own work with their knowledge and skills. (McMillan, 2004, p. 198)

Similarly, Gronlund (1998) defines performance assessment as "requiring students to demonstrate their achievement of understanding and skills by actually performing a task or set of tasks (e.g., writing a story, giving a speech, conducting an experiment, operating a machine" (p. 3).

From these definitions, we conclude that performance assessment is very authentic, calls to constructivist methodological perspectives, and serves as an alternative to more traditional paper-and-pencil assessment activities. According to Palm (2008):

> the idea was to measure individuals' proficiency in certain task situations of interest. It was acknowledged that the correlation between facts and knowledge, on the one hand, and performance based on these facts and knowledge, on the other, were not always highly correlated. Judgment of the performance in the actual situation was therefore desirable. (from Brief History section, n.p.)

Airasian (1991) suggests that performance assessments help in diagnosing behaviours, learning styles, and specific talents (or lack of talents) of a student. In order to judge, grade, or assess any presentation, a criterion of reference or perhaps inference must be first established. To the best of my knowledge a norm-referenced standardised multiple choice test probably does not exist. Therefore, by beginning with the creation of a series of characteristics within the performance assessment phenomenon, a possible norm reference test could be contrived. Palm (2008) presents a possibility: "cognitive processes required by students, contextualised tasks, judgmental marking … cognitive complexity, communication, real world applications, instructionally meaningful tasks, significant commitments of student time and effort, and qualitative judgments in the marking process" (from Characteristics section, n.p.).

These characteristics go far beyond regurgitation or an execution of a mime-like exercise. Looking at them more closely in light of the Mosca monologue, the criteria of these characteristics could appear as:

1. Cognitive processes required by students: The student must be able to perceive the needs of Mosca and Mosca's position as a servant of Volpone and his purview that he is to act like Volpone to his class of people;
2. Contextualised tasks: The student must understand the historical constructs of class and gender chauvinisms of the time along with the political innuendos and parodies of Elizabethan times;
3. Judgmental marking: The student realises that his/her performance is being adjudicated on context influence as shown through body gestures, vocal interpretation, and dramatic, theatrical elucidation;
4. Cognitive complexity: The student must work through and demonstrate the interactions and inter-weavings of the verisimilitude of the Mosca character whilst simultaneously interpreting the literary content and context;
5. Communication: The student must succeed in conveying Mosca's beliefs and ideas that are believable to the audience;
6. Real world application: The student must understand that his/her presence and ability to successfully communicate will be one characteristic of how he/she will be judged in their future;
7. Instructionally meaningful tasks: The student must connect between his instructions and execution of tasks. They must be meaningful in terms of logic, performability and attainability;
8. Significant commitments of student time and effort: The student must believe that the allotment of his/her time/effort has been or will be justified towards the completion of the presentation; and
9. Qualitative judgments in the marking process: the student must understand and accept that the teacher's adjudication and assessment of his/her performance will contain qualitative bias in terms of tradition, expectation and teacher personal belief.

Having such criteria for assessment expands the scope of student learning. It also stretches the teacher's cognitive and assessment abilities. Airasian et al. (2007) state that performance assessment criteria should:

1. have a clear purpose that identifies the decision to be made from the performance assessment;
2. identify observable aspects of the student's performance or product that can be judged;
3. provide an appropriate setting for eliciting and judging the performance product; and
4. provide a judgment or score to describe performance. (p. 151)

Within these criteria, there may also be a proposed sequence of actions, physical gesture and vocal execution expectations, line interpretation, and presentation denouement. There might also be a co-operation with teacher factor. For example, did the student follow directorial instructions and/or expectations? This may also include the student's participatory involvement with other students. In other words, within an artistic/aesthetic context: did it work? Was it believable? And did the student fulfil the expectations of the presentation?

From a curricular point of view (Popham, 2003, p. 16) were the accustomed curricular outcomes of: (a) the acquisition of cognitive skills, (b) the acquisition of bodies of knowledge, and (c) their effect on values – spiritual, actual, and theoretical – realised? Have the performance standards, those that refer to the requisite proficiency that students are expected to exhibit when they have mastered a content standard, been successfully demonstrated?

Is performance assessment also authentic assessment? Gronlund (1998) defines authentic assessment as, "performance assessment that stresses the importance of focusing on the application of understandings and skills to real problems in 'real world' contextual settings" (p. 2). Tanner (2001) includes in a list of authentic assessment characteristics the following: criterion based standards, multiple indicators of quality, judgment reliability, assessment relevance and consequential validity, and student diversity influences (pp. 25–26).

Through performance assessment, as demonstrated in Mosca's third act opening monolog, the Arts opens an entirely different view towards assessment and student academic success from typical academic subject assessment protocols. The Arts teacher also considers the "quality" of parameter of the assignment presentation in terms of historical presentation beliefs, accepted performance behaviours, and believed or inferred artistic and aesthetic values (more than likely biased in some way). The Arts teacher considers these quality parameters very seriously via the following assessment questions:

- What do I want my students to learn from this evaluative experience?
- What do I want to learn about my students?
- How will I successfully link the goals of the lesson or project with the outcomes that will be demonstrated or executed by the students?
- Does this lesson have value in terms of content and applicability?
- Will the adjudication process be fair, equal or equitable with all students?
- Is participation only a goal?
- How much does talent (or lack of) affect the assessment process?

Answering all these questions can be daunting to say the least. Inevitably, many Arts teachers look for a rubric of some kind to assist towards successfully adjudicating a performance assessment activity.

Many teachers often create rubrics; yet, a performance assessment rubric can present troublesome considerations. First, should it be detailed and task specific, or holistic and consider all presentation characteristics more as a mélange than as item specific? Second, is it more important to build student confidence than student competence? Third, are the short term needs of technique busy, but necessary exercises, less or more critical than an eventual end product. Fourth, how do we measure long-term growth and process as opposed to product? Fifth, is the end product more important than the process?

These five issues are critical to understanding performance assessment. There are no patented answers. More than likely – and I know this from a life time of performing, directing and teaching – every class and every student within an Art discipline class changes in growth, attitude, and psychological perspective moment by moment. This in itself is both a joy and a hardship. I have heard many Arts' teachers argue and debate these questions in terms of academic versus artistic worth.

There are some who believe that assessment can only serve as an end product when the arts activity is presented or created because it is only at this time when all the aspects of its production and/or fabrication come together and be finalised. In this position, some teachers believe that there are those participants who only come alive when the presentation is on – and not in the practice room, or rehearsal period, or in the sketchbook. There are others who take the opposite view that it is the process of continual success and failure in the production and fabrication stages of an Arts or Performance-based activity is where the only learning occurs. They also argue that students can spend hours and/or days preparing and fabricating a project or work and that its culminating presentation is merely as icing on a cake. What is real or authentic, and what is not? Yes, it is truly an assessment dilemma.

It would be so much easier, some would say, to assess things or activities that are written as opposed to attempting to assess things that are not written. Perhaps the words, *performance* and *authentic,* are not the most useful words to use in assessment practice. Eliot's (1994) definitions may be useful. He defines these as "*performance emphasises a student's active generation of a response* and highlights the fact that the response is observable either directly or indirectly via a permanent product ... the term *authentic* refers to the nature of the *task* and *context* in which the assessment occurs" (p. 3). He argues that these terms are useful because most teachers deem the more life like tasks as more appealing than they would be to students. Secondly, more authentic or realistic tasks cross over to many skill sets in many disciples and hence are more useful in the long-term of student learning and real-life knowledge applications.

On the other side of things, the term *performance* is also used to discuss success or failure in terms of outcomes, as in *the performance of this grade* or *the overall performance of the province's Grade 2 students* which illustrates that teachers tend to use such terms in respect of an individual or activity setting. There are variations as well. There are low and high level performance objectives within activities. Some are product-oriented and some are more process-oriented. If one were to create a scale of sorts, a guideline might be that low level performance activities might be such activities that students simply have to pick and choose objects for identification. The high end performance activities require students to construct specific item(s) with these objects.

Performance assessments require a variety of activities to be useful and successful. However it does require some specific areas of dedication on the part of teachers. It requires this dedication because students must *construct* rather than *select* solutions to questions or queries. Teachers must not only observe these constructions, they must also:

- evaluate students' work in a manner that is fair to all students realising talent and time restrictions;
- create scoring and evaluation schemes that reflect curricular goals;
- be in harmony with provincially stated learning objectives and outcomes;
- craft rubrics that are logical and scalable to be successfully measurable; and
- be able to explain in a peaceful manner to those irate parents who may believe that their child is being undervalued compared to other students.

Whether or not teachers approve or disapprove of rubrics and their employment, the fact is they exist. We continually use and revise them in our assessment practices. We will proceed to examine the issues of rubrics in both visual and performing arts programs of study and, following that, performance assessment issues in non-visual and performing arts areas. Many rubrics and rubric schematics are available: simply go online and search 'rubrics' for any subject area and dozens of sites will pop up. Many of these are from provincial and state departments of education.

The critical element here is to be aware of conflicting issues of use with any assessment protocol. Mehrens, Popham, and Ryan (1998) offer the following six guidelines for what they call "proper preparation of students for performance assessments" (p. 19):

1. Determine whether the interpretation to be drawn from the student's performance is related only to the specific task or whether an inference is to be made to a broader domain of performance tasks.
2. When the inference is to the broader domain, one should not instruct in any fashion that would minimise the accuracy of the inference to the broader domain.
3. Make sure that the student is not surprised, and hence confused, by the performance assessment's format.
4. Identify evaluative criteria in advance of instructional planning, and communicate these to students.
5. Stress transferability of the skills and knowledge assessed by performance tests.
6. Foster students' self-evaluation skills.

These guidelines suggest a number of items to keep in mind. Most important is whether or not the individual tasks required for success in the activity are more important than the holistic end product of the activity's resolution. In other words, are the individual tasks more valid from a qualitative perspective than the end-product – the presentation itself? Many individual tasks are involved within a presentation. In the Mosca dialog these are:

- vocal mechanics such as diction clarity, timing, inner line rhythm;
- memorisation;
- physical mechanics such as bodily gestures, facial gestures;
- body spacing;
- from the theatrical side there is the use of space, dramatic denouement (the final resolution: in a presentational sense how the voice ends a line);
- dramatic interpretation of text in light of the characterisation of the character with the actuality and persona of the actor; and
- the connection the actor makes with the audience.

These are only a few of the individual characteristics. Together, and not necessarily equally, when executed, they form a unified presentation – an end-product – performance. And, all Arts assessors must answer one question: did it work?

What kind of a question is that, "did it work?" I respond with, "Did it work successfully as a dramatic presentation?" It is a holistic response assessment. From a rubric perspective, I could use a real or fabricated checklist of the above stated items. But I might judge certain *moments* of those executable tasks more valid than others.

Notice I used the concept of time here. I may see certain *moments* as more complete than from the combination of individual tasks or within, compared, or opposed to other moments presented in the assignment. From a theatrical perspective, I know that in this monologue there are several key places where the actor, as Mosca, must engage the audience. The actor must lure the audience into his/her belief that parasites are the smartest folk on the planet and that by the end of the monolog, Mosca must have successfully ensnared the audience members into believing that they are all fools or clowns. How do I as an adjudicator and as an observer make this assessment? Does my view on the presentation characteristics have preference over those of the students?

One could argue that there is no accountability within my bias. Do I require a checklist of quantitative minutia to qualify my score using such criteria as: the amount of words dropped or mispronounced; the number of perceived appropriate or inappropriate gestures; the number of times the student has made eye contact with audience members? These would indeed make scoring an easier task. However, I would argue in the overall façade of the presentation, these details would only be considered small factors. In my view, the critical score would be based on the success of the student's ability to convince me that he or she actually believes that he or she is Mosca. Now I ask, can you put that on a rubric?

So we create an incontestable, generic rubric that may look something like Fig. 5.1 designed by Dr Joe Norris (formerly of StFX, presently of Brock University).

Or like Fig. 5.2 downloaded from the Internet at http://stouffer.pbwiki.com/Drama-rubric.

You will note that in both of these rubrics (see Figs. 5.1 and 5.2) the criteria are laid out in a holistic categorised manner. They lack scoring scales; herein lies the challenge of the Performance Arts assessment.

How detailed should that scoring scale be? It could be a numerical rating scale with lowest to highest. It also could be a graphic scale such as Fig. 5.3.

Similarly, it could be a descriptive scale with definitions for each of these items. Or it could be a combination of any of the above. Value laden descriptors can also be terms such as *excellent, good, fair,* and *poor*.

Review Musical Theatre (Saskatchewan Education) rubric's anecdotal criteria scale (see Table 5.1).

> Performance Rubric (Individual or Group)*
>
> Concentration/Precision/Focus
> Smoothness of presentation (timing)
> Tight picturisation (maintain character and setting)
> Belief/Sincerity
> Memorisation (Degree)
>
> Voice
> Audibility
> Clarity/articulation
> Expressiveness
> Unison, antiphonal, cumulative, solo considerations
>
> Body
> Appropriate gestures
> Variety
> Clear body movements (no wandering)
> Blocking (Relationship with others)
>
> Interpretation
> Variety
> Vocal selections
> Picturisations
> Unity of Form and Content
> Picturisation
> Creation of mood and atmosphere
> Appropriate for audience
> Creativity/Uniqueness
>
> Overall Effectiveness
> Ability to hold an audience
> Extras (props, costumes, sound effects, lighting, set etc.)
>
> *used by permission

Fig. 5.1 Performance rubric

Notice the flexibility in magnitude of interpretation in the following scale:

$$\text{never} \rightarrow \text{rarely} \rightarrow \text{usually} \rightarrow \text{always}$$

Drama Rubric

Attitude 20
Positive
Encouraging
Respectful

Presentation 20
Voice
Good use of props
Establish strong character

Participation 20
Prepared
Organised
On time

Effort 20
110%
Participate in all activities

Creativity 20
Understand your role
Colourful
Audience understands your role

Fig. 5.2 Drama rubric

Fig. 5.3 Graphic scale

| always | usually | seldom | never |

5 Arts-Inspired Performance Assessment Considerations for Educational Leaders

Table 5.1 Rubric for musical theatre (Saskatchewan education)

Grade 4–8	D	C	B	A	
Grade 1–3	Beginning	Satisfactory	Proficient	Excellent	Mark
Stage presence	Never aware of audience and others on stage	Rarely aware of audience and others on stage	Sometimes aware of audience and others on stage	Always aware of audience and others on stage	1.
	Inappropriate or negative body language	At times, good use of body language	Good use of body language	Outstanding use of body language	
Choreography	No knowledge of choreography	Demonstrates some knowledge of choreography	Demonstrates good knowledge of choreography	Demonstrates excellent knowledge of choreography	2.
	Style of dance is not reflective of character	Style of dance is rarely reflective of character	Style of dance is occasionally reflective of character	Style of dance is always reflective of character	
	Unenthusiastic participation	Rarely portrays enthusiasm in movement	Occasionally portrays enthusiasm in movement	Always portrays enthusiasm in movement	
Vocals	Never sings/speaks clearly with good enunciation and varied dynamics	Rarely sings/speaks clearly with good enunciation and varied dynamics	Usually sings/speaks clearly with good enunciation and varied dynamics	Always sings/speaks clearly with good enunciation and varied dynamics	3.
	Never blends	When reminded, will blend	Usually knows how and when to blend	Always knows how and when to blend	
Direction	Unwilling to accept direction, does not follow direction, and responds with negative attitude	Rarely willing to accept direction, unclear of direction, and responds with poor attitude	Usually willing to accept direction, understands most directions and complies with a positive attitude	Always willing to accept direction, understands that direction is required and complies with a positive attitude	4.

How many times, and to what does, *rarely* and *usually* refer? Similarly, such ranges as: "willing to accept" versus "usually willing to accept" require very personal and challenging interpretations by the teacher and may be equally challenging for students to completely understand and believe. A subsequent issue, going back to Mehrens et al. (1998) six item list is the acknowledged goals and indicators of identifiable instruction, skills, and knowledge level expectations for success. In other words, how much of "*a whatever*" is a **never → rarely → usually → always**? In my view the issue of scale, whether point specific, holistic or floating, is the critical bias issue of these rubrics.

The following is another rubric that is in the more integrated realm, and perhaps more applicable in some eyes.[1]

5.2.1.1 Minnesota State University, Mankato

Category 6: Humanities and the Arts
Goal:

Produce students who understand and appreciate the connection between the Arts and Humanities and society.

Objectives/Outcomes:

Following the Completion of Category 6 of the General Education Programme, students can:
Create and/or critique artistic performances
Demonstrate awareness of the scope and variety of works in the Arts and Humanities
Describe the relationship between the Arts and Humanities and society

Population:

O/O 1-3:
Sample sections of Category 6 general education courses

Who does the Assessment?

O/O 1-3:

Category 6 Course Instructor's Assessment Group
Assessment Rubric for O/O #1: Create and/or Critique artistic performances:

1. Student observed a work of art or a work in the Humanities
2. Student can create a work of art or work in the Humanities, or can critique a work of art or a work in the Humanities
3. Student can create a work in the Arts and/or Humanities, and critique a work of art and/or evaluate a work in the Humanities
4. Student can create a work in the arts and/or Humanities, and can develop and use acceptable criteria to critique a work of art and/or evaluate a work in the Humanities

Level of Mastery

For year 1, baseline data will be gathered

---

[1] At the time of writing, the following rubrics were found on the Internet in a simple search using "arts rubrics" as a starting search phrase.

5.2.2 Minnesota State University, Mankato

Assessment Rubric for O/O #2: Knowledge of scope and variety
GE Category 6 Rubric –

1. Student can list works in the Arts or Humanities from different eras, or list works that deal with different issues from the same era.
2. Student can describe works in the Arts or Humanities from different eras, and discuss works that deal with different issues from the same era.
3. Student can compare and contrast works in the Arts or Humanities from different eras, and compare and contrast works that deal with different issues from the same era. Student comparison shows a depth of knowledge concerning the works compared.
4. Student can compare and contrast works in the Arts and Humanities from different eras, and compare and contrast works that deal with different issues from the same era. Student comparison shows a depth of knowledge concerning the works compared.

Level of Mastery

For year 1, baseline data will be gathered

Assessment Rubric for O/O #3: Relationship

1. Student can identify a relationship or a connection between a work in the Arts and/or Humanities and society.
2. Student can explain a relationship connection between a work in the Arts and/or Humanities and society.
3. Student can explain how works in the Arts and Humanities help to define, create, recreate, change or sustain a society, or how that society creates conditions or constraints for the creation of works in the Arts and Humanities.
4. Student can explain how works in the Arts and Humanities help to define, create, recreate, change or sustain a society, and how that society creates conditions or constraints for the creation of works in the Arts and Humanities.

The criterion is generalised but again there is no true scale. Notice the words that are used in the objectives sections: *create, demonstrate, describe* as opposed to *will* or *will demonstrate*, and in the assessment rubric, *can explain*. These are more of a conditional construction rather than a demonstration action. Table 5.2 is another rubric for which the scale is highly descriptive in detail.

Here is one that I use (see Fig. 5.4) quite a bit for group projects, adjusting as necessary.

Many authors and scholars have spent much time developing rubrics and their applications including Airasian, Engemann, and Gallagher (2007), McMillan (2004), Popham (2008), Moskal (2003), and Tierney and Simon (2004). The important issues in rubric formation are to remember that criteria must be clearly stated, focused on tasks, consistent in execution, and clear on expectations. Also, the scoring

Table 5.2 Descriptive analytical grid rubric

LES in drama – secondary (cycle one) www.learnquebec.ca/.../analytical_grid_all_arts_evaluation.doc

Coherent relationship between the stimulus for creation, the development process of ideas, and the result of his/her creative efforts	Varied use of the elements of the language of drama	Coherent organisation of dramaturgical components	Original use of elements of the language of drama	Effective use of elements of the language and technique of drama	Integration of periods of reflection and review into the creative experience
❺ Excellent	❺ Excellent	❺ Excellent	❺ Excellent	❺ Excellent	❺ Excellent
The production, which is based on an indepth search for new ideas, is entirely consistent with the stimulus for creation	The production uses a variety of elements of the language of drama, resulting in a clear understanding of the story	The production uses the characters' intentions to create a sense of dramatic progression	The production demonstrates frequent original treatment of characters, dramatic structure, set design and stage directions	The production uses a number of elements of performance, playwriting and theatricality that enhance the initial creative idea in a precise and well adapted way	A number of ideas are recorded throughout the process and the student presents a clear description of what he or she learned and the methods he or she used, using the appropriate drama vocabulary
❹ Very good	❹ Very good	❹ Very good	❹ Very good	❹ Very good	❹ Very good
The production makes good use of the elements of the stimulus for creation	The production uses several elements of the language of drama that facilitate understanding of the story	The time, space and location components of the production are all appropriate to the dramatic action	The production offers distinctively drawn characters, a coherent dramatic structure and some original touches in its set design	The production makes appropriate use of certain elements of performance, playwriting and theatricality that accurately reflect the initial creative idea	Several ideas are included in the recording tool and some of them clearly contributed to the creative development of the production

5 Arts-Inspired Performance Assessment Considerations for Educational Leaders

❸ Satisfactory	❸ Satisfactory	❸ Satisfactory	❸ Satisfactory	❸ Satisfactory	❸ Satisfactory
The production takes into account the elements of the stimulus for creation	The production uses those elements of the language of drama that are essential for understanding the story	The production demonstrates attention to the coherent development of characters and situations	The production includes a few elements of the language of drama that demonstrate a degree of originality	The production conveys the initial creative idea through an acceptable use of elements of the language and technique of drama	Elements of the creative experience were incorporated into the production
❷ Poor	❷ Poor	❷ Poor	❷ Poor	❷ Poor	❷ Poor
The production is the result of a simplification of the stimulus for creation	The production uses a few elements of the language of drama, but in an incomplete, repetitive or awkward manner	The production presents some inconsistencies in the characters' actions or in the storyline	The production borrows one or more elements from dramatic works	Most of the elements of performance, playwriting and theatricality used in the production are adequately effective	Very few ideas from the periods of reflection and review can be recognised, either in the production or in the recording tool
❶ Unsatisfactory	❶ Unsatisfactory	❶ Unsatisfactory	❶ Unsatisfactory	❶ Unsatisfactory	❶ Unsatisfactory
The production is not at all consistent with the stimulus for creation	The production uses only one or two elements of the language of drama, which contribute little to the understanding of the story	The production presents characters and actions that are plainly inconsistent	The production consists almost exclusively of borrowings from other dramatic works	The production shows awkward or inadequate use of the elements of the language and technique of drama	The recording tools contain no ideas that can be used in a period of reflection and review

Group Project Performance /Presentation Rubric

Group members: _____ Date: _____

_____

_____ Topic/Title: _____

	Criteria				Points
Scale →	10–9	8–7	6–4	3–0	
Topic/scene	Student(s) provide **much** thematic depth and understanding of content matter or practice	Student(s) provide **some insight** and understanding in content matter or practice.	Student(s) **require prompts** to further information on the content matter or practice	Presentation **lacked** depth, little understanding of content matter or practice.	___
Course Themes Reached	**Numerous** detailed connections are reached and evidence was presented.	**Several** detailed connections reached from the evidence offered.	**Some** detailed connections are provided from the evidence offered.	**A connection** was made from the evidence offered.	___
Presentation	Well organized, demonstrates **much** logical use of performance requirements, was well sequenced, and the audience was engaged.	Well organized, but demonstrates only **some** flow of sequencing or structure.	**A sensible** presentation, but demonstrates little to no engagement of audience.	**Weakly** organized, no involvement at any level.	___
Sense of Ensemble	**Well connected** to topic and themes	There is **some** evidence of connection to topic and themes	There were **limited** evidence of connection to topic and themes	There was **no** evidence of connection to topic and themes.	___
				Total --->	/40

Comments:

Fig. 5.4 Group project performance rubric

on such rubrics – whether using a holistic score or analytic scale – must be clear in its scoring criteria and definitions. This can actually be fun. Gaze upon any provincial curricula expectations for learners and you will see such words and or phrases as "demonstrate" or "students will", "the student will be able to do", and so on.

The challenge here is develop value scales that correspond to such area level words as *excellent, good, poor* or equivalent numerical notations. Airasian et al. (2007) give detail on the exact working of such scoring rubrics. Clarity is the issue. Clarity will also assist in the accountability facet of assessment. In other words, a well-constructed rubric attempts to minimise a teacher's personal bias towards both the student and/or the art form whether based on students' talent versus non talent abilities; students' individual demonstrated positive or negative behaviours; or teacher, cultural, or art form beliefs.

The uniqueness of specific art forms whether visual, performing, or in combination of media often conflict with each other in form, texture, and performance values. Hence individual likes and dislikes are part of the human condition. There can be conflicts in terms of values and ethics between students, teachers, and perhaps even parents of what is acceptable or not acceptable Art forms to be employed as teaching/learning activities in the classroom. Of course much of this depends on age, knowledge, grade level, and student(s) maturity. Nevertheless, some activities will be deemed appropriate or inappropriate regardless of the levels of formality, informality, openness, flexibility of thought, and courage of the classroom teacher.

There are many who believe some forms of contemporary art and music have no form or artistic merit; hence, they will not be used in classes except perhaps to discredit them. Similarly there are icons, chants, beliefs, and visual and performing rituals that may have political, religious, social, or spiritual belief underpinnings that are counter to a teacher's or community's set of mores. And, even though one may feel open to change, and use such items or assignments, prudence may come before radicalism.

As a music major in my earlier days, I recall vividly one professor who had a vision of modern classical music; he believed there was no music before Stravinsky – only organised noise. This was in complete opposition to another professor who staunchly believed that modern music was a curse, and if there was no melody, then it was only noise. This became quite problematic in the assessment of a music major's performance – who was faced with the plight of putting together a recital knowing full well that the adjudication committee was in conflict over the definition of the art form itself.

This is not unique in education and it is a way of life in the Arts. I began this section exploring the uniqueness of the Arts in education and, in part, the way we look at performance assessment in the Arts. Yet there is one daunting assessment question which many fear to ask and answer. Where does the participation fall into assessment? Is it simply enough to get a student to perform or present, knowing full well they may have little or no ability in the art form? Is, however, the courage to participate and put themselves perhaps, in emotional jeopardy worth giving them some sort of grade? In effect, does this create assessment criteria that have virtually nothing to do with the actual growth – either artistically or academically – of the student? It is certainly a dilemma. Is it encouragement, compassion, or support? Ultimately, performance assessment faces a true test of fairness and equity, but not necessarily equality between students. This is also unique to the Arts.

5.2.3 *Instructional Leadership in the Arts*

Instructional leadership in the Arts is a highly controversial subject area. Is a person with a proven performance talent in an area equated to being an instructional leader in that area? This is also not exceptional to the Arts; however, it is many times very prevalent. The literature on administration preparation for assessment is not vast and for performance assessment or the Arts in general is scattered. However, McMillan (2000) did review some research and offers a number of insights regarding some general assessment principles that are easily understandable within an Arts performance influenced protocol. He details the following:

- Assessment is inherently a process of professional judgment
- Assessment is based on separate but related principles of measurement evidence and evaluation
- Assessment decision-making is influenced by a series of tensions
- Assessment influences student motivation and learning
- Learning vs. auditing
- Formative (informal and on-going) vs. summative (formal and at the end)
- Criterion-referenced vs. absolute standards
- Traditional vs. alternative
- Authentic vs. contrived
- Speeded tests vs. power tests
- Standardised tests vs. classroom tests
- Assessment contains error
- Good assessment enhances instruction
- Good assessment is valid
- Good assessment is fair and ethical
- Good assessments use multiple methods
- Good assessment is efficient and feasible
- Good assessment appropriately incorporates technology (subheadings)

None of these points are unique. However, in the performance context, they cannot be generalised. This may lead to issues of validity and consistency. I say "may" because within the individual teacher's belief system, it may only be consistent within a personal psychological logic. However, they may be brought into question if these do not seem logical within a given school or department's evaluation protocols.

So, obtaining administrative support is paramount for performance based assessment to be successful (Gigante & Firestone, 2007). In referring to teacher leaders, Gigante and Firestone acknowledged that those personnel were working with administrators who recognised the power of distributive leadership in both permitting their subordinates to be creative and in taking on responsibility. So from this we can infer that the high degree of trust on the part of an administrator was vital in affecting positive and successful outcomes of performance assessment. This, of course, also infers that administrators will probably encourage alternative assessment protocols in their schools. Along with the benefit of helping in the evolution of teacher leaders, administrators directly and indirectly encourage these teacher leaders to further their professional development and to create strong collegial relationships within a school environment (p. 318).

If we accept the possibility that administrators can encourage their teaching staffs to expand and include performance assessment practices within their teaching pedagogies, we can assume that several organisational engagements would occur.

Highlighting such a change would mean that the distributive leadership construction of truly permitting teachers to take the lead role in assessment within their classrooms would be the first step. Copland (2003), in analysing Elmore's leadership domains' theory, outlines several "domains" of distributive leadership that we can adapt to our discussion (p. 377). Distributed leadership, in our interpretation of its employment of performance assessment, would:

- expand the teacher's roles and responsibilities and alter (hopefully positively) the power/control limitations in classroom assessment;
- bring together teachers in their individual and collective professional development efforts;
- expand teachers' individual and collective expertise in both content matter and assessment practices.

There is no doubt that the school's administration team – especially the principal – would play a key role in leading both the supervision of instruction and personnel. It would behoove any administrator to be knowledgeable on all assessment issues.

Realistically, it is a challenge for the principal to capture and know all that there is to know regarding assessment protocols. As Stiggins (2001) states, "the principal's role is to advocate on behalf of balanced development and use of assessment" (p. 15). This is based on what Stiggins sees as a state (or province's) "obsessive belief that the path to school improvement is paved with better and more frequent standardized tests" (p. 14). Stiggins lists several other "barriers" that may impede effective assessment and argues that it is the principal's responsibility to break down these barriers. For this author, some barriers to assessment are:

- the educator's fear of being accountable (p. 15);
- parents who define sound assessment practices in terms of their own experiences during their youth (p. 15);
- the collective lack of clarity about achievement targets high school graduates should be expected to hit (p. 16); and
- the tradition of naïve assumptions about the relationship between assessment and student motivation (p. 16).

It is the responsibility of the principal to provide leadership and role-modelling to all school constituencies in the explanation, instruction, and execution of all assessment strategies and to further evolve the collective learning and teaching capacities of all.

These actions would dutifully and expeditiously forge a more complete professional learning community within the school. This would then create a school culture and climate that builds trust and a sense of solidarity between administration and faculty, thus furthering their school mission. This, hopefully, will resolve curricular issues that challenge the success of the school, especially in light of today's encroaching external accountability bodies, school improvement plans, school accreditation plans, and evolving use (rightly or wrongly) of high stakes testing for stated provincial outcomes. Not only would teacher behaviours change, but student academic and discipline behaviours would also change for the better.

In their study, Firestone and Mayrowetz (1998) theorised that, "under some circumstances, performance-based assessments can change specific behaviours and procedures in the classroom more easily than general paradigms for teaching a subject" (p. 111). In our Canadian classroom context, such changes can assist students of all academic ability levels, especially in those classrooms where differentiated learning is abundant. Their second theory revolves around the notion that high-stakes assessments (in their view, American federal and local state authorities) are forces that by their nature and funding power promote (rightly or wrongly) both pedagogical assessment policies and procedures.

Do teachers teach to an annual exam or foster optimum learning situations in their classrooms? The following is an example of such a teaching moment that could challenge assessment use. In a high stakes test there would exist questions of pure content. A performance assessment would have another maxim. Here's an excerpt from former Canadian Prime Minister Pierre Elliot Trudeau's national broadcast on October 16, 1970 when he announced the Canadian War Measures Act:

> I am speaking to you at a moment of grave crisis, when violent and fanatical men are attempting to destroy the unity and the freedom of Canada. One aspect of that crisis is the threat which has been made on the lives of two innocent men. These are matters of the utmost gravity and I want to tell you what the Government is doing to deal with them.
>
> What has taken place in Montreal in the past two weeks is not unprecedented. It has happened elsewhere in the world on several recent occasions; it could happen elsewhere within Canada. But Canadians have always assumed that it could not happen here and as a result we are doubly shocked that it has.
>
> Our assumption may have been naive, but it was understandable; understandable because democracy flourishes in Canada; understandable because individual liberty is cherished in Canada.
>
> Notwithstanding these conditions - partly because of them - it has now been demonstrated to us by a few misguided persons just how fragile a democratic society can be, if democracy is not prepared to defend itself, and just how vulnerable to blackmail are tolerant, compassionate people.
>
> Because the kidnappings and the blackmail are most familiar to you, I shall deal with them first.
>
> The governments of Canada and Quebec have been told by groups of self-styled revolutionaries that they intend to murder in cold blood two innocent men unless their demands are met. The kidnappers claim they act as they do in order to draw attention to instances of social injustice. But I ask them whose attention are they seeking to attract? The Government of Canada? The Government of Quebec? Every government in this country is well aware of the existence of deep and important social problems. And every government to the limit of its resources and ability is deeply committed to their solution. But not by kidnappings and bombings; by hard work. And if any doubt exists about the good faith or the ability of any government, there are opposition parties ready and willing to be given an opportunity to govern. In short, there is available everywhere in Canada an effective mechanism to change governments by peaceful means. It has been employed by disenchanted voters again and again. (CBC Archives retrieved from: www.cbc.ca/archives)

This speech shook the foundations of Canada almost 40 years ago. Using this excerpt as a platform, a performance-based activity can be designed to accentuate how this moment in history changed the course of Canadian nationalism, the quest for Quebec nationalism and served as one of the defining moments in the maturity of Canada as a nation.

From this excerpt alone, lessons can be constructed that concern themselves with the literary language that was employed, the political posturing and decision making courage Trudeau demonstrated, and the panic and uncertainty of the people of the time. A group creation dramatic project could be created at any academic level employing several academic areas. Students could explore the financial and economic considerations, create mathematical and statistical models to gage public opinion, create strategy sessions from a number of views: the Federal government, the FLQ (Front de libération du QuébecFLQ; English: Quebec Liberation Front); local and provincial police departments, and so on. This creation and learning experience alone would clearly engage students, bring history to life and give those moments credibility in those students' lives.

Let us recall Moon and Callahan's (2001) words mentioned previously, "Performance assessments are built on the belief that curriculum, instruction, and assessments are intricately intertwined. By focusing on what students need to know, understand, and be able to do, teachers are more aware of what to teach" (p. 52). In these exercises, instructors are relentlessly, unfailingly and simultaneously interweaving content, pedagogy and assessment protocols in their teaching. Likewise, the following exercise further tasks an instructor. It is quite different than a typical pencil/paper standard multiple choice test on the subject matter; and yes, it does take up much time. But clearly students would be engaged.

5.2.4 The October Crisis Exercise

5.2.4.1 Context

Inspired by Prime Minister Pierre Elliot Trudeau's speech of Oct 17, 1970, you are to create a scenario (of 8–10 min) which depicts one of the involved faction's strategy sessions. It can occur before or after the actual kidnapping event. After researching the event and gathering information about your involved faction, your group must do the following:

1. Develop characters and personality roles of the involved individuals. At least two of your characters must be actual involved persons;
2. You must create a scenario that is based on at least 10 actual facts;
3. Your scenario must have a casual theme that is resolved by the end of the scenario.

Your story line can only have two scenes maximum

5.2.4.2 Evaluation Criteria

Written submitted work
  Your project will be evaluated according to the following criteria:
  Script (30 marks):

- Historical accuracy;
- The accuracy of the faction's point of view;
- The degree of persuasiveness of your characters; and
- The plotline's logic, script's dialog, accuracy of character's personalities within the context of the scenario.

  Four page background document (30 marks)

- Your group will submit a fully referenced document that explains the historical background and rationale for your scenario. It will list all your bibliographic sources in APA 6th edition format.

  The Group Project Performance/Presentation Rubric will be used for assessment (see Fig. 5.5).

5.3 Policy and Research

We now return to the four paradigms that were mentioned earlier from the Alberta Student Assessment study (Webber et al., 2008):

1. the assessment of knowledge;
2. the view that schools should prepare students for their place in society and to manifest "good citizenship";
3. that schools should "prepare students for the world of work"; and
4. schools should further strive in "developing the natural talents of students".

Intellectually, experientially, and theoretically school leaders – whether administrators or classroom teachers – must further their understanding and experiences in teaching and learning specifically with our topic of Arts-based performance assessment. The policy construct here is to expand the use of the Arts, aesthetics, and other such philosophical and theoretical underpinnings of our social and educational-political structures in our curriculum to further solidify the intellectual needs and demands of our complex society.

We need to research and experiment with teaching and learning models of pedagogy in both the linear standards mode and in the more constructivist experiential mode. As Madeja (1977) has written, "Evaluation has two major purposes … One is to determine the effectiveness of the instructional programme and all its components; the other is to assess students' progress and to diagnose their problems" (p. 70). These basic tenets call for us administrators and educators to explore such aesthetic cultural components that excite our individual and communal senses of

Group Project Performance / Presentation Rubric (50 marks)

Group members:

Student: Character:

Date:

Topic/Title: October Crisis

	Criteria				Points
Scale →	10–9	8–7	6–4	3–0	
Topic/scene	Script shows **much** clarity and logic in construction; characters showed much accuracy in construction and presentation	Script shows **some** clarity and logic in construction; characters showed much accuracy in construction and presentation	Script shows **little** clarity and logic in construction; characters showed much accuracy in construction and presentation	Script shows **very little** clarity and logic in construction; characters showed much accuracy in construction and presentation	____
Course Themes Reached	**Numerous** detailed connections are reached and evidence was presented.	**Several** detailed connections reached from the evidence offered.	**Some** detailed connections are provided from the evidence offered.	**A connection** was made from the evidence offered.	____
Presentation	Well organized, demonstrates **much** logical use of performance requirements, was well sequenced, and the audience was engaged.	Well organized, but demonstrates only **some** flow of sequencing or structure.	**A sensible** presentation, but demonstrates little to no engagement of audience.	**Weakly** organized, no involvement at any level.	____
Sense of ensemble	Presentation was well connected scenario's themes	Presentation was **somewhat** connected scenario's themes	Presentation was **little** connected scenario's themes	Presentation was **very little** connected scenario's themes	____
				Total---->	/50

Comments:

Fig. 5.5 Group project performance/presentation rubric

perception, exploration, observation, theorisation, and experimentation in our pedagogies and assessment schemes.

In regard to the paradigms, we can discern Paradigm 1, in that, the assessment of knowledge is ongoing. In our pedagogies and assessment protocols we must continue to expand all forms of knowledge: content, experiential, and applied. We must forge assessment systems and mechanisms than bring content and theory on the applied reality of daily life. Paradigm 2 requires pedagogies and assessment schemes that foster dialog, debate, and discussion amongst our students and constituent school community members in order to create citizens who embrace the democratic ideals upon which our nation is founded. Paradigm 3 implies that our pedagogies must fulfil content knowledge and application modalities for our students to survive and prosper in today's highly complex society.

In my opinion, Paradigm 4 – schooling should further strive in developing the natural talent of students – is the most challenging. We must continue to create pedagogies and assessment systems that unleash our students' learning, emotive, and applied life skill talents in order for them to evolve as thinkers, listeners, and potential contributing members to our work force. Talents can be latent as well as obvious. Using assessments to further open the minds of our students is one of many paths that can help them become happy, successful, contributing members of society.

5.4 Advocacy Is Leadership in the Arts

At the beginning of this chapter, along with instructional leadership in the Arts, the following entrenched issues of Arts assessment were presented: leadership preparation implications, professional development implications for educators, implications for student-parent-community communication, and governance policy implications for Arts programmes' administration. There is an additional embedded issue that I label as cultural and political socialisation. From a more international perspective let us assume that all nations (in their own individual manner and all levels of governance from local to national) employ the Arts to further their cultural, moral and social mores, and national identity. Whether it is a national anthem, historical vignette, or pieces of visual art such as paintings or statues, the Arts are tools of nationalism to some degree. Similarly, the manner in which Arts education is deployed is as varied as one can imagine even within an individual country to further such nationalism. In North America Arts education may be mandated by state or provincial legislatures but not necessarily with a common curriculum. In many cases Arts are considered only as an *extra-curricular activity* and are not funded within a particular school. In Great Britain many Arts programs do not exist at all in public education but do exist outside of the public sector in independent schools or academies. In Australia, Arts education is nationally looked upon as a required content component. In other countries a more folkloric national perspective is taken employing Arts as a cultural integration tool within the general curriculum – in other words to promote a national political agenda.

More generally, in many elementary programs, Visual and Performing Arts are employed as curricular tools for specific non-Arts content areas. At the secondary level, an even greater complication is the ageless conflict of whether or not Arts education is intended to create and prepare future visual and performing artists, or simply only to be employed to bring an Arts awareness and appreciation of the Arts to students. Educational leaders and educational policy makers must now take a more pragmatic view of Visual and Performing Arts education and further expand their understanding and utilisation of the realities of the escalating world of employment opportunities in social, entertainment, and electronic media. This could lead to the expansion of the creative abilities of all students and also provide future employment possibilities for students in the varied communications fields. The assessment of Visual and Performing Arts curricula must reflect these growths and realities. Both preservice teaching programmes and inservice professional development programs must be expanded to accommodate these present and future demands.

As in all times, there are phenomena that change our course of action. Currently this phenomena is technology ranging from robotics, MP3 players, smart boards, tablets and smartphones to media communication devices that shrink our universe exponentially by the moment. We must harness such technologies with the same spirit as Galileo in investigating physics, or Michelangelo in discovering paint chemistries, or Bill Gates in discovering computer programs. I truly believe that Arts, aesthetics, and their exploration are part of our pathway to understanding our presence in the universe. We should be open and courageous in welcoming them into our teaching pedagogies.

References

Airasian, P. (1991). *Classroom assessment* (3rd ed.). New York, NY: McGraw-Hill.

Airasian, P., Engemann, J., & Gallagher, T. (2007). *Classroom assessment: Concepts and applications* (Canadian ed.). Toronto, ON, Canada: McGraw Hill.

Copland, M. (2003). Leadership of inquiry: Building and sustaining capacity for school improvement. *Educational Evaluation and Policy Analysis, 25*(4), 375–395.

Elliot, S. N. (1994). *Creating meaningful performance assessments: Fundamental concepts product #P5059*. Reston, VA: The Council for Exceptional Children.

Firestone, W., & Mayrowetz, F. (1998). Performance-based assessment and instructional change: The effects of testing in Maine and Maryland. *Educational Evaluation and Policy Analysis, 20*(2), 95–113.

Gigante, N., & Firestone, W. (2007). Administrative support and teacher leadership in schools implementing reform. *Journal of Educational Administration, 46*(3), 302–331.

Gronlund, N. E. (1998). *Assessment of student achievement* (6th ed.). Boston, MA: Allyn & Bacon.

Johnson, B. (1606/2013 updated). *Volpone; Or, The Fox*. The Project Gutenberg Ebook of Volpone. Act 3, scene 3.1. Retrieved from http://www.gutenberg.org/files/4039/4039-h/4039-h.htm#link2H_4_0008

Madeja, S. (1977). Structuring a research agenda for the arts and aesthetics. *Journal of Aesthetic Education, 11*(2), 67–86.

McMillan, J. (2000). Fundamental assessment principles for teachers and school administrators. *Practical Assessment, Research & Evaluation, 7*(8). Retrieved from: http://parconline.net/getvn.asp? v=7&n=8

McMillan, J. (2004). *Classroom assessment: Principles and practice for effective instruction* (3rd ed.). Boston, MA: Pearson Education.

Mehrens, W., Popham, W. J., & Ryan, J. (1998). How to prepare students for performance assessments. *Educational Measurement: Issues and Practice, 17*(1), 19–22.

Moon, T., & Callahan, C. (2001). Classroom performance assessment: What should it look like in a standards-based classroom? *NASSP Bulletin, 85*(622), 48–58. doi:10.1177/019263650108562207.

Moskal, B. (2003). Recommendations for developing classroom performance assessments and scoring rubrics. *Practical Assessment, Research & Evaluation, 9*(2). Retrieved from: http://parconline.net/getvn.asp? v=8&n=14

Palm, T. (2008). Performance assessment and authentic assessment: A conceptual analysis of the literature. *Practical Assessment, Research & Evaluation, 8*(14). Retrieved from: http://parconline.net/getvn.asp? v=13&n=4

Popham, W. J. (2003). *Test better, teach better: The instructional role of assessment*. Alexandria, VA: ASCD.

Popham, W. J. (2008). *Classroom assessment: What teachers need to know* (5th ed.). Boston, MA: Allyn & Bacon.
Stein, J. (Ed.). (1971). *The random house dictionary of the English language*. New York, NY: Random House.
Stiggins, R. (2001). The principal's leadership role in assessment. *NASSP Bulletin, 85*(621), 13–26.
Tanner, D. (2001). Authentic assessment: A solution, or part of the problem? *The High School Journal, 85*(1), 24–29.
Tierney, R., & Simon, M. (2004). What's still wrong with rubrics: Focusing on the consistency of performance criteria across scale levels. *Practical Assessment, Research & Evaluation, 9*(2). Retrieved from: http://PAREonline.net/getvn.asp? v=9&n=2
Webber, C., Aitken, N., Lupart, J., Runté, R., & Scott, S. (2008). *The Alberta student assessment study: Stage one findings.* Paper presented at the annual meeting of the Canadian Association for the Study of Educational Administration, Vancouver, BC, Canada.

Chapter 6
Assessment for Learning in a Math Classroom

Sharon Friesen

Abstract A design-based research (DBR) approach was used to investigate how a mathematics geometry study which employed the principles of universal design for learning (UDL) within a discipline-based inquiry which embedded assessment for learning impacted student learning, and teacher learning and instructional designs. Qualitative and quantitative data informed the research findings and indicated: (i) all students showed significant improvement in achievement, (ii) all students made gains in the five strands of mathematical proficiency, (iii) all students can engage with difficult mathematical ideas when they are provided with assessment for learning, (iv) the principles of UDL permit teachers to break the stranglehold of the procedural script for teaching mathematics, (v) access to technology is a critical factor in an accessible mathematics classroom, (vi) introducing UDL and assessment for learning into the mathematics classroom is a disruptive innovation, and (vii) creating accessible mathematics classrooms, consistent with UDL and assessment for learning principles and practices, requires increased teacher knowledge and support for on-going professional development.

Keywords Discipline-based inquiry • Assessment for learning • Mathematics learning • Student-centred leadership

> *Math.* The bane of my existence for as many years as I can count. I cannot relate it to my life or become interested in what I'm learning. I find it boring and cannot find any way to apply myself to it since I rarely understand it. (ATA, 2003, p. 28)
>
> Was ever a human activity preached so differently from how it was practiced, taught so clumsily, learned so grudgingly, its light buried beneath so many bushels, as mathematics? (Kaplan & Kaplan, 2007, p. 117)

S. Friesen (✉)
Werklund School of Education, University of Calgary,
2500 University Drive NW, Calgary, AB T2N 1N4, Canada
e-mail: sfriesen@ucalgary.ca

© Springer International Publishing Switzerland 2016
S. Scott et al. (eds.), *Leadership of Assessment, Inclusion, and Learning*,
The Enabling Power of Assessment 3, DOI 10.1007/978-3-319-23347-5_6

6.1 Introduction

For the past 10 years, researchers and consultants from the University of Calgary, Werklund School of Education, Galileo Educational Network (Galileo) have been committed to partnering with teachers and administrators in schools in Alberta, Canada. These are sites in which the reflexive relationship between theory and practice is worked out and studied using design-based research methodologies. Within these sites researchers, consultants, teachers and administrators come together in a common inquiry into what it means to design contemporary learning environments. The classroom described in this chapter is in one of the schools within the larger study that was undertaken in Mountain View School Division.[1] I have selected to focus on one classroom as it represents at the micro level what is being worked out at the macro level of this ambitious initiative.

The work of researchers, teachers and administrators involves the creation and study of discipline-based inquiry (see Galileo Educational Network, 2013; Newmann, Bryk, & Nagaoka, 2001) approaches to instructional design and practices. Inquiry approaches consist of problem-based, project-based or design-based instructional designs (Darling-Hammond, 2008).

Discipline-based inquiry is a dynamic process of coming to know and understand the world in genuine and authentic ways. It encompasses the processes of posing questions, problems or issues; gathering information; thinking creatively about possibilities; becoming proficient in providing evidence; making decisions; justifying conclusions; and learning the ways of challenging, building upon, and improving knowledge of a topic or field of study. Discipline-based inquiry can encompass a range of instructional design practices including problem-based learning, project-based learning and design-based learning. It enables the teacher to design learning that provides students with the opportunity to ask genuine questions of the disciplines. It provides learners, all learners novice and expert alike, with the opportunity to engage in disciplinary ways of knowing, doing and being in order to build deep understanding.

Within this learning milieu, teachers develop a repertoire of contemporary instructional practices which some researchers currently refer to as twenty-first century learning practices (Clifford & Marinucci, 2008; Jardine, Clifford, & Friesen, 2002, 2008; Rose & Meyer, 2002; Sawyer, 2006; Scardamalia, 2001). Contemporary instructional practices demand full attention be given to: (i) designing the inquiry study to ensure that students are learning their way into disciplinary ways of knowing, doing and being, (ii) understanding fully what the student knows and understands, that is, where he or she is on their learning journey and what they, the teacher, needs to do to help the student make progress, (iii) ensuring students have clear, explicit, criteria to guide and direct their learning, (iv) providing many opportunities from many different sources for specific feedback and feed forward along the way, and (v) providing students with multiple, flexible representations of concepts and

---

[1] Mountain View School Division is a pseudonym.

enabling them to express their understandings and engage in multiple, flexible ways (Friesen, 2009). That is, the teaching, learning and thinking are visible and conform to the learners in personalised ways (Hattie, 2009; Ritchhart, Church, & Morrison, 2011).

This chapter details the nature of mathematics learning in one classroom. It highlights the student-centred leadership implications, leadership that makes a difference to the equity and excellence of student outcomes (Robinson, 2011).

6.2 A Look at the Literature

Fuson, Kalchman, and Bransford (2005), Mighton (2003, 2007), Stigler and Hiebert (1999), and Swain and Swan (2007) argue that new approaches are needed to help students learn mathematics.

> Today, mathematics education faces two major challenges: raising the floor by expanding achievement for all, and lifting the ceiling of achievement to better prepare future leaders in mathematics, as well as in science, engineering, and technology. At first glance, these appear to be mutually exclusive. (Research Points, 2006, p. 1)

Is it really possible to achieve both excellence and equity in mathematics learning?

6.2.1 Universal Design for Learning (UDL)

"Recent educational innovations, such as differentiated instruction and universal design for learning, offer insights into proactively planning instruction that embraces academic diversity" characteristic of most ordinary classrooms (Edyburn, 2006, p. 21). UDL is grounded in emerging insights about brain development, learning, and digital media. Rose and Meyer (2002, 2006) and Rose, Meyer, and Hitchcock (2005) observed that the disconnect between an increasingly diverse student population and a "one-size-fits-all" curriculum will not produce the desired academic achievement gains expected in the twenty-first century. Drawing on the historical application of universal design in architecture, they advance UDL as a means of focusing educational research, development, and practice on understanding diversity, technology, and learning.

Universal Design for Learning is being taken up more seriously in special education where issues of access to high quality learning experiences for variously identified special needs students carry a particular urgency (Firchow, 2002; Meo, 2005). But all proponents of UDL actually make much larger claims for their ideas:

- that diversity in the classroom is the norm rather than a problem to be fixed;
- that paying attention to what does – and does not – work for students generally relegated to the margins will improve learning for all;

- that all students can meet similar learning goals if curricula, instruction and assessment are radically reconceptualised; and
- that effective use of technology enables all students to represent, express and engage with ideas in multiple ways not generally seen in conventional classrooms.

To the extent that principles of UDL are increasingly familiar within the educational community, I will draw on the following key principles as they provide a focus for developing mathematical proficiency for all.

1. Procedural approaches to the teaching of mathematics privilege naked independence (Edyburn, 2006) – "the notion that completing tasks without performance-enhancing access to technology is superior to performance that is enhanced through technology" (p. 22). This out-dated formulation of what it means to be an educated person ensures that academic achievement is reserved only for able-bodied individuals, and only for those individuals who are able to succeed without external support, resources or technology. For many students, "technology can be the difference between students with special needs sitting in a classroom watching others participate and all students participating fully" (Bausch & Hasselbring, 2005, p. 9).
2. And for all, access to a wide variety of digital media permits mathematical explorations that are difficult or impossible with only pencil and paper. These media include (but are not limited to) spreadsheets and databases, simulations, software such as dynamic geometry, computer assisted design, programming, interactive games, etc. Accessible classrooms are media rich (Friesen, 2006).
3. Disability can be conceived as a mismatch between the learner's needs and the education offered (Rothberg & Treviranus, 2006). Rather than conceptualised as a personal trait, disability can be seen as an artifact of the way children are taught (Mighton, 2007).
4. UDL design principles focus on creating clear goals, flexible methods and materials, and embedded assessments that enable all learners including those with disabilities to access knowledge, participate and progress.
5. Learning is about deep understanding, constructing knowledge and developing skills and thus requires a careful balance of support, challenge and opportunity. "But the most fundamental change will come in our understanding of goals. The ultimate educational goals will no longer be about the mastery of content (content will be available everywhere, anytime, electronically) but about the mastery of learning" (Rose & Meyer, 2002, p. 7).
6. UDL calls for:

   - *Multiple means of representation,* to give learners various ways of acquiring information and knowledge,
   - *Multiple means of expression,* to provide learners alternatives for demonstrating what they know,
   - *Multiple means of engagement,* to tap into learners' interests, offer appropriate challenges, and increase motivation. (CAST, 2013)

A teacher working with the principles of UDL in the classroom has the ability to represent any mathematical concept in multiple ways. It is the conceptual understanding, which involves an understanding of concepts, operations and relations, and the development of procedural fluency that is focus of the instruction.

Teaching for mathematical proficiency (i.e., conceptual understanding, procedural fluency, strategic competence, adaptive reasoning and a productive disposition) requires that the teachers design a learning environment that provides "a solid foundation of detailed knowledge and clarity about the core concepts around which that knowledge is organized to support effective learning" (Donovan & Bransford, 2005, p. 569). The type of practice that builds mathematical proficiency requires that students be brought into a collaborative "relationship between different facts students are learning, between the procedures they are learning, and the underlying concepts" through robust, rich problems and investigations (Shanker Institute, 2005, p. 7). It is to this type of mathematical learning environment that the instructional principles of UDL need to be tethered.

6.2.2 Assessment for Learning

Effective classroom assessment is known internationally as assessment for learning, a term made popular by Stiggins (see http://ati.pearson.com/downloads/afldefined.pdf also Wiliam, 2011, p. 39) and also as embedded formative assessment (Wiliam, 2011), "has as its primary focus the ongoing improvement of learning for all students" (Chappuis & Stiggins, 2002, p. 39). Hattie (2009, 2012) refers to assessment for learning as formative evaluation, indicating that this is assessment that occurs before and during the learning process itself. Embedded formative assessments for learning allow all students to demonstrate their progress and understanding in multiple ways (Wiliam, 2011). In a UDL classroom, classroom assessment practices also acknowledge and attend to the fact that traditional print-based assessments often block a true picture of the learning (Rose et al., 2005). In a UDL classroom it is imperative that students are able to draw upon strategic networks to provide multiple ways to enact and express their understanding.

The value of assessment *for* learning is becoming more widely recognised (Black & Wiliam, 1998; Bransford, Brown, & Cocking, 2000; Carver, 2006; Davies, 2002–2003; Hattie, 2009; Stiggins, Arter, Chappuis, & Chappius, 2004; Wiliam, 2011).

> Professors Paul Black and Dylan Wiliam synthesised evidence from over 250 studies linking assessment and learning. The outcome was a clear and incontrovertible message: that initiatives designed to enhance effectiveness of the way assessment is used in the classroom to promote learning can raise pupil achievement. (Assessment Reform Group, 1999, p. 4)

More recently, Hattie's (2009) synthesis of over 800 meta-analyses related to achievement demonstrated the power of feedback in improving student achievement.

> However, one should not start immediately providing feedback and then await the magical increases in achievement. …increasing the amount of feedback to have a positive effect on achievement requires a change in the conception of what it means to be a teacher; it is the feedback to the teacher about what students can and cannot do that is more powerful than feedback to the student, and it necessitates a different way of interacting and respecting students. (p. 4)

Black (2004) reported that much confusion exists regarding the type of assessment that actually increases student learning and achievement. He noted that misunderstandings arise when teachers think that teacher-made tests and student portfolio assessments can be used to improve student learning. They cannot because they are put together at the end of a piece of learning. Assessment for learning occurs while the learning is taking place.

Wiliam (2011) identifies five strategies that form the basis of effective classroom assessment:

1. Clarifying, sharing, and understanding learning intentions and criteria for success.
2. Engineering effective classroom discussions, activities, and learning tasks that elicit evidence of learning.
3. Providing feedback that moves learning forward.
4. Activating learners as instructional resources for one another.
5. Activating learners as owners of their own learning. (p. 46)

Hattie (2009) found that students made significant learning gains when the following features of classroom assessment were incorporated in instruction: (i) self-reported grades, effect size = 1.44; (ii) providing formative evaluation, effect size = 0.9; and (iii) feedback, effect size = 0.73.

Researchers at Boston College found that when students were given access to computers to digitally compose their answers to written portions of tests, they scored significantly higher than those using paper and pencil (Dolan & Hall, 2001). Digital tools and expressive media give students a wide range of opportunities to represent and express what they are learning. When such media have built-in capacities for interaction, they also provide immediate feedback and feed forward to students on their performance. Consider, for example, how engaging a computer game can be as players strive to develop the skills they need to move to the next level of play. The learning environment, itself, is designed to give precise feedback. No gamer needs to wait for a Friday morning quiz to see if she is progressing.

Inflexible assessments that do not meet the learning needs of students confound the measurement of knowledge and abilities (Dolan & Hall, 2001), even when that assessment is computer-based. If assessment practices remain a one-size-fits-all method of sorting out ability hierarchies in the classroom, they will give incomplete pictures of the multiple ways in which individuals develop their proficiencies, while well-designed, embedded, assessment for learning practices built upon the principles of UDL have the potential to ensure both learning excellence and equity (OECD, 2005; Wiliam, 2011), removing many of the barriers to learning in many mathematics classrooms.

6.2.3 Student-Centred Leadership

Leadership practice focused on improving student learning and achievement for all students is what Robinson (2011) calls student-centred leadership. Robinson, drawing upon a rigorous meta-analysis, identified five dimensions of leadership that were focused on improved student learning and achievement. She and her research team found these five dimensions to have the highest effect sizes: (i) establishing goals and expectations, effect size = 0.42; (ii) resourcing strategically, effect size = 0.31; (iii) ensuring quality teaching, effect size = 0.42; (iv) leading teacher learning and development, effect size = 0.84; and (v) ensuring an orderly and safe environment, effect size = 0.27.

Three of Robinson's (2011) leadership dimensions were particularly important for the principal of the school in which this study occurred: establishing goals and expectations, ensuring quality teaching, and leading teacher learning and development.

6.3 Research Design and Methodology

Principles of design-based research informed both the design and the methods used throughout this study. "Design-based research can help create and extend knowledge about developing, enacting, and sustaining innovative learning environments" (Design-Based Research Collective, 2003, p. 5). Design-based research uses both qualitative and quantitative methodologies. It is used when the purpose of the research endeavour is towards sustained innovation, to envision what is not yet, what might be possible in real education settings (Kelly, Lesh, & Baek, 2008).

Design-based research is interventionist. Design researchers are trying to make things happen; therefore, there is no claim of objectivity, and the lines between actor and observer are intentionally crossed. "The best design research has a visionary quality that cannot be derived from these other kinds of research, nor does it often arise from practice. It requires a research community driven by potentiality" (Bereiter, 2002, p. 324).

The particular strength of design-based research is its ability to increase the capacity of participants to make evidence-based decisions that feedback to change practice while the study is in progress. This is a significant difference from more conventional research designs in which findings emerge primarily at the end of the study when participants have no opportunity to act on them within the context of the stated goals of the project.

In designing the pedagogical interactions in this study, the research team placed a strong emphasis on assessment for learning, defined as:

> any assessment for which the first priority in its design and practice is to serve the purpose of promoting pupils' learning. It thus differs from assessment designed primarily to serve the purposes of accountability, or of ranking, or of certifying competence. An assessment activity can help learning if it provides information to be used as feedback, by teachers, and by their pupils in assessing themselves and each other, to modify the teaching and learning activities in which they are engaged. Such assessment becomes 'formative assessment' when the evidence is actually used to adapt the teaching work to meet learning needs. (Black, Harrison, Lee, Marshall, & Wiliam, 2002, pp. 2–3)

The research team employed various forms of assessment for learning:

- Sustained dialogue with students. A great deal of effort went into examining the geometric mathematical territory by the teachers and me so they could engage

students in dialogue around questions that were worthy mathematically and which could assist students in making connections, developing reasoning and building mathematical proficiency.
- An analytic trait rubric made available to the students before the study started and constantly available to the students throughout the study at (www.iomembership.com/1993).
- Specific daily feedback, both written and oral from the research and teaching team and from each other around identified criteria that were open and readily available.
- The dynamic geometry application also provided the students with feedback. Students got immediate feedback from the dynamic geometry application when a construction wasn't working as they had intended it to.
- Daily meetings by the research and teaching team to review emerging student understanding and design the next day's instruction.

The research team created a number of environments and ways to record the students' written work. Because so much of that work was digital, the research team created a wiki (http://gr7math.wikispaces.com). They also requested that the school jurisdiction's information technology department provide the students with email accounts. In this way, teachers and I, as well as other members of the class, could provide the students with additional written feedback and respond to the students' reflections.

Teachers and I focused strongly on providing strong, ongoing oral and written feedback individually and to small groups. Large group conversation was built into each class so students could test out their ideas, identify shared problems or gaps in understanding, listen to other students' emerging understandings, build on other students' ideas in order to advance understanding beyond the level of the individual and seek clarification.

The analytic trait rubric that was used to guide the student learning was also used at the end of learning as summative assessment. Students worked with their team members to assess their final task performance. Having worked with the rubric throughout the learning task, they knew what criteria they were working towards. Students were able to accurately self-assess their work.

6.3.1 Data Collection

Students whose parents signed consent forms wrote a pre-test and post-test. The pre-test was administered before the intervention began. The post-test was administered at the conclusion of the 4-week intervention. Students were given 45 min for both administrations of four sample task geometry related test questions selected from PISA 2000, 2003, 2006: Continent Area, Carpenter, Farms and Twisted Building.[2]

---

[2] These tasks were released in December 2006 in a document called PISA Released Items for Mathematics which can be found at www.oecd.org/dataoecd/14/10/38709418.pdf

6 Assessment for Learning in a Math Classroom

Table 6.1 Types of special codes

Special education code	Meaning of code	Number of students
51	Mild cognitive disability	1
54	Learning disability	7
80	Gifted and talented	2
38	Assigned by school jurisdiction	1
		11

Table 6.2 Overall participation

Students	Students in classroom	Signed consents	Valid pre-test data	Valid post-test data	Valid data for both	Participation rate
Learning disabilities	9	6	6	6	6	67 %
Gifted	2	2	2	2	2	100 %
Regular	25	18	18	21	20	72 %
	36	26	26	26	26	72 %

While the students in this study were younger than students selected to write PISA mathematics examinations, I was interested in finding test items that were:

1. reliability and validity tested (Adams & Wu, 2002);
2. designed to assess conceptual understanding and procedural fluency; and
3. organised contextually in order to facilitate problem solving or strategic competence.

The study was conducted in a rural school board in Alberta. There were a total of 36 students in the classroom. This group was composed of nine students, eight boys and one girl, who were (1) coded with social, emotional or academic disabilities and (2) had Individual Programme Plans (IPPs) in place. There were also two students who were coded as gifted. These two students also had IPPs in place.

Table 6.1 shows the eligibility special education code assigned to 11 of the 36 students in this class and the meaning of this code. It also shows the number of students in the class assigned that particular code.

Table 6.2 shows that, of the available sample of 36 Grade 7 students, 72 % (N=26) signed consent forms and produced data from both administrations of the four task questions.

In addition to the pre-test and post-test, observational data was collected from two sources: video observations of classroom interactions and field notes from classroom observations. Samples of student work were collected throughout the intervention from students whose parents had provided consent. The research team interviewed the teacher and the principal. This consisted of a semi-structured interview conducted at the end of the research study. We recorded and transcribed interviews and provided each of the interviewees with an opportunity to review and edit their transcript.

6.3.1.1 Data Analysis

Members of the research team collected both qualitative and quantitative data. All audio data, observational data, and field notes went through an iterative process of reading, rereading and review. Pre- and post-test data were statistically analysed using SPSS.

6.3.1.2 Transcripts

Transcripts from interviews were initially read in their entirety to a get a sense of their content and context, without imposing a specific analytic lens. In the second stage, members of the research team independently read the same text and coded it independently to determine descriptive categories and criteria. We then compared our coding to establish consistency. These were not a priori categories and criteria; rather, they emerged from the analysis of the transcripts themselves. The aim of this level of analysis was to map out the data, review it for further analysis, and become more familiar with its content.

The research team also analysed the transcripts to discern patterns of experience. We coded the transcripts, noting all data that related to the patterns. The identified patterns were then expounded on and combined. We defined themes derived from patterns such as conversation topics, recurring vocabulary, recurring activities, meanings, and/or feelings. Themes that emerged from the participants' accounts formed a comprehensive picture of their collective experience. In this way, we were able to establish which themes and sub-themes fit together in a meaningful way (Leininger, 1985).

6.3.1.3 Observational Analysis

Members of the research team collected observational data in two ways. Video footage was collected during math classes. The video data was transcribed. One researcher conducted focused observational notes during the 16 classes. These notes were analysed to discern patterns.

6.3.1.4 Pre-test/Post-test Design and Analysis

Part of the study is a one-group pre-test post-test design. Twenty-seven students were pre-tested. They then participated in the intervention, and then were post-tested at the conclusion of the intervention. Students who did not participate in both the pre-test and the post-test were not included in the analysis.

The success of the treatment was determined by comparing the results of the pre-test and post-test scores. The paired-sample t-test for non-independent samples was used to determine if there was a significant difference between the means of each sub-unit of instruction and the total scores. By requiring a higher value to reject the null hypothesis, the t-test makes adjustments for smaller sample size (Gay, Mills, & Airasian, 2006). An alpha level of .05 was used for all statistical tests.

6.4 Findings

Seven findings emerged from a close analysis of the data, which it is hoped will provide guidance to teachers, school jurisdiction leaders, policy makers and subsequent researchers as they consider:

- Building mathematical proficiency for *all* students by employing UDL and assessment for learning principles and practices;
- Creating a curriculum that is accessible to all students;
- Improving the achievement of special needs students; and
- Building the capacity of teachers to change mathematics teaching practices.

These findings are:

1. All students showed significant improvement in achievement.
2. All students demonstrated gains in the five strands of mathematical proficiency.
3. All students can engage with difficult mathematical ideas when they are provided with assessment for learning.
4. The principles of UDL permit teachers to break the stranglehold of the procedural script for teaching mathematics.
5. Access to technology is a critical factor in an accessible mathematics classroom.
6. Introducing UDL and assessment for learning into the mathematics classroom is a disruptive innovation.
7. Creating accessible mathematics classrooms, consistent with UDL and assessment for learning principles and practices, requires increased teacher knowledge and support for on-going professional development.

6.4.1 All Students Showed Significant Improvement in Achievement

The PISA test items used for pre- and post-tests were chosen (1) for their validity and reliability, and (2) for their ability to measure mathematical proficiency. The four items had levels of difficulty from middle to highest range. The instructional intervention was not designed to 'teach to the test'. Rather, all elements were designed to build mathematical proficiency that would transfer to a number of contexts, one of which is standardised testing of the highest international calibre.

I selected four task questions from PISA 2000, 2003, 2006: Continent Area, Carpenter, Farms and Twisted Building.[3] While the students in this study were younger than students selected to write PISA mathematics examinations, I was interested in finding test items that were:

- reliability and validity tested (Adams & Wu, 2002);
- designed to assess conceptual understanding and procedural fluency; and
- organised contextually in order to facilitate problem solving or strategic competence.

PISA tests are designed to test various mathematical competencies:

- Mathematical thinking and reasoning;
- Mathematical argumentation;
- Mathematical communication;
- Modelling;
- Problem posing and solving;
- Representation;
- Using symbolic, formal and technical language and operations; and
- Use of aids and tools.

> PISA does not use tasks that access the above competencies individually. When doing 'real mathematics' it is necessary to draw simultaneously upon many of these skills (OECD, 2000, p. 83).

The following is an analysis of student performance on each of the task questions and an analysis of their total performance on the pre-test and post-test. Our analysis consisted of calculating the mean, standard deviation and standard error. We compared the pre-test to the post-test on each of these measures. To determine the size of the variation within vthe group of students taking the same test, we ran a paired-sample t-test for non-independent samples. This was used to determine if there was a significant difference between the means of each sub-unit of instruction and the total scores. The t-test tests the statistical significance of the difference in the two means. Specifically, instead of treating each group separately, and analysing raw scores, the paired-sample t-test for non-independent samples allowed us to look only at the differences between the two measures, the pre-test and post-test for each of the groups of students to determine whether we had a statistically significant difference in achievement between the pre-test and post-test results. By subtracting the first score from the second for each subject and then analysing only those 'pure (paired) differences', we were able to exclude the entire part of the variation in our data set that results from unequal base levels of individual students. By requiring a higher value to reject the null hypothesis, the t-test makes adjustments for smaller sample size (Gay et al., 2006). Members of the research team selected an alpha level of .05 for all statistical tests.

---

[3] These tasks were released in December 2006 in a document called PISA Released Items for Mathematics which can be found at www.oecd.org/dataoecd/14/10/38709418.pdf

Table 6.3 Mean scores for continent area task

Paired sample – continent area task	N	Mean	Std. deviation	Std. error mean
Identified students pre-test	7	1.00	0.82	0.31
Identified LD students post-test	7	1.29	0.95	0.36
Regular students pre-test	20	1.10	0.85	0.19
Regular students post-test	20	2.10	1.33	0.30
All students pre-test	27	1.07	0.83	0.16
All students post-test	27	1.89	1.28	0.25

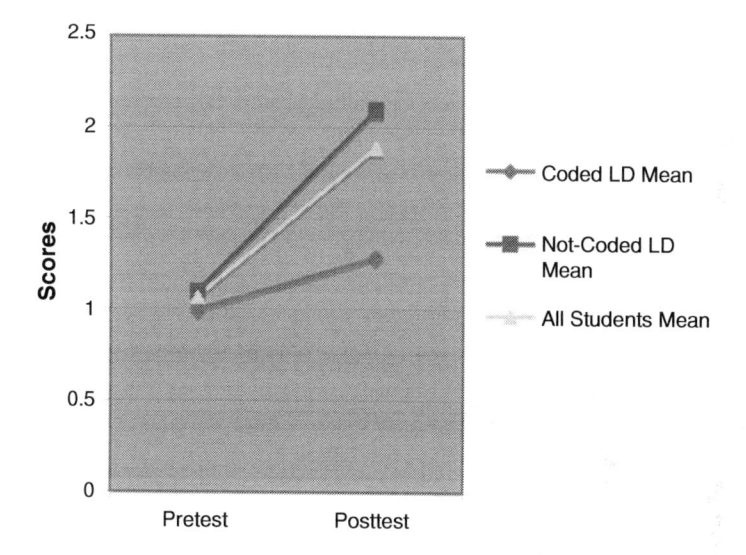

Fig. 6.1 Mean scores for pre-test-post-test for continent area task

1. Task One: *Continent Area Task*

   The Continent Area task requires students to identify an appropriate strategy and method for estimating the area of an irregular and unfamiliar shape, and to select and apply the appropriate mathematical tools in an unfamiliar context. Students need to choose a suitable shape or shapes with which to model the irregular area (for example, approximating parts of the map with rectangle(s), circle(s), triangle(s). Students need to know and apply the appropriate formulae for the shapes they use; to work with scale; to estimate length; and to carry out a computation involving a few steps.

   Table 6.3 shows how the students performed on the *Continent Area Task* pre-test and post-test.

   The graph above (Fig. 6.1) shows an increase in mean scores between *Continent Area Task* pre-test and post-test.

   The data in Table 6.4 indicates that the mean on *Continent Area Task* scores was significantly different for regular students (Not Coded LD student) and for all students. However there was not a significant difference between the pre-test and post-test

Table 6.4 Paired sample t-test results for continent area task

Paired sample t-test	T	df	Sig. (2 tailed)	Mean difference
Identified LD students	−1.00	6	0.36	−0.29
Regular students	−3.34	19	0.00	−1.00
All students	−3.41	26	0.00	−0.82

scores for the identified LD students (Coded LD students). This difference on the pre-test and post-test scores represents a significant improvement in achievement for the regular students and for the class as a whole.

The *Continent Area Task* is particularly difficult, demanding a high level of competency, including the ability to calculate area by using scales. In the PISA test, this task is given a difficulty level of 712, one of the highest levels assigned to tasks. The teachers and I were impressed that all students demonstrated at least some degree of increased ability to perform such a demanding task after the 4-week study.

During the study, some students worked with scale while measuring some of the images they took. Many students did not. Many students chose to measure the actual object rather than determine the scale represented on their image. In addition to scale, this task required students to calculate the area of an irregular shape – the continent of Australia. Students were required to analyse this shape by deconstructing it into constituent shapes: triangles, rectangles and squares to calculate the area. Once this was accomplished they needed to calculate measures of all the constituent shapes, adding them together to arrive at a reasonable estimate of land area.

As the following *Farm Task* indicates, the identified LD students developed proficiency in calculating area; however they may have experienced confusion in recognising that all the smaller shapes needed to be added together to determine the whole. When examining the actual tests, the teacher and I noted that all students divided the irregular landmass into smaller shapes. On further examination of the actual tests, it is obvious that scale caused these students difficulty.

2. Task Two: *Farm Task*

Students are given a mathematical model (in the form of a diagram) and a written mathematical description of a real-world object (a pyramid-shaped roof) and asked to calculate one of the lengths in the diagram. This task requires students to work with a familiar geometric model and to link information in verbal and symbolic form to a diagram. Students need to visually "disembed" a triangle from a two-dimensional representation of a three-dimensional object; to select the appropriate information about side length relationships; and to use knowledge of similar triangles in order to solve the problem.

Table 6.5 shows how the students performed on the *Farm Task* pre-test and post-test.

The graph below (Fig. 6.2) shows an increase in mean scores between *Farm Task* pre-test and post-test.

6 Assessment for Learning in a Math Classroom

Table 6.5 Mean scores for farm task

	N	Mean	Std. deviation	Std. error mean
LD coded pre-test	7	0.57	0.54	0.20
LD coded post-test	7	1.14	0.69	0.26
Not-coded LD pre-test	20	0.95	0.83	0.19
Not-coded LD post-test	20	1.15	0.59	0.13
All students pre-test	27	0.85	0.77	0.15
All students post-test	27	1.15	0.60	0.12

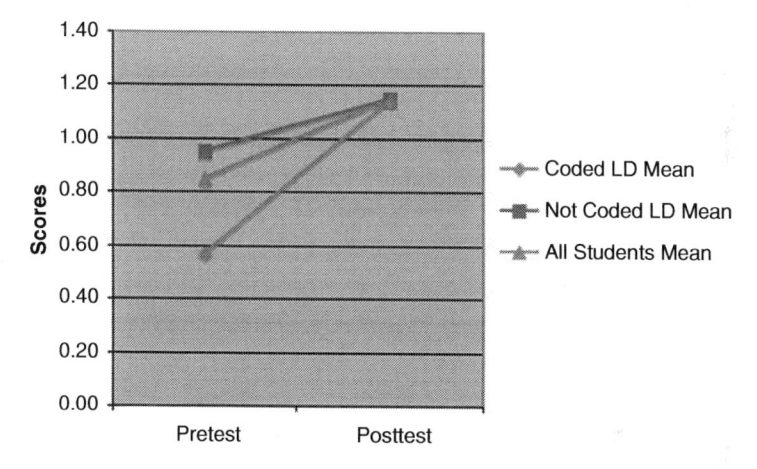

Fig. 6.2 Mean scores for pre-test post-test for farm task

Table 6.6 Paired samples t-test for farm task

Paired-sample t-test	t	df	Sig. (2 tailed)	Mean difference
Coded LD	−2.83	6	0.03	−0.57
Not coded LD	−1.07	19	0.30	−0.20
All students	−1.99	26	0.06	−0.30

The data in Table 6.6 indicates that the mean of scores on the *Farm Task* is significantly different for Coded LD students, but not for Not Coded LD students. This represents a significant improvement in achievement for the Coded LD students, but not the Not Coded LD students. Overall, the class did not demonstrate significant improvement.

This task receives a task difficulty level of 492 on the PISA test. 492 is within the middle range of task difficulty. While still demanding for 12 year olds, this was a more familiar task given the type of tasks and activities students had engaged in throughout the study. It is clear that all students were able to transfer the learning gained during the study into this new context. What is worth attending to is the level of performance attained by Coded LD students. These students attained a level of performance comparable to the Not Coded LD students.

3. Task 3: *Carpenter Task*

This task requires students to interpret and link text and diagrams representing a real-world situation; show insight in 2-D geometrical properties; extract information from geometrical representation; calculate perimeters for compound and irregular shapes; apply routine procedures.

Table 6.7 shows how the students performed on the *Carpenter Task* pre-test and post-test.

The graph in Fig. 6.3 shows an increase in mean scores between *Carpenter Task* pre-test and post-test.

The data in Table 6.8 below indicates that the mean of *Carpenter Task* scores is significantly different for the Coded LD students, for Not Coded LD students and for all participating students. This represents a significant improvement in achievement for the Coded LD students and the Not Coded LD students. Overall, the class demonstrated significant improvement.

Table 6.7 Mean scores for carpenter task

	N	Mean	Std. deviation	Std. error mean
LD coded pre-test	7	1.29	0.76	0.29
LD coded post-test	7	3.14	1.22	0.46
Not-coded LD pre-test	20	2.00	1.08	0.24
Not-coded LD post-test	20	2.65	0.93	0.21
All students pre-test	27	1.81	1.04	0.20
All students post-test	27	2.78	1.01	0.20

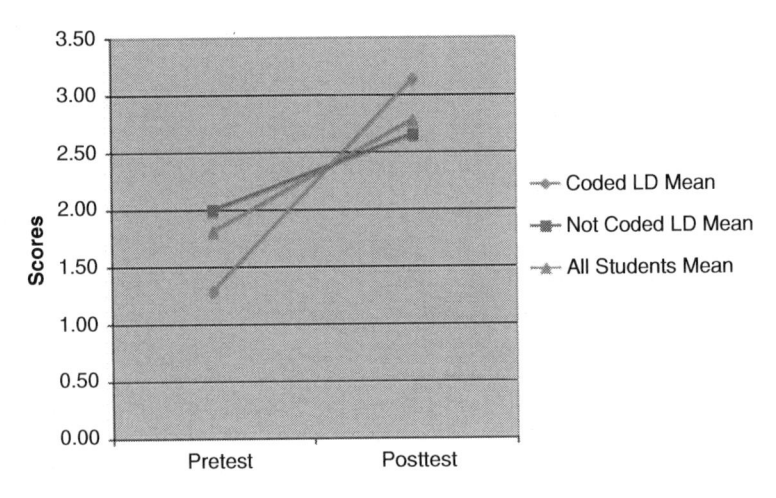

Fig. 6.3 Mean scores for pre-test post-test for carpenter task

Table 6.8 Paired samples t-test for carpenter task

Paired-sample t-test	t	df	Sig. (2 tailed)	Mean difference
Coded LD	−4.04	6	0.01	−1.86
Not coded LD	−2.80	19	0.01	−0.65
All students	−4.20	26	0.00	−0.96

Table 6.9 Mean scores for twisted building task

	N	Mean	Std. deviation	Std. error mean
LD coded pre-test	7	1.86	1.46	0.55
LD coded post-test	7	4.00	0.00	0.00
Not-coded LD pre-test	20	2.20	1.94	0.43
Not-coded LD post-test	20	4.00	0.00	0.00
All students pre-test	27	2.11	1.81	0.35
All students post-test	27	4.00	0.00	0.00

This task receives a task difficulty level of 687, at the highest level within the middle range of task difficulty. Like the Farm Task, this is a demanding task for 12 year olds, requiring a high degree of mathematical proficiency. Again it is clear that the tasks and activities students had engaged in throughout the study helped them develop this proficiency. While students did not work on tasks like this one, they did calculate perimeters for compound and irregular shapes and applied routine procedures. The Coded LD students' performance on this question shows that they can reach high levels of mathematical proficiency.

4. Task Four: *Twisted Building Task*

This task requires students to imagine the cumulative effect of the twisting phenomenon over a number of steps and to construct a graphic representation of those turns. They are required to extract information from geometrical representation; calculate degrees of rotation and determine orientation following a number of turns.

Table 6.9 shows how the students performed on the *Twisted Building Task* pre-test and post-test.

The graph in Fig. 6.4 shows an increase in mean scores between *Twisted Building Task* pre-test and post-test.

Table 6.10 indicates that the mean of *Twisted Building Task* scores is significantly different for Coded LD students, for Not Coded LD students and for all participating students. This represents a significant improvement in achievement for the Coded LD students and the Not Coded LD students. Overall, the class demonstrated significant improvement.

This is a demanding task for 12 year olds, requiring a high degree of mathematical proficiency. Again, tasks and activities students had engaged in throughout the study helped all students increase their mathematical proficiency. While students did not work on tasks like this one, they did calculate angles of many different types of lines within 1-D, 2-D and 3-D. While all students demonstrated a significant difference,

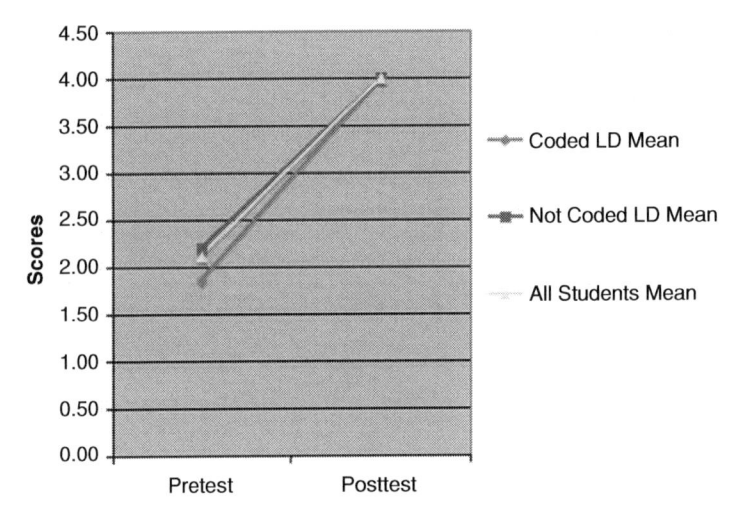

Fig. 6.4 Mean scores for pre-test – post-test for twisted building task

Table 6.10 Paired samples t-test for twisted building task

Paired-sample t-test	t	df	Sig. (2 tailed)	Mean difference
Coded LD	−3.87	6	0.01	−2.14
Not coded LD	−4.16	19	0.01	−1.80
All students	−5.44	26	0.00	−1.89

Table 6.11 Mean scores for all tasks

	N	Mean	Std. deviation	Std. error mean
LD coded pre-test	7	5.00	1.63	0.62
LD coded post-test	7	9.57	1.13	0.43
Not-coded LD pre-test	20	6.25	2.75	0.62
Not-coded LD post-test	20	9.90	1.89	0.42
All students pre-test	27	5.93	2.54	0.49
All students post-test	27	9.81	1.71	0.33

the teachers and I felt it was once again important to emphasise that the Coded LD students' performance on this task question shows that they can reach high levels of mathematical proficiency.

What changes occurred in overall achievement after administration of the UDL intervention?

Table 6.11 indicates how the students performed as a total on pre-test and post-test.

The graph in Fig. 6.5 shows an increase in the overall mean scores between pre-tests and post-tests on all items combined.

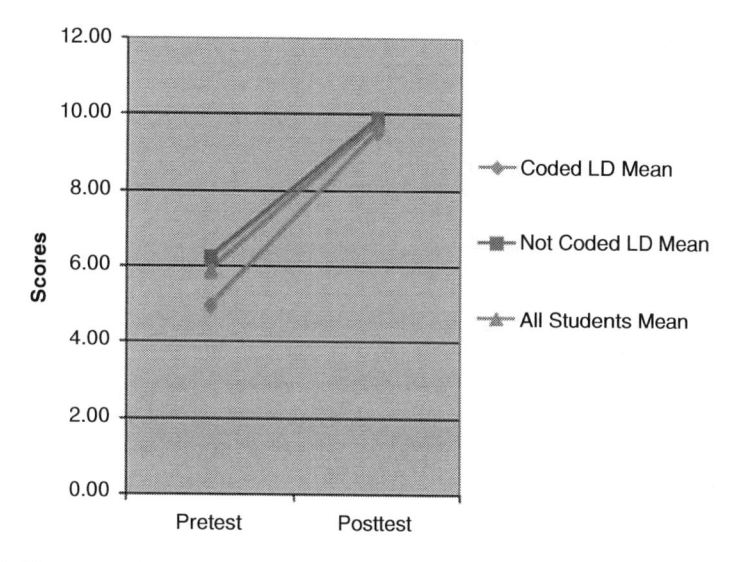

Fig. 6.5 Mean scores for pre-test – post-test for overall performance

Table 6.12 Paired samples t-test for overall achievement

Paired-sample t-test	t	df	Sig. (2 tailed)	Mean difference
Coded LD	−10.67	6	0.00	−4.57
Not coded LD	−5.84	19	0.00	−3.65
All students	−8.13	26	0.00	−3.89

Table 6.12 indicates that the mean of overall scores is significantly different for Coded LD students, for Not Coded LD students and for all participating students. This represents a significant improvement in achievement for the Coded LD students and the Not Coded LD students. Overall, the class demonstrated significant improvement.

Commonsense worries about changing mathematics instruction to better meet the needs of special needs students were not realised. All students improved on all items. Mean scores for all tasks demonstrate statistically significant improvement for students identified with learning disabilities (coded LD students), for 'regular' students (not-coded LD students) and for the class as a whole. Thus, it is possible to raise both the ceiling and the floor of student achievement by incorporating UDL and assessment for learning principles and practices into the design of classroom mathematics curricula.

All students achieved a high level of mathematical proficiency as measured by these four PISA test items. This led the research team to conclude that designing mathematical learning for students as outlined in this study, leads to significantly increased student achievement.

6.4.2 All Students Demonstrated Gains in the Five Strands of Mathematical Proficiency

Analysis of the qualitative data reveals the developing mathematical proficiency of students in this Grade 7 classroom as evidenced in their ability to dialogue with each other, to explore concepts indepth, to think and reason, to test conjectures, and justify solutions.

When considering the power of UDL and assessment for learning principles and practices to change the dominant facts and procedures script of mathematics teaching, it is especially important to note that the instructional intervention involved five essential and connected elements: (1) mathematical content knowledge; (2) pedagogical content knowledge for mathematics; (3) UDL principles; (4) assessment for learning; and (5) an instructional design process that supports the effective integration of mathematics strands as identified in the Programme of Studies (Alberta Education, 2007).

6.4.3 All Students Can Engage with Difficult Mathematical Ideas When They Are Provided with Assessment for Learning

Assessment for learning places teachers and students in a design environment in which constant feedback informs the next teaching and learning steps. As Black (2004) indicates, there is a great deal of confusion about the kinds of assessment that build proficiency and improve achievement. In this study, students received dynamic feedback in a number of ways:

- From teachers, in response to their individual work;
- From teachers, in response to the emergent design of lessons and activities to address misconceptions;
- From peers as they worked and talked together; and
- From the learning environment, particularly in the case of the dynamic geometry software.

It is important to emphasise the difference between assessment for learning and more conventional forms of assessment through tests, quizzes and assignments is that the latter are designed solely for purposes of accountability, ranking of students, or certifying competence. The latter assessment practices are particularly damaging to students "with low attainments who are led to believe they lack 'ability' and are not able to learn" (Black, 2004, p. 1).

Learning goals remained the same for all students throughout the study. What changed was the instruction was designed to conform to the learner. The instructional design included multiple means of representation and encouraged multiple means of expression. When (1) the learning task was mathematically robust; (2) the representation of concepts was varied in pedagogically sound ways; and (3) students were given a range of opportunities to express their emerging understandings, then all students were able to engage deeply. They volunteered their attention to and interest in the learning task.

6.4.4 The Principles of UDL Permit Teachers to Break the Stranglehold of the Procedural Script for Teaching Mathematics

Creating more robust and interesting mathematical tasks, problems or inquiries is a necessary component of the design for accessible classrooms. However, it is not sufficient to provide more robust, complex problems intended to create mathematical proficiency (Shanker Institute, 2005; Stigler & Hiebert, 1999). The dominant North American script for teaching mathematics is so ingrained that teachers turn even the best problems into routine, procedural exercises.

Incorporating UDL principles into instructional design has the potential to change instruction at its root, disrupting the processes by which many students come to be labelled as unable to learn mathematics.

Members of the research team and teachers designed a number of representations to help the students describe, analyse and measure lines, shapes and solids. They wanted the students (1) to investigate the similarities and differences among shapes and objects, (2) to analyse the components of form, and (3) to recognise different representations of shapes in ways that made sense and created connections.

One of the activities they designed involved using the tools that were important and available to the ancient Greeks. They had the students construct line segments, construct circles using the length of the line segments, and identify diameters and radii using only a compass and straight edge. For some students this was exactly the representation that they needed to make sense of the concepts related to circles. In fact, these students went far beyond the demands of the activity.

While intrigued with the exercise, some of the students didn't make the necessary conceptual connections. In fact, many students, particularly, but not exclusively, the students with identified learning disabilities, found working with a compass and straight edge quite frustrating. These students didn't have the manual dexterity needed to work with a compass. For other students, the compasses posed a significant problem because the school-issue tools lacked screws that would hold the pencils securely.

As researchers and teachers had anticipated that this might happen, we had prepared a similar activity using a dynamic geometry application called Geometers Sketchpad™. First, we knew we would likely need to accommodate learning difficulties. Geometers Sketchpad™ is, in this sense, a powerful assistive technology (AT) for special needs students who lack either the manual dexterity or the patience to create precise and accurate constructions. And in other contexts, we have seen teachers give some students access to Sketchpad as an enrichment activity to engage them while the rest of the class caught up.

But the use of this application was more than adapting to learning differences (or even to the poor quality of compasses provided for students). It introduced opportunities for students to explore different representations and to make connections between them. And this is a key element of mathematical proficiency:

> A significant indicator of conceptual understanding is being able to represent mathematical situations in different ways and knowing how different representations can be useful for different purposes. To find one's way around the mathematical terrain, it is important to see how the various representations connect with each other, how they are similar, and how they are different. The degree of students' conceptual understanding is related to the richness and extent of the connections they have made. (Kilpatrick, Swafford, & Findell, 2001, p. 119)

We also provided the students with the option of using MathsNet (http://www.mathsnet.net/campus/construction/circleonly.html) or Virtual Manipulatives (http://nlvm.usu.edu/en/nav/frames_asid_282_g_3_t_3.html) to work through the various activities.

It is important to keep in mind here that the concepts were not, themselves, changing or being in any sense "dumbed down" in this variety of representation. That is, the learning goals remained constant for all students. Rather, by representing these concepts in different ways, students were given opportunities to use different solution methods, and thus to develop multiple, flexible expressions. The variations in their approaches, solutions and ideas would provide an opportunity for the class to discuss the similarities and differences of the representations and expressions, the advantages of each, and how they must be connected if they yield the same answers.

The teachers and I taught alongside the students as they worked through their various problems. In this way we were able to:

- address misconceptions as they arose;
- provide specific, dynamic feedback to guide the students' learning;
- provide a different representation should they be having unproductive difficulty with the one they were using;
- make connections between the representation they were currently using and one they had used before or one that the team next to them was using;
- engage students in dialogue to advance their ability to reason mathematically;
- discern what needed to be brought forward to the entire class for discussion; and
- determine our next day's teaching activities.

An unexpected outcome of building in such flexibility was that students were initially uncomfortable working with the different representations. As they looked across the classroom, they saw some students using geoboards; others using the virtual manipulatives online site; others using compass, protractor and straight edge; and still others using Geometers Sketchpad™.

Welcoming multiple expressions yields insight into individuals' number sense, not just their procedural fluency. And it provides the opportunity for discussion and debate about the underlying concepts represented by each of the different methods.

6.4.4.1 That Is How Understanding Is Built

Increasingly, students need to develop sophisticated and multiple ways to express solutions to problems. When one solution is a barrier to knowledge building, whether through an individual's disability or through the inadequacy of the medium to meet the complexity and richness of the idea under construction, then students need to know that they can find more effective ways to build mathematical proficiency.

6.4.4.2 It Was Not Initially Easy for the Students to Live This Tension

During the second week, the students started to realise that we actually wanted to hear how they were making sense of the mathematical ideas. Questions such as *"Tell us how you solved that problem?"* was not a criticism. Instead, it was a question that would be taken up with all seriousness for the benefit of all.

In working with technology-rich, multiple and varied representations and expressions, we wanted students to recognise that a mathematical community is one in which differences are valued because of the opportunities they provide for explanation, justification, debate and exploration. Being good at math had come to include care and respect for others: listening, hearing, seeing; collaborating, building on, and challenging each other's ideas.

Being good at math was starting to mean far more, now, than finding the right answer quickly and in the way that everyone else found it, too.

Students who were engaged have volunteered to give their attention and interest to the learning task (Rose & Meyer, 2002). The teachers and I were interested in looking at the extent to which students became engaged and volunteered to give their attention and interest to geometry.

Too often, students with learning difficulties collapse under the strain of the unexpected. For them, ambiguity is a threat, not a charm. What is needed is what Kaplan and Kaplan, (2007) call "attention without tension":

> walking through an inviting landscape, taking in its foggy valleys and cloudy peaks, pausing for views that seem to unify and views where everything falls or rises away. Like good explorers, we're willing to put up with a bit of uncertainty in our situation for the adventure of it all. (p. 48)

Student interest and engagement increased in precisely these ways throughout the study.

6.4.5 Access to Technology Is a Critical Factor in an Accessible Mathematics Classroom

Currently the use of technology in UDL emphasises the role of assistive technologies that permit students with identified needs to adapt to the pervasively print environment of most classrooms. AT has a definite role to play in creating more accessible learning opportunities for all students. However, AT alone may leave untouched the procedural script for teaching mathematics if it leaves assumptions about the effective development of mathematical proficiency unchallenged. We can easily imagine classrooms in which, for example, technology is introduced so that weaker students can in some sense keep up with the demands of fast-right-answer-giving, or where modifications that "dumb down" or fragment experiences are provided in the name of assistance.

What this study demonstrates is the inherent nature of digital environments such as Geometer's Sketchpad™ and IO to represent and express mathematical concepts in dynamic ways. Introducing UDL and assessment for learning into the mathematics classroom is a disruptive innovation.

6.4.6 Introducing UDL and Assessment for Learning into the Mathematics Classroom Is a Disruptive Innovation

While the goal of creating increasingly accessible classrooms seems incontrovertible, actually creating the changes that make a difference for students disrupts the status quo. Members of the research team and teachers had not anticipated the extent to which the increased proficiency of students with identified learning disabilities disrupted the social hierarchies of the classroom. Students who considered themselves (or were considered by others) to be better at math were initially very uncomfortable with the emerging confidence and ability of students they thought were less able.

During our class discussions, particularly towards the end of the second week, something quite unexpected surfaced. As we anticipated, it was becoming increasingly difficult to identify the eleven students who were identified as having learning disabilities. They accessed the same learning curriculum, were given the choice and support to express their learning using methods of their choice and they were not isolated from their peers.

Many of the questions during the open discussion times came from the students with learning disabilities. Concepts such as Pi, circumference, area and perimeter intrigued them. They questioned with confidence, added their thoughts to the general discussions, and became active participants in their own learning. That is, students who typically had difficulty understanding mathematics, those for whom mathematics typically didn't make much sense, started to speak up.

What we did not anticipate was the extent to which their increasing proficiency temporarily bothered some of the students who saw themselves, or were seen by others as being good at math. They protested: "Hey, how do you know that?" "You don't get math." Then in quiet, hushed conversations, out of what they thought were the ears of the teachers and I, their complaints grew.

It wasn't fair that the "coded kids" were getting math. Fortunately, this attitude changed, with some quick interventions by the research and teaching team, as they realised that learning in this way was not a competition. Too often, when marks are used as a sorting device, achievement becomes a zero sum game: the advance of some is gained at the expense of others. As students' engagement increased, they lost this fear.

Initially, the academic order of the classroom was disrupted, a social order created by conventional educational structures and processes and their organising principles and assumptions. It is beyond the scope of this chapter to determine whether the reactions of these students would be in any way typical of other classrooms when those who "everyone knows" are left behind suddenly emerge as equally able and engaged. For now, however, we are comfortable to note two things. First, "equality is – and must continue to be – a key goal of any public education system"; however, "we need new ways of thinking about equality, ways that do not involve sameness, or one-size-fits-all approaches" (Gilbert, 2005, p. 102). And it would appear that one of those new ways of thinking may involve re-interpreting the unintended consequences of meeting individual needs by identifying some students as inherently less able than others when, in fact, their perceived disabilities are to some extent artefacts of our own structures and pedagogies. UDL and assessment for learning have the potential and the possibility of being one of these new ways.

Second, it may be important to examine the history of mathematics as a gatekeeper subject that has traditionally been used to separate the academically able sheep from the less talented goats. Some members of the community of mathematics educators and researchers (Kaplan & Kaplan, 2007; Mighton, 2007; Swain & Swan, 2007) have been working to expose what they call the myth of mathematical talent as the primary way to explain why some students "get" math and others do not.

Our study demonstrates that in a short time, even in a classroom with a disproportionately large number of students with learning disabilities, it is possible to raise both ceiling and floor simultaneously.

Disruptions of the kind just discussed point, perhaps, to the tenacity of conventional teaching scripts. When teachers and students experience initial discomfort at the introduction of innovation, it is tempting to retreat to familiar ground.

It is easy to pen the words that describe access for all to high levels of mathematical proficiency. It will be more challenging to live with the inevitable pressures that such a goal will place on taken-for-granted, everyday structures and experiences.

Choosing to do so becomes, then, a matter of policy. How badly do we want equality for all students, and are we prepared to weather what may be inevitable storms from the highest levels right down to the playground?

6.4.7 Creating Accessible Mathematics Classrooms Consistent with UDL and Assessment for Learning Principles and Practices Requires Increased Teacher Knowledge and Support for On-Going Professional Development

Changing teaching practices and school, jurisdiction and classroom structures will require significant investment in professional development.

Progress will require the active engagement of mathematicians and math educators to design pedagogical content knowledge that is mathematically sound. More math courses of the procedural sort will not get teachers out of their current dilemma.

While most need more mathematics, it is mathematics of a particular sort: the kind that permits them to design instruction that gives students access to complex ideas.

6.5 Recommendations

The primary recommendation forwarded from this study highlights the need to establish a network of teachers who are dedicated to creating universal design for learning mathematics classrooms which effectively embed assessment for learning practices.

Conventionally, new curricula are developed by some and delivered by others. In the US we have seen the failure of this approach, even to the creation and dissemination of mathematically robust problems. This recommendation suggests that the development of a mathematics curriculum based on UDL will require design research in which teachers are involved from the outset in multiple ways: in dialogue with mathematicians and math educators; in working through robust problems to increase their own mathematical understandings; to dialogue as they work in their classrooms; and to make their practice public so that others in the network can build their own mathematical and pedagogical proficiency. In essence, we are suggesting a new approach to developing curriculum by prototyping the innovation as it is being created.

In this report, we have suggested the potential pitfalls of attaching UDL principles to tenacious procedural scripts for the teaching of mathematics. It is easy to read about such principles and quickly assume that one knows how to teach with them. We anticipate, for example, educators who will dismiss their power by saying, "They are just good practice. There's nothing really new in all this."

If that happens, then the province will suffer a rash of "multiples" stuck on to existing resources and procedures. We do not underestimate the danger of this, nor the care with which one must proceed to develop innovations that will actually take hold effectively.

The support and active involvement of teachers willing to do what Mrs Jamieson did – to try unfamiliar approaches over an extended period of time – will be key to the innovation's success.

Alberta has the technological broadband infrastructure through SuperNet to permit teachers to connect in both synchronous and asynchronous ways. The community of practice does not need to be geographically limited. In fact, in terms of addressing issues of diversity, the capacity to have teachers from across the globe working on the same issues is essential.

6.5.1 *Implications for Principals*

- Develop the student-centred leadership practices to direct work at the school level. Few principals will have taught in these ways, and it cannot be assumed that they will know how to effectively establish goals and expectations; ensure

quality teaching that focuses on UDL principles and embeds assessment for learning; and lead teacher learning and development. It would do a disservice to principals and to teachers to establish a myth that UDL principles are just like all the other good things they have always done. Leaders must understand and be able to act on the dimensions that make a difference to student learning and achievement (Robinson, 2011).
- Disruptions to the status quo are bound to occur. Of necessity, for example,
  - the need for new timetables may emerge.
  - understanding the dynamics of anticipated and unanticipated resistance that puts pressure on teachers to revert to conventional practices.

6.5.2 *Implications for Teachers*

- Active participation in a teacher-researcher network will take time for participating teachers. It is unreasonable to ask people to do pioneering work without providing additional time and resources they find meaningful.
- Participants will be asked to demonstrate willingness to:
  - increase their own mathematical proficiency
  - learn the principles of UDL and understand their application to mathematics in particular
  - learn the five strategies that form the basis of effective classroom assessment
  - use technology both to represent concepts to students and to permit students to express knowledge in multiple ways
  - collaborate with others in ways that build new knowledge and "next practice"
  - make their practice increasingly visible and public by sharing video clips; student responses to the work; struggles and successes in developing next practices, etc.

6.6 Conclusion

Robust discipline-based inquiry affords the teacher, students, and leaders with the opportunity to investigate genuine questions of mathematics. Powerful learning and increased student achievement results when: (i) the inquiry design reflects disciplinary ways of knowing, doing and being, (ii) the principles and practices of universal design for learning (UDL) are used to guide the instructional design, and (iii) assessment for learning is used to make teaching and learning visible thereby guiding the day-to-day teaching and learning decisions. Student-centred leadership focused on the five dimensions of leadership ensures that leadership practices are focused on improving learning and achievement for all students.

References

Adams, R., & Wu, M. (Eds.). (2002). *PISA 2000 technical report*. Paris, France: Organisation for Economic Co-operation and Development (OECD). Retrieved from: http://www.pisa.oecd.org/dataoecd/53/19/33688233.pdf

Alberta Education. (2007). *Mathematics kindergarten to grade 9 program of studies*. Alberta Education. Retrieved from: http://education.alberta.ca/media/645594/kto9math.pdf

Assessment Reform Group. (1999). *Assessment for learning: Beyond the black box*. Cambridge, UK: Cambridge School of Education. Retrieved from: http://k1.ioe.ac.uk/tlrp/arg/AssessInsides.pdf

Bausch, M., & Hasselbring, T. (2005). Using AT: Is it working? *Threshold, 2*(1), 7–9.

Bereiter, C. (2002). Design research for sustained innovation. *Cognitive Studies: Bulletin of the Japanese Cognitive Science Society, 9*(3), 321–327.

Black, P. (2004). *The nature and value of formative assessment for learning. Assessment for Learning Group*. Retrieved from: http://www.kcl.ac.uk/content/1/c4/73/57/formative.pdf

Black, P., Harrison, C., Lee, C., Marshall, B., & Wiliam, D. (2002). *Working inside the black box: Assessment for learning in the classroom*. London, UK: King's College London School of Education.

Black, P., & Wiliam, D. (1998). Assessment and classroom learning. *Assessment in Education, 5*(1), 7–71.

Bransford, J., Brown, A., & Cocking, R. (Eds.). (2000). *How people learn: Brain, mind, experience and school*. Washington, DC: National Academies Press.

Carver, S. (2006). Assessing for deep understanding. In K. Sawyer (Ed.), *The Cambridge handbook of the learning sciences* (pp. 205–224). New York, NY: Cambridge University Press.

CAST. (2013). Retrieved from: http://www.cast.org

Chappuis, S., & Stiggins, R. (2002). Classroom assessment for learning. *Educational Leadership, 60*(1), 30–43.

Clifford, P., & Marinucci, S. (2008). Testing the waters: Three elements of classroom inquiry. *Harvard Educational Review, 78*(4), 675–688.

Darling-Hammond, L. (2008). *Powerful learning: What we know about teaching for understanding*. San Francisco, CA: Jossey-Bass.

Davies, A. (2002–2003). *Finding proof of learning in a one-to-one computing classroom*. Courtenay, BC, Canada: Connections Publishing.

Design-Based Research Collective. (2003). Design-based research: An emerging paradigm for educational inquiry. *Educational Researcher, 32*(1), 5–8.

Dolan, R. P., & Hall, T. E. (2001). Universal design for learning: Implications for large-scale assessment. *IDA Perspectives, 27*(4), 22–25.

Donovan, M. S., & Bransford, J. (2005). Pulling threads. In M. S. Donovan & J. Bransford (Eds.), *How students learn: Mathematics in the classroom* (pp. 569–590). Washington, DC: National Academies Press.

Edyburn, D. (2006). Failure is not an option: Collecting, reviewing, and acting on evidence for using technology to enhance academic performance. *Learning and Leading with Technology, 34*(1), 20–23.

Firchow, N. (2002). *Universal design for learning: Improved access for all*. Retrieved from: SchwabLearning.org http://www.schwablearning.org/articles.aspx?r=490

Friesen, S. (2006). *Inside an accessible classroom*. Unpublished manuscript.

Friesen, S. (2009). *Teaching effectiveness: A framework and rubric*. Toronto, ON, Canada: Canadian Education Association. Retrieved from: http://www.cea-ace.ca/sites/cea-ace.ca/files/cea-2009-wdydist-teaching.pdf

Fuson, K., Kalchman, M., & Bransford, J. (2005). Mathematical understanding: An introduction. In M. S. Donovan & J. Bransford (Eds.), *How students learn: Mathematics in the classroom* (pp. 217–256). Washington, DC: National Academies Press.

Galileo Educational Network. (2013). *Discipline-based inquiry rubric*. Retrieved from: http://www.galileo.org/research/publications/rubric.pdf

Gay, L., Mills, G., & Airasian, P. (2006). *Educational research: Competencies for analysis and applications* (8th ed.). New Jersey, NY: Pearson.

Gilbert, J. (2005). *Catching the knowledge wave? The knowledge society and the future of education.* Wellington, New Zealand: NZCER Press.

Hattie, J. (2009). *Visible learning: A synthesis of over 800 meta analyses.* New York, NY: Routledge Press.

Hattie, J. (2012). *Visible learning for teachers: Maximizing impact on learning.* New York, NY: Routledge Press.

Jardine, D., Clifford, P., & Friesen, S. (2002). *Back to the basics of teaching and learning.* Mahwah, NJ: Lawrence Erlbaum and Associates.

Jardine, D., Clifford, P., & Friesen, S. (2008). *Back to the basics of teaching and learning* (2nd ed.). New York, NY: Routledge Press.

Kaplan, R., & Kaplan, E. (2007). *Out of the labyrinth: Setting mathematics free.* New York, NY: Oxford University Press.

Kelly, A., Lesh, R., & Baek, J. (Eds.). (2008). *Handbook of design research methods in education.* New York, NY: Routledge.

Kilpatrick, J., Swafford, J., & Findell, B. (Eds.). (2001). *Adding it up: Helping children learn mathematics.* Washington, DC: National Academy Press.

Leininger, M. M. (1985). Ethnography and ethnonursing: Models and modes of qualitative data analysis. In M. M. Leininger (Ed.), *Qualitative research methods in nursing* (pp. 33–72). Orlando, FL: Grune & Stratton.

Meo, G. (2005). Curriculum access for all: Universal design for learning. *Harvard Education Letter, 21*(5). Retrieved from: http://www.edletter.org/past/issues/2005-nd/meo.shtml

Mighton, J. (2003). *The myth of ability: Nurturing mathematical talent in every child.* Toronto, ON, Canada: House of Anansi Press.

Mighton, J. (2007). *The end of ignorance: Multiplying our human potential.* Toronto, ON, Canada: Knopf Canada.

Newmann, F., Bryk, A., & Nagaoka, J. (2001). *Authentic intellectual work and standardized tests: Conflict or coexistence?* Chicago, IL: Consortium on Chicago School Research. Retrieved from: http://ccsr.uchicago.edu/sites/default/files/publications/p0a02.pdf

Organisation for Economic Cooperation and Development (OECD). (2000). *Programme for international student assessment: Sample tasks from the PISA 2000 assessment: Reading, mathematical and scientific literacy.* OECD Publishing.

Organisation for Economic Cooperation and Development (OECD). (2005). *Formative assessment: Improving learning in secondary classrooms. Policy brief.* OECD Publishing. Retrieved from: http://www.oecd.org/edu/ceri/35661078.pdf

Research Points. (2006). Do the math: Cognitive demand makes a difference. *Research Points, 4*(2). AERA.

Ritchhart, R., Church, M., & Morrison, K. (2011). *Making thinking visible: How to promote engagement, understanding, and independence for all learners.* San Francisco, CA: Wiley.

Robinson, V. (2011). *Student-centered leadership.* San Francisco, CA: Wiley.

Rose, D., & Meyer, A. (2002). *Teaching every student in the digital age: Universal design for learning.* ASCD. Retrieved from: http://www.cast.org/teachingeverystudent/ideas/tes/

Rose, D., Meyer, A., & Hitchcock, C. (Eds.). (2005). *The universally designed classroom: Accessible curriculum and digital technologies.* Cambridge, MA: Harvard University Press.

Rose, D. H., & Meyer, A. (2006). *A practical reader in universal design for learning.* Cambridge, MA: Harvard Education Press.

Rothberg, M., & Treviranus, J. (2006). Accessible e-learning demonstrations using IMS accessibility specifications. In *ATIA National Conference*, Orlando, FL. Retrieved from: http://ncdae.org/activities/atia06/presentations.cfm

Sawyer, K. (2006). *The Cambridge handbook of the learning sciences.* New York, NY: Cambridge University Press.

Scardamalia, M. (2001). Getting real about 21st century education. *The Journal of Educational Change, 2,* 171–176. Retrieved from: http://ikit.org/fulltext/2001getting_real.pdf

Shanker Institute. (2005, May 5). *From best research to what works: Improving the teaching and learning of mathematics: A forum.* Washington, DC.

Stiggins, R., Arter, J., Chappuis, J., & Chappius, S. (2004). *Classroom assessment for student achievement: Doing it right – Using it well.* Portland, OR: Assessment Training Institute.

Stigler, J., & Hiebert, J. (1999). *The teaching gap: Best ideas from the world's teachers for improving education in the classroom.* New York, NY: The Free Press.

Swain, J., & Swan, M. (2007). *Thinking through mathematics: Research report.* NRDC. Retrieved from: http://www.maths4life.org/uploads/documents/doc_296.pdf

The Alberta Teachers' Association (ATA). (2003). *Trying to teaching, trying to learn: Listening to students.* Edmonton, AB, Canada: The Alberta Teachers Association.

Wiliam, D. (2011). *Embedded formative assessment.* Bloomington, IN: Solution Tree Press.

Chapter 7
Supporting Optimal Student Assessment Practices in Science as a Core Subject Area

Ann Sherman and Leo MacDonald

Abstract This chapter discusses assessment in inquiry-based science classrooms. Three classroom scenarios are examined for ways that they support assessment for learning. Implications are provided for teachers and school leaders to consider when seeking to implement effective assessment approaches in science classrooms. We suggest that school leaders can enable assessment for learning by having focused conversations with teachers about their science lessons. Teachers, who are encouraged to create learning environments where students take ownership and control of their learning, open up their classrooms in ways that allow them to engage in meaningful conversations and observations with their students. Classroom teachers will then be better able to carry out the kinds of assessment that provide the most powerful feedback for students and help them develop accurate interpretations of their students' science learning. We argue that teaching science through an inquiry-based approach offers substantial opportunity for enacting assessment for learning strategies.

Keywords Science assessment • Formative • Assessment for learning • Preservice • Motivation and assessment • Performance assessment • Assessment of conversation • Self-assessment • Peer assessment • Success • Leadership

7.1 Introduction

With the current trends and changes in instructional approaches and practices, including more individualised approaches, differentiated instruction, and inclusionary practices, have come changes in thinking about how we create and use assessment strategies and techniques in our classrooms (Black & Wiliam, 1998a; Darling-Hammond,

---

A. Sherman (✉)
Faculty of Education, University of New Brunswick,
3 Bailey Drive, Fredericton, NB, Canada E3B 5A3
e-mail: shermana@unb.ca

L. MacDonald
Faculty of Education, St. Francis Xavier University,
PO Box 5000, Antigonish, NS, Canada B2G 2W5
e-mail: lxmacdon@stfx.ca

© Springer International Publishing Switzerland 2016
S. Scott et al (eds.), *Leadership of Assessment, Inclusion, and Learning*,
The Enabling Power of Assessment 3, DOI 10.1007/978-3-319-23347-5_7

1997, 2004; Davies, 2011; Tomlinson, 1999). Although there remains a great deal of pressure to use standardised tests and concern is often focused on meeting international standards, there exists a growing movement that is focusing on formative assessment at the classroom level (Black, Harrison, Lee, Marshall, & Wiliam, 2003; Harrison, 2005; Lee & Wiliam, 2005) and strategies that help students grow and learn from these experiences. For instance, ministries of education from a variety of countries such as Canada, Great Britain, New Zealand, and the United States provide web-based resources for inservice and preservice teachers focused on classroom-based assessment that supports learning.

Instead of assessment OF learning, teachers are being encouraged to assess FOR learning (Chappuis & Stiggins, 2002; Chappuis, Stiggins, Arter, & Chappuis, 2004) and we understand more fully the idea that assessment involves learning and learning involves assessment (Shavelson et al., 2008; White & Gunstone, 1992) for all core subject areas. This has huge implications for the way teachers think about and approach both instruction and assessment with their students. It also has implications for principals in schools supervising teachers, teacher preparation programs, inservice teacher professional development programs, and the work of the various ministries of education who create the curriculum and make recommendations about how to teach and assess it.

Why should we think about new approaches to assessment? There are many things to consider. Approaches to instruction and formative assessment can contribute to viewing learning as a process of constructing knowledge and as such, both need to have personal coherence and relevance for the students. In the past, some approaches to assessment have left students with a distinct disconnect between what they learned and how it can be applied (Saliu, 2005). Approaches to assessment have sometimes been very different to the instructional approaches used with the same material, often leaving students confused and unclear as to what is expected. In an effort to help students better connect what is learned within the classroom with what they need to know outside the classroom, instructional strategies and assessment strategies are being developed that focus on connection and coherence (Brookhart, 2013; Duran, Duran, Haney, & Scheuermann, 2011; Keely, Eherle, & Farrin, 2005; Leahy, Lyon, Thompson, & Wiliam, 2005; Zembal-Saul, 2012). At the same time, these approaches to assessment enable students to self-assess more often and gain stronger feedback from teachers about ways to improve their achievement (Hattie & Timperley, 2007). As a result, assessment for learning can contribute to student motivation and confidence as students experience progress and achievement with increased relevance (Butler, 1988). This is a key element to consider when using assessment for learning in a way that is supportive of increased student success.

Approaches to assessment that focus on learning can be used to increase both teacher and student awareness of knowledge, skills, and beliefs that students brings to a task, thus allowing all involved to become better able to use that knowledge to construct new understandings (Black & Wiliam, 1998b). Strategies that focus on assessment for learning can help students learn more about their own level of understanding while helping the teacher understand student understanding in general.

Knowledge gained through continuous and formative assessment can be the starting point of new instruction and can help teachers lead students to greater understandings in their core subject areas.

When thinking about subject specific assessment, we need to think about several questions related to the learning of that particular subject. Questions about subject specific assessment include: (1) What approach to assessment will generate effective learning of the subject area I teach?; (2) What specific content knowledge or pedagogical content knowledge do I have as a teacher and what more do I need?; and (3) How do I plan my instruction so that my students and I can develop a shared understanding of what the learning goal is and how feedback can be used to help achieve that goal? In this chapter, we will focus specifically on assessment practices in science as a core subject area.

7.2 Conceptual Framework

As we consider assessment in a science classroom, we bear in mind several core understandings about teaching and assessment for learning. In the following section we identify key beliefs and concepts that we believe are essential in thinking about assessment in science classrooms. They will be further elaborated on and discussed in depth in the rest of the chapter.

7.2.1 Assessment for Learning

Assessment for learning shifts assessment from a process of monitoring student's learning to a process that is designed to enhance their learning. Assessment for learning involves teachers in helping their students develop a clear goal for their learning by sharing learning targets that are written in student-friendly language and are accompanied by exemplars of quality student work. In the classroom episodes that follow, students are engaged in learning activities that provide them with manageable amounts of descriptive feedback from the teacher, their peers, and themselves on a continuous basis over time. The students' role is to use the feedback gathered from each assessment to measure where their achievement lies in relation to their goal and plot a course on how to close the gap the next time. As students become increasingly proficient, they learn to generate their own descriptive feedback and set their own goals (Stiggins, 2007, p. 23).

With the international obsession with standardised testing, Stiggins (2002) suggests we are failing our students by not focusing on ways to ensure that our approaches to assessment are improving student learning. He describes a crisis in schools where little assessment for learning exists. Instead, he suggests, teachers have focused on the assessment OF learning, with end of unit tests and projects. Term tests and end of year projects do little to encourage students to want to learn and feel able to learn. Perhaps the strongest argument in favour of an assessment for learning approach is that it has a significant positive impact on student achievement (Black & Wiliam, 1998b; Wiliam, Lee, Harrison, & Black, 2004). Hutchinson (2008) reports on the status of assessment for learning approaches across several countries including Australia, Canada, Finland, Ireland, Scotland, and the United States. While the assessment approaches in each context are different, there are some similarities. For instance, Canada and Finland each have systems in place to provide early support for students as soon as teachers' assessments show they are having difficulty learning. In addition, Canada, Finland, Ireland, and Scotland have placed emphasis on professional development for teachers that is focused on assessment for learning. Finally, countries such as Australia, Canada, and Scotland have emphasised the importance of students engaging in self-assessment and self-maintenance of their own learning (Hutchinson, 2008, pp. 45–47).

7.2.2 Link Between Instructional and Assessment Strategies

Activities created as good instructional or pedagogical activities are also good assessment activities (White & Gunstone, 1992), providing the opportunities for students to learn from the assessments in ways that support their interest and desire to learn more. Assessment approaches that do this will help students begin to understand how they learn, potentially enabling them to improve their learning and understanding about the subject area content and processes. "In a classroom that uses assessment to support learning, the divide between instruction and assessment blurs" (Leahy et al., 2005, p. 22).

7.2.3 Link Between Leadership and Assessment

School leadership can play an important role in the improvement of assessment strategies (Absolum, Flockton, Hattie, Hipkins, & Reid, 2009; Robinson, Hohepa, & Lloyd, 2009). Absolum et al. (2009) argue that school leadership plays a central role in the development of teachers' assessment capabilities and recommend that both teachers and leaders should participate in professional development aimed to develop their understanding of assessment strategies. Robinson et al. (2009, pp. 106–140) present six dimensions of leadership that are important in developing effective teaching: (1) setting clear educational goals; (2) obtaining and allocating resources aligned to pedagogic goals; (3) creating educationally powerful connections; (4) creating a community that learns how to improve student success; (5) engaging in constructive problem talk; and (6) selecting, developing and using smart tools. In addition, Robinson et al. (pp. 94–96) have shown that school leadership can have a positive impact on student learning. Each of these dimensions can lead to improvements when they are adopted individually, but they become most powerful when implemented collectively. Other research has demonstrated a range of impact of school leadership on student learning, from a small but important impact (Hallinger & Heck, 1998) to a substantial impact (Marzano, Waters, & McNulty, 2005). Robinson et al. present a synthesis of 27 international studies across nine countries. A common thread in all of these studies is that leadership has the greatest impact on teaching and learning when it is pedagogical in nature i.e., focused on improving classroom pedagogy, rather than transformational i.e., focused on establishing leader-follower relationships.

7.2.4 Content Knowledge and Pedagogical Content Knowledge

When thinking about science instruction and assessment, there is a need for teachers to have content knowledge and pedagogical content knowledge. Our own research (MacDonald & Sherman, 2001, 2006, 2007; Sherman & MacDonald, 2008, 2009) in the area of elementary science has shown this to be particularly significant. Many elementary teachers and principals have little content knowledge or pedagogical content knowledge in the area of science. Many enter their BEd without a science degree and have only the required number of science courses when entering their Bachelor of Education programs (which in the case of some universities is none) (MacDonald & Sherman, 2007). Elementary principals suggest that with the current instructional leadership expectations they are often left asking themselves: "How do I support subject areas where I lack knowledge?" (Sherman & MacDonald, 2008).

Teachers express concern about their own lack of confidence and content knowledge when approaching science in elementary schools. In our work with inservice teachers, we have found this to be the case (MacDonald & Sherman, 2001). In addition to having limited content knowledge in science, we also find many preservice teachers have a wariness about the teaching of science, believing they do not have the content knowledge needed to teach even lower elementary grades (MacDonald & Sherman, 2007). Principals have also expressed concern about their ability to support teachers in the teaching and assessing of science when, as administrators, they have little or no content knowledge in the sciences (Sherman & MacDonald, 2008).

This lack of knowledge is also a concern in middle schools and high schools, where teachers are being asked to teach outside of their science expertise. Childs and McNicholl (2007) highlighted the challenges secondary science teachers faced to their pedagogical practice when teaching unfamiliar areas of the science curriculum or being asked to teach outside of their subject specialisation. Studies link student achievement in science with teacher preparation in science (Clymer & Wiliam, 2007). Wenglinsky and Silverstien (2007) suggest that classroom science teachers should focus on developing skills in the following content or pedagogical content areas: (1) laboratory skills; (2) hands-on approaches to learning science; (3) integrating instructional technology into science classes; and (4) the use of frequent formative assessment. While many preservice and inservice programs do include many of these issues, challenges still exist in classrooms where constraints create challenges that include finding and maintaining resources and large class sizes. In a core subject area like science, both these concerns are emphasised when teachers are trying to include a variety of hands-on, experiential activities with their students; as a result, the lack of science content knowledge and science pedagogical content knowledge in schools has instructional and assessment implications for both teachers and school leaders.

7.2.5 Formative Assessment and Uncovering Student Thinking

Formative assessment is directly connected to the idea of ongoing and continuous assessment. It requires a teacher to provide many opportunities to engage in learning activities where they generate artefacts of their learning, e.g., things they say or do, things they create, that can be interpreted by the teacher (Shavelson et al., 1992). Formative assessment involves a teacher interpreting this evidence of learning and comparing it to their goals of what they would like their students to know and be able to do, and then making decisions about how to proceed next in a teaching and learning sequence. For instance, a teacher may provide students with suggestions on how they could improve their performance in a just completed task and engage them with a new learning activity as a result of the interpretation of the thinking that was displayed in the completed task.

Keely et al. (2005) discuss the value of formative assessment in uncovering student thinking. Formative assessment has a flexibility that can allow a teacher to probe students' thinking in ways that can uncover misconceptions and incomplete ideas. Formative assessment based on evidence gathered from classroom activities such as discussions, journals, and science notebooks can be used to trace back to where a gap may have occurred in the student's opportunity to learn. This is essential in science where a misconception can result in future problems for students' understanding of increasingly complex material.

Formative assessments can arise out of instructional strategies that allow students to create representations of thinking, which also enable a greater uncovering of student thinking. It can also open space for students to talk about what they think and this is a foundational piece of assessing student thinking.

7.2.6 Use of Inquiry-Based Approaches

Teaching science as an inquiry process stresses active student learning and the importance of deep understanding. The strategies used in an inquiry approach classroom focus on empowering students to construct their own understanding through investigations, often extended over a period of time, in order to arrive at explanations which help them understand fundamental science concepts within many relevant contexts that relate to students' lives (Collette & Chiappetta, 1994).

However, scientific inquiry goes beyond constructing knowledge through hands-on activities. Much of the inquiry that scientists and engineers engage in involves reading and communicating with others. In the same way, science teachers must create conditions where students can also engage in researching literature and communicating about their thinking and learning (Chiappetta, 1997).

The following classroom example shows an inquiry-based approach in a Grade 8 classroom.

7.2.6.1 Tim and Mark's CO_2 Powered Car

Tim and Mark's idea was to build a rocket-powered car. Tim wanted to make something that could go fast and carry a load. Mark wanted to do something original. The fact that they were the only students who planned to use rocket power was important to them. Ms B., their teacher, liked their idea but was concerned about the safety of using solid rocket fuel. She asked the boys to think of some other ways they could power their car and suggested that they talk to Mr T. (the industrial arts teacher). Mr T. suggested a safe alternative. He told the boys that he knew of CO_2 powered cars that could go just as fast as most solid fuel devices. That was good enough for Tim and Mark and they began thinking about how to build a rocket-powered car using CO_2 cartridges.

The materials for building the car were provided by Mark. He had a collection of plastic building blocks known as "Constructs" at home that he brought to school. Tim, who already had some expertise with using hobby rocket engines, provided several CO_2 cartridges.

The building began immediately. Attaching a CO_2 cartridge onto the plastic chassis became the most pressing problem. At first they tried taping it to the outside of the car. When they tested this design they found that it was difficult to keep the CO_2 cartridge securely fastened to their car because a wet condensation formed on the cylinder as it discharged its gas. They decided to embed the cylinder inside the plastic frame. A lot of time was spent making adjustments to accommodate this design change. They built and rebuilt their car several times as they attempted to improve their design. Three areas needed attention: (1) getting the car to travel in a straight line; (2) making the car go as fast as possible while carrying a load; and (3) incorporating a third simple machine into the design. Tim and Mark attempted to solve problems (1) and (3) together. They tried using a tightly stretched string looped through a pulley which was attached to their car as a guide to keep it moving along a line. While this attracted a lot of attention from the class, it did not work. Getting the car to travel in a straight line remained an unresolved problem.

Mark discovered how to incorporate a third machine. In a conversation with Ms B., he learned that an aerodynamic wing could be thought of as a kind of wedge. He adapted the "Constructs" to develop an air foil by covering the front section of the car with construction paper. He referred to it as a "wind wedge". Mark seemed pleased with this contribution and experimented with many slight modifications to its design. These explorations continued even after the car was demonstrated to the class (Fig. 7.1).

Meanwhile, Tim focused on solving the problem of increasing the car's speed and distance travelled. As he discharged several CO_2 canisters he discovered that the amount of thrust generated depended on the size of the hole made in the end of the cylinder. Tim made these holes with the end of a sharp pin. First, he tried using pins with different diameters before settling on one that seemed to work best. Second, he found that the size of the hole depended on how he hit the end of the CO_2 cylinder with the pin. He continued to explore ideas about how to improve this process even after the class demonstration.

When demonstrated to the class, the car did not perform as well as it had in earlier tests. The boys were only slightly disappointed by this result. Tim and Mark continued to talk about how they could extend this project further.

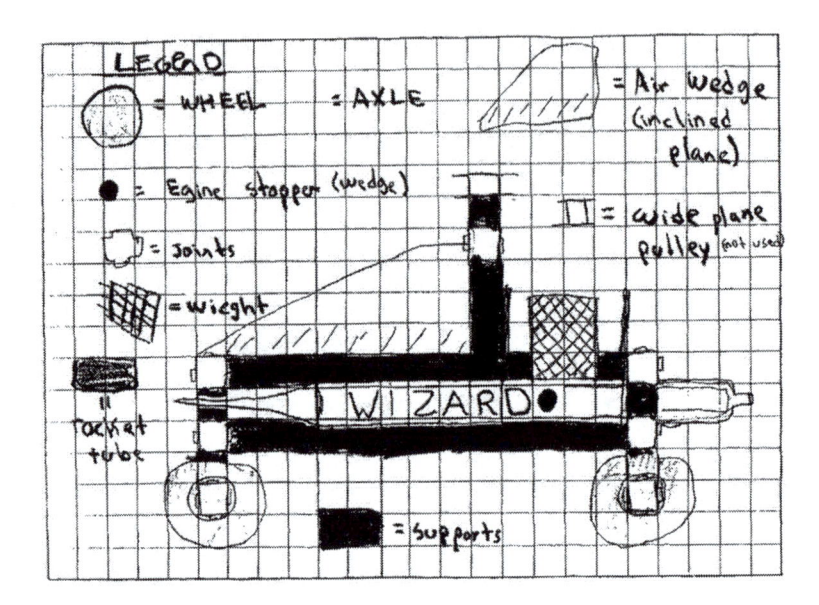

Fig. 7.1 Tim and Mark's depiction of their car design

This case demonstrates many elements of an inquiry approach. The students engaged in an extended investigation that included design and revision processes. They created models and ran trials with their cars, observing and recording their data to draw conclusions.

One of the students reflected, in his science journal, on the inquiry-based experience of building the car:

> We worked really hard in class. Like we never fooled around. I have this memorized now. I could make a drawing of this after not seeing it for a long time and I could get every joint or piece of plastic on this in the right place. I have such a good feeling for it because I know it and I also have developed knowledge of it, like how you work with CO_2 cartridges. I know why it didn't go well [in the class presentation] and I know why it did go well the first time [in an early test].

This example also illustrates how students can generate evidence of their learning in multiple forms. For instance, the students built a physical working model; they gave each other verbal feedback on the viability of the various designs that led up to the final model and they engaged in conversations with their teacher during the design process; they drew sketches of their models; they kept a written journal where they reflected on their thinking over time. Finally, the students gave a presentation to their peers and the teacher as a culmination to their work. All of these actions by the students allowed the teacher to gather multiple forms of evidence over the period of the project and enabled her to more accurately assess the quality of their thinking and learning. The model car the students built did not perform up to the expectations of the students in their culminating class presentation. If the teacher had based her evaluation on this final outcome, it would not have reflected the high quality of the thinking that led to the final design.

Nichol and Macfarlane-Dick (2006) describe feedback as being effective when it supports students' capacities to take control of their own learning, in that it builds their abilities to assess their own work and generate their own feedback. This teacher was able to provide effective feedback for these students through many brief conversations she had with them throughout this building project. Each conversation focused on where the students were in relation to their goal and what their next steps would be to make improvements in the design of their car. She was able to make a more informed and accurate judgment about the quality of their thinking because she had gathered many forms of evidence over the extended timeline of the project.

How does this example inform leadership in assessment? In this case, one of the authors participated in the classroom as a team-teacher and worked with students and the teacher in the classroom on a daily basis for the entire instructional sequence. The teacher viewed this project as an opportunity for her to explore new ways of learning with her students. A strong professional relationship developed that enabled productive conversations between one of the authors and the teacher about students' learning and the collection of many different kinds of evidence of student learning. Participating with a teacher in her classroom, even as an observer, and in focused talk about classroom events and student achievement can help enable powerful learning by the teacher about how assessment for learning can be enacted (Black & Wiliam, 2004; Gardner, Harlen, Hayward, & Stobart, 2008).

7.3 Review of the Literature

A variety of assessment issues and approaches are described across educational literature. Researchers are identifying differences in educational approaches to gathering student data, including tendencies to rely on daily impressions versus more systematically collected evidence, and on formative versus summative assessment (Gipps, 1999, cited in Gearhart et al., 2006). Formative assessment and assessment for learning, in particular, have become topics of much focus in educational literature and we use these terms to mean the same thing in this chapter.

7.3.1 Formative Assessment

Formative assessment is carried out with the explicit goal of re-shaping both the teaching and the learning that is happening in a classroom so that both can be improved in an ongoing way (Sadler, 1989; Shepard, 2003). Formative assessment refers to assessment that is specifically intended to generate feedback on performance to improve learning (Sadler, 1998) and can only occur while a teaching and learning sequence is still in progress. Formative assessment is assessment for learning, not assessment of learning (Black, 1993). When teachers know how students are progressing and where they are having difficulties, the teachers can use this information to make necessary instructional adjustments, such as re-teaching, trying alternative instructional approaches, or offering more opportunities for practice. These activities can lead to improved student success. Leahy et al. (2005) suggest five strategies that support assessment for learning. These strategies are: (1) clarifying and sharing intentions and criteria; (2) engineering effective classroom discussion; (3) providing feedback that moves learners forward; (4) activating students as owners of their learning; and (5) activating students as instructional resources for one another (p. 20).

The use of formative assessment can have dramatic effects on student achievement, especially for struggling learners (Black & Wiliam, 1998). Clymer and Wiliam (2007) suggest that formative assessment can double the rate of student achievement and Wiliam and Thompson (2007) assert that formative assessment produces greater increases in student achievement than reductions in class-size or increases in teacher content knowledge. Research evidence has shown that embedding formative assessments within science curricula has a positive impact on students' achievement (Black & Wiliam, 1998a) and motivation (Butler, 1988). Shavelson et al. (2008) have shown that teachers' understanding of ways to employ formative assessment in their classrooms is a critical factor in the effect that such assessment approaches can have on students' achievement in science.

7.3.2 Formal vs. Informal Formative Assessment

Formal formative assessment usually begins with students engaging in activities designed or selected in advance by the teacher with the direct purpose of collecting assessment information. Typically, formal formative assessments take the form of curriculum-embedded assessments and they focus on some specific aspects of learning (e.g., students' knowledge about how atoms and molecules are related), but they may also be direct questioning, quizzes, brainstorming, and generation of questions (Bell & Cowie, 2001). A formal formative assessment activity enables teachers to step back at certain points during instruction, allows them to check student understanding (interpreting), and then plan on the next steps that must be taken to move their students' learning forward (acting). Teachers' planning of this type of formative assessment may occur at the initial stage of planning, during the teaching of the unit, or at the end of a unit.

Alternatively, informal formative assessment is more improvisational and can take place in any student – teacher interaction at the whole class, small – group, or one-on-one level. It can arise out of any instructional/learning activity at hand, and it is "embedded and strongly linked to learning and teaching activities" (Bell & Cowie, 2001, p. 86). The information gathered during informal formative assessment is transient (Bell & Cowie, 2001; e.g., students' comments, responses, and students' questions) and many times goes unrecorded. It can also be nonverbal, e.g., based on a teacher's observations of students during the course of an activity (Davies, 2011).

The time-frame for interpreting and acting is more immediate when compared with formal formative assessments. A student's response, question, or unexpected action can initiate an assessment event by making a teacher aware of the nature of a student's thinking.

Ruiz-Primo and Furtak (2007) focus on informal formative assessment. They suggest that informal formative assessment can be distinguished from formal formative assessment by three factors: (1) the premeditation of the assessment moment; (2) the formality of the ways used to make explicit what students know and can do; and (3) the nature of the action taken by the teacher (the characteristics of the feedback). Ruiz-Primo and Furtak go on to describe informal assessment practices as 'ESRU' cycles – the teacher Elicits a question; the Student responds; the teacher Recognises the student's response; and then Uses the information collected to support student learning.

ESRU cycles are similar to formal formative assessment strategies where teachers gather (i.e., collect or bring together) information from all the students in groups at a planned time; however, the word eliciting means evoking, educing, bringing out, or developing. To describe a teacher's actions as eliciting during informal formative assessment is thus a more complete description, as teachers are listening/watching for a reaction, clarification, elaboration, or explanation from students. During formal formative assessment, teachers have the time to step back to analyse and interpret the information gathered. Based on this interpretation, an action can be planned (e.g., re-teaching a concept). However, during informal formative assessment, teachers must react on the fly by recognising whether a student's response is a scientifically accepted idea and then use the information from the response in a way that the general flow of the classroom narrative is not interrupted (e.g., calling students in the class to start a discussion, shaping students' ideas). A teacher acting in response to ideas elicited from a student needs to be quick, spontaneous, and flexible, because gathering and prompting these responses can take different forms (e.g., responding with a question, eliciting other points of view from other students, conducting a demonstration when appropriate, repeating an activity). No matter what format a teacher chooses to use, they need to be prepared for a number of possible responses from their students with an understanding of the many possible responses they can, in return, provide the student.

7.3.3 Examples of Formative Assessment in Science

Formative assessment involves specific strategies like concept maps and science notebooks, or writing as an assessment tool, on a continuous basis, allowing students to demonstrate their understanding on a daily basis. Just as student-centred teaching is recommended, student-centred assessments are also recommended (Angelo & Cross, 1993). For instance, using portfolios, competency-based assessments, and multiple opportunities to demonstrate learning are ways that faculty can implement authentic, student-centred assessment activities (Angelo & Cross, 1993). This allows not only the teacher to monitor the students learning regularly, but also allows the teacher to think about the ways to approach their own teaching each day. In classrooms that use assessment to support learning, teachers continually adapt instruction to meet student needs (Leahy et al., 2005, p. 19). When assessment consists of end of term tests and activities, the information is too late for teachers to change their classroom instructional practices. While an end of term test can contribute to what we know about a student's overall level of achievement, it provides little information about specific weaknesses.

Student-centred assessment techniques that create an active environment with cooperative groups and authentic learning are recommended as ways to help students actively construct science knowledge (Yanowitz & Hahs-Vaughn, 2007). Science educators have been encouraged to increase their use of instructional and assessment strategies and approaches that promote deep conceptual understanding instead of rote memorisation (National Research Council, 1997). Approaches that more fully engage the students in the 'doing' of science contribute to a deeper understanding of the content and processes involved in science.

Klassen (2006, p. 820) describes the importance of considering context when thinking about assessment in science. In the past science assessment was driven by assumptions of decomposition and decontextualisation of knowledge, resulting in low-inference testing systems. With new research on learning and the requirement for science assessment to meet the goals of the individual, the classroom, and society, more contextualised forms of assessment are being implemented. These forms of assessment (Davies, 2011) include assessment of conversations, performances, and student generated products, such as portfolios, to name a few. Introducing these types of assessment is a role that instructional leaders can support. An effective instructional leader will find ways to extend autonomy to their teachers in a way that allows teachers to gain control over their professional responsibilities (Blase & Blase, 2004) including assessment, and the encouragement and support of the principal can go a long way in enabling teachers' willingness to try new approaches to assessment. Instructional leaders who are more science-aware can help teachers make informed choices about the kind of assessment that is appropriate in the science classroom.

Using writing, in the form of science notebooks or journals, can also provide an avenue for feedback and self-evaluation for students (Rockrow, 2008). The idea of using science notebooks is not new and they allow teachers to assess students' conceptual and procedural understanding while allowing teachers to provide the feedback students need for improving their learning (Ruiz-Primo, Li, Ayala, & Shavelson, 2004, p. 1477). In their study, Ruiz-Primo et al. demonstrated that notebooks can be reliably scored and they help teachers evaluate how well they, as teachers, have implemented curriculum, as well as providing another way to collect data about student learning.

Assessing practice and performance in science is another key element to be considered. Often students are left to report on their own practice or laboratory work in a structured formatted 'lab report' which limits what a teacher is able to understand about the student's thinking and understanding of the practice and performance in science (Roberts & Gott, 2006). Approaches to better gathering data from student performance include written performance tests, rubrics completed by teachers through observation (with criteria set ahead for student use), students writing about their experiences, and assessment conversations.

Involving students in discourse or conversations aimed at improving learning is an approach that can also contribute to improving the ways they understand and engage with science. Anderson, Zuiker, Tassoobshiri, and Hickey (2007), examined an innovative approach to coordinating and enhancing multiple levels of assessment and discursive feedback in a science learning activity. Their work suggests that participation in social forms of scientific engagement including discursive practices supports learning and subsequent performance in more formal contexts (p. 1721). The use of feedback is essential (Clymer & Wiliam, 2007) and can be a tool for helping students take ownership of their own learning in a substantial way. The feedback need not only come from the teacher. Both peer assessment and feedback amongst students can be an important part of effective instruction (Leahy et al., 2005, p. 21). Also, teachers who endeavour to understand students' perception of the learning and assessment processes can better serve their students. Dhindsa, Omar, and Waldrip (2007) suggest that ascertaining student perceptions about assessment and allowing students a voice can help students feel ownership over their learning in a more extensive way. The work of Cowie (2005) also suggested this:

> increased understanding of the link between learning and assessment combined with a shift to view learning as more a social than individual process have contributed to an appreciation of the role that classroom assessment can play in enhancing student learning and achievement. Student commentary indicated that assessment shaped what it means to be a student and to learn and know science. (p. 199)

An important part of discourse, questioning, particularly open ended questions, can enable deeper thinking and understanding in students. Black and Wiliam (1998b) encourage teachers to use questioning and classroom discussion as an opportunity to increase their students' knowledge and improve understanding. They caution, however, that teachers need to make sure to ask thoughtful, reflective questions rather than simple, factual ones and then give students adequate time to respond, enabling effective conversations about learning to occur.

Ongoing formative assessment occurs in a learning environment where teachers are able to acquire information on a continuing and informal basis, such as within the course of daily classroom talk. This type of classroom talk has been termed an assessment conversation (Duschl, 2008; Duschl & Gitomer, 1997). Assessment conversations permit teachers to better recognise and understand students' conceptions, mental models, strategies, language use, or communication skills, and allow teachers to use this information to guide instruction. In learning environments where assessment conversations take place, the boundaries of curriculum, instruction, and assessment should blur (Duschl & Gitomer, 1997). For example, an instructional activity suggested by a curriculum, such as discussion of the results of an investigation, can be viewed by the teachers as an assessment conversation to find out how students evaluate the quality of evidence and how they use evidence in explanations.

Assessment conversations have the three characteristics of informal assessment previously described: eliciting, recognising, and using information. Eliciting information employs strategies that allow students to share and make visible or explicit their understanding as completely as possible (e.g., sharing their thinking with the class, in overheads or posters).

In this context of informal formative assessment, Ruiz-Primo and Furtak (2007) use the terms eliciting, recognising, and using to describe the teacher's activities. Assessment conversations, then, require teachers to be facilitators and mediators of student learning, rather than providers or evaluators of correct or acceptable answers. In summary, successful classrooms emphasise not only the management of actions, materials, and behaviour, but also stress the management of reasoning, ideas, and communication (Duschl & Gitomer, 1997).

Wiliam and Thompson (2007) have identified five key strategies that teachers should be aware of for formal assessment to work well. In order to address where the learner is going, teachers and students need to come to a common understanding of the learning goals and the criteria for success. Ascertaining where the learner is in their learning at any moment in time is accomplished by the teacher engineering effective classroom discussions and opportunities for students to elicit evidence of their learning, by activating learners as instructional resources for one another and by encouraging students to take ownership of their own learning. Finally, teachers should seek to move their students forward in their learning with effective feedback during their learning activities.

A key characteristic of effective informal formative assessment is to promote frequent assessment conversations that may allow teachers to listen to inquiry (Duschl, 2003). Listening to inquiry as part of an assessment conversation should focus on helping students "examine how scientists have come to know what they believe to be scientific knowledge and why they believe this knowledge over other competing knowledge claims" (Duschl, 2003, p. 53). Therefore, assessment conversations that facilitate listening to inquiry should: (1) involve discussions in which students share their thinking, beliefs, ideas, and products (eliciting); (2) allow teachers to acknowledge student participation (recognising); and (3) allow teachers to use students' participation as the springboard to develop questions and/or activities that can promote their learning (using).

7.3.3.1 Looking Closely at an Assessment Conversation

The following portrayal, entitled Jill's Investigation, of a classroom episode involving students' investigation heat and energy flow is intended as an example of an assessment conversation in which the teacher seeks to elicit student ideas (in the form of student actions and discourse), recognise and respond to the students' ideas, and then use this information to support new learning. The teacher's comments are in bold font.

7.3.3.2 Jill's Investigation

Jill is a Grade 9 student with a question. It involves the convection box (Fig. 7.2) she is exploring. Other students have already experienced phenomena arising from this piece of equipment that she has yet to experiment with. They have told Jill that when they placed their hands just above (10–15 cm) the chimney, a sensation of intense heat was felt immediately, whereas it took longer to experience a sensation of similar intensity when the chimney was covered with their hands.

Jill disagrees. She has apparently had the opposite experience. And why not? Heat is more concentrated near its source (just above the chimney) as opposed to further away (about 10–15 cm above). Jill resumes her explorations with the convection box while the other students work together doing seat work. Jill lights the candle in the box and puts her hand over the chimney as she had done before. She leaves it there for a little while before crying out, "See it's hotter here (top of the chimney) than here" (moves her hand 10–15 cm further up). Another student joins her and tries the same actions. She disagrees with Jill and points out that the heat begins to go out the "cool" chimney when the "hot" chimney is covered. Jill decides an explanation must involve her hand sensing heat differently and talks about the distribution of nerves in her hand.

Jill continues her exploration. First, she observes smoke from the burning "touch paper" going down into the "cool" chimney when both chimneys are left open. Second, she observes the smoke changing direction by going up the "cool" chimney after she blocks the "hot" chimney with her hand. "But that's only telling me where the air is going ... heat rises", she announces in frustration.

A couple of other students join Jill and she explains her dilemma to them. One student suggests that it takes a few seconds for the covering hand (over the chimney) to get hot because the act of covering pushes cool air down into the chimney. He demonstrates this by moving his hand up and down over the chimney a couple of times. Another student joins them and says, "OK, do it like this", and moves his hand back and forth horizontally over the chimney. "See, I don't push any air this way."

Jill steps back, her gaze focussed on the apparatus. She appears to be thinking hard about the other explanations. "But heat rises", she protests. Another student suggests tilting the box on edge so that the "cool" chimney is higher than the "hot" chimney to see if smoke will go out the cool chimney even though both chimneys are open. They try it. Smoke goes out the hot chimney as before.

Jill announces that she's still not satisfied with any of the explanations put forward. When asked by another student about the tilted box attempt, Jill replies "Oh, that's Cam's idea."

Fig. 7.2 Schematic drawing of convection box apparatus

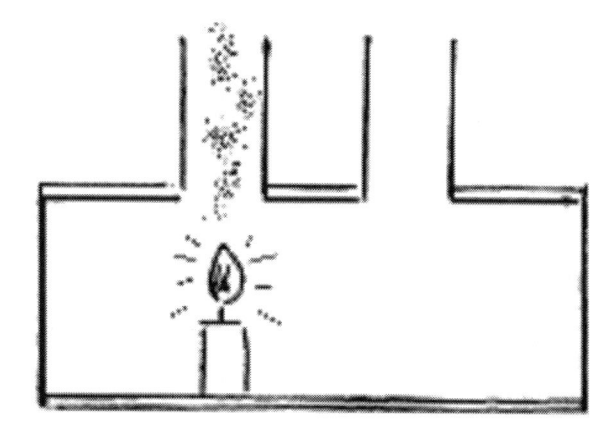

Jill's teacher notices her at work and she asks Jill "**What are you planning to do?**"

Jill responds: "I'm just working on this because I don't understand it ... when you put your hand on top of this (points to the "hot" glass chimney above the candle) really close you can't feel anything ... like it's not really warm ... the other kids said that the explanation was because the heat can't get out of there so it goes out the other one ("cool" chimney) ... but the heat is going to rise ... because heat rises ... and it doesn't know that the hand is on top." The teacher sits down nearby and says, "**OK, well you go ahead and do what you were going to do. I'll just sit here and watch.**"

Jill lights the candle and Karen joins in the activity. The teacher stands nearby and watches quietly as they work. She is not sure what they are trying to do. Their hands move up and down over the "hot" chimney and they pause briefly to rub the palms of their hands and stare at them intently. Similar actions are repeated several times. There seems to be more complexity to their experiences than just a sensation of heat. "**What was that thing you were trying to understand Jill?**" asks the teacher.

Jill takes her hands off the convection box and looks up at the teacher and says: "OK, well I didn't do this activity before but when Karen and her group did it they said when they put their hand right there ... just touching it (puts her hand directly above "hot" chimney) ... it was not as hot as when they felt it up here (her hand moves about 15 centimetres above the same chimney) and so we started discussing it and the conclusion was that the heat can't travel out the top so it goes out the other one (points to the "cool" chimney), but heat rises and the heat has to get to the top of this chimney (points to the "hot" chimney) before it can go out the other one." The teacher's curiosity overwhelms her and she asks Jill: "**Can I try it?**"

Karen and Jill look up, surprised by the teacher's request. "Yeah", they say in unison and make a space for the teacher to get close to the box. As the teacher puts her hand over the "hot" chimney, she reminds herself to be careful not to "steamroll" Jill or Karen by her actions. However, she still feels a need to get "in touch" with this phenomenon. The teacher pulls her hand away and asks for help: "**Tell me what I need to do.**"

Jill acts out instructions with her hand as Karen gives verbal directions: "Well first of all put your hand right there (about 10–15 cm above) and feel how hot it is ... then just kind of go, just put it down to see if it gets hotter ... you don't have to keep it there or anything." The teacher seeks to understand the girls thinking by following their instructions. She puts her hand, palm down, at the upper location above the chimney and waits. It feels painfully hot almost immediately. Then she repeats this action at the lower location. It takes a few seconds longer before her hand feels the same sensation of heat as in the upper location. The teacher suggests: "**It seems not quite as hot down here.**"

Karen adds complexity and their paths of thinking diverge: "Yeah, well, if you hold it down long enough it will be." Jill doesn't agree: "But I think it's because of your hand", she says. Jill places her hand at the spot where the teacher's had been just before.

Several cycles of action and explanation take place before the teacher gains a clearer picture of how Jill has been thinking. Jill considers the movement of smoke to indicate the direction of air movement but not the direction of heat transfer. Jill seems to consider the flow of heat to be independent of the flow of smoke or air. In Jill's opinion, heat can only rise and, therefore, it can only move out through the "hot" chimney. Explanations suggesting that heat moves out the "cool" chimney when the "hot" one is covered do not make sense to Jill. The teacher can now begin to understand why and can plan for a follow-up experience for Jill and Karen.

The teacher suggests that they might try taking apart the apparatus and experiencing the phenomena with various pieces missing. As the two students continue to work they notice that the smoke and the heat move together. When they report this to their teacher, the teacher asks them to draw a picture showing the movement of heat and smoke through the convection box and to annotate their drawing with an explanation of what they felt was happening.

This episode illustrates a sequence in which a teacher was actively making decisions on the fly based on evidence that she was gathering about the students' thinking. She elicited information from the students by having them guide her through the activity and, in allowing them the occasion to guide her actions, was better able to understand the nature of their thinking in the activity and, thus, able to make informed decisions on how to further support learning through an assessment conversation. The conversation was one in which students were guiding the teacher and, in so doing, helping the teacher engage in formative assessment.

In addition, this episode illustrates a teacher taking time to participate in a conversation with her students that was more indepth and extended in time than would typically be the case in her classroom. This opportunity was partly enabled (from the perspective of the teacher) by the presence of a second adult (one of the authors) in the classroom. The exchange between the students and teacher took only a few minutes but helped the teacher see classroom conversations as a new way to assess student thinking. When a school leader expresses genuine interest in learning episodes from a teacher's classroom, even if they are relatively brief, it can help enable positive new directions in assessment for learning (Black & Wiliam, 2004; Gardner et al., 2008). This does not mean that a school leader needs to be physically present in a teacher's classroom in order to provide effective support. A focused conversation preceding and following a lesson can be an important dimension to provide effective support for a teacher (Robinson et al., 2009, pp. 128–132).

7.4 Discussion and Implications

Given the amount of research and literature about assessment, there is much to consider with regard to assessment specific to science as a core subject area. Science assessment should reflect the science that all students need to know and be about enhancing the science learning. Assessment strategies and approaches should promote valid inferences about science learning.

Several general principles can be applied to assessment in all core subject areas. Assessment should promote the philosophy of equity, including using different assessment strategies that cut across learning styles, allowing all students to best demonstrate their learning. Assessment should be an open and transparent process where students know what is expected of them, and their learning can be improved through the process because they can see where they grow and where they need to focus more attention. This helps students focus on what they know, not on what they don't know and won't label children as failures because of unrealistic expectations (Briars, 1998).

Assessment strategies should include the idea of revision with products so that the products are not typically viewed as end products but are viewed as products under development. One of the most important things for a teacher to listen for as students talk about their work or their products is around the idea of "where do I go next?" or "what do I do next?" – it is an indicator of a certain degree of engagement with the task and a certain degree of ownership for the process and products.

Assessment should be a coherent process where the assessment strategies mirror the instructional strategies and both are linked to the curriculum. This way the assessment is integral to instruction and doesn't detract from student opportunities to continue to learn.

Assessment that promotes learning is assessment that allows students to learn at their own pace. Time is a limiting factor in many activities for students. This doesn't mean students shouldn't be challenged to strive for timely processing and analysis of data; however, too often timetable restrictions mean that science classes are cut short, or teachers resort to demonstrations to save time. Students need to have the time to explore and analyse, to evaluate the information provided, and synthesise or apply the information. Greater student success is possible when students are not rushed.

Effective assessment in science classes communicates to students, teachers, and parents that most real problems in science can't be solved quickly. Effective assessment in science classes doesn't use time as a factor, since speed is almost never relevant in scientific effectiveness. What do we need to assess in science class? When thinking specifically about science assessment, teachers must continually ask themselves what they want all students to learn, how they will know each student has learned it, and what should be done when students experience difficulty (Dufour, 2004). We need to observe and determine how students' use of science to make sense of complex situations. This is often best done through providing students with the opportunity to participate in extended science investigations. While many discrepant events used in science class are quick and attention grabbing, they are best used to prompt questions and initiate a more extended investigation. It is during more extended science investigations that we can, as teachers, better evaluate and assess the ability of students to formulate and refine hypotheses, collect and organise information, and demonstrate this through providing explanations about their thinking. When students have opportunities to generate evidence of their learning in multiple forms (i.e., products, conversations, performances), and receive feedback on numerous occasions (e.g., from peers and teacher), powerful and enduring learning can result (Davies, 2011).

Instructional strategies that enable the teacher to engage and interact more closely with individual students are important in increasing the amount and kind of formative assessment teachers can develop in their classrooms. In a recent research project (Sherman, MacDonald, & Schaeffer, 2011), teachers were observed and interviewed about using science resource kits (also referred to as crates) that contained the materials and ideas for centre-based activities. These activities were inquiry-based where students engaged in hand-on activities while endeavouring to answer some questions posed to them by their teacher and others that emerged from small group discussions with classmates about the activities they were completing.

The way the activities were created allowed children more time to explore, and the fact that small groups of students were engaged in actively figuring out the answers to the challenges presented in the activities meant the teachers were able to really get to see what individuals or small groups were doing. As one teacher explains:

> When they're doing a crate, I'm usually observing, I'm listening to the questions, I'll keep anecdotal notes, I'm looking for group interaction, so I'll look at that and I'll look at the kind of questions that they're asking each other, listen to the questions they ask me, and their use of science vocabulary, how they're asking and answering those questions, if they're using their terminology, if they're really trying to figure it out, and demonstrating their knowledge (teacher interview, May, 2009).

Through their close involvement, teachers were able to engage in formative forms of assessment to support their students' learning as students interacted with the science resources relatively autonomously in the learning centres. Teachers used the time to listen to the conversations and questions of their students, taking anecdotal notes, and recording information on rubrics. Teachers stated that they felt they had increased opportunity to provide effective feedback, recognise and identify misconceptions, and know their students better. The way the centres were used meant students could take the time they needed to complete their investigations, generate detailed responses as evidence of their learning, and provide peer feedback to one another. The science resource kits in this example helped to enable conditions for pedagogic change to take place around assessment practices by the classroom teacher. Effective leadership that supports assessment for learning practices can be enabled simply by providing aligned pedagogic resources that help a teacher focus on her students' in new ways (Robinson et al., 2009, pp. 111–116). The opportunity to talk about and reflect on the experience of using the science kits was also an important dimension of the leadership provided in this case.

7.5 Future Directions and Recommendations for Teacher Preparation and Professional Development

There are many implications for the preparation of teachers and professional development of practicing teachers with regards to both instruction and assessment of science. It is particularly important to reflect on the level of preparation of BEd students to teach science in elementary classrooms (Loughran, 1994; Russell, 2001). Finding ways to help elementary preservice teachers learn how to teach science effectively is a challenge faced by teacher education programs. One of the challenges faced by teacher educators of science involves how the prior science experiences of many preservice teachers can lead to a low sense of self-efficacy to teach science which reminds us of the roles of content knowledge and pedagogical content knowledge.

Bianchini, Johnston, Oram, and Cavazos (2003) described the challenges faced by first-year science teachers as they tried to teach in contemporary and equitable ways. Overcoming pre-conceived notions of the nature of effective science teaching was, perhaps, the greatest challenge. Preservice teachers find it difficult to describe successful and engaging science experiences they had as children in school

(MacDonald & Sherman, 2007). Poor experiences with science and/or a general lack of engaging science experiences, affect the belief system each preservice teacher has about her/his own science teaching and assessment abilities (Bryan, 2003). Previous science experiences, or lack thereof, are very influential on preservice teachers' abilities to be confident in the teaching of science (Cheng, 2002). This suggests that the provision of typical science experiences within the context of instruction and assessment will help preservice teachers develop understanding from the perspective of a learner of science and as well as a teacher of science.

Without content knowledge, teachers are not able to teach students to understand topics indepth, nor are they able to assess the quality of student understanding. Given the: (1) lack of content knowledge many elementary teachers have and (2) the challenges faced by those in higher grades when asked to teach outside of their subject specific expertise, development of content knowledge and pedagogical content knowledge must be an essential element of teacher preparation and inservice professional development if we are to improve instruction and assessment in science classrooms. Irving, Dickson, and Keyser (1999) demonstrated the connection between professional development learning courses in science content and improved knowledge in the classroom. The augmented content knowledge of the teachers participating in the university led professional development provided teachers with additional pedagogical content knowledge for the classroom.

Pedagogical content knowledge, the content specific knowledge that embodies the aspects of content most germane to its teachability and which is most likely to distinguish the understanding of the content specialist from the pedagogue, has been widely regarded as important for effective instruction and assessment of complex subject matter such as science (Magnusson & Krajcik, 1993). Without pedagogical content knowledge, teachers are unable to know what makes a topic easy or hard. Making judgments about what misconceptions students have becomes more difficult and there may be a lack of knowledge about what strategies might help students overcome misconceptions. These are other key aspects that need to be considered in teacher preparation and inservice professional development, with implications for teachers and principals.

As teachers develop their knowledge both of content and pedagogical approaches in science, they should continually ask themselves questions regarding a variety of context related standards which affect the teaching, learning and assessment of science. Given the general lack of content knowledge in science it is important that teachers ask what they need to know about the science content area that will foster deeper student understanding and what are ways that they can learn these concepts in order to be better able to work with students. It is also important for teachers to think about what students need to know in life that relates to the science content area. This allows for greater relevance to be incorporated into the teaching and assessment of science. Teachers need to think about what has come before and what will come after their instruction, either in a previous grade or unit in their own classroom. This not only allows for their teaching to build on previous knowledge the students bring, but to draw connections to that knowledge. And because of the implications research shows for using hands-on activities in science, teachers must also ask themselves what they know about the most effective and engaging materials that can be used to support the science content area (Emberger, 2007). Our own research has shown that many teachers in elementary and middle schools find it difficult to collect and maintain appropriate materials and equipment and many are at a loss to know where to be in gathering what is needed for inquiry-based, hands-on learning activities in science (Sherman & MacDonald, 2009). An important feature in science, resources are not just for the student, but the appropriate use of resources open up a space for teachers to be able to listen to and gather information about their students to make better assessments of their students. Well designed and utilised resources allow students to participate in a kind of assessment that is more contextualised, continuous and is focused on process rather than only products. Informed instructional leaders may also help improve access to resources and provide teachers with help in using those resources. These science-aware administrators will be also better able to interact with their provincial departments of education with regard to the content, resources and approaches used in science teaching.

Preservice and inservice teachers need a great deal of integrated understanding of the role of assessment, in the ways that instructional strategies and assessment strategies support each other and work together, often within the same activity. For instance, simply providing new teachers with several opportunities to engage in and later reflect upon assessment conversations with individual and small groups of students may help them more easily adopt an assessment for learning perspective, especially if they can talk about the experience with a lead teacher. Enabling such an experience may require that managing some of the regular classroom concerns are relaxed by the presence of another teacher. Such professional development does not occur quickly and needs to take place through long-term engagement in professional discussion and research (Loucks-Horsley, Love, Stiles, Mundy, & Hewson, 2003). Strong professional development in science assessment will help teachers focus on the interpretation of student work in sound and equitable ways (Gearhart et al., 2006; Mamiok-Naamn, Hofstein, & Penick, 2007). Professional development programs and teacher preparation courses that help teachers focus on creative and diverse instructional strategies can encourage a more diverse and open approach to assessment (Mamiok-Naamn, Hofstein, & Penick, 2007). Again, this is best achieved when the teachers receive sustained support for new ideas and approaches.

Teachers who are knowledgeable and confident in their content knowledge and pedagogical content knowledge will be able to better ensure they use assessment strategies that will contribute to the way students not only engage with science, but how they understand it. These same assessment strategies should also help teachers engage with students and help us understand what our students are thinking and experiencing. Teachers who have the knowledge and confidence needed to assess students in this way will be empowered by thinking like assessors, design strategies for instruction and assessment that are not mutually exclusive, engage in discourse with their students using a vocabulary of assessment while collecting strong evidence of student thinking and understanding.

Teachers who create learning environments where students take ownership and control of their learning open up their classrooms in ways that allow them to engage in meaningful conversations and observation with their students will be better able to carry out the kinds of assessments that provide the most powerful feedback for students and accurate interpretations of their learning. Content knowledge and pedagogical content knowledge help teachers to accomplish this. School leaders who focus their efforts around supporting the growth of teachers' professional development, especially in the context of classroom-based teaching and learning activity will realise powerful and sustainable results (Davies, Herbst, & Parrott Reynolds, 2011).

References

Absolum, M., Flockton, L., Hattie, J., Hipkins, R., & Reid, I. (Eds.). (2009). *Directions for assessment in New Zealand: Developing students' assessment capabilities.* Retrieved from: Te Kete Ipurangi http://www.tki.org.nz/r/assessment/research/mainpage/directions/

Anderson, K. T., Zuiker, S. J., Taasoobshirazi, G., & Hickey, D. (2007). Classroom discourse as a tool to enhance formative assessment and practise in science. *International Journal of Science Education, 29*(14), 1721–1744.

Angelo, T. A., & Cross, K. P. (1993). *Classroom assessment techniques: A handbook for college teachers* (2nd ed.). San Francisco, CA: Jossey Bass.

Bell, B., & Cowie, B. (2001). *Formative assessment and science education.* Dordrecht, The Netherlands: Kluwer.

Bianchini, J. A., Johnston, C. C., Oram, S. Y., & Cavazos, L. M. (2003). Learning to teach science in contemporary and equitable ways: The successes and struggles of first-year science teachers. *Science Education, 87*(3), 419–443.

Black, P. (1993). Formative and summative assessment by teachers. *Studies in Science Education, 21*, 49–97.

Black, P., Harrison, C., Lee, C., Marshall, B., & Wiliam, D. (2003). *Assessment for learning – Putting it into practice.* Buckingham, UK: Open University Press.

Black, P. J., & Wiliam, D. (1998a). Assessment and classroom learning. *Assessment in Education, 5*(1), 7–74.

Black, P. J., & Wiliam, D. (1998b). Inside the black box: Raising standards through classroom assessment. *Phi Delta Kappan, 80*, 139–148.

Black, P., & Wiliam, D. (2004). Working inside the black box: Assessment for learning in the classroom. *Phi Delta Kappan, 86*(1), 8–21.

Blase, J., & Blase, J. (2004). *Handbook of instructional leadership.* Thousand Oaks, CA: Corwin Press.

Briars, D. J. (1998). Implementing standards-based classroom assessment practices. In G. W. Bright & J. M. Joyner (Eds.), *Classroom assessment in mathematics: Views from a national science foundation working conference* (pp. 81–90). New York, NY: University Press of America.

Brookhart, S. (2013). Assessing creativity. *Educational Leadership, 70*(5), 28–34.

Bryan, L. A. (2003). Nestedness of beliefs: Examining a prospective elementary teacher's belief system about science teaching and learning. *Journal of Research in Science Teaching, 40*(9), 835–868.

Butler, R. (1988). Enhancing and undermining intrinsic motivation: The effects of task-involving and ego-involving evaluation on interest and performance. *British Journal of Educational Psychology, 58*, 1–14.

Chappuis, S., & Stiggins, R. (2002). Classroom assessment for learning. *Educational Leadership, 60*(1), 40–44.

Chappuis, S., Stiggins, R., Arter, J., & Chappuis, J. (2004). *Assessment for learning: An action guide for school leaders*. Upper Saddle River, NJ: Pearson Education.

Cheng, M. H. (2002, April 1–5). *Becoming confident teachers of science: Changes of science teaching efficacy beliefs*. Paper presented at the annual meeting of the national Association for the Research in Science Teaching, New Orleans, LA.

Chiappetta, E. L. (1997). Inquiry-based science: Strategies and techniques for encouraging inquiry in the classroom. *The Science Teacher, 2*, 22–26.

Childs, A., & McNicholl, J. (2007). Science teaching outside of subject specialism: Issues and challenges for teacher education. *Teacher Development, 11*(1), 1–20.

Clymer, J. B., & Wiliam, D. (2007). Improving the way we grade science. *Educational Leadership, 64*(4), 36–42.

Collette, A. T., & Chiappette, E. L. (1994). *Science instruction in the middle and secondary schools*. Columbus, OH: Merrill.

Cowie, B. (2005). Student commentary on classroom assessment in science: A sociocultural interpretation. *International Journal of Science Education, 27*(2), 199–214.

Darling-Hammond, L. (1997). *The right to learn: A blueprint for creating schools that work*. San Francisco, CA: Jossey-Bass Publishers.

Darling-Hammond, L. (2004). Performance-based assessment and educational equity. *Harvard Educational Review, 64*(1), 5–31.

Davies, A. (2011). *Making classroom assessment work*. Courtenay, BC, Canada: Connections Publishing.

Davies, A., Herbst, S., & Parrott Reynolds, B. (2011). *Leading the way to assessment for learning: A practical guide*. Courtenay, BC, Canada: Connections Publishing.

Dhindsa, H. S., Omar, K., & Waldrip, B. (2007). Upper secondary Bruneian science students' perceptions of assessment. *International Journal of Science Education, 29*(10), 1261–1280.

Dufour, R. (2004). Are you looking out the window or in a mirror? *Journal of Staff Development, 25*(3), 63–64.

Duran, E., Duran, L., Haney, J., & Scheuermann, A. (2011). A learning cycle for all students: Modifying the 5E instructional model to address the needs of all learners. *The Science Teacher, 78*(3), 56–60.

Duschl, R. (2003). Assessment of inquiry. In J. M. Atkin & J. Coffey (Eds.), *Everyday assessment in science classrooms*. Washington, DC: NSTA Press.

Duschl, R. A. (2008). Science education in three part harmony: Balancing conceptual, epistemic, and social learning goals. *Review of Research in Education, 32*(1), 268–291.

Duschl, R. A., & Gitomer, D. H. (1997). Strategies and challenges to changing the focus of assessment and instruction in science classrooms. *Educational Assessment, 4*(1), 37–73. doi:10.1207/s15326977ea0401_2.

Emberger, M. (2007). Helping teachers improve classroom assessments. *Principal Leadership, 7*(9), 24–29.

Gardner, J., Harlen, W., Hayward, L., & Stobart, G. (2008). *Changing assessment practice: Process, principles and standards*. Cambridge, UK: Assessment Reform Group, University of Cambridge School of Education.

Gearhart, M., Nagashima, S., Pfotenhauer, J., Clark, S., Schwab, C., Vendlinski, T., … Bernbaum, J. (2006). Classroom assessment in K–12 science: Learning to interpret student work. Interim findings from a 2-year study. *Educational Assessment, 11*(3 & 4), 238–263.

Hallinger, P., & Heck, R. H. (1998). Exploring the principal's contribution to school effectiveness: 1980–1995. *School Effectiveness and School Improvement, 9*(2), 157–191.

Harrison, C. (2005). Teachers developing assessment for learning: Mapping teacher change. *Teacher Development, 9*, 255–264.

Hattie, J., & Timperley, H. (2007). The power of feedback. *Review of Educational Research, 77*(1), 81–112.

Hutchinson, C. (2008). *Assessment systems in small countries and states*. Learning and Teaching Scotland. Retrieved from: http://assessment.tki.org.nz/Media/Files/Hutchinson-C.-Assessment-systems-in-small-countries-and-states-Learning-and-Teaching-Scotland

Irving, M. M., Dickson, L. A., & Keyser, J. (1999). Retraining public secondary science teachers by upgrading their content knowledge and pedagogical skills. *Journal of Negro Education, 68*(3), 409–418.

Keeley, P., Eberle, F., & Farrin, L. (2005). *Uncovering student ideas in science, volume 1: 25 formative assessment probes*. Arlington, VA: NSTA Press.

Klassen, S. (2006). Contextual assessment in science education: Background, issues, and policy. *Science Education, 90*(5), 820–851.

Leahy, S., Lyon, C., Thompson, M., & Wiliam, D. (2005). Classroom assessment: Minute-by-minute, day-by-day. *Educational Leadership, 63*(3), 18–24.

Lee, C., & Wiliam, D. (2005). Studying changes in the practice of two teachers developing assessment for learning. *Teacher Development, 9*, 265–283.

Loucks-Horsley, S., Love, N., Stiles, K. E., Mundy, S., & Hewson, P. (2003). *Designing professional development for teachers of science and mathematics*. Thousand Oaks, CA: Sage.

Loughran, J. (1994). Bridging the gap – An analysis of the needs of 2nd year science teachers. *Science Education, 78*(4), 365–386.

MacDonald, A. L., & Sherman, A. (2001). Encouraging extended science investigations in elementary classrooms. *Alberta Teachers' Association Early Childhood Education Journal, Autumn, 38*(2), 15–18.

MacDonald, A. L., & Sherman, A. (2006). Children's perspectives on building science models. *Education 3 to 13, 34*(1), 89–98.

MacDonald, A. L., & Sherman, A. (2007). Preservice teachers' experiences with a science education module. *Journal of Science Teacher Education, 18*(4), 525–541, Springer Publishing.

Magnusson, S., & Krajcik, J. S. (1993, April). *Teacher knowledge and representation of content in instruction about heat energy and temperature*. Paper presented at the Annual meeting of National Association for Research in Science Teaching, Atlanta, GA.

Mamiok-Naamn, R., Hofstein, A., & Penick, J. (2007). Science teachers developing assessment tools for "science and technology for all" programs. *Journal of Science Teachers Education, 18*, 427–524.

Marzano, R. J., Waters, T., & McNulty, B. (2005). *School leadership that works: From research to results*. Alexandria, VA: ASCD and McREL.

National Research Council. (1997). *Science teaching reconsidered*. Washington, DC: National Academics' Press.

Nicol, D. J., & Macfarlane-Dick, D. (2006). Formative assessment and self-regulated learning: A model and seven principles of good feedback practice. *Studies in Higher Education, 31*(2), 199–218.

Roberts, R., & Gott, R. (2006). Assessment of performance in practical science and pupil attributes. *Assessment in Education, 13*(1), 45–67.

Robinson, V., Hohepa, M., & Lloyd, C. (2009). *School leadership and student outcomes: Identifying what works and why*. Auckland, New Zealand: New Zealand Ministry of Education. Retrieved from: http://www.educationcounts.govt.nz/__data/assets/pdf_file/0015/60180/BES-Leadership-Web.pdf

Rockrow, M. (2008). This isn't English class: Using writing as an assessment tool in science. *Science Scope, 31*(5), 22–26.

Ruiz-Primo, M. A., & Furtak, E. M. (2007). Exploring teachers' informal formative assessment practices and students' understanding in the context of scientific inquiry. *Journal of Research in Science Teaching, 44*(1), 57–84.

Ruiz-Primo, M. A., Li, M., Ayala, C., & Shavelson, R. J. (2004). Evaluating students' science notebooks as an assessment tool. *International Journal of Science Education, 26*(12), 1477–1506.

Russell, T. (2001, April). *Radical program change in preservice teacher education: What and how we learn from personal and institutional experience*. Paper presented at the annual meeting of the American Educational Research Association, Seattle, WA.

Sadler, D. R. (1989). Formative assessment and the design of instructional systems. *Instructional Science, 18*, 119–144.

Sadler, D. R. (1998). Formative assessment: Revisiting the territory. *Assessment in Education, 5*(1), 77–84.

Saliu, S. (2005). Constrained subjective assessment of student learning. *Journal of Science Education and Technology, 14*(3), 271–284.

Shavelson, R. J, Baxter, G. P., & Pine, J. (1992, May). What we've learned about assessing hands-on science. *Educational Leadership, 21*(4), 20–25.

Shavelson, R. J., Yin, Y., Furtak, E. M., Ruiz-Primo, M. A., Ayala, C. C., Young, D. B., … Pottenger III, F. M. (2008). In J. Coffey, R. Douglas, & C. Stearns (Eds.), *Assessing science learning: Perspectives from research and practice* (pp. 17–31). Arlington, VA: National Science Teachers' Association Press.

Shepard, L. (2003). Reconsidering large-scale assessment to heighten its relevance to learning. In J. M. Atkin & J. E. Coffey (Eds.), *Everyday assessment in the science classroom* (pp. 121–146). Washington, DC: National Science Teachers' Association Press.

Sherman, A., & MacDonald, L. (2008). Instructional leadership in elementary school science: How can I be an instructional leader in a content area, like science, where I have little to no background experience or knowledge? *International Electronic Journal for Leadership in Learning (IEJLL), 12*, Article 12. Retrieved from: http://www.ucalgary.ca/iejll/sherman

Sherman, A., & MacDonald, A. L. (2009). The use of science kits in professional development for rural elementary school teachers. *The Science Education Review, 7*(2), 41–48.

Sherman, A., MacDonald, A. L., & Schaeffer, H. (2011, June). Crates in the classroom – Enabling inquiry based science. *Alberta Teachers Association Science Council Journal*.

Stiggins, R. (2007). Assessment through the student's eyes. *Educational Leadership, 64*(8), 22–26.

Stiggins, R. J. (2002). Assessment crisis: The absence of assessment FOR learning. *Phi Delta Kappan, 83*(10), 758–765.

Tomlinson, C. A. (1999). *The differentiated classroom: Responding to the needs of all learners*. Alexandria, VA: Association for Supervision and Curriculum Development.

Wenglinsky, H., & Silverstien, S. C. (2007). The science training teachers need. *Educational Leadership, 64*(4), 24–29.

White, R. T., & Gunstone, R. F. (1992). *Probing understanding*. London, UK: Falmer Press.

Wiliam, D., Lee, C., Harrison, C., & Black, P. (2004). Teachers developing assessment for learning: Impact on student achievement. *Assessment in Education, 11*(1), 49–65.

Wiliam, D., & Thompson, M. (2007). Integrating assessment with instruction: What will it take to make it work? In C. A. Dwyer (Ed.), *The future of assessment: Shaping teaching and learning*. Mahwah, NJ: Lawrence Erlbaum Associates.

Yanowitz, K. L., & Hahs-Vaughn, D. L. (2007). Changes in student-centred assessment by post-secondary science and non-science faculty. *Teaching in Higher Education, 12*(2), 171–184.

Zembal-Saul, C. L. (2012). *What's your evidence? Engaging K-5 children in constructing explanation in Science*. Toronto, ON, Canada: Pearson.

Part III
Pragmatics of Assessment Leadership for Inclusion

Chapter 8
Effective Leadership for Inclusionary Practice: Assessment Considerations for Cognitively Challenged Students

Elaine Fournier, Shelleyann Scott, and Donald E. Scott

Abstract This chapter focuses on leadership for effective inclusion for students with cognitive challenges. As leadership is pivotal to enhancing student outcomes, we explore how leaders influence teachers and promote inclusionary practices in terms of facilitating professional development and differentiation in instruction and assessment. Deconstructing two case studies in relation to the literature, we illustrate the complexities in addressing teaching and learning for inclusion, and highlight the importance of principals having an ethic of care and an appreciation of diversity. An inclusive leadership framework is proposed which articulates the essential knowledge, skills, and attitudes/beliefs principals and system leaders must acquire and refine in order to effectively lead in diverse schools and systems. In the exploration of the research, it was overtly evident that educators are grappling with differentiation and its implications for them as leaders of learning due to an inherent lack of preparation and pragmatic professional development. We therefore created two models designed to address the demand for building leadership capacity at the system and school levels that encompass leaders, educators, as well as paraprofessionals in the pursuit of enhanced outcomes for students with special needs. The foundation of the capacity building models is the development of a pool of expert leaders who can engage in peer coaching relationships, thereby influencing professional development and team-based case management. We advocate for closer community engagement between university experts and school systems, as well as a greater nexus between inclusion theory and practical pedagogical differentiation in preservice programmes.

Keywords Inclusion • Disabilities • Exceptionalities • Differentiated instruction • Differentiated assessment • Authentic assessment • Differentiation • Leadership

---

E. Fournier (✉)
1835 South Baptiste Lake Road, RR#2, Bancroft, ON, Canada, K0L 1C0
e-mail: Elaine.Fournier@TLDSB.ON.CA

S. Scott (✉) • D.E. Scott
Werklund School of Education, University of Calgary,
2500 University Drive NW, Calgary, AB, Canada, T2N 1N4
e-mail: sscott@ucalgary.ca; descott@ucalgary.ca

development • Professional development • Knowledge, skills and attributes/values • Capacity building • Peer coaching • System leadership • School leadership • Principals • Community partnerships • Case management • Student voice • Paraprofessionals • Advocacy • Ethic of care • Appreciation of diversity

8.1 Introduction

The United Nations' (1989) 'Convention on the Rights of the Child' clearly states that all children have the right to an education including, or maybe especially, those with special needs. Inclusion, where special needs students are integrated into general education classrooms for at least part of the school day, is the norm in schools in many countries around the world. Inclusion presents increased complexity in the classroom for many teachers who have not been adequately prepared for teaching and managing special needs students. We know that appropriate preparation and professional development makes a difference to teachers in their efficacy in teaching within the inclusive classroom (Al-Zyoudi, 2006; Gwernan-Jones & Burden, 2010; Hue, 2012). Additionally, we know from leadership studies that principals have a significant impact on school culture and teacher capacity, which in this case can influence teachers' attitudes towards special needs students and their competence in addressing the instructional approaches needed for effective learning outcomes for all (Leithwood, Seashore Louis, Anderson, & Wahlstrom, 2004). The purpose of this chapter therefore, is to focus specifically on the leadership implications from the findings of Fournier's (2012) doctoral study with regards to supporting students with cognitive challenges. We also drew upon our previous studies in assessment and leadership preparation and development (Scott & Webber, 2008; Webber, Aitken, Lupart, & Scott, 2009; Webber & Scott, 2013; Webber, Scott, Aitken, Lupart, & Scott, 2013). Fournier's findings illustrate the relationship between novice teachers' self-efficacy, teaching special needs students in an inclusive setting, and the leadership support that teachers experience at both the school and district levels. The leadership implications described throughout the chapter references the knowledge, skills, and attitudes/beliefs of both school and district level leaders for effective inclusionary practices (see Fig. 8.1). We present pragmatic insights designed to guide leaders' beliefs and approaches and we propose models for capacity building (see Figs. 8.2 and 8.3) that district leaders may find valuable. These models articulate the establishment of a pool of expertise at the leadership level that can in turn support more informed inclusionary practices.

8.2 Conceptualising Inclusion

> Teachers face increasingly diverse classes of students. The heterogeneity of the student population is the result of numerous influences: changes in immigration patterns and population demographics; advances in medicine that increase the survival rates of children;

8 Effective Leadership for Inclusionary Practice: Assessment Considerations... 201

School & System Leaders (KSAs for Inclusion)

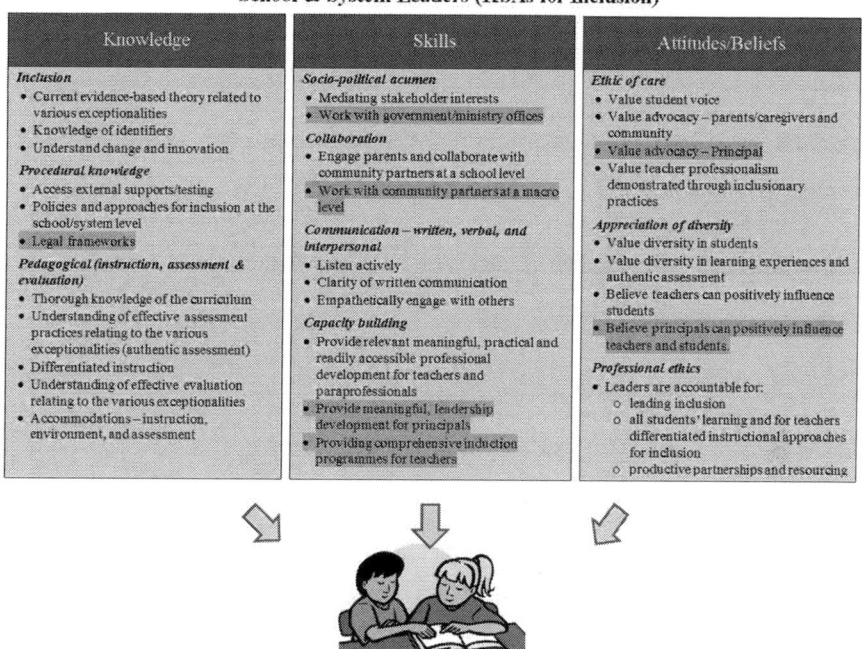

Knowledge	Skills	Attitudes/Beliefs

Inclusion
• Current evidence-based theory related to various exceptionalities
• Knowledge of identifiers
• Understand change and innovation
Procedural knowledge
• Access external supports/testing
• Policies and approaches for inclusion at the school/system level
• Legal frameworks
Pedagogical (instruction, assessment & evaluation)
• Thorough knowledge of the curriculum
• Understanding of effective assessment practices relating to the various exceptionalities (authentic assessment)
• Differentiated instruction
• Understanding of effective evaluation relating to the various exceptionalities
• Accommodations – instruction, environment, and assessment
	Socio-political acumen
	• Mediating stakeholder interests
	• Work with government/ministry offices
	Collaboration
	• Engage parents and collaborate with community partners at a school level
	• Work with community partners at a macro level
	Communication – written, verbal, and interpersonal
	• Listen actively
	• Clarity of written communication
	• Empathetically engage with others
	Capacity building
	• Provide relevant meaningful, practical and readily accessible professional development for teachers and paraprofessionals
	• Provide meaningful, leadership development for principals
	• Providing comprehensive induction programmes for teachers
		Ethic of care
		• Value student voice
		• Value advocacy – parents/caregivers and community
		• Value advocacy – Principal
		• Value teacher professionalism demonstrated through inclusionary practices
		Appreciation of diversity
		• Value diversity in students
		• Value diversity in learning experiences and authentic assessment
		• Believe teachers can positively influence students
		• Believe principals can positively influence teachers and students.
		Professional ethics
		• Leaders are accountable for:
		  o leading inclusion
		  o all students' learning and for teachers differentiated instructional approaches for inclusion
		  o productive partnerships and resourcing

Fig. 8.1 Inclusive leadership framework

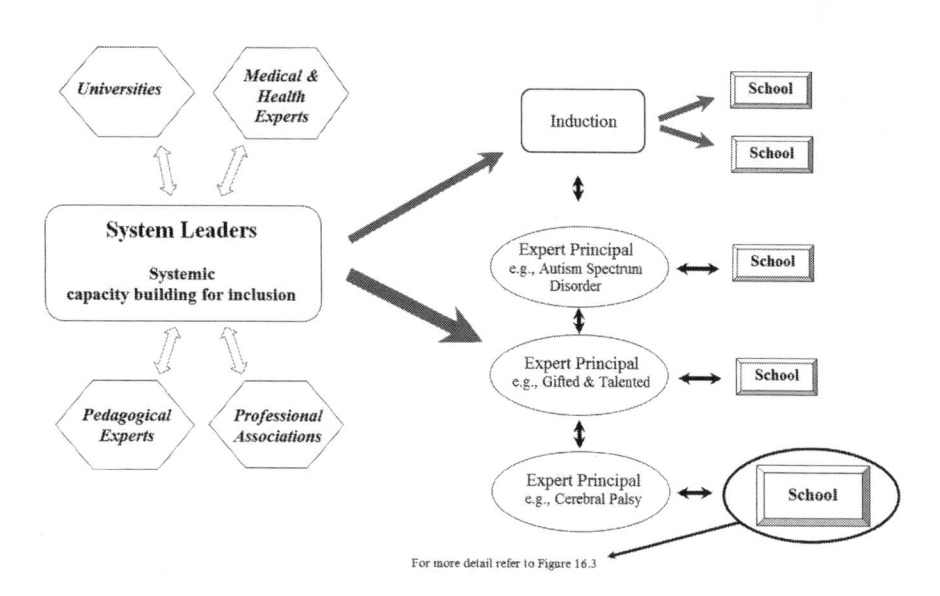

Fig. 8.2 Building capacity for inclusion (system level)

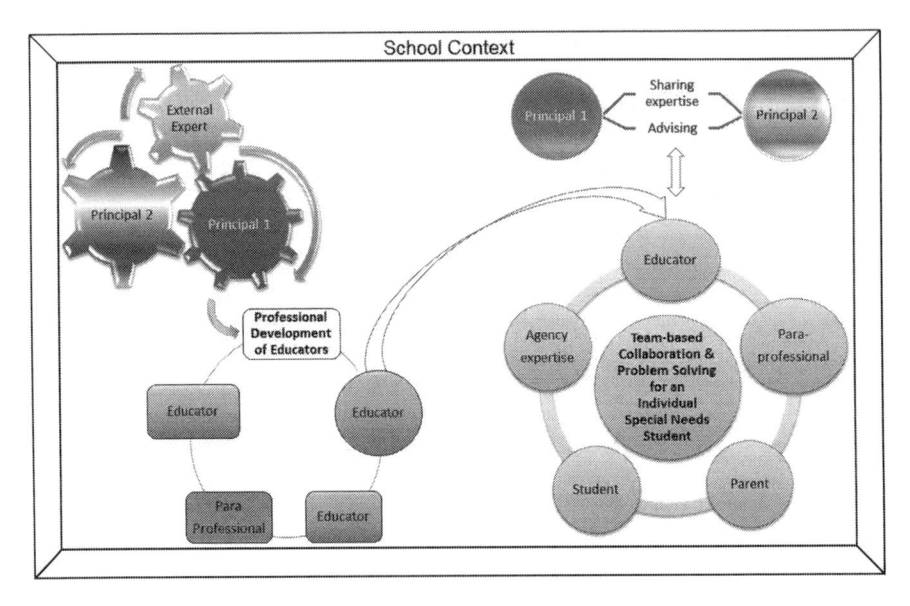

Fig. 8.3 Peer coaching leadership in building capacity (school level)

social programs that are no longer delivered in segregated locations but are integrated into the community; an increase in the numbers and types of disabilities being diagnosed and numbers of students identified as having a disability; and changes to legislation that recognize the rights of people to access educational resources and services in the mainstream of society. (Jordan, 2007, p. xi)

Students with special needs have always been in society but how different societies have responded to their learning needs has varied dramatically over the past three decades. For example, two to three decades ago in Canada many students were either not placed in school or placed in 'special' schools that were separate from the regular education system (Webber & Lupart, 2011). In other countries, students with disabilities had no access to schooling and some were placed in asylums and essentially largely forgotten by their families and society (Montessori, 1967; Webber & Scott, 2009). Many nations around the world have responded to the United Nations' (1989) "Declaration of the Rights of the Child" Principle 5, which stated: "The child who is physically, mentally or socially handicapped shall be given the special treatment, education and care required by his particular condition", by examining their policy frameworks related to special needs children and youth. Most Western nations, such as Australia, Canada, England, and the US, as well as many others in Eastern Europe and Asia have addressed these negative practices and have instituted policies to ensure special needs children can receive access to education much like their more able counterparts (Aspland, Datta, & Talukdar, 2012; Robertson, 2012; Webber & Scott, 2009). Even so, there remains criticism of many nations including Australia, Hong Kong, and many European countries, which are lagging in their proactiveness in effectively providing for 'disabled' children with the extent and quality of the education they receive still questionable (Aspland et al., 2012; Hue, 2012; Lundy, 2012). As educational understandings about students with exceptionalities has progressed, so too has the attention to meeting these students' learning and socialisation skills, which has led to inclusion policies and practices where students with special needs spend some or all of their school day within a mainstream classroom (Jordan, 2007). With the implementation of inclusion policies in many educational systems throughout the world, an ever increasing number of special needs students are entering regular education classrooms and teachers and school leaders are attempting as best they can to meet the needs of students with special education needs (Aspland et al., 2012). This raises issues with how effective inclusion has been, with Baroness Warnock's wry conclusions about inclusion in the UK indicating that:

> The concept of inclusion springs from hearts in the right place. Its meaning however, is far from clear, and in practice it often means that children are physically included but emotionally excluded … Inclusion should mean being involved in a common enterprise of learning, rather than being necessarily under the same roof. (2005, cited in Robertson, 2012, p. 79)

8.2.1 International Definitions of Special Needs

The term inclusion is defined differently by educators, administrators, and academics (Weber & Bennett, 2004). As Carroll and her associates (2011) identified "inclusion is not a legal term", rather is a "philosophy," and references the US IDEIA Act's articulation of "the least restrictive environment" (p. 120). They offered though, a rather intriguing concept of situated learning based upon Lave and Wenger's (1991) research, whereby students with significant support needs have the opportunity to learn within communities of practice, where their interaction is "legitimately peripheral initially, but which increases in degree of involvement and complexity over time" (p. 120).

Many nations and states/provinces provide definitions of special needs within their policy frameworks and a sample of these definitions from different cultural contexts are outlined below. For example, Ontario Ministry of Education defined categories of exceptionalities as follows:

- Behaviour;
- Communication (includes autism, deaf and hard of hearing, speech impairment and learning disability);
- Intellectual (includes giftedness, mild intellectual disability, and developmental disability);
- Physical (includes blind and low vision); and
- Multiple (a combination of learning or other disorders, impairments, or physical disabilities). (Ontario Education Act, 1990)

For purposes of special education support, the US Government defines a cognitively challenged student as an individual with a significantly limited, impaired, or delayed learning capacity of a young child (3–9 years old), exhibited by difficulties in one or more of the following areas: receptive and/or expressive language, cognitive abilities, physical functioning, social emotional, or adaptive functioning, and/or self-help skills (IDEIA, 2004).

The Department of Education, Western Australia, has had a long-term policy direction for caring for students with special needs and recently redrafted their "Disability Access and Inclusion Plan 2012–2017" in response to the 2004 amendments to the Western Australian Disability Services Act 1993. The Act defines students with disabilities as a condition:

- which is attributable to an intellectual, psychiatric, cognitive, neurological, sensory or physical impairment or a combination of those impairments;
- which is permanent or likely to be permanent;
- which may or may not be of a chronic or episodic nature; and
- which results in –
  (i) a substantially reduced capacity of a person for communication, social interaction, learning or mobility; and
  (ii) the need for continuing support services. (Government of Western Australia, 1999, p. 3)

The Federal Republic of Nigeria offers a broader definition of special needs students as those with a "learning difficulty because of different categories of handicaps, such as blindness, deafness, hardness of hearing, social maladjustment, among others, due to circumstances of birth inheritance, social position, mental and physical health pattern, or accident in later life" (Eskay & Oboegbulem, 2013, p. 253).

The terminology used to describe students with special needs also varies around the world. For example, the Ontario Ministry policies refer to special needs students as those with "exceptionalities" – a positive connotation; contrastingly, the Western Australian Department of Education policy refers to these students as those with "disabilities", which tends to reinforce the deficit perception. This deficit phraseology is similar to that in Nigeria's policy which referred to special needs students as those with "handicaps". Even more curious is that Nigeria's policy definition included "social maladjustment" and "social position". To further reinforce the differential within categorisation of students with special needs or exceptionalities, the Western Australian Department of Education Policy Framework (2001) and the Nigerian policy definition separates students with "disabilities" or "handicaps" from the "gifted and talented" (G&T) even though many G&T students also present with disabilities which masks and confuses identification and the appropriate servicing of their learning needs.

For purposes of clarity, the working definition of inclusion throughout this chapter refers to a student who may or may not have been formally identified through an identification, placement, and review process, and who is in a regular (inclusive) education classroom setting for all or most of the day (Jordan, 2007). The definition of special needs is open to interpretation but frequently means students who have physical, cognitive, psychological, and/or emotional challenges and may also include the gifted disabled student (Weber & Bennett, 2004). Despite these differences around the world there is a general understanding and acceptance of inclusion as a part of an educator's classroom life however it is defined.

Further compounding the confusion within terminology use in discussion about inclusion, Jones and Bender (1993) noted that authors use a variety of terms to describe support personnel working with special needs students in an educational setting (e.g., teacher's aide and/or instructional support aide) but the majority of the literature does not distinguish amongst the terms or the differences in the roles. The model in much of the literature refers to these positions as paraprofessional. For the purposes of this chapter a paraprofessional refers to any one of the following: a teacher's aide, an educational assistant, a child and youth worker, and/or a designated early childhood educator.

8.2.2 Societal Expectations

The discussion in this chapter is founded largely upon the findings from Fournier's (2012) doctoral study set in Ontario, Canada, exploring novice teachers' perceptions of working with special needs students in their inclusive (mainstream) classrooms. In examining the societal demands regarding inclusionary practices with special needs students, Fournier noted that on average 15 % of elementary students per school required some special education support (People for Education, 2007). In 2007, the Government of Ontario also introduced two significant pieces of legislation which directly related to special needs students: *Bill 212 – the Amended Safe Schools Act* (Ontario Education Act, 2007); this Bill required educators to be extremely cognisant of the needs of special education students with regard to discipline; and *The Public Policy Memorandum (PPM) 140* (Policy/Programme Memorandum, 2007) which mandated that boards of education offer programmes based on the principles of Applied Behaviour Analysis (ABA) to all students within a board of education who are diagnosed as autistic. As a result of these political moves, the legislative and moral responsibilities placed on teachers became quite daunting, further complicating their already complex role (Browder & Spooner, 2006).

As previously stated, inclusive classrooms, where students with and without special needs learn alongside one another, have become the norm rather than the exception in many school systems throughout the world. These policy shifts were purportedly for the purposes of providing better educational access to a range of programming, as well as greater access to social environments that more closely mirrored wider society. However, some may argue that during an era of managerialism and marketisation applied to education, this was a cost cutting mechanism designed to shut down expensive special schools and programmes that had entire staff with extensive experience and expertise in meeting the specific and targeted needs of these students, although this has simply moved the expense into regular schools (California Postsecondary Education Commission, 2008; Hadderman, 2001; Tearle & Spandagou, 2012). As a result many students were placed in schools where teachers had little expertise or experience to effectively teach to the range of exceptionalities now found in their inclusive classrooms (Cooper, Kurtts, Baber, & Vallecorsa, 2008; Gwernan-Jones & Burden, 2010; Lombardi & Hunka, 2001). Even now some decades later, many novice and experienced teachers still feel inadequately prepared to cope with teaching special needs children and youth (Killoran et al., 2013; McCray & McHatton, 2011; Woodcock, Hemmings, & Kay, 2012). Additionally, as Gökdere (2012) stated, teachers indicated inclusion "causes extra work and intra-class problems for the teacher" (p. 2804). This means that there is a need for insightful and informed leadership at the school and district levels to ensure that novice and experienced teachers have the knowledge and expertise to effectively teach and assess all students within their care (Eskay & Oboegbulem, 2013; Fournier, 2012).

8.3 The Cognitively Challenged Student

Students with cognitive challenges require significant modifications to the regular curriculum in order to be successful. Many students who have significant cognitive delay also need a great deal of support to facilitate their socialisation and to manage problem behaviours (Cooper, 1996). Therefore in many cases, these special needs students are unable to follow the regular curricula approaches that teachers prepare for the class and so, in many Western countries, teachers are expected to create and follow a plan that has been uniquely designed for the particular instructional and assessment needs of an individual student. These plans are commonly referred to as Individual Programme/Education Plans (IPP/IEP) and entail specific, measurable, and realistic objectives and outcomes tailored to the student but also aligned with the curricula guidelines (Jordan, 2007). Indeed, some countries such as the US actually mandate IPP/IEP for special needs students as an approach to ensuring students are overtly considered in the classroom and that teachers are making every effort to support their educational needs (Cooper, 1996).

Effective programme implementation and assessment for cognitively challenged students begins with the principal's ability to ensure that the instructional, environmental, and assessment accommodations and modifications are planned for, and implemented by, the teacher and paraprofessional in consultation with the student, parents, and other experts who can support the student's learning and socialisation outcomes (Bausch, Quinn, Chung, Ault, & Behrmann, 2009). Indeed, as principals are held accountable for the learning outcomes of all students in their schools, they therefore must monitor and report on the implementation of differentiated learning and assessment for these special needs students. A well-articulated IPP/IEP is, however, only effective if the educators (classroom teachers and/or paraprofessionals) are capable of implementing and assessing these programme plans. Fournier's (2012) teachers expressed great dismay at not being prepared at university to write and implement these plans, with 68 % reporting feeling overwhelmed and unprepared for the challenge of writing an IPP/IEP. They stated that writing an IPP/IEP was "the worst experience ever … because I had no idea at all what I'm supposed to write in these documents" with many of them having to complete seven or eight in their first year. The other concern with IPP/IEPs is that considerable time is expended in creating these, which in many cases could be time better spent actually engaging with the student in a learning activity. Unfortunately there is the risk that the emphasis of provision is on the plan rather than on the implementation of differentiated instructional strategies tailored to meet the needs of the child or youth (Frankl, 2005). Another common criticism of the IPP/IEP is the tendency for teachers to prepare these in isolation and without collaboration with important stakeholders such as the parent, and more importantly, the student him/herself (Goepel, 2009; Peters, 1990).

It is also important to note that as an instructional leader, principals need to be reasonably conversant with the curriculum in order to fully understand how the curriculum can and should be modified in order to meet the unique educational and social needs of students with cognitive challenges. Traditional assessment methods frequently are inappropriate or simply do not meet the needs of students with cognitive challenges; therefore, principals must also be able to model creative, real world applications for assessment purposes (Frankl, 2005). It is imperative that leaders and educators must understand that goal attainment for students with cognitive challenges is, in many cases, a multi-year long process reliant upon educators' having a deep understanding of skill acquisition and the capacity to effectively and appropriately scaffold students' learning, with aligned assessment that is realistic and relevant. Identifying what students will need to know, be able to do, and value by the end of their school career and backward map from that endpoint to the present (the planning stage), ensuring to integrate continuous assessment that will provide essential feedback for improvement, is critical for the ongoing success of a student with a cognitive challenge. Educators' ability to link this knowledge and skill acquisition to pragmatic, real world applications and authentic assessment tasks, is a key element to the successful implementation of a student's individual education plan. The following real case study illustrates some of the challenges experienced by a child with a cognitive delay in a regular elementary classroom setting.

8.3.1 Case Study 1 – Meeting Carlos' Needs

Carlos, a 12 year old boy, was enrolled in a regular Grade 7 classroom. He struggled with all aspects of school throughout the primary grades. In Grade 4, he underwent a psycho-educational assessment. This assessment, which included evaluation of Carlos' cognitive functioning, his academic abilities, and his adaptive behaviours, provided an important starting point from which to begin planning for Carlos' individualised programme. The assessment indicated that Carlos was functioning cognitively below the first percentile. During the junior grades, Carlos received a considerably modified programme and was placed with the same teacher for two consecutive years because the teacher understood and was responsive to Carlos' needs. She received ongoing professional development specific to Carlos' programme and assessment needs. Additionally, he received additional support from a paraprofessional who was a valued member of the overall team supporting him. Throughout the junior grades Carlos had a small peer group that transitioned with him as a cohort from year-to-year. Carlos' peer group knew him well, and liked and accepted him and these combined factors attributed to Carlos' relative academic and social success throughout his junior grade years.

This year Carlos entered Grade 7 at the local community middle school. He now has more than one teacher throughout the day and his peer group is no longer an intact cohort.

Not all of his teachers fully understand how to modify the curriculum appropriately for him. The paraprofessional at Carlos' new school supports several students throughout the day. Carlos is struggling. He is displaying a number of negative behaviours (swearing, hitting, and running away) that have not been present since his early primary years. Carlos' parents are frustrated and angry. They fear that he will not make further academic gains and they worry about his safety. Carlos' teachers feel stressed and defensive and are concerned that they will not be able to effectively teach and assess Carlos while also addressing the needs of all of their other students.

Carlos' teachers need effective leadership from their principal. As an instructional leader, the principal should be supporting and advising his/her teachers about how to provide high quality programming and appropriate assessments to facilitate Carlos' academic success. Equally important he/she must model the belief that all students can learn given the right supports. So what do principals need to know and be able to do in order to enact instructional leadership for optimal inclusive education?

8.4 Implications for School/District Level Leadership

> Inclusive education for students with significant support needs requires a philosophical shift in the beliefs, values, habits and assumed ways of doing things within a school community … Likewise, inclusive practices … must be located within the culture of the school … where … differences [are] celebrated, and diversity maximized. … and access require school organizations to recognize, value, and provide for diversity in new ways. … educators will need to collaboratively address the challenges brought by these students and reflectively problem-solve to provide standards-based education in inclusive settings. This inclusive school culture exudes a sense of belonging, where all children are accepted and valued. (Carroll et al., 2011, p. 121)

Carlos' case clearly indicates that a student with a cognitive delay may pose many unique challenges for teachers regarding programming and assessment. These challenges require effective leadership to make a difference in the life of the student and his/her family. Illustrating this leadership issue, Fullan (2003) passionately made a plea for the moral imperative of school leadership when he stated:

> As the main institution for fostering social cohesion in an increasingly diverse society, publicly funded schools must serve all children not simply those with the loudest or most powerful advocates. This means addressing the cognitive and social needs of all children, with an emphasis on including those who may not have been well served in the past. (p. 3)

In this chapter we propose the *Inclusive Leadership Framework* (see Fig. 8.1), which offers insights into the knowledge, skills, and attitudes/beliefs that enable school and district/ministerial leaders to effectively support inclusion. In the diagram the highlighted text indicates KSAs that are specific to system leaders rather than principals and represent the different expectations and responsibilities these have from their counterparts at the school level.

8.4.1 Knowledge

School level leaders require sufficient broad *research-based knowledge* about a range of different exceptionalities in order to suspect an underlying special need (knowledge of the *identifiers* of particular disorders, syndromes, or gifts etc.) in a student that warrants further testing and *identification* by an expert; however, this does not mean that a principal must be an expert in all exceptionalities. Furthermore, leaders need to demonstrate their procedural knowledge of the *agencies, university experts, and services* within the community that can provide identification, advice, support, and professional development for educators and families. Additionally, they should understand inclusion and the pragmatics of how to facilitate inclusionary approaches, which would encompass: the specifics of *differentiated instruction and assessment* that support learning, as well as the "why" and "what" of accommodations and modifications that assist particular special needs students. System and school leaders must also be conversant with the *legal frameworks* that regulate inclusion and understand how the *policies* can and should be implemented. Additionally, they must know how to bring about *change and innovation* in their school in order to create optimal inclusionary environments and to confront educators' inappropriate belief systems.

As an instructional leader, the principal must know and understand pedagogically and developmentally sound programming options for students with cognitive challenges. These include the importance of functional skills and practical academics. The elementary/primary principal must be well versed in the *curriculum* in order to understand how to modify it appropriately; whereas, secondary leaders lead the inclusionary efforts by collaborating with heads of subject areas, who have deep discipline-specific curriculum knowledge, to ensure differentiated approaches within that discipline. Regardless of the level of the school, the leader needs to be well versed in differentiated instruction and assessment in order to lead innovation in inclusion; for example, promoting different *learning strategies* and *authentic assessment* opportunities, as well as informatively monitoring the effectiveness of teachers' instructional approaches. Both school and system leaders must understand the importance of *evaluation* in monitoring programmes and initiatives designed to support particular exceptionalities, as the data from evaluation informs future implementation efforts and programming innovations.

Leaders need to understand the types of *accommodations* that are possible, which include: *instructional* – grouping work into smaller segments, scaffolding tasks to ensure foundational building blocks have been acquired etc.; *environmental* – preferential seating, breaks if needed, various types of classroom furniture, for example, therapeutic chairs, standing desks, fidget tools etc.; and *assessment* – provisions for increased time allotments for various tasks, scribing, oral dictation etc. Additionally, technology can be an accommodation that encompasses all three categories of accommodation and can be a valuable tool for student engagement.

8.4.2 Skills

Principals must refine a range of skills such as collaboration; communication – interpersonal, verbal, and written; and capacity building in order to effectively integrate inclusion in their schools. They must also have *socio-politicalacumen* in being able to mediate the sometimes competing *interests of different stakeholders*, for example, negotiating the demands of parents and educators while protecting the vulnerable student. Similarly, system leaders must also mediate these competitive interests at the societal level between government, community leaders, and professional associations etc., to ensure appropriate education that maximises student outcomes. Therefore, *collaboration* is essential in genuinely and respectfully engaging with stakeholders to solve problems and create optimal educational opportunities; a vital part of collaboration is the capacity to effectively communicate. *Communication* entails having interpersonal strengths which enable leaders to *empathise and understand different perspectives*, as well as to *actively listen* and effectively interact with others. *Written communication* can be effective in reducing power differentials if it is jargon-free and accessible to parents and teachers. Principals will *build the capacity* of their staff by encouraging teacher engagement in *pragmatic and informative professional development*. A well-educated staff will more effectively facilitate informed, practical inclusionary approaches. Similarly, system leaders must ensure principals have access to evidence-based and pragmatic *leadership development*. As part of the succession planning system, leaders will also establish induction programmes for novice and new-to-the-district educators with the view to creating capacity in the next generation of leaders.

8.4.3 Attitudes/Beliefs

Leaders' attitudes and beliefs are frequently not addressed within frameworks, potentially because the assumption is made that these are already positive or are too difficult to accommodate and change within leadership development. They are however, too important to ignore or neglect as they underpin the actions and agency of leaders. In our framework we identified the *ethic of care* as a crucial foundational attitude which should pervade leaders' interactions with others. The ethic of care will influence leaders' perceptions about *parentaladvocacy*. Leaders who value advocacy will foster an atmosphere of trust, respect, and courtesy avoiding patronisation and remaining mindful of the power differential inherent in schools. An ethic of care will mean leaders' *value 'student voice'*, understanding that student motivation is increased when they have 'a say' about their learning and assessment tasks, as well as through active input in the development of their IEP/IPPs. Leaders who value professionalism related to inclusion will actively promote teacher/paraprofessional engagement with professional development that will increase educator efficacy and capacity in differentiated instruction and assessment. System leaders' ethic of care is demonstrated by valuing principals' advocacy for inclusionary efforts.

Another value or attitude is the *appreciation of diversity*, namely: the (1) *belief that all children can learn* – principals must interrogate their beliefs about learning and ensure the conditions for learning are met; (2) *value diversity in students and ensure all are integrated within their school community* – leaders must recognise that diversity is not something to be suffered or tolerated, but rather celebrated and embraced, ensuring students with exceptionalities are an integral part of the school; and (3) *appreciating the importance of diversity in learning experiences and authentic assessment* – principals promote the implementation of creative and alternative activities and assessments, and leaders must remove barriers to innovation. These three foundational "values" are underpinned by the *recognition of teachers* as crucial influencers on students' learning. Indeed, leaders must have faith in the research that noted "teachers have such fine abilities to learn" (Joyce & Calhoun, 2010, n.p.) and when leaders discern weaknesses in educator capacity they must proactively remedy these deficits. Likewise, system leaders must overtly *value principals* and recognise them as significant influencers on educators and students.

Professional ethics encompasses conceptualisations of leaders' sense of accountability and responsibility to stakeholders and society. Our framework highlights the importance of leaders' accountability for *leading inclusion*; responsibility for ensuring *all students can and do learn* to the best of their ability, and that all *teachers are using appropriate differentiated approaches* to support learning and assessment; as well as the expectation on leaders to effectively establish productive partnerships, and garner resources, for constructive inclusion.

8.4.3.1 Deconstructing Carlos' Case

The principal in Carlos' case needed to ensure that the teachers felt confident writing and implementing Carlos' IEP in a meaningful and appropriate way; however, Carlos' teachers felt stressed and defensive, indicating they were concerned about whether or not they would be able to meet his academic and social needs. In order to address these issues, Carlos' principal needed to recognise the challenges faced by his teachers and not assume that all his teachers knew how to effectively modify and assess the curriculum. Additionally, the principal should have considered what professional development would facilitate teachers' and paraprofessionals' instructional effectiveness and ensured they had access to such programmes. Giancreco, Edelman, Broer, and Doyle (2001) warned of the 'training gap', where many paraprofessionals were untrained or undertrained, resulting in students with the greatest learning challenges in the classroom receiving exclusive instruction and support from the least qualified staff member.

Table 8.1 outlines a set of practical 'Do's and Don'ts' which offer guidance regarding the type of programming and assessment supports principals might consider for students with cognitive challenges.

So what might this programming and assessment chart look like in practice when the principal begins to structure collaborative planning and assessment PD for Carlos' teachers and the paraprofessional who support him? Communicating

Table 8.1 Do's and Don'ts for programming and assessment

Do	Don't
Take into account student interest (pay attention to student voice)	Give apparently 'easy' or 'easy looking' work to older students
Consider the authenticity of the task (represent real life)	Create 'make work' or 'busy work' projects that aren't purposeful
Link assessment tasks to the curriculum	Assess concepts that are beyond the student's cognitive capability (even if the tasks have been reduced in number and volume)
Align assessment tasks with daily work and the goals of the IPP/IEP	Solely rely on peer tutors (other students) to support the student's needs

effectively with Carlos' family was a pivotal starting point. Meaningful dialogue with the family revealed that Carlos always showed an interest in cooking (*student voice*) – he was engaged and enthusiastic (*student motivation*) at home during meal preparations and especially during special occasions (*authentic task and assessment*). Furthermore, Carlos enjoyed feeling needed and displayed pride when his family praised his cooking (*authentic assessment and reinforcement*).

Carlos' middle school runs a breakfast programme; hence, the educator-team thought creatively and collaborated with one another so that this breakfast programme constituted an excellent platform upon which to base Carlos' individualised curricular goals (*student interest*). The team started by backward mapping a number of goals in both numeracy and literacy (*planning*). In this scenario, Carlos was now part of a team that planned daily nutritious snacks for over 100 students (*authentic task linked to curriculum*). This required Carlos to read supermarket flyers for weekly specials, formulate shopping lists, budget for the week, shop, prepare recipes, and track student responses to various breakfast options, all of which were monitored for quality by the teacher (*authentic assessment*).

Carlos' homeroom teacher began to share ideas with the other teachers and as a result the civics teacher has now included the chef from a local restaurant and the produce manager of a nearby supermarket to make presentations at an upcoming career fair (*relevant and authentic programming*). Overall this approach has been positive as Carlos is now beginning to feel like a valuable contributing member of his new school community (*positive student efficacy*).

8.5 Issues with Professional Development

Similar to Carlos' teachers, Fournier's (2012) participants described many challenges in teaching special needs students in an inclusive classroom setting. They felt overwhelmed, intimidated, frustrated, and distracted. Findings emphasised the importance of principals building the capacity of their teachers through the provision or enabling them access to professional development on inclusionary practices. Teachers valued the professional development if it met their very specific needs.

One participant described why professional development that included a collegial mentoring aspect was a key component to his success:

> I think that while workshops can be useful, … for first year teachers the hands-on experience does definitely outweigh that and if we have a chance to see that [the strategy] modelled, see examples of what other teachers are doing, has been much more effective for me.

The opposite was also true in that if the relevance was not apparent, teachers rejected it:

> Our principal gave a little presentation on autism but when you can't really relate to something – I don't have any autistic students so for me it … wasn't very effective. It's bad of me to say but I wasn't listening because I couldn't relate to what she was talking about.

Accessibility was an equally important aspect of professional development which emerged from the study:

> The most effective for me was having the special education resource teacher in the school, who was … a mentor, but it wasn't an official role. For me that was the most effective. Having somebody with a lot of knowledge and experience in the field who was accessible, willingly accessible, and it was just widely known that you could go to that person.

Therefore, Carlos' principal needed to: understand the curriculum (knowledge), build the capacity of his staff in terms of differentiated instruction and assessment (skills); possess an unwavering ethic of care, and value parent advocacy and student voice (attitude/belief). However, just as important as providing professional development is the type, relevance, and accessibility of it.

Having considered school leaders, educators, and paraprofessionals we should at this juncture explore other stakeholder perspectives and avenues available to educators to support special needs students.

8.5.1 Community Partnerships

The importance of community partnerships cannot be underestimated; hence, school leaders must also be skilful at working with a variety of other people; for example, students, parents, educators, paraprofessionals, and experts. Leaders need to meaningfully engage parents and outside agencies (including psychological services, occupational therapists, and physiotherapists etc.) acknowledging that each stakeholder contributes unique knowledge, expertise, and resources that can supplement the school-based support for special needs students. Blue-Banning, Summers, Frankland, Lord Nelson, and Beegle (2004) asserted that forging supportive relationships between parents and professionals is key to successful collaborative partnerships. These authors explored the specific indicators that professionals and parents identified as indicative to them of 'effective collaborative partnerships': from the perspective of educators these involved improved academic achievement and functional life skills; whereas, for families the ultimate goal was improved overall quality of life for their children with disabilities and for themselves and was linked with the quality of their partnerships with service providers.

Blue-Banning and associates (2004) also identified the disparity of power as a problem for parents who were frequently not perceived as equal partners by professionals who continued to maintain overall control. Indeed, other authors have categorically advocated for parents as integral partners in their child's education with some indicating that IEP/IPP should be written in jargon-free language in order to make this accessible and understandable to parents and students (Frankl, 2005; Goepel, 2009; Robertson, 2012). As an extension of their *ethic of care* and *appreciation for diversity* (see Fig. 8.1), leaders play a pivotal liaison role in assisting parents in accessing agency and district support. As Blue-Banning and associates found, families indicated it was stressful having to fight for services, cope with humiliating or disrespectful regulations, and poor provider attitudes.

The following real account describes a parent's experience with an education system in trying to find the right placement for her developmentally delayed autistic daughter. It illustrates leadership issues when there is a lack of an ethic of care and appreciation for diversity, which exacerbated the parent's stress.

8.5.1.1 Case Study 2 – Accessing Support for Jennifer: A Mother's Anguish

> I feel like all eyes are always on me; always blaming me without ever really saying it. I mean I had services in place [in the city]. I know what my daughter needs but life happens. It throws you the raw end of the stick sometimes. I moved up here [to the rural area] because this is where my parents live and they needed me. I'm all they had. My father was diagnosed with cancer so I came here to help my mother care for him but then she died and it was just us! I tried to enrol Jennifer in the school closest to my parents' home but I was told that we are out of area and they don't have to accept her. The school was only fifteen minutes away from my home. I never imagined that I was literally on the wrong side of the street [the school boundary was on the other side of the street].
>
> So I came here [school in her jurisdiction] but you folks [the principal and his staff] keep telling me that the only programme that the district has for developmentally delayed students is more than fifty minutes away so Jennifer will have to go there. Jennifer could never manage a bus ride like that [*this mother put her head down on the table and cried*]. I hear so much about meeting every child's needs but it's just one door after another slamming in my face! I can't keep her [Jennifer] at home any longer and yet it seems like no one is willing to bend, or change the rules just a little bit. All I've heard is what the schools can't do for her; can't find her an educational assistant, can't find her a place to call her own. All I want is for you to make it possible for my daughter to attend school, and learn and have friends. Is that asking too much?

Clearly Jennifer's mother was experiencing understandable anguish in the tensions between needing to assist her aging ill parents and finding the right support for her daughter – needs which appeared to be mutually exclusive in the perception of the principal. This case epitomised what leaders 'should not do'. Indeed, when considering this mother's turmoil it highlights the importance of establishing trusting, collaborative, empowering relationships between families and educators in the facilitation of inclusion. Constructive relationships contribute to the elimination of the type of horrific experience Jennifer's mother encountered in trying to advocate for her child within a rigid, uncaring, and impersonal education system. Blue-

Banning and her associates' (2004) propose a model for successful collaborative family-professional partnerships founded on six key themes that provide a useful approach for leaders:

- Communication;
- Commitment;
- Equality;
- Skills;
- Trust; and
- Respect.

Effective communication meant that all members of the partnership needed to maintain respectful lines of communication. In order for the members to feel that there was *genuine commitment*, all parties had to be loyal to children and families and to each other's commitment to the goals of the partnership. *Equality* entailed maintaining a sense of equity amongst all members especially with regard to decision-making and feeling "equally powerful in their ability to influence outcomes for children and families" (p. 174). Recognising the respective *skill sets* of all members of the partnership as competent was also described as very important. *Trust*, honesty, and mutual *respect* were important characteristics and behaviours crucial in these partnerships which ensured each member regarded the others with high esteem. Lawson, Claiborne, Hardman, Austin, and Surko (2007) made a powerful yet simple statement when they proclaimed "Partnerships involve people working together to solve important problems and to achieve important goals" (p. 36). In Jennifer's case, if the principal had been committed to the principles outlined by Blue-Banning et al. (2004) he would have respected this mother's lived experience without passing negative judgment. Jennifer's mother brought valuable information to the table, as she knew her daughter's capacities and understood that such a long bus ride would deleteriously affect her child. If this mother had been viewed as an equal partner in Jennifer's education then perhaps more creative solutions could have been proposed instead of the raising of barriers.

Our Inclusive Leadership Framework (Fig. 8.1) provides leaders with a valuable reflective tool enabling them to critically evaluate their actions/decision-making when faced with providing educational support for special needs students. If a principal genuinely takes into account all three areas of the framework; their knowledge, skills, and attitudes/beliefs and been able to liaise with community partners (parent and mental health agencies), then there would have been real potential for a more positive outcome in a case such as Jennifer's. Goor, Schwenn, and Boyer (1997) asserted that the principal is the key instructional leader for all programmes within the school, including special education. The principal's attitude (*ethic of care* and *appreciation for diversity*) toward special education and his/her concern expressed for special needs students influences the success of these programmes (p. 133). In Jennifer's case, the principal was more concerned about the impact that accepting this new student would have on his existing programming and the problems that might arise as a result, for example, the need to find and hire specialised staff, rearrange existing timetables, and educate the school community about

Jennifer's unique needs. The principal's lack of a strong ethic of care and a willingness to take a moral stance created further barriers for Jennifer and her family which was contrary to the tenets of inclusionary leadership.

Similar to the reports by the teachers in Fournier's (2012) study, principals frequently feel unprepared for their role in the administration of special programmes in their schools (Irvine, Lupart, Loreman, & McGhie-Richmond, 2010). They may be unaware of the extent of their legal and educational responsibilities, or uncaring regarding their moral responsibilities to serve the needs of their communities, or they may simply delegate their responsibilities to other potentially less qualified personnel. Previous inclusive leadership programmes have focused solely on knowledge and skills without addressing the beliefs and values that underpin and influence leadership behaviours (Lindsey, 1986). They also frequently neglect the importance of self-reflection (Lindsey, 1986). Furthermore, there is a dearth of research about inclusive leadership, as well as a gap in provision of appropriate leadership development which compounds principals' inability to access support for their instructional leadership role (Irvine et al., 2010). Therefore we propose our leadership framework for inclusive leaders which includes the knowledge, skills, attributes/attitudes principals must have in order to be successful within contemporary inclusive environments. This framework can inform the selection of content and skills for leadership development and provides a valuable reflective tool for principals in their metacognition on the quality of their leadership for inclusion.

8.6 Building Capacity for Inclusion

System leaders, at the district and/or ministerial level, play a significant role in supporting the school principal. Providing ongoing, pedagogically sound leadership development for principals means they will have exposure to current evidence-based theory and approaches for inclusion. Many principals have not had personal experience teaching in an inclusive classroom, which may be further compounded by a lack of foundational knowledge about differentiated teaching and assessment in their own preservice preparation. This lack of preparation can lead to situations where the principal may know his legal responsibilities and be familiar with the pertinent legislation and policies related to special needs students but may not be able to ensure that, not only the letter of the law is followed, but also the principles of the law. System leaders are in a position to create a systemic infrastructure that allows for genuine collaboration and problem-solving with a variety of community partners, such as mental health agencies, local hospitals, and private and publicly funded occupational- and physio-therapists. Lawson et al. (2007) argued that system leaders are core partner-leaders as they help facilitate strategic bridge-building between community partners and school districts. System leaders are able to ameliorate bureaucratic barriers including budgetary constraints, thereby enabling school leaders greater flexibility to find creative solutions for students with exceptional needs.

8.6.1 Building Capacity for Inclusion (System Level)

In considering the need to build capacity for inclusion (Fig. 8.2) we identified that system leaders – district and/or ministerial – are pivotal in promoting the development of inclusive school leaders, as well as ensuring that novice and new-to-the-district educators are inducted into inclusionary approaches expected in their schools. In the model *Building Capacity for Inclusion (system level)*, system leaders are depicted as conduits in the flow of knowledge and expertise by accessing internal and external agencies, experts, and community stakeholders who can provide professional development and services to school leaders. We identified these networks as encompassing *university scholars* who provide the evidence-based research strengths in curriculum, instruction and assessment strategies, differentiation, and identification in specific exceptionalities; *medical and health experts* would be important not only for providing indepth information about the psycho-social and physical health aspects of student needs, but also in identification and guidance for educators in programming for these students; *pedagogical experts* may include teacher-leaders, special education educators, or university professors who have expertise in tailoring teaching and learning for students with specific disabilities and/or exceptionalities; *professional associations* may include other community groups or stakeholders and their associated networks who can inform special needs services and advocate for particular exceptionalities. We propose that system leaders can draw upon the expertise residing within these different 'expert' groups to provide valuable leadership development for principals to ensure they have a broad knowledge about a range of disabilities and exceptionalities, as well as comprehensive understandings of differentiation in curriculum, instruction, and assessment.

In this model (Fig. 8.2) we advocate for a pooling of expertise across a district/region. This means each principal would become an expert in one particular disability/exceptionality. For example, a principal could specialise in Autism Spectrum Disorder attaining a deep understanding of the range of characteristics that would aid identification, the psycho-social aspects of the disorder, the educational approaches that support students with this disorder, behavioural management strategies that work to promote enhanced student engagement, and the accommodations necessary for optimal student performance. Similarly, another principal could become an expert in 'gifted and talented' education, while another may become an expert in cerebral palsy. Hence, principals would 'know a little about a lot' in relation to inclusion but be experts in one particular disability/exceptionality. Therefore, at the system level inclusive leadership would be widespread, creating a pool of experts that could serve inclusive leadership across the system. This pool of experts would ensure the distribution of excellence in inclusion without risking leader burnout in expecting each principal to be an expert in all manner of disabilities/exceptionalities. Additionally, this model acts as a protection mechanism against the devastating loss of expertise with principal attrition as only part of the collective knowledge base would be lost at any given time. The foundational concept in this model is peer coaching, which research indicates is highly effective professional development (Joyce & Calhoun, 2010; Showers & Joyce, 1996); therefore, it can be expected that this approach would facilitate an overall increase in leadership capacity for inclusion across all exceptionalities over time.

Mirroring the leadership development approach, system leaders would focus on incoming novice and experienced new-to-the-district educators. As the literature notes, most educators have significant deficits in terms of the pragmatics of inclusion (Cooper et al., 2008; Gwernan-Jones & Burden, 2010; Killoran et al., 2013; Lombardi & Hunka, 2001; McCray & McHatton, 2011; Woodcock et al., 2012). Therefore, system leaders have the responsibility to provide theoretically sound and pragmatically-oriented professional development to address the current gaps in pedagogical knowledge and expertise. Considering that novice teachers are the leaders of the future, it is crucial to provide them with appropriate professional development, along with positive experiences with special needs students, at the commencement of their career that will nurture the knowledge, skills, and values that are essential for inclusionary leadership in the future. Effective induction models have the potential to act as a bridge between inadequate university preparation and the realities of the inclusive classroom. To this end, we propose in the model that the expert principals could also work with the induction programme facilitators, sharing their expertise and bridging the gap between theory and practice in teaching novice teachers about particular exceptionalities and the optimal approaches to inclusion to meet the needs of exceptional students.

8.6.2 *Inclusionary Leadership for Building Capacity (School Level)*

The second model (Fig. 8.3) depicts inclusionary leadership for building capacity at the school level. Two key aspects are included in the school-based model: first, principals leading professional development for their staff; and second, their leadership and support of team-based case management for special needs individuals.

8.6.2.1 Leading Professional Development

In the system model (Fig. 8.2), we highlighted the importance of developing a pool of expert leaders with individual specialisations. In the school-level model (Fig. 8.3) we envisaged that this pool of leaders could provide peer-to-peer support for each other thereby providing expert consultancy in the provision of professional development at the school level, as well as the sharing of their particular expertise and the consultancy advice in case management for individual students. Considering that many school populations have students with varied disabilities/exceptionalities, it creates complications for a principal to effectively lead across this diversity. Hence, these models are designed to promote expertise across a district without overwhelming any one principal. The school-level model (Fig. 8.3) proposes that when a principal (Principal 1) encounters a deficit in knowledge and skills in his/her staff regarding a particular disability/exceptionality, he/she can call upon the expertise of a peer-expert (Principal 2) and potentially an external expert (either a teacher-leader or other expert) to work with him/her (Principal 1) in providing targeted professional development for the staff. This peer coaching support would be reciprocated if Principal 2 needed the expertise of Principal 1. In addition to the professional development of entire staff, the peer coaching collaboration could be extended into the team-based case management cycle.

8.6.2.2 Inclusive Leadership in Team-Based Case Management

As previously highlighted in this chapter, effective inclusion of students with disabilities requires collaboration amongst a team which could include the classroom teacher, special educator, paraprofessional, the student and parents, outside agencies (if appropriate), and the principal. These team collaborations involve co-planning ways to most effectively meet the student's needs in the learning environment. Therefore, the principal must have confidence in teachers' instructional effectiveness for students with disabilities, and teachers must feel efficacious in working with, and making the most of, the impact of a paraprofessional's support. The principal must also feel confident in his/her own capacity to provide instructional leadership for effective case management; hence, if Principal 1 lacks the expertise needed in this case then he/she can draw upon the expertise of Principal 2. This peer coaching relationship facilitates the sharing of information and expertise among the team thereby ensuring optimal approaches for the case management. This peer coaching also results in increased knowledge and efficacy across the team.

8.7 Future Directions for University Stakeholders

This chapter resonates with the issues of educator and leadership preparedness in effectively supporting the learning of special needs students. Al-Zyoudi (2006), Fournier (2012), Gwernan-Jones and Burden (2010), and Hue (2012) all iterate that teachers' effectiveness in teaching special needs students is influenced by their prior experiences with students with disabilities/exceptionalities, and the relevancy of their training in differentiated instruction and assessment. Hence, it is imperative that university preservice programmes overtly address not only the philosophies and theories related to inclusion but also the pragmatic specifics of differentiated teaching and assessment. Furthermore, leadership development programming should enable teacher-leaders and principals to achieve a nexus between inclusion theory and differentiated practices.

University programmes focused on school psychology, counselling and psychological testing services are advised to forge stronger professional community engagement networks so that school and system leaders and their community stakeholders can readily access their expertise and services. This means that psychology departments can provide pragmatic support to parents and educators in identification, accommodations, and pedagogical advice in the service of children and youth with disabilities/exceptionalities.

8.8 Conclusion

This chapter explored the importance of knowledgeable and skilled leadership in promoting more effective inclusion for cognitively challenged students. Although there is contention in defining inclusion, there is no doubt that the expectation to integrate individuals with special needs into regular classrooms is a global phenomenon. Accompanying this phenomenon is the concern with educator preparedness for the practicalities of differentiating their instructional approaches and assessment strategies in order to meet the unique needs of their students. Moreover, leaders at the school and district/ministerial levels are also grappling with the demands of instructional leadership for inclusion. Fournier's study showed that if teachers felt well supported by their leaders, the likelihood that they would feel a greater sense of self-efficacy teaching special needs students in an inclusive setting increased.

An inclusive leadership framework was proposed to identify specific knowledge – inclusion, procedural, and pedagogical; skills – socio-politicalacumen, collaboration, communication and capacity building; and attitudes/beliefs/values – a strong ethic of care, appreciation of diversity, and professional ethics. This framework is designed to provide guidance for leadership development.

We identified the pivotal importance of capacity building at both the leadership and educator levels within educational systems and posited two models designed to promote capacity for inclusion. The first model focused on district/ministerial leadership wherein leaders can facilitate networks with key experts in the provision of leadership development and induction programmes. This system model was founded on the principles of peer coaching to create a pool of expert principals with specialisations in a range of disabilities and exceptionalities, with the peer coaching dimension focussed on the sharing of expertise and support across the system. A second model, nested at the school level, envisaged how leaders could utilise the pool of expertise in providing ongoing leader peer-to-peer support and leadership development, as well as consultancy and professional development for teachers and team-based case management cycles.

When principals and system leaders provide a strong support network for all teachers, students, and parents, the result will be greater teacher efficacy and ultimately, and most importantly, greater positive outcomes for all students with special needs.

References

Al-Zyoudi, M. (2006). Teachers' attitudes towards inclusive education in Jordanian schools. *International Journal of Special Education, 21*(2), 55–62.

Aspland, T., Datta, P., & Talukdar, J. (2012). Curriculum policies for students with special needs in Australia. *International Journal of Special Education, 27*(3), 36–44.

Bausch, M. E., Quinn, B. S., Chung, Y., Ault, M. J., & Behrmann, M. M. (2009). Assistive technology in the individualized education plan: Analysis of policies across ten states. *Journal of Special Education Leadership, 22*(1), 9–23.

Blue-Banning, M., Summers, J. A., Frankland, C. H., Lord Nelson, L., & Beegle, G. (2004). Dimensions of family and professional partnerships: Constructive guidelines for collaboration. *Exceptional Children, 70*(2), 167–184.

Browder, D. M., & Spooner, F. (2006). *Teaching language arts, math, and science to students with significant cognitive disabilities*. Baltimore, MD: Brookes Publishing Company.

California Postsecondary Education Commission. (2008). *Overview of Governor Schwarzenegger's proposed 2008–09 state budget* (Commission Report 08-02, pp. 1–6). Sacramento, CA: California Postsecondary Education Commission.

Carroll, D., Fulmer, C., Sobel, D., Garrison-Wade, D., Aragon, L., & Coval, L. (2011). School culture for students with significant support needs: Belonging is not enough. *International Journal of Special Education, 26*(2), 120–127.

Cooper, P. (1996). Are individual education plans a waste of paper? *British Journal of Special Education, 23*(3), 115–119.

Cooper, J. E., Kurtts, S., Baber, C. R., & Vallecorsa, A. (2008). A model for examining teacher preparation curricula for inclusion. *Teacher Education Quarterly, 35*(4), 155–176.

Eskay, M., & Oboegbulem, A. (2013). Designing appropriate curriculum for special education in urban school in Nigeria: Implication for administrators. *US-China Education Review, 3*(4), 252–258.

Fournier, E. (2012). *Novice elementary teachers' perspectives teaching mainstreamed special needs students: Implications for leadership, preservice education, and professional development*. Unpublished Doctor of Education (EdD) thesis, University of Calgary.

Frankl, C. (2005). Managing Individual Education Plans: Reducing the load of the special educational needs coordinator. *Support for Learning, 20*(2), 77–82.

Fullan, M. (2003). *The moral imperative of school leadership*. Thousand Oaks, CA: Corwin Press.

Giancreco, M. F., Edelman, S. W., Broer, S. M., & Doyle, M. B. (2001). Paraprofessional support of students with disabilities: Literature from the past decade. *Exceptional Children, 68*, 45–63.

Goepel, J. (2009). Constructing the individual education plan: Confusion or collaboration? *Support for Learning, 24*(3), 126–132.

Gökdere, M. (2012). A comparative study of the attitude, concern, and interaction levels of elementary school teachers and teacher candidates towards inclusive education. *Educational Sciences: Theory and Practice, 12*(4), 2800–2806.

Goor, M. B., Schwenn, J. O., & Boyer, L. (1997). Preparing principals for leadership in special education. *Intervention in School and Clinic, 32*(3), 133–141.

Government of Western Australia. (1999). *Western Australian School Education Act, 1999*. Perth, Australia: Western Australia Government Press.

Gwernan-Jones, R., & Burden, R. L. (2010). "Are they just lazy?" Student teachers' attitudes about dyslexia. *Dyslexia, 16*(1), 66–86. doi:10.1002/dys.393.

Hadderman, M. (2001). *School finance. Trends and issues* (pp. 1–50). Washington, DC: Office of Educational Research and Improvement.

Hue, M. (2012). Inclusion practices with special educational needs students in a Hong Kong secondary school: Teachers' narratives from a school guidance perspective. *British Journal of Guidance & Counselling, 40*(2), 143–156. doi:10.1080/03069885.2011.646950.

Individuals with Disabilities Education Improvement Act of 2004, PL-108-446, 20 U.S.C. §§ 1400 et.seq.

Irvine, A., Lupart, J., Loreman, T., & McGhie-Richmond, D. (2010). Educational leadership to create authentic inclusive schools: The experiences of principals in a Canadian rural school district. *Exceptionality Education International, 20*(2), 70–88.

Jones, K., & Bender, W. N. (1993). Utilization of paraprofessionals in special education: A review of the literature. *Remedial and Special Education, 14*(1), 7–14. doi:10.1177/074193259301400103.

Jordan, A. (2007). *Introduction to inclusive education*. Mississauga, ON, Canada: Wiley.

Joyce, B., & Calhoun, E. (2010). *Models of professional development. A celebration of educators*. Thousand Oaks, CA: Corwin.

Killoran, I., Zaretsky, H., Jordan, A., Smith, D., Allard, C., & Moloney, J. (2013). Supporting teachers to work with children with exceptionalities. *Canadian Journal of Education, 36*(1), 240–270.

Lave, J., & Wenger, E. (1991). *Situated learning. Legitimate peripheral participation*. Cambridge, MA: University of Cambridge Press.

Lawson, H. A., Claiborne, N., Hardman, E., Austin, S., & Surko, M. (2007). Deriving theories of change from successful community development partnerships for youths: Implications for school improvement. *American Journal of Education, 114*(1), 1–40.

Leithwood, K., Seashore Louis, K., Anderson, S., & Wahlstrom, K. (2004). *How leadership influences student learning*. New York, NY: Wallace Foundation.

Lindsey, B. (1986). *PRIDE: Principals, resources, information and direction for excellence in special education*. Paper presented at the 11th annual meeting of the National Council of States on Inservice Education, Nashville, TN.

Lombardi, T. P., & Hunka, N. J. (2001). Preparing general education teachers for inclusive classrooms: Assessing the process. *Teacher Education and Special Education, 24*(3), 183–197. doi:10.1177/088840640102400303.

Lundy, L. (2012). Children's rights and educational policy in Europe: The implementation of the United Nations Convention on the Rights of the Child. *Oxford Review of Education, 38*(4), 393–411. doi:10.1080/03054985.2012.704874.

McCray, E. D., & McHatton, P. A. (2011). "Less afraid to have them in my classroom": Understanding preservice general educators' perceptions about inclusion. *Teacher Education Quarterly, 38*(4), 135.

Montessori, M. (1967). *The discovery of the child*. New York, NY: Ballantine Books.

Ontario Education Act, R.S.O., CE.2, s.8 (3), Categories of Exceptionalities (1990).

Ontario Education Act, R.S.O., CE.2 1990, c.7, Sch 9 AM (2007).

People for Education. (2007). *Annual report on Ontario's publicly funded schools*. Retrieved from: http://www.peopleforeducation.ca

Peters, M. T. (1990). Someone's missing: The student as an overlooked participant in the IEP process. *Preventing School Failure, 34*(4), 32–36.

Policy/Programme Memorandum No. 140. (2007). *Incorporating methods of Applied Behaviour Analysis (ABA) into programmes for students with Autism Spectrum Disorder*. Retrieved from: http://www.edu.gov.on.ca/extra/eng/ppm/140.html

Robertson, C. (2012). Special educational needs and disability co-ordination in a changing policy landscape: Making sense of policy from a SENCo's perspective. *British Journal of Learning Support, 27*(2), 77–83. doi:10.1111/j.1467-9604.2012.01517.x.

Scott, S., & Webber, C. F. (2008). Evidence-based leadership development: The 4L framework. *Journal of Educational Administration, 46*(6), 762–776.

Showers, B., & Joyce, B. (1996). The evolution of peer coaching. *Educational Leadership, 53*(6), 12–16.

Tearle, K., & Spandagou, I. (2012). *Learning support policy in Australia (New South Wales) and New Zealand; Discourses of influence* (pp. 1–14). Sydney, Australia: Australian Association for Research in Education.

United Nations. (1989). *UN Convention on the Rights of the Child*. Geneva, Switzerland: United Nations.

Webber, C. F., Aitken, N., Lupart, J., & Scott, S. (2009). *The Alberta student assessment study: Final report*. Edmonton, AB, Canada: The Government of Alberta.

Webber, C. F., & Lupart, J. (2011). Leading intercultural inclusive schools: An international perspective. *International Studies in Educational Administration, 39*(1), 3–18.

Webber, C. F., & Scott, S. (2009). Leadership development in support of inclusive education in Ukraine. *Leading and Managing, 15*(2), 88–103.

Webber, C. F., & Scott, S. (2013). Principles for principal preparation. In C. L. Slater & S. Nelson (Eds.), *Understanding the principalship: An international guide to principal preparation* (pp. 73–100). Bingley, UK: Emerald.

Webber, C. F., Scott, S., Aitken, N., Lupart, J., & Scott, D. E. (2013). Leading assessment for enhanced student outcomes. *School Leadership & Management.* doi:10.1080/13632434.2013.773885.

Weber, K., & Bennett, S. (2004). *Special education in Ontario schools.* Palgrave, ON, Canada: Highland Press.

Western Australia Department of Education, Policy Framework. (2001). *Students at educational risk.* Retrieved from: http://det.wa.edu.au/policies/detcms/policy-planning-and-accountability/policies-framework/policies/students-at-educational-risk.en?oid=au.edu.wa.det.cms.content-types.Policy-id-3785047

Woodcock, S., Hemmings, B., & Kay, R. (2012). Does study of an inclusive education subject influence preservice teachers' concerns and self-efficacy about inclusion? *Australian Journal of Teacher Education, 37*(6), 1–11.

Chapter 9
Assessing Bilingual and Multilingual Learners in Mainstream Classrooms

Sylvie Roy

Abstract This chapter looks at how we should not assess bilingual and multilingual learners the same way as we assess students with one language. By providing a view that bilinguals and multilinguals have specific linguistics systems of their own, and by showing that some assessments are not equitable for some students and cause them fail, this chapter presents ideas for leaders and teachers on how to assess bilingual and multilingual learners in classrooms. We recommend accommodation as a useful strategy but employing alternative assessments might also be preferable to meet the needs of this diverse clientele.

Keywords Monolingual bias • Assessment • Bilinguals and multilinguals • Accommodation • Leaders • English language learners

9.1 Introduction

Every assessment is an assessment of language. (García, 2009)

More and more students in our schools possess multiple languages and cultural competencies. In some countries, multilingualism has existed for several years. Other countries have recently started to acknowledge diversity. For example, many students in Canada speak neither English nor French – the two official languages – when they begin school. Some students do not possess the linguistic capital or the linguistic variety that the school expects them to have, even if their first language is English or French. Linguistic capital (Bourdieu, 1982) refers to the right kind of language that students will possess when entering schools. If a child speaks a different variety (some call it dialect or slang) than the school, that child will have less chance to succeed or might be behind others who possess the language of the school. The complexity of language competencies and language varieties becomes more problematic when it is time to assess students with different linguistic and cultural

---

S. Roy (✉)
Werklund School of Education, University of Calgary,
2500 University Drive NW, Calgary, AB, Canada, T2N 1N4
e-mail: syroy@ucalgary.ca

© Springer International Publishing Switzerland 2016
S. Scott et al. (eds.), *Leadership of Assessment, Inclusion, and Learning*,
The Enabling Power of Assessment 3, DOI 10.1007/978-3-319-23347-5_9

backgrounds. The need to evaluate these students differently is essential; we cannot assess students from multiple backgrounds in the same way that we do monolinguals (speakers of one language) because they don't use their language(s) the same way (Cruz-Ferreira, 2010). If we do, these students receive remediation when they don't need it, they are assigned in lower curriculum pathways, they have higher dropout and lower graduation rates, and they are disproportionately referred to special education classes (García & Kleifgen, 2010; Martín Rojo, 2010). The problem, as several studies have demonstrated, is that bilingual and multilingual students are often assessed from a monolingual point of view (García & Baetens Beardsmore, 2009). This means that we often assess all our students in the same way, giving them the same tests or exams as if they were all speaking, reading, and understanding one language as a native speaker or as if they possess the language variety of the school, which is often a defined standard of a particular language. Even native speakers can experience challenges in school if their linguistic capital or their language variation is not aligned with that considered legitimate in the school system (Bourdieu & Passeron, 1977; Davies, 2001). As Brown (2013) pointed out: in assessment, Davies (2001) noted "a loss of nerve about the native speaker goal among language testers" (p. 91), emphasising the challenges in determining native language use and even in defining who native speakers are. These trends are reflected to some extent in assessment scales for the Common European Framework for Reference for Languages (CEFR), in which the goal of native speaker attainment in production is absent from some areas.

Changes are slowly coming into place, especially in Europe where languages are both taught and extensively used. The monolingual bias is still very strong though. When researchers use native speakers' criteria to measure bilinguals in vocabulary, for example, with a question, such as: how do bilinguals perform relative to monolinguals? It is difficult not to continue to use monolingual norms to examine bilinguals and multilinguals when researchers are doing so (Stadthagen-Gonzàles, Mueller Gathercole, Pérez-Tattam, & Yavas, 2013, p. 126). Even if Stadthagen-Gonzàles, Mueller Gathercole, Pérez-Tattam, and Yavas acknowledged the differences between native speakers and bilinguals, very few use a different research approach or examine criteria created for bilinguals or multilinguals when it is time to measure multiple languages in one person. In classrooms, these concerns are sometimes addressed by allowing the student to consult a dictionary, by providing aids to help the student read or understand the questions, or by allowing the student extra time to complete the test. These practices do help students but they do not solve issues of assessing students with different linguistic and cultural competencies; indeed, we have to examine the system that is failing them and the actors that work in that system.

Standardised tests and assessment play an important role in the day-to-day lives of teachers and students and also play a role in marginalising and keeping some students at the lower levels of society. Assessment confirms the competency of individuals in a particular society, and, based on their level of competency the assessment facilitates the selection of an individual into higher levels of education or precludes them from further education thereby leaving them at a lower end of career options within society. Assessment can therefore reinforce an unegalitarian educational experience, and it can disadvantage students whose culture or socioeconomic class is not consistent with schools' prevailing values and traditional education practices. It can also disadvantage leaders and teachers. As García and Kleifgen (2010) noted in US schools:

> Scores on assessments are driving not only the kinds of instruction and programmatic opportunities that emergent bilinguals can access, but also the salary that their teachers receive, the funding that their schools and the states in which they reside obtain, and the real estate value of the communities in which they live. (p. 117)

In this chapter, issues related to assessing bilingual and multilingual students in mainstream classrooms will be scrutinised. First, I propose a theoretical framework that states that assessment is a political act that marginalises bilingual and multilingual students. These students do not have a monolingual way of learning and understanding the world; they possess different linguistic backgrounds that might not be congruent with the ways in which we evaluate them. We will also see how research continues to explore the issues of the emergence of bilinguals in comparison to native speakers (García & Kleifgen, 2010). Next, I will discuss some of the relevant research undertaken on assessment of bilingual and multilingual students, especially in the field of English as an additional language or ELL (English Language Learners). In the literature, we see that different terms are used to describe learners of English as an additional language (EAL) or English as a second language (ESL). For the purposes of consistency, I use the term ELL in this paper even when authors have used another term when conducting their research. This literature review presents some of the research in the field of large-scale assessment for ELL students and shares insights on how some research that examines assessment of these students cannot be valid because of the way it has been constructed. We will also discuss how accommodations have been accomplished; and how measuring content and language separately constitutes good practice. Finally, I present the implications for leaders and teachers and suggest ways to assess students with different linguistic and cultural needs in the school system.

9.2 Assessment as a Political Act

Assessment is a political act because it is under the control of official, national, or regional authorities and it is based on specific cultural and pedagogical traditions (García & Baetens Beardsmore, 2009). Shohamy (2001) also maintained that testing is endowed with power because of the following features: tests are administrated by powerful institutions; they rely on documentation; and they use objective formats, the language of science and numbers, and the written form of communication. For García (2009), the original aim of tests was to sort out and rank students for purposes of comparison and placement: "Testing has been used, and continues to be used, to allocate educational and employment benefits, rather than as a means for informing teaching and developing learning" (p. 368). From the student's point of view, Martín Rojo (2010) found that in Spain immigrant children lost trust in the educational system because that system placed them in a lower rank and, after a while, they became aware that they were not progressing as they should. They felt isolated in mainstream classes, which resulted in some dropping out of school. In Spain, one of the schools studied was reputed to be a 'special school' with 90 % of the school population being from an immigrant background. This school had a lot of programmes to manage diversity, "but the higher secondary education courses (after the ESO, the compulsory secondary education) were not offered" (Martín Rojo, 2010, p. 360). After a while, the school had difficulties in changing its image, few students still attended school, and teachers indicated that the government intended to close the school. This illustrates how bilinguals and multilinguals often find themselves marginalised and betrayed by the society that gave them the freedom to be a citizen in the first place, because we assess them for a specific purpose and find them incompetent within mainstream.

As Cook (2012) outlined, the progression that has occurred within the field of linguistics research articulating that linguistics has progressively refused to classify speakers in terms of groups of which they are not, and never could be members: first, granting independence to primitive languages (Boas, 1920/1940); then freeing children's language from that of adults (the independent grammar assumption); then liberating black English speakers from white English speakers (Labov, 1969); working-class restricted code from middle-class elaborated code (Bernstein, 1971); and women's language from men's. The only group still to be judged by the standards of another is that of second language users. But they too have the right to use language appropriately for their needs, not for those of a native speaker group to which they can never belong.

Even as a political act, sometimes the discourse is seen as something that will allow children to be included. For example, with the US *No Child Left Behind* Act, a key goal is that all children will be proficient in English. However, those at the bottom of the achievement curve will receive little help while those at the top won't be challenged intellectually because their scores will not make a difference for the school. Only students in the middle will benefit from the policy (García & Kleifgen, 2010).

9.3 Bilinguals and Multilinguals Are Not Monolinguals

It is possible to measure ducks in terms of swans. But when everything has to satisfy the swan criteria, the unique qualities of ducks will always elude the observer – just as black English, working-class English, and women's language were once seen as pale shadows of a 'true' variety. Uniquely bilingual functions of language like code-switching and translation will never show up in a native speaker model; unique grammatical forms of second language users like the rules of the Basic Variety (Klein & Perdue, 1997) will just appear as mistakes (Cook, 2012).

The idea of perceiving bilinguals as 'deficient' has a long history. In the nineteenth century, bilingualism was a matter of public debate because it was regarded as a potential threat to the establishment of nation-states and the maintenance of their boundaries (Heller, 2007). Heller argued that in the context of nations that were focusing on developing standard monolingual forms and practices underpinning the nation-state, there was a need to evaluate and explain bilingualism:

> Sometimes, it was integrated into the dominant model as a special case of multiple monolingualism (see Bloomfield, 1933). Sometimes it was pathologized, its consequences for the health of "normal" individuals, groups and political entities weighed and positions taken as to what, if anything, needed to be done about it ... And sometimes it was brought to bear on broader concerns about the regulation of diversity and about the nature of language, culture and society. (p. 5)

Grosjean (2008) and Mondada and Gajo (2001) argued that not only the public in general but also researchers have a misconception of what it means to be bilingual. Many view bilinguals as people who separately possess two languages – the equivalent of two monolinguals. The fractional or monolingual view of bilingualism was developed because the language sciences expanded primarily through the study of monolinguals, who had served as models of "normal" speaker-hearers (Grosjean, 2008). Blommaert (2005) maintained that native speakers are usually regarded as the "ideal" members of any ethnolinguistic community, and that the discourse of a homogeneous common language is used to define an equally normalising notion of common identity. Such discourses have helped to construct group identities (who is part of the group) and categorical identities (who is not part of the group). Often, bilinguals are not included in an ethnolinguistic community that is considered homogeneous, unless they are able to highly competently manage both languages separately (Roy, 2010).

Seeing bilinguals and multilinguals as a problem is a historical and social phenomenon that researchers continue to produce and reproduce today. The terms *dominant, unbalanced, semilingual,* and *alingual* were and are still used to talk about bilinguals who have not reached a true or balanced bilingualism (Skutnabb-Kangas, 1984). These views of bilinguals continue to have negative effects on how we perceive bilinguals and multilinguals. These effects result from studies that compare bilinguals to monolinguals, and also from the field of assessment and testing, in which students' language proficiency is compared to that of native speakers. According to Appel and Muysken (1987):

> Empirical support for the concept of semilingualism is largely derived from the assessment of language skills by means of language tests. From such tests it is concluded that semilingual children know less of each of their languages than monolingual students. (p. 108)

Appel and Muysken (1987), along with other authors (e.g., Ortega, 2010), have argued that the bilingual's repertoire should be seen as different, not as deficient, and that the quantitative monolingual norm should not be applied as the standard. According to these authors, students with multiple linguistic repertoires have unique code-switching abilities that give them the opportunity to convey messages in a very sophisticated way, but such abilities are usually not highly valued in schools.

Similarly, Grosjean (2008) noted that the tests used with bilinguals rarely take into account the differential needs for the two languages or the different social functions of these languages:

> It would appear that much of the controversy surrounding so-called "semilingualism" or "alingualism" in children is affected by the prevalence of the monolingual viewpoint and by the monolingual tests which have been used. These may be appropriate for monolingual children but not for other kinds of children: those who are monolingual in the other language, those who are in the process of becoming bilingual, or those who have attained a stable level of bilingualism. Monolingual tests are, for the most part, quite inappropriate to evaluate language skills of bilinguals. (p. 11)

In his experimental research, Grosjean (2008) discussed the complementary principle, whereby speakers acquire and use their languages for different purposes, in different domains of life, with different people. Consequently, bilinguals are rarely equally fluent in all language skills in both languages. Additionally, some bilinguals may still be in the process of acquiring a language skill, while others have attained a certain level of stability. Finally, the language repertoire of bilinguals may change over time; bilinguals will interact with both monolinguals and other bilinguals, and their language mode will change accordingly. The problem is that bilinguals continue to be evaluated in terms of fluency in both languages and the balance between the two languages (and, in the case of multilinguals, in more than two languages).

As early as 1982, Grosjean (2008) advocated testing bilinguals in terms of social and occupational demands of a practical nature in a particular society; he was mainly concerned with purpose and function. More recently, he proposed a holistic view of bilingualism, and we can add multilingualism that recognises bilinguals' unique linguistic configuration:

> The coexistence and the use of two or more languages has produced a different but complete language system of a fully competent speaker-hearer; he or she has developed competencies (in the two languages and possibly in a third system that is a combination of the first two) to the extent required by his or her needs and those of the environment. (p. 14)

Grosjean argued that we cannot evaluate speakers of different languages correctly though, only one language. He suggested that we must study a bilingual and a multilingual through the individual's total language repertoire as it is used in his or her everyday life.

According to Grosjean, traditional testing put more stress on the form of the language, rather than the speaker's ability to communicate in context:

> In the long run, the really interesting question of language learning and language forgetting is how the human communicator adjusts to and uses one, two, or more languages – separately or together – to maintain a necessary level of communicative competence, and not what level of grammatical competence is reached in each language taken individually and out of context. Unfortunately, too much stress has been put on the latter in bilingual research, especially when children are being studied. (p. 17)

Cook (1992) expressed the same concerns as Grosjean and introduced the concept of 'multicompetency', which is the knowledge of two or more languages in the same mind. In teaching, the goal will then be to produce a successful second language user instead of imitating the native speakers.

9.3.1 Assessing Students: An Overview of ELL Studies

I chose to look at English particularly because there are a lot of varieties of English in different cultural contexts, English being learned in several countries. For English learners around the world, varieties of English are shaped by interactions between communities, porous national boundaries, and hybrid languages and cultures. For Canagarajah (2006), English is now a heterogeneous language with multiple forms and diverse grammars. Several studies were conducted to assess the English proficiency of English as second language learners. Marks (2005) investigated the contribution of socioeconomic factors (parents' education and employment), sociocultural factors (parents' aspirations for their children's education and students' attitudes toward education), and school factors (location of school) to the relative performance of first- and second-generation immigrant students in 20 countries, using data from the Programme for International Student Assessment survey conducted by the OECD in 2000. Marks's results indicated that in most countries, socioeconomic factors substantially accounted for the weaker performance of immigrant students, whereas sociocultural factors contributed little and school factors were important in only a limited number of instances. According to Marks, policies that reduced the impact of socioeconomic background on educational performance would improve educational and socioeconomic outcomes of immigrant groups. This research presented additional information regarding English language learners being at the lower level of a society and staying there unless we help them to succeed in schools.

Other studies investigated how to assess students for more specific purposes or for particular subjects. Okhee (2005) focused on how students who are learning English are assessed in the sciences, because assessment usually concentrates on the literacy and numeracy skills of students. In addition, science usually does not count toward accountability measures even when it is tested, and therefore research on assessment accommodations in science for ELLs is sparse. Assessment for ELLs ideally should distinguish science knowledge from English language proficiency, although this is rarely done in research and assessment programs. As we will demonstrate later, the separation of language and content may well present solutions to the deficit approach in assessing these students. Shaw (1997) also examined the use of science performance assessment with ELL high school students. Shaw's study focused specifically on a performance assessment task in a sheltered science instruction programme taught by two teachers fluent in both English and Spanish. The results indicated that only the inquiry procedure (the most text-dependent item) was significantly affected by students' level of English proficiency. Conversely, graphs, calculations using an equation and a data table, and final summary questions were significantly affected by students' level of science knowledge. Thus there was no simple answer to the question of whether performance assessments accurately measured ELLs' science knowledge; instead, the answer depended on the assessment task in question.

In the context of increasing numbers of second language (L2) learners in Canadian schools and expanding standards-driven testing frameworks, a passing score on the Ontario Secondary School Literacy Test (OSSLT) was imposed as a secondary school graduation requirement in the province of Ontario. There is evidence that tests designed for first language (L1) populations may have lower reliability and validity for L2 students. A study by Fox and Cheng (2007) elicited accounts of the OSSLT from 33 focus groups prior to and immediately after the March 2006 test administration. The focus groups comprised a total of 22 L1 students and 136 L2 students, attending seven Ontario secondary schools. The results suggested important differences in L1 and L2 accounts of test constructs, and a gap between what was valued as literacy on the test and what was valued in classroom literacy practice, which consequently raised some concerns regarding the test's validity. By examining how different groups of test-takers interpret test constructs, and the interaction between these interpretations, test design, and accounts of classroom practice, we may better address issues of fidelity in test construct representation (i.e., what may constitute construct underrepresentation and construct-irrelevant variance). Fox and Cheng's study highlighted what may make a test more L2 friendly – that is, what supported (or impeded) L2 test performance. Although test-taker accounts of tests have been the least researched in the washback literature, Fox and Cheng's findings suggested that such accounts have the potential to increase test fairness, enhance the validity of inferences drawn from test performance, improve the effectiveness of accommodation strategies, and promote positive feedback.

Another study (Lee, Maerten-Rivera, Penfield, LeRoy, & Secada, 2008) entailed a 5-year professional development intervention aimed at improving science and literacy achievement of ELLs in urban elementary schools, within an environment increasingly driven by high-stakes testing and accountability. Specifically, the study examined students' science achievement at the end of the intervention's first-year implementation, which consisted of developing and adapting curriculum units and teacher workshops. The study involved 1134 third-grade students at seven treatment schools and 966 third-grade students at eight comparison schools. Nine curriculum units were developed with the collaboration of science educators, bilingual-ELL educators, mathematics educators, and district administrators in science education. They followed the state curriculum recommendations and covered the Grade 3–5 science curriculum. The goal was to integrate English language and literacy development as part of science instruction. The teachers' guide for each unit promoted students' science inquiry and understanding of key science concepts and big ideas, how to incorporate English language and literacy development as part of science instruction and how to incorporate mathematics to support science instruction (although the curriculum was based on sciences and literacy, the units also considered mathematics). The units were designed to move progressively from being teacher-led to student-initiated continuum to promote science inquiry. Teachers' guides provided content-specific teaching strategies and suggestions to promote literacy development, such as, students writing expository paragraphs describing the scientific process of the investigations of experiments conducted in class. The units also addressed the needs of ELL students by providing guidance to promote English proficiency. The authors (Lee et al., 2008) gave the following example:

science terms in Spanish and Haitian Creole are provided to support communication and comprehension. Language load for students at varying levels of English proficiency is increasingly more demanding from grades 3 through 5. The units introduce key vocabulary in the beginning and encourage students to practice the vocabulary in a variety of settings to enhance their understanding throughout the lesson and over the course of the unit. Additionally, the units use multiple modes of communication and representation (verbal, gestural, written, graphic) to enhance students' understanding of science. Teachers' guides also emphasize the importance of linguistic scaffolding to promote ELL students' comprehension and understanding of science. (p. 37)

Teachers in the treatment group had five full day workshops in order to familiarise themselves with the science content, hands-on activities, and potential learning problems. During the workshops, teachers also identified students' cultural and linguistic experiences from their home that could serve as intellectual resources to learn school science, and the difficulties they encountered with science concepts and inquiry. The workshops focused on incorporating English language and literacy development into specific science lessons by adjusting the level and mode of communication to enhance students' understanding of science, to recognise the diversity of students' levels of language proficiency, and use language to match students' levels of communicative competence language proficiency and adjust the language load required. At the fourth workshop, teachers worked to incorporate ESOL strategies in selected lessons.

The results of this study looking at science achievement for ELL students and students with low English proficiency led to three main findings. First, treatment students displayed a statistically significant increase in science achievement. Second, there was no statistically significant difference in achievement gains between students at English-to-Speakers-of-Other-Languages (ESOL) levels 1–4 and students who had exited from ESOL or never been in ESOL. Similarly, there was no significant difference in achievement gains between students who had been retained on the basis of state wide reading test scores and students who had never been retained. Third, treatment students showed a higher score on a state wide mathematics test – particularly on the measurement strand emphasised in the intervention – than comparison students. The results indicated that through the professional development intervention, ELL students and others in the intervention learned to think and reason scientifically while also performing well on high-stakes testing.

A Los Angeles study by Flores, Painter, and Pachon (2009) demonstrated that fluency in English was one of the factors most strongly associated with higher performance in every academic outcome. In turn, English language learning and reclassification as English proficient were two of the most influential processes shaping the educational trajectories of language minority students. Being reclassified from an ELL to English proficient in elementary school or middle school was a significant predictor of educational success. It was essential that provision of resources to English language learners should begin early and continue through elementary and middle school, for two reasons: first, early English language learning and later reclassification are associated with improved academic outcomes; second, 76 % of students not reclassified as English proficient by eighth grade had entered the school system before the first grade. Of these students who were not reclassified by the end of middle school, roughly half failed the ninth grade. Furthermore, the majority of these students were born in the United States. Flores et al. emphasised the need to investigate why these students remained in the system for so long without being reclassified. This particular research demonstrates how students who do not have Standard English are failing in the educational system.

Finally, there seem to be two opposing perspectives on valid and equitable assessment of ELLs. Traditionally, the focus was on eliminating the effects of students' home language and culture as a way to ensure test validity. Lately, an emerging approach has advocated that an understanding of the home language and culture should guide the entire assessment process (Solano-Flores & Nelson-Barber, 2001). Solano-Flores and Trumbull (2003) maintain that it is difficult to remove cultural biases, because tests are cultural devices, therefore teachers and testers need to understand the cultural beliefs of the students with whom they work.

In summary, various factors can contribute to differences in test and assessment results of diverse students: socioeconomic factors, the way we design tests, what knowledge the students already have, and students' cultural beliefs and practices, as well as how we take all these factors into account. Given the limited research, it is difficult to draw conclusions about how to ensure valid and equitable assessment of science knowledge with English language learners (ELLs). It is also unclear whether new assessment technologies and innovations will provide these students with new hope or more obstacles. In light of all of these challenges, assessment of ELLs remains one of the thorniest problems in educational policy and practice.

To improve assessment tools and methods, it is important to focus on two distinct aspects of assessment: language and content. These topics are discussed in the next section.

9.3.2 Language Proficiency and Content Proficiency

Whereas assessments of language proficiency test language skills such as vocabulary, grammar, and sound system, content proficiency is more about subject knowledge. Testing language and content proficiency is a complex task. As García (2009) pointed out, "The difficulty in offering fair and equitable assessment for bilinguals has to do with being able to understand the interrelationship between language proficiency and content proficiency – two important objectives in all testing" (p. 370).

Content proficiency is defined as the knowledge of the subject matter. Content knowledge is often left to mainstream content teachers and whether content is tested with academic English. For emergent bilinguals, both language and content proficiency are entangled and the assessment lacks validity (García & Kleifgen, 2010). Students who are not English speakers will often be evaluated alongside others whose first language is English. One way to assess bilinguals is to translate the test into the native language of the student; however, schools often lack bilingual teachers who speak the students' languages. Sometimes these students will go to an ESL class for a few hours each day and come back to the regular classes for the complement of the day. Various researchers (Collier & Thomas, 1998; García & Pearson, 1994; Gottlieb, 2006) have argued that we should assess these students' academic progress on the basis of ongoing documentation and combined instruction, such as student portfolios, rather than tests. According to Dong (2004):

> Some mainstream content teachers may have concerns over whether it is fair to evaluate a new English language learner differently from the rest of the class. While I respect these teachers' efforts to treat all students equally, I believe that blind equality can run the risk of not recognizing that all students are unique individuals and may have different needs and backgrounds. (p. 42)

Dong further stated that it is preferable to allow these students to become familiar with the learning environment, and to provide opportunities for them to express what they know. He advised not giving these students passing or failing grades, because good assessment also has the goal of motivating and informing students of their learning and teachers of their instruction. Thus it is necessary to consider multiple measures for students with diverse backgrounds. In addition, assessment and evaluation should be ongoing, so that teachers can adjust their expectations and raise their standards accordingly. Language learning and content learning do not always develop at equal rates; teachers should not have low expectations for ELL students or students who are learning a second language. Students' knowledge of the language will change and expand, so it is important to periodically re-evaluate what they know.

There is also a need to assess the language and literacy skills of learners who seem to be doing well, and to use the findings to help teachers. Often, these students have developed basic communication skills and seem to be fluent in the target language but they are still learning specific and important aspects of the language. However, their writing and reading skills or their academic competency could be at a lower level than their teachers realise. Reading skills in particular can be difficult to evaluate, and problems in this area might go unnoticed.

The performance of bilinguals should be seen as a continuum that is related to language acquisition, and the language of assessment should be adapted according to where the student is in the continuum (Shepard, 1996). Duverger (2005) argued for a double set of criteria, with one set related to the discipline (content knowledge) and the other related to the language. Depending on the goal of the assessment, one of the scales could have a higher coefficient. For example, if the purpose of the bilingual education programme is to teach a second language, the language criteria would be more important.

Another suggestion is that in order to assess bilinguals, we should assess them in both languages. If not, we will get an incomplete picture of the bilingual's knowledge. The assessment of both languages should be based on bilingual norms. Bilinguals shouldn't be tested in English nor should the test be translated from English to the native language, because sometimes the student might not be strong enough in his/her native language to understand, especially if he or she is educated in English.

9.4 Implications for Leaders

Leaders are essential in bilingual and multilingual education. Baker (2009) mentioned that it was important that the leaders have some kind of expertise in bilingual education, bilingualism, language learning, and a fine understanding of the community, even extending their leadership into the community in order to connect with families and community leaders. Hunt (2011) noted four essential components for leadership in bilingual and multilingual schools: mission, collaborative and shared leadership, flexibility, and trust. It is a shared responsibility in learning communities that teachers, leaders, and students work together and support each other, especially in bilingual and multilingual clientele schools and where diversity is at the centre of the school mission. It is also important that multilingualism and bilingualism is not perceived as a problem to be solved. One way to do that is to include the languages and cultures of students and their parents in the school community. In Hunt's research in New York, creating a shared mission in the school and the value of being bilingual were placed at the centre of the work. Principals and teachers made sure that the mission was understood and they trusted each other. The goal was to ensure that their students grew linguistically and academically. Hunt mentioned that in order to:

> promote students' academic achievement and bilingual language and literacy development over time, school leadership must view multiple languages and cultures as resources and find creative ways to both build on and promote them within children's schooling. Second, identifying ways to build capacity within a learning community so that leadership is collaborative and shared allows any organization to move beyond dependence on any one individual. (p. 204)

This happens only if principals and teachers work together. Family and community engagement is another way to work with bilinguals and multilinguals in mainstream schools. Parents and community leaders have linguistic and cultural knowledge that the students' possess and which are different from the prevailing cultural knowledge in the school. Leaders should take advantage of that knowledge to promote an equitable education for diverse students. Leaders should know who their clientele are, build on the dynamic bilingualism, incorporate multilingual pedagogies, embrace challenge and care, recreate the school community, and account for fair assessment (García & Kleifgen, 2010). García and Kleifgen also proposed translanguaging pedagogies which mean that teachers will teach English using the home language as a scaffold for students' learning. The next section offers suggestions for teachers and leaders regarding how to better understand linguistic differences between monolingual and multilingual speakers. It is important to be on familiar terms with these linguistic differences in order to support a dynamic bilingualism and multilingual pedagogies.

9.4.1 Linguistics Differences

Brown (2013) noted linguistic differences between a monolingual person to a multicompetent person, using Cook's definition of multicompetent. She noted that students who spoke several languages needed more time for word recognition in order to produce and comprehend the language. For a multilingual person, it takes more time to read and comprehend text; therefore, more time should be allowed for them to finish a task. She suggested that teachers should not expect bilingual students to reach the precise reading or listening speeds of a monolingual student. In terms of pronunciation, this is one of the linguistic domains that is most accepted as speakers' variation. Vocabulary is also a domain that differs between a multilingual individual and a monolingual. A multilingual has less vocabulary in each language but if we count both languages, they will have more words than a monolingual. Brown noted that:

> In either case, language assessors should not consider language switches to be categorically nontarget-like but rather characteristic of multicompetent language use. Unfortunately, evidence already attests to the negative impact of codes witching in assessments of language and even academic potential (Berthele, 2011). Although such negative evaluations would be considered inaccurate from the perspective of the multicompetent target, more research is needed, particularly in naturalistic contexts, to determine norms in, for example, the frequency of language switching in multicompetent discourse. (p. 227)

This quote presupposes that there is a lot of research that needs to be done to better understand multilingual speakers in several linguistic domains. Brown (2013) presented some ideas about how we could develop assessments for multilingual students. She mentioned that, in practice, multicompetent benchmarks might already be in place. She gave the example of a Japanese-French speaker teaching French in Japan. The teacher's multicompetent profile matched the developing profile of her students and the bilingual French performance of the teacher could be used as an appropriate target for the second language learning of French performance from the students. Brown described that a monolingual native speaker of French with no Japanese would not constitute the appropriate target; in that case, the teacher could seek advice from bilingual colleagues with the relevant combination of languages in constructing and scoring assessments. However, it is not always the case that teachers have the same language profile as their students.

9.4.2 For Classrooms: Alternative Assessments

Ralph (2008) proposed some key features and practices of authentic assessment in a second language classroom. First, the key principles for authentic assessment emerged from constructivist learning, whereby learners engage alone or with others in various assessment activities that require personal meaning-making and reflective self-regulated interpretation. In this approach, communicative tasks engage students in specific functional-notional scenarios appropriate for their age, interests, and level of linguistic competence. Second, teaching, learning, and assessment are linked together:

> Because the cognitivist-constructivist approaches emphasizes learners' performance of tasks that demonstrate what they know and are able to do in real-life situations (or meaningful simulations of the same), then it follows that any of these tasks – whether they take the form of informal practice-sessions, or of more formal performances, projects, portfolios, or tests – are eligible to be evaluated in any second language class period. (Ralph, 2008, p. 496)

Ralph advised that students should be informed of how and why they will be assessed, and that teachers should know clearly what the particular content and performance outcomes are for each task. A third principle is that authentic assessment should be linked to the curriculum or the field of study.

For the range of proficiencies in languages, Canagarajah (2006) suggested choosing:

> multitask, multirater and multicandidate tests. The multiple tasks would help assess the candidate's skills in different communicative activities. The multiple raters would help assess the candidate according to a range of holistic and discrete-item criteria. The multiple candidates would create a communicative interaction where language use has to be negotiated. Such a format would also involve a spoken component with the possibility of face-to-face interactions between examiners and candidates. (p. 238)

A study of 543 South African university freshmen examined testing issues in relation to use of English as a first or second language (Miller, Bradbury, & Wessels, 1997). Results suggested that multiple-choice tests yielded higher grades than essay tests for both native and non-native speakers, performance on essay questions varied depending on the type of question, and open-ended tutorial assessments were reasonable predictors of academic success. Other alternative approaches to assessment can then powerfully shape students and teachers on a daily basis (Moore, 2001). They can be used to assess all students in schools, especially students with multiple languages and cultural competencies. Moore also reviewed ESL assessment in Australia, and found that alternative means of assessment can be successfully applied in practice. She suggested alternatives such as:

1. the use of portfolios;
2. learner self-assessment;
3. longitudinal classroom-based record-keeping or profiling; and
4. criterion-referenced (curriculum-embedded) performance-based assessment.

The purpose of portfolios is to collect students' work in a longitudinal approach created in relation to specific instructional objectives and evaluated in relation to the same criteria. Self-assessment could be, for example, the use of rating scales, check lists and questionnaires. Performance-based assessment demonstrates the scope of knowledge that students have acquired on a subject, such as, through a poster presentation.

García and Kleifgen (2010) proposed additional ideas to assess students. For example, in terms of accommodation, they suggested the following: presentations, responses, setting, timing/scheduling, and reinforcement. Their ideas reiterated suggestions previously described. The term presentations referred to allowing more repetition, explanation, simplification, test translation for students, and assessing students in their home language if the language was well developed. Response involved allowing students to dictate their answers or display knowledge using alternative forms of representation. Setting included individual or small group administration of the test or multiple testing sessions. Timing referred to allowing more time to finish the test. Reinforcement indicated the use of dictionaries and glossaries were allowable, hence, these ideas added to the discussion. One of the main ways to understand and assess bilingual and multilingual students was to observe and listen to them for a long period of time. This form of assessment also permitted the development of a multidimensional portrait of bilingual students.

9.5 Conclusion

Students with multiple competencies are not like monolinguals. We need to consider them differently within the school system. However, assessing students with bilingual and multilingual competencies is very complex, especially given the variety of programs and schools (and also because schools usually promote a certain standard or norm that only a few students can attain). One of the major themes of this chapter was that teachers should not assume that all students in their classrooms are the same; heterogeneity exists in every classroom, even if students appear to possess the same language competency. In a multilingual school, more focus should be put on alternative assessments such as portfolios, self-assessment, and long-term profiling. Assessment is a political act, and if the people in power do not want to change the way it is conducted, students will find it more difficult to achieve. But everybody will win if we decide to look at this issue differently. Students will do better on provincial tests, and they will be more likely to succeed in terms of continuing their education and finding good jobs. In return, every multilingual society will comprise linguistically and culturally diverse people who are well educated and who can contribute to the advancement of the society. There is a lot to be done in this line of research in order to offer equitable and fair assessments of bilingual and multilingual children.

References

Appel, R., & Muysken, P. (1987). *Language contact and bilingualism*. New York, NY: Edward Arnold.
Baker, C. (2009). Becoming bilingual through bilingual education. In P. Auer & L. Wei (Eds.), *Handbook of multilingualism and multilingual communication* (pp. 131–152). Berlin, NY: Mouton de Gruyter.
Bernstein, B. (1971). *Class, codes and control: Volume 1*. London, UK: Routledge & Kegan Paul.

Berthele, R. (2011). The influence of code-mixing and speaker information on perception and assessment of foreign language proficiency: An experimental study. *International Journal of Bilingualism*. doi:10.1177/1367006911429514.

Blommaert, J. (2005). *Discourse*. Cambridge, UK: Cambridge University Press.

Bloomfield, J. (1933). *Language*. New York, NY: Holt, Rinehart and Winston.

Boas, F. (1920/1940). The methods of ethnology. *American Anthropologist, 22*, 311–322. Reprinted in F. Boas (1940). *Race, language and culture* (pp. 281–289). New York, NY: Free Press.

Bourdieu, P. (1982). *Ce que parler veut dire*. Paris, France: Fayard.

Bourdieu, P., & Passeron, J. C. (1977). *Reproduction in education, society and culture*. London, UK: Sage.

Brown, A. (2013). Multicompetence and second language assessment. *Language Assessment Quarterly, 10*(2), 219–235.

Canagarajah, S. (2006). Changing communicative needs, revised assessment objectives: Testing English as an international language. *Language Assessment Quarterly, 3*(3), 229–242.

Collier, V. P., & Thomas, W. P. (1998). Assessment and evaluation. In C. J. Ovando & V. P. Collier (Eds.), *Bilingual and ESL classrooms: Teaching in multicultural contexts* (pp. 240–268). Boston, MA: McGraw-Hill.

Cook, V. (1992). Evidence for multicompetence. *Language Learning, 42*, 557–591.

Cook, V. (2012). *Multi-competence*. Retrieved from: http://homepage.ntlworld.com/vivian.c/Writings/Papers/MCentry.htm

Cruz-Ferreira, M. (Ed.). (2010). *Multilingual norms*. Frankfurt, Germany: Peter Lang.

Davies, A. (2001). What second language learners can tell us about the native speaker: Identifying and describing exceptions. In R. Cooper, L. E. Shohamy, & J. Walters (Eds.), *New perspectives and issues in educational language policy* (pp. 91–112). Philadelphia, PA: John Benjamins.

Dong, Y. R. (2004). *Teaching language and content to linguistically and culturally diverse students*. Greenwich, CT: Information Age Publishing.

Duverger, J. (2005). *L'enseignement en classe bilingue*. Paris, France: Hachette.

Flores, E., Painter, G., & Pachon, H. (2009). *Qué pasa? Are ELL students remaining in English learning classes too long?* Los Angeles, CA: Tomás Rivera Policy Institute.

Fox, J., & Cheng, L. (2007). Did we take the same test? Differing accounts of the Ontario Secondary School Literacy Test by first and second language test-takers. *Assessment in Education: Principles, Policy & Practice, 14*(1), 9–26.

García, O. (2009). *Bilingual education in the 21st century: A global perspective*. Oxford, UK: Wiley-Blackwell.

García, O., & Baetens Beardsmore, H. (2009). Assessment of bilinguals. In O. García (Ed.), *Bilingual education in the 21st century: A global perspective* (pp. 336–380). Oxford, UK: Wiley-Blackwell.

García, O., & Kleifgen, J. A. (2010). *Emergent bilinguals. Policies, programs, and practices for English language learners*. New York, NY: Teachers College Press, Columbia University.

García, G., & Pearson, P. (1994). Assessment and diversity. In L. Darling-Hammond (Ed.), *Review of research in education* (Vol. 20, pp. 337–391). Washington, DC: American Educational Research Association.

Gottlieb, M. (2006). *Assessing English language learners: Bridge from language proficiency to academic achievement*. Thousand Oaks, CA: Corwin Press.

Grosjean, F. (2008). *Studying bilinguals*. Oxford, UK: Oxford University Press.

Heller, M. (Ed.). (2007). *Bilingualism: A social approach*. London, UK: Palgrave Macmillan.

Hunt, V. (2011). Learning from success stories: Leadership structures that support dual language programs over time in New York City. *International Journal of Bilingual Education and Bilingualism, 14*(2), 187–206.

Klein, W., & Perdue, C. (1997). The basic variety (or: Couldn't natural languages be much simpler?). *Second Language Research, 13*(4), 301–347. doi:10.1191/026765897666879396.

Labov, W. (1969). The logic of non-standard English. *Georgetown Monographs on Language and Linguistics, 22*, 1–31.

Lee, O., Maerten-Rivera, J., Penfield, R. D., LeRoy, K., & Secada, W. G. (2008). Science achievement of English language learners in urban elementary schools: Results of a first-year professional development intervention. *Journal of Research in Science Teaching, 45*(1), 31–52. doi:10.1002/tea.20209.

Marks, G. (2005). Accounting for immigrant non-immigrant differences in reading and mathematics in twenty countries. *Ethnic & Racial Studies, 28*(5), 925–946.

Martín Rojo, L. (2010). *Constructing inequality in multilingual classrooms*. Berlin, NY: Mouton de Gruyter.

Miller, R., Bradbury, J., & Wessels, S. L. (1997). Academic performance of first and second language students: Kinds of assessment. *South African Journal of Higher Education, 11*(2), 70–79.

Mondada, L., & Gajo, L. (2001). Classroom interaction and the bilingual resources of migrant students in Switzerland. In M. Heller & M. Martin-Jones (Eds.), *Voices of authority: Education and linguistic difference* (pp. 235–267). Westport, CT: Ablex.

Moore, H. (2001). Telling what is real: Competing views in assessing ESL development in Australia. In M. Heller & M. Martin-Jones (Eds.), *Voices of authority: Education and linguistic difference* (pp. 335–379). Westport, CT: Ablex.

O'Sullivan, C. Y., Lauko, M. A., Grigg, W. S., Qian, J., & Zhang, J. (2003). *The nation's report card: Science 2000*. Washington, DC: U.S. Department of Education, Institution of Education Sciences.

Ortega, L. (2010, March). *The bilingual turn in SLA*. Paper presented at the annual conference of the American Association of Applied Linguistics, Atlanta, GA.

Okhee, L. (2005). Science education with English language learners: Synthesis and research agenda. *Review of Educational Research, 75*(4), 491–530.

Ralph, E. G. (2008). Teaching to the test: Principles of authentic assessment for second-language education. In A. Mollica (Ed.), *Teaching and learning languages* (pp. 493–504). Welland, ON, Canada: Soleil.

Roy, S. (2010). Not truly, not entirely. Pas comme les francophones. *Canadian Journal of Education. Special Issue on Language, Identity and Educational Policies, 33*(3), 541–563.

Shaw, J. M. (1997). Threats to the validity of science performance assessments for English language learners. *Journal of Research in Science Teaching, 34*(7), 721–743.

Shepard, L. A. (1996, September). *Research framework for investigating accommodations for language minority students*. Paper presented at the CRESST Assessment Conference, Los Angeles, CA.

Shohamy, E. (2001). *The power of tests: A critical perspective on the uses of language tests*. Harlow, UK: Longman.

Skutnabb-Kangas, T. (1984). *Bilingualism or not: The education of minorities*. Clevedon, UK: Multilingual Matters.

Solano-Flores, G., & Nelson-Barber, S. (2001). On the cultural validity of science assessments. *Journal of Research in Science Teaching, 38*(5), 553–573.

Solano-Flores, G., & Trumbull, E. (2003). Examining language in context: The need for new research and practice paradigms in the testing of English-language learners. *Educational Researcher, 32*(2), 3–13.

Stadthagen-Gonzàles, H., Mueller Gathercole, V., Pérez-Tattam, R., & Yavas, F. (2013). Vocabulary assessment of bilingual adults. To cognate or not to cognate. In V. Mueller Gathercole (Ed.), *Solutions for the assessment of bilinguals* (pp. 125–145). Bristol, NY: Multilingual Matters.

Chapter 10
Leading Assessment for Gifted and Talented Students: The Pursuit of Mediocrity of Excellence?

Shelleyann Scott, Donald E. Scott, and Leanne Longmire

> When our gifted students are the future scientists, inventors, and political leaders of our country, we are doing our society a grave injustice by not encouraging them towards excellence.
>
> (Burton-Szabo, 1996, p. 17)

Abstract This chapter highlights the socio-political egalitarian versus meritocratic tensions that overtly or covertly underpin educational policies and educator philosophies for gifted education. We provide theoretical and pragmatic information, and guidance to inform the inclusive leadership practices of principals and district leaders in relation to meeting the special needs of the gifted and talented. We explore issues for gifted and talented (G&T) students in terms of conceptualising giftedness and talents, identification, and the values and philosophies that influence policies, provisions, and practices across the international context. We present a case study from Australia and explore the implications in terms of educators, parents and family, and programmes. We examine features of differentiated instruction and assessment, characteristics of the "right teacher" for the gifted class, partnerships with external agencies/supports and advocacy for the gifted, and other leadership implications. We emphasise that meeting the needs of G&T students is a fundamental issue of social justice as opposed to elitism, and we advocate for equity not equality.

S. Scott (✉) • D.E. Scott
Werklund School of Education, University of Calgary,
2500 University Drive NW, Calgary, AB, Canada, T2N 1N4
e-mail: sscott@ucalgary.ca; descott@ucalgary.ca

L. Longmire
Department of Education Western Australia, Perth, Australia
e-mail: llongmire@westnet.com.au

Throughout the chapter we highlight the need for leaders to interrogate prevailing assumptions about the capacity of G&T students to be successful without specialised programming and instruction. Leaders must take action within their sphere of influence to more effectively support these at-risk individuals, otherwise leaders risk reinforcing the pursuit of mediocrity rather than equity.

Keywords Gifted and talented • Equity • Equality • Differentiated instruction • Differentiated assessment • Excellence or mediocrity • Gifted and talented programmes • Leadership • Inclusion • Policy • District leaders • Principals • G&T teachers • Advocacy • Ethic of care

10.1 Introduction

Inclusion in contemporary schools is a well understood concept that is backed by legislation in most countries. Inclusion policies are aimed at ensuring the needs of physically and intellectually challenged students and those with a range of exceptionalities are met within the regular classroom environment. Frequently, gifted and talented (G&T) students are grouped within inclusion policies even though their needs are quite different to those of their less able peers. Indeed, some may argue that G&T students are more at-risk than other special needs students as their exceptionalities frequently go undetected, educators and leaders assume that their abilities will ensure they thrive within schools without support, and/or their giftedness may be masked due to other complications, such as being coupled with other exceptionalities or because of problematic behaviour (Nicpon, Assouline, Colangelo, & O'Brien, 2008; Orendorff, 2009). Additionally, giftedness and talents are not always well understood by educators and parents and there is contention over how to define and identify these concepts which continues as more research identifies the complexities of intelligence and talents (Gardner, 1983, 1993). What is readily accepted is that IQ tests are too limited and fall short in identifying multiple intelligences and creative talents (Pfeiffer, 2012; Sternberg, 2010). In fact, when researching this topic we identified a range of debates within the field of G&T which included:

- ideological debates revolving around elitism or equity in providing specialised G&T programming (Braggett, 1997a, 1997b; Mandelman, Tan, Aljughaiman, & Grigorenko, 2010);
- issues in the provision of appropriate educational instruction and assessment (Maker, 2005);
- expanding understandings of the complexities of intelligence and talents (Thompson & Oehlert, 2010);
- difficulties in accessing psychometric assessments for identification (Sternberg, 2010);

- contentions from different countries over what measures should be used in identification of G&T abilities (Maker, 2005; Sibaya, Hlongwane, & Makunga, 2002);
- concerns over racial, gender, or linguistic bias in identification of G&T students (Erwin & Worrell, 2011; Lidz & Macrine, 2002);
- lack of funding or imperatives to provide appropriate programming within school systems (Subotnik & Rickoff, 2010); and
- a lack of teacher preparation and/or professional development focused on the appropriate knowledge, skills, and attitudes teachers must have to effectively address the unique learning needs of these students (LeTendre, Baker, Akiba, Goesling, & Wiseman, 2002; Reis & Renzulli, 2010), and the isolation experienced by teachers of special needs students (Henley et al., 2010).

While acknowledging these interesting and sometimes worrying debates, as well as recognising that we do not claim to be experts in the fields of psychology or gifted education, we designed this chapter to highlight what leaders must know about G&T students and what actions they should take in order to lead enhanced student assessment for gifted special needs students. We have approached this by exploring the literature to draw together experts' research and advice providing a brief exploration of: definitions and conceptualisations of G&T that can guide educators' identification efforts; international trends in gifted education; an actual case from Australia of a family's struggle with their gifted child debriefing what made a difference in their case; and what leaders need to understand about differentiated instruction and assessment in meeting the needs of G&T students. Finally, we explore what leaders at the school and district levels need to consider to ensure they are promoting equity and the pursuit of excellence, rather than pursuing mediocrity and equality.

This chapter is really focused on the leaders – whether they be teacher-leaders, formal school leaders, or district leaders – rather than being an exhaustive account about gifted and talented students. We endorse Robinson's (2003) statement that research that explores administrators' "philosophies, beliefs, and actions … toward talented students is largely nonexistent" (n.p.) and we seek to consolidate insights in the literature regarding G&T and differentiated instruction and assessment to provide guidance to school leaders who we know are so influential in supporting student success and effective schools (Leithwood, Patten, & Jantzi, 2010; Leithwood, Seashore Louis, Anderson, & Wahlstrom, 2004).

10.2 Conceptualisations of Gifted and Talented Students

When discussing with educators whether a student may be gifted and talented, you encounter many characteristics or criteria that they perceive to be relevant in identifying students' giftedness. Teacher observations generally come into play, identifying a student's concentration and attention levels, the sophistication of their language and vocabulary use, their memory and retention capacity, task commitment, and sometimes their motivation as significant giftedness attributes (Heller, Perleth, & Lim, 2005, cited in Reis & Renzulli, 2010, p. 308). The most common identifier cited is the intelligence quotient (IQ) originally identified by Binet and Simon in 1905 as a measure of intelligence and further investigated as a measure of giftedness by Terman (1925, cited in Reis & Renzulli, 2010). A common misnomer is that high IQ is synonymous with giftedness, and is a fixed, highly stable, embedded characteristic of the individual which will exhibit itself with little encouragement or development (Borland, 2009; Sternberg, 2010). Even though IQ has remained the recognised measure for giftedness for approximately 100 years, many scholars and knowledgeable educators feel that IQ is insufficient in explaining children and youth's range of exceptionalities and talents; however, it remains a pervasive myth amongst the uninformed (Pfeiffer, 2012). Indeed as research has continued about the nature and expression of giftedness, there has been a shift of understanding about what comprises giftedness with the inclusion of the concept of talents, how these exhibit, and what supports are needed for these students to realise their G&T potential, as well as the cultural nuances that are bound with these conceptualisations (Borland, 2009; Pfeiffer, 2012). Gardner's (1983, 1993) multiple intelligence research has been a significant contribution to the expansion of conceptualisations of gifts and talents.

Maker (2005) noted that there is an "emerging paradigm" in the G&T field that conceptualises G&T as "multiple forms, being developmental and process-oriented, based on performance, collaborative at all levels, and field-oriented" (p. ix). Sternberg and Davidson (2005), similar to Gardner, identified that giftedness was frequently culturally bound, was exhibited in multidimensional ways, and needed development in order to realise an individual's full potential. Reis and Renzulli (2010) indicated that some definitions articulate "specific actions, products, or abilities within domains" (p. 308), whereas Pfeiffer (2012) cited higher level cognitive skills including advanced reasoning and the capacity of the student to articulate their thinking, their capacity to see relationships and link sophisticated ideas, interests and reading that were far in advance of their chronological age group, curiosity that must be satisfied, and enhanced sensitivity (Robinson, 2003; Pfeiffer, 2009, cited in Pfeiffer, 2012). Gifted and talented students may prefer reading alone, are drawn to more adult material, and select books and resources that are highly sophisticated and factual, for example, biographies, encyclopaedias, historical accounts of important events, atlases, and science and technology manuals (Maker, 2005). Sternberg and Davidson went further describing actual intellectual capacity and the potential for intellectual ability, identifying motivation, creativity, and self-concept as features that are crucial to the realisation of giftedness and talent.

A significant proviso when determining whether a child or young person may be gifted or talented is that they may demonstrate some but not all of these characteristics or capacities previously identified. For example, they may be voraciously curious, with interests well beyond their peers who are the same age, but may not complete assessment tasks or only partially complete these to the point that their own curiosity is satisfied before moving on to the next topic of interest, therefore not providing educators with sufficient documentary evidence of their intelligence or talents. This means that educators and leaders must be keen observers and forge interactive warm relationships so they can observe and/or discern the signs of gifted or talent potential in these students' whose behaviours may mask their giftedness.

Programmes that promoted G&T development were initiated during the 1960s and 1970s and were spurred on by the demands of international competition, such as, the Cold War, Sputnik and the space race, and the advancements of technology, highlighting the societal and commercial importance of nurturing intelligence, creativity, and innovation (Mandelman et al., 2010; Ushakov, 2010). Even so, with policies on inclusion emerging around the world in the 1980s and 1990s that frequently focused on students with challenges, with gifted exceptionalities as an afterthought, there has been a lessening in the attention given to, and funding for, educational programmes specific to meeting the needs of G&T students. Where G&T programmes exist, Maker stated they are no longer focused on elitism but on the pursuit of excellence and realising potential, with diversity (frequently racial, linguistic, and socioeconomic) being an important goal. Mandelman et al. advocated for a resurgence in the focus on, and quality of, gifted education worldwide: "the failure to do so results in the loss of egregious amounts of human capital, which has a direct economic impact on all. The current system lacks vision" (p. 294). So this leads us to consider what is happening internationally regarding G&T education.

10.3 Background

What we do categorically know is that giftedness and talent are aspects of the human condition regardless of race and cultural contexts, although cultural values may influence the development of certain gifts and talents. Gardner's research on multiple intelligences drew upon subjects from many different cultures and the acceptance of his theories around the world indicates that his expanded construction of intelligence resonates across cultural and national boundaries. Similarly, Sternberg's (2010) research on intelligence over five continents found that the "general principles seem to hold, although the content used to assess abilities need to differ from one locale to another" (p. 335).

In this section we seek to provide some examples of countries that have been exploring gifted and talented educational programmes and we cite some policy examples that have had considerable impact in the country of origin, and in some cases, a ripple effect across countries. We do not profess this section to be a comprehensive coverage of the international context as this is beyond the scope and aims of the chapter, but we hope that it will provide a sample of flavour, focus, attention, and political actions that have been taken within G&T education in order to extract some common lessons learned across the international context.

10.3.1 Australia

Following the release of the Marland (1972) report in the US, Great Britain and Australia followed in implementing G&T programmes in the subsequent decade. However, Braggett (1985, 1997a) and other researchers acknowledged the concern over so little Australian research in the field of gifted education (McCann, 2005). International developments in G&T were reflected at both the Australian federal and state levels (the 1983 *Report of the Review Committee: Intellectually Talented Students Programme of Western Australia*) resulting in two senate reports the first of which was *The Australia Parliament Senate Select Committee on the Education of Gifted and Talented Children* (1988). The establishment of the Gifted Education Research, Resource and Information Centre (GERRIC) and other limited teacher education and research programmes ensured the continuance of the issue in the domain of educational research (Gross, 2002). Using minimal resourcing, schools were expected to be accountable for the provision of extensive gifted programmes which met the policy guidelines and included enrichment, acceleration, and extension activities (explained later in the chapter). Private schools closely watched these developments and either matched them, or attempted to anticipate them, to ensure the high quality of provision for their students. The *Senate Employment, Workplace Relations, Small Business and Education References Committee* report (2001) summarised an audit of teacher training for G&T education and bemoaned a dearth of opportunity for the interested teacher (or preservice teacher).

During the 1980s and 1990s there was boom in policies and programmes for G&T and in the provision of professional development for educators; however, at the conclusion of the 1990s this interest and effort waned and programmes were shut down, policies revoked, and funding discontinued (McCann, 2005). In 2005, the Federal Government tendered the development of *Gifted and Talented Education, Professional Development Package for Teachers* to GERRIC with a 'computer-based course' being distributed on disk to all teachers across all education systems as a result of this government funding. Although it appears that there has been significant focus on G&T policies and research, the lack of ongoing focus on teacher professional development at the inservice and preservice levels has resulted in: a lack of identification of students and dedicated funding for G&T specialist programmes, as well as issues surrounding ethnic diversity in programmes (Beattie, Watters, Stewart, & Devlin, 2006). In Beattie et al.'s (2006) *Submission to the House Standing Committee on Education and Vocational Training*, the Australian Association for the Education of the Gifted and Talented identified that even with all the policies and senate reports, change was not occurring and suggested strategies were not being implemented: "untrained teachers are more likely to see giftedness in well-behaved children of the dominant culture, and tend to miss underachievers, divergent thinkers, visual-spatial learners, and children who mask their ability" (p. 2).

A more worrying issue in Australia is that there is a serious ideological contention that Plunkett and Kronborg (2007) identified as an education system that is "characterised by an almost evangelical zeal for principles supporting inclusiveness and egalitarianism" (p. 72), wherein the theory and Australian practice of gifted education is the source of "elitism" (McCann, 2005) and "is inequitable, undemocratic and even eugenic by intention" (Mandelman et al., 2010, p. 293). In describing the tension between egalitarian and meritocracy national ideologies, Mandelman et al. noted that the Senate Committee report (2001) stated that "denying the need for services of gifted children on the grounds that these children are already privileged, or that such services created inequity, was both misguided and misleading" (p. 293). Therefore, Australia's heavily egalitarian paradigm places G&T students more at-risk than others.

10.3.2 United States

In the 1970s Sydney Marland was commissioned to undertake a report for US Congress on education for the gifted wherein he defined and codified six areas as domains of giftedness. This report focused the US Government's spotlight on ensuring gifted students were a priority within education in the 1970s and 1980s. Even though this report has been widely criticised due to the limitations of Marland's definition of giftedness and his statistics on the prevalence of G&T students in the population, it had a ripple effect influence around the world (Kao, 2012). The famous *A Nation at Risk* report (National Commission on Educational Excellence, 1983) highlighted the lack of expertise within the teaching profession to effectively cater for the G&T demographic. Even though this report was tabled in 1983, the concerns over the lack of educator pedagogical expertise with differentiated instructional approaches for G&T programming, resonates throughout the literature to the present day (Maker, 2005; Sternberg, 2010; VanTassel-Baska & Wood, 2010). Reis and Renzulli (2010) reiterated the critical need within contemporary US education systems for gifted education programmes, "when our nation's creative productivity is being challenged by European and Asian nations" (p. 308). Milligan, Neal, and Singleton (2012) stated that with no federal mandate covering gifted children the responsibility for G&T programmes and funding falls to the state level, which frequently means this has become a neglected area of special needs.

10.3.3 Canada

Most likely due to its proximity with the United States, Canada was influenced by many of the reports to emerge from the US, such as the *Marland* and *A Nation at Risk* reports. In Canada during the 1900–1950 era, concerns were raised about how students with disabilities and challenges were treated and this period saw changes in programming whereby special programmes for gifted students were introduced in North America (Lupart & Webber, 2002). From the 1950s through to the 1970s there was widespread concern over the Soviet technological supremacy demonstrated with the launch of Sputnik, which resulted in funding being provided for initiatives focused on Science and Mathematics. Additionally, as part of this focus on national competition, future prosperity, and security for the nation, there was "new appreciation for the educational nurturing of gifted students" which continued throughout the 1960s and onwards (p. 16). However, there were and continue to be many concerns, about how well educators can effectively teach in inclusive classrooms and meet the needs of gifted students. Advocates for the gifted were concerned that the fight for funding for specialist G&T programmes would be lost due to inclusion.

In contemporary Canada, as the provincial governments have jurisdiction over education and budgets, the provision for gifted students varies across the provinces and territories. For example, in Alberta G&T provisions encompass whole-school G&T programmes in private or charter schools, advanced placement programmes, the International Baccalaureate (IB) programme, and individual G&T programmes within regular schools. Unfortunately, with the focus on inclusion in many provinces there is no overt citation of G&T students as they are simply clustered under the various legislations related to "students with special needs" (e.g., Alberta School Act revised statutes, 2000; Ontario Education Act, 1990). The main issues with G&T programmes in Canada revolve around: the consistency of identification and the definitions used for identification; funding of these programmes; identification and inclusion of ethnic, linguistic, and socioeconomically diverse students into programmes; and concerns with the adequacy of educators to effectively teach and assess G&T students (Scott, Webber, Aitken, & Lupart, 2011, Scott, Webber, Lupart, Aitken, & Scott, 2013).

10.3.4 New Zealand

Unlike Australia, New Zealand (NZ) has not had a long history of G&T programmes or policies, with Moltzen (1996, cited in Apted, Macnee, Court, & Riley, 2007, n.p.) describing G&T students as being a low priority with provisions being inconsistent and patchy, uneven and weak. Similar to the findings in Australia, Riley and her team (2004, cited in Apted et al., 2007) identified that there was a dearth of NZ literature and research on G&T programmes. In 2005, the NZ Ministry of Education specified that it was a requirement for schools to identify and meet the needs of G&T students. Interestingly, the 2005 Government mandate specifically targeted school leaders as the ones charged with ensuring that G&T students' needs were met within their schools. Similar to other national settings, Apted et al. found that there were misconceptions by parents and staff about G&T students and initiatives. Their study recommended focusing on embedding support for G&T programmes, the importance of positive school cultures, distributing leadership amongst expert teachers, providing school-wide professional development for all teachers, and the need for educators to engage in wider G&T networks.

10.3.5 *Russia*

Russia has a long history of identifying students who are exceptional and supporting them to reach excellence, although Ushakov (2010) identified that for many, education was not the usual for all, so "special programs for the gifted arises only when education becomes available to the masses and the variance of abilities among students increases" (p. 338). Since 1945 until the 1990s there were a lot of changes in G&T education including greater flexibility for individuals and organisations to adapt curriculum and education processes to meet students' needs. This meant that the construct of education as a "social contract" gave way to goals driven by "self-realization" (p. 337). In line with Russia's socialist history, Ushakov described the main goals of G&T programmes as supporting "social benefits (development of scientific research, technologies, etc.)", as well as to fulfil individual development and finally to "obtain spectacular results" (p. 337).

10.3.6 *Taiwan*

Kao (2012) indicated that the G&T focus in Taiwan was initiated in the early 1960s and was significantly influenced by the US *Marland* report. Taiwan's "Special Education" legislation was passed in 1984 and was a milestone for G&T education. Kao reflected that in Taiwan G&T programming was highly desirable as education was perceived as a key mechanism to upward social mobility and financial security; however, their system has a pervasive acceptance of standardised testing which he described as "victimising" gifted students. He indicated G&T programmes include pull-out and self-contained classes although the latter is mainly for the Arts and Music.

Overall, from this limited review of various nations' approaches to addressing the needs of G&T students, it is clear that most have some policies outlining the expectation of service for G&T students and acknowledge them as 'special needs' students. They identify that they require particular curricula and assessment strategies to promote the realisation of potential, and yet there remains a gap between policy and practice in most education systems which must be addressed. One of the most poignant features is that educators are not prepared in preservice education and many have only limited inservice opportunities to become competent to identify and/or teach G&T students; hence, many students are not receiving the educational support required to realise their potential. This is a loss to not only the student, but also to these nations. As Aljughaiman (2010) stated:

> At the close of the first decade of the 21st Century nothing significantly changed in the school environment; teaching methods did not change significantly and the school system did not keep pace with the sweeping changes that occurred outside of the schools. (p. 285)

The preceding section discussed G&T from a macro-societal perspective which can be somewhat impersonal and mask the emotional impact of G&T issues;

therefore, in the next section we present an actual case study from Australia which describes one young man's experience through the K-12 system and includes the attitudes and approaches of teachers, his parents' concerns in advocating for their son, the difference that expert educators make to a G&T student, and finally, a positive outcome.

10.4 Advocacy for Equity: Justin's Case

10.4.1 *Justin's Case*

This case describes Mr and Mrs Smith's advocacy journey with their son, Justin, and follows their trials and tribulations in seeking appropriate educational support to meet their son's needs within the Australian educational system.

At 5 years of age, Justin started school a little earlier than most of his year group due to his birthday being late in the year and in some cases he was almost a year younger than some of his peers. He was happy though to start school as this represented new and interesting activities and the opportunity to make new friends. Before long, the teacher noticed that Justin was a bit different to the others as he liked to pursue his own interests which frequently did not align with her classroom schedule of learning activities. While many of his peers were learning to write their names, count, and start to read, Justin was interested in physical activities, socialising, and creative work. The teacher expressed her concerns to Mr and Mrs Smith and indicated that it was possible that Justin was really too immature to start school and had fallen behind his peers. Nevertheless Mr and Mrs Smith, who were also educators but at the secondary school level, felt that Justin was coping well and enjoying the mental stimulation of his pre-primary year. As he continued through his early primary schooling, Justin enjoyed school activities, particularly when they offered him the freedom to investigate or explore new ideas, develop physical skills, and to engage in sports in which he excelled. The state literacy and numeracy tests undertaken in Year 3, 5, and 7 revealed that Justin was performing well in advance of his chronological year group in literacy, and in Year 3 slightly below his cohort in numeracy, but not so much that remedial action was deemed useful. Justin's precocious language skills and quick humour often led him into conflict with his teachers and resulted in frequent disciplinary action causing them to remove him from the class. By Year 4, his teacher indicated that he was too far behind to catch up in his mathematics and recommended he repeat the year. Mr and Mrs Smith did not find Justin to be a problem at home and he appeared to be well-adjusted socially in his out-of-school music and sporting activities, but they were increasingly worried about the consistent negative commentary from teachers about their son including routine negative behavioural reports and his seemingly lagging academic performance. The Year 4 teacher indicated there was a need to have Justin tested for ADHD because "he can't seem to sit still and never sits up straight with his feet on the floor like the girls do", so in her view there was clearly something wrong with him. She told Mrs Smith that Justin's problems were her fault for indulging her son too much and not encouraging him to become more independent. As educators, Mr and Mrs Smith felt conflicted as they deeply loved their son, perceived him to be bright and full of potential, admired his many talents and engaging personality but felt torn with their sense of loyalty to their professional colleagues. They also did not want to cause too much trouble in advocating too strongly for him with the school administrators. They became increasingly worried that their son was not progressing at the speed they felt he could, so they followed the educators' advice and kept their son back a year. Repeating Year 4 did little to assist Justin's overall academic progress, although there was a marginal increase in his mathematics skills; but curiously staying back a year did not negatively affect him socially as Justin had considerable interpersonal skills and a friendly, funny persona which enabled him to easily make new friends. The pattern of educator insistence that Justin was ADHD continued throughout the following years and although Mr and Mrs Smith did not believe that Justin was ADHD, they eventually sought psychological testing to obtain a definitive answer. Psychological tests undertaken by a private psychological clinic revealed Justin was not ADHD or learning disabled with any recognised syndrome or disorder. Even with this evidence, teacher opinion across the school (including the views of the vice principal and principal) did not change and their negative views of Justin bled into the playground, sports field, and other extra-curricular activities, in which he excelled and relished. Justin was frequently barred by teachers from engaging in school-based extra-curricular activities such as representing the school in sports competitions, joining the choir, or participating in music productions as he was deemed a 'discipline problem'.

He continued to experience problems with school into high school but by this time Mr and Mrs Smith were becoming increasingly concerned with his negative perceptions of school, teachers, and more worryingly about himself. They recalled one occasion when he claimed their loyalties were to their colleagues and not to him, and that it did not matter what his perspective was as they would always side with the teachers against him. This comment caused them to seriously reflect on their views and they realised that their tension over collegial loyalty was creating a schism with their son where he felt he no longer had advocates at home. This was unacceptable and they decided to ensure that he was aware of their unconditional support and love. Unfortunately, by this time his primary school experiences had seriously deleteriously influenced his self-esteem to such a point that they had real concerns that he may actually consider taking his own life. He now believed teachers' constant value-laden commentary that he was "useless", "stupid", "a troublemaker", and "dumb" even though Mr and Mrs Smith had made every attempt to counteract these aspersions. In an attempt to provide Justin with a fresh start, his parents enrolled him in a different high school to that in his home locale.

During his Year 8 (his first year of high school) Justin found that some of his teachers were drawn to his quick mind and clever rhetoric while others continued the primary school educators' pattern of labelling him as "cheeky", "rude", "challenging authority" or "disruptive". However, he developed an excellent relationship with his social studies teacher, Mr James, and as a result of Mr James's positive and somewhat flexible (more independence oriented) classroom environment, Justin excelled in his assignments and project work for this teacher. Conversely, Justin experienced many conflicts with other teachers to the point where Mr and Mrs Smith, in their frustration with the school, system, and poor leadership, considered home schooling Justin even though they were ideologically opposed to this approach. During the Year 8 parent interviews, Mr James informed Mr and Mrs Smith that through his indepth conversations with Justin and the intensive project work that Justin had undertaken in class, he felt Justin was gifted:

> Justin does not think the same way as others. I think he must be a lateral thinker. He approaches problems and inquiry in very different ways to other students and yet his conclusions and arguments are deeper and more insightful than his cohort peers. I would recommend he is tested for giftedness.

This surprising suggestion resulted in Mr and Mrs Smith seeking advice from a professional colleague and family friend, Mrs Heart, who was coordinator of a gifted and talented school programme. She agreed with Mr James's estimation and organised to have Justin tested. Even though Justin experienced boredom with the tests and did not complete them, they revealed that he was gifted in Language, Literacy, and Humanities, identifying his cognitive functioning at a level that exceeded 18+ years of age even though he was just 12 years old.

10.4.1.1 Features of the G&T Classroom

On the prompting of Mr James and Mrs Heart, Justin was moved to Mrs Heart's gifted and talented programme in another school. In 1 year, Justin made rapid progress, not only academically but also in terms of his self-efficacy and confidence. Features of Mrs Heart's programme included some direct teaching of foundational concepts with the majority of class time engaged at higher cognitive levels. Her routine teaching approach included classroom and group discussions, debates, critical analyses, inquiry projects etc. Her classroom was filled with visual and aural stimuli with continual music playing in the background. Provided they were on task, students had the freedom to move around, to work in groups, and to talk and challenge each other in their exploration of the topics. Mrs Heart's class was an exemplar of inclusion as many of the students were 'gifted learning disabled', so Justin gained experience in exercising tolerance and respect for diversity within this overtly supportive classroom. Indeed, many of the students were very protective of their disabled peers and looked out for them in other classes and in extra-curricular contexts. One aspect that made a significant different to Justin's achievement was that all assessment rubrics were developed in a whole class – teacher collaboration so all students understood the expectations, assignment formats, deadlines, and frequently topics (although always aligned with curricula outcomes) were individually negotiated with the teacher. This created greater relevance for Justin and meant he actually submitted his assignments for marking which in turn resulted in increases in his marks. As part of the whole – school approach to the G&T programme, Mrs Heart also mediated problems between her G&T students and teachers in other disciplines and encouraged her students' engagement in arts, music, and sports which aligned with their interests and talents. Her focus was on caring for the 'entire' personality and intellectual development of the young adults in her class.

10.4.1.2 Extra-Curricular Activities That Promoted Self-Efficacy and Skill Acquisition

Concurrent with his move to the specialist G&T programme, Justin commenced basketball referee training, about which he was passionate. Refereeing meant he had to hone a range of skills such as interpersonal communication, mediation and conflict resolution, and swift evaluation and judgment, as well as engage in self-reflection and be receptive to constructive criticism – all of which matured him and increased his self-confidence. At the conclusion of his Year 9, he received the state Basketball Association's award for "talented 'rookie' referee of the year". He had forged new friendships with a group of Year 12 boys who were also involved in the basketball team at his school (where he also served as referee). However, even with Mrs Heart's support Justin still lagged in many of his academic subjects due to the missed foundational content as a result of the time spent out of class for misbehaviour throughout his primary school years, so his parents hired tutors to provide direct teaching and individual academic support.

Justin's Year 8–9 year went extremely well; then the government shut the school down due to declining numbers. There were no G&T programmes available within the district so he went to another local school. Even with no programme in place, Justin developed an excellent rapport with his new principal who took a personal interest in him and assisted in negotiations between Justin and his teachers (who frequently did not understand his needs as a G&T student). Justin achieved high school graduation but did not find the same level of acceptance, structure, and ideal programming that he had in the specialist G&T programme, although he appreciated and valued his principal. While he did obtain university entrance his marks were mediocre which limited his career choices.

Justin enrolled in a university programme and worked with his parents to learn the study skills and foundational writing skills so necessary for success in university which he had missed in his early K-12 learning. Over a period of 3 years, he upgraded his university marks and strategically transferred from low ranked institutions to higher ranked ones. He is now in an elite university programme in a top-ranked institution, is maintaining a high distinction average, regularly engages in intense academic debates with his professors outside of class time, and is planning on undertaking a law degree to prepare him for his ultimate desire to engage in Human Rights advocacy or ambassadorial services. His motivation is intrinsic; he wants to "make a difference to society" and to "be an advocate for those who do not a have a strong enough voice". His closest friend is a gifted learning disabled individual and Justin actively assists him in his studies and, more importantly, in advising him in navigating the human interactions his friend, with his syndrome, finds too complex and challenging. Justin still referees for a state association and is a member of the university debating team. His professors like and respect his intellect and his engaging sense of humour, and he is deriving considerable satisfaction from finally achieving his academic and personal potential.

When we asked Mr and Mrs Smith to reflect on the turning points in Justin's education, they indicated it encompassed: (1) getting the psychological reports to refute his teachers' ingrained belief that there was something seriously wrong with Justin (and more advantageously confirmed their own beliefs in their son's capacities while also being a relief to Justin himself); (2) the positive impact of a select few knowledgeable and caring high school teachers and leaders who went out of their way to develop warm and caring relationships with Justin and who were able to advocate for him within the school context; (3) the unconditional love and pragmatic support of his parents who had the social and political acumen to advocate for their son, and the academic skills to teach him what he needed to know for academic success in university; (4) encouraging him to engage in sporting activities that promoted high self-esteem and the development of competence across a range of skills that would serve him well in later studies and real life. They mused about the successful outcome in their own family history but were distressed as to what would happen to children and youths who had less educated parents, and those families with less social and political acumen, who did not have the financial capacity to engage private tutors, or who lost faith in their child and the system.

10.4.2 Debriefing Justin's Case

> The natural distribution is neither just nor unjust; nor is it unjust that persons are born into society at some particular position. These are simply natural facts. What is just and unjust is the way that institutions deal with these facts. (Rawls, 1999, p. 87)

10.4.2.1 Educators

There were three main features worthy of scrutiny in this case: the educators, the parents, and the G&T programme. It was disturbing that the primary school educators involved in Justin's early education did not engage with Justin sufficiently to note his giftedness. Their lack of knowledge about G&T meant that Justin's K-7 years were largely wasted, or worse, destructive, particularly in relation to his self-esteem and self-concept. Considering that many educators make the claim that primary teachers are "teachers of the whole child" as opposed to their secondary counterparts who perceive themselves as "teachers of subjects", it was surprising that the crucial intervention and educational support in Justin's case arose from secondary educators. This case illustrates the importance of ***all*** educators' having a knowledge of G&T characteristics, how to accommodate their learning needs, as well as displaying an ethic of care and the capacity to create relationships with students, in order to actually get to know them as people, rather than simply as one of the masses. There was a failure of leadership in Justin's primary school where the leaders should have put a stop to the negative labelling of him particularly in the face of psychological reports that refuted staff conceptions of his "problem". Additionally, there appeared to be an inappropriate coalescence of teacher assessments of Justin's behaviour and his academic performance. On a positive note, it was gratifying to note that there were some educators and leaders who did care enough to get to know Justin, and one who was sufficiently expert in G&T to revoke much of the damage done to Justin's psyche; even so, the damage done to his academic knowledge-base was so extensive it required many years of intensive tutoring and personal study to "catch up" on missing content and the study skills required for success.

10.4.2.2 Parent and Family Support

Justin was fortunate in many ways to have been born into this particular family. His parents were devoted and supportive but also had the social and political acumen to advocate for him, teach him the requisite functional English composition and study skills, and the financial capacity to obtain tutors. As Freeman (2000) indicated, the time Mr and Mrs Smith spent with Justin may have had a significant impact on his intellectual development. They consistently articulated trust in his abilities and tried to counteract the negative messaging from teachers. Contrastingly, their professional loyalty deleteriously impacted their relationship with their son and resulted in their misplaced trust in professional colleagues, which actively impeded Justin's education and the development of his gifts. It was interesting that Justin's active involvement in sports and other extra-curricular activities which his parents organised and encouraged was a key factor in recovering Justin's self-esteem and efficacy. This endorsed Freeman's statements that self-esteem is influenced by family and is a crucial component to gifted students' development.

10.4.2.3 Effective Programming

Justin clearly thrived within the specialist G&T programming and the caring and scaffolded classroom environment. The features that made the most impact on Justin were the level of independence and trust that was extended: being finally treated like an intelligent adult and finding acceptance within the group even with his advanced cognition; the interesting and engaging project work; the clarity of expectations and negotiation of assessment task criteria; the stimulating classroom; the cooperative and collaborative orientation; and the support in the school from a coordinator who buffered her G&T cohort in their interactions with other teachers. The impact of 1 year of specialised programming was sufficient to revoke much of the damage done to Justin's self-concept and efficacy from his K-7 experience. Imagine what could have been achieved by this student by the conclusion of his schooling if this G&T programme had continued throughout his senior secondary life.

So what are the lessons leaders can extract from this account and from the other sections? In the following sections we articulate what leaders need to know about differentiated instruction, differentiated assessment, as well as what to look for in optimal teachers for G&T programmes.

10.5 Differentiated Instruction and Assessment for the Gifted: Implications for Leaders

Leaders are frequently faced with highly complex environments so to expect an average principal to be an expert on gifted education, psychological testing for giftedness, or to be highly competent in teaching G&T students him or herself is unreasonable. What we do expect is for principals to know enough about differentiated instruction and assessment to be able to select the optimal teacher to support these students within the school. It is important for principals to: care enough about these students; believe that they are as at-risk as other at-risk categories (e.g., students with autism, ADHD, cerebral palsy etc.); understand that appropriate G&T programmes are not elitist but are an expression of equity (meeting the needs of the individual even if these are different to other students) not equality (treating all students the same); and to know enough to ascertain if the teacher's programming in the classroom is likely to promote academic and social engagement for these advanced children and youth (Hansen, 2000; Maker, 2005; Silverman, 2000). Additionally, as Robinson pointed out from Feldhusen, Haeger, and Pellegrino's (1989, cited in Robinson, 2003) work "informed administrators are more supportive of teachers engaged in differentiated instruction and are more likely to make decisions with positive outcomes for high-ability learners" (n.p.). Indeed, the principles we outline here would work for most classes and certainly for students of moderate to high abilities.

As instructional leaders, principals need to understand that G&T students (including those with disabilities) who are not identified and served tend to encounter emotional trauma, need to seek counselling, and tend to drop out of school (Reis & Renzulli, 2010); whereas students who are identified and placed in specialised G&T programmes enjoy greater social development, "greater popularity, greater social competence, more mature social relations, earlier psychological maturity, and fewer indications of psychological problems than their less gifted peers" (Silverman, 2000, p. 31).

10.5.1 Differentiated Instruction

There is considerable talk within schools and undergraduate preparation programmes about differentiated instruction but there is a lack of understanding of what it is and why it is crucial to G&T students. In fact, in their large-scale study in the US, Reis and Renzulli (2010) identified that "gifted students rarely received instruction in homogeneous groups (only 21 % of the time), and more alarmingly, the target gifted students experienced no instructional or curricular differentiation in 84 % of the instructional activities in which they participated" (p. 309).

So let us deconstruct what differentiated instruction is and what it would look like. Moon and her colleagues, drawing upon Tomlinson's (1995, 2001) definition indicated it is "purposeful instruction" that takes into account student differences in their "readiness, interests, and learning profiles" (Moon, Brighton, Callahan, & Robinson, 2005, p. 121). They continued indicating that "drill and practice on discrete, unconnected, or isolated factual knowledge" is inappropriate and disengaging for G&T students (p. 119). Similarly, Maker (2005) identified that differentiated instruction was characterised by:

> (a) integrated, interdisciplinary content; (b) higher-order thinking, appropriate pacing, self-directed learning, and complex problem solving processes; (c) development of unique products for real audiences (authentic assessment); and (d) student interaction, interaction with experts, and learning environments with physical and psychological flexibility, openness, and safety. The environment is rich in resources, and the teacher usually acts as a guide rather than a dispenser of knowledge as the students make choices based on interest and ability. (p. x)

Clearly there is a need for variety in learning experiences and greater freedom for students to work "independently, in pairs, with peers, in larger groups, and with the teacher" (Honigsfeld, 2002, p. 82) while educators maintain high expectations (VanTassel-Baska & Wood, 2010, p. 354). Honigsfeld also indicated that there was a relationship between G&T students and "tactual-perceptual preference", meaning they learned more effectively and remembered information when they had manipulated it in some way "using their hands for drawing, illustrating or note taking during lectures or reading assignments" (p. 82). Neber and Schommer-Aikins (2002, cited in Thompson & Oehlert, 2010) indicated gifted students need to explore their individual interests in their "rage to master", while De Groot (1990, cited in Thompson & Oehlert, 2010) found self-regulation was bound with self-efficacy along with intrinsic value of the activity and were predictors of academic performance (p. 305).

Acceleration, enrichment and curriculum enhancement, and curricular compacting and pull-out classes are also useful strategies for leaders to consider (Reis & Renzulli, 2010; VanTassel-Baska & Wood, 2010). *Acceleration* indicates that teachers determine the level at which a student is functioning and then moves them to more advanced work that is commensurate with their abilities – this is sometimes achieved through the skipping of grades or with higher order approaches within a specialised programme of study. *Enrichment* is usually undertaken with students who are within usual or mainstream classes and can involve different activities and project work. Unfortunately, this is sometimes interpreted as simply giving G&T students **more** work which they perceive to be punishment. *Pull-out classes* is where students are generally with their usual mainstream class but spend some of their time in a specialised gifted class undertaking curriculum pitched to a more advanced level or engaged in critical and creative thinking activities. *Curricular compacting* is where a teacher pretests a G&T student to establish what content skills he/she has already mastered with the intent to skip work, and to progress them to deeper concepts or different topics with the view to avoid unnecessary repetition and boredom.

10.5.2 A Cheat Sheet for Leaders: Features of Differentiated Instruction

Programmes

- Specialised programming is best (when students are learning with others with similar advanced abilities as well as with gifted learning disabled students teachers can ensure all learning activities and instruction is designed for greater challenge and cognitive demand)
- May include acceleration, enrichment, curricular compacting, pull-out classes, and specialised programmes

Classroom Environment

- Caring, friendly, and psychologically safe (acceptance)
- Interactions characterised by maturity and respect (adult learning principles – Knowles, Holton, & Swanson, 2005; Merriam & Grace, 2011)
- Visually and aurally stimulating
- Encourage negotiation between teacher-student, and student-student
- Promotes tolerance for difference (interactions with gifted learning disabled peers)

Learning Experiences

- Encompass high expectations
- Encourage deeper exploration of the content (depth)
- Extend and challenge students (breadth)
- Learning of content and skills within a domain of inquiry using deliberate instructional approaches and ensuring that learning experiences are organised around major themes, ideas, issues that enable students to identify relationships and linkages within and across disciplines (inter-disciplinarity and trans-disciplinarity)
- Involve problem-solving, higher order thinking, research and inquiry
- Incorporate student interaction with experts, materials, resources, and technologies
- Provide for increased flexibility, choice, and the opportunity to pursue personal interests
- Variety in learning tasks and avoid repetition (avoidance of boredom)
- Encourage hands-on activities (tactile preference)
- Include opportunities for work that is independent, peer-to-peer, group, and in collaboration with the teacher

- Variability in complex instructional strategies (e.g., Models of Teaching [Joyce, Weil, & Calhoun, 2009], cooperative learning e.g., Jigsaw, [Aronson, 1997], Student Teams Achievement Divisions [Slavin, Sharan, Hertz-Lazarowitz, Webb, & Schmuck, 1985], Group Investigation [Sharan & Sharan, 1992])

10.6 Differentiated Assessment

Instruction is guided by assessment and vice versa. Students and teachers align with assessment expectations so ensuring the inclusion of differentiated assessment into G&T programming is essential in driving positive motivation and student engagement that will not only enhance the quality of their learning but also will reveal demonstrable and measureable student outcomes. This means that principals must also understand differentiated assessment.

We know that many students, much less G&T students, find no challenge, interest, or use in many assessments. These perceptions are heightened for G&T students and as Maker (2005) stated with poor and meaningless assessment, students "were so totally frustrated and disillusioned that they simply 'gave up' and started to act out or doodle" (p. 7); therefore engagement with the assessment process is crucial for G&T students. Maker along with Moon et al. (2005) recommended the use of performance-based assessment, which represents a significant challenge to students, provides them opportunities to demonstrate their knowledge and talents, and are open-ended utilising multiple approaches. It is also hands-on which links with Honigsfeld's (2002) findings that G&T students prefer tactile activity. She continued by identifying that gifted students desired more freedom – less adult supervision, preferred self-designed objectives and learning tasks, and self-paced progress.

Another form of assessment that is deemed useful with G&T students is authentic assessment – tasks that are undertaken for real audiences, serve real purposes, and that are judged by experts for which the product was designed and crafted. They may include performances, demonstrations, debates, website development, simulations, presentations, publications, practical tests etc. Moon and her associates (2005) indicated that authentic assessment focuses on macro thinking and the quality of the product, is indepth, is completed in class time, includes explicit criteria negotiated with the teacher, provides scope for interpretation and multiple representations and perspectives, and is marked using the criteria and weighted on the complexity of the criteria.

Self- and peer-assessment is also a reasonable and useful assessment format for G&T students. Self-reflection which includes metacognition (the ability to understand, regulate, and use one's cognitive processes in a constructive manner) is a key capacity in experts which enables them to "organize greater amounts of knowledge in a more effective manner, use more appropriate strategies, and regulate their thinking and performance more effectively than non-experts" (Snyder, Nietfeld, & Linnenbrink-Garcia, 2011, p. 181). Snyder and her associates also found that G&T students were more accurate in making judgments of their peers and their own work than typical students.

A common misconception is that gifted students will complete their assessment and project work more quickly than others; however, Snyder et al. did not find this but they did identify that G&T students expended more time in the planning stages of the task, therefore accuracy is more important to them than speed.

Overall as Thompson and Oehlert (2010) stated "the best strategy for nurturing this varied expression of high cognitive ability appears to be to offer a very broad range of opportunity and encourage each individual to find their preferred path for expressing their gift" (p. 305). Maker (2005) reported that evaluation of student learning could include students themselves, administrators, teachers, and parents. This assessment involves information on student strengths with considerable detail on problem solving behaviours, core competencies, creativity and task commitment, which provides useful information for parents and students to discuss future development.

10.6.1 A Cheat Sheet for Leaders: Features of Differentiated Assessment

- Higher order thinking including problem solving
- Alignment with curriculum outcomes
- Authentic tasks and/or performance-based assessment (educative assessment)
- Complexity and challenge
- Variability in expression and demonstration (e.g., potentially using a range of technologies, performances, artwork, etc.)
- Encompasses students' interests and is engaging
- Explicit and negotiated criteria
- Opportunities for periodic feedback with the view to developing a quality product
- Peer and self-reflection (metacognition)

10.7 Selecting the Right Teacher for Gifted Programs

There is an almost worldwide expectation that all teachers can teach the inclusive classroom; however, studies have identified that this is simply not the case (Braggett, 1997a, 1997b; Fournier, 2012; Lupart & Webber, 2002; McCann, 2005). This is not to say that teachers who adopt the many strategies of differentiated instruction and assessment can only use these for G&T classes, rather, these are optimal approaches for meeting the needs of the diverse class but are most impactful for G&T students who frequently do not thrive in transmissive (teacher-led rather than student-centred and constructivist oriented) classrooms. Acceleration, curriculum compacting, curricular enhancement or enrichment also require specialised pedagogical understandings and expertise which means that leaders who are selecting staff for inclusive classrooms or for specialist programmes must ensure teachers have this specialisation as part of the instructional repertoire. There is a common misconception that G&T students are bright so they will be successful anywhere and in any classroom environment because they can learn by themselves with little or no support. This is a myth and is not only untrue, but dangerous, as it denies acknowledging these students as 'at-risk' needing specialised instruction and assessment approaches in order to reach their potential and to demonstrate their abilities in ways that are acceptable to themselves and the system that accredits and documents their achievement. Therefore, leaders have the moral and legal responsibility to examine the selection of teachers and consider the "right placement" of the "right teacher" in particular classes and programmes to ensure G&T students' needs will be met. But this then raises the question: "what is the right teacher for G&T programs?"

Hansen (2000) and David (2011) identified a number of key qualities, capacities, and characteristics of teachers for the gifted. Teachers must have the pedagogical *knowledge of gifted education* and, more importantly, *positive philosophical orientations* towards gifted students, and the *willingness to accelerate* student learning and assessment. They should be able to *identify the signs of giftedness and talent* and know how to nurture students' intellect and creativity.

Not surprisingly, they both stated they had to have *high intelligence* – at least commensurate with their students, as this will assist in building mutual respect. They must understand *higher level thinking* and be able to scaffold these cognitive capacities for students, as well as routinely engage them at these higher levels. *Deep curriculum and/or subject specialist knowledge* is also important considering they may have to compact or directly teach concepts and skills that are foundational in order to accelerate students through other less vital aspects. They must have a *deep theoretical understanding* which encourages students to engage with the complexities, relationships, and linkages within and across theories. Without strong curricular understandings their *flexibility* will be significantly reduced and students will lose respect in their *competence*. They need to have a *broad cultured background* as this will enable them to express wisdom across diverse topics and the *confidence* to promote a world or 'big picture' perspective, and to provide activities that facilitate indepth exploration. Teachers must have a *passion for teaching* as well as their subject matter which is contagious for students. *Networking* is also a key function for a teacher where they should encourage and facilitate the interaction between students and experts, which enables students to receive *authentic feedback* and exposure to expert views.

They must have *high expectations* for students and integrate strategies that will encourage and promote students' pursuit of excellence, but also facilitate *resilience and perseverance*. They need to be open to *individualised attention* and negotiation with a student which will *expand students' interests* and be prepared to accept *responsibility for their [the teacher's] influence* on students. Along a similar vein, teachers need to be able to forge *caring, warm relationships* and create classroom environments that *foster a sense of positive identity and belonging* in G&T students. They should model humility, honesty, and courage – potentially advocating for G&T students even if this is not a popular or easy task (Hansen, 2000, pp. 14 & 19).

Teachers can assist G&T students to be more successful by scaffolding political acumen. This means teachers describe and explain how students can be respectful and knowledgeable self-advocates, and how to navigate their learning needs, and demonstrate their learning outcomes within a restrictive educational system. Within this concept teachers would explain the demands and expectations that educators must meet in grading and reporting students' achievement, and negotiate with and explain how students can align with their assessment outcome expectations with curriculum outcome criteria. This enables students to develop political acumen and proactivity to engage with learning that will maximise their grades/marks.

Maker (2005) recommended that principals interview or find ways to explore teachers' beliefs of giftedness and talents, identify if their teaching philosophy is one that is aligned with new paradigms of teaching (constructivist), and to identify their teaching competence in specific strategies that will promote optimal learning environments for G&T students.

Where principals do not have the luxury of selecting the 'right' teacher for an inclusive classroom or for a specialised programme, we recommend professional development on specific strategies for G&T programming is sought and provided for teachers who have appropriate philosophical orientations that will enable them to create positive classroom environments for these at-risk students. Moon et al. (2005) advocated for professional development related to assessment as this was deemed a crucial component in any national system due to its importance in providing "valid and reliable" information about student performance; yet she states, there has been a failure in providing teachers with the necessary professional development to support their capacity to develop effective and valid assessment for gifted programming, which can in turn, provide useful information to inform instructional practice.

Another leadership consideration with G&T education is that of advocacy. The next section explores some of these issues and provides some guidance.

10.7.1 Partnerships and Advocacy

We know that a key factor in effective schools is involved and interested parents or caregivers and the incidence of involved parents is generally greater in high SES schools (McCoach et al., 2010; Rapp & Duncan, 2012). Parental involvement is an important consideration for administrators as it can make a real difference to student achievement, which in turn influences school results. However, increased parental involvement, sometimes referred to as "helicopter parents", increases the potential for teacher-parent conflict. One avenue where parents and teacher or leader may come into conflict is in the identification of an individual's gifts and talents, therefore effective leaders will have network with other agencies that can assess students' gifts and talents, as well as identify if there are multiple exceptionalities that may be masking their giftedness. Hornby and Lafaele (2011) identified that there are barriers to parental involvement (PI) which can have serious effects on student engagement and success:

barriers to effective PI can be evident when parents consider their children are academically gifted if this view is not shared by teachers (Montgomery, 2009). Parents in this situation tend to lose confidence in the school and therefore reduce their involvement with teachers. Also, many children who are academically (sic) gifted become frustrated at school, typically because they are being insufficiently (sic) challenged, and either begin to underachieve or develop behaviour problems. Either situation is likely to lead to conflict between parents and teachers which then acts as a barrier to effective PI. (p. 43)

Maker (2005) continued this theme of the importance of leaders forging positive relationships with parents and respect for their advocacy, noting that schools that actively encouraged this involvement "outperform schools without strong parent involvement programs" (p. 23). Similar to Kelly's (2000) sentiments, Maker reported that students who have caring and involved parents tend to perform better at school, are more engaged, have more positive attitudes, complete school and go on to university and other postsecondary education, than children without these home supports. This means that even though we acknowledge that administrators are busy and frequently bombarded with a myriad of issues, parent advocacy is an important factor in forging positive relationships with school and educators and should not be side-lined, ignored, or ridiculed by leaders and educators. Robinson (2003) noted that administration was a complex job that required leaders to balance many competing demands for their time and attention, but she recommended that it was important for principals to encourage parent advocates to come to the table to discuss issues and seek solutions.

Advocates for G&T students may include others aside from parents; for example, Lewis, Cruzeiro, and Hall (2007) identified that advocacy may be presented by teachers and the students themselves particularly when these students are functioning at intellectual levels commensurate of adults. They stressed that leaders should be open to this advocacy and be prepared to collaborate with these different advocates – including students – to ensure that service for these special needs are coherent, accessible, and educationally sound.

10.7.2 Other Leadership Implications

As the focus on this chapter is on what leaders need to understand, be able to do, and appreciate or value, it may appear odd to have a section on 'other leadership implications'; however, we felt that it was important to provide an overview of leadership implications which would provide an opportunity for readers to step back and look at how all the pieces we have examined and discussed coalesce. This section touches on reflection, educator philosophies, school culture, leadership development, establishing programmes and practices, building teacher capacity, and productive partnerships.

Examination of Values and Beliefs Leaders need to engage in honest reflection to consider if they believe gifted students to be at-risk, if they perceive the provision of G&T programming to be "elitist," if they truly understand the nuances of equity versus equality in the case of gifted students, and whether or not they have the courage to argue for a 'social justice' stance for G&T education with their school stakeholders. Additionally, they must interrogate their beliefs about the prevalence or occurrence of G&T capacities in certain demographics; for example, G&T students are in minority groups, refugee students, and low socio-economic localities.

Establish School Cultures on Sound Values Truly inclusive leadership seeks to establish a school culture where educators do not simply tolerate difference but celebrate student uniqueness, gifts, and talents. This may translate into actively addressing the common misconceptions about G&T including beliefs that nurture mediocrity.

Engage in G&T Leadership Development Inclusive leaders need to know enough to identify, lead, monitor, and evaluate differentiated approaches in their school. They must be sufficiently knowledgeable to suspect G&T potential in students or at least ensure there are teachers in the school with the expertise to advise them.

Investigate Behavioural Issues We know that many unidentified G&T students disengage and become frustrated with school and teachers so it is important for leaders to put aside their irritation with students who present as behaviour problems to entertain the possibility that a 'problem student' may be gifted or have multiple exceptionalities.

Monitor and Scrutinise Teaching and Learning Leaders need to ask themselves "do I have sufficient knowledge and expertise to evaluate the effectiveness of inclusionary practices and special programmes?" If not, then leadership development is needed. Specialised programmes must be evaluated like all other programmes of instruction in the school to ensure they are meeting (and hopefully exceeding) the expectations of the system (Lewis et al., 2007).

Establish Specialised Programmes Even though G&T students can thrive in inclusive classrooms if there is differentiated instruction and assessment they learn best, and teachers can be more effective and less stressed, if G&T students are clustered in specific programmes or classes that can focus on acceleration, enrichment, curriculum compacting and so on. Effective leaders are creative in managing their resources and timetabling to ensure appropriate programmes are in place for these students.

Build Teacher Capacity Teachers rarely are adequately prepared for differentiated instruction and assessment, hence leaders must actively encourage and promote the professional development of teachers and teacher-leaders in order to ensure optimal learning conditions for these special needs students. We recommend the principal invest in the professional growth of teacher-leaders who can share their expertise with colleagues.

Productive Partnership Leaders will form constructive partnerships with parents, psychologists, and other experts to identify and support continued academic and social success for students with exceptionality.

10.7.2.1 Recommendations for District/Regional or Ministerial Levels

As regional or district leadership entails different responsibilities it was important to consider what district directors or superintendents, and ministry leaders should consider in promoting learning for *all* students and the pursuit of excellence not mediocrity for G&T students.

Policies and Funding It is clear that many countries have revoked or simply not developed policies that overtly serve the needs of G&T students. All too often they are either aggregated with students with other exceptionalities or physical and cognitive challenges with an underlying assumption that they too will have their needs met through 'inclusion approaches. Occasionally, G&T students do not appear within policy frameworks at all – in many countries they are simply the "lost boys (and girls)" of the special needs category. It is important therefore to overtly include G&T students within policy frameworks, as much of the work in schools is undertaken to ensure alignment with policy expectations, so this is a crucial missing piece of the provision jigsaw because if G&T considerations are not in policy it is highly unlikely that it will be perceived as a priority. Policy also provides clear direction to school leaders and educators that these students are also a priority amongst the larger group of students with exceptionalities.

Funding for Programmes Many schools may have too small a population to provide special programmes or entire classes of G&T students, therefore, it would be useful for district leaders to consider ensuring there are specialised programmes available to students across a district with expert teachers who are best able to meet the needs of these students.

Identification Services System leaders need to consider developing partnerships with psychological testing services and other agencies that can support schools and educators in the identification of exceptionalities. As part of the social justice philosophy, systems should consider establishing or subsidising these services to ensure accessibility to all children including those within lower SES areas. Identification is only the first step; it is then about how best to support teachers in providing optimal instructional and assessment in the classroom. Hence, it is also important that these partnerships also translate into professional development whereby educators can access expertise in interpreting psychological assessment reports and obtain advice on how and what strategies and approaches will be successful within the classroom to meet G&T students' needs.

Leadership Development Leadership development programmes designed to assist leaders in understanding differentiated instruction and assessment is crucial – not in vague policy terms – but in the pragmatics of what these actually are and how to identify these in teachers' practice. This may mean that district leaders establish a pool of expert school leaders who have specialised in a particular exceptionality who can be released from part of their leadership responsibilities to support leader-peers with specific problems related to inclusionary matters within the peer's school. This would mean that the instructional leadership expertise for specific exceptionalities would be distributed around the district while ensuring all leaders have access to this expertise and advice through this peer coaching model – representing maximum impact for the leadership development expenditure (in time and money).

Building Teacher-Leader Capacity District leaders should ensure there is appropriate professional development available for teachers related to G&T needs. We recommend that system leaders provide incentives for teacher-leaders who wish to specialise in this field and provide career pathways for them so that their efforts in increasing their expertise is rewarded through formal recognition mechanism rather than just more work.

Using Evidence to Monitor G&T Responsiveness Systems are accountable to society and generally use data to report back to stakeholders; gifted programmes should not be treated differently. Leaders who have programmes should evaluate the effectiveness of these programmes to promote the justification of system focus and expenditure. Additionally, schools that do not appear to be identifying or serving G&T students should be scrutinised to determine why as this may be an artefact of skewed values, lack of expertise, or misconceptions related to student demographics in particular socio-economic areas, all of which need to be addressed by district leaders.

10.8 Concluding Thoughts

In undertaking the research for this chapter we found a plethora of disturbing issues within the field of gifted education. Some of these issues involved: the lack of governmental policy and priority for G&T programmes and students in this contemporary era; the lack of funding for specialist programmes with expert teachers; a lack of attention to the identification of gifted students within schools; and a lack of pragmatic preparation regarding differentiated instruction and assessment for gifted students within undergraduate teacher education programmes compounded by a dearth of pragmatic inservice programming in this field. Most terrifying was the apparent negative philosophical stance underpinning the lack of expertise and provision for gifted and talented students – that identifying and providing for G&T students' needs constitutes elitism at best, and the undermining of 'egalitarian' societal mores at its worst, rather than an issue of social justice and equity for a different category of special needs students. We described a case of a gifted young man's educational journey and discussed the barriers and constraints he and his family encountered, along with what made a difference to him in his educational journey through K-12 and beyond. We sought to provide some practical guidance for school leaders based upon scholarly evidence in relation to: the identification and characteristics of G&T students; understanding the features of differentiated instruction and assessment; and what knowledge, skills, and attributes/attitudes an optimal teacher of G&T students should have and exemplify. We noted the importance of advocacy for these students which is particularly poignant considering so many countries have limited or no policy priority for these students.

Our final comment is that leaders and educators need to reflect on their own professional beliefs to consider if they align with the philosophy that *all* children should be treated equally or should have educational opportunities that will meet their unique needs, that is be treated with equity. If it is the latter then it behoves leaders to learn about G&T students and the pragmatics of differentiated instruction and assessment in order to ensure that these at-risk students can thrive. Considering G&T students who realise their potential will become the next generation of creative influencers, leaders, and innovators, we, as leaders, can conceive our leadership of optimal G&T education as being the pursuit of excellence for a better society, rather than in pursuit of mediocrity (Subotnik & Rickoff, 2010).

References

Aljughaiman, A. M. (2010). New dimensions: Gifted education in the 21st century. *Learning and Individual Differences, 20*(4), 285–286. doi:10.1016/j.lindif.2010.06.001.

Apted, K., Macnee, K., Court, M. R., & Riley, T. L. (2006). The development of schoolwide programmes in gifted and talented education: What can we learn from other schools? *New Zealand Principal, 21*(1), 19–23.

Aronson, E. (1997). *The Jigsaw classroom: Building cooperation in the classroom* (2nd ed.). New York, NY: Longman.

Australia Parliament Senate Select Committee on the Education of Gifted and Talented Children. (1988). *The education of gifted and talented children* (pp. 1–197). Canberra, ACT, Australia: Australian Government Publishing Services.

Beattie, J., Watters, J., Stewart, W., & Devlin, N. (2006). *Submission to the House Standing Committee on Education and Vocational Training* (pp. 1–20). Hobart, Tasmania, Australia: Australian Association for the Education of the Gifted and Talented Ltd.

Borland, J. H. (2009). Myth 2: The gifted constitute 3% to 5% of the population. Moreover, giftedness equals high IQ, which is a stable measure of aptitude. *Gifted Child Quarterly, 53*(4), 236–238. doi:10.1177/0016986209346825.

Braggett, E. J. (1985). *Education of gifted and talented children from populations with special needs: Discussion documents*. Canberra, ACT, Australia: Commonwealth Schools Commission.

Braggett, E. J. (1997a). *Differentiating programs for secondary schools*. Sydney, Australia: Hawker Brownlow.

Braggett, E. J. (1997b). A developmental concept of giftedness: Implications for the regular classroom. *Gifted Education International, 12*(2), 64–71.

Burton-Szabo, S. (1996). Special classes for gifted students? Absolutely! *Our Gifted Children, 3*(7), 17–20.

David, H. (2011). The importance of teachers' attitude in nurturing and educating gifted children. *Gifted and Talented International, 26*(1–2), 71–80.

Erwin, J. O., & Worrell, F. C. (2011). Assessment practices and the underrepresentation of minority students in gifted and talented education. *Journal of Psychoeducational Assessment, 30*(1), 74–87. doi:10.1177/0734282911428197.

Fournier, E. (2012). *Novice elementary teachers' perspectives teaching mainstreamed special needs students: Implications for leadership, preservice education, and professional development*. Unpublished Doctor of Education (EdD) thesis, University of Calgary.

Freeman, J. (2000). Families: The source of gifts. *Mensa Research Journal, 43*(Winter), 52–59.

Gardner, H. (1983). *Frames of mind: The theory of multiple intelligences*. New York, NY: Basic Books.

Gardner, H. (1993). *Multiple intelligences: The theory into practice*. New York, NY: Basic Books.

Gross, M. U. M. (2002). Gifted and talented students: Advantaged or disadvantaged? *Show Cause, 7*, 36–37.

Hansen, J. B. (2000). The ideal teacher for highly gifted students. *Mensa Research Journal, 43*(Winter), 12–21.

Henley, J., Milligan, J., McBride, J., Neal, G., Nichols, J., & Singleton, J. (2010). Outsiders looking in? Ensuring that teachers of the gifted and talented education and teachers of students with disabilities are part of the 'in-crowd'. *Journal of Instructional Psychology, 37*(3), 203–209.

Honigsfeld, A. (2002). The learning styles of high-achieving and creative adolescents in Hungary. *Mensa Research Journal, 33*(Winter), 72–89.

Hornby, G., & Lafaele, R. (2011). Barriers to parental involvement in education: An explanatory model. *Educational Review, 63*(1), 37–52. doi:10.1080/00131911.2010.488049.

Joyce, B., Weil, M., & Calhoun, E. (2009). *Models of teaching* (8th ed.). New York, NY: Allyn & Bacon.

Kao, C. (2012). The educational predicament confronting Taiwan's gifted programs: An evaluation of current practices and future challenges. *Roeper Review, 34*(4), 234–243. doi:10.1080/02783193.2012.715335.

Kelly, K. R. (2000). Understanding the career development of talented adolescents and adults. *Mensa Research Journal, 43*(Winter), 22–30.

Knowles, M. S., Holton, E. F., III, & Swanson, R. A. (2005). *The adult learner: The definitive classic in adult education and human resource development* (6th ed.). Amsterdam, The Netherlands: Elsevier.

Leithwood, K., Patten, S., & Jantzi, D. (2010). Testing a conception of how school leadership influences student learning. *Educational Administration Quarterly, 46*(5), 671–706. doi:10.1177/0013161x10377347.

Leithwood, K., Seashore Louis, K., Anderson, S., & Wahlstrom, K. (2004). *How leadership influences student learning*. New York, NY: Wallace Foundation.

LeTendre, G. K., Baker, D. P., Akiba, M., Goesling, B., & Wiseman, A. (2002). Teachers' work: International isomorphism and cultural variation in the U.S., Germany, and Japan. *Mensa Research Journal, 33*(Winter), 46–71.

Lewis, J. D., Cruzeiro, P. A., & Hall, C. A. (2007). Leadership on gifted education: Impact of two elementary school principals' in their building leadership. *Gifted Child Today, 30*(2), 56–62.

Lidz, C. S., & Macrine, S. L. (2002). The contribution of dynamic assessment. *Mensa Research Journal, 33*(Winter), 12–33.

Lupart, J., & Webber, C. F. (2002). Canadian schools in transition: Moving from dual education systems to inclusive schools. *Exceptionality Education Canada, 12*(2&3), 7–52.

Maker, C. J. (2005). *The "Discover" Project: Improving assessment and curriculum for diverse gifted learners* (pp. 1–223). Storrs, CT: National Research Center on the Gifted and Talented.

Mandelman, S. D., Tan, M., Aljughaiman, A. M., & Grigorenko, E. L. (2010). Intellectual giftedness: Economic, political, cultural, and psychological considerations. *Learning and Individual Differences, 20*(4), 287–297. doi:10.1016/j.lindif.2010.04.014.

Marland, S. P., Jr. (1972). *Education of the gifted and talented: Report to the Congress of the United States*. Washington, DC: U.S. Office of Education.

McCann, M. (2005). Our greatest natural resource: Gifted education in Australia. *Gifted Education International, 19*(2), 90–106.

McCoach, D. B., Goldstein, J., Behuniak, P., Reis, S. M., Black, A. C., Sullivan, E. E., et al. (2010). Examining the unexpected: Outlier analyses of factors affecting student achievement. *Journal of Advanced Academics, 21*(3), 426–468.

Merriam, S. B., & Grace, A. P. (Eds.). (2011). *Contemporary issues in adult education*. San Francisco, CA: Jossey-Bass.

Milligan, J., Neal, G., & Singleton, J. (2012). Administrators of special and gifted education: Preparing them for the challenge. *Education, 133*(1), 171–180.

Minister's Review Committee. (1983). *Intellectually talented students programme – Report of the Review Committee*. Perth, WA, Australia: Education Department of Western Australia.

Moon, T. R., Brighton, C. M., Callahan, C. M., & Robinson, A. (2005). Development of authentic assessments for the middle school classroom. *Journal of Secondary Gifted Education, 16*(2–3), 119–135.

National Commission on Educational Excellence. (1983). *A nation at risk: The imperative for educational reform.* Washington, DC: U.S. Government Printing Office.

Nicpon, M. F., Assouline, S. G., Colangelo, N., & O'Brien, M. (2008). *The paradox of giftedness and autism: Packet of information for families* (pp. 1–40). Iowa City, IA: Connie Belin & Jacqueline N. Blank International Center for Gifted Education and Talent Development, Iowa University.

Orendorff, K. A. (2009). *The relationship between ADHD and giftedness.* Unpublished Master of Science in Education School of Education, Dominican University of California. Online Submission.

Pfeiffer, S. I. (2012). Current perspectives on the identification and assessment of gifted students. *Journal of Psychoeducational Assessment, 30*(1), 3–9. doi:10.1177/0734282911428192.

Plunkett, M., & Kronborg, L. (2007). Gifted education in Australia: A story of striving for balance. *Gifted Education International, 23*(1), 72–83.

Rapp, N., & Duncan, H. (2012). Multi-dimensional parental involvement in schools: A principal's guide. *International Journal of Educational Leadership Preparation, 7*(1), 1–14.

Rawls, J. (1999). *A theory of justice* (Revised ed.). Cambridge, MA: Harvard University Press.

Reis, S. M., & Renzulli, J. S. (2010). Is there still a need for gifted education? An examination of current research. *Learning and Individual Differences, 20*(4), 308–317. doi:10.1016/j.lindif.2009.10.012.

Robinson, A. (2003). Collaborating and advocating with administrators: The Arkansas gifted education administrators' story. *Gifted Child Today, 26*(4), 20–25.

Scott, S., Webber, C. F., Aitken, N., & Lupart, J. (2011). Developing teachers' knowledge, beliefs, and expertise findings from the Alberta Student Assessment Study. *The Educational Forum, 75*(2), 96–113. doi:10.1080/00131725.2011.552594.

Scott, S., Webber, C. F., Lupart, J. L., Aitken, N., & Scott, D. E. (2013). Fair and equitable assessment practices for all students. *Assessment in Education: Principles, Policy & Practice.* doi:10.1080/0969594X.2013.776943.

Sharan, Y., & Sharan, S. (1992). *Expanding cooperative learning through group investigation.* New York, NY: Teachers College Press.

Sibaya, P. T., Hlongwane, M., & Makunga, N. (2002). Giftedness and intelligence, assessment in a third world country: Constraints and alternatives. *Mensa Research Journal, 33*(Winter), 34–45.

Silverman, L. K. (2000). Social development in the gifted. *Mensa Research Journal, 43*(Winter), 31–38.

Slavin, R., Sharan, S., Hertz-Lazarowitz, R., Webb, C., & Schmuck, R. (Eds.). (1985). *Learning to cooperate, cooperating to learn.* New York, NY: Plenum Press.

Snyder, K. E., Nietfeld, J. L., & Linnenbrink-Garcia, L. (2011). Giftedness and metacognition. A short-term longitudinal investigation of metacognitive monitoring in the classroom. *Gifted Child Quarterly, 55*(3), 181–193. doi:10.1177/0016986211412769.

Sternberg, R. J. (2010). Assessment of gifted students for identification purposes: New techniques for a new millennium. *Learning and Individual Differences, 20*(4), 327–336. doi:10.1016/j.lindif.2009.08.003.

Sternberg, R. J., & Davidson, J. E. (2005). *Conceptions of giftedness* (2nd ed.). Boston, MA: Cambridge University Press.

Subotnik, R. F., & Rickoff, R. (2010). Should eminence based on outstanding innovation be the goal of gifted education and talent development? Implications for policy and research. *Learning and Individual Differences, 20*(4), 358–364. doi:10.1016/j.lindif.2009.12.005.

Thompson, L. A., & Oehlert, J. (2010). The etiology of giftedness. *Learning and Individual Differences, 20*(4), 298–307. doi:10.1016/j.lindif.2009.11.004.

Tomlinson, C. A. (1995). *How to differentiate instruction in mixed-ability classrooms.* Alexandria, VA: Association for Supervision and Curriculum Development.

Tomlinson, C. A. (2001). *How to differentiate instruction in mixed-ability classrooms* (2nd ed.). Alexandria, VA: Association for Supervision and Curriculum Development.

Ushakov, D. V. (2010). Olympics of the mind as a method to identify giftedness: Soviet and Russian experience. *Learning and Individual Differences, 20*(4), 337–344. doi:10.1016/j.lindif.2010.04.012.

VanTassel-Baska, J., & Wood, S. (2010). The Integrated Curriculum Model (ICM). *Learning and Individual Differences, 20*(4), 345–357. doi:10.1016/j.lindif.2009.12.006.

Chapter 11
Fairer Assessment for Indigenous Students: An Australian Perspective

Val Klenowski

Abstract Drawing on the largest collection and analysis of empirical data on multiple facets of Aboriginal and Torres Strait Islander education in state schools to date, this chapter critically analyses the systemic push for standardised testing and improved scores in Australia, and argues for a greater balance of assessment types. Alternative, inclusive, participatory approaches to student assessment are recommended. Research evidence from a major evaluation of the Stronger Smarter Learning Communities (SSLC) project conducted by a Core Evaluation Team based at the Queensland University of Technology (QUT), Faculty of Education underpins this argument for fairer assessment and ethical leadership. This evaluation presents the first large-scale picture of what is occurring in classroom assessment and pedagogy for Indigenous students; however the focus in this chapter remains on leadership and student assessment. Additional evidence is drawn from an Australian Research Council Linkage project that sought to explore ways to improve learning outcomes for Aboriginal and Torres Strait Islander students through fairer assessment practices. At a time of unrelenting high-stakes, standardised testing in Australia with a dominance of secondary as opposed to primary uses of student achievement data by systems, schools and leaders, formative as well as summative purposes of assessment are called for with more alternative student assessment incorporated in teachers' pedagogic practices to cater for increased student diversity and to recognise the cultural needs of Indigenous students.

Keywords Student assessment • Fairness • Accountability • Testing • Indigenous education

---

This chapter reflects the views of the author and in no way represents the views of the Department of Education, Employment and Workplace Relations, the Queensland University of Technology or the Stronger Smarter Institute and Stronger Smarter Learning Communities Project.

V. Klenowski (✉)
School of Learning and Professional Studies, Faculty of Education, Queensland University of Technology, GPO Box 2434, Brisbane, QLD, Australia, 4001
e-mail: val.klenowski@qut.edu.au

© Springer International Publishing Switzerland 2016
S. Scott et al. (eds.), *Leadership of Assessment, Inclusion, and Learning*,
The Enabling Power of Assessment 3, DOI 10.1007/978-3-319-23347-5_11

11.1 Introduction

The increasing diversity of the Australian student population, culturally, ethnically, socially and linguistically has major implications for school leaders in their considerations of fairer assessment relative to teachers' classroom practices and to systems of examination and assessment. The purpose of this chapter is to contribute to thinking about fairness in assessment from a social justice perspective, to stimulate further consideration of what fair assessment means and to raise the ethical implications for school leadership. Fairness in assessment practice is conceptualised and discussed in terms of how fairer assessment practice might be attempted in the Australian context as found from empirical research into attempts to improve learning outcomes for Indigenous[1] students. The implications of fairer approaches to assessment for wider international application are made explicit.

11.2 Context

In 2008, Prime Minister Kevin Rudd gave the Apology to Australia's Indigenous Peoples. All Australian governments "adopted a new approach and committed to six ambitious, long-term, Closing the Gap targets which aim to bridge the divide between Indigenous and non-Indigenous Australians in life expectancy, educational achievement and employment opportunities" (DEEWR, 2008, p. iii). Four of the six targets are the responsibility of the Department of Education, Employment and Workplace Relations (DEEWR). These are to:

1. ensure all Indigenous 4 year olds in remote communities have access to early childhood education within 5 years;
2. halve the gap in reading, writing and numeracy achievements for Indigenous children within a decade;
3. halve the gap for Indigenous students in Year 12 attainment or equivalent attainment rates by 2020; and
4. halve the gap in employment outcomes between Indigenous and non-Indigenous Australians within a decade. (DEEWR, 2012)

These 'Closing the Gap' targets were introduced in Australia at a time of increased summative testing and accountability that in 2008 took the form of the National Australian Programme – Literacy and Numeracy (NAPLAN) annual testing of students in Years 3, 5, 7 and 9, on the same days, using national tests in Reading, Writing, Language Conventions (Spelling, Grammar and Punctuation) and Numeracy. Accountability testing in Australian public education policy has become a priority. In 2010 the NAPLAN results were published on the MySchool

---

[1] Throughout this chapter I will use a capital for the word Indigenous as a mark of respect and as is protocol.

website (www.myschool.edu.au) and the high stakes nature of the national testing programme was confirmed. The government argued that publishing the results of NAPLAN testing would give parents access to achievement data to decide on the best school for their child/ren. The issue of equity and fairness in assessment was not raised yet patterns of under-achievement by Indigenous students were reflected not only in national benchmark data (NAPLAN) but also international testing programs like the Trends in International Mathematics and Science Study (TIMSS) and the Programme for International Student Assessment (PISA).

11.3 Background

The research that informs this chapter is derived from a major evaluation conducted by a Core Evaluation Team based at the Queensland University of Technology (QUT) Faculty of Education (Luke et al., 2013) of the Stronger Smarter Learning Communities (SSLC) project. This team was charged with independent formative and summative evaluations. The research design of this study was qualitative and quantitative, cross-sectional and longitudinal. Data was gathered from interviews (n=525) with Indigenous community members (75), community and regional staff (14), students (147) and school workers (54); interviews with and observations of school leaders (80), head teachers and co-ordinators (31), teachers (119), administrative staff (3), counsellors (2) and key school staff (31); field observation visits to selected SSLC schools over a 3-year period; survey responses and self-reports by a large sample of SSLC and non-SSLC schools; multilevel statistical analysis of 2009/2010 systemic data on test score achievement, attendance and other school profile indicators provided by state and territory governments.

Further relevant empirical evidence emerged from an Australian Research Council (ARC) Linkage project that took the form of a design experiment and was conducted in seven Catholic and Independent primary schools in northern Queensland. This research design has been used extensively by educators in medium-scale curriculum innovation in United States schools (Cobb, Confrey, di Sessa, Lehrer, & Schauble, 2003) and was developed at Vanderbilt, Washington and University of California, Berkeley. It combines a rigorous approach to data collected on the effects of an intervention from the stage of programme development through to the action research. The intervention in this study was a professional development programme of pedagogical and assessment change that was reviewed and revised in light of new empirical evidence of the intended and unintended effects. The data collection involved semi-structured focus group interviews with Year 4 and 6 Indigenous students, principals, teachers and Indigenous Teacher Assistants,[2] classroom observations and document analyses. The number of Indigenous students in relation to the rest of the school's student population in these

---

[2] Indigenous Teacher Assistant (ITA) is used throughout this chapter; however, other terms frequently used are Indigenous Education Worker (IEW) and Indigenous Education Aide (IEA).

research schools varied from 5 %, 6 %, 7 % (in two schools), 13 %, 21 %, to 100 %. In the latter school, 92 % of these Indigenous students had Languages Other Than English (inclusive of a mix of first, second and possibly third languages). This corpus of data was analysed using a sociocultural theoretical lens, which helped to identify cultural influences, values and Indigenous students' funds of knowledge. The information from this analysis was made explicit to teachers to demonstrate how they could enhance their pedagogic and assessment practices by embracing and extending the cultural spaces for learning and teaching of Indigenous students.

From the findings of these two projects, focused on how classroom teachers' pedagogy and assessment practice could be fairer for Indigenous students in a context of increased summative testing and accountability, it is apparent the concepts of validity and fairness in assessment are not universally understood. Many leaders and teachers are unaware that there is no cultural neutrality in assessment or in the selection of what is assessed. The findings highlight the importance of cultural difference and equity concerns. Equity relates to cultural difference and issues of access and what is just; it does not mean treating students all the same or equality of outcomes. What needs to be understood in a discussion of fairness in assessment is that students from different cultures, ethnic backgrounds or social circumstances will have different qualities and experiences that they bring to classroom learning contexts. Fairness then relates to the students' access to the curriculum and educational opportunities (Gipps & Stobart, 2009).

11.4 Conceptual Framework

A framework for social justice in education as developed by Courtney Cazden (2012) underpins the conceptualisation of fairness in assessment as presented in this chapter. Nancy Fraser's "theory of social justice" with three dimensions: redistribution (economic), recognition (cultural) and representation (political) is central to Cazden's framework. In addition, the thesis presented here for fairer assessment aligns with Onora O'Neill's persuasive case for more "intelligent accountability in education" (2013). O'Neill (2002) has indicated that if "we want greater accountability without damaging professional performance we need intelligent accountability" (p. 58). Regulating performance through standardisation and provision of detailed regulation for total control she claimed were damaging. Intelligent accountability, O'Neill stated:

> requires more attention to good governance and fewer fantasies about total control. Good governance is possible only if institutions are allowed some margin for self-governance of a form appropriate to their particular tasks, within a framework of financial and other reporting. Such reporting ... is not improved by being wholly standardised or relentlessly detailed, and since much that has to be accounted for is not easily measured it cannot be boiled down to a set of stock performance indicators. Those who are called to account should give an account of what they have done and of their successes or failures to others who have sufficient time and experience to assess the evidence and report on it. Real accountability provides substantive and knowledgeable independent judgement of an institution's or professional's work. (p. 58)

While Australia is experiencing escalating diversity, more accountability is being demanded of leaders and teachers than ever before. Here, O'Neill's (2013) warning that "processes of holding to account can impose high costs without securing substantial benefits" becomes relevant and instructive (p. 4). O'Neill, in her call for more intelligent accountability systems, has clearly articulated how "secondary use of assessment evidence to hold teachers and schools to account can damage primary, educational use of that assessment" (p. 5). She claims that, assessment systems that use the same evidence to hold to account the students who are being assessed as well as to hold their teachers to account deserve greater scrutiny. This is because knowing that one is held to account for others' performance, as measured by a given system of assessment, may well impact on "the action of those who do the preparation" (p. 5). While systems may aim to increase standards of student achievement by holding teachers and schools to account, in reality such second-order uses may result in teachers and schools responding to such accountability in ways that impact negatively on the performance being measured.

Currently in Australia standardised NAPLAN testing has diverted time away from teaching to preparation for the summative tests with teachers providing opportunities for their students to rehearse or practice performances in preparation for the tests. Klenowski and Wyatt-Smith (2012) have reported elsewhere how unintended consequences are emerging, such as:

> pressures on leaders to lift performance, threats to their jobs if results do not improve, more attention given to those students who are more likely to achieve better grades, neglect of those students who have the greatest need for support, the emergence of commercial tests that have not been quality assured, increased absenteeism for low performing students on the day of the test and increased instances of cheating. (p. 70)

Further negative impacts reported from the second-order use of results include: the pressure on principals from their line managers to improve their test results at all costs without acknowledging the school's efforts to improve the students' performance and the factors that have inhibited progress. Leaders have reported how they have felt "unfairly 'threatened' if they failed to treat raising the average test performance as their absolute goal. It was implied that their job would be on the line if the school's results did not improve" (p. 71).

Other examples of the distorted effects of second order use of achievement evidence include: the practice by some schools of encouraging parents to keep their children at home on test day if the school judged that the student would not perform well in the tests, teacher assistance provided to students while sitting the tests to improve their test results and the requirement by some line managers for some schools to lift their results by a certain percentage. These schools identified the students most likely to show improvement if given extra assistance and allocated resources to this select group of students. Students with greater needs did not receive as much attention for the first 5 months of the year until the completion of the NAPLAN tests. As O'Neill (2013) suggests, "more accountability is not always better" (p. 4). As is evident in Australia, damaging consequences or perverse effects have resulted from an assessment system that holds teachers to account and results in the reuse of assessment data for "second-order purposes". O'Neill (2013) cites

Strathern's (1997, p. 308) formulation of Goodhart's law, which warns against such reuse of assessment data to hold third parties to account, "when a measure becomes a target it ceases to be a good measure".

11.5 Fairness in Assessment

Increasing financial uncertainties and the consequential differences in economic status, combined with the differences in both social and cultural capital for the full range of students, give rise to important questions of how assessment systems can be fairer and what the implications are for leader and teacher development particularly as this applies to assessment capability. Here, as indicated by Cazden, the redistribution and recognition dimensions of Nancy Fraser's theory of social justice become important for "'closing the gap' in academic achievement". Cazden (2012) adds that "representation is [also] important for school and community relations" (p. 178). In pursuing fairness and equity in assessment, it is important that all students are given the opportunity to demonstrate learning and that the form of the assessment does not override the knowledge to be assessed (Gipps & Stobart, 2009). It is important therefore to acknowledge that students from different cultures, ethnic backgrounds or social circumstances will have different qualities and experiences that they bring to the classroom learning contexts. In the interest of fairness to "treat all students the same", as expressed by many teachers who were interviewed, illustrates a limited understanding of the concept and of validity.

Fairness in assessment requires then a consideration of the social contexts of assessment and, as defined more broadly by Gipps and Stobart (2009), moves beyond the technical definition of a concern with test construction to a more encompassing view of "what precedes an assessment (for example, access and resources)" (p. 105) or recognitive and redistributive justice as expressed in Cazden's framework. Fairness in assessment from this view includes "its consequences (for example, interpretations of results and impact) as well as aspects of the assessment design itself" (Gipps & Stobart, p. 105). As discussed, O'Neill (2013) case for more intelligent forms of accountability is significant as the perverse effects of current accountability systems can result in damaging influences on students' future learning trajectories. As was seen, such effects are evident when a system of accountability "creates incentives for pupils and institutions to gravitate to subjects where adequate or good scores or points are perceived as more readily available" and students are displaced "… into courses that are less educationally desirable for them" (p. 8).

The hallmark of quality in the context of education and measurement is validity, the "single most important criterion" for evaluating an assessment method (Koretz, 2008, p. 215). Ultimately, "validity and validation are concerned with the quality or potential of an assessment method" (Newton & Shaw, in press). When an assessment method is declared as valid then its potential for supporting good measurement and decision-making is claimed. The differences in students' performances on standardised tests for many students from diverse backgrounds arise because of problems with access or opportunities to demonstrate learning. Hipwell and

Klenowski (2011) argue that all students should have access to the literacy demands of the test and should not be disadvantaged by the fact that they may not have Standard Australian English as their first language. Assessment capable leaders and teachers understand and practice the fundamental principles of assessment design such as ensuring that the assessments they design are fit for purpose and that the mode of assessment impacts positively on teaching and learning (Gipps, 1994).

11.6   Ethical Leadership

Given the issues associated with fairness in assessment that have been identified for leaders and teachers in times of increasing accountability associated with improved learning outcomes and equity demands, it is important to raise the ethical questions that leaders face. Leaders are obligated to meet the needs of the system but also have to make defensible judgments that support the diversity of the students and their local communities. Ehrich et al. (2013) make the case for moral accountability, recognising the moral dimension and purpose of education (Fullan & Hargreaves, 1992). Ehrich et al. define ethical leaders as:

> those who act justly, fairly and professionally and in the best interests of students and staff. They are socially responsive and adhere to and act upon values of justice and equity (Duignan, 2012). … [they] promote the achievement of all students, especially those who have been previously marginalised or disadvantaged. We take the position that there are multiple account-abilities facing school leaders, and ethical leaders are those who balance these accountabilities in professional and responsive ways to support the inclusion of all students. (p. 4)

Leaders hold key roles in organisations and, as made clear by Ehrich et al. (2013), are involved in decision making that draws on values that relate to what is fair and just. They go on to define ethical leadership as:

> a social, relational practice concerned with the moral accountability and moral purpose of education (Angus, 2006). It thus promotes core values of inclusion, trust, respect, collaboration, and social justice when working with staff and students in school communities. Ethical schools are those that have inclusive structures and cultures and where teachers, students, parents and staff have a voice and are treated respectfully (Carrington, 1999; Dyson, Howes, & Roberts, 2002). Teachers and leaders are involved in ongoing inquiries about student learning. (Comber & Kamler, 2009, p. 179)

The key findings from the research evidence support the argument for greater ethical leadership in these times of increased accountability and the need for fairer assessment practices. It is to these findings that this chapter now turns.

11.7   Findings

The first of the key findings derived from these studies relates to leaders and teachers in both studies who demonstrated limited expertise and training in the analysis and the use of test score and other performance data. Although principals reported and were observed attempting to use test score data as evidence for decision-making, there were very few instances where school leaders had specialised training or relevant expertise in data analysis. There were only isolated instances observed where principals used test data for developmental, diagnostic purposes and for the selection of specific curriculum interventions, particularly for attending to the learning needs of diverse student cohorts.

Second, with the changing accountability context in Australia it has become apparent that a dominant influence on school planning, policy and pedagogy is the improvement of NAPLAN test scores. A consistent systemic push to improve NAPLAN scores was reported by leaders. Current emergent assessment practices are focused strongly on NAPLAN complemented by a dominant pedagogical concentration on basic skills and vocational education.

Third, the picture painted is one of a system concerned with deficit and pull-out remediation programs, testing, streaming and tracking with attention to basic skills instruction. Streaming and ability grouping are common at all levels of primary and secondary education and this would appear to be yet another perverse effect of the approach to accountability. Accompanying such measures are test preparation lessons, retailoring pedagogy by schools and teachers and, in some instances, whole school programs and timetabling in what was viewed as efforts to improve test score results. At the same time, streaming and tracking practices are ubiquitous in the teaching of Indigenous students. This consists of a combination of ability grouping in primary basic skills instruction, whole class homogeneous grouping for stated purposes of behaviour management and targeted teaching, pull-out programs and special education remediation models, and tracking into vocational and non-academic programs in the middle and secondary years. Again these are some of the perverse effects of secondary uses of assessment data to call teachers and schools to account.

Fourth, there is very little evidence of innovation or the building of teacher expertise in classroom assessment (e.g., task-based assessment, high quality assessment). The lack of expertise and innovation with little explicit discussion of dominant practices of streaming and ability grouping constitute major issues for fairness in assessment. Teacher proficiency in assessment and/or innovation with classroom-based assessment and use of models of authentic assessment, assessment-for-learning, or task-based assessment are important for inclusive education.

Fifth, the use of Personal Learning Plans[3] (PLPs) provides a viable approach to authentic and negotiated assessment and planning, but it is also clear that these require training and systematic implementation. The use of Personal Learning Plans is mandated for Indigenous students in several states of Australia. Samples of PLPs that were analysed reflected different levels and degrees of rigour and implementation. Where they were focused on negotiation and engagement of Indigenous parents and students in dialogue over aspirations, pathways, cultural resources and

---

[3] 'Personal Learning Plans' should not be confused with terms such as 'Individualised Education Programme' as used in the United States, or the Canadian term 'Individual Education Plan' which refer to support programmes or plans for 'exceptional pupils' or students with special needs.

challenges, PLPs had value in addressing issues raised by communities and students about teacher and school knowledge of Indigenous families and cultures.

11.8 Assessment and Learning

It is important to illustrate why more authentic and negotiated assessment and planning provides a viable alternative to present assessment practice prior to a discussion of the policy implications for leaders and systems. Overall the findings relate to the ways in which schools and leaders are using assessment data for a range of purposes, which in some cases constitute second-order purposes.

A greater balance between formative and summative purposes and alternatives to an over reliance on standardised assessment has recently been recommended in the Organisation for Economic Co-operation and Development's (OECD) review on Evaluation and Assessment Frameworks for Improving School Outcomes. The policy advice recommends that the student is placed at the centre of the evaluation and assessment framework, and that a variety of assessment types be used to develop a more holistic view of student learning (OECD, 2013). There is also a clear priority for systems to focus on improving classroom practices to optimise the potential of evaluation and assessment to improve student learning with the recommendation that policy makers promote regular use of evaluation and assessment results for improvements in the classroom.

In the United States, The Gordon Commission on the Future of Assessment in Education established by the Educational Testing Service in January 2011, has recommended that systems of assessment include methods "that provide teachers with actionable information about their students and their practice in real time" (Gordon Commission, 2013, p. 8). The Commission also reported how the emphasis on "measuring student performance at a single point in time with assessments whose primary purpose is to provide information to constituencies external to the classroom has, to a large extent, neglected the other purposes of assessment" (p. 10). Therefore "radically different forms of assessments" and "challenging performance tasks" that better represent the learning activities that will help students develop the competencies needed to succeed in the twenty-first century have been called for (p. 10).

Such international reviews and recommendations are significant to the findings as principals and teachers demonstrated only limited expertise and training in the analysis and the use of test score and other performance data to improve student learning. Although leaders reported and were observed attempting to use test score data as evidence for decision-making, there were very few instances where they had specialised training or relevant expertise in data analysis. We observed only isolated instances where principals used test data for developmental, diagnostic purposes and for the selection of specific curriculum interventions, particularly for attending to the learning needs of diverse student cohorts. Very limited use of a variety of assessment types to gain a more holistic view of student learning was observed.

11.9 Discussion

When leaders and teachers are supported to understand the importance of cultural awareness, intercultural relationships, code-switching to access for example mathematical language, or use cultural examples of mathematical concepts, this combination of understandings promotes cultural responsive pedagogy for more socially just outcomes. The potential for more culturally responsive pedagogy and assessment requires productive working relationships with the students first and foremost, and second with the Indigenous community via the Indigenous Teacher Assistant. Productive working relationships comprise processes and pedagogic practices to support learning and include content knowledge, knowledge of learners, diagnostic strategies, high expectations, and ethical leadership, which includes an ethic of care. The role of the Indigenous Teacher Assistant is little understood in Australia and requires systems and teachers to rethink their working relationships in classrooms and with their communities. Teachers with good intentions may strive to include students in the cultural literacy and culturally specific funds of knowledge of the classroom, but have not had the professional training or the cultural experience to provide for effective or proficient inclusion processes within the classroom. There are degrees of proficiency and experience but on the whole teachers' classroom practices are mediated by an audit culture, are largely driven by dispositions external to classroom settings, and consequently are falling short of full empathetic recognition, acceptance and inclusion of students from non-dominant cultural backgrounds in the classroom.

A shift from deficit views of cultural difference to more considered understandings of how teachers, schools and systems can take responsibility for more culturally and socially responsive models and quality teaching and assessment practices (Ainscow, 2010; Bishop, O'Sullivan, & Berryman, 2010; Comber & Kamler, 2004; Mahuika, Berryman, & Bishop, 2011) is developing. Too often teachers and school leaders indicate that very little can be done to improve the achievement of students from different social or cultural backgrounds with explanations for low achievement directed at the student, the student's home circumstances or outside of school experiences. Schools and teachers need to develop their capacity to identify deficit views of difference (Ainscow 2010) which position students as 'lacking in something'. These assumptions that relate to notions of deficit regarding difference are challenged from sociocultural perspectives of learning and assessment, which give greater respect to the valuing of difference. This view of learning and assessment is reflected by some authors (Murphy, Hall, McCormick, & Drury, 2008) who have presented views of how assessment can become more enabling and appreciative of the knowledge, skills and understanding that the students bring to the classroom.

Teachers can support students from diverse groups through the use of inclusive assessment and pedagogic practices that recognise the agency of learners. Such practices call for a different teacher–student relationship where both are learners, gaining important knowledge from interactions and exchanges during assessment processes. Where systemic opportunities are opened up for students to be brought into assessment practice as a shared enterprise, together with their parents, teachers and aides, aspirations and expectations can be facilitated and raised (Luke et al., 2013). Here *the use of analyses* of students' achievement data is crucial for diagnostic and planning purposes. However, school leaders and teachers need support and resources to make informed decisions based on the monitoring and analysis of assessment data.

The involvement of parents in discursive assessment practices helps to develop useful and productive relationships, which can only be beneficial to both the students and their teachers. Educational justice as articulated by Cazden (2012) requires "recognition and inclusion in the school curriculum of their [Indigenous] histories, cultures and knowledges" (p. 182). The PLP process is seen as a way of involving community and parents in the assessment and learning practices of the school and has been a way of extending teacher participation into the communities with home visits to families. From the empirical research related to these assessment practices it became apparent that this process had the potential to engage the teacher, the ITA, the student and his/her parents in constructive dialogue. It is here that Cazden's (p. 183) framework for social justice in education becomes significant. In her interpretation of recognition she cites Fraser (2000) and her alternative 'social status' interpretation of recognition. That is,

> What requires recognition is not group-specific identity but the status of individual members as full partners in social interaction (p. 4)… Redressing misrecognition now means changing social institutions – or, more specifically, changing the interaction-regulating values that impede participation at all relevant institutional sites. (p. 5)

In Cazden's framework for social justice in education the meaning of 'identity' applies to 'what' is taught as in the curriculum, and the meaning of 'status' applies to 'how' it is taught, the quality of the teaching, particularly through the moment-to-moment teacher-student interactions (Cazden, 2001, 2012, p. 183). In the PLP assessment process the interactions extend beyond the teacher-student interactions to include interactions with the parents and the ITA. This process challenges the existing 'interaction-regulating values' that impede participation by providing for inclusion and decision-making for Indigenous families, thereby attending to the social justice dimensions of recognition and representation. At this school level of decision-making the Personalised Learning Planning teacher, student, parent and ITA are all involved. As expressed by a provincial Hub school leader:

> *Building relationships with the community is core to the PLP process* for this school. It promotes parents' engagement with their child's learning through participation in the development of the plan with their child's teacher. *The focus for the classroom teacher is to provide a range of quality teaching and learning strategies* to develop students' confidence and competence, accommodate different learning styles and paces of learning. The focus for the PLP is on basic skills and giving opportunities for enrichment extension.

This is one way that more respectful and positive relationships between the stakeholders can be developed and "expertise … pooled to achieve objectives that are consistent with the aspirations of community members" (Heslop, 1998 cited by Cazden, 2012, p. 185). These constitute small steps towards fairer assessment practices for more equitable outcomes.

In this chapter the argument for more intelligent and moral accountability systems has been developed. Such systems acknowledge the value of quality culture-inclusive teaching and assessment practices to develop the role of the learner through mutual engagement in a community of practice that includes parents, carers and community members. Intelligent accountability and ethical leadership require support, such as helpful policies and resources, to allow leaders and teachers to develop the necessary capabilities to facilitate the implementation and development of major curriculum and assessment reform in these times of increased accountability and diversity.

Acknowledgements The author would like to acknowledge the joint funding arrangement between the Australian Research Council, Queensland University of Technology, the Independent Schools of Queensland and the Catholic Education Diocese of Townsville.

Acknowledgement is also made for the funding received from the Australian Government Department of Education, Employment and Workplace Relations for the evaluation and research completed by the members of the Core Research Team.

References

Ainscow, M. (2010). Achieving excellence and equity: Reflections on the development of practices in one local district over 10 years. *School Effectiveness and School Improvement, 21*(1), 75–91.

Angus, L. (2006). Educational leadership and the imperative of including student voices, student interest, and students' lives in the mainstream. *International Journal of Leadership in Education, 9*(4), 369–379.

Bishop, R., O'Sullivan, D., & Berryman, M. (2010). *Scaling up education reform: Addressing the politics of disparity*. Wellington, New Zealand: NZCER Press.

Carrington, S. B. (1999). Inclusion needs a different school culture. *International Journal of Inclusive Education, 3*(3), 257–268.

Cazden, C. B. (2001). *Classroom discourse: The language of teaching and learning*. Portsmouth, NH: Heinemann.

Cazden, C. (2012). A framework for social justice in education. *International Journal of Educational Psychology, 1*(3), 178–198. doi:10.4471/ijep.2012.11.

Cobb, P., Confrey, J., diSessa, A., Lehrer, R., & Schauble, L. (2003). Design experiments in educational research. *Educational Researcher, 32*(1), 9–13.

Comber, B., & Kamler, B. (2004). Getting out of deficit: Pedagogies of reconnection. *Teaching Education, 15*(3), 293–310.

Comber, B., & Kamler, B. (2009). Sustaining the next generation of teacher-researchers to work for social justice. In B. Somekh & S. Noffke (Eds.), *Handbook of educational action research* (pp. 177–185). London, UK: Sage Publications.

Department of Education, Employment and Workplace Relations (DEEWR). (2008). *National report to parliament on Indigenous education and training, 2006*. Canberra, Australia: Australian Government.

DEEWR. (2012). *Indigenous overview*. Retrieved from http://www.deewr.gov.au/indigenous/Pages/Overview.aspx

Duignan, P. (2012). *Educational leadership: Together creating ethical learning environments* (2nd ed.). Cambridge, UK: Cambridge University Press.

Dyson, A., Howes, A., & Roberts, B. (2002). *A systematic review of the effectiveness of school-level actions for promoting participation by all students* (EPPI-Centre Review, version 1.1). Research Evidence in Education Library. London, UK: EPPI-Centre, Social Science Research Unit, Institute of Education.

Ehrich, L., Klenowski, V., Harris, J., Smeed, J., Carrington, S., & Ainscow, M. (2013, September 3–5). *Ethical leadership in a time of increasing accountability*. Paper presented at British Educational Research Association annual conference. Brighton, England.

Fraser, N. (2000). Rethinking recognition. *New left review, 3*(May–June), 107–119. Retrieved from http://newleftreview.org/II/3/nancy-fraser-rethinking-recognition

Fullan, M., & Hargreaves, A. (1992). *What's worth fighting for in your school?* Buckingham, UK: Open University Press.

Gipps, C. (1994). *Beyond testing*. London, UK: Falmer Press.

Gipps, C., & Stobart, G. (2009). Fairness in assessment. In C. Wyatt-Smith & J. J. Cumming (Eds.), *Educational assessment in the 21st century: Connecting theory and practice* (pp. 105–118). Dordrecht, The Netherlands: Springer. doi:10.1007/978-1-4020-9964-9.

Gordon Commission. (2013). A public policy statement, *The Gordon Commission on the Future of Assessment in Education*. Retrieved from www.gordoncommission.org

Hipwell, P., & Klenowski, V. (2011). A case for addressing the literacy demands of student assessment. *Australian Journal of Language and Literacy, 34*(2), 127–146.

Klenowski, V., & Wyatt-Smith, C. (2012). The impact of high stakes testing: The Australian story. *Assessment in Education: Principles, Policy and Practice, 19*(1), 65–79.

Koretz, D. (2008). *Measuring up: What educational testing really tells us*. Cambridge, MA: Harvard University Press.

Luke, A., Cazden, C., Coopes, R., Klenowski, V., Ladwig, J., Lester, J., … Woods, A. (2013, March). *A summative evaluation of the stronger smarter learning communities project*, Report (Vol. 1). Queensland University of Technology, Brisbane, Australia.

Mahuika, R., Berryman, M., & Bishop, R. (2011). Issues of culture and assessment in New Zealand education pertaining to Māori students. *Assessment Matters, 3*, 183–198.

Murphy, P., Hall, K., McCormick, R., & Drury, R. (2008). *Curriculum, learning and society: Investigating practice* (Study guide, masters in education). Maidenhall, UK: Open University.

O'Neill, O. (2002). *A question of trust: The BBC Reith Lectures*. Cambridge, UK: Cambridge University Press.

O'Neill, O. (2013). Intelligent accountability in education. *Oxford Review of Education, 39*(1), 4–16. doi:10.1080/03054985.2013.764761.

OECD. (2013). *Synergies for better learning: An international perspective on evaluation and assessment, pointers for policy development*. Retrieved from http://www.oecd.org/edu/school/synergies-for-better-learning.htm

Strathern, M. (1997). Improving ratings: Audit in the British university system. *European Review, 5*, 305–321.

Chapter 12
Challenges, Tensions and Possibilities: An Analysis of Assessment Policy and Practice in New Zealand

Bronwen Cowie and Dawn Penney

Abstract This chapter draws on insights from education policy sociology to explore the dynamics between international, national, and institutional arenas of assessment and assessment systems. It interrogates the interactions between curriculum, pedagogy and assessment and explores the enabling constraints at different levels of the assessment system. Attention is drawn to the ways in which tensions offer spaces for creative action in relation to current policies and practices in New Zealand.

Keywords Equity • Enabling constraints • Policy • Curriculum • Pedagogy • Formative assessment • Standards • Assessment literacy

12.1 Introduction

This chapter describes and discusses assessment policy and practice in primary and secondary education in New Zealand with a particular emphasis on the synergies and tensions in assessment within and across the various levels and aspects of the assessment system. The formative potential of assessment has long been accorded priority in policy (Ministerial Working Party on Assessment for Better Learning, 1990; Ministry of Education, 1994), professional development provision (Crooks, 2011; Gilmore, 2002), and practice (Bell & Cowie, 2001). From 2002 secondary student exit qualifications have been standards based, with credits awarded via a

---

B. Cowie (✉)
Faculty of Education, The University of Waikato, Knighton Rd, Hamilton 3240, New Zealand
e-mail: bcowie@waikato.ac.nz

D. Penney
Faculty of Education, Monash University,
Building A, Peninsula Campus, McMahons Road, Frankston, VIC 3199, Australia
e-mail: Dawn.Penney@monash.edu

combination of externally set and supervised and teacher designed and administered assessment tasks. There was no mandated national assessment for primary students until 2009 when national standards in reading, writing, and mathematics were introduced. Importantly, student achievement relative to the standards is assessed based on an 'overall teacher judgment'. For this teachers draw on and apply a range of evidence (observation, conversation, formal assessment tools) to make a judgment about whether a student is *above*, at, *below*, and well-*below the expected standard.* Overall, by international standards, accountability pressures on New Zealand teachers and schools are comparatively minor (Crooks, 2011) although these are on the rise. As in many Western countries, teacher professionalism is sometimes called into question through political and media commentary and schools are increasingly being subject to accountability pressures. In this chapter we explore the dynamics within and between the arenas of classroom, school, and national assessment to interrogate the interactions between assessment, curriculum, pedagogy and learning. Our focus is on how any constraints felt amidst various policy initiatives, and between aspects of policy and practice, might also be construed as enabling. Attention is thus drawn to the ways in which tensions offer spaces for creative action in relation to current policies and practices in New Zealand. Necessarily we first provide an overview of the New Zealand context.

12.2 The New Zealand Curriculum, Assessment and Pedagogy Policy Context

Since the administrative restructuring of the *Tomorrow's Schools* reforms in 1988 (Minister of Education, 1988), the management of individual schools has been devolved to Boards of Trustees. These are constituted of members elected from within the school community. Boards of Trustees, together with the school principal and teachers, are responsible for developing and implementing the curriculum as set out in the *New Zealand curriculum* document (Ministry of Education [MOE], 2007) in a manner that is responsive to local needs, interests and circumstances. The *New Zealand Curriculum*, hereafter referred to as NZC, sets out achievement objectives for eight learning areas and defines five 'key competencies'. The competencies were introduced for the first time in the 2007 curriculum and are described as the skills and attributes that "are critical to sustained learning and effective participation in society and that underline the emphasis on lifelong learning" (MOE, 2007, p. 4). The NZC includes a list of principles to guide curriculum decision making: high expectations, Treaty of Waitangi, cultural diversity, inclusion, learning to learn, community engagement, coherence and future focus (MOE, 2007, p. 11). Of these the Treaty of Waitangi principle is distinctive. It accords a central role to the principles of partnership between the crown and Māori (the indigenous people of New Zealand) that are detailed in Te Tiriti o Waitangi. The Treaty established the bicultural foundations of Aotearoa New Zealand. Other principles emphasise that all students need access to opportunities to learn that are appropriate to them, and to their communities.

The NZC describes effective teaching as a process of inquiry in which assessment plays a pivotal role. In relation to assessment, the NZC states that: "the primary purpose of assessment is to improve students' learning and teachers' teaching as both student and teacher respond to the information that it provides" (p. 42). This emphasis can be seen across various government policy documents preceding and following publication of the NZC (e.g. Department of Education, 1989; Ministry of Education, 2011). Assessment for the purpose of improving student learning is described as best understood as an ongoing process that arises out of the interaction between teachers and students and involving the generation, interpretation, and action on multiple sources of information about student learning and progress. Other purposes for and forms of assessment detailed in NZC include school-wide assessment and assessment for qualifications. School-wide assessment information allows schools to monitor the impact of their programmes on student learning with the information to be used to inform changes to policies and/or programmes and/or teaching practices as well as to report to school Boards of Trustees, parents, and the Ministry of Education.

In the international arena, New Zealand participates in the Trends in International Mathematics and Science Study (TIMSS) and the Programme for International Student Assessment (PISA). Findings from these studies have consistently indicated that a substantial proportion of New Zealand students are performing to a high standard but that there are significant differentials in achievement across student groups, with Māori and Pasifika students over-represented in the lower performing group in all subjects and both studies. As has been the case elsewhere, the results of these studies have invoked considerable concern and influenced the allocation of resources and priorities. Further useful insights into trends in educational achievement have been generated from a National Educational Monitoring Programme [NEMP]. From 1995 to 2010 this provided a national 'snapshot' at the system level of students' knowledge, skills, and attitudes across the curriculum learning areas. The different curriculum areas were assessed in 4-year cycles through a randomly selected sample of around 3000 students in school years 4 and 8 using a combination of one-to-one interviews, team, 'hands on', and independent assessment tasks. These were administered and marked by teachers recruited and trained by the NEMP team. A new system for national monitoring (National Monitoring Study of Student Achievement), also based on light sampling, was implemented for the first time in 2013. This has a focus on the identification of trends in educational performance, factors that influence achievement, and the provision of robust information to policy makers, curriculum specialists, educators, and the public. Thus, New Zealand is actively complementing the data generated from international assessment systems to inform national assessment policy and practice.

From 2002 assessment for student exit qualifications has been undertaken via achievement and/or unit standards registered on the National Qualifications Framework. Students accumulate credits towards a "National Certificate of Educational Achievement (NCEA)" at Levels 1, 2, or 3 and other national certificates that schools may choose to offer to their students in school years 11–13 (at which time students are aged 15–18 years). From 2010, primary aged students have been assessed against National Standards in reading, writing, and mathematics. As explained above, these assessments are based on an overall teacher judgment of a student's progress and achievement. This information is reported annually to the Board of Trustees and the Ministry of Education, and, since 2012 school-level information has been made available to the public via the Ministry website.

In the sections that follow we set out our theoretical framework and discuss some of the tensions, challenges, and opportunities that have emerged within the assessment system in New Zealand.

12.2.1 A Focus on a Balanced, Coherent and Responsive System

Our chapter is underpinned by a view of assessment as a complex, multifaceted, and multilayered system that, ideally, balances the need for assessment to monitor student learning with a concern to improve student learning (Clarke, 2012; UNESCO, 2007). This requires consideration of the full range of assessment purposes and uses, and needs of users at the classroom, programme, institutional, and policy levels (MOE, 2011; Stiggins, 2008). We also recognise the central influence of the dynamic relationships between curriculum, pedagogy, and assessment (Hay & Penney, 2013). As Bernstein (1971, 1990) articulated, curriculum, pedagogy and evaluation constitute three powerful and inter-related "message systems" of schooling that serve to shape and frame students' experiences of schooling and of themselves as learners and active members of society. Simultaneously, they shape teacher priorities, and societal expectations of schooling. The message system of evaluation can be seen as encompassing assessment systems, requirements, approaches and data. As others have argued (Hay & Penney, 2013), alignment between curriculum, pedagogy, and assessment is critical to the coherence of education systems. We reaffirm the need for such alignment together with the need for assessment to value and validate the full breadth of learning outcomes that are desired. In the chapter we use the notion of enabling constraints to consider how the multiple and potentially contradictory agendas of different stakeholders and the various demands of curriculum, pedagogy, and assessment interact and might play out. As Davis, Sumara, and Luce-Kapler (2000, p. 193) explain, "Enabling constraints are not prescriptive; they don't dictate what MUST be done, rather they are expansive, indicating what MIGHT be done" (emphasis in original). This notion allows us to consider how tensions and contradictions within and across different levels of the assessment system might offer spaces for productive local engagement with curriculum, assessment, and pedagogy (Penney & Cowie, 2014).

12.3 Examining Assessment Challenges, Tensions and Possibilities

12.3.1 Assessment for and Within a Flexible and Responsive Curriculum

The NZC provides a flexible framework within which schools are expected to design and implement a curriculum that meets local needs and builds on local strengths (MOE, 2007). School and teacher response to NZC has been largely positive with school implementation processes tending to begin with a focus on reconstructing the school vision and/or developing a local interpretation of the key competencies (Cowie et al., 2009). The imperative towards a local response has prompted schools to look more closely at how they are interacting with families and communities in relation to curriculum design and implementation, and also to analyse and revise their reporting on student achievement. Principals, often with the active support of Boards of Trustees, have surveyed and held meetings with parents to elicit their vision for their child's education. What the key competencies might 'look, sound and feel like' in a particular community has been a subject of discussion by teacher groups and school communities. These activities have opened up productive spaces and foci for communication and partnership across the curriculum and assessment interface.

A number of debates and tensions have emerged to do with whether and/or how to formally assess and monitor the development of the key competencies. Specific issues include the breadth of assessment strategies, tasks, and occasions needed to generate a trustworthy representation of these complex learning outcomes (Hipkins, 2008) and the appropriate unit of analysis for assessment – should the focus be on individual students and their development, should it be on the student in context, and/or on students as a group or whole class? (Cowie & Carr, forthcoming). Teacher, principal, and parent groups, together with researchers, have variously raised matters to do with the potential for assessments to make visible and validate achievement and/or to limit and even narrow what is valued and seen as possible (Hipkins, Cowie, Boyd, Keown, & McGee, 2011). Teachers who were early adopters of NZC have expressed a desire to foster key competency development with a life-long and life-wide emphasis. They were interested in how competency might develop and be expressed, assessed, and supported in the classroom, in the school grounds, and in the community. As teachers have continued to discuss and implement the curriculum their attention has turned to consider how the key competency outcomes interface with and may be integral to conventional learning areas (Hipkins et al., 2011). At this time, the challenge of how to assess and communicate complex outcomes in a manner that supports the NZC vision is a substantial project in which researchers and teachers are beginning to collaborate (see Teachers and Curriculum, Volume X, 2013).

Illustrative Example 1 As part of a project aiming to develop rich examples of ways to embed the key competencies into the curriculum learning areas, Hipkins, Cowie, McDowell, and Carr (2013) came to appreciate that there were some deep layers to aspects of each key competency that could be expressed in different ways in the different learning areas, and that often several competencies were needed in combination to meet a specific type of learning challenge. The research team, in collaboration with a group of teachers, developed examples to illustrate how the key competencies were both end and means for learning (MOE, 2007, p. 38). The project generated a set of self-audit questions and illustrative classroom examples to assist teachers to identify the competencies and their development (see http://www.keycompetencies.tki.org.nz/Key-competencies-and-effective-pedagogy).

The principles for curriculum design in the NZC emphasise that curriculum design and practice should begin with the premise that all students can learn and succeed (the high expectations principle) and recognise and respect students' diverse identities, languages, abilities, and talents (the cultural diversity and inclusion principle). The implication of these principles, and other policies (Ministry of Education, 2008) is that school and teacher assessment practices need to be responsive to the curriculum learning needs of *all* students and, furthermore, students' wider sense of who they are and might become, and of students' links with their families/whānau and communities. In *Ka Hikitia – Managing for success 2008–2012* (MOE, 2008) this notion is discussed as helping Māori students succeed as Māori, and as citizens of the world. The prospective tension here is that when a teacher's assessment converges on the goals of the curriculum (Torrance & Pryor, 1998), the ideas, experiences, and value positions that students actually have in relation to an idea, event, or phenomena may be overlooked. On the other hand, assessment that is responsive to the diversity of students' knowledge, experiences, values, and worldviews holds out the prospect that this diversity will serve as a resource for learning. Studies by Glyn, Cowie, and Otrel-Cass (Glynn, Cowie, Otrel-Cass, & MacFarlane, 2010; Cowie, Otrel-Cass, et al. 2011) have demonstrated the value of teachers accessing and inviting student funds of knowledge and experience (González & Moll, 2002) into the curriculum as a resource for individual and collective learning. Their work has also demonstrated the value of providing students with multiple modes, media, and audiences as part of both formative and summative assessment (Cowie & Otrel-Cass, 2011). Somewhat problematically, their work also indicates assessment practice with an equity and culturally responsive agenda places considerable demands on teacher content, pedagogical, and pedagogical content knowledge (Cowie, Moreland, & Otrel-Cass, 2013). Culturally responsive pedagogy and assessment places substantial demands on teacher cultural knowledge and relationships with people in the local school community who could be approached to contribute to the curriculum and to engage with students in formative dialogue (Cowie & Glynn, 2012). The work of Mahuika, Berryman, and Bishop (2011) highlights the extent that culture influences how we interpret information, the importance we attach to different types of information, and also what outcomes we value (see also Gipps & Murphy, 1994). They note, "compatibility between the home and school environments will better facilitate effective learning and assessment" (p. 185) but caution that Māori students are by no means a homogenous group. The wider implication here is that both formative and summative assessment need to be responsive to diversity amongst learners and, even more importantly in the New Zealand context, it needs to find effective ways of assisting educators at all levels of the system to address the disparities in achievement amongst different student subgroups, especially Māori and Pasifica. For this to become possible, all those involved need to develop assessment literacy and capability.

12.3.2 The Need for All Participants and Audiences to Be Assessment Literate/Capable

The devolution of the New Zealand education system means that individuals and groups at all levels of the system need to be assessment capable/literate (Crooks, 2011; Ministry of Education, 2011; Nusche, Laveault, MacBeath, & Santiago, 2012). Given their responsibilities for school governance, Board of Trustee members need to be able to make sense of student assessment data to ensure their resourcing decisions are well informed and judged. Principals and teachers need to be able to design their own assessment processes and to use data generated through nationally provided assessment tools to inform their teaching and student learning. They need to know when it is reasonable and how to collate and combine information on student learning and learning progress from a range of sources in order to reach an "overall teacher judgment" on what a student has achieved. They need to be able to report on student learning to Board of Trustee members, family/whānau, and students in ways that support the willingness and ability of each of these groups to take informed and productive action.

New Zealand curriculum and assessment policy establishes parents, families/whānau as key stakeholders and partners in the process of improving learning, as the following statement in the Ministry assessment policy position paper (MOE, 2011) indicates:

> The key contributors to learning classrooms are teachers, students, and parents and whānau. These contributors need to maintain close dialogue, share information, and work together if students are to be fully supported in their learning. The interactions students have with their peers, teachers, and families and whānau are important in the process of improved learning. Teachers have a key role in shaping these interactions and in encouraging reciprocal conversations with parents and whānau. (p. 29)

This statement reminds us that parents and whānau are legitimate audiences for the demonstration of knowing and sources of valid feedback on student learning, both throughout and at the end of a period of learning work. However, as might be expected, parents have been found to vary in their confidence and capacity to partner with teachers in their children's learning (Cowie et al., 2009) with some parents, and especially those who have English as a second language and/or were educated in a different country, finding this situation challenging (Thrupp, in preparation).

In the New Zealand setting *Tātaiako: Cultural competencies for teachers of Māori learners* (MOE, 2011) positions ako or teachers taking responsibility for their own learning and that of Māori learners as a pedagogical competency.

The Ministry position paper on assessment describes ako or the collaborative exchange of information as important in responsive assessment as follows:

> Effective assessment is not only concerned with high-quality technical processes in the collection and interpretation of assessment information. It also requires a high level of responsiveness to unique learning and learner contexts. It includes collaborative exchanges of information between participants in a process of reciprocal learning or ako. (p. 4)

Key aspects of ako include: (i) language, identity, and culture counts, and so it is important to know where students come from and build on what they bring with them, and (ii) productive partnerships where Māori students, whānau, and educators share knowledge and experiences with each other to produce better outcomes (MOE, 2008). This construct, along with that of "tuakana-teina" (the more informed and more skilled teaching the less-informed and less skilled), provides a distinct context for the demonstration of expertise through sharing as reciprocal learning. Studies working with this orientation have demonstrated the value of teachers making available multiple media, modes, and audiences for student learning, including engaging parents early on in teaching, learning, and assessment, as the next example illustrates.

Illustrative Example 2 Jude invited families into class to talk about the upcoming science unit on Matariki (astronomy) so they knew what learning was planned and could support their child at home. During this event parents shared and checked out what of their experiences might be relevant. Subsequently, Jude used a class website and individual student 'home learning' books to support two-way communication between home and school about what students were doing and learning. The unit concluded with a class presentation to families on what students' had learned. The families at this event expressed their appreciation at having been told about what their children would be learning; they considered that with this knowledge they were more able to support their child's learning.

Ako or reciprocal learning is necessary at all levels of the assessment system: "It has a role to play in classroom practice, professional dialogue, school review, and the development of school-based policy and practices, system monitoring and evaluation and review, and development of system-wide policy and practices" (MOE, 2011, p. 4). Policy makers and government officials along with politicians need to be assessment literate for them to be able to effectively guide assessment policy and practice development and to take assessment informed action on national and international assessment data. We would add that the media also needs these assessment capabilities to ensure reporting of data contributes to, and does not undermine, the goals of education for a better society. Even more importantly, as the Ministry position paper states, students need to be at the centre of curriculum, pedagogy and assessment practices (see also the NZC); a position that is generally supported by the teaching profession (McGee et al., 2004). The implication of this is that students need high levels of assessment literacy: student capacity and inclination to monitor and assess their own learning progress and outcomes is central to the development of students as "confident, connected, actively involved, lifelong learners" (MOE, 2007, p. 8). Arguably it is not possible to leverage the full potential for lifelong or lifewide (Hay & Penney, 2013) learning, in the absence of a strategic awareness of how to develop, access and activate resources and practices that support learning (Hipkins & Cowie, 2014). The students that Cowie (2005) spoke to were very clear about the different purposes and consequences of classroom assessment for their learning, their self-esteem and their standing with their peers. Their comments endorsed the need for teacher feedback to move beyond praise and affirmation to the provision of information they could use to move their learning forward. More recently, Harris and Brown (2013), also researching with New Zealand students, documented differences in teacher and student perspectives of, and purposes for, peer and student self-assessment. Their data indicated that both teachers and students need a deep understanding of how to use peer and self-assessment for improvement and self-regulation purposes. Hence, while support for student agency and authority within learning and assessment are policy goals and have the espoused support of teachers, there is still much to be done to realise this in practice.

In considering opportunities for educators to develop assessment literacy, it is notable that since 1995 the New Zealand Ministry of Education has allocated substantial resources to assessment-focused professional development programmes for teachers. These usually involve 2 years of professional development support, the main focus of which has been the development of individual teacher assessment *for* learning practices. Over the same period the government, amongst other organisations, has produced and made available a range of assessment tools for teachers to use, some of which come with marking and analysis support. The challenge for teachers remains, however, how to construct their own assessments from these resources to meet their own and their students' needs and interests. It seems that teacher capacity to design and select assessment tasks is variable (Poskitt & Taylor, 2008), something that is cause for concern given the extensive range of assessment tasks New Zealand teachers access and use (McGee et al., 2004). Moreover, despite the sustained focus on formative assessment, it seems New Zealand teachers hold conceptions of the purposes of assessment ranging from improvement of teaching and learning to school accountability or student accountability and, in a few cases, view assessment as irrelevant (Harris & Brown, 2009a). More recently, Harris and Brown (2013) have documented differences in teacher and student perspectives of and purposes for peer- and student self-assessment. Their data indicated teachers and students need a deep understanding of how to use peer- and self-assessment for improvement and self-regulation purposes. Dixon, Hawe, and Parr (2011) have reported that even teachers who articulate similar beliefs with regard to the importance of developing student autonomy and who had described similar practices to develop self-monitoring behaviour engage in very different classroom assessment practices. These studies indicate, as others have (James & Pedder, 2006), that there is a need to attend to the interaction of teacher beliefs and national and local policy and practices, alerting us to the challenge of coherence between these aspects.

Returning to the point about the need to build commitment at all levels of the system, Timperley and Parr (2009) provide evidence of the collaborative use of assessment data by clusters of teachers or by all staff at a school. The Ministry has recently begun funding assessment-focused professional development for school leaders. The work of McKinley and colleagues illustrates the possible impact of this approach.

Illustrative Example 3 Starpath, an extended research and development study driven by a concern that low-income, Māori and Pacific students did not have an equal opportunity to enter and succeed in tertiary education, which provides evidence of the value of a school-wide focus on data generation and use. Working with Year 11–13 students, their project has demonstrated the benefits of systematic whole-school data utilisation; of regular academic counselling, target setting and progress reviews by students in conversation with a trained teacher, and of student-parent-teacher conferences that provide opportunities for evidence-based discussion on progress and plans with parents/whānau (Madjar & McKinley, 2010).

McKinley has been clear, however, that school change is challenging, time-consuming and requires commitment. Taken together, these New Zealand policies and studies suggest constraints and enablers arise from many sources, including the teaching resources that teachers have access to and/or are familiar with, and teachers' personal values and interests. This suggests the need to move beyond a focus on assessment in interaction with curriculum and pedagogy as an individual teacher or even individual school concern. He endorses the need for a systems view of assessment and the provision of space for greater cross stakeholder collaboration and development.

12.4 Assessment and Accountability: To Whom and for What

In New Zealand, as elsewhere, there has been an increase in assessment discourses to do with accountability. Hay and Penney (2013) note that the intersection of assessment and accountability can be understood in a number of ways. Assessment can be seen to provide a means for students to develop an account of their learning progress and to take account of how *they* best learn. In one sense, being able to account for what and how one learns is central to the development of learning capacity and so this form of accountability can be seen to be productive and broadly aligned with assessment *for* lifelong learning (formative assessment). Developing an account of learning can also have a quite different orientation and prime purpose, broadly aligning with assessment *of* learning and summative assessment, and focusing on the communication of what has been accomplished. The extent to which systems, schools, teachers, and students are held to account for fixed and predetermined outcomes is critical here. Where there is tight prescription, the teacher and student orientation to assessment can become one of performativity (Ball, 2003) and criteria compliance (Torrance, 2007) rather than learning. The tensions between these various functions of accountability in and through assessment are discussed next in relation to the challenges and potentials associated with the use of nationally prescribed standards for student learning and achievement as part of the National Standards regime in schooling years 1–8 and NCEA in schooling years 11–13.

In relation to accountability in schooling Years 1–8, the introduction of the National Standards programme of assessment has been hotly contested, in part because it represents a break from longstanding practices where the focus has been on formative assessment and in part because of limited teacher and principal consultation during its preparation (Thrupp, 2010). On the other hand, advocates for its introduction argue that the use of standards, rather than a national test, and the way teachers are expected to combine multiple sources of information in making Overall Teacher Judgments (OTJs) against National Standards avoids the problem of "teaching to the test". It was also proposed that schools reporting against the standards in 'plain language' would lead to more consistent and comprehensible reporting to parents. An indepth school-based study by Thrupp and Easter (2013) found that schools have responded to the Standards in very different and incremental ways, strongly related to school-specific contextual factors. These include long-term and situated thinking about how assessment and reporting should be done in and for the particular school community and the personal preferences of the principal/ influential staff member. Some parents are reporting they do not understand National Standards-based reporting, others are concerned that their children are being labelled as below standard from an early age (Thrupp, 2013).

The introduction of National Standards has highlighted the challenge of collecting comprehensive data on complex outcomes as well as the role and importance of moderation, both within and between schools (Ward & Thomas, 2012). Moderation is a process whereby teachers share interpretations and implementation of criteria and standards to assure consistency and comparability in teacher evidence-based judgments on student achievement (Klenowski & Wyatt-Smith, 2010). Consistency and moderation within and between schools has not traditionally featured as a concern for teachers because of the independence accorded schools by Tomorrow's Schools and, more recently, the emphasis on local interpretation of the NZC. Schools have developed their own policies and practices around curriculum, assessment and reporting. Whether or not the tensions inherent in the need to assess against prescribed standards within a flexible curriculum will drive greater collaboration and networking aimed at overall improvement in teaching, learning and assessment or whether they will foster competition that limits the sharing of effective practice and diminishes the exercise of collective responsibility for the learning of all students is yet to be seen. Just as problematically, anecdotal evidence suggests that school and teacher curriculum design response to the Standards has been to direct increased curriculum time to reading, writing, and mathematics (the focus of the Standards) at the expense of other curriculum areas. Here again future developments could be generative, with curriculum planning focused on leveraging and enriching students' capacities in these aspects through learning in other curriculum areas, or the curriculum could narrow further on to these three aspects. Encouragingly, there have been some reports of teachers coming together as a whole staff to consider student achievement data and plan for individual and joint action, with student learning moving from an individual to a collective responsibility (Hipkins et al., 2013). Such an approach opens the door to shared learning amidst what can be construed as a constraining mechanism.

Internationally it is recognised that exit qualifications are frequently where discourses of accountability and standardisation can be seen to come to the fore, and where it is sometimes a challenge to ensure that discourses of equity and inclusion are not marginalised. In New Zealand the National Certificate of Educational Achievement (NCEA) is intended to provide pathways towards appropriate qualification for students with very different interests and capabilities. Established and vocational secondary school subjects are subdivided into several (usually 5–8) Achievement Standards, each of which has a 'failing or not achieved level' and three passing levels (achieved, merit, and excellence), and a specified number of 'credits' (usually 3–6). Students are assessed through a combination of internal and external assessment tasks. In addition, there are Unit Standards, most of which are assessed on a pass/fail (not achieved/achieved) basis. For the 'internally assessed' credits teachers may choose to use or adapt existing assessment tasks that are available in various banks of tasks. They need to follow national specifications for the assessment processes, criteria, and performance levels. Students are allowed to re-sit some tasks. Most schools require teachers to engage in some form of internal moderation to help ensure consistency across different teachers and classes. A national external moderation process monitors at least 10 % of internally assessed standards each year. This national moderation includes checks on the suitability of the assessment task or tasks, as well as the application of the marking criteria and standards. Most externally assessed Achievement Standards are assessed through written national examinations. In a few cases, such as art works, musical compositions, dance or drama performances, external standards are used for work accumulated into portfolios during the school year. There is some evidence that students and teachers view and experience the internally and externally assessed standards differently. External standards are accorded greater status and seen as harder to achieve but teachers and students collaborate to support student achievement. The potential for conflict between assessment *of* and assessment *for* learning and the teacher roles as judges of and supporters for student learning are considerable when students are being prepared and assessed for internally assessed Achievement Standards or Unit Standards. Indeed, there is some evidence that student preparation for internally assessed tasks might undermine the validity of any summative grade they are awarded (Hume & Coll, 2009), which poses a challenge to the trustworthiness of the NCEA system and to the proposal that the NCEA system might support quality formative and summative assessment. On the other hand, Sheehan's (2013) research examining the contribution of internally assessed NCEA course work indicates that it has made a substantial contribution to students' motivation and learning to think historically, to adjudicate between competing versions of historical authenticity, and to understand how second order concepts operate in the discipline. Teacher understanding of the discipline of history was crucial in their providing specific feedback to students and assisting students to think critically about the past, all the more so because developing the ability to think historically is counter-intuitive. Students especially valued the personal autonomy of course work and they committed to the substantial workload required to investigate historical questions that were of personal interest.

In NCEA, accountability operates at three levels: students, teachers, and schools. Students are held to direct account for their results on individual standards and on accumulation of credits towards an NCEA certificate as they progress to higher level qualifications. New Zealand does not have a system of high school graduation and so students' educational standing when they leave school depends largely on what NCEA qualifications they have gained. The results for all secondary schools are publicly available, and schools and teachers can develop reputations based on how well their students do in the NCEA. Crooks (2011) points out student decisions about which Standards they work on can have a major influence on their future learning and employment. Research in the Starpath Project at the University of Auckland (Madyar, McKinley, Jensen, & van der Merwe, 2009) has shown that school-guided choices of subjects and Standards often significantly constrain future academic options for students, and this can perpetuate existing disadvantages and stereotypes for particular ethnic or socio-economic subgroups in the school population.

A notable recent development in New Zealand is a major project to align NCEA with the NZC. This process is intended to ensure that whatever their qualification goals, all senior secondary students can benefit from the flexible pathways that NCEA offers. This initiative provides for the intent of the NZC to be expressed in senior secondary curriculum although the relationship between the NZC and NCEA is evolving, as understandings in both areas are evolving. As Hipkins and Spiller (2012) have recognised, the flexibility that both the NZC and NCEA promote in relation to assessment, and the move to alignment, can be constructively exploited to support innovative developments that address individual student learning needs, challenges, and potential. Yet, it is also the case that such innovation is far from assured in all schools and classrooms.

The National Standards and NCEA, as two accountability mechanisms, embody the ever-present tension between formative and summative assessment and they highlight issues around externally and internally designed tasks and teacher assessment task design capacity. Teacher responses indicate National Standards provide a high stakes arena where teachers face the dilemma of balancing what they "feel is best for their students versus what is deemed necessary for school accountability" (Harris & Brown, 2009b, p. 365).

12.5 Implications and Conclusion

In this chapter we have scoped out some of the challenges, tensions, and possibilities that arise for the various stakeholders (children/youth and their families, teachers, schools, policy makers) in the New Zealand education system. The system is one in which traditionally, significant responsibility for curriculum programme planning, pedagogy, assessment, and reporting has been devolved to schools but where there is currently notable policy and political pressure for schools to engage with more prescriptive assessment regimes. The clear challenge in responding to such pressures is to ensure that the rhetoric of improved educational outcomes for all students becomes a meaningful discourse that is integral to discourses of assessment for learning. Embedding notions of quality, authentic and equitable assessment into the ongoing implementation of NZC, NCEA, and National Standards, remains a significant challenge for teachers throughout the education system in New Zealand.

Like their international colleagues, they feel policy tensions in a very real sense as they seek to enact a set of policy requirements and initiatives that speak to a complex mix of discourses. Arguably, aspects of both the history and culture of education in New Zealand position teachers well in terms of their capacity to generate innovative and inclusive assessmentpractices amidst what has been described as a "policy soup" (Braun, Maguire, & Ball, 2010). We would argue that they are operating in a policy and practice soup – national policies, historical practices and many aspects of individual school and community contexts all variously inform local policies and practices. School community aspirations for *their* students rightly shape and frame the planned and enacted curriculum and the nature of the assessment practices deemed most appropriate and possible within that school context albeit curriculum, pedagogy, and assessment are also influenced by national imperatives. As is indicated in recent scholarship on assessment (Stiggins, 2008), coherence across these systems is important. In New Zealand as elsewhere, current policies present the scope for this coherency to be advanced amidst interpretation and implementation, or in contrast, jeopardised.

The implications of the New Zealand experience for policy makers as leaders of reform include the need to consider carefully how new policies will interface and interact with prior policies and resourcing (materials and professional development), and the local policy and practices that schools have developed to enact earlier policies within their setting. There is strong evidence that local policies and practices tend to be slow to change, all the more so if new policies are contradictory and/or their deeper implications are not clear (Thrupp & Easter, 2013). As Brown (2012) points out: "New Zealand has prioritised formative assessment and committed resources to enabling teachers to implement the policy, kept consequences for schools and teachers relatively low, and safe-guarded the professionalism of its teachers" (n.p.). This approach comes with substantial challenges to teacher content and pedagogical content knowledge as well as to their assessment literacy including how to design robust assessment tasks and make quality judgments. Within any future developments it will therefore be important for policy makers to continue to provide the support schools and teachers need to enable them to enact and use assessment to ameliorate disparity and enhance equity of opportunity and outcomes for *all* students. At this time there is a distinct lack of assessment resources for Māori-medium education and of resources that allow teachers to take the diversity in student linguistic, cultural and special educational needs into account.

The implication for school leaders, and teachers – as leaders of learning in classrooms – is that there is value in clearly articulating their own policies, principles, and practices and in focusing on the spaces for change and innovation offered by new policies and associated support materials and programmes. Studies of innovative schools (Cowie et al., 2009) indicate that there would be value in schools sharing the practices they have found to be effective; and, as was the case when schools were first working to integrate the use of laptops (Cowie, Jones, & Harlow, 2006), in small schools sharing resources and expertise (see also the recommendations from Nusche et al., 2012). The imperative to place students at the centre of their own assessment (MOE, 2011) has implications for teachers' understanding of their professional role and responsibilities, with ample evidence that for teachers the reconceptualisation of their role is a challenge (James & Pedder, 2006). If teachers and schools are to explore this shift, there will need to be societal and school community support for the exploration and risk taking by teachers and students. The variability in teacher assessment and moderation practices (Wylie & Hodgen, 2010) indicates a need for teacher development to ensure overall teacher judgments are reliable and nationally comparable. This development comes with the potential to develop teacher understanding of learning goals, assessment criteria (National Standards), and formative responses and strategies.

The New Zealand context is one of possibilities and constraints. We have illustrated here that there is merit in viewing any potential constraint as an enabling constraint – while it delimits possibilities it does not completely close these off. However, we also acknowledge that the possibilities that are open for any individual to leverage are not the same and are influenced by many factors. Leaders at all levels of the system need to be proactive in collaborative endeavours to optimise the spaces for action that the policy and practice context presents.

References

Baker, R., & Jones, A. (2005). How can international studies such as TIMSS and the PISA be used to inform practice, policy and future research in science education in New Zealand? *International Journal of Science Education, 27*(2), 145–157.

Ball, S. (2003). The teacher's sole and the terror of performativity. *Journal of Educational Philosophy, 18*(2), 215–228.

Ball, S., Maguire, M., Braun, A., with Hoskins, K., & Perryman, J. (2012). *How schools do policy. Policy enactment in secondary schools*. Abingdon, UK: Routledge.

Bell, B., & Cowie, B. (2001). *Formative assessment in science education*. Dordrecht, The Netherlands: Kluwer.

Bernstein, B. (1971). On the classification and framing of educational knowledge. In M. F. D. Young (Ed.), *Knowledge and control: New directions for the sociology of education*. London, UK: Collier Macmillan.

Bernstein, B. (1990). *The structuring of pedagogic discourse* (Class, codes and control, Vol. IV). London, UK: Routledge.

Braun, A., Maguire, M., & Ball, S. (2010). Policy enactments in the UK secondary school: Examining policy, practice and school positioning. *Journal of Education Policy, 25*(4), 547–560.

Brown, G. (2012, November 2–4). *National testing: Promises and pitfalls – The NZ perspective*. Presentation to International Forum on Achievement Assessment and Evaluation, Shanghai, China.

Clarke, M. (2012). *What matters most for student assessment systems: A framework paper*. Washington, DC: The World Bank, The International Bank for Reconstruction and Development.

Cowie, B. (2005). Pupil commentary on assessment for learning. *The Curriculum Journal, 16*(2), 137–151.

Cowie, B., & Carr, M. (forthcoming). Assessing a connected person-plus learner. In M. Morton (Ed.), *Supporting inclusive education: Learning from narrative assessment*. Rotterdam, The Netherlands: Sense.

Cowie, B., & Glynn, T. (2012, November). *The role of affordance networks in supporting teachers to become culturally responsive*. Paper presented at the second Culturally responsive research and pedagogy conference, Hamilton, New Zealand.

Cowie, B., Hipkins, R., Boyd, S., Bull, A., Keown, P., McGee, C., et al. (2009). *Curriculum implementation exploratory studies: Final report*. Wellington, New Zealand: New Zealand Ministry of Education.

Cowie, B., Hipkins, R., Keown, P., & Boyd, S. (2011). *The shape of curriculum change*. Wellington, New Zealand: Ministry of Education.

Cowie, B., Jones, A., & Harlow, A. (2006). The digital horizons: Laptops for teachers policy initiative: Impacts and consequences. *New Zealand Annual Review of Education, 15*, 111–132.

Cowie, B., Moreland, J., & Otrel-Cass, K. (2013). *Expanding notions of assessment for learning: Inside science and technology primary classrooms*. Rotterdam, The Netherlands: Sense.

Cowie, B., & Otrel-Cass, K. (2011). Exploring the value of 'horizontal' learning in early years science classrooms. *Early Years, 31*(3), 285–295.

Cowie, B., Otrel-Cass, K., Glynn, T., Kara, H., Anderson, M., Doyle, J., …, Te Kiri, C. (2011). *Culturally responsive pedagogy and assessment in primary science classrooms: Whakamana tamariki. Summary Report*. Wellington, New Zealand: Teaching and Learning Research Initiative.

Crooks, T. (2011). Assessment for learning in the accountability era: New Zealand. *Studies in Educational Evaluation, 37*(1), 71–77. doi:10.1016/j.stueduc.2011.03.002.

Crooks, T., & Flockton, L. (1993). *Some proposals for national monitoring of education outcomes*. Unpublished paper. Dunedin, New Zealand: University of Otago.

Davis, B., Sumara, D., & Luce-Kapler, R. (2000). *Engaging minds: Changing teaching in complex times*. Mahwah, NJ: Lawrence Erlbaum Associates.

Department of Education. (1989). *Assessment for better learning: A public discussion document*. Wellington, New Zealand: Department of Education.

Dixon, H., Hawe, E., & Parr, J. (2011). Enacting assessment for learning: The beliefs practice nexus. *Assessment in Education, 18*(4), 365–379. doi:10.1080/0969594X.2010.526587.

Flockton, L. (1999). Connecting theory and practice in national monitoring assessment. *Teachers and Curriculum, 3*, 23–30.

Gilmore, A. (2002). Large-scale assessment and teachers' capacity: Learning opportunities for teachers in the National Education Monitoring Project in New Zealand. *Assessment in Education, 9*(3), 343–361.

Gipps, C., & Murphy, P. (1994). *A fair test? Assessment, achievement and equity*. Buckingham, UK: Open University Press.

Glynn, T., Cowie, B., & Otrel-Cass, K. (2008). *Quality Teaching Research and Development Science Hub (Waikato): Connecting New Zealand teachers of science with their Māori students. Report to Ministry of Education*. Hamilton, New Zealand: Wilf Malcolm Institute of Educational Research, University of Waikato.

Glynn, T., Cowie, B., Otrel-Cass, K., & MacFarlane, A. (2010). Culturally responsive pedagogy: Connecting New Zealand teachers of science with their Māori students. *Australian Journal of Indigenous Education, 39*, 118–127.

González, N., & Moll, L. (2002). Cruzando el puente: Building bridges to funds of knowledge. *Journal of Educational Policy, 16*(4), 623–641.

Harris, L., & Brown, G. (2009a). Opportunities and obstacles to consider when using peer- and self-assessment to improve student learning: Case studies into teachers' implementation. *Teaching and Teacher Education, 36*, 101–111.

Harris, L., & Brown, G. (2009b). The complexity of teachers' conceptions of assessment: Tensions between the needs of schools and students. *Assessment in Education, 16*(3), 365–381.

Harris, L., & Brown, G. (2013). Opportunities and obstacles to consider when using peer- and self-assessment to improve student learning: Case studies into teachers' implementation. *Teaching and Teacher Education, 36*, 101–111. doi:10.1016/j.tate.2013.07.008.

Hay, P. J., & Penney, D. (2013). *Assessment in physical education. A socio-cultural perspective*. Abingdon, UK: Routledge.
Hipkins, R. (2008). *Assessing key competencies: Why would we? How could we?* Wellington, New Zealand: Ministry of Education.
Hipkins, R. (2013). *NCEA one decade on: Views and experiences from the 2012 NZCER National Survey of Secondary Schools*. Wellington, New Zealand: NZCER.
Hipkins, R., & Cowie, B. (2014). Learning to learn, lifewide and lifelong learning: Reflections on the New Zealand experience. In R. Deakin Crick, C. Stringher, & K. Ren (Eds.), *Learning to learn: International perspectives from theory and practice*. Abingdon, UK: Routlege.
Hipkins, R., Cowie, B., Boyd, S., Keown, P., & McGee, C. (2011). *Curriculum Implementation Exploratory Studies 2*. Ministry of Education. Retrieved from Ministry of Education's website Education Counts: www.educationcounts.govt.nz/publications
Hipkins, R., Cowie, B., McDowell, S., & Carr, M. (2013). *Key competencies and effective pedagogy*. Retrieved from http://keycompetencies.tki.org.nz/Key-competencies-and-effective-pedagogy
Hipkins, R., & Spiller, L. (2012). *NCEA and curriculum innovation: Learning from change in three schools*. Wellington, New Zealand: New Zealand Council for Educational Research.
Hume, A., & Coll, R. (2009). Assessment of learning, for learning, and as learning: New Zealand case studies. *Assessment in Education, 16*(3), 263–268.
James, M., & Pedder, D. (2006). Beyond method: Assessment and learning practices and values. *Curriculum Journal, 17*(2), 109–138.
Klenowski, V., & Wyatt-Smith, C. M. (2010). Standards, teacher judgement and moderation in the contexts of national curriculum and assessment reform. *Assessment Matters, 2*, 107–131.
Madjar, I., & McKinley, E. (2010). *Understanding NCEA: A relatively short and very useful guide for secondary students and their parents*. Wellington, New Zealand: NZCER.
Madyar, J., McKinley, E., Jensen, S., & van der Merwe, A. (2009). *Towards university: Navigating NCEA course choices in low-mid decile schools*. Retrieved from http://www.education.ac.nz/uoa/home/about/research/starpath-home/starpath-research/towards-university
Mahuika, R., Berryman, M., & Bishop, R. (2011). Issues of culture and assessment in New Zealand education pertaining to Māori students. *Assessment Matters, 3*, 183–198.
McGee, C., Harlow, A., Miller, T., Cowie, B., Hill, M., Jones, A., et al. (2004). *Teachers' experiences in curriculum implementation: General curriculum, the arts, and health and physical education* (Report to the Ministry of Education). Wellington, New Zealand: Ministry of Education.
Minister of Education. (1988). *Tomorrow's schools: The reform of education administration in New Zealand*. Wellington, New Zealand: Government Printer.
Ministerial Working Party on Assessment for Better Learning. (1990). *Tomorrow's standards*. Wellington, New Zealand: Learning Media.
Ministry of Education. (1993). *The New Zealand curriculum framework*. Wellington, New Zealand: Learning Media.
Ministry of Education. (1994). *Assessment: Policy to practice*. Wellington, New Zealand: Learning Media.
Ministry of Education. (2007). *New Zealand curriculum*. Wellington, New Zealand: Learning Media.
Ministry of Education. (2008). *Ka Hikitia – Managing for success 2008–2012*. Wellington, New Zealand: Learning Media.
Ministry of Education. (2011). *Ministry of Education position paper: Assessment (schooling sector)*. Wellington, New Zealand: Learning Media.
Nusche, D., Laveault, D., MacBeath, J., & Santiago, P. (2012). *OECD reviews of evaluation and assessment in education: New Zealand 2011*. OECD Publishing. doi:10.1787/9789264116917-en
Penney, D., & Cowie, B. (2014). Assessment: Power relations, political influences, and pedagogical change. In A. St. George, S. Brown, & J. O'Neill (Eds.), *Facing the big questions in teaching: Purpose, power, and learning* (2nd ed., pp. 73-80). Melbourne, Australia: Cengage.

Poskitt, J., & Taylor, K. (2008). *National education findings of Assess to Learn (AtoL) report.* Wellington, New Zealand: Ministry of Education.

Sheehan, M. (2013). *"Better to do than receive": Learning to think historically through internally assessed course work.* Wellington, New Zealand: Teaching and Learning Research Initiative.

Stiggins, R. J. (2008). *Assessment manifesto: A call for the development of balanced assessment systems. A position paper.* Portland, OR: ETS Assessment Training Institute.

Thrupp, M. (2010). Emerging school-level education policy under National 2008–9. *New Zealand Annual Review of Education, 19,* 30–51.

Thrupp, M. (2013). National standards for student achievement: Is New Zealand's idiosyncratic approach any better? *Australian Journal of Language and Literacy, 36*(2), 99-110.

Thrupp, M., & Easter, A. (2013). 'Tell me about your school': Researching local responses to New Zealand's National Standards policy. *Assessment Matters, 5.* Retrieved from http://www.nzcer.org.nz/nzcerpress/assessment-matters/articles/tell-me-about-your-school-researching-local-responses-new-ze

Timperley, H., & Parr, J. (2009). Chain of influence from policy to practice in the New Zealand literacy strategy. *Research Papers in Education, 24*(2), 135–154.

Torrance, H. (2007). Assessment as learning? How the use of explicit learning objectives, assessment criteria and feedback in post-secondary education and training can come to dominate learning. *Assessment in Education, 14*(3), 281–294.

Torrance, H., & Pryor, J. (1998). *Investigating formative assessment: Teaching, learning and assessment in the classroom.* Philadelphia, PA: Open University Press.

United Nations Educational Scientific, and Cultural Organization (UNESCO). (2007). *Education for all global monitoring report 2008: Education for all by 2015. Will we make it?* Paris, France: Oxford University Press.

Ward, J., & Thomas, G. (2012). *National Standards; School sample monitoring and evaluation project 2011.* Reporting to the Ministry of Education. Wellington, New Zealand: Learning Media.

Wylie, C., & Hodgen, E. (2010). *NZCER 2010 primary and intermediate schools national survey: A snapshot of overall patterns and findings related to national standards.* Wellington, New Zealand: NZCER.

Chapter 13
First Nations Assessment Issues

David F. Philpott

Abstract This chapter delves into the challenges and discussion around identifying and supporting disabilities in Aboriginal youth. Despite the global paradigm of inclusion, educators and service providers continue to struggle to understand children's developmental needs so as to inform programs. This process is increasingly complicated by cultural and linguistic differences, in an increasingly diverse student population. Like many regions of the world, Canada has a shifting demographic base and there is growing concern for the cultural appropriateness of traditional approaches to assessment and special education practices. Canada is not alone in struggling to meet the educational needs of its indigenous people and proven practice from one country can help inform the international community. This chapter presents three factors driving this debate in Canada: growing sensitivity to multicultural/multi-linguistic differences in our schools; the impact of inclusive education; and recognised criticisms of traditional psycho-educational assessment practices. While the author recognises a place in education for standardised assessment, an argument is presented that current practice, which strives to fit children into funded support categories, has resulted in an overreliance on test scores and a devaluing of teacher and parent perspectives. Certainly, there is growing recognition that such approaches have failed to empower teachers to adapt programs and create effective instruction. Instead the author argues to keep "testing" separate from "teaching" and presents existing culturally sensitive models in Canada which are succeeding in this practice. As such, emerging practice for Canada's Aboriginal population offers food for thought in other regions of the world that are struggling with similar issues. The chapter concludes with a discussion of the implications of this discussion and these models on educational leadership.

Keywords Indigenous people • Aboriginal education • Cultural diversity • Assessment • Classroom-based assessment • Empowerment • Educational leadership

D.F. Philpott (✉)
Faculty of Education, Memorial University of Newfoundland,
230 Elizabeth Ave, St. John's, NL, Canada A1B 3X9
e-mail: philpott@mun.ca

13.1 Introduction

Recent discourse in education has been dominated by the effects of the school reform movement which placed greater emphasis on enhancing school curriculum and improving student achievement. Globally, the school reform movement, to various degrees, changed the organisational structure of schools with a shift toward site-based management. It redesigned curriculum by calling for quality instruction and higher academic standards. It heralded increased assessment practices so as to monitor student performance and hold educators accountable; and it brought heightened scrutiny of special education, which was often viewed as being a separate system with a lower standard (Lipsky & Gartner, 1997). While the reforms in education have been dramatic, for special education it resulted in an increased blending of special and regular education into one set of educational standards for all children (Hockenbury, Kauffman, & Hallahan, 2000; Zigmond & Baker, 1995). In fact, establishing higher educational standards with tighter performance measures for students in special education quickly became a global trend. In Britain, the 1988 Educational Reform Act introduced a common national curriculum with standardised instruction for all students (Armstrong, Armstrong, & Barton, 2000). This shift was welcomed by Mittler (2000) who referred to it as a "major watershed" for inclusion. He stated "a school curriculum that is accessible and that provides all pupils without exception with opportunities to participate fully and to experience success is an essential foundation for inclusion" (p. 111). He documented this trend as being increasingly popular in countries as diverse as Bangladesh, Denmark, Italy, and Lesotho and referenced international organisations such as *UNESCO* and the newly-formed *European Agency for Special Needs Education* as being instrumental in promoting this reform.

While Canadian educational systems were attempting to raise the standards of achievement and blend curriculum for all children who were deemed "regular" or "special", the experience of Aboriginal youth would prove to be another example of the need for reform. Concern for the education of Canada's Aboriginal population has been well identified, though it continues to go relatively unaddressed. As early as the 1960s Aboriginal people were voicing concern about inequities in educational services for their children (Hawthorne, 1967). As a result, a federal government policy paper titled *The White Paper* (Government of Canada, 1969) presented a response plan that would assign the individual provinces sole responsibility for the education of Aboriginal children. Philpott, Nesbit, Cahill, and Jeffery (2004a) argue that while the "intention may have been the development of equity in educational opportunities for all children, many Aboriginal leaders interpreted it as an attempt to facilitate assimilation" (p. 52). Goulet (2001) supports this and views this history of Aboriginal education as being reflective of the struggle for self-determination against the effects of colonisation: "Aboriginal education has a legacy of assimilationist policies that were guided by the ideology of cultural deprivation and deficit" (p. 69). In discussing the inappropriateness of this approach and the resulting oppression, Goulet writes:

> Social struggles are enacted in classroom practice where Aboriginal students can encounter an ethnocentric curriculum, authoritative relationships, racist attitudes, and prejudicial beliefs about inferiority or deficits. Conditions such as these are intolerable for Aboriginal children, who are made to feel stupid when they cannot learn under these circumstances and fail in school. Some resist the oppression and so do not participate and drop out of school. (p. 68)

Following *The White Paper*, and certainly long before the school reform movement began, The National Indian Brotherhood (1972), in a report titled *Indian Control of Indian Education*, outlined its own plan to reform education by assuming self-management of its schools. That report heralded the establishment of an Aboriginal version of site-based management, which was band managed education, which sought to establish culturally appropriate and language-sensitive educational models. However noble the goal, the ensuing years did not bring about change as significant as the school reform movement would herald, and by 2004 the effects of this separate model of education led the Council of Ministers of Education (2004) to conclude:

> There is recognition in all educational jurisdictions that the achievement rates of Aboriginal children, including the completion of secondary school, must be improved. Studies have shown that some of the factors contributing to this low level of academic achievement are that Aboriginals in Canada have the lowest income and thus the highest rates of poverty, the highest rate of drop-outs from formal education, and the lowest health indicators of any group. (p. 22)

That same year, the Office of the Auditor General of Canada (2004) also voiced concern, stating: "We remain concerned that a significant education gap exists between First Nations people living on reserves and the Canadian population as a whole and that the time estimated to close this gap has increased slightly, from about 27 to 28 years" (Section 5.2).

While educational practices in dominant cultures were attempting to bridge the divisions between "regular" children and those identified as "special", the division for children identified as "Aboriginal" would continue. Philpott (2007) speaks to this parallel between special education, where difference is labelled based on assessment, and Aboriginal education, where difference is labelled based on ethnicity. He cites Wotherspoon (2001) who, in examining the history of Aboriginal education in Canada, illustrates the impact of a deficit-based model on a people's identity.

> Schooling has contributed to the subjugation and marginalization of Aboriginal people but is regarded as a critical agency for their future social, economic and political success... The realities and struggles associated with Aboriginal self-determination, in conjunction with Aboriginal people's participation in broader societal contexts, demonstrate how exclusionary processes operate in the absence of 'inclusive spaces'. (p. 2)

It is against this background of growing concern about models of education, which separated children based on label, that we begin a debate on how students are identified as "different". As schools move toward "inclusive spaces" and the negative effects of labelling children to rationalise separate approaches become increasingly evident, how do schools face the challenge of identifying needs so as to inform effective programs? More pertinent to this current debate is how educators can identify individual need in an increasingly diverse population. Canada's Aboriginal population may well exemplify the effects of being labelled and treated as different, while at the same time failed assimilative practice speaks to the need for individualised response. Central to this struggle to find efficacious ways of identifying need, optimising support and empowering people is the field of educational assessment. We begin this dialogue by examining reasons why this issue is quickly moving to the forefront of educational discourse in Canada.

13.1.1 Demographic Concerns

A dominant reason to begin this debate in Canada is rather pragmatic: *need*. The 2006 census outlined what Canadians had suspected for some time: that the population base is shifting radically toward greater cultural and linguistic diversity. In fact, there are 200 languages spoken in Canadian schools and today 20 % of our population is from a visible minority and reports a first language other than English. This represents an 18.5 % increase since 2001 and predictions are that by 2017, 23 % of Canada's population will be from a visible minority. While two-thirds of this growth is due to immigration, the Aboriginal population has exploded with a 45 % increase in the last decade. The 2006 census outlines that the Aboriginal population now stands at nearly 1.2 million with a projected growth rate of 34 % in the next 20 years. Of greater concern to educators is the age of this population, where 48 % of the Aboriginal population is school aged (Statistics Canada, 2007, 2008). Responsibility for educating the Aboriginal population rests with the federal department of Indian and Northern Affairs (INAC) which operated 515 schools, with a budget of 1.2 billion dollars, for 109,000 students in the 2007–2008 school year. While 60 % of those students were enrolled in reserve-based, band-run schools, 11.65 % were identified as "special education", an increase of 3.65 % in 2 years (INAC, Personal communication, October, 2008).

The impact of this population shift is being felt in schools across the country and teachers, especially those in urban or northern communities, are quickly discovering a much broader interpretation of what is meant by diverse classrooms. Hutchinson (2007), commenting on this increasing diversity, concluded: "inclusive education is an issue within the context of Canadian society, not just within the context of Canadian schools … In Canada, if we choose to teach, we are choosing to teach in inclusive settings" (p. xxv). Consequently, the impact on teacher training, curriculum, and instruction is significant. Equally significant, given the push toward enhanced achievement and assessment, is the impact on recognising individual need within such a pluralistic population, given the well-documented concern for the accuracy of standardised assessment for students of diverse cultural backgrounds (Armour-Thomas, 1992; Cummins, 1984; Gopaul-McNichol & Armour-Thomas, 2002; Lewis, 1998; Samunda, 1975, 1998). While assessment practices may likely be "an inescapable reality of the educational, social, and economic enterprise of any modern society" (Samunda, 1998, p. 1), their use in this diverse Canadian context is concerning. Approaches to assessment, which is often the gate-keeper to support services, are at the forefront of this concern.

13.1.2 Diversity Concerns

While concern for assessing Aboriginal youth is evident, there is also growing concern for why we assess children at all. The global shift towards inclusive education has shifted our view of diversity, as well as how we accommodate individual need. It certainly has fostered a debate as to why a child must be labelled as "disabled" before supports are provided. In fact, the school reform movement has expedited this shift away from segregated sites and alternate curriculum by fuelling much criticism of special education practices. Hockenbury et al. (2000) summarise current criticisms of special education as clustering around seven emergent themes:

- It is a place that should become a service;
- It is a separate system but should be an integrated system;
- It identifies and stigmatises students but should be offered without labels;
- It has no particularly effective methods and could be replaced by good general education;
- It returns few students to general education but should return most;
- It has changed incrementally but should be radically reformed; and
- It is needed now but should not be needed if general education is reformed. (p. 4)

Moreover, Skrtic (1995) criticises that special education is based in a "theory of human pathology" where difference is measured and pathologised so as to rationalise an organisational approach to accommodating it, despite the impact of being marginalised by a label. Concern for labelling children is shared by Lipsky and Gartner (1997), who call for a model that is based on displayed need rather than a prescribed label. Foucault (1977) questions the social construction of "disability" while Fulcher (1989) refers to this practice of testing and labelling as a "discursive social practice" that is designed to marginalise and disempower. Danforth (1999) calls for a shift toward creating democratic approaches to enhancing dignity. He challenges educators to "demystify the power of the professional" so that children are not labelled via psychological testing. Sergiovanni (1994) references the resultant perspective and approach as community building, where diversity is valued as part of the social fabric of the community. Noddings (1992) endorses this view of diversity, stressing that schools have a responsibility to promote an "ethic of caring" in communities via positive classroom experiences for children. Subsequently, the need for testing children for "disability status" is being replaced by inclusive education, anchored in a more democratic school system with programs that strive to create environments which embrace all differences (Sands, Kozelski, & French, 2001; Smith, 1998; Stainback & Stainback, 1992; Thomas, 1997).

This paradigm shift is raising scepticism about existing practices of "testing" students to determine whether they fit a label. In part, this scepticism stems from recognition that a disproportionate number of students are being labelled as disabled (Lupart, 1999; Philpott & Dibbon, 2008) *especially* among minority groups (Duren-Green, McIntosh, Cook-Morales, & Robinson, 2005). Given the shift in demographics and a push toward democratic, inclusive schools, the need and the effectiveness of "testing" students is being questioned. These questions become more critical as educational practices for Aboriginal groups move under closer scrutiny.

In fact, there is also a growing recognition of an inherent preference for inclusive models of education within Aboriginal schools themselves. Hurton (2002) identified this preference towards inclusion among Aboriginals stating that, "education of First Nations students is inclusive and culturally relevant"; this preference "has its historical roots from the residential schools era, but is also influenced by the lack of special education funding" (p. 13). Philpott et al. (2004a) report that inclusion is a core cultural value of Aboriginal people: "Instead of viewing differences as something to be tolerated and accepted, Aboriginal culture sees difference as being essential to the group's survival and as such are to be celebrated" (p. 64). This is supported by Ross (1992), who argues that individual differences are respected and valued, as being essential to the group's survival and central to Aboriginal faith. What emerges, Ross argues, is "a kind of mandatory egalitarianism, not only in terms of possessions but in all other respects as well, including criticism, praise, advice-giving, censure" (p. 39). Similarly, Henriksen (1993) comments upon this innate attribute of inclusivity among First Nations people. He argues that difference does not divide the people but rather unites them into a stronger repertoire of skills and attributes with which to face daily life and achieve group success.

13.1.3 Assessment Concerns

Long before shifting demographics necessitated a re-examination of assessment practices for Aboriginal students, concern had been growing for the very nature of assessment itself. Ysseldyke, Algozzine, and Thurlow (1991) articulated this by concluding: "a major issue in assessment is the link between assessment information and instruction… Unfortunately much that goes on in the assessment of students with disabilities has very limited relevance to intervention" (p. 24). Well before then, Ysseldyke and Shinn (1981) raised concern, reporting that "13.5 % of teachers claimed that these [psychoeducational] assessments were *slightly helpful* or better, and 77.3 % claimed that these [psychoeducational] assessments were *not relevant, no help,* or *detrimental*". They went on to report that teachers and parents both viewed psychologists' reports as being very difficult to comprehend and, therefore, having little impact on interventions.

These concerns have persisted over the years and the very appropriateness of standardised testing has remained a hotly debated issue (Grobe & McCall, 2004; Holdnack & Weiss, 2006; Lipsky & Gartner, 1998; Zigmond & Baker, 1995). Ashman and Conway (1993) elaborated on the history of this concern:

> These tests have come under considerable criticism over the past two decades because of three characteristics: their bias against minority groups and those with identifiable learning difficulties; their inability to partial out the contributions of motivation, personality and setting; and their inability to provide information that can be translated into instructional practice. (p. 25)

These sentiments were echoed by Black and William (1998) who postulated that the more removed from the classroom assessment is, the less impact it has on instruction. McLaughlin (1991) also commented that few tests measure attributes or variables that are directly related to learning, higher order thinking, or problem solving. Because tests do not tap complex cognitive processes, they do not support classroom practices that are directed toward teaching them. Ashman and Conway (1993) added:

> In our view, it is unrealistic to make instructional decisions that are unrelated to, or removed from, the context in which learning occurs. It is for this reason we believe that information derived from assessment processes must be linked explicitly with classroom instruction practices. (p. 35)

They went on to say:

> As educational policy and practice has moved toward greater inclusion of children with special needs in mainstream classes, teachers have come under greater pressure to provide an appropriate education for all children under their care. Perhaps more than ever before, there is now a need for all information relevant to the teaching and remediation of students to be accessible to, and useable by, teachers. Up to the present time, much data collected by clinicians and other specialists have not been of assistance in program planning or instructional design. (p. 41)

In addition to the appropriateness and the effectiveness of assessment practices, there is a recognised disconnect between the assessor and the teacher. Contemporary educational practices are collaborative in nature and when a child with a unique learning need is identified, this collaboration becomes more essential. However, Ashman and Conway (1993) concluded:

> Clinicians, such as school psychologists and counsellors, spend a considerable part of their professional lives administering and scoring standardised psychological and achievement tests with the objective of identifying, screening and classifying students, and teachers also spend a good part of their professional lives preparing students for assessment, and administering and scoring tests that provide evidence of mastery over the curriculum: it indeed seems that there is an inherent inefficiency in testing for classification and testing again to establish goals for instruction or remediation (p. 25) [and]... Without doubt, clinicians have been reluctant to involve themselves in classroom remediation or instruction, but teachers also have been less than enthusiastic about the ability of psychologists and counsellors to collaborate with them. (p. 33)

These concerns become heightened when we consider students of Aboriginal backgrounds. In fact, there is little debate at all over the validity of standardised approaches to "diagnose" Aboriginal children, much less inform their programs. Gopaul-McNichol and Armour-Thomas (2002) concluded "that standardized tests are invalid for students of non-dominant cultures" (p. 5). They went on to suggest that attempts to assess these children:

> reflect Western/Anglo/Euro epistemological traditions [in which] there is a tendency to generalize findings to other groups that do not share those perspectives. Often, studies do not include operationally definable constructs of culture and when they do, terms like *culturally disadvantaged* or *cultural deprivation* betray an ethnocentric bias. (p. 9)

Samunda (1998) cautioned that ensuring accuracy of assessment findings for minority children is not as simple as selecting an instrument that is marketed as culture-fair. He stated that "even the so-called culture-fair tests are really only culture-reduced because they assume that examinees have been socialized and educated in the culture in which the test originated" (p. 17). He called for a broader view of assessment that moves beyond measurement to facilitating individual development. While assessment practices have an important role in education, an over-reliance on standardised instruments for children of diverse cultural backgrounds has had a negative effect. Samunda concluded that:

> the issue of test results and their interpretation extends beyond concerns that relate to their use in the school systems. Tests can have dire social and economic consequences for those individuals who are labelled and placed in minimal curricular programs, and thus curtailed from further secondary or tertiary education. Tests and their results, therefore, can bring disastrous outcomes affecting the lives and aspirations of minorities in any society. (p. 3)

Again, caution and concern dominate the discourse on assessment practices among Aboriginal students with a preference towards optimising instruction and opportunity versus attempting to measure ability. While *culturally fairer* assessment practices are being recognised, the need for such is being lessened by a model of education which aspires toward a reduced need to label children.

Collectively, this debate challenges educators to reflect upon and reconsider models for identifying individualised need, certainly to re-examine the disconnect between assessing and informing programs. Perhaps it calls for a return to the very nature of *assessment* itself which, as noted by Wiggins (1993), is derived from the Latin *assidere*, meaning "to sit beside or with". Sattler (2001) articulated this process approach of identifying need with a limited and specific role for testing. He referenced "the four pillars of assessment" as being observation, interviews, informal assessment and testing. The current debate clearly identifies practice which moves to testing as an initial step in identifying need.

Perhaps the problem is rooted as much in a disconnect between policy and practice as in a disconnect between assessment and instruction. Too often practice is concerned with screening and classification of students rather than finding ways to improve their performance in the classroom. Current policy is indeed inclusionary in its language, but the actuality of current models of education is exclusionary at best, as it requires students to be diagnosed first in order to qualify for resources. Earl (2003) commented that the theoretical model which assessment is based on is supposed to be a process-oriented practice that is driven by parents and teachers. In this model, struggling students are supposed to be monitored and the teacher consults with team members and adapts the programme accordingly *before* formalised testing is even considered. Earl identified that what happens in current models of education is that assessment becomes driven by a need to have students 'qualify for service'. She outlined that this approach serves to undervalue the importance of observations and opinions and leads to assessment which is, as described earlier, separate from instruction.

All these criticisms are based on what was described by Philpott (2007) as the 'old paradigm of assessment' consisting of practice which is summative, quantitative, deficit-based, prescriptive, expert-centred, and static. This constitutes a linear view of ability and individualistic focus on curriculum goals under which differences are merely tolerated. Conversely, Philpott argued for a 'new paradigm of assessment', one which is more formative, qualitative, strengths-based, descriptive, child/family centred, and fluid. It has multiple views of ability and a holistic focus on lifespan goals under which differences are embraced. This approach reflects what Ashman and Conway (1993) outlined:

> All classroom teachers are continually involved in the assessment of students' learning outcomes. Typically, the classroom teacher will become aware of problems being experienced by individual students when they are unable to complete assignments or through discussion with parents. How the teacher deals with this situation will depend upon their ability to provide individualized assistance within the context of the teaching day. In other words, the way in which instruction and remediation is provided is a function of program. (p. 35)

A focus on process, classroom-based assessment doesn't remove the need for "testing" children but it lessens it. It places it in a continuum of approaches to inform programs, in a system that empowers practitioners, in an environment that values diversity. However, if we have learned anything from this debate it is the urgent need for less rhetoric and more concrete examples. Luckily, there are at least three which stand to inform practitioners.

13.2 Suggested Models

13.2.1 The Innu of Labrador

The task of developing a model of assessment for Aboriginal students which reflects the cautions identified in the literature, balances cultural perspectives, and strives to empower teachers, was undertaken by a team of researchers involved with the Innu of Labrador. Although educational institutions, including those in Labrador, had struggled to earn a place in many Aboriginal communities, for the Innu of Labrador the failure was dramatically more significant (Press, 1995; Samson, 2000/2001). These people were perhaps the last to make contact with the dominant Canadian culture (Mailhot, 1997) and their conflict with Western institutions would become so pronounced that they would be eventually referred to in contemporary media as "Canada's Tibet" (Samson, 2000/2001). At the start of the new millennium they were well into negotiations with the federal government for self-management of their own communities, including assuming charge of their school system. To this end, a team of researchers was invited to conduct a large-scale assessment project, the largest ever completed on Canada's Aboriginal youth, so as to identify the needs of these children and inform a more effective model of education. Assessment was done on 908 school aged students from two isolated coastal communities in Labrador and the final report articulated the creation of a bi-cultural model of education (Philpott, Nesbit, Cahill, & Jeffery, 2004b, 2005). The methodology used by this team affords an opportunity for reflection of those engaged in similar work with Aboriginal youth.

Innu communities had a long-standing concern about educational outcomes, and provincial public documents showed that in the 10 years prior to the study only seven youths graduated high school (Philpott et al., 2004b). Likewise, provincial records also showed alarmingly low attendance rates of less than 50 %. There was also significant concern about a perceived high rate of Foetal Alcohol Spectrum Disorder and the social issues surrounding it. Despite this, the Innu people felt that their children were well behaved, cooperative, intellectually capable and eager to achieve in school. The dominant concerns were about a culturally insensitive model of education and a clash with language where English was the language of instruction, despite Statistics Canada (2001) identifying the Innu as being the most successful Aboriginal group in Canada at retaining its native language. Literally, Innu children arrived at school speaking only Innu-aimun (their native language) and met English speaking teachers who then proceeded to teach them the provincial curriculum in English.

The research team, recognising these linguistic and cultural sensitivities, developed a model of assessment that blended qualitative approaches with carefully selected quantitative instruments in an effort to "focus on the identification of the strengths of Innu children as well as the conditions that enable or impede the application of these strengths when learning" (Philpott et al., 2004b, p. 10).

> The goal was not to diagnose learner diversity but rather articulate a base line for intervention, identify areas where support was needed, and document student need against the reality of the Innu experience with education. The researchers wanted to identify current levels of need within the authentic context that education occurs in these communities. (Philpott, 2006a, p. 371)

Teachers were inserviced on authentic assessment practices and encouraged to share their observations of their students. Qualitative indictors included individual interviews with community leaders, educators, teachers and students. A number of focus groups were also conducted and researchers recorded observations on visits to the schools and communities. Surveys were conducted with teachers, students and parents to gather their perceptions and aspirations on issues ranging from student ability, achievement levels and language proficiency to attendance patterns and career aspirations.

Following extensive reviews of quantitative instruments, the students were assessed using formalised measures that were seen as *culturally fairer*, but used only as a general indicator of functioning. A number of instruments were reviewed for consideration with the majority being discarded as inappropriate for reasons such as content bias, language of administration, limited norm group and lack of cultural relevance to the Innu experience. Qualified professionals were hired to administer selected instruments, with preference being given to individuals who were familiar to the Innu children. Parental consent forms were translated and obtained for all children assessed on cognitive ability measures. The researchers combined data from statistical analyses with the qualitative data collected to provide a comprehensive view of students' needs and strengths. "The findings of the study were not used to categorise students but rather to indicate possible paths that might be used to develop more effective teaching methods and a more appropriate curriculum model" (Philpott, 2006a, p. 372).

What emerged from this data collection and analysis was a dramatic match between the qualitative and the quantitative data:

> Perhaps the most significant finding of the study is that the results validate the perceptions and impressions that key informants – Innu leaders and educators – reported at the outset: Innu youth are of average ability, consistently display diverse strengths and abilities, and lag in formal school achievement levels due, in large part, to poor attendance. This report serves to synthesize and validate these perceptions and articulate a baseline for intervention. It reveals the magnitude of educational need and, at the same time, begins to chart a course for change. (Philpott et al., 2004b, p. 23)

The 2-year study yielded a wealth of data that has gone on to serve as the baseline of an enhanced model of Innu education (Philpott et al., 2005). A 2-year follow-up study on the needs of students in one of these two Innu communities, Natuashish, (Philpott, 2006b) identified dramatic improvements in reading, writing, attendance and school participation. That report concluded that "children who only know school as it exists now in Natuashish, have attendance and achievement levels remarkably close to provincial averages" (p. 22).

The study on Innu children has offered educators of children from culturally and linguistically diverse backgrounds an assessment alternative. It reflects the debate on culturally fair assessment and supports authentic approaches to identifying need and enhancing teaching and learning versus labelling children within a diagnostic/prescriptive model. It reflects the call for authentic assessment that leads to enhanced learning opportunities for children (Burns, 1995; Chappuis, 2005; Hargrove, 2000; Stanley, 2003). More appropriate to this debate is that in the 4 years since the initial study on the Innu children and the implementation of a new model of education, not one Innu child was labelled.

13.2.2 Nunavut's Articulation

While the Innu assessment project validated how carefully conducted assessment can inform programs, the model used in Canada's newest territory, Nunavut, outlines approaches to creating a model of education which has a limited need for assessment.

Like other people of Aboriginal ancestry, the people of Nunavut were successful in assuming autonomy and in 1999 Canada's newest territory was established. In short order the newly established government prioritised a renewed model of education by passing the Education Act as the first piece of legislation. With four official languages, the highest birth rate in Canada, and 96 % of the school-aged population being Inuk, the territory boasts wide use of first language instruction with immersion into English instruction beginning in the elementary grades (Philpott, 2007). It is, however, their articulation of accommodating learner diversity which is particularly intriguing.

Secured in core cultural beliefs, Nunavut views education as stemming "from a foundation of culture, tradition, heritage and language" (Department of Education, Curriculum & School Service, 2002, p. iii). As a result, all educational practices and discourse reflect a mandate to establish curriculum that will solidify culture and education while meeting the needs of all children. Subsequently, the Nunavut Schools Act references *Inuit Qaujimajatuqangit*, the worldview of Inuit culture, as being the foundation of education in Nunavut. A 1999 Council of Nunavut Elders explains this as including:

1. The long-practiced tradition of passing Inuit knowledge, values and teachings from elders to the younger generations,
2. Inuit knowledge in all areas of life,
3. A system of laws, values and consultations before making important decisions that affect the community. (Department of Education, Curriculum & School Service, 2002, p. 9)

To this end, they follow a highly inclusive model of education which strives to empower the classroom teacher with the knowledge, training and skills to accommodate all students. They define inclusion as being:

an attitude and a belief. It is a way of life, a way of living and working together, based on the belief that each individual is valued and does belong. ... Critical to the concept of inclusion is the fact that student support is for all students and not just for those commonly referred to as having special needs. All students may require some form of support at some time in their education. (Department of Education, Curriculum & School Services, 2002, p. 10)

Philpott (2007) outlines this articulation of inclusion:

In a 2006 document entitled *Inclusive Education in Nunavut Schools: Student Support Handbook* (Department of Education, Curriculum & School Service, 2006), a model is proposed to support regular classroom placement by building teacher capacity and knowledge. While 75–80 % of students are envisioned as having their needs met by classroom teachers trained in diverse methodologies, 20 % are seen as needing periodic support that is outlined in an Individual Accommodations Plan, developed by the teacher with input from consultants. It is further imagined that 5–7 % of the population may require more intensive supports for severe learning disabilities, social/emotional issues and/or *high need* issues. These five support options are referenced as *Tumits* which are described as:

pathways/footprints of support. The objective of this support model is to improve the learning environment so as to increase the number of students who can meet the learning outcomes of Nunavut curricula with minimal support and to decrease the number of students who now require intense levels of support because of academic or social/ emotional/ behavioural challenges. The institution of many best practices in the system as a whole should go a long way to increase the number of students who are successful in their learning. There will always be, in any given school population, a small proportion of students who require individualized programs and multiple supports on an ongoing basis in order to meet their learning and life goals. This small group of high needs students requires collaborative, interagency, support service delivery in order to enhance their learning and prepare them for transition to life as contributing adults in their community. (p. 106)

Subsequently, assessment is not seen as having a strong role in Nunavut's model. Paralleling the use of cultural understandings of practice, Nunavut define assessment practice as:

In Nunavut the term *ilitauvalliajunik qaujinasungniq* has been used to describe the process of assessment in schools. This term refers to assessment as a method of "monitoring" students...it represents the dynamic interaction of teaching, learning and assessment.

Assessment should be seen as a process that improves both teaching and learning. The assessment process begins on the day that the students enter the classroom and we, as teachers, begin to learn who they are, what they know, and what they want to know …it is linked closely to goal setting and learning outcomes. It is a collaborative process that involves all the partners in a learning/teaching community – those in the classroom and those in the home and community. It is a process that evolves over time, involving interaction between teaching and learning, and teacher and student. (Department of Education, Curriculum & School Services, 2005, p. 3)

They go on to outline seven key principles of culturally appropriate assessment. It:

1. supports continuous learning for all students;
2. shows respect for all learners;
3. recognises each student's unique talents and skills;
4. emphasises the interdependence, growth, and success of the group;
5. needs to be outcome-based;
6. has different purposes; and
7. is authentic, meaningful, and builds on student strengths. (p. 7)

Nunavut's refusal to label children as different by focusing instead on creating supportive learning environments with empowered teachers does echo the global discourse of inclusive education. Its articulation of culturally defined practice stands in radical contrast to policy and programs in Western schools which tend to use the language of inclusion yet continue to hold to the practice of special education. Yet Nunavut's preference for classroom-based identification of need is reflective of a growing trend toward authentic assessment that will result in enhanced instruction.

13.2.3 Classroom-Based Assessment

Recognition of the role of the classroom teacher in identifying learner need and in developing accommodations is hardly new. In fact, most education systems throughout Western society include some type of pre-referral service that is mandated to occur before any more formalised assessment or intervention begins. This "pre-referral stage" recognises that assessment begins when the teacher/parent first becomes aware of a concern and initiates steps to address it. The goal of the pre-referral stage is to adjust the instructional process to enable the student to be successful, yet appropriately challenged by the curriculum. While the importance of the pre-referral stage cannot be overstated, as outlined earlier in this paper, it is often overlooked or given cursory attention in favour of more formalised testing. It is further hampered by diverse levels of training among classroom teachers.

Nonetheless, it is possible to make pre-referral intervention work by incorporating both dynamic and authentic assessment into the process. Dynamic assessment has been proposed by Moore-Brown, Huerta, Uranga-Hernandez, and Pena (2006) "as a way of distinguishing between culturally and linguistically based learning disabilities and true learning disabilities" (p. 210). The authors go on to state:

In the traditional approach, each team member typically completed the assessment independently and then shared the results with the others. Because of the nature of this study, the team members shared the same experiences by conducting the assessment while the others observed. In doing so, their conversations about how the students performed on various tasks became richer, because the experience was a shared experience and not one reported by only one member. (p. 215)

Authentic assessment is an essential tool at the pre-referral stage which allows for more accurate and informed assessment of the barriers to student achievement. Wiggins (1993) defined authentic assessment as:

engaging and worthy problems or questions of importance, in which students must use knowledge to fashion performances effectively and creatively. The tasks are either replicas of or analogous to the kinds of problems faced by adult citizens and consumers or professionals in the field. (p. 229)

Other articulations of this pre-referral, authentic approach to assessment exist. Lerner and Johns (2009) describe an approach called *clinical teaching* which Lerner has developed and promoted over the past decades.

The goal of clinical teaching is to tailor the learning experiences for the unique needs of the individual student. By using information gathered through the evaluation of the student, along with an analysis of the student's specific learning characteristics, the clinical teacher designs a plan of instruction for that student. Assessment does not stop when teaching begins. In fact, the essence of clinical teaching is that assessment and instruction are interwoven. The clinical teacher modifies the teaching as new needs become apparent. (p. 88)

Likewise, Stanovich and Jordan (2000) describe a similar approach to classroom assessment. They refer to this as creating *interventionist teachers*, who recognise and embrace the ...

increasing classroom diversity resulting from changes in the socio-cultural conditions and educational policy, engage in more academic interactions with their students and are more persistent in actively assisting students to construct understanding, and demonstrate more effective teaching behaviors. (pp. 236–237)

Differentiated instruction has been presented as yet another conceptualisation of this focus of assessment as a part of the teaching process. Cox (2008) offers an explanation of this approach:

This requires individualizing learning for each student by arranging the classroom and the entire school for small group, large group and individualized learning. The goal is to maximize the capacity of each learner by teaching in ways that help all learners bridge gaps in understanding and skill and help each learner grow as much and as quickly as he or she can. (p. 53)

Currently, this recognition of the teacher as initial assessor and as support planner is being re-conceptualised, this time as *Response to Intervention* (*RTI*). Danielson, Doolittle, and Bradley (2005) outline that this approach reinforces "a more direct link between assessment procedures and instructional interventions, which will be more useful than current practices to teachers making instructional and curriculum decisions" (p. 138). Gibbons (2004) stated that:

RTI is a problem solving approach that involves providing quality interventions to at-risk students and providing special education services to those students who fail to respond to well-designed interventions, and do not demonstrate evidence for exclusionary criteria. RTI approaches share three essential components (1) emphasis on universal screening of all students for achievement difficulties, (2) placement in early intervention programs, and (3) careful monitoring of progress and accountability for results. (p. 1)

Gibbons (2004) hailed this approach as avoiding the pitfalls of our current "diagnose first" practice and outlined numerous advantages. She stated:

> There are many advantages to an RTI. First the "Wait to Fail" model is eliminated, and schools can operate under a preventative model focused on early intervention. Second, there is a clear link between assessment and intervention. Third, the emphasis in special education is shifted away from eligibility and focused toward getting children the interventions they need to be successful. Fourth, the model is conceptual as well as practical. Fifth, the model is multidisciplinary and increases teaming. By creating a language of skills and instruction as opposed to disability and pathology, barriers between general and special education may be removed. Sixth, school psychologists will have increased time to focus on functional assessment activities that are directly linked to intervention planning. Finally, the model emphasises serving students in the Least Restrictive Environment. (p. 2)

Bradley, Danielson, and Doolittle (2007) echoed these strengths, stating that teachers would be empowered to intervene earlier for students by focusing on support versus label. They stated: "RTI begins with the implementation of scientifically based, school-wide instructional interventions and promotes intervention at the first indication of non-response to traditional classroom instruction…shift of emphasis from process to outcomes" (p. 8).

The consideration of RTI however, does not come without cautions. First and foremost is the need for appropriate teacher training and professional development. Danielson et al. (2005) acknowledged that: "In order to successfully modify the curriculum with the use of universal design or other evidence-based strategies, general education teachers will need appropriate training or, at least, access to special education teachers who have received high-quality training" (p. 138). Stanovich and Jordan (2000) also stated that, "it is especially important that we determine what characteristics of teachers, classrooms, and schools are most important for the effective inclusion of students with learning disabilities. Clearly, the general education classroom teacher is the key to successful inclusion" (p. 237).

Would such an approach work in an Aboriginal context? This question was explored by Gee (2001), who commented specifically on the appropriateness of RTI for children from minority backgrounds. He cautioned that "research based interventions must be culturally, linguistically and socially appropriate. One size does not fit all, especially as it applies to language/reading difficulties." Klingner and Edwards (2006) also explored the usefulness of this approach across cultures and also stressed a need for caution in using any approach to identification/intervention for minority status children, including RTI. They cautioned that family values and linguistic/culturally sensitive interventions must be the hallmark of a culturally appropriate interpretation of RTI. They also cautioned that interventions must be "relevant to the contextualized experiences, knowledge and culture of the child, including explicit intense training in underlying skills and pre-requisite concepts and multi-faceted approaches with frequent opportunities to practice skills in meaningful contexts" (p. 112).

A final caution in the considered implementation of an RTI approach for Aboriginal students is that it doesn't negate a place for more formalised assessment approaches. "At best the RTI model can only infer that a processing deficit exists and, without direct assessment, there is no way to determine if a student may possess SLD [specific learning disability] as currently conceptualized" (Kavale, Holdnack, & Mostert, 2006, p. 115). Though a place remains for psycho-educational assessment, Klassen (2002) noted that "Consultation and whole-school intervention may become more germane for most school psychologists; classroom and special education teachers may assume a greater role in the assessment and identification process" (p. 214).

Summarily, Danielson et al. (2005) stated that:

> Although numerous questions remain regarding broad implementation of RTI, this process currently reflects the best thinking on how to better link assessment and instruction for children with SLD [specific learning disabilities], and holds the most promise, with further study and refinement, for a more effective method of ensuring that the appropriate children are identified in an efficient manner. (p. 138)

13.3 Conclusion

13.3.1 Implications for Educational Leaders

The need for Canadian education leaders to encourage a debate on assessment practices for all children is clear. As contemporary schools move through shifting paradigms of instruction, curriculum and diversity, methods of screening children for individualised service are being examined much more critically. Along with this re-examination will be a discussion of the language which is used to articulate children's needs. This is especially so as we view inclusive practice as including different cultures, values, faiths and abilities. Traditional models, which labelled difference, are growing increasingly antiquated as the focus shifts toward empowering classroom teachers.

However, it is imperative that educational leaders ensure that debate is guided by a pragmatic acceptance of the importance of a place for clinical assessment, a place where qualitative and quantitative approaches to collecting indicators of need are carefully blended. The three models presented herein, Nunavut's articulation of assessment, the model used with the Innu of Labrador, and the Response to Intervention model, all acknowledge such a place for some formalised approaches, especially for children with complex, multiple needs. Even though, the models used in Nunavut and Labrador are not transferable to other regions, they do stand as strong examples of alternative, culturally sensitive practice. Educational leaders can use them as examples of innovation that balances good practice with local context. Effective assessment, especially culturally sensitive assessment, must be seen as being a teacher-driven process to optimise a child's learning opportunities. It relies on standardised approaches and "outside" clinicians not as a means to *allow* the child to receive supports but rather to *complement* the services already underway. It is a preventative model that builds capacity in the classroom without risking the ill effects of labelling difference.

It is also imperative that educational leaders create collaborative environments that recognise a more complex and expanded role for classroom teachers and team decision making. Dettmer, Dyck, and Thurston (2005) discussed the critical nature of establishing clear understandings of collaboration when attempting to identify and respond to complex student needs. They defined effective school collaboration as "interaction in which school personnel and families confer, consult and collaborate as a team to identify learning and behavioural needs and to plan, implement, evaluate and revise as needed the educational programs that are expected to serve those needs" (p. 6). Morse (1996) suggested that such would be the reality of inclusive schools and an absolute necessity to effectively respond to the needs of diverse students. He wrote:

> We either find a better way to relate to each other in solving our problems or we go down to defeat. Rejecting collaboration is not an option. Collaboration is a step up in democratic process, going beyond compromise and cooperation to shared understanding and shared meaning in decision making. This is not a simple upgrading: It is a transformation. (p. xii)

Friend (2000) supported this call for a transformation in assessment approaches, as well as models of care, and suggested training and leadership to ensure it occurs:

> the increased complexity of educating students with special needs, the deluge of new information being produced and disseminated about teaching and learning, and the ongoing school reform efforts suggest that for professionals to manage their jobs, collaboration must keep pace with the increasing demand for its practice. (p. 132)

Leaders must accept responsibility to ensure that, in order for this to happen, assessors, certainly clinicians who work outside the classroom space, must shift from consultation to collaboration. Friend and Cook (2003) commented on this and differentiated the term *consultation* (which is, in their view, often characterised by an unequal relationship between participants) from *collaboration*. Their rather precise definition of *collaboration* spelled out the difference: "Interpersonal collaboration is a style for direct interaction between at least two *co-equal parties* voluntarily engaged in shared decision-making as they work toward a common goal" (p. 5). This promotion of equality of perspective, shared input, and sensitivity to others, anchors both the model used in Nunavut, as well as the RTI model.

> In much the same way that the teaching and learning process is a collaborative activity between the teacher and student, so clinicians must work with classroom teachers to ensure that the information collected in the psychologist's office will contribute to the use of more efficient and relevant instructional strategies within the classroom. (Ashman & Conway, 1993. p. 27)

This shift in thinking toward effecting change by focusing on collaboration and innovative leadership is highly relevant in any context, not just Canadian, given how quickly change is occurring. In fact, it has been argued that at no point in our history has the need for effective leadership to embrace and accommodate differences been more urgent (Philpott, Furey, & Penney, 2010). Today, educational leaders must understand the importance of classroom teachers being well trained on differing abilities and differing cultures to ensure teaching aligns with student specific accommodations and prevents stereotypes/discrimination (Golder, Jones, & Quinn, 2009). In order for this to happen, educational leaders must be innovative in establishing professional development on both acquiring and using teaching strategies for instructional differentiation (Griffin, Jitendra, & League, 2009; Jenkins & Ornelles,

2009). Classroom teachers must be supported in understanding student abilities, in assuming greater responsibility, and in integrating effective teaching strategies (Golder et al., 2009; Jenkins & Ornelles, 2009; Lohrmann, Boggs, & Bambara, 2006). Professional development opportunities must respond to the needs of teachers and promote indepth, empirically-validated teaching strategies for specific curricular areas, as well as social/emotional needs (Baker & Martin, 2008; Forlin & Hopewell, 2006; Leko & Browneil, 2009).

Providing leadership for this shift in practice is predicated by a re-examination of preservice training for teachers and school administrators. Crocker and Dibbon (2008), in a national study on teacher readiness to identify or respond to diverse learning needs, reported that while 81 % of school principals ranked training in diversity as being important to new teachers, only 8 % felt that current graduates were prepared to face the realities of today's classrooms. More pertinent to a debate on shifting assessment models, they reported that while 90 % of Canadian school principals ranked training in educational assessment as very important, only 7 % of them reported that current graduates were well prepared in this area.

Nonetheless, there is little doubt that existing models, where students either have to "wait to fail" or be "labelled" before they can qualify for specialised services, offer little for those exploring assessment paradigms for Aboriginal youth. A new model is emerging which attempts to strike a balance between this call for higher achievement, a strengthened curriculum, a philosophy of inclusion, and an active promoting of Aboriginal identity. As this continues to emerge, preservice teacher training will evolve as a factor for lasting change. Although this "may seem a Herculean task, it is politically more optimistic than the pessimism of structural approaches which in education have not offered policy makers a viable agenda" (Fulcher, 1989, p. 16). Ironically, in this difficult process, Aboriginal people, who have long been impacted by structural approaches, ineffective policy, and the stigma of being "labelled" to qualify for support services, may well display leadership in establishing this viable agenda.

References

Armour-Thomas, E. (1992). Intellectual assessment of children from culturally diverse backgrounds. *School Psychology Review, 21*(4), 552–565.

Armstrong, F., Armstrong, D., & Barton, L. (2000). *Inclusive education: Policy, contexts and comparative perspectives.* London, UK: David Fulton. Blackwell Press.

Ashman, A. F., & Conway, R. N. F. (1993). Examining the links between psychoeducational assessment, instruction and remediation. *International Journal of Disability, Development and Education, 40*(1), 23–44.

Baker, C., & Martin, B. (2008). An examination of stakeholders' perceptions of the collaborative process utilized within a school-linked integrated partnership. *Journal of School Public Relations, 29*(1), 15–43.

Black, P., & William, D. (1998). Inside the black box: Raising standards through classroom assessment. *Phi Delta Kappan, 80*(2), 139–148.

Bradley, R., Danielson, L., & Doolittle, J. (2007, May/June). Responsiveness to intervention: 1997–2007. *Teaching Exceptional Children, 39*, 8–12.

Burns, G. E. (1995). Factors and themes in native education and school boards/First Nations tuition negations and tuition agreement schooling. *Canadian Journal of Native Education, 22*(1), 53–67.

Chappuis, J. (2005, November). Helping students understand assessment. *Educational Leadership, 63*, 39–43.

Council of Ministers of Education. (2004). *Quality education for all young people: Challenges, trends, and priorities.* Retrieved from: www.cmec.ca/international/unesco/ice47.en.stm

Cox, S. G. (2008). Differentiated instruction in the elementary classroom. *The Education Digest, 73*(9), 52–54.

Crocker, R., & Dibbon, D. (2008). *Teacher education in Canada.* Kelowna, BC, Canada: Society of the Advancement of Excellence in Education.

Cummins, J. (1984). *Bilingualism and special education: Issues in assessment and pedagogy.* San Diego, CA: College Hill.

Danforth, S. (1999). Pragmatism and the scientific validation of professional practices in American special education. *Disability & Society, 14*(6), 733–751.

Danielson, L., Doolittle, J., & Bradley, R. (2005). Past accomplishments and future challenges. *Learning Disability Quarterly, 28*(2), 137–139.

Department of Education, Curriculum & School Services. (2002). *Supporting inclusion in Nunavut: A discussion paper on inclusive education and student support.* Iqaluit, NU, Canada: Government of Nunavut.

Department of Education, Curriculum & School Services. (2005). *School enrollment report for 2005/06.* Iqaluit, NU, Canada: Government of Nunavut.

Dettmer, P. A., Dyck, N. T., & Thurston, L. P. (2005). *Consultation, collaboration and team work for students with special needs* (5th ed.). New York, NY: Pearson Education.

Duren-Green, T., McIntosh, A. S., Cook-Morales, V. J., & Robinson, Z. C. (2005). From old schools to tomorrow's schools: Psychoeducational assessment of African-American students. *Remedial and Special Education, 26*(2), 82–92.

Earl, L. M. (2003). *Assessment as learning: Using classroom assessment to maximize student learning* (2nd ed.). Thousand Oaks, CA: Corwin Press.

Forlin, C., & Hopewell, T. (2006). Inclusion – The heart of the matter: Trainee teachers' perceptions of a parent's journey. *British Journal of Special Education, 33*(2), 55–61.

Foucault, M. (1977). Intellectuals and power: A conversation between Michael Foucault and Giles Deleuze. In D. Bouchard (Ed.), *Language, counter-memory, practice: Selected essays and interviews by Michael Foucault* (pp. 205–217). Oxford, UK: Basil Blackwell Press.

Friend, M. (2000). Myths and misunderstandings about professional collaboration. *Remedial and Special Education, 21*(3), 130–132.

Friend, M., & Cook, L. (2003). *Interactions: Collaboration skills for school professionals* (4th ed.). White Plains, NY: Longman.

Fulcher, G. (1989). *Disabling policies? A comparative approach to education policy and disability.* London, UK: The Farmer Press.

Gee, J. P. (2001). A socio-cultural perspective on early literacy development. In S. B. Newman & D. K. Dickinson (Eds.), *Handbook of early literacy research* (pp. 30–42). New York, NY: Guildford Press.

Gibbons, K. (2004). *Frequently asked questions (FAQ) regarding response to intervention (RTI) and upcoming idea reauthorization.* Retrieved from: http://www.mnase.org

Golder, G., Jones, N., & Quinn, E. E. (2009). Strengthening the special educational needs element of initial teacher training and education. *British Journal of Special Education, 36*(4), 183–190.

Gopaul-McNichol, S., & Armour-Thomas, E. (2002). *Assessment and culture: Psychological tests with minority populations.* San Diego, CA: Academic.

Goulet, L. (2001). Two teachers of Aboriginal students: Effective practice in sociohistorical realities. *Canadian Journal of Native Education, 25*(1), 68–81.

Government of Canada. (1969). *Statement of the Government of Canada on Indian Policy.* Ottawa, ON, Canada: Published under the authority of the Hon. Jean Chrétien, Minister of Indian Affairs and Northern Development. Also known as *The White Paper.*

Griffin, C. C., Jitendra, A. K., & League, M. B. (2009). Novice special educators' instructional practices, communication patterns, and content knowledge for teaching mathematics. *Teacher Education and Special Education, 32*(4), 319–336.

Grobe, W. J., & McCall, D. (2004). Valid uses of student testing as part of authentic and comprehensive student assessment, school reports, and school system accountability: A statement of concern from the International Confederation of Principals. *Educational Horizons, 82*(2), 131–142.

Hargrove, L. J. (2000). Assessment and inclusion: A teacher's perspective. *Preventing School Failure, 45*(1), 18–21.

Hawthorne, H. B. (1967). *A survey of the contemporary Indians of Canada: Economic, political, educational needs and policies.* Ottawa, ON, Canada: Queen's Printer.

Henriksen, G. (1993). *Life and death among the Mushuau Innu of northern Labrador.* St. John's, NL, Canada: ISER.

Hockenbury, J. C., Kauffman, J. M., & Hallahan, D. P. (2000). What is right about special education. *Exceptionality, 8*(1), 3–11.

Holdnack, J. A., & Weiss, L. G. (2006). IDEA 2004: Anticipated implications for clinical practice – Integrating assessment and intervention. *Psychology in the Schools, 43*(8), 871–882.

Hurton, G. (2002). *A review of First Nations special education policies and funding directions within the Canadian context: Minister's national working group on education. Final report.* Ottawa, ON, Canada: Government of Canada.

Hutchinson, N. L. (2007). *Inclusion of exceptional learners in Canadian schools.* Toronto, ON, Canada: Pearson Canada.

Jenkins, A., & Ornelles, C. (2009). Determining professional development needs of general educators in teaching students with disabilities in Hawaii. *Professional Development in Education, 35*(4), 635–654.

Kavale, K. A., Holdnack, J. A., & Mostert, M. P. (2006). Responsiveness to intervention and the identification of specific learning disabilities: A critique and alternative proposal. *Learning Disabilities Quarterly, 29*(2), 113–127.

Klassen, B. (2002). The changing landscape of learning disabilities in Canada: Definitions and practice from 1989–2000. *School Psychology International, 23*(2), 199–219.

Klingner, J. K., & Edwards, P. A. (2006). Cultural considerations with response to intervention models. *Reading Research Quarterly, 41*(1), 108–117.

Leko, M. M., & Browneil, M. T. (2009). Crafting quality professional development for special educators what school leaders should know. *Teaching Exceptional Children, 42*(1), 64–70.

Lerner, J., & Johns, B. (2009). *Learning disabilities and related mild disabilities: Characteristics, teaching strategies, and new directions* (11th ed.). Boston, MA: Houghton/Mifflin.

Lewis, J. E. (1998). Nontraditional uses of traditional aptitude tests. In R. J. Samunda, R. Feuerstein, A. S. Kauffman, J. E. Lewis, R. J. Sternberg, & Associates (Eds.), *Advances in cross-cultural assessment* (pp. 218–241). Thousand Oaks, CA: Sage.

Lipsky, D. K., & Gartner, A. (1997). *Inclusion and school reform.* Baltimore, MD: Paul H. Brookes Publishing Company.

Lipsky, D. K., & Gartner, A. (1998). Taking inclusion into the future. *Educational Leadership, 30*(2), 198–203.

Lohrmann, S., Boggs, E. M., & Bambara, L. M. (2006). Elementary education teachers' beliefs about essential supports needed to successfully include students with developmental disabilities who engage in challenging behaviors. *Research and Practice for Persons with Severe Disabilities, 31*(2), 157–173.

Lupart, J. L. (1999, February 16–17). *Inching toward inclusion: The excellence/equity dilemma in our schools.* Paper presented at PCERA symposium, Ottawa, ON, Canada.

Mailhot, J. (1997). *In the land of the Innu: The people of Sheshatshit* (A. Harvey, Trans.). St. John's, NL, Canada: ISER Books.

McLaughlin, M. W. (1991). Test-based account as a reform strategy. *Phi Delta Kappan, 73*, 248–251.

Mittler, P. (2000). *Working towards inclusive education: Social contexts.* London, UK: David Fulton.

Moore-Brown, B., Huerta, M., Uranga-Hernandez, Y., & Pena, E. D. (2006). Using dynamic assessment to evaluate children with suspected learning disabilities. *Intervention in School and Clinic, 41*(4), 209–217.

Morse, W. C. (1996). Forward. In M. Friend & L. Cook (Eds.), *Interactions: Collaboration skills for school professionals* (pp. xiii–xvii). White Plains, NY: Longman.

National Indian Brotherhood (now the Assembly of First Nations). (1972). *Indian control of Indian education*. Ottawa, ON, Canada: Author.

Noddings, N. (1992). *The challenge to care in schools: An alternative to care in schools*. New York, NY: Teachers College Press.

Office of the Auditor General of Canada. (2004, November). *Indian and Northern Affairs Canada- educational program and post-secondary student support* (sect. 5.2). Retrieved from: http://www.oag-bvg.gc.ca/domino.reports.nsf/html/20041105.ce.html

Philpott, D. F. (2006a). Identifying the learning needs of Innu students: Creating a model of culturally appropriate assessment. *Canadian Journal of Native Studies, 26*(2), 361–381.

Philpott, D. F. (2006b). *Updated achievement/attendance indicators on Natuashish students*. Goose Bay, NL: Canada Report to the Labrador School District. Principal Researcher.

Philpott, D. F. (2007). Assessing without labels: Inclusive education in the Canadian context. *Exceptionality Education Canada, 17*(3), 3–34.

Philpott, D. F., & Dibbon, D. (2008). The evolution of disability studies amidst school reform in Newfoundland and Labrador. *The Morning Watch, 36*(1–22), 1–30.

Philpott, D. F., Furey, E., & Penney, S. C. (2010). Promoting leadership in the ongoing professional development of teachers: Responding to globalization and inclusion. *Exceptionality Education International, 20*(2), 38–54.

Philpott, D. F., Nesbit, W., Cahill, M., & Jeffery, G. (2004a). Supporting learner diversity in aboriginal schools: The emergence of a cultural paradigm of inclusion. In W. C. Nesbit (Ed.), *Cultural diversity and education: Interface issues* (pp. 51–75). St. John's, NL, Canada: Memorial University of Newfoundland.

Philpott, D. F., Nesbit, W. C., Cahill, M., & Jeffery, G. H. (2004b). *An educational profile of the learning needs of Innu youth*. St. John's, NL, Canada: Memorial University of Newfoundland.

Philpott, D. F., Nesbit, W. C., Cahill, M., & Jeffery, G. H. (2005). *Enhancing Innu education: A report to the Education Steering Committee*. St. John's, NL, Canada: Memorial University of Newfoundland.

Press, H. (1995). Davis Inlet in crisis: Will the lessons ever be learned? *Canadian Journal of Native Studies, 15*(2), 187–209.

Ross, R. (1992). *Dancing with a ghost*. Toronto, ON, Canada: Reed Books.

Samson, C. (2000/2001). Teaching lies: The Innu experience of schooling. *London Journal of Canadian Studies, 16*, 84–102.

Samunda, R. J. (1975). From ethnocentrism to a multicultural perspective in educational testing. *Journal of Afro-American Issues, 3*(1), 4–17.

Samunda, R. J. (1998). Cross-cultural assessment: Issues and alternatives. In R. J. Samunda, R. Feuerstein, A. S. Kauffman, J. E. Lewis, R. J. Sternberg, & Associates (Eds.), *Advances in cross-cultural assessment* (pp. 1–19). Thousand Oaks, CA: Sage.

Sands, D. S., Kozelski, E., & French, N. (2001). *Inclusive education for the 21st century*. Canada Wadsworth Thomson Learning. Toronto, Canada.

Sattler, J. M. (2001). *Assessment of children: Cognitive applications* (4th ed.). San Diego, CA: Jerome M. Sattler, Publisher.

Sergiovanni, T. (1994). *Building community in schools*. San Francisco, CA: Jossey-Bass.

Skrtic, T. M. (1995). The special education knowledge tradition: Crisis and opportunity. In E. L. Meyen & T. M. Skrtic (Eds.), *Special education and student disability: An introduction – Traditional, emerging, and alternative perspectives*. Denver, CO: Love Publishing Company.

Smith, J. D. (1998). *Inclusion: Schools for all students*. New York, NY: Wadsworth Publishing Company.

Stainback, S., & Stainback, W. (1992). *Curriculum considerations in inclusive schools: Facilitating learning in inclusive classrooms*. Toronto, ON, Canada: Paul H. Brookes Publishing Co.

Stanley, L. D. (2003). Developments in curriculum-based measurement. *The Journal of Special Education, 37*(3), 184–192.

Stanovich, P. J., & Jordan, A. (2000). Effective teaching as effective intervention. *Learning Disabilities: A Multidisciplinary Journal, 10*(4), 235–238.

Statistics Canada. (2001). *2001 community profiles (St. John's, Newfoundland and Labrador, Canada)*. Retrieved from: http://www.statcan.ca/

Statistics Canada. (2007). *Portrait of the Canadian population 2006*. Retrieved from: http://www12.statcan.ca/english/census06/analysis/popdwell/highlights.cfm

Statistics Canada. (2008). *The Daily*. Retrieved from: http://www12.statcan.ca/english/070426/d070426a.html

Thomas, G. (1997). Inclusive schools for an inclusive society. *British Journal of Special Education, 24*(3), 103–107.

Wiggins, G. P. (1993). *Assessing student performance: Exploring the purpose and limits of testing*. San Francisco, CA: Jossey-Bass.

Wotherspoon, T. (2001, March 8–9). *The dynamics of social inclusion and exclusion in public education in Canada*. Paper presented at The Canadian Council on Social Development. Retrieved from: http://www.ccsd.ca/subsites/inclusion/bp/tw.htm

Ysseldyke, J. E., Algozzine, B., & Thurlow, M. L. (1991). *Critical issues in special education* (2nd ed.). Boston, MA: Houghton Mifflin.

Ysseldyke, J. E., & Shinn, M. R. (1981). Psychoeducational evaluation: Procedures, considerations, and limitations. In D. Hallahan & J. Kauffman (Eds.), *The handbook of special education*. Englewood Cliffs, NJ: Prentice Hall.

Zigmond, N., & Baker, J. M. (1995). Concluding comments: Current and future practices in inclusive schooling. *The Journal of Special Education, 29*(2), 245–250.

Chapter 14
Assessment Practices and Aboriginal Students

Jacqueline Ottmann and Joan Jeary

Abstract Aboriginal or Indigenous student achievement is multidimensional and complex in Canada and in an international context. Although successes are experienced by Aboriginal students, there continue to be barriers and challenges (e.g., socio-cultural factors, school and community perceptions that determine policy and practice) that have negative implications. Statistically, Aboriginal student graduation rates in Canada continue to be disproportional when compared to non-Aboriginal students (a reflection of academic achievement), and Aboriginal students continue to be over-represented in terms of requiring special education programs and services and under-represented in the gifted and talented categories. Since academic achievement and the allocation of Aboriginal students to special education programs are influenced and/or determined by assessment practices implemented by teachers and educational psychologists, the validity and effectiveness (this including the cultural relevance; the knowledge and skill level, and affective orientation of teachers and educational psychologists) of the assessment practices should be critically examined and improved on a regular basis. Disproportionality in special education becomes an issue when it perpetuates the deficit view of Aboriginal students and/or when the precursors or outcomes of special education are biased or inadequate.

The possibilities for improving the school experiences and achievement of Aboriginal or Indigenous students at a local, district, provincial/state, national and global context are endless. It needs to begin, however, with educators examining their beliefs, assumptions, biases and judgments and by using culturally sensitive instructional practice, including materials and assessment tools. Effective assessment must be embedded in authentic learning activities based on higher order thinking and problem solving. It is through these authentic learning experiences that the feelings of disconnect that Aboriginal students experience in traditional Western schools will be minimised. The life experiences that Aboriginal students bring to the classroom will be validated and subsequently contribute to their learning and achievement.

J. Ottmann (✉) • J. Jeary
Werklund School of Education, University of Calgary,
2500 University Drive NW, Calgary, AB, Canada, T2N1N4
e-mail: jottmann@ucalgary.ca; jottmann@ucalgary.ca

Keywords Aboriginal • First Nations • Métis and Inuit • Special education • Assessment practices • Affective domain • Promising practices

14.1 Introduction

Although this chapter focuses on the Canadian context as it relates to Aboriginal student achievement and educational assessment practices, the challenging experiences with schooling and the resultant consequences (e.g., disparity, and the persistent education gap between Indigenous students and the general student population) are also evident in countries such as Australia, the United States, and New Zealand (Education Week, 2013; Hughes & Hughes, 2012; Klenowski, 2009; New Zealand Government, 2013; National Center for Education Statistics, 2012); hence the professional development or learning suggested for educators and the recommendations that are suggested in this chapter could be adapted and delivered in contexts that have Indigenous populations and/or minority students.

Ottmann and Jeary's (2006) study provides a snapshot of the overall Canadian experience for Aboriginal students. In the study on Aboriginal students and assessment practices in Alberta, Canada Ottmann and Jeary noted that in 2003–2004 there were 6547 First Nations students enrolled (Grades 1–12) in provincial and First Nations managed schools (Indian and Northern Affairs Canada, 2004a, p. 39) whereas, the total number of students in Alberta numbered 592,731 (Alberta Learning, 2004, p. 123). Overall, the Aboriginal student population was 1.1 % of the total student population. The number of Aboriginal students who graduated from high school, however, was disproportional when compared to the number of non-Aboriginal students who graduated. Furthermore, Ottmann and Jeary's study revealed that Aboriginal students were significantly over-represented in terms of requiring special education programmes and services and under-represented in the gifted and talented categories. Aboriginal student achievement and success is multidimensional and complex. This chapter will review literature relevant to student achievement and issues of assessment in schools. It will examine socio-cultural factors that influence student achievement and the assessment of ability, and provide a context to better understand Aboriginal learners. Although the mental health and emotional wellbeing of Aboriginal children and youth is of extreme importance, the focus of this chapter will be assessment practices linked to academic achievement.

14.2 The Context: The Experiences Outside the School

> A common concern of parents is when schooling becomes a threat to their developing child's identity, primarily when the values and world view that prevail at school contradict or ignore the existence of a different perspective the child lives with at home – Elsie Wuttunee. (Indian and Northern Affairs Canada, Royal Commission on Aboriginal Peoples, Volume 3, Gathering Strength, Chapter 5, Education, 2004b)

Chief Seattle once said, "We did not weave the web of life, we are merely a strand in it. What we do to the web, we do to ourselves" (cited in Jeffers, 1991, p. 21). Martin Luther King (1998) echoed this belief in his letter from Birmingham Jail, "We are caught in an inescapable network of mutuality, tied in a single garment of destiny. Whatever affects one directly, affects all indirectly" (pp. 187–204). These quotations capture the interconnectedness of all things and the school environment is no exception. Students are deeply connected to a culture and environment outside the school. What does this environment look like for Aboriginal students? Generalisations are difficult to make as Aboriginal people are diverse in language, culture, and traditions; however, there are common threads that bind all Aboriginal people.

Before one can proceed, a backward glance into our past is necessary. Since the British North America Act, the First Nations have been cited in Canadian legislation as one group, and as a result have shared the dire consequences of legislation that was unilateral and prescriptive. This history bound all Aboriginal people to a common reality and future, and because everything is connected it has impacted learning and teaching in today's classroom. The Indian Act (1876) and residential school system have had resounding effects on the lives of many Aboriginal people. Because of systematic events and federal legislation, issues of poverty, abuse, and societal marginalisation emerged in higher concentrations within the Aboriginal populations.

The Aboriginal population is experiencing greater population growth than the general population. According to Statistics Canada 2006 Census, 1,172,790 people self-identified as Aboriginal – this is 3.8 % of the total Canadian population. In 10 years (1996–2006) the Aboriginal population increased by 45 % (Statistics Canada, 2006a). In addition, the median age of Canada's Aboriginal population was 27 compared to 40 years of age for the general population with 48 % of the total Aboriginal population being under the age of 25, and 19 % under the age of 10 (Statistics Canada, 2006b). Interestingly, more than 600,000 Aboriginal youth will turn 15 between 2001 and 2026 (Hull, 2005). These statistical findings have significant implications for education and provide an idea of the societal and systemic issues to which organisations, in partnership with Aboriginal people, will have to respond.

Aboriginal people in Canada experience poverty to a greater extent than the general population, and poverty has proven to have dramatic and invasive effects for Aboriginal people. According to Campaign 2000, *2010 Report Card on Child and Family Poverty in Canada: 1989–2010* (2010a), "Across Canada, self-identified First Nations, Métis, and Inuit peoples account for 12 % of food bank usage. This has steadily increased over the past three years" (p. 3). *Revisiting Family Security in Unsecure Times: 2011 Report Card on Child and Family Poverty in Canada* also disclosed:

1. 117 First Nations communities are under drinking water advisories.
2. There were three times the number of First Nations children in care in 2010 (27,500) than at the height of the residential schools during the 1940s, yet First Nations Child Welfare agencies receive 22 % less per capita funding than provincial agencies. The Auditor General of Canada reported in 2008 that the funding formula [for First Nations communities] has not been reviewed since 1988 nor adjusted for inflation since 1995.

3. Children on-reserve receive about $2000–3000 less funding per year for elementary and secondary school than children who live off-reserve.
4. Youth suicide is more prevalent in First Nations communities than among all youth in Canada. While the suicide rates vary widely among First Nations communities, the suicide rate in these communities is between three and seven times greater than in Canada overall. (Campaign 2000, 2010b, p. 9)

A common concern for parents is when the values and worldview that prevail at school contradict or ignore the existence of the different perspective the child lives with at home.

Furthermore, people who live in poverty experience a higher incidence of inadequate housing conditions and increased health problems. Allard, Wilkins, and Berthelot (2004) explained:

> Aboriginal populations worldwide have undergone major social, economic and cultural changes in the past several decades, some of which may have negatively affected their health status. In Canada, as in other countries, Aboriginal peoples bear a disproportionate burden of disease and die younger and at higher rates than do members of the non-Aboriginal population. (p. 51)

O'Donnell and Tait (2004) reported that "non-Reserve Aboriginal people are more likely to live in crowded conditions" (p. 22) and that "crowded living conditions can lead to transmission of infectious diseases such as tuberculosis and hepatitis A, and can increase risk for injuries, mental health problems, family tensions and violence" (p. 22). Inuit Tapiriit Kanatami (the national voice of 55,000 Inuit living in 53 communities across the Inuvialuit Settlement Region, Nunavut, Nunavik, and Nunatsiavut land claims regions) released the following statement:

> The tuberculosis rate among Inuit has doubled in the past four years – to 185 times the rate of Canadian-born non-aboriginals – at a time when the national rate is declining, according to 2008 figures recently made public by the Public Health Agency of Canada.
>
> This compares with an Inuit rate 90 times higher than the non-aboriginal, Canadian-born population as recently as 2004. The rate among First Nations is also climbing, from 29 times the non-aboriginal, Canadian-born rate in 2004 to a rate now 31 times higher. (Inuit Tapiriit Kanatami, 2010, n.p.)

Poor nutrition, overcrowded housing conditions, and lack of access to health care contribute to the higher rates of diseases, this included H1N1, among First Nations and Inuit communities. It is clear that poverty affects every area of a person's life, and it does not exclude children. In this context, "Aboriginal children experience higher rates of malnutrition; disabilities; drug and alcohol abuse" (Canadian Council of Child and Youth Advocates, 2011, p. 4); and issues related to education and substandard housing (p. 3). Aboriginal children who live in poverty also become more involved in the youth criminal justice and child protection systems (Standing Senate Committee on Human Rights, 2007).

The primary source of income for many Aboriginal people continues to be government transfer payments. Howe (2004) stated, "An Aboriginal dropout lives an economically marginalised life in which the male earns only a little more than a third of a million dollars, and the female earns less than ninety thousand dollars. That is over an entire lifetime" (p. 187). Wilson and Macdonald (2010) stated:

"Not only has the legacy of colonialism left Aboriginal peoples disproportionately ranked among the poorest of Canadians", their study that measured "the income gap between Aboriginal peoples and the rest of Canadians" (p. 3) over three Canadian censuses (1996, 2001, and 2006) discovered "disturbing levels of income inequality" (p. 3). The Wilson and Macdonald study revealed the following:

> In 2006, the median income for Aboriginal peoples was $18,962 – 30 % lower than the $27,097 median income for the rest of Canadians. The difference of $8135 that existed in 2006, however, was marginally smaller than the difference of $9045 in 2001 or $9428 in 1996. While income disparity between Aboriginal peoples and the rest of Canadians narrowed slightly between 1996 and 2006, at this rate it would take 63 years for the gap to be erased. Ironically, if and when parity with other Canadians is reached, Aboriginal peoples will achieve the same level of income inequality as the rest of the country, which is getting worse, not better. The study reveals income inequality persists no matter where Aboriginal peoples live in Canada. The income gap in urban settings is $7083 higher in urban settings and $4492 higher in rural settings. Non-Aboriginal people working on urban reserves earn 34 % more than First Nation workers. On rural reserves, non-Aboriginal Canadians make 88 % more than their First Nation colleagues. The study also reveals income inequality persists despite rapid increases in educational attainment for Aboriginal people over the past 10 years, with one exception. Aboriginal peoples with university degrees have overcome much of the income gap between them and the rest of Canadians. (pp. 3–4)

Despite the dismal statistics, Wilson and Macdonald posited that their findings garner "reason for hope … [as] new approaches and solutions" (p. 4) can emerge with the inclusion and active involvement of Aboriginal peoples in the planning and decision-making process. Wilson and Macdonald also suggested the first step to a solution: "Though demanding, poverty among Aboriginal peoples in Canada must be understood within its historical context" (p. 5).

Studies have consistently shown that Aboriginal children experience significantly higher levels of poverty than the general population. British Columbia's Representative for Children and Youth, and former Saskatchewan judge, Mary Ellen Turpel-Lafond commented, "The disparities among Indigenous and non-indigenous children are alarming" (2007, p. 172). The Canadian Teachers' Federation 2009 report, *Supporting education … building Canada: Child poverty and schools* begins, "Child poverty is a tragic and shameful fact of life in a nation as wealthy as ours. The child poverty rate remains at 1989 levels, the year of the all-party House of Commons resolution to end child poverty in Canada by the year 2000" (p. 1). In relation to Aboriginal children the report declares:

- Children in racialised, new Canadian and Aboriginal families as well as children with disabilities are at greater risk of living in poverty.
- Poverty rates are a formidable barrier in Aboriginal communities. Almost one in two Aboriginal children (49 %) under the age of 6 (not living in First Nations communities) lives in a low-income family. (p. 1)

The Canadian Council on Social Development (CCSD) also found that Aboriginal children had the highest rate of poverty in the three equity groups that include visible minorities and children with disabilities. CCSD also discovered that Aboriginal children were four times more likely to be hungry and, in general, had more health problems (2003). A report by the Ontario Federation of Indian Friendship Centres

(OFIF) declared, "The distinct nature of Aboriginal child and family poverty is rooted in cultural fragmentation, multi-generational effects of residential schools, wardship through the child welfare system, and socio-economic marginalization" (OFIF, 2000, n.p.).

The educational realm is not immune to effects of poverty. Combating child poverty is important as there is a "strong correlation between socio-economic status and children's academic performance" (Canadian Teachers' Federation, 2009, p. 2) and "children from lower income families were less ready to learn than children from more affluent households" (p. 2). In the opening statement to the Standing Senate Committee on Aboriginal Peoples, the Auditor General of Canada, Sheila Fraser shared the following:

> We … found a significant gap in educational achievement between Indian students and non-Indian students. The education gap refers to the proportion of First Nations people living on reserves over the age of 15 with at least a high school diploma, compared with the proportion in the overall Canadian population. We recommended that an action plan be implemented to close the gap.
>
> In 2004, we followed up on recommendations and observations from our 2000 audit and also included the Post-Secondary Student Support Program in our audit scope. We found that the situation had not improved since 2000. By 2004, the education gap had not narrowed, and the time estimated to close that gap had actually increased from 27 to 28 years. (Office of the Auditor General of Canada, 2010, n.p.)

With statistics like these, educators are posed with significant challenges – and opportunities.

14.3 School Experiences for Aboriginal Students

Aboriginal students in Canada may attend either provincial schools or schools located on reserve and it is not uncommon for students to move between these two educational systems during their school years. Aboriginal students, particularly on reserve and in Nunavut, are attending and completing high school at much lower rates than the non-Aboriginal population. In 2006, 56.3 % of Aboriginal students (15 and older) completed high school, compared to 76.9 % of the non-Aboriginal population (Community Foundations of Canada, 2009a). Of the total Aboriginal student population, approximately 40 % of on-reserve and Inuit students complete high school, whereas 60 % of off-reserve students finish high school. In addition, Aboriginal youth attended school at a lower rate (71.3 %) compared to the general student population (81 %). *Canada's Vital Signs 2009: Research Findings* also documented, "High school is the highest completed level of education for more Aboriginal Canadians (38.5 %) than non-Aboriginal Canadians (24.8 %)" (Community Foundations of Canada, 2009b, n.p.). The societal consequences of statistics such as these are significant.

The Government of Canada's Royal Commission on Aboriginal Peoples (RCAP) Final Report (1996) in *Gathering Strength* (Volume 3) documented Aboriginal students' feelings related to schooling:

> Aboriginal youth today straddle two worlds. The non-Aboriginal world has become a fast-paced, competitive, changing environment in which ever higher levels of education and new skills are required to survive. These are powerful cultural forces that necessitate a secure, solid identity to balance the conflicting messages and demands created where the Aboriginal and non-Aboriginal worlds meet ... the vast majority of Aboriginal youth, however, are simply struggling to survive. They are caught between the expectations, values and demands of two worlds, unable to find a point of balance. Their despair is manifested in early school leaving, substance abuse, suicide attempts, defiance of the law, and teen pregnancies. (Indian and Northern Affairs Canada, n.p.)

Many Aboriginal youth who communicated with the Commission expressed a desire to be heard at their schools and in their communities, to become less marginalised. RCAP Commissioners recommended that all Aboriginal children have access to dynamic, culture-based early childhood education. For elementary education they proposed the following:

1. All schools, whether or not they serve mainly Aboriginal students, adopt curriculums that reflect Aboriginal cultures and realities;
2. Governments allocate resources such that Aboriginal language instruction can be given high priority, where numbers warrant; and
3. Provincial and territorial schools make greater efforts to involve Aboriginal parents in decision making. (Indian and Northern Affairs Canada, 1996)

On a provincial level, Alberta has prioritised Aboriginal education as one of the top five areas of focus. Initiatives such as the First Nations, Metis, and Inuit Education Project have brought attention to Aboriginal students, resulting in school-wide efforts to change the experience of Aboriginal students with the goal of improving educational achievement and establishing the foundation for sustained school success.

14.4 Assessment

Assessment is a process of information gathering using a variety of techniques and strategies. Testing is only one aspect of assessment; however, it often becomes an end in itself. Assessment, in contrast, seeks to form a more complete picture of the student by integrating multiple types of data from multiple sources. Assessment in schools serves different purposes – to determine eligibility for special programs and services; to have progress monitored; and to aid in making instructional and educational decisions about programs. Information obtained through the assessment process contributes to educational decision-making for students and therefore should be fair and free from bias. For the purposes of this report, assessment is conceived as: formal assessment, informal assessment, and authentic assessment. These types of assessments and the implications of these evaluations with Aboriginal students will be discussed.

14.4.1 Formal Assessment

Formal assessment strategies typically involve the use of a standardised test instrument and provide detailed guidelines for administration, scoring, and interpretation, as well as statistical data related to validity, reliability, and standardisation procedures (Smith et al., 2006). Standardised testing can be either norm-referenced or criterion-referenced. Norm-referenced tests provide measures of performance that compare scores and may include the Wechsler Intelligence Scale for Children – Fourth Edition (WISC-IV), Wechsler Individual Achievement Test – Second Edition (WIAT-II), and the Woodcock-Johnson Test of Education Achievement – Third Edition. Criterion-referenced testing compares a student's performance with a specific level of skill mastery (McLoughlin & Lewis, 2001).

14.4.2 Psychological Tests

Standardised psychological tests are commonly given as part of a process to evaluate students' special education needs and can be group or individually administered. They may be used to determine eligibility for special services, programs, and supports, and may include a recommendation to code or label a student with a particular special learning need.

Sternberg (2004) stated that "intelligence cannot be fully or even meaningfully understood outside its cultural context" and that there is no one overall conception of intelligence (p. 325). Okagaki and Sternberg (1993) found that different ethnic groups in San Jose, California, had different conceptions of intelligence. In some groups the importance of social-competency overrides cognitive skills. Sternberg (2004) concluded that when cultural context is taken into account, individuals are better recognised for their talents, and schools assess and teach children better. He cautioned that care must be taken when attempting to measure the intelligence of various cultural groups and to carefully examine whether test scores mean the same thing for various groups.

Group administered standardised tests also have potential limitations. Friend and Bursuck (1996) commented on the following:

1. Students may not have the opportunity to ask the teacher questions about directions or to clarify test questions.
2. Many group tests are timed, which may limit the responses of children who take longer to process information or for whom English is a second language.
3. National norms may not match actual distribution of classroom achievement.
4. The results of standardised tests may not provide useful information to guide instruction.
5. The content of the test may not match what is being taught in a particular classroom.

6. Due to the difficulty in administering standardised tests it is not practical to give them frequently enough to be used as a tool for evaluating day-to-day instruction.

It is possible that standardised tests may underestimate the potential of Aboriginal students. Beiser and Gotowiec (2000) studied the 'biopsychosocial' factors underlying inter-ethnic discrepancies in IQ scores in order to help resolve discrepancies in academic achievement scores. Their study was part of a longitudinal study that began in the 1980s. Results from the earlier investigation found that the IQ scores of Native children were lower than non-Native children (Beiser, 1989). The difference was more pronounced for the WISC-R's Verbal than Performance scores. Native children's Verbal IQ scores were nearly 1.5 standard deviations lower than non-Native children; the Performance sub-scale differential was slightly greater than 0.5 standard deviation units. Beiser and Gotowiec's (2000) work focused upon the various social, cultural, and environmental factors, hypothesised as explanatory variables to account for Native/non-Native IQ score differentials. The addition of explanatory variables reduced Native/non-Native Verbal scores differences from a spread of 22 points to only 9.5 points. Performance scores differences were reduced from an initial difference of 7.9 points to an estimated 2.6 points. The independent variables in the investigation included information on mother's prenatal health care, mother's prenatal health, hearing problem of the child, parent education, household amenities, satisfaction with school, cultural separation attitudes, and life events. The ninth-independent variable was the child's English language skills and this was obtained through teacher ratings. The findings were that biopsychosocial variables including maternal and child health, socio-economic status, parental attitudes toward school, and toward cultural separation, and children's English-language skills accounted for 67 % of the Native/non-Native difference on the Performance score and 57 % of the Verbal score difference. The authors noted that while the instrument used for comparison (WISC-R) has been revised with a better standardisation sample it is likely that the use of the WISC-III would "probably not have altered patterns of findings" (p. 249).

Variables that may compromise the validity of standardised measures include failure to account for the use of languages other than English (Suzuki & Valencia, 1997); failure to account for culturally-based differences in cognitive styles (Beiser, Sack, Manson, Redshirt, & Dion, 1998); failure to account for factors such as poverty and parental education (Neisser et al., 1996; Suzuki & Valencia, 1997); and biases in test content (Greenfield, 1997; Suzuki & Valencia, 1997). Friend and Bursuck (1996) discussed six ways in which psychological tests may discriminate against students from culturally different or disadvantaged backgrounds (p. 263):

1. Inappropriate content. Students from minority populations may lack exposure to certain items on the instrument.
2. Inappropriate standardisation samples. Cultural and ethnic minorities may not have been represented in the normative sample.

3. **Misunderstood examiner or language.** Anglo, English-speaking examiners may be unable to establish rapport with minority students and students from different linguistic backgrounds.
4. **Inequitable social consequences.** As the result of discriminatory assessment practices, minority students may be relegated to lower educational placements, with the ultimate result that they obtain lower-paying jobs.
5. **Ineffective measurement of constructs.** Test developers design instruments assumed to measure academic or cognitive ability for all students. When used with minority students, however, the instruments may measure only the degree to which the students have absorbed middle-class culture.
6. **Different predictive validity.** Instruments designed to predict the educational or academic outcomes or potential for students of the majority culture may not do so for minority students. (p. 263)

14.4.3 Informal Assessment

Informal assessment refers to direct measures of student performance and progress in academic or behavioural tasks, and includes teacher observation, informal inventories of reading and mathematics skills, teacher-made tests, and curriculum-based measurement. The two purposes of informal assessment are formative assessment and summative assessment. Formative assessment takes place during teaching. Summative assessment typically occurs at the end of a unit or term to convey student progress. In *Rethinking Classroom Assessment with Purpose in Mind* (2006), a document of the Western and Northern Canadian Protocol for Collaboration in Education, the authors, Earl and Katz (2006) highlighted five quality issues that are important in classroom assessment: reliability, reference points, validity, record-keeping, and reporting. It is possible that many teachers do not understand the importance of these five issues, especially as they relate to minority students.

Students from culturally-diverse backgrounds, particularly Aboriginal children, often encounter difficulties in school. Most teachers are from the Anglo-European culture and may not be knowledgeable about Aboriginal cultures or culturally-relevant curriculum. Aboriginal issues are distinct from multicultural issues. First Nations people did not make a choice to immigrate with an expectation to change; rather the country that they inhabited changed and they were forced to assimilate. The preservation of almost-extinct languages, traditions, and culture has become a real issue for Aboriginal people, who have a holistic perspective and believe in the connectedness of education, culture, language, and in the importance of community. Teachers must become aware of their own assumptions, biases, expectations, and judgments related to Aboriginal children and the way in which they assess this learning. Hargreaves and Fullan (cited in Yero, 2002b) stated, "It is what teachers think, what teachers believe, and what teachers do at the level of the classroom that ultimately shapes the kind of learning that young people get" (p. 4). Costa (1997) also contended that "all school education depends totally upon the views… of teachers" (p. 2).

In many cases, teachers are not aware of the invasive impact that their values and belief systems have on student learning and wellbeing. According to Yero (2002b), the beliefs, values, and actions that teachers bring to the classroom "generally exist outside of conscious awareness" (p. 6) and "are largely unexamined" (Yero, 2002a, p. 12) by both the teacher and the educational system. In such cases 'reflective practitioner' practices are encouraged to unveil potentially harmful classroom practices. Richards, Brown, and Forde (2007) posited:

> Teacher self-reflection is an important part of the personal dimension. By honestly examining their attitudes and beliefs about themselves and others, teachers begin to discover why they are who they are, and can confront biases that have influenced their values system (Villegas & Lucas, 2007). Because teachers' values impact relationships with students and their families, teachers must reconcile negative feelings towards any cultural, language, or ethnic group. Often teachers are resistant to the notion that their values might reflect prejudices or even racism towards certain groups. When teachers are able to rid themselves of such biases, they help to create an atmosphere of trust and acceptance for students and their families, resulting in greater opportunity for students' success ... Another important aspect of the personal dimension is exploration. It is crucial that teachers explore their personal histories and experiences, as well as the history and current experiences of their students and families. With knowledge comes understanding of self and others, and greater appreciation of differences. When teachers are unbiased in their instruction and knowledgeable about themselves and their students, they can better respond to the needs of all their students. (p. 65)

These introspective practices have the potential to strengthen both teacher and student identity, to develop positive classroom culture and climate, and foster quality teacher-student- community relationships.

Harry, Klingner, Sturges, and Moore (2002) investigated the roles that teachers' informal diagnoses play in the assessment and found that teachers' judgments displayed gender and ethnicity biases. It is possible that teachers' informal explanations of the causes of children's difficulties actually influence the assessment process and subsequent decisions about placement.

It is critical that assessment strategies adhere to principles of fairness. Alberta Education (2002) identified 13 principles of assessment for teachers of Aboriginal Studies 10-20-30 that can be applied to any assessment situation:

1. Assessment should reflect the philosophy of the school, the community and the culture;
2. Assessment should reflect the students' growth across all aspects of the curriculum;
3. Assessment should be performed consistently over time;
4. A variety of assessment strategies and tools should be used;
5. The assessment strategy should suit the skill in question;
6. Assessment tools should be developmentally appropriate;
7. Students should be aware of how and when their knowledge and abilities are assessed;
8. Students should be given opportunities to participate in the assessment process;
9. Students should have a positive attitude towards assessment;
10. The information gathered should be used to plan future instruction;

11. The results of assessment should be clear and easily understood;
12. The results of assessment should be shared with students and parents on a regular basis; and
13. How results are shared should depend on who they are shared with and why.

The *Principles for Fair Student Assessment Practices for Education in Canada* (Joint Advisory Working Group Committee, 1993) contain a set of principles and related guidelines accepted by professional organisations as indicative of fair assessment practice within the Canadian education context. As assessments depend on professional judgments, the principles and guidelines identify issues to consider in exercising professional judgment and in striving for fair and equitable assessment of all students.

14.4.4 Alternative/Authentic Assessment

Alternative assessment methods have resulted from dissatisfaction with individual and group-administered standardised tests and include authentic assessment, performance assessment, portfolio assessment, and ecological assessment. These assessments use similar techniques such as requiring students to construct, produce, perform, or demonstrate a task. The goal is to evaluate a student's critical-thinking and problem-solving ability in real-life situations. Wiggins (1993) identified four characteristics of authentic assessment:

1. Performance on engaging and important problems;
2. Performance on a contextualised task that represents those expected in the adult world;
3. Real problems with a number of steps that require more than formulaic solutions; and
4. Tasks that demand students produce a quality product or performance.

Performance assessments enable students to show what they can do; such assessments do not rely exclusively on reading and writing and have no time constraints. They provide opportunities for students to demonstrate their knowledge, skills, and habits of mind (Harper, O'Connor, & Simpson, 1999). A portfolio assessment is a collection of student work that represents a sampling of achievements, provides evidence of learning over time, and contains evidence of student reflection and self-evaluation. Ecological assessment compares the child's performance to the demands and expectations of activities and tasks in the child's environments. A child might be assessed in the classroom, in the playground, during one-to-one interaction, and at home. Parents/caregivers are included as part of the assessment team.

The use of alternative assessment methods is a best practice in the assessment of minority students. The evaluation of students is more representative and comprehensive when teachers use multiple ways of demonstrating knowledge and learning. As the number of students from diverse cultures increases, the challenge of ensuring fair and equitable assessment procedures will continue to be important.

14.5 Disproportionality in Special Education

A number of authors have reported on disproportionate enrolments in special education categories (Agbenyega & Jiggetts, 1999; Artiles, 1998; Daniels, 1998; Ford, 1998; Harry et al., 2002; Losen & Orfield, 2002; MacMillan & Reschly, 1998; Oswald, Coutinho, & Best, 2002; Suzuki & Valencia, 1997; Valles, 1998). The disproportionality is found in the over-representation of minority students in special education programs and the under-representation in gifted programs. The issue of over-representation was mentioned as early as the 1960s by Dunn (1968), when he described the children in classes for the educable mentally retarded as follows:

> In my best judgment, about 60 to 80 percent of the pupils taught by these teachers are children from low-status backgrounds – including Afro-Americans, American Indians, Mexicans, and Puerto Rican Americans; those from nonstandard English speaking, broken, disorganized, and inadequate homes; and children from other non-middle class environments. (p. 5)

That was almost 30 years ago but the issues persist today. In 1998, approximately 1.5 million minority children were identified as having mental retardation, emotional disturbance, or a specific learning disability. More than 876,000 of these were black or Native American, and black students were nearly three times as likely as white students to be labelled mentally retarded (Losen & Orfield, 2002). In the United States, black students account for 14.8 % of the school-aged population but 19.8 % of the special education population. American Indian students remain over-represented in special education services as well (U.S. Department of Education, 2002).

Another report that affirmed that Aboriginal students were disproportionately represented in all special education categories except the gifted category was released by the British Columbia Ministry of Education (2001). The report indicated that unexamined beliefs about Aboriginal children and a lack of culturally-sensitive assessment tools may lead to inappropriate labelling. An attempt was made to access similar statistics from Alberta Education but was unsuccessful. As a result a survey was sent to 60 school boards and 60 band schools in Alberta (Ottmann & Jeary, 2006). Twenty surveys were returned and the results were similar to those of British Columbia – Aboriginal students were twice as likely to be identified as requiring special educational services.

Why are some culturally-diverse groups over-represented as requiring special education services and under-represented in the gifted population? There are a number of possible explanations. First, the way children are referred for assessment and special education services is a subjective process performed by the teacher and dependent upon local norms. MacMillan, Gresham, Lopez, and Bocian (1996) demonstrated that teachers refer children with significant behaviour and academic problems and appear to not refer students who are performing well. The teacher's understanding of cultural and linguistic differences, their expectations, and ability to differentiate instruction may affect their judgment about who is referred for assessment.

Second, the use of assessment instruments may be culturally biased. Misperceptions between the student and the evaluator, cross-cultural stereotyping, and item bias can lead to poor performance, particularly by students who may have limited proficiency in English (U.S. Department of Education, 2001). Assessment methods that are closely linked to classroom practice – performance-based assessments and curriculum-based assessments – are better tools to determine students' knowledge, skills, and attitudes.

Third, individual and societal biases, values and belief systems related to 'difference' may negatively influence school policy and practice. Artiles (1998) framed the over-representation of minority students in special education as a "dilemma of difference" (p. 32). He took a socio-historical point of view and maintained that minority people are seen as "different" and the way we treat difference requires examination. He argued that we must comprehend the local understandings of difference and the local values, beliefs, constraints, and resources that are embedded in the school's programs and student population. He cautioned that the notions of culture and difference that we have used in the past are simplistic and that we must learn about our own professional identity in order to unravel the issues of disproportionate representation.

Daniels (1998) suggested that we need educational reform in policy, programming, and instructional practices that focuses on the educational and related service needs of at-risk and underachieving students, rather than diagnostic classifications for underachievement that fit nearly under the umbrella of special education. She argued that the majority of "knowledge producers" are of Euro-American heritage and therefore current educational practices perpetuate disproportionate minority representation in gifted and special education programs. She maintained that present educational goals and practices require clarification in order to restructure an education system that lends itself to educational equity for all students.

While educational reform may be needed, it will take time to make major changes. In the meantime the importance of ensuring fair and equitable assessment procedures cannot be overemphasised. Many sources of possible bias can be found in the assessment process. Standardised administration procedures, cultural and ethnic prejudice, linguistic variance and test item bias can influence the validity of the assessment results. The best practices section of this paper will provide suggestions for fair and equitable assessment methods.

14.6 Achievement Gap

The achievement gap between the general student population and the Aboriginal/indigenous/minority population has been substantially presented in research literature (Olszewski-Kubilius, Lee, Ngoi, & Ngoi, 2004; Reid, 2002; Rothstein, 2004). Olszewski-Kubilius et al. (2004) suggested that many minority children succumb to low expectations, negative ramifications of success, and survival guilt for surpassing peers and family. McShane (1983a) listed the following factors that hinder the academic achievement of First Nations children:

1. Disadvantage – detrimental environmental conditions that disadvantage them, e.g., poverty, inadequate health care, poor housing;
2. Deficits – alcoholism, FASD, vision problems, ear infections;
3. Deprivation – illness, increased absenteeism, poor nutrition leading to less energy;
4. Disorganisation and disruption – pressure to assimilate, pressure to reject their culture, leads to them becoming marginalised;
5. Dependence – on systems leads to lack of motivation to progress and to learn; and
6. Differences – in language, culture, values, behaviour, interpretation of behaviour, can lead to academic difficulties.

McShane believed that these factors may account for the variance in achievement scores between First Nations and Anglo children. In his research, the patterns of performance on ability tests revealed a significant discrepancy between verbal and non-verbal abilities between the two groups; non-verbal ability was equal or above that of the Anglo group. He also indicated that the performance on intellectual tests such as the Wechsler scales may be influenced by language acquisition and culturally-transmitted values and behaviours (McShane, 1983b). Parker, Rubalcava, and Teruel (2005) affirmed the influence that language, especially if a student is unilingual, has on school achievement, and, that bilingual primary schools may help narrow the gap. These results support the hypothesis that language or related indigenous cultural barriers are factors in the achievement of indigenous children. In his article, McShane labels the 'Crossover Effect' as the achievement gap that begins to take shape in elementary school – indigenous children enter school at relatively the same or slightly lower achievement levels than non-indigenous children, then the discrepancy widens by third or fourth grade across all subject areas.

Reid (2002) discovered that the gap in standard achievement testing performance has lasting consequences on meaningful postsecondary choices. To combat barriers and improve postsecondary enrolment and success, programs like "Project EXCITE" – a collaboration between a university-based gifted centre and local school districts (Olszewski-Kubilius et al., 2004) – prepare minority children for advanced track mathematics and science high school programs. After 2 years of the programme, there has been a 30 % increase of minority children qualifying for advanced mathematics class in Grade 6.

In relation to Aboriginal students in Alberta, Alberta Learning (2002) has noted the following:

> The existing measurement data from Alberta Learning indicates that the percentage of Alberta students with registered Indian status who participated in the Achievement Testing Program in a band-operated school in 2000 was approximately 75 % in grades 3 and 6, and approximately 60 % in grade 9. The participation of students with registered-Indian status in other school systems, especially at the grade 9 level, was greater than the participation of students in band-operated schools but was still below the overall participation rate in the province (approximately 90 %). The strongest performance by students with registered Indian status who wrote the Achievement Test was in grade 3. Over the past two years approximately 40 % of grade 3 students in band-operated schools and 50–70 % of students in other school systems met the Acceptable Standard in English language arts and mathematics. The weakest performance was in grade 9. In the past three years, fewer than 15 %

of grade 9 students in band-operated schools and fewer than 50 % of students in other school systems met the Acceptable Standard in mathematics, science and social studies. While this measurement data exists, these observations cannot be generalized to all students with registered Indian status in the province due to the low participation rate of these students in the Achievement Testing Program, especially at the grade 9 level. (p. 21)

In response to the Aboriginal student Provincial Achievement Testing scores, Alberta Education has prioritised programming that includes language and cultural development for Aboriginal students.

Closing the achievement gap is complex. Rothstein (2004) commented that "closing the achievement gap requires more than just improving schools" and suggested other factors to consider include mobility rates (e.g., in 1994, 30 % of the poorest students had attended at least three different schools by Grade 3, compared to 10 % of middle-class students), health needs, and socio-economic status. To address the achievement gap, concerted efforts, that include the voices of Aboriginal educators, parents, and students, need to be organised. Education and community initiatives that directly focus on the systematic issues that contribute to conditions in the development and maintenance of an achievement gap should be implemented and frequently evaluated for effectiveness.

14.7 Education Variables

Education variables reported in literature that contribute to the success of Aboriginal/indigenous students were: committed and effective teachers, particularly Native teachers; and programming that addressed the increasing diversity in the classroom. Meece and Kurtz-Costes (2001) concluded that schools were ill prepared for the increased diversity, and race and ethnic differences were consistently found in achievement, test scores, grades, course enrolment, and school completion rates. The following limitations to previous research on the schooling of ethnic minority children were highlighted by Meece and Kurtz-Costes:

1. Pervasiveness of race comparisons. This "approach too often [led] to a deficit model in which ethnic minority children are viewed as inferior to the majority group" (p. 4);
2. A focus on negative outcomes. A focus on negative outcomes led researchers to overlook the factors that led minority youth to succeed academically (p. 4);
3. Lack of examination of contexts and factors outside the school. The contexts and factors outside the school are just as important to a child's cognitive development and academic progress (p. 5);
4. Failure to view children from a developmental perspective. There is a need for more longitudinal studies as opposed to single-age studies that are a mere snapshot in time; children are continually changing and researchers should not treat children's outcomes in a "static" way (p. 5); and
5. School culture. More research needs to be done on ways in which school cultures can change in order to be more supportive of cultural diversity (p. 5).

After conducting research that included indigenous students from Canada, the United States, and Australia, McInerney and McInerney (1996) concluded that the motivational profiles of the groups were more similar than different, and that motivational goals influencing school performance appear to be more related to a child's perception of their role as a student. They found that many children were not effectively socialised into existing school frameworks, and an individual's integration into academic systems appears to be related to school achievement and continuance of school attendance. They suggested that effective socialisation of indigenous students regarding the school environment would increase motivation and academic achievement.

Manuelito (2003) discussed the need for a well-prepared Native teaching force:

1. Learning is enhanced when teacher and student share the same culture;
2. There is an increased relationship between student and teacher, affecting student desire to stay in school;
3. Native teachers serve as important role models;
4. There is an increased connectivity to the Native community; and
5. There may be an increased awareness of Native learning styles and thus more likely to use this information in instructional planning.

Manuelito's suggestions have significant implications for the recruitment process, curriculum development, and course content of teacher preparation programs, as well as hiring practices.

The last variable identified in this section is poverty. Howley and Bickel (2000) studied the effects of poverty and school size on academic achievement and found that as schools become larger, the negative effect of poverty on achievement increases. The correlation between poverty and school size appeared ten times stronger in larger schools than in smaller schools and the benefits of smaller schools appeared to be more important at the middle grade level. They concluded that while all children were potentially affected by the relationship between poverty and school size, minority children were more at risk because they often attended large schools.

14.8 Culture and Community Factors

The significant influence that culture has on student achievement has increasingly gained attention. Vygotsky's (1963) Zone of Proximal Learning and Feuerstein's Mediated Learning supports the impact of the 'culture factor' in the classroom. These theories acknowledge, value, and utilise the knowledge, beliefs, values, and cultural traditions that children experience prior to and in conjunction with formal schooling. Along with issues related to poverty, many Aboriginal children bring to the classroom an indigenous worldview that may include a second language and knowledge of cultural traditions. Oftentimes, the 'school world' and the 'home world' are very different realms (Battiste, 2000; Little Bear, 2000). The 'disconnect' that Aboriginal students experience in traditional Western schools contributes to negative perceptions that directly affect educational achievement.

The literature that was compiled for this review supported the socio-cultural learning theory and encouraged awareness of indigenous "ways of knowing" and "ways of being". Nelson-Barber and Estrin (1995) stressed that assessment of cognition should consider the "ways of knowing" of a group to which an individual belongs; otherwise, the outcomes should not be considered valid (p. 14). Ardila and Moreno (2001) conducted an exploratory study that focused on the neuropsychological test performance on Aruaco Indians of Colombia. They concluded, "Cognitive abilities measured by neuropsychological test represent, at least in their contents, culturally learned abilities … Culture prescribes what should be learned and at what age" (p. 510). The authors stated that "basic cognitive processes are universal" and that differences lie more in the testing situations than in the particular cognitive processes of the individual (p. 510).

The study indicated a significant correlation between neuropsychological test performance and years of school, which supported the assumption that ability that is typically measured in neuropsychological testing is to a large extent, school-trained ability. Ostrosky-Solis, Ramirez, Lozano, Picasso, and Velez (2004) investigated the differential effect of the level of education and culture on performance with cognitive ability tests between indigenous (Mayan) and non-indigenous groups. They discovered that the indigenous group showed better results in visuospatial tasks but lower scores on verbal memory tasks, suggesting that the cultural environment influences the development and expression of specific cognitive skills over others.

Okagaki (2001) emphasised three factors that influence the school achievement of minority children. The first factor is the role of the school along with its form and perceived function. Okagaki believed that the role, form, and function of a school have the potential to elicit resistance from ethnic minority children if the culture of the school is not congruous with their own culture. The second factor encompasses the role of the family and recognises that ethnic minority children experience two distinct cultural contexts, home and school. The tension and dichotomy between these contexts may contribute to underachievement. The third factor is the role of the child and that the conflict between one's cultural identity and one's academic identity can result in resistance to academic achievement.

Running Wolf et al. (2002) stated that American Indian-Alaskan Native students that are at a higher risk for dropping out of school are in need of social and mental services, but determining these needs is full of challenges. A challenge mentioned by the authors is the view that psychological and evaluation processes are based in Western psychological theory, which is in contrast to the values of the tribal communities involved (pp. 32–33). They also acknowledged the tension between traditional educational formal assessment practices and cultural values contributes to educational achievement results.

Stairs (1995) identified the cultural basis of learning and teaching in Native education and listed the varying depth of First Nations content and curriculum implementation in schools. Table 14.1 outlines the various educational approaches to Aboriginal education.

Native ecology refers to the 'traditional material culture' and the acknowledgment, examination, and implementation of historic and traditional learning experiences

Table 14.1 The cultural base of learning and teaching in Native education

Limited cultural inclusion	Cultural inclusion	Narrow cultural base	Expanding cultural base	Broad cultural base
Native language	Native language	Native language	Native language	Native language
	Content material	Content material	Content material	Content material
		Ecological context	Ecological context	Ecological context
			Social process	Social process
				Cognitive process

and styles. It includes opportunities for extended observation, "backward chaining" (p. 140) and repetition of tasks. Backward chaining involves the deliberate incompletion of tasks by adults for children to complete. The goal is to involve the child in important and necessary tasks with the purpose of instilling a sense of community. The social process refers to the individual responsibility for group wellbeing. Education and learning are valued for both individual and group development. Finally, the cognitive process relates to the organisation of knowledge. Stairs (1995) encouraged educators to understand that First Nations students may perceive and organise information in a culturally distinct manner.

14.8.1 Trust

Reyna (2000) stated that numerous factors produce achievement discrepancies in minority students. Positive or negative expectations and beliefs about groups can affect how minority students are treated and can contribute to achievement discrepancies. Reyna also commented that stereotypes have attributional structures and that the attributions a teacher makes for a student's behaviour or performance can impact the student's own beliefs about his/her outcomes, which can positively or negatively influence motivation and future achievement strategies. Reyna's conclusions call attention to the potential impact that a teacher's subtle behaviour can have on student motivation and learning, and the need to address and challenge verbal and nonverbal behaviours that are barriers to student growth.

In their studies, Aakhus and Hoover (1998) and Albertini (2004) highlighted the importance for establishing trust. Aakhus and Hoover stated that for indigenous peoples, comfort level with service professionals (including teachers) was a key factor in ensuring programme success and that lack of trust toward non-Native professionals was a key obstacle. Albertini supported these conclusions with the following findings: "35 to 50 % of the students reported perceptions of moderate to high levels or unfavourable levels of racial mistrust towards their white teachers and whites in general" (p. 324). Albertine suggested that racial mistrust is an understudied area of school work, research, and practice.

14.9 Successful Initiatives and Promising Practices

> Like successful athletic coaches, the best teachers recognize the importance of ongoing assessments and continual adjustments on the part of both teacher and student as the means to achieve maximum performance. (McTighe & O'Conner, 2005, p. 10)

The assessment process should begin with the teacher gathering information to adapt instruction and support students in their learning. It may be necessary to involve parents and other professionals in the process. It is for this reason that a large portion of the best practices section of this paper will focus upon the knowledge, skills, and attitudes that teachers require in order to engage in fair, equitable, and quality assessments. These skills can be acquired in teacher preparation programs and through professional development opportunities. The need to recruit teachers of First Nation descent will also be addressed.

The second section of best practices will discuss assessment practices linked to goal setting and instructional planning; as well as assessment practices that motivate and assist students' meta-cognitive development and self-assessment. The need for assessment to be authentic, purposeful, and involve contextualized tasks will be elaborated upon.

The last section will address other important factors related to assessment such as parent support, relationships and trust, and community factors. When assessing Aboriginal students it is particularly important to form trusting relationships, and to be able to both gather information from parents as well as discuss assessment results. In order to truly understand the student and their learning it is necessary to understand the community in which they belong.

14.9.1 Teachers – Assessment and Instructional Response

Assessment is a dynamic process that contributes information to the decisions that are made about programs. Smith et al. (2006) believed that teachers play four major roles in school-based assessment as: consumers of assessment information; producers of assessment information; communicators of assessment information; and developers of assessment instruments. It is critical that they have a deep understanding of assessment which includes creating assessment techniques, and understanding test information, as well as the strengths and limitations of assessment strategies, and communicating assessment results with parents, students, and other professionals.

Smith et al. (2006) identified six ways that teachers can be involved in assessment:

1. Ask questions about the assessment process;
2. Seek help as needed in conveying information to parents;
3. Provide input. Formal test data should add to observations in the classroom about a student's ability, achievement, and learning patterns. A valid assessment should bring together multiple sources of information;

4. Observe assessment procedures whenever possible;
5. Consider issues of possible bias; and
6. Avoid viewing assessment as a means of confirming a set of observations or conclusions. Assessment is exploratory and may not lead to expected results. The purpose is to elicit useful information to help the student through effective programming, not to arrive at a foregone decision about eligibility for specific programs. (p. 19)

Teachers must become aware of their own assumptions, biases, expectations, and judgments. Thirteen principles of assessment for teachers of Aboriginal Studies 10-20-30 were outlined by Alberta Education and stated earlier in this paper (p. 15). These principles can be applied to the learning and achievement of all students, but resonate particularly well with Aboriginal students.

Assessment does not have to look the same for all students. As Hutchinson (2002) explained, fairness can be complex. She gives examples of students in wheelchairs who are not tested on running and blind students who are tested in braille. These examples of differentiated assessment strategies obviously make sense but are sometimes difficult to explain to parents and students. It is therefore important that teachers consistently reiterate their commitment to meeting individual needs.

Leahy, Lyon, Thompson, and William (2005) encouraged teachers to make a shift in their assessment practices from "quality control" to "quality assurance" (p. 18). The quality assurance approach is assessment *for* learning and involves adjustments to teaching while the learning is taking place. It requires a shift from 'attention to teaching' to 'attention to learning'. Research findings support the notion that using assessment for learning improves students' achievement. Leahy et al. (2005) developed five broad assessment strategies:

> clarifying and sharing learning intentions and criteria for success; engineering effective classroom discussions, questions, and learning tasks; providing feedback that moves learners forward; activating students as the owners of their own learning; and activating students as instructional resources for one another. (p. 20)

Another best practice is to link formative assessment to scaffolding. Shepard (2005) described scaffolding as teacher support to the learner during problem-solving – in the form of reminders, hints, and encouragement – to ensure successful completion of a task. Shepard stated that formative assessment uses insights about a learner's current understanding to alter the course of instruction and thus support the development of greater competence. She believed that formative assessment – like scaffolding – is a collaborative process and involves negotiation of meaning between teacher and learner about expectations and how best to improve performance. Shepard discussed four strategies that she believed are required before teachers realise the benefits of formative assessment. The first strategy is to elicit prior knowledge from students, as students understand new information only when it has been integrated into existing systems of meanings. The second strategy is to provide effective feedback to students to maintain motivation and self-confidence while focusing on learning goals and standards. The third strategy is to teach for transfer of knowledge to allow students to extend their knowledge to new situations.

The reality is that much of school learning is compartmentalised and is not applied to real-life situations. The fourth strategy is to teach students how to self-assess. By engaging students in self-critique, thinking deepens and both meta-cognitive and motivational purposes can be served.

In the Alberta Education resource titled *Our Words, Our Ways: Teaching First Nations, Métis and InuitLearners* (2005), the point is made that effective assessment is not removed from the learning experience, but is embedded in authentic learning activities based on higher-order thinking skills, such as problem-solving and analysis. The document described authentic assessments as comprising the following characteristics:

1. reflect understandings and abilities that matter in life;
2. are educational and engaging;
3. grow out of curriculum studies and are designed to do much more than provide a grade;
4. present real-life, interdisciplinary situations;
5. pose complex, open-ended challenges that require integration of knowledge and skills; and
6. often result in performances or presentations. (p. 111)

This resource underscores the need for teachers to be competent in 'assessment literacy' including: understanding and using multiple assessment methods to ensure that the information gathered about students' learning is complete and accurate; that individual students have the opportunity to demonstrate their learning in a variety of ways; communicating assessment criteria and results effectively; and involving students as partners in the assessment process.

In *Our Words, Our Ways: TeachingFirst Nations, Métis and Inuit Learners* attention is drawn to the fact that Aboriginal students may bring a set of life experiences to the classroom. "Aligning assessment approaches to match students' life experiences and culturally-based responses ensures that assessment practices are fair, inclusive and authentic, and that they contribute to students learning and overall sense of connection to learning" (p. 113). The document described a number of assessment practices that may penalise Aboriginal students:

1. single rather than multiple assessment methods;
2. inflexible deadlines (with late penalties);
3. time-limited assignments;
4. marks awarded for class participation and effort;
5. awarding zeroes for incomplete or missing assignments;
6. failure to match testing to teaching;
7. surprising students with pop quizzes; and
8. grading first efforts rather than providing ample time for teaching, practice and feedback before evaluating products.

The document suggested that Aboriginal students may struggle with handing assignments in on time and that lesser penalties (a 1 % or 2 % reduction) are more effective in encouraging on-time work while still accurately reflecting student achievement. It was suggested that Aboriginal approaches to education provide a student with repeated opportunities to observe, practice, and master a skill, much like an apprenticeship model. Reflecting this approach in assignments and tests offers students a second chance at being assessed. Teachers can support Aboriginal students by choosing to emphasise content rather than timing and by allowing students to complete missed tests and assignments. A third area of consideration was the assignment of grades on personal and social characteristics such as marks for participation. Personal and social characteristics such as effort, participation, and attitude may be related to cultural values. Aboriginal students may be quieter and less assertive and, as a result, may receive lower grades when these characteristics are part of an assessment. It was suggested that the learning needs and strengths of Aboriginal students can be most effectively supported by assessment practices that: offer multiple methods of assessment; state expectations and timelines clearly; and include elements of self-evaluation. It is important to note that the principles and practices that are outlined in the *Our Words, Our Ways* document are not only beneficial for Aboriginal students, but all students can benefit from their implementation.

14.9.2 Teachers – Professional Development

Generally, assessment practices are directly and indirectly influenced by many factors. This section will explore specific factors, particularly cognitive (i.e., knowledge and skill development) and affective (i.e., 'attitude', value, belief exploration and development) aspects of professional development, that influence the quality of assessment practiced on Aboriginal students. Increasingly, authentic Aboriginal content and materials are being developed and being made available for teachers. Quality content and materials are needed for meaningful knowledge and skill development and are representative of the cognitive domain. Authentic Aboriginal materials are an important component of an overall programme; 'how' teachers deliver the content (i.e., to what degree, with what attitude, the tone of both verbal and non-verbal communication – all aspects of the affective domain) is another critical component. With this in mind, a balanced teacher preparation and professional development programme should include both cognitive and affective exploration and learning.

In Aboriginal Perspectives Action Research Project: A Review of Literature, Ottmann and Pritchard (2009) stated:

> With the advent of globalization and significant population shifts and migration, there is a need for teacher preparation programs and professional development initiatives to address cultural diversity, specifically Aboriginal diversity. Gilchrist (2005) explains, 'In a study on teacher education, Johnston and Carson (2000) found that the curriculum of teacher education focused theories on learning, evaluation, normal child development, curriculum, and unit and lesson planning. There was very little in the curriculum that prepared teachers to teach in a multicultural setting'. (p. 25)

Leonard and Leonard (2006) supported Gilchrist, while specifically identifying the affective dimension when they wrote: "evidence is steadily growing of the need for preservice and inservice teachers to acquire the attitudes, values, and beliefs that will enable them to better serve the needs of an increasingly diverse student population" (p. 32). These authors encouraged educational organisations to address both the cognitive and affective aspects of learning to better prepare teachers for diverse and multicultural settings. Overall:

> Professional development in our changing world should be strategic, culturally- and contextually-relevant, interactive (e.g., action learning), multi-modal in delivery, continuous, and multi-faceted in consideration of complex needs, issues, and responsibilities of school leaders and educators – all with the goal of enhancing student achievement and overall student wellbeing. (Ottmann, 2010, p. 19)

There is evidence of educational organisations that are addressing the 'affective domain' of teaching and learning. In the Alberta Teachers Association (ATA) publication *Education is Our Buffalo* (2006) the following statement was made:

> In recent years, teachers have become more aware of prejudice toward, stereotyping of, and outright discrimination toward Aboriginal peoples in this society. Teachers can do their part to address this issue by increasing their awareness and understanding of Aboriginal histories, cultures, and perspectives. In doing so, they will be better able to implement instructional programs that support Aboriginal students and teacher Aboriginal learning outcomes to all students. (p. vii)

The ATA developed a full-day workshop titled *First Nations, Métis and InuitEducation – Taking Root, Branching Out* to complement the publication. In this workshop teachers examine the history, worldviews, cultures, and current perspectives of Alberta's First Nations, Metis, and Inuit peoples. Delving into the affective domain can be 'messy' and difficult as the learning shifts to more second-order change aspects; therefore, professional development of this kind requires a skilled facilitator and a process-oriented approach to delivery – time and support are key to growth at this level. Ottmann and Pritchard (2010) commented:

> It is important to reiterate that classroom practice is contextual, so there is no correct prescriptive method to teaching Aboriginal Perspectives. Meaningful learning happens when a teacher intimately knows himself or herself, and knows his or her students – where they come from and from what worldview they interpret their environment. Reaching this state of intimate understanding, may require deep, second-order change processes. In this respect, second-order change constitutes the seeking of personal understanding in relation to the environment. This process of discovery is a courageous movement, a shift to a place below the surface, to a more protective place, a place where the affective domain resides – a place where values and beliefs evolve. It is in a sense, a vision quest. If conscious, deliberate changes happen for an educator at this level, the chances of sustainability for those changes increase – the desired changes are captured for the future … second-order, deep seated changes in both the cognitive (the way Aboriginal peoples are known) and affective (the beliefs and feelings towards Aboriginal peoples) domains are needed for meaningful and 'effective' teaching of Aboriginal Perspectives … they are needed to perhaps address what the Elder indicated … to move towards 'something more right' for Aboriginal students, for all students. (p. 41)

As the Elder shared, professional development of this nature will benefit all teachers and their students. The components of a professional development programme that focuses on affective learning and Aboriginal perspectives may include cross-cultural learning and emphasise the importance of the educator's role as a cultural broker. Banks (1997) promoted the development of "cross-cultural competencies". He defined "cross-cultural competencies" as the skills, attitudes, and abilities that are needed in order to interact effectively and function competently within different cultural settings. He identified seven specific capacities:

1. to communicate respect in observable, tangible and appropriate ways;
2. to be non-judgmental;
3. to personalise knowledge and perceptions;
4. to display empathy to understand the feelings or ideas of another person;
5. for role flexibility;
6. to demonstrate reciprocal concern; and
7. to tolerate ambiguity.

While it is critical for teachers to increase their knowledge about Aboriginal peoples and to develop skills to meet the needs of an increasingly diverse group of students, it is also necessary to confront personal attitudes and values. This process of becoming aware of the internalised racism and stereotypes as well as institutional racism can be both challenging and rewarding but is a necessary prerequisite to fully understanding Aboriginal students, their families, and their communities.

The role of teacher as cultural broker can also be explored in a professional development process. Stairs (1995) stated that teachers act as cultural brokers between the 'Native and non-Native' and are consciously and unconsciously "selecting and transmitting to students a personal synthesis of knowledge, values, and human relationships gleaned from cultures in contact" (p. 147). For this reason, Stairs encouraged the intentional recruitment of Aboriginal people in teacher education programs. However, with intentional, strategic, continuous and supportive learning processes, both Aboriginal and non-Aboriginal teachers may be able to 'broker' and decipher the cultural and language nuances that influence learning while positively influencing Aboriginal student learning.

Quality, process-oriented, holistic teacher development, one that incorporates both cognitive and affective learning, is important to ensure that assessment practiced on Aboriginal students is respectful, meaningful, and culturally-appropriate. It requires both individual and societal examination of structures (i.e., laws, policies, rules etc.) and the values and belief systems that determine them. In this respect, professional development should include exercises that will lead the learner to either affirm or challenge existing assessment practices. Ultimately, the goal should be to intentionally and continually improve assessment practiced on Aboriginal students by considering the factors that positively or negatively influence the development and implementation of assessment.

14.9.3 School and Community

School and community collaboration and partnerships can be developed with the purpose of supporting Aboriginal student wellbeing which, in turn, may positively affect teacher assessment practices and influence positive academic achievement. Increasingly, there are examples of schools 'reaching out' to the community and to parents in order to further understand and support the students within the school. By understanding students' histories and backgrounds (e.g., worldviews), teachers are better able to develop programs, lesson plans, and implement assessment models that support student learning. Students have difficulty learning when their primary needs are not met and when they lack stability and safety in their families and communities. In a publication of Saskatchewan Education titled *Building Communities of Hope: Best Practices for Meeting the Learning Needs of At-Risk and Indian and Metis Students* (2004), the community school's framework is described as a comprehensive approach that has the "potential to create the holistic, preventive, caring and empowering educational environment required by all children, youth, and their families" (p. 2). The "communities of hope" are described as "responsive, inclusive, culturally affirming and academically challenging" (p. 4) and they "use collaborative approaches to achieve learning excellence and wellbeing for the entire community" (p. 8).

Another example of community involvement is from Parrett's (2005) research focused on an Idaho Nez Perce reservation school's success in turning around a history of underachievement and low performance. Factors of success included a focus on improving community collaboration, the hiring of a multicultural coordinator, a leadership team, alignment of curriculum with state standards, and administrators committed to established goals and vision. In addition, the stakeholders created and implemented eight components of improvement:

1. Ensure that effective district and school leadership eliminates failed policies and practices, and continually strives to establish successful interventions;
2. Understand the culture of poverty and its pervasive influences on student learning and academic achievement. The goal was to address the classroom (learning and teaching) challenges related to poverty;
3. Target low performing students, particularly in reading;
4. Early intervention; starting as early as possible with learning needs, and extending instructional hours to address student needs;
5. Institute and mandate curriculum and instructional improvements;
6. Build data and foster assessment literacy; understand how to use assessment data in order to foster a culture of assessment literacy; teachers need to develop clear targets and assessments to use as benchmarks;
7. Engage parents, schools and community; and
8. Support effective teaching; teachers must reflect a sincere belief that every student will achieve.

Emekauwa (2004) described a concerted effort to positively influence the Alaska state achievement scores for Alaskan Native Indians. The Alaska Rural Systems Initiative (AKRSI) included five major initiatives intended to create culturally-responsive education practices designed to help advance the achievement of Native children. An intent of the "Culturally Assigned Curriculum Adaptations" was to develop assessment practices that would be culturally appropriate, and that this aspect would be given as much attention as classroom content and teaching methods. As a result, non-traditional means of testing in state achievement tests were acceptable. Students could demonstrate their competence through projects, exhibitions, and portfolios. Emekauwa commented that AKRSI schools demonstrated positive gains in many of the state achievement tests, decreased dropout rates, and increased university enrolment.

There are growing examples of successful school practices for Aboriginal students. In 1987, Williams began the Feuerstein Mediated Learning pilot programme at a Vancouver inner-city school that had a 40 % Aboriginal population. Williams (2000, cited in Brant Castellano et al., 2000) wrote:

> At the end of the first year students scored higher in three cognitive abilities tests than they did at the beginning of the year (Vavrik, 1986). The program had a positive impact on student's self-esteem and confidence … First Nations learners in the FIE (Feuerstein Instrumental Enriched) program improved their ability to grasp the lessons and completed tasks more successfully than those who were not in the program. … Through the pilot project, we confirmed one of our suspicions: that teachers have to believe that the students are capable of learning demanding and abstract ideas. Without that belief, teachers are likely to give up on the students too quickly. The FIE curriculum gives teachers and students the opportunity to see that the latter can achieve and that their efforts will pay off. (p. 139)

In 1997, the FIE programme, comprised of "problem solving skills and exercises that are grouped into fourteen areas of cognitive development" (p. 141), won the Canada Award for the video *Mind of the Child*. The documentary highlighted the theory and practice supporting the FIE programme.

Joe Duquette High School (Regnier, 1995) mission statement reads:

> The Joe Duquette High School is a healing place which nurtures the mind, body and soul of its students. The school offers a program of studies which affirms the contemporary worldview of Indian people. The school supports the uniqueness and creativity of the individual and fosters self-actualization in a cooperative environment. (p. 314)

The philosophical foundation of the high school is based on the Sacred Circle. Regnier (1995) stated, "The Sacred Circle offered a healing approach to education based on holistic spiritual perspective on students and their place in the world" (p. 315). Teachers within the school attempt to address and academically stimulate the whole student with culturally relevant and meaningful school experiences.

Sharing our Success: *Ten Case Studies in Aboriginal Schooling* (Bell et al., 2004) provided findings from the case studies of ten schools located throughout British Columbia, Alberta, Saskatchewan, Manitoba, and the Yukon. The schools had diverse Aboriginal populations (ranging from 30 to 100 %) and varying governance structures (provincial, First Nations, and provincial-private partnerships). The academic programs implemented to improve student achievement also varied. For instance, Princess Alexandra, an inner-city elementary school in Saskatoon, discovered that school climate, community and parental relationships, teacher and staff-efficacy, and academic achievement improved after the Restitution Self-Management Programme was implemented. This programme encourages, among other things, problem solving, and internal-over-external reward motivators. Overall, analysis of the case studies revealed that the ten schools shared the following components:

1. Strong leadership and governance structures, often with long tenure;
2. High expectations for students;
3. Focus on academic achievement and long-term success;

4. Secure and welcoming climates for children and families;
5. Respect for Aboriginal culture and traditions to make learning relevant;
6. Quality staff development; and
7. Provision of a wide range of programs/supports for learning (Bell et al., 2004, p. 13).

Supporting Aboriginal students within the school is important in helping to increase student achievement; however, parental support is essential. Jeynes (2003) examined 21 previous studies to determine the impact of parental involvement on minority students' academic achievement. The results indicated that parental involvement positively affects academic achievement of minority students. Establishing and maintaining a strong home-school relationship contributes to a student's overall wellbeing and school success.

14.10 Conclusion: Possibilities

Ethnic disproportionality in special education refers to the fact that students from certain minority groups have been identified and placed in special education programs at rates that are disproportionate to the incidence of those minority students in the student population as a whole. In a province-wide survey conducted by Ottmann and Jeary in 2006, it was found that Aboriginal students were significantly over-represented in special education categories denoting both moderate and severe disabilities and under-represented in the gifted and talented category. While it is an established fact that achievement levels of Aboriginal students fall below those of non-Aboriginal peers, the point at which low achievement comes to be interpreted as "disability" is not as clear. The reasons for this low achievement are multiple and complex and comprise of socio-cultural factors, the dominant cultural impact on assessment, as well as factors related to the individual student and teacher.

Although special education provides costly and specialised services for those students with disabilities it is based on a deficit model, and the effectiveness of special education programs has been questioned over the last 30 years. Special education placement has historically meant removal from the mainstream into segregated programs and classrooms and there has been a societal stigma to the concept of "disability".

Disproportionality in special education becomes an issue when it perpetuates the deficit view of minority students and/or when the precursors or outcomes of special education are biased or inadequate (Harry, 2007). Three critical factors to be considered before students are identified with special education needs are: the quality of instruction prior to referral, possible bias in the referral process and inappropriate or biased assessment. Despite the fact that school personnel believe that the psychological evaluation process provides a scientific pathway to special education placement, Harry and Klingner (2006, cited in Harry, 2007), identified six sources of influence on the assessment. They identified the following: the influence of teachers' informal diagnoses of children's problems; school personnel's negative perceptions of children's families; external pressure for placement, such as the desire to remove low achievers from state-wide testing; the exclusion of information on classroom ecology, variable choice and implementation of assessment instruments; and psychologists' varying philosophical orientations. The researchers concluded that the power of 'unofficial practice and influences' undermined the belief that the assessment was either scientific or objective (p. 79).

There is overwhelming evidence that many Aboriginal children live in poverty and there is also overwhelming evidence of the correlation between socio-economic status and children's academic performance. In a report titled *Nurturing the Learning Spirit of First Nations Students* (National Panel on First Nation Elementary and Secondary Education for Students on Reserve, 2012) seven priorities for action were identified at the school level. Although the focus of the report was on schools on Reserves, it is equally important that these issues be addressed in provincial schools. The essential issues that were documented in the report align closely with the content of this chapter and for this reason some of the recommendations of the report are provided here. The report of the National Panel identified the following factors that correlate strongly with First Nation student success and must be addressed in improving the achievement of Aboriginal students: increasing school attendance; recruiting and retaining strong and effective principals to provide leadership in schools; recruiting well-qualified and effective teachers and ensuring the quality of instruction; creating safe and healthy learning environments; establishing a primary focus on developing basic literacy and numeracy skills; supporting extra-curricular activities in sports, art and music; and the provision of trades programs for high school students. The report also recognised three other important areas of investment: exposing students to their own language and culture in order to promote cultural awareness and pride; developing accurate ways to assess special needs, especially at the early primary level; and providing connectivity and technology equipment, training and content.

The possibilities for improving the school experiences and achievement of Aboriginal students are endless. It needs to begin however with educators examining their beliefs, assumptions, biases and judgments and using culturally sensitive instructional practice, including materials and assessment tools. Effective assessment must be embedded in authentic learning activities based on higher order thinking and problem solving. It is through these authentic learning experiences that the feelings of disconnect that Aboriginal students experience in traditional Western schools will be minimised. The life experiences that Aboriginal students bring to the classroom will be validated and subsequently contribute to their learning and achievement.

14.10.1 The Role of the Educational Leader

Strong leadership is essential in creating and sustaining first- and second-order change within an organisation, and it is apparent that policy, programme, curriculum, strategy and teacher and leadership professional development changes are necessary to better support Aboriginal students. Aboriginal educational scholars and leaders are providing recommendations that aim to strengthen First Nations, Métis and Inuit student learning and overall wellbeing. In 2005, the Assembly of First Nations (a national Indigenous organisation that represents 633 First Nations chiefs and their communities) in the document *First Nations Education Action Plan* made the following recommendations to educational leaders:

1. "Education that embodies and support the strengthening of a First Nation's identity through an emphasis on language, cultural and traditional knowledge, and the effective reincorporation of First Nation elders and women in educating younger generation" (p. 3).
2. "First Nations have opportunities to design and develop appropriate institutions to deliver essential professional and administrative support to their schools and communities in areas such as curriculum development, specialized services [and] assessment" (p. 6).
3. "Full involvement of First Nations people in the decision-making process as related to First Nations education" (p. 5).
4. "Enhanced relationships … between First Nations and provincial/territorial ministries, school boards, and schools to support First Nations participation in governance and to develop culturally appropriate programming, teacher recruitment and retention strategies and methods for tracking First Nations student progress and rates of success in the provincial/territorial systems" (p. 8).

The Assembly of First Nations encouraged the participation of Aboriginal peoples in designing authentic, culturally-appropriate programs and curricula; this included special education programs, for Aboriginal students. In order to make this a reality, educational leaders need to be intentional about developing collaborative partnerships with Aboriginal parents, Elders and leadership.

Dupuis (2012), in the study entitled *Supporting Urban Aboriginal Social Justice in Education: A Case Study of the Educational Leaders' Roles, Responsibilities, and Relationships as Care Providers* supports the Assembly of First Nations recommendations and she also highlights the importance of the ethic of care when working with Aboriginal students. Dupuis concluded:

> More conscious efforts by educational leaders across Canada are needed for the advocacy for change that leads to Aboriginal student success in schools systems; specifically, for educational leaders at the system level to address the most current community issues (ranging from educational attainment, to self-esteem, to mental wellness, to poverty), so educational leaders at the local level are empowered to address the academic, cultural, social, and economic needs of the Aboriginal students in a caring manner, in a manner that ultimately establishes relationships and school-family-community partnerships. The result is that educational leader's need adequate time and support to provide up-to-date programming for Aboriginal students and at every step of this process, they need to work together with all committed stakeholders to build respectful, innovative partnerships that are sustainable. (p. 193)

Based on her literature and research findings, which included interviewing educational leaders within an urban school division, Dupuis made the following suggestions for educational leaders:

1. Aim to build holistic, caring, and collaborative school-family-community relationships and networks to improve the urban Aboriginal learners' wellbeing that identify with Aboriginal beliefs and values to inspire, motivate, and support Aboriginal student success.
 2. Take the time to observe and actively listen to the Aboriginal students and their families. Ask essential questions to understand their individual needs, appreciate their way of thinking, and honour their stories and experiences.
 3. Demonstrate a genuine willingness to provide a high level of care and support so the concepts of harmony, balance, and interconnectedness within the collaborative relationship will be realised.
 4. Develop a well-thought out 'individualised care and support plan' that involves the participation of a collaborative network of school-family-community partners who are willing to selflessly commit themselves throughout the duration of the programme experience.
 5. The plan needs to look at identifying the following: (a) the individual needs of Aboriginal students and their families; (b) the existing barriers and challenges; (c) goals, strategies, and programming that addresses academic, cultural, social, and economic needs; (d) authentic ways to explore Aboriginal student identity, heritage and culture (i.e., including methods of communication, diverse traditions, practices, belief and value systems); (e) roles and responsibilities of the caregivers based on area of expertise; and (f) next steps for student success and/or student transitions.
 6. Take time to identify approaches to implement quality professional development activities and professional development networking opportunities, and identification of culturally relevant curriculum resource and support materials that are aligned with the Ministry of Education requirements and the needs of the Aboriginal communities.
 7. Monitor Aboriginal student success by establishing benchmark goals with measurables and assessing the effectiveness of the supports in place.
 8. It is likely that a caregiving relationship that promotes harmony, balance, and interconnectedness among the worldviews has likely been achieved by following the recommended approaches.
 9. Take time to honour and share the success stories of the school-family-community partners involved.
 10. Provide encouragement for educational leaders to continue to build on their own educational pedagogies to include knowledge and understanding of urban Aboriginal peoples (i.e., traditions, practices, and philosophies), varied realities, as well as their existing issues and challenges, so they can work to generate a shared purpose. (p. 200)

Finally, Dupuis proposed a holistic model for change that educational leaders can refer to when working with Aboriginal students and their communities.

Both cognitive (knowledge and skill acquisition) and affective (perceptions, values and beliefs systems) professional development as it relates to Aboriginal peoples (their histories, epistemologies, ontologies, philosophies, cultures and traditions that are very dependent on the location) is important for educational leaders, and their staff, for the purpose of strengthening programming and curriculum for Aboriginal students. Aboriginal students' reality needs to be understood, and one way of doing this is to seek and secure meaningful partnerships with Aboriginal parents, Elders, scholars and leadership. Next, assessment practices and teacher and leader perceptions and practices have to be questioned, evaluated and strengthened if meaningful and sustainable change is to be experienced by Aboriginal students in Canada and in other contexts. Ultimately, change begins with the ethic and exercise of care.

References

Aakhus, B. P., & Hoover, H. (1998). *Rural Ojibwe mothers' experiences with early childhood special education services*. North Dakota, ND: Clearinghouse on Rural Education and Small Schools.
Agbenyega, S., & Jiggetts, J. (1999). Minority children & their overrepresentation in special education. *Education, 119*(4), 619–632.
Alberta Education. (2002). *Aboriginal studies 10-20-30 guide to implementation, section 4: Assessment*. Edmonton, AB, Canada: Alberta Learning.
Alberta Education. (2005). *Our words, our ways: Teaching First Nations, Métis and Inuit learners*. Edmonton, AB, Canada: Alberta Government. Retrieved from: www.education.gov.ab.ca/k_12/curriculum/OurWords.asp
Alberta Learning. (2002). *First Nations, Métis and Inuit policy framework*. Edmonton, AB, Canada: Government of Alberta. Retrieved from: http://education.alberta.ca/media/164126/framework.pdf
Alberta Learning. (2004). *Student population by grade, school and authority in Alberta: 2003/2004 school year*. Edmonton, AB, Canada: Government of Alberta. Retrieved from: http://education.alberta.ca/apps/eireports/pdf_files/eis1004_2004/eis1004.pdf
Alberta Teachers' Association. (2006). *Education is our buffalo: A teachers' resource for First Nations, Métis and Inuit education in Alberta*. Edmonton, AB, Canada: Alberta Teachers' Association.
Albertini, V. L. (2004). Racial mistrust among immigrant minority students. *Child and Adolescent Social Work Journal, 21*(4), 311–331.
Allard, Y., Wilkins, R., & Berthelot, J. (2004). Premature mortality in health regions with Aboriginal populations. *Health Reports, 15*(1), 51–60. Ottawa, ON, Canada: Statistics Canada. Retrieved from: http://www.statcan.gc.ca/pub/82-003-x/2003001/article/6765-eng.pdf
Ardila, A., & Moreno, S. (2001). Neuropsychological test performance on Aruaco Indians: An exploratory study. *Journal of the International Neuropsychological Society, 7*(4), 510–515.
Artiles, A. J. (1998). The dilemma of difference: Enriching the disproportionality discourse with theory and context. *Journal of Special Education, 32*(1), 32–36.
Assembly of First Nations. (2005). *First Nations education action plan, May 2005*. Retrieved from: http://www.afn.ca/cmslib/general/Education-Action%20Plan.pdf
Banks, J. A. (1997). Multicultural education: Characteristics and goals. In J. A. Banks & C. A. McGee Banks (Eds.), *Multicultural education: Issues and perspectives* (3rd ed., pp. 3–31). Boston, MA: Allyn and Bacon.
Battiste, M. (Ed.). (2000). *Reclaiming indigenous voice and vision*. Vancouver, BC, Canada: UBC Press.
Beiser, M. (1989). *Flower of two soils: Final report for NIMH Grant No MH 36678-04*. Rockville, MD: National Institute of Mental Health.

Beiser, M., & Gotowiec, A. (2000). Accounting for native/non-native differences in IQ scores. *Psychology in the Schools, 37*(3), 237–252.

Beiser, M., Sack, W., Manson, S. M., Redshirt, R., & Dion, R. (1998, July). Mental health and the academic performance of First Nations and majority-culture children. *American Journal of Orthopsychiatry, 63*(3), 455–468.

Bell, D., Anderson, K., Fortin, T., Ottmann, J., Rose, S., Simard, L., ... Raham, H. (2004). *Sharing our success: Ten case studies in Aboriginal schooling*. Kelowna, BC, Canada: Society for the Advancement of Excellence in Education.

British Columbia Ministry of Education. (2001). *Over-representation of Aboriginal students reported with behaviour disorders*. Victoria, BC, Canada: Government of British Columbia, Aboriginal Education Branch and Special Program Branch. Retrieved from: http://www.bced.gov.bc.ca/abed/abed_over.pdf

Campaign 2000. (2010a). *2010 report card on child and family poverty in Canada: 1989–2010*. Toronto, ON, Canada: Thistle Printing.

Campaign 2000. (2010b). *Revisiting family security in unsecure times: 2011 report card on child and family poverty in Canada*. Toronto, ON, Canada: Thistle Printing.

Canadian Council of Child and Youth Advocates. (2011). *Special report, Aboriginal children, Canada must do better: Today and tomorrow*. Retrieved from: http://www.rcybc.ca/Images/PDFs/Reports/CCCYA_UN_Report-FINAL%20oct%2027.pdf

Canadian Council on Social Development. (2003). *Aboriginal children in poverty in urban communities: Social exclusion and the growing racialization of poverty in Canada*. Ottawa, ON, Canada: CCSD. Retrieved from: http://www.ccsd.ca/pr/2003/aboriginal.htm

Canadian Teachers' Federation. (2009). *Supporting education ... building Canada: Child poverty and schools*. Ottawa, ON, Canada: Canadian Teachers' Federation. Retrieved from: http://www.ctf-fce.ca/publications/Briefs/FINAL_Hilldayleavebehind_eng.pdf

Community Foundations of Canada. (2009a). *Vital signs: Community foundations taking the pulse of Canadian communities, executive summary*. Retrieved from: http://www.vitalsignscanada.ca/nr-2009-intro-e.html

Community Foundations of Canada. (2009b). *Canada's vital signs 2009: Research findings*. Retrieved from: http://www.vitalsignscanada.ca/nr-2009-research-findings-e.html

Costa, X. B. (1997). Intercultural education and teacher training. In D. Woodrow, G. K. Verma, M. B. Rocha-Trindade, G. Campani, & C. Bagley (Eds.), *Intercultural education: Theories, policies and practice* (pp. 183–201). Aldershot, UK: Ashgate Publishing.

Daniels, V. I. (1998). Minority students in gifted and special education programs: The case for educational equity. *The Journal of Special Education, 32*(1), 41–43.

Dunn, L. M. (1968). Special education for the mildly retarded – Is much of it justifiable? *Exceptional Children, 35*, 5–22.

Dupuis, J. (2012). *Supporting urban Aboriginal social justice in education: A case study of the educational leaders' roles, responsibilities, and relationships as care providers*. Unpublished doctoral dissertation, University of Calgary, Calgary, AB, Canada.

Earl, L., & Katz, S. (2006). *Rethinking classroom assessment with purpose in mind: Assessment for learning, assessment as learning, assessment of learning*. Winnipeg, MN, Canada: Manitoba Education, Citizenship and Youth. Retrieved from: http://www.edu.gov.mb.ca/k12/assess/wncp/rethinking_assess_mb.pdf

Education Week. (2013, November 7). *Achievement gap*. Bethesda, MD: Editorial Projects in Education. Retrieved from: http://www.edweek.org/ew/issues/achievement-gap/

Emekauwa, E. (2004). *The star with my name: The Alaska rural systemic initiative and the impact of place-based education on native student achievement*. Washington, DC: Rural School and Community Trust.

Ford, D. Y. (1998). The underrepresentation of minority students in gifted education: Problems and promises in recruitment and retention. *Journal of Special Education, 32*(1), 4–14.

Friend, M., & Bursuck, W. (1996). *Including students with special needs: A practical guide for classroom teachers*. Toronto, ON, Canada: Allyn & Bacon.

Gilchrist, B. (2005). *Integrating aboriginal content and perspectives: The experience of four elementary school teachers*. Unpublished master's thesis, University of Saskatchewan, Saskatoon, Saskatchewan, Canada.

Government of Canada. (1996). *Report of the Royal Commission on Aboriginal peoples* (Vol. 3). Retrieved from: http://www.collectionscanada.gc.ca/webarchives/20071211053327/http://www.ainc-inac.gc.ca/ch/rcap/sg/si45_e.html#4. Youth.

Greenfield, P. M. (1997). You can't take it with you: Why ability assessments don't cross cultures. *American Psychologist, 52*(10), 1115–1124.

Harper, M., O'Connor, K., & Simpson, M. (1999). *Quality assessment: Fitting the pieces together*. Toronto, ON, Canada: Ontario Secondary School Teachers Federation.

Harry, B. (2007). The disproportionate placement of ethnic minorities in special education. In L. Florian (Ed.), *The sage handbook of special education* (pp. 67–84). Thousand Oaks, CA: Sage.

Harry, B., Klingner, J. K., Sturges, K. M., & Moore, R. F. (2002). Of rock and soft places: Using qualitative methods to investigate disproportionality. In D. J. Losen & G. Orfield (Eds.), *Racial inequity in special education* (pp. 71–92). Cambridge, MA: Harvard Education Press.

Howe, E. (2004). Education and lifetime income for Aboriginal people in Saskatchewan. In J. P. White, P. Maxim, & D. Beavon (Eds.), *Aboriginal policy research: Setting the agenda for change* (Vol. 1). Toronto, ON, Canada: Thompson Educational Publishing.

Howley, C. B., & Bickel, R. (2000). *When it comes to schooling … small works: School size, poverty, and student achievement*. Randolph, VT: Clearinghouse on Rural Education and Small Schools.

Hughes, H., & Hughes, M. (2012). *Indigenous education 2012*. St. Leonards, NSW, Australia: The Centre for Independent Studies. Retrieved from: http://www.cis.org.au/images/stories/policy-monographs/pm-129.pdf

Hull, J. (2005, June 15). *Post-secondary education and labour market outcomes Canada, 2001*. Ottawa, ON, Canada: Minister of Indian Affairs and Northern Development.

Hutchinson, N. (2002). *Inclusion of exceptional learners in Canadian schools: A practical handbook for teachers*. Toronto, ON, Canada: Pearson.

Indian and Northern Affairs Canada. (1996). *Royal Commission on Aboriginal peoples, Volume 3, Gathering strength, youth*. Retrieved from: http://www.collectionscanada.gc.ca/webarchives/20071115053257/http://www.ainc-inac.gc.ca/ch/rcap/sg/sgmm_e.html

Indian and Northern Affairs Canada. (2004a). *Basic departmental data 2004*. Canada: Author. Retrieved from: http://www.collectionscanada.gc.ca/webarchives/20071125233054/http://www.ainc-inac.gc.ca/pr/sts/bdd04/bdd04_e.pdf

Indian and Northern Affairs Canada. (2004b). *Royal Commission on Aboriginal peoples, Volume 3, Gathering strength, education*. Canada: Author. Retrieved from: http://www.collectionscanada.gc.ca/webarchives/20060205104115/http://www.aincinac.gc.ca/ch/rcap/sg/si43_e.html

Inuit Tapiriit Kanatami. (2010). *Inuit TB rates double to 185 times the rate of Canadian-born non-Aboriginals: First Nations rate 31 times higher*. Ottawa, ON, Canada. Retrieved from: http://www.itk.ca/media-release/inuit-tb-rate-doubles-185-times-rate-canadian-born-nonaboriginals-first-nations-rate-

Jeffers, S. (1991). *Brother eagle and sister sky*. New York, NY: Dial Books.

Jeynes, W. H. (2003). A meta-analysis: The effects of parental involvement on minority children's academic achievement. *Education and Urban Society, 35*(2), 202–218.

Joint Advisory Working Group Committee. (1993). *Principles for fair student assessment practices for education in Canada*. Edmonton, AB, Canada: Joint Advisory Committee. Retrieved from: http://www2.education.ualberta.ca/educ/psych/crame/files/eng_prin.pdf

King, M. L. (1998). Letter from Birmingham jail. In C. Carson (Ed.), *The autobiography of Martin Luther King Jr* (pp. 187–204). New York, NY: Intellectual Properties Management in Association with Warner Books.

Klenowski, V. (2009). Australian indigenous students: Addressing equity issues in assessment. *Teaching Education, 20*(1), 77–93.

Leahy, S., Lyon, C., Thompson, M., & William, D. (2005). Classroom assessment: Minute-by-minute and day-by-day. *Educational Leadership, 63*(3), 18–24.

Leonard, P., & Leonard, L. (2006). Teachers and tolerance: Discriminating diversity dispositions. *The Teacher Educator, 42*(1), 30–62.

Little Bear, L. (2000). Jagged worldviews colliding. In M. Battiste (Ed.), *Reclaiming Indigenous voice and vision* (pp. 77–85). Vancouver, BC, Canada: UBC Press.

Losen, D. J., & Orfield, G. (Eds.). (2002). *Racial inequity in special education*. Cambridge, MA: Harvard Education Press.

MacMillan, D. L., Gresham, F. M., Lopez, M. F., & Bocian, K. M. (1996). Comparison of students nominated for prereferral interventions by ethnicity and gender. *The Journal of Special Education, 30*, 133–151.

MacMillan, D. L., & Reschly, D. J. (1998). Overrepresentation of minority students: The case for greater specificity or reconsideration of the variables examined. *Journal of Special Education, 32*(1), 15–24.

Manuelito, K. D. (2003). *Building a native teaching force: Important considerations*. Charleston, WV: Clearinghouse on Rural Education and Small Schools.

McInerney, D. M., & McInerney, V. (1996). *Schools, socialization, and the goals of schooling: What counts in classrooms characterised by cultural diversity*. New South Wales, Australia: Clearinghouse on Teaching and Teacher Education.

McLoughlin, J. A., & Lewis, R. B. (2001). *Assessing students with special needs* (5th ed.). Columbus, OH: Merrill/Prentice Hall.

McShane, D. A. (1983a). Explaining achievement patterns of American Indian children: A transcultural and developmental model. *Peabody Journal of Education, 61*(1), 34–48.

McShane, D. A. (1983b). The transcultural education of American Indian and Alaska Native children: Teachers and students in transaction. *Peabody Journal of Education, 61*(1), 1–5.

McTighe, J., & O'Conner, J. (2005, November). Seven principles for effective learning. *Educational Leadership, 63*(3), 10–17.

Meece, J. L., & Kurtz-Costes, B. (2001). Introduction: The schooling of ethnic minority children and youth. *Educational Psychologist, 36*(1), 1–7.

National Center for Education Statistics. (2012). *National Indian education study 2011. The educational experiences of American Indian and Alaska Native students at grades 4 and 8*. Institute of Educational Sciences: U.S. Department of Education, Washington, DC. Retrieved from: http://niea.org/data/files/Policy/nationsreportcardaian2012.pdf

National Panel on First Nation Elementary and Secondary Education for Students on Reserve. (2012). *Nurturing the learning spirit of First Nations students*. Ottawa, ON, Canada: Aboriginal Affairs and Northern Development. Retrieved from: http://firstnationeducation.ca/wp-content/themes/clf3/pdfs/Report_02_2012.pdf

Neisser, U., Boodoo, G., Bouchard Jr. T. J., Boykin, A. W., Brody, N., … Urbina, S. (1996). Intelligence: Knowns and unknowns. *American Psychologist, 51*(2), 77–101.

Nelson-Barber, S., & Estrin, E. T. (1995). *Culturally responsive mathematics and science education for native students*. Washington, DC: Clearinghouse on Rural Education and Small Schools.

New Zealand Government. (2013). *Effective governance: Supporting education success as Māori*. Wellington, NZ, New Zealand: Ministry of Education. Retrieved from: http://www.minedu.govt.nz/~/media/MinEdu/Files/Boards/EffectiveGovernance/SupportingEducationSuccessAsMaori.pdf

O'Donnell, V., & Tait, H. (2004). Well-being of the non-reserve Aboriginal population (Catalogue no. 11-008). *Canadian Social Trends*. Ottawa, ON, Canada: Statistics Canada. Retrieved from: http://thornlea.sharpschool.com/UserFiles/Servers/Server_119514/File/Library%20Classes%20Documents/Gr.%209%20Geography/wellbeingofnonaboriginalpopulation.pdf

Office of the Auditor General of Canada. (2010). *Opening statement to the standing senate committee on Aboriginal peoples: Indian and Northern affairs Canada – Education program and post-secondary student support*. Retrieved from: http://www.oag-bvg.gc.ca/internet/English/oss_20100512_e_33879.html

Okagaki, L. (2001). Triarchic model of minority children's school achievement. *Educational Psychologist, 36*(1), 9–20.

Okagaki, L., & Sternberg, R. J. (1993). Parental beliefs and children's school performance. *Child Development, 64,* 36–56.

Olszewski-Kubilius, P., Lee, S. Y., Ngoi, M., & Ngoi, D. (2004). Addressing the achievement gap between minority and nonminority children by increasing access to gifted programs. *Journal for the Education of the Gifted, 28*(2), 127–158.

Ontario Federation of Indian Friendship Centres. (2000). *Urban Aboriginal child poverty: A status report on Aboriginal children and their families in Ontario.* Retrieved from: http://www.spcottawa.on.ca/EOCPRN/PDFs/FSAboriginal.pdf

Ostrosky-Solis, F., Ramirez, M., Lozano, A., Picasso, H., & Velez, A. (2004). Culture or education? Neuropsychological test performance of a Maya indigenous population. *International Journal of Psychology, 39*(1), 34–46.

Oswald, D. P., Coutinho, M. J., & Best, L. M. (2002). Community and school predictors of overrepresentation of minority children in special education. In D. J. Losen & G. Orfield (Eds.), *Racial inequity in special education* (pp. 1–13). Cambridge, MA: Harvard Education Press.

Ottmann, J. (2010). *"Our way is a valid way": A professional development resource and "Our way is a valid way". A Professional Development Resource for Teachers K-12: A Literature Review.* Edmonton, AB, Canada: Alberta Education, FNMI Services Branch.

Ottmann, J., & Jeary, J. (2006). *Aboriginal students and assessment practices.* Unpublished manuscript.

Ottmann, J., & Pritchard, L. (2009). *Aboriginal perspectives action research project: A review of literature.* Calgary, AB, Canada: Calgary Regional Consortium.

Ottmann, J., & Pritchard, L. (2010). Aboriginal perspectives and the social studies curriculum. *First Nations Perspectives: The Journal of the Manitoba First Nations Education Resource Centre Inc., 3,* 21–46.

Parker, S. W., Rubalcava, L., & Teruel, G. (2005). Schooling inequality and language barriers. *Economic Development and Cultural Change, 54*(1), 71–94.

Parrett, W. H. (2005). Against all odds. *School Administrator, 62*(1), 26–29.

Regnier, R. (1995). The sacred circle: An Aboriginal approach to healing education at a urban high school. In M. Battiste & J. Barman (Eds.), *First Nations education in Canada: The circle unfolds* (pp. 313–329). Vancouver, BC, Canada: UBC Press.

Reid, S. (2002). *The achievement gap 2002: How minority students are faring in North Carolina's public schools. An update.* Raleigh, NC: Clearinghouse on Urban Education.

Reyna, C. (2000). Lazy, dumb, or industrious: When stereotypes convey attribution information in the classroom. *Educational Psychology Review, 12*(1), 85–110.

Richards, H. V., Brown, A. F., & Forde, T. B. (2007). Addressing diversity in schools: Culturally responsive pedagogy. *Teaching Exceptional Children, 39*(3), 64–68.

Rothstein, R. (2004). The achievement gap: A broader picture. *Educational Leadership, 62*(3), 40–43.

Running Wolf, P., Soler, R., Manteuffel, B., Sondheimer, D., Rolando, L., & Erickson, J. S. (2002). *Cultural competence approaches to evaluation in tribal communities.* New Mexico, USA: Clearinghouse on Rural Education and Small Schools.

Saskatchewan Learning. (2004). *Building communities of hope: Best practices for meeting the learning needs of at-risk and Indian and Metis students.* Regina, SK, Canada: Children's Services and Program Branch. Retrieved from: http://www.education.gov.sk.ca/building-communities-of-hope

Shepard, L. A. (2005). Linking formative assessment to scaffolding. *Educational Leadership, 63*(3), 66–70.

Smith, T. E., Polloway, E. A., Patton, J. K., Dowdy, C. A., Heath, N., McIntyre, L. J., & Francis, G. C. (2006). *Teaching students with special needs in inclusive settings.* Toronto, ON, Canada: Pearson.

Stairs, A. (1995). Learning processes and teaching roles in Native education: Cultural base and cultural brokerage. In M. Battiste & J. Barman (Eds.), *First Nations education in Canada: The circle unfolds* (pp. 139–153). Vancouver, BC, Canada: UBC Press.

Standing Senate Committee on Human Rights. (2007). *Children: The silenced citizens. Effective implementation of Canada's international obligations with respect to the rights of children.* Ottawa, ON, Canada. Retrieved from: http://www.parl.gc.ca/Content/SEN/Committee/391/huma/rep/rep10apr07-e.pdf

Statistics Canada. (2006a). *Aboriginal peoples in Canada in 2006: Inuit, Metis and First Nations, 2006 census.* Retrieved from: Statistics Canada: http://www.statcan.gc.ca/daily-quotidien/080115/dq080115a-eng.htm

Statistics Canada. (2006b). *Aboriginal people are younger on average than non-Aboriginal people.* Retrieved from: Statistics Canada: http://www.statcan.gc.ca/pub/89-645-x/2010001/median-age-eng.htm

Sternberg, R. (2004). Culture and intelligence. *American Psychologist, 59*(5), 325–338.

Suzuki, L. A., & Valencia, R. R. (1997). Race-ethnicity and measured intelligence: Educational implications. *American Psychologist, 52*(10), 1103–1114.

Turpel-Lafond, M. (2007). More than words: Promoting and protecting the rights of indigenous children with international human rights instruments. In J. Hartley, P. Joffe, & J. Preston (Eds.), *Realizing the UN declaration on the rights of Indigenous peoples: Triumph, hope, and action* (pp. 169–188). Saskatoon, SK, Canada: Purich Publishing Ltd.

U.S. Department of Education. (2001). *American Indian and Alaska native education research agenda.* Washington, DC: U.S. Department of Education.

U.S. Department of Education. (2002). *Twenty-fourth annual report to Congress on the implementation of the individuals with disabilities Education Act.* Washington, DC: U.S. Department of Education.

Valles, B. C. (1998). The disproportionate representation of minority students in special education: Responding to the problem. *The Journal of Special Education, 32*(1), 52–54.

Villegas, A. M., & Lucas, T. (2007). The culturally responsive teacher. *Educational Leadership, 64*(6), 28–33.

Vygotsky, L. S. (1963). Learning and mental development at school age. In J. Simon & B. Simons (Eds.), *Educational psychology in the USSR* (pp. 21–34). Stanford, CA: Stanford University Press.

Wiggins, G. (1993). Assessment: Authenticity, context, and validity. *Phi Delta Kappan, 75*(3), 200–214.

Williams, L. (2000). Urban Aboriginal education: The Vancouver experience. In M. Brant Castellano, L. Davis, & L. Lahache (Eds.), *Aboriginal education: Fulfilling the promise* (pp. 129–146). Vancouver, BC, Canada: UBC Press.

Wilson, D., & Macdonald, D. (2010, April). *The income gap between Aboriginal peoples and the rest of Canada.* Ottawa, ON, Canada: Canadian Centre for Policy Alternatives. Retrieved from: http://www.policyalternatives.ca/sites/default/files/uploads/publications/reports/docs/Aboriginal%20Income%20Gap.pdf

Yero, J. L. (2002a). *If we should, why don't we?* Teacher's mind resources. Retrieved from: http://www.teachersmind.com/pdfdirectory/Should.PDF

Yero, J. L. (2002b). *Teaching in mind: How teacher thinking shapes education.* Hamilton, MO, Canada: MindFlight Publishing.

Index

A
Accountability, 7, 8, 15, 17–18, 39, 54, 71, 72, 94, 147, 211, 276, 278, 296–299
Assessment
 alternative, 38–39
 authentic, 28, 37, 119, 207, 209, 237, 238, 259, 280, 314, 318, 333, 338, 348
 classroom-based, 313, 317–320
 contemporary, 31
 of conversation, 182
 criterion-referenced, 238, 334
 debates, 35, 89, 91, 95, 97–101, 229, 244, 291, 307, 309, 311, 312, 315
 diagnostic, 39
 dynamic, 39–40
 formative, 179–187
 function of, 32, 35
 integrative, 40
 for learning, 29, 33, 68, 70–74, 104, 145–147, 160, 164–165, 174, 298, 336, 347
 of learning, 29, 34, 50, 56, 68, 70, 71, 82, 172, 179
 literacy, 293–296
 norm-referenced, 117, 334
 paradigm, 322
 peer, 101, 104, 183
 performance, 37, 38, 90, 100, 112, 114, 117, 119, 121, 133, 135, 231, 338
 policy, 287, 289, 293, 294
 practices, 106, 112, 121, 132, 146, 160, 173, 181, 189, 276, 280, 283, 292, 295, 300, 306, 310–312, 320, 328, 336, 344, 346, 348, 349, 351, 352, 358
 purpose of, 29, 32, 289
 self-assessment, 40, 105
 standardised testing, 90, 95, 132, 172, 173, 226, 251, 278, 334
 terminology, 25–26, 28, 36–41, 189, 204
Assessment philosophy
 appreciation of diversity, 211, 220
 equality, 131, 165, 215, 245, 258, 266, 276, 321
 equity, 131, 143, 187, 215, 244, 245, 252–258, 268, 275, 278, 292, 297, 300, 306, 340
 ethic of care, 210, 213, 220, 256, 282, 356
 fairness, 232, 274–276, 278, 279, 337, 347
Australia, 105, 138, 174, 202, 248–249, 328, 343

B
Bangladesh, 306
Beliefs, 90, 119, 130, 172, 184, 200, 208, 210–212, 216, 234, 245, 264, 265, 269, 295, 307, 315, 337, 340, 343, 345, 350, 357

C
Canada, 79, 134, 174, 202, 225, 249–250, 308, 329, 332, 343
 Canadian education, 306, 320, 338
Change
 Concerns Based Adoption Model (CBAM), 48, 75
Community partnerships, 213–216, 356
Cultural diversity
 bilinguals and multilinguals, 228–236
 English language learners (ELL), 231, 233, 234
 monolingual bias, 226

D

Decision-making, 215, 278, 280, 281, 283, 321, 331, 333, 356
Differentiation
 assessment, 258, 261–262, 347
 instruction, 81, 207, 210, 213, 219, 245, 249, 258–261, 267, 268, 318
Disciplines
 mathematics learning, 143
 science assessment, 114, 182, 187, 191
 visual and performing arts, 112, 114, 116, 121, 138

E

Efficacy, 64
 self, 15–16, 255–256, 259
 student, 2, 15, 212, 254
 teacher collective, 6
 teachers, 6, 17, 47, 48, 189, 200, 210, 220
England, 202
Evaluation, 40–41
 formative, 262, 275
 programme, 27, 28
 purpose of, 25, 28–34, 136, 209, 235, 290, 345
 resistance to evaluation, 167, 344
 self-evaluation (*see* Assessment, self-assessment)
 summative, 275

F

Finland, 105, 174

G

Germany, 48, 79
Gifted and talented (G&T)
 programmes, 247, 248, 250, 256, 268
 students, 244, 245, 249, 250, 258, 261, 266–268
 teacher, 262–264
Globalisation, 3, 12, 349
Great Britain, 138, 172, 248

H

Hong Kong, 105, 202

I

Inclusion
 accommodation, 206, 209, 217, 227, 231, 232, 238, 317, 321
 advocacy, 210, 213, 252, 264–265, 268
 case management, 218, 220
 disabilities, 144, 159, 161, 165, 202, 203, 217, 220, 258, 310, 317, 330, 354
 diversity, 94, 119, 233, 236, 247, 248, 254, 274, 284, 288, 292, 293, 309, 313, 315, 320, 322, 342
 exceptionalities, 203–205, 209, 211, 218–220, 244, 246, 247, 264, 266–268
 inclusive assessment, 282, 300
 paraprofessionals, 205, 206, 211, 213
 special education, 143, 149, 203, 215, 226, 300, 306, 308, 309, 317, 328, 334, 339–340, 354
 special needs, 14, 143, 151, 159, 161, 200, 202–206, 209, 212, 215, 218, 219, 244, 249, 251, 266, 268, 311, 321
Indigenous students
 Australian Aboriginals, 273–284
 First Nations, 306–322, 328–358
 Māori, 289, 292, 294, 296
 Métis and Inuit, 348, 350, 356
Instructional approaches
 classroom practices, 274, 281, 282, 311, 337
 cooperative learning, 45–83
 discipline-based inquiry, 142
 group work, 46, 52–54, 56, 58, 60, 61, 63, 64, 66, 71–74, 81, 82
Instructional design, 8–10, 12, 16–17, 19
 planning, 59, 89, 121, 180, 186, 207, 211, 219, 280, 283, 297, 299, 343, 346
 universal design for learning (UDL), 143–145
Ireland, 48, 51, 79, 174

J

Japan, 237

K

Korea, 105

L

Leadership
 commitment, 215, 245
 courage, 131, 135, 139, 263, 266
 instructional, 2–9, 46, 79, 83, 112, 131–135, 138, 175, 182, 208, 216, 220
 principal's role, 133
 student-centred leadership, 143, 146–147, 167

Index

M
Moderation, 105, 297, 301
Motivation, 14–17, 60, 90, 180, 261
Motivation and assessment
  affective domain, 349, 350
  empowerment, 103
  leader, 6, 8
  student, 6, 8, 14–16, 100, 132, 133, 172, 210, 212, 298, 341, 343, 345
  teacher, 6, 8, 15, 17, 20

N
New Zealand, 105, 106, 172, 250, 287–301, 328

P
Political dimensions
  democracy, 60, 68, 134
  policy maker, 138, 281, 289, 294, 299, 300, 322
  political acumen, 210, 220, 256, 257, 264
  public education, 138, 274
  socio-political, 5, 9, 15, 17–18, 103, 210, 220
  stakeholders, 52, 207, 210, 211, 217, 219–220
  tensions, 287, 290, 296, 297, 299, 330
Power of assessment, 19, 20
Professional development, 5–9, 13, 15, 17, 18, 79
  capacity building, 64, 172, 174, 189–192, 200, 210–216, 218, 220, 248, 295, 321, 349–351
  peer coaching, 63, 66, 79, 82, 202, 217, 219, 220, 268
Professionalism, 210, 288, 300
Programme for International Student Assessment (PISA), 148, 152, 154, 155, 289

R
Reform, 51, 300, 340

Reporting
  communicating assessment, 30, 41, 101, 211, 276, 291, 294, 297, 299, 336, 346, 348
  standards-based reporting, 89, 208, 297
Rubrics, 81, 89–107, 119, 121, 122, 125, 127, 183, 189
Russia, 251

S
Scotland, 174
South Africa, 238
Spain, 228
Special needs. *See* Inclusion
Student
  learning, 2, 5, 6, 12, 14, 15, 19, 28, 31, 34, 35, 39, 47, 48, 50, 51, 55, 57, 61, 64, 66, 73–75, 82, 100, 118, 120, 145, 146, 148, 167, 173, 174, 176, 179, 181–183, 263, 279, 281, 289, 290, 293, 294, 296–299, 337, 351, 352, 356
  voice, 183, 210, 212, 213

T
Taiwan, 251–252
Teacher judgment, 288, 297

U
United States, 172, 174, 202, 248, 249, 275, 281, 328, 339, 343
University
  preservice, 58, 59, 64, 74, 81, 138, 172, 175, 189, 191, 322

V
Validity, 26, 41, 89, 92, 93, 95–97, 99, 100, 119, 132, 149, 151, 152, 234, 276, 278, 298, 311, 334, 335, 340
Values. *See* Beliefs

Made in the USA
Middletown, DE
05 December 2017